THE ENCYCLOPEDIA OF THE MUSIC BUSINESS

Harvey Rachlin

THE ENCYCLOPEDIA OF THE MUSIC BUSINESS

1817

HARPER & ROW, PUBLISHERS, New York
Cambridge, Philadelphia, San Francisco, London
Mexico City, São Paulo, Sydney

Photo credits appear on page 523.

FIRST EDITION

Designer: Sidney Feinberg

Library of Congress Cataloging in Publication Data

Rachlin, Harvey.
   The encyclopedia of the music business.
   1. Music trade—Dictionaries. I. Title.
ML102.M85R3   338.4′778′0973   81–47235
   ISBN 0–06–014913–2   AACR2

81 82 83 84 85 10 9 8 7 6 5 4 3 2 1

For My Parents,
Philip and Mazie Rachlin

Contents

Contents

Contents

Acknowledgments

Celebrated persons often say, in making their brief speech as they collect an award at a presentation ceremony, that they would like to thank . . . (they then give a few names) . . . because without these people's help their achievement would not have been possible. To the reader, I would like to echo that sentiment (without passing myself off as a celebrity or award winner) before conveying my gratitude to those who helped me. I hope that the reader appreciates their efforts in making this book a comprehensive and accurate reference volume on the music business.

I would like to express my very special gratitude to Lawrence Lighter, who served as the general legal editor of this book. His experience in so many areas eased the burden of this difficult task. In addition, Mr. Lighter's enthusiasm for, and love of, the music business was a constant source of personal inspiration.

Of more help than I can describe is one of the nicest persons I have ever had the privilege of knowing—C. Victor Campos. Mr. Campos helped out with many of the technical sections in this book and is a genius in his own right. To him, I am most indebted.

I was most fortunate to have the copyright material in the manuscript proofread, and errors therein corrected as well as information supplemented, by two brilliant and kind attorneys from the United States Copyright Office: Charlotte Givens, Attorney Adviser for the Performing Arts Section, and Marybeth Peters, Chief of Examining Division. Charlotte Givens also spent many hours on the telephone with me, answering questions, explaining regulations, and providing insight. She was always delightful and patient.

I am especially grateful to Maxine Chrein and Ben Rizzi for their generous assistance in many areas. Besides being well informed, Maxine is incredibly sweet and working with her was always fun.

On a sad note, I'd like to pay tribute to one of my dearest friends and colleagues, Joel Goldstein, who passed away while this book was being written. A recording engineer, Joel was an inspiration to everyone he encountered in the music business. He died in his prime at the age of 33.

There is a substantial portion of the text devoted to the radio field and to this end I express my deepest appreciation to Loring Fisher, an independent consultant, who is undoubtedly one of the most knowledgeable persons in communications.

No single person has done more to help the recording industry reduce the amount of piracy, counterfeiting, and bootlegging in this era than Jules Yarnell, head of RIAA's Anti-Piracy Intelligence Bureau and I was most privileged to have his assistance with respect to the text in these areas. Steven J. D'Onofrio and Robin Goold of the same unit compiled the data on state anti-piracy laws.

I am heavily indebted to the many attorneys who gave freely of their valuable time to peruse the legal sections of my manuscript and make corrections and annotations. I was fortunate to have the assistance of some of the finest attorneys in the music business:

For the entry on the Dramatists Guild Dramatico-Musical Production Contract, I am indebted to Donald C. Farber. Mr. Farber is a foremost authority in the area of theatrical production contracts and was instrumental in helping me simplify this difficult area.

Another intricate and legal area is limited partnerships and to that end I am grateful to Seth Schapiro for his kind assistance and also to Patricia A. Rogowski.

Trademark law is a fascinating but again complex subject but I was fortunate to have my manuscript proofread and corrected by two experts—Myron Cohen and Marie V. Driscoll.

Immigration law is important to the music business as it is under a federal statute and regulation of federal agencies that various performers enter the U.S. to perform or otherwise work. Much help in that area was provided by Allen E. Kaye, a specialist in immigration law.

Foreign licensing of musical compositions and sound recordings is an intricate area and Richard H. Roemer, an expert, provided the important information in that area.

Special thanks is due to Neville L. Johnson for his contribution to the section on international publishing agreements. For the entry on the music publisher and related areas I am grateful to William Calderwood, Wayne D. Rooks and Kim Guggenheim for their generous assistance.

For the section on international copyright relations I am most grateful for the assistance of Lawrence E. Abelman, an authority in this area.

I am indebted to Richard N. Winfield for his help in the areas of defamation and rights of privacy and publicity. His associate, David A. Thurm, clarified other legal areas.

Elliot L. Hoffman criticized and improved various sections and I was fortunate to have the benefit of his many years of legal experience and keen insight.

Other attorneys who made valuable contributions were Nicholas Arcomano, Gary F. Roth, John A. Giroux, Irwin Robinson, Robert C. Harris, Michael F. Sukin, Robert Flax, Howard L. Wattenberg, James Gianopulos,

Albert F. Ciancimino, Joseph L. Latwin, and Lawrence I. Kaplan.

Two of the most knowledgeable accountants in the business are Marshall M. Gelfand and Wayne Coleman, who generously assisted with the manuscript. Also of valuable help related to this field were Alan S. Honig, Leo Strauss, Stephen Tenenbaum, and Steven White.

Albert Berman and Howard Balsam of The Harry Fox Agency were most helpful in the area of mechanical rights. After I interviewed Mr. Berman for several hours one afternoon, carefully jotting down every bit of information, he told me I could now start my own Harry Fox Agency.

It is no wonder that CBS Records is the giant record company it is, employing so many kind and professional people. Those interviewed provided wonderful insight into the record business. In particular I'd like to express gratitude to Al DeMarino (artist development), Bruce Harris (artists and repertoire), Susan Blond (publicity), and Robin Sloane (publicity). In addition, many thanks to Rosemary Mina, Marvin Cohn, Jim Charne, Jerry Shulman, Tom McGuiness, Ralph F. Colin, Jr., Leon Graham, Robert Altshuler, Yvonne Ericson, and Bonnie McCourt. Lois Marino is the writer of the "publicity plans" that appear in the RECORD COMPANY entry.

Bill Wardlow, associate publisher of *Billboard*, is in my opinion the "'king of the charts" and I am grateful for his generous assistance in that area. Thanks also to Ron Willman, Dennis Hyland, and Mike Feierstein of *Billboard*.

In the music publishing field I am grateful to Frank J. Hackinson for his contribution to the printed music and print licensing sections. Melanie Orlinick was also of much help in these areas; both work together and were always cooperative. Norman Weiser is a brilliant music publisher and a willing interviewee.

Public relations is an exciting aspect of any area of the entertainment business and I was fortunate to get information from the cream of the crop here. Joe Dera is a solid pro and can make anyone famous. And there's Carol Ross, who's a wizard.

In the print music retailing field, I interviewed the best, Danyale English-Klein. She has to become a legend in New York's retail music center on West 48th Street.

Many thanks to Jeanne Smookler for her fine drawings illustrating "How Some Multi-Track 'Pop' Recordings Are Made." She is as kind as she is talented and to her I am indebted.

I am grateful to Sid Davis and *Music Retailer* for their kind assistance and permission to reproduce various materials. It is an excellent magazine and recommended reading for anyone interested in the music business.

Some individuals who deserve special recognition are Eddy Manson, Agnes Dubin, Max Dubin, Dr. David Rachman, Larry Abel, John F. Knapp, Lou Stevens, Susan Elliott, Randy Roberts, Tony Camillo, Rick Kives, Richard Lavsky, Sidney Bernstein, Michael A. Kerker, Richard Lewis, Jay Sonin, James D. Liddane, Jack Grossman, Peter Albu, and Claude Masouyé, of the World Intellectual Property Organization.

Individuals at trade and professional associations and unions who helped are Christine M. Farnon, Leonard Feist, Victor W. Fuentealba, Robert Crothers, Edward Peters, Lew Mancini, Stephen Traiman, Lewis Bachman, Heather D. Connor, Richard D. Freed, Henry Brief, Leo A. Droste, Kat Brady, Delloyd Tibbs, Mickey Granberg, David Grossman, Ralph Black, Lisa Gonzalez, William Spencer Reilly, Trudy Wilson, Josephine Walter, Jules Malamud, Eileen Turbow, George Wachtel, Jack Segal, and Dorothy Fey (of the United States Trademark Association).

In the concert promotion and booking agency field I owe gratitude to Larry Vaughn and Anne Astuto (who conveyed the excitement of a concert by generously supplying me and an entourage with backstage passes to a concert at Nassau Coliseum) and Amy Polan who diligently proofread the manuscript, as well as Stuart Weintraub, Debbi Federoff, Carl S. Hirsh, Joe Tuchs, Marci Weber, and Hank McCann.

Record company operations were also explained or manuscript sections thereof proofread by Ronnie Edmonston, Herb Goldfarb, William Levy, Elliot Goldman, Robert Feiden, Herb Helman, Roxy Myzal, Bernard Boorstein, and Ben Karol.

Songwriters are among my favorite people and grateful(acknowledgment is due to some of the best: Sammy Cahn, Marvin Hamlisch, Ervin Drake, Philip J. Lang, Oscar Brand, Larry Weiss, Johnny Marks, and Max Morath.

There is considerable material devoted to Canada and special gratitude is due Barbara Bloor (Acting Registrar of Copyrights), Paul M. Berry, John V. Mills, Nancy Gyokeris, Craig Parks, R. G. Gordon, Harriet Miller, and C. C. Devereaux.

In no small way were each of the following helpful: Morris Ballen, Harry Gershon, Henrietta Gershon, Al Dargis, Rita M. Chambers, Frank Millburn, Elliot Gorlin, Bruce Clear, Thomas J. Valentino, Sr., Ross Wetzsteon, Rosemary Davey, Dan Rau, Mike Scalzi, Sarah Basbas, Judie Janowski, Mike Vallone, Ken Kirkwood, Constance Anthes, Sherman Broday, Ed Fox, Mitch Plotkin, Gordon Elliott, P. J. Cummings, Seli Groves, Frankie MacCormick, Mike Roe, Larry Sonin, Herbert A. Linsky, Robert L. Gur-Arie, Albert B. Grundy, Donald J. Plunkett, Rick Mitz, Alexander Gordon, Roddy S. Shashoua, Trish Rother, Laura Harth, George Biello, Jr., Leo Artiles, Sta'sh, Keith Ripka, David Enders, Dana Webster, Traugott Rohner, Charles E. McGee, Clifton B. Knight, Jr., and Susan Stoller.

I have taught music business and songwriting courses over the past few years at Five Towns College in Merrick, New York, and have learned much from both students and faculty. I'd like to specially thank Dr. Stenley Cohen, Martin Crafton, William Nosofsky, and Michele Cervoni.

My gratitude is also expressed to Marianne Schlesinger, Hanna Berkovitz, Jay Cohen, Steven Schulman, Alan Goodman, Jeff Luckman, Phil Trugman, Barbara Masry, Shirley Tiffen, Howard Posin, Jack Lipsky, Bonnie Schachter, Sandy Banks, Helene Goldberg, David Copper, Brenda Murphy, Doria Sussman, Pam Ott, Jim Ott, Ann Costabile, and Paula Schack.

Special thanks are also due to Cliff Share, Alan Leventhal, Phyllis Levine, Lonnie Grosewald, Diane Wittpenn, Pearl Bernstein, Sally Rachlin, and Joseph Costanzo.

I have always been appreciative of the competence of excellent typists, and I was fortunate to have two of Brooklyn's finest—Eileen Rohleder and Audrey Pekar—who typed and retyped and.... Margaret Dyke efficiently provided the finishing touches. To all, my special thanks not only for your services but also for spending almost as much time trying to decipher my handwriting.

Without the support of my brother, Dr. Steven Rachlin, I do not think I would have been able to complete this book. Craig and Gary provided humor to many a hectic night, as well as my first sister-in-law, Sharon.

My everlasting gratitude is given to those who helped me get started in the music business: Syde Berman, Robert Banks, and Alfred Haber.

If anyone has been responsible for helping and guiding me in my career as a writer, it is the editor of this book, Bernard Skydell. He is my "Max Perkins" as well as trusted friend and advisor. I owe a great debt to him and I hope he is aware of my gratitude and appreciation. I am also specially grateful to Marjorie Horvitz, copyeditor of this book, for her patience and excellent work as well as to Ellen Royer, production editor at Harper & Row.

The writing of this book was often more than a full-time pursuit; it involved round-the-clock work for the greater part of almost three years. During intense periods of stress, people tend to engage in excessive habits such as overeating. I developed an enormous appetite too, but not for food. Rather, I became a fanatic for ragtime music. In closing, then, I would like to pay homage to the master of ragtime composers, Scott Joplin, whose rags I played almost every day during this period, and which provided a tremendous sense of relief and much relaxation from the frustrations I endured while writing this book.

Introduction

In the north region of the valley of the Euphrates River in southwest Asia thousands of years ago, a group of villagers gathered in the town square to hear a local musician perform on a crude string instrument. After the "concert," many people, pleased by his performance, piled food, pottery, and other valuables next to him. Musicians in other villages throughout the region earned their livelihood in much the same way.

What you have just read is a fictional story, but may very well be an example of the seeds from which organized forms of music business later sprouted. No one can say exactly when or where the first form of music business began, but it would be safe to say that it revolved around payments to musicians for their services. In some ancient civilizations such as Sumeria, Egypt, Babylonia and Greece, music was a highly regarded profession and musicians were treated as privileged members of the community. In many societies, composers, dancers, singers, and instrument makers also flourished.

Through the millennia the "music business" has changed dramatically in many ways. Yet its basic goal—that of bringing musical enjoyment to people—has remained the same. It is said that music is almost as old as man himself. Indeed, the music business may be the world's oldest *respected* profession.

Quite simply, the music business may be defined as "the business of selling music." Music, today, is essentially "sold" in two forms. One is *product*, which as used here refers to the material objects that store and reproduce sound and/or audiovisual programs such as LPs, 45s, cassettes, eight-track cartridges, videocassettes, and videodiscs, as well as other objects from which music can be communicated such as sheet music, fakebooks, and folios.

As music is by its nature a performing art, *live performances* represent another medium for selling music. Here again, music is "sold" in many different ways, depending upon the nature of the music. There are symphonic concerts, recitals, operas, musical shows, rock concerts and festivals, among others.

In accordance with the definition above, there are numerous types of persons, companies, and other entities comprising the music business. These may be categorized as follows:

Talent: songwriters, musicians, singers, recording artists, record producers, arrangers, orchestrators, conductors, dancers, choreographers, film composers, jingle writers.

Talent representatives: personal managers, agents, attorneys, business managers, accountants, contractors, leaders, public relations firms, artist management agencies, road managers.

Companies: record companies, distributors (branch and independent), rack jobbers, one-stops, record and tape retailers, music publishers, print music licensees and selling agents, music jobbers, print music retailers, jukebox operators, record and tape clubs, mail-order firms, record merchandisers, record/tape importers and exporters, video production companies, musical instrument rental firms, rehearsal studios, recording studios, mastering facilities, plating plants, pressing plants, tape duplicators, album packaging suppliers, record and tape care accessories manufacturers, cartridge and cassette parts manufacturers, tape manufacturers, independent record promoters, player piano roll manufacturers, music box manufacturers, musical instrument manufacturers, typographers, sheet music and folio printers, music copying services, advertising agencies, sound and lighting firms.

Licensing organizations: performing rights organizations (e.g., American Society of Composers, Authors and Publishers; Broadcast Music, Inc.; and SESAC Inc.) and mechanical rights agencies (e.g., The Harry Fox Agency, Inc.).

Trade associations: e.g., Recording Industry Association of America, Inc., National Music Publishers Association, National Association of Recording Merchandisers.

Professional and educational organizations: e.g., National Academy of Recording Arts and Sciences, American Music Conference, Country Music Association, American Guild of Authors and Composers, Music Educators National Conference.

Unions: e.g., American Federation of Musicians of the United States and Canada, American Federation of Television and Radio Artists, American Guild of Musical Artists, Screen Actors Guild.

Talent "buyers" and venues: concert promoters, clubs, discos, concert halls, stadiums, arenas, theaters.

Trade publications: e.g., *Billboard, Cash Box, Record World, Variety.*

In this world of modern communication, the music business partially embraces (or is itself embraced by) other industries where music plays an integral role—radio, television, and motion pictures chief among them. Thus, the music business also touches upon various entities in *communications:* radio stations, television stations, motion picture companies, programming consultants, program suppliers and syndicators, broadcast measurement services.

About this book

In many entries, a word, term, or phrase is used which requires further explanation or

whose own entry will amplify the information given at that point. These are capitalized and the reader should refer to the entry of such a cross-reference.

Use of pronouns is another area of clarification. In most cases "he" is used but doesn't necessarily mean the majority of persons using that title or in a particular position or profession are male; it may actually refer to *anyone*.

Much attention in this encyclopedia has been paid to the copyright law. This is because it is this law, essentially, that provides the foundation upon which the music business runs. By granting creators of musical works exclusive rights, it enables them to earn a living which consequently enables the industry to exist. Thus, because it is so important, it is the author's intention to give the reader an understanding and appreciation of the law, and so historical analyses are contained in various entries (also those of a noncopyright nature for the same reason). Likewise, because of the copyright law's importance to those in the music business, there are separate entries for many terms found in the statute (e.g., anonymous work, copies, phonorecords, pseudonymous work, sound recording and work made-for-hire). Many of these terms are legalese and not used by most professionals in the music business, but it has been necessary to give them separate entries in order to be complete in this book's explanation of the copyright law and, at the same time, fit in with its format. All references in this book to the U.S. copyright law refer to Public Law 94–553 (90 Stat. 2541), commonly known as the Copyright Act of 1976, unless otherwise specified.

Great care has been taken so that the material in this book is as up-to-date as possible. Included here are discussions or listings of various trade, professional, and educational associations. These are by no means exhaustive. New ones are constantly forming to represent the collective interests of groups as deemed necessary, and usually for good reason. But many soon terminate, after much initial excitement and fanfare, for any of various reasons. To eliminate chances for outdating in this respect also, this book generally contains the names of those associations in existence as of 1970 or earlier. This is not a reflection on the merit or status of any other association.

I have included in the *Encyclopedia* discussions of other industries insofar as they relate to the music business. A text on the subject of this book would be incomplete, for example, without touching upon the radio, television, and motion picture industries. The music business is strongly integrated with others; hence the reason for such discussions.

There also follows a discussion of popular music and its various genres. Writing about popular music was the most subjective part of this book. It is difficult to convey in words an aesthetic art form that means different things to different people.

In conclusion, this book contains many diverse entries. Learning about the music business is an education in many different areas such as copyright law, record distribution, music publishing, recording, and unions. These are all separate and different disciplines but, as treated here, have one binding element— the bringing of music to the public. Music is that intangible art form that I trust we all love and is the ultimate reason for anyone reading this book.

—Harvey Rachlin
June 1981

A

A & R (Artists and Repertoire). *See* RECORD COMPANY.

A Side. *See* SINGLE.

Academy Awards. Prizes of merit given annually in the United States by the Academy of Motion Picture Arts and Sciences for outstanding achievements in motion pictures. The Academy Awards have worldwide prestige and are highly valued by those who work in the film medium. Among the many awards conferred are those in the music categories, to composers, adapters, and songwriters.

Music Categories. The categories for Music Awards have varied over the years (*see* Appendix G), but have been in the areas of Best Original Score, Best Adaptation Score, and Best Original Song. In its special rules for the Music Awards, the academy makes the following definitions: an Original Score is "a body of music or a substantial body of songs (consisting of music and lyrics), in either case originating solely with the submitting composer(s) or songwriter(s), specifically created for the feature motion picture for which eligibility is claimed." An Adaptation Score is "a work consisting *primarily* of thematic and connective musical material based either on pre-existing musical material or on musical material specifically created for the eligible film (not original with the adapter)." An Original Song "consists of original words and music specifically created for the feature motion picture for which eligibility is claimed. There must be a substantive rendition (not necessarily visual) of both lyric and melody in the body of the film."

Nominating a Work. For an achievement to be considered for nomination, the creator(s) must present an Official Submission Form. Certain materials must accompany the form, such as a music cue sheet and a lead sheet of a song. These required materials vary, depending on the category in which the work is being considered.

Voting. Final voting for awards is restricted to active members of the academy. Voting is conducted by secret ballot and tallied by an impartial auditing firm.

History of Music Categories. Although the first Academy Awards ceremony was held on May 16, 1929, to honor works from the 1927–28 season, the first music awards weren't presented until 1934. Through the years, awards have been added, deleted, or redefined.

History of Academy. The Academy of Motion Picture Arts and Sciences was organized in May 1927 by 36 people from various segments of the motion picture industry. It was organized as a nonprofit corporation, chartered under the laws of California, "dedicated to the ideal of enhancing the cultural, educational, and technical progress of motion pictures." (Its first president was Douglas Fairbanks, Sr.) The Academy has grown as a professional honorary organization through the years and had over 3,900 members in 1980.

The "Oscar." Winners of an Academy Award receive a golden statuette, described by the academy as "a stalwart man standing on a reel of film and holding a crusader's sword."

This statuette is nicknamed "Oscar." Art director Cedric Gibbons originally sketched the figure and it was molded by sculptor George Stanley.

See also AWARDS.

Accountant, Certified Public. *See* AUDIT, ROYALTY; BUSINESS MANAGER.

Acetate. A disc whose grooves are inscribed on a cutting lathe by a cutting head driven by the audio signal from a recording. Acetates are often cut from MASTER mix tapes to evaluate how a final disc pressing will sound. Acetates are also cut from disc or other tape recordings and used for demo purposes. The method of cutting an acetate is substantially identical to the manner in which a master lacquer is cut (metal parts for the pressing of a commercial record are made from the master lacquer—*see* RECORD MANUFACTURING).

Acetates can be cut in mono or stereo and made to play at speeds of 33⅓ rpm or 45 rpm. They are available in standard sizes of 7, 10, or 12 inches and may be single-faced (grooved on one side, thereby containing one or more selections on that side) or double-faced (grooved on both sides, thereby containing one or more selections on each side).

An acetate is thicker than a commercially pressed record, but since its surface material is softer and less elastic, it wears out more quickly with repeated playings. Many recording studios have the equipment to play either a tape or a disc recording and simultaneously inscribe an acetate dub.

Act. A decree of a legislative body. Congress is the legislative body of the United States and consists of two houses—the Senate and the House of Representatives. The approval of both houses is necessary to pass a bill on to the President for his approval, which, if given, causes the bill to become law.

Congress is empowered by the U.S. Consti-

tution to make, or enact, *copyright* laws. The present U.S. copyright law is commonly referred to as the Copyright Act of 1976. Congress has also enacted various statutes aimed at regulating business practices.

"Act" also refers to a performing or recording group.

See BUSINESS LAWS, FEDERAL AND STATE; COPYRIGHT LAW OF THE UNITED STATES; RECORDING ARTIST.

Actors' Equity Association (AEA or Equity). Labor union that represents actors, singers, dancers, chorus members, and all professional performers and stage managers who work in the LEGITIMATE THEATER in the United States.

Eligibility for Membership. Membership in Equity is open to citizens of the United States or resident aliens of the U.S. Performers admitted into the U.S. pursuant to its immigration laws for the purpose of performing in a theatrical production may, at the discretion of the union's council, be elected as alien members.

Fees and Dues. There is an initiation fee for all Equity members and annual dues for resident members, based upon their gross annual earnings from employment within the union's jurisdiction. Alien members pay a small percentage of their income for services rendered in fields within the jurisdiction of Equity.

Affiliation. AEA is a branch of ASSOCIATED ACTORS AND ARTISTES OF AMERICA (FOUR A's) and is affiliated with AFL-CIO and the International Federation of Actors (FIA).

Areas of Agreements. Equity is the exclusive bargaining representative of its members for dealing, negotiating, and contracting with producers, managers, agents, packagers, impresarios, and other employers. The union has specific agreements and rules governing employment in various types of legitimate theater: Broadway, Off Broadway, stock resident dramatic, stock nonresident dramatic, indoor musical, outdoor musical, resident theater, dinner theater, theater for young audiences, and industrial shows. These agreements provide the UNION SCALE and terms of employment for Equity members working in these various areas. Members of AEA are not allowed to perform in non-Equity shows unless special permission is granted by the union's council.

Arbitration. Any dispute between an employer and Equity or an Equity member relating to the interpretation or application of any agreement between Equity and the employer may be submitted to ARBITRATION at the request of either party and such decision is deemed the exclusive remedy for the resolution or adjustment of disputes. Procedures for the request and regulations regarding arbitration are provided for in Equity's various agreements, as stated above. These agreements either name a permanent board of arbitrators or call for the dispute to be submitted to arbitration pursuant to the voluntary Arbitration Rules of the American Arbitration Association.

History. Actors' Equity Association was founded May 26, 1913, in New York City by a group of actors wishing to create standard employment agreements in the industry in order to protect themselves from prevalent exploitative practices. Standard agreements have been established by Equity in the various areas of legitimate theater, providing for minimum wages, overtime compensation, rehearsal money, insurance pension and welfare plans, and safe working and travel conditions. Equity's membership grew from 112 at its conception to approximately 30,000 in 1980. Its headquarters is in New York; regional offices are located in Hollywood, San Francisco, and Chicago.

See also UNIONS.

Administration of a Music Publisher's Catalog.
Musical compositions are intangible properties whose owners are granted certain exclusive rights by the copyright law. In practice, commercial uses of musical works (songs) are authorized by the granting of licenses. Transfers (assignments) of ownership of musical compositions are executed and bound by the terms of negotiated contracts. Full protection for a copyright is achieved by compliance with both domestic and international laws. The management of music copyrights is special, complex, and involves many responsibilities. Clearly, *administration* is an important facet of the MUSIC PUBLISHER's operation.

The administration of a music publisher's catalog falls into three general areas: *copyright*, *contractual*, and *financial*. A music publisher generally maintains separate (but interrelated) departments to handle the various administration areas. Careful supervision of activities is necessary, as improper administration can result in a loss of income for both writer and publisher, the songwriter terminating the agreement because of the publisher being in default with the contract terms, or, in a rare instance, the copyright falling into the PUBLIC DOMAIN.

Duties. Stated above are the three areas in which administrative tasks are performed on behalf of a copyright or catalog. The following is a breakdown of the responsibilities that generally fall into the domain of each area:

Copyright Administration
- Makes copyright registrations in the United States Copyright Office for musical compositions and arrangements and adaptations
- Satisfies the mandatory deposit provisions with respect to published works, by sending copies of published works to the Library of Congress
- Records transfers of copyright ownership (assignments, mortgages, exclusive licenses) and other documents dealing with copyright ownership at the Copyright Office
- Registers copyright renewal claims in the U.S. Copyright Office (for certain pre-1978 works)
- Prepares copyright notices for publication of the works
- Secures international copyright protection for the work by:
    (1) printing "All Rights Reserved" under the

copyright notice for protection in contracting nations of the Buenos Aires Convention;

(2) publishing the work "simultaneously" in a Berne Union country for protection in countries that are signatories to that convention;

(3) using the UCC notice (see INTERNATIONAL COPYRIGHT RELATIONS)

- Searches or authorizes searches of Copyright Office records when necessary
- Maintains orderly records of administrative activities
- Keeps abreast of emerging copyright legislation

Contractual Administration

- Prepares contracts for assignments or transfers of copyrights from writers and other owners
- Prepares contracts providing for co-ownership of copyrights with other music publishers
- Prepares contracts to administer other publishers' catalogs
- Prepares contracts for subpublishing agreements
- Joins or affiliates with a performing rights organization and "clears" songs with it (licenses for nondramatic performances of works are issued through the performing rights organization the publisher is a member or affiliate of)
- Issues licenses for uses of the copyrights, such as in records, tapes, films, videodiscs, videocassettes, plays, jingles, and print (if the publisher is affiliated with a mechanical rights agency, various types of licenses are issued on the publisher's behalf by such organization)

Financial Administration

- Collects income and records information received regarding earnings generated by the copyrights both domestically and internationally
- Prepares writer royalty statements in accordance with writer contracts
- Sends accurate royalty statements and checks to writers on a periodic basis
- Prepares business accountings for other publishers whose catalogs the supervising publisher administers or copublishes and sends these statements with checks corresponding to the publishers' earnings (after writer royalties, administration fees, and contractually provided expenses are deducted) on a periodic basis

Administration Deals. Many music publishers do not handle the administration of the catalogs they own but rather enter into agreements with other publishing companies to have this function performed for them for a percentage of their receipts. Such an agreement is known as an *administration deal*.

Songwriters, recording artists, producers, and others often form publishing companies for the musical compositions they write or acquire an ownership interest in. These individuals are frequently more concerned and occupied with creative pursuits, however, than with conducting the business affairs of a publishing company. Consequently they have other publishers administer their catalogs.

The commission charged by administering publishers varies. It may range from 10% of the engaging publisher's share of income to 25% of its gross collections. After an administration deal is executed, generally all moneys payable by licensees are directed to the administering publisher, which periodically renders a statement of accounting of all royalties collected to the other publisher with a remittance, after deducting its administration fee, contractually provided expenses, and writers' royalties. Occasionally the owner-publisher receives a net share directly from the source. The duration of administration deals varies widely; for example, they may be made for an initial period of 1, 2, 3, or more years.

Before a publishing company assumes an administrative role for another music publisher, it generally examines certain criteria: the amount of income the catalog is earning (it must be substantial), the volume of copyrights in the catalog, and the activity (primarily in terms of recordings and performances) a number of the copyrights are currently having.

In an administration agreement, there is no ownership interest in the copyrights on behalf of the supervising publisher. Other publisher services, such as exploitation of copyrights or promotion of the catalog, are normally not provided. The administering publisher negotiates all deals regarding uses of the copyrights, such as mechanical, synchronization, and print licenses. If foreign rights are not to be controlled by the administering publisher, this should be specified in the agreement. Some agreements provide for the administering publisher to obtain a copyright interest in a composition if it obtains one or more "covers" (*see* COVER RECORD) or generates a certain amount of income.

Catalog administration is also handled for music publishers by attorneys, accountants, business managers, and others. The AMERICAN GUILD OF AUTHORS AND COMPOSERS (AGAC) offers a plan to administer the catalogs of its writer/publisher members and those in the estates of its deceased members.

Advance. A prepayment of royalties to an individual or company that enters into a royalty contract, the equivalent of which is recoupable (recoverable) from future royalties earned and payable. Advances are generally deemed nonreturnable where royalties fail to accrue to the equivalent of the advance.

In the music business, advances are given by various entities to individuals and companies. Such advances include:

Music Publisher/Songwriter Advance. A music publisher may give a songwriter an advance for transferring an unpublished composition to it or for reassigning a composition whose term of assignment to the publisher is due to expire. Songwriters who are signatories to "exclusive writer agreements" normally receive weekly or monthly salaries, which are deemed advances recoupable from earnings of all or certain compositions created under and covered by the agreement.

Performing Rights Organization/Writer, Publisher Advance. ASCAP, BMI, and SESAC may give an advance to a writer or publisher upon the signing or renewal of a membership or affiliation agreement, or prior to the release of a recording of their work.

Factors that are considered in determining if an advance for joining or affiliating is justified, and if so, what amount it should be, include the writer's or publisher's track record and past earnings, current activity, forthcoming record releases, competitive offers from another performing rights organization, and what the organization thinks the writer or publisher will earn over a future period of time. In determining whether an advance should be given for a record release, and if so, how much, the following may be considered: the artist, the record company, whether the selection will be a single or an album cut, and other relevant indicia of the likelihood of performing rights income.

Record Company/Recording Artist Advance. Recording artists enter into agreements with record companies to record a certain number of masters within a specified period of time and such agreements normally provide for advances to the artist.

Other Advances. Other advances in the music industry include the following (indicated as: payer of the advance/recipient): record company/record producer; record company/associated label; record and tape club/record company; record merchandising company/record company; record merchandising company/music publisher; concert promoter/performing artist; print licensee/music publisher; foreign record licensee/domestic record licensor; subpublisher/domestic music publisher.

See BONUS.

Advertising. The practice of sponsoring paid public announcements for the purpose of stimulating the sale of products or use of a service. Advertising is a regular and important part of business practice for many companies in the music industry. Advertisements are geared to attract business from industry sources, from the general public, or from both. Consumers are often the target audience of ads or campaigns sponsored by record manufacturers, record/tape retailers, record/tape clubs, record merchandisers, mail order firms, and concert promoters. This entry presents some general aspects of advertising, but its main area of concentration is the advertising of records and tapes to consumers.

In the recording industry, getting airplay

may be the most effective way of bringing a record to public attention. Advertising functions to support airplay but for many artists (particularly those who aren't receiving much airplay) or records (such as jazz or folk), it plays a more important role. (The term "record" here designates a single or an LP and its counterpart on prerecorded tape.)

Advertising may also serve the purpose of developing an artist's image. Ideally, then, an ad should do more than just bring attention to a PRODUCT. It should attempt to build the artist's *career*. For example, for an experienced artist, it could show the growth and success the artist has had and any new direction taken; for a new artist, the ad could concentrate on any success attained to date or the "freshness" of the artist. An ad campaign should represent the artist creatively, interestingly, and honestly, and be designed to reach the target audience—existing fans and particular segments of the public not previously aware of or interested in the artist and his/her product. Ads should also reflect the image of the label. All this is transmitted through both copy and artwork, and an ad's media placement.

Advertising Media. The means to communicate advertisments is via the media. Among the various media are the following: newspapers (daily, Sunday, weekly, life-style, alternative, underground, organization, shoppers' guides, college and high school); magazines (general and "fanzines"); trade publications; programs (for concerts and theatrical production); direct mail; radio (different formats on AM and FM); television (local, network, cable, and pay TV); movie theaters (motion picture commercials or lobby displays); outdoor (billboards, posters, signs, electric displays); transportation (buses, trains, subways, streetcars, taxicabs, airports, bus/train stations); in-store/point of purchase (window and wall displays, signs, literature, in-store play); miscellaneous (handbills, fliers, bumper stickers, T-shirts, Frisbees, backs of concert tickets).

Record Company Advertising. Some of the larger record manufacturers have in-house ad agencies which plan and create advertisements as well as place them in various media. Other companies engage the services of independent advertising agencies (see below). In-house and private ad agencies function very much alike—they plan their clients' advertising for particular record releases and attempt to reach the most people possible at the most efficient cost levels.

Advertisements in consumer media are strategically placed to reach "target" audiences. An artist may have a selective audience profile (particularly in the case of new artists) or, as with superstars, a broad audience profile. Consequently the various media are constantly evaluated by media directors.

A magazine, for example, will be evaluated in terms of its circulation, audience demographics, slant, and editorial content. Likewise, the artist will be evaluated—in terms of image, type of music performed, and target audience. If it is determined that the artist and his music will appeal to a large cross section of the magazine's audience, ads may be placed. In planning, care must be taken to ensure that they are timed properly—that is, synchronized to release dates, radio promotion campaigns, and/or concert appearances. Ads may be closely related to or built upon ideas and approaches that come out of the company's marketing departments (i.e., merchandising, sales, publicity, artist development, A & R, and promotion).

To advertise effectively, the advertiser must be knowledgeable about the target audience—their tastes, buying habits, whether they will purchase product by new artists, where they shop, etc. Finding out the answers to these and other questions regarding consumers and their buying habits is known as *market research*. (Market research is often in the form of DEMOGRAPHIC SURVEYS.) Some companies have their own market research departments, while others employ independent research firms.

Record companies place consumer advertisements on national and local levels. Large-circulation magazines are mostly utilized for national advertising. Local advertising, where the majority of advertising dollars are spent, is done in newspapers and on local radio and television.

Record companies sponsor local advertisements by paying for ads run by their retail accounts which feature their records and tapes. In contrast to other industries, where manufacturers and retailers split the cost of ad dollars (referred to as "co-op" advertising), record companies actually pay the full costs for ads that feature their product. For "major" record companies, local advertising is coordinated through their distribution branches, which have budgets for advertising the label's product in their territory.

Record company advertising funds are also made available for local advertisements in special situations. If an artist is touring, for example, his label might set up a fund to sponsor advertisements in the localities where he performs (such advertisements would be coordinated through the branch operations in conjunction with the national headquarters). The branches may in addition initiate promotions by supplying local promoters of the artist's concerts with albums to be given away on the radio spots they run.

Other forms of advertising at the retail level include the following:

Institutional advertising—This is an advertisement sponsored and paid for by the merchant, with no financial support from a label. Institutional advertising often features heavily discounted product, with the intention that this will draw people into the outlet and result in the purchase of other merchandise. Product offered at large discounts is known as *loss leaders* or *traffic builders* and the advertising of such product is basically a promotion for the retailer.

In-store advertising—There are various ways a manufacturer can advertise in a retail outlet. A retailer may rent wall space, window space, airplay on the store's stereo system, time on the outlet's videotape machine, or even play time when the store's telephone is put on hold.

Direct mail—Some retailers compile master lists of their customers' names and addresses. When such retailers have a special sale or promotion, are featuring a new release, or are having an artist appear at the store, they may notify their customers by mail. Such mail may also contain discount coupons.

Information in Advertisements. Advertisements by local retailers should indicate the name of the store, its location and hours, and the names and prices of the products being advertised. Generally, as much recognizable product should be featured as possible. Several versions of advertising particular products and frequent run of them are the most effective ways to reach consumers.

Advertising by Retailers. A retail operation may handle its advertising in any of the following ways: it may have an in-house agency that handles all media or have one that is responsible for certain media, such as radio and television, with an outside agency handling other media; or the retailer may use the services of an independent agency for all its advertising.

Advertising Agency. Record manufacturers, record/tape retailers, and many other businesses often engage independent advertising agencies to handle their advertising. This is because not only is the running of an in-house agency costly, but successful advertising is specialized and complex.

Once an agency's services are acquired for an account, the agency researches the product, devises a creative strategy, plans a campaign, produces the ads or commercials (or employs free-lancers to do this), and inserts them into the media. An advertising agency is typically composed of various departments to perform these specialized services. They include the following:

Account management area—Account executives develop advertising and marketing programs for clients. They study the client's sales and public image and devise a program that will satisfy the client's needs. They coordinate all agency functions for the client and are the liaison between the client and the agency.

Research department—Research personnel study the client's product (or service). They develop market information and suggest ways of reaching potential buyers.

Creative department—This department prepares the written copy and designs the ads. It employs copywriters, who create the text and sales message to be used in the ads, and art directors and layout workers, who design print ads by selecting photographs, illustrations, and typography.

Production department—Production personnel physically prepare the advertisement for print or broadcast. For print production, the typographer sets the copy in type, the photoengraver makes the engravings for illustrations, and the electrotypist prepares electrotypes, mats, and other materials. Type is proofread and engravings, mats, and the other materials are checked.

Media department—Media personnel determine where the advertisement would be most effective and execute the purchase of that space or time. They attempt to reach the largest section of the target audience at the lowest cost.

Traffic department—There are deadlines for the insertion of ads and commercials into the media and it is the function of this department to see that copy, artwork, plates, electrotype, music, etc., are prepared on time and that the final product is available by the deadline. The traffic department channels interdepartmental communication.

Agency Income. In most cases, an advertising agency's main source of income is the commissions allowed by the media for inserting ads and commercials. Such income is earned as follows: It is first determined in which media to advertise and how much space or time should be bought. After the advertiser approves a budget, the ads or commercials are created and inserted. Contracts are usually taken out between the media and the agency.

For an insertion, the agency is billed by the medium for the cost of the ad less usually 15%, and any other discounts. The agency in turn bills the client at the full rate. This 15% of the insertion cost is the agency's income. If an agency does production, it will typically charge the client for all expenses incurred, plus a markup.

While the commission system is the most common one used for agency remuneration, there are also other systems used for billing clients or obtaining compensation:

Fee system—This is where the agency charges fees (usually on a monthly or an annual basis) for its services.

Reduced commission system—An agency that places a considerable amount of advertising for its client may reduce its commission, as little new work may be required. The commission may be reduced, for example, where the agency runs the same ad over a long period of time.

Incentive system—A client may offer an advertising agency a bonus or a "piece of the action" if its sales increase substantially.

An agency can also be paid in a combination of any of these ways. Other income for an agency might come from music publishing revenues (*see* ADVERTISING MUSIC).

See also POINT-OF-PURCHASE MERCHANDISING.

Advertising Music. Music is virtually synonymous with advertising on radio and television. This is because the musical advertising message is perhaps the most effective device known to promote a product. A clever musical catch phrase can create a unique identification for a product, which is critical for competing manufacturers who want to distinguish their brands from others. Furthermore, a phrase set to a catchy tune is easier to remember than a nonmusical one, and a memorable message serves as a constant reminder of the wonderful virtues of the product it extols.

Advertising music is commonly associated with the jingle. A *jingle* is a melodic catch phrase (or "hook"), with or without accompanying lyrics, that was written or adapted for advertising. A jingle may be in the form of a full theme, or an opening (the "front") and closing (the "tag") to a COMMERCIAL (the gap in the music for the spoken announcement is sometimes referred to as a "doughnut"). In general, jingles may be characterized as being light and peppy, and having the effect of creating a happy feeling, though not all conform to this description.

Advertising Agency Aspects. Sponsors often retain an advertising agency to handle their campaigns. It is the responsibility of an advertising agency to present its client's product or service to its best advantage to the public. The agency, in conjunction with its client, devises a creative strategy and media campaign (agency commissions and fees are discussed in ADVERTISING).

Music (for reasons stated above) is often a part of advertising campaigns. While some agencies create advertising music in-house, for national campaigns an agency usually commissions original music or licenses preexisting compositions on behalf of its client. National account clients commonly include manufacturers of automobiles, household cleaning products, health products, cosmetics, and beauty aids; producers of food, beverages, and pet products; and companies selling transportation, communication and banking services.

When it has been decided that a jingle should be used in a particular campaign and is to be created by an outside source, the creative head, producer, or music director at the agency will invite jingle composers and music production houses (which employ composers, arrangers, and producers) to create jingles and submit demos. In recent years an average of 3 composers/music houses have competed for an account (with the losers receiving nominal production and "work" fees). Previously, "cattle calls" existed, free competitions for numerous submissions (sometimes up to 50 or more). Underscores (background music) today are assigned to writers on a noncompetitive basis.

In commissioning a jingle, the agency may provide a fact sheet describing the product or service and have the writer create his own words, or it may furnish a lyric previously written. In any case, the agency (at a briefing) provides the composers and/or music houses with essential information: the name of the sponsor, name of the product and all its uses, research reports (if any) on the product, demographics of the target market, strategy of the campaign, how the commercial will be used (i.e., local or network radio and/or television and times of broadcast), a description of the old ad campaign and how it should be changed, and the kind of musical sound wanted. The agency will provide the slogan or hook of the campaign.

After the agency decides which submission to use in its media campaign (sometimes all the jingles are rejected), it gives the "go-ahead" to the composer to produce the jingle. For television commercials, the composer will often have the actors lip-sync the vocals to a guide track during the filming or videotaping, and later synchronize to the video portion a sound track made in a recording studio. Contracts are usually negotiated with the agency's business affairs department.

Production Responsibilities. Where a composer or music house's reponsibility is to provide a complete jingle package, his/its duties include composing the jingle (subject to the agency's approval) and producing the track. Production responsibilities include taking footage counts, arranging the music, copying the charts, hiring the musicians and singers, booking studio time, conferring with the engineer (regarding the instrumentation, overdubs, sound effects, "sound" desired, number of tracks to be used, and microphone placements), mixing and synchronizing the track with visual sequences if the commercial is to be used for television broadcast.

Composer's Fees. Jingle writers (or music houses) receive a one-time fee for creating and producing a jingle (for a national account, this can range from $3,500 to $10,000). If the jingle is used in certain other ways, the composer may contractually provide for additional fees. There are:

Reuse fees—Money earned if the jingle (commercial) is tested or used beyond a specified time period.

Conversion fees—Money earned if the jingle was written for TV broadcast and is then used in radio, or vice versa.

Lift fees—Money earned if a jingle used in a particular commercial is transferred to a different track, as for example, a television commercial with a different visual sequence.

Copyright Ownership of Original Works. When an advertising agency requests original music to be created for a commercial advertisement, the ownership of the copyright may be as follows:

1. Under an express Work Made for Hire agreement, the advertising agency (or its client) owns the copyright. For this reason, an agency or company may own its own music publishing company. In certain work-for-hire agreements, the composer may negotiate to retain the performance royalties.

2. The advertising agency and composer may jointly own the copyright.

3. The composer may retain complete ownership of the copyright. In such a case, the composer will normally license all rights to the advertiser for use of the jingle and reserve ownership rights for all other uses. The copyright owner is free to put new words to the jingle (unless contractually restricted) and fashion it into a popular song.

Licensing Preexisting Music. It is often desirable or advantageous for a particular ad campaign to use a tune that has already achieved popularity and acceptance with the public. To use an existing copyright in advertising—whether in an original form or with adapted lyrics—a license must be obtained from the copyright owner (advertising music does not fall under the compulsory license provisions of the law). Unauthorized use of copyrighted music for advertising is an infringement under U.S. copyright law and violators are subject to legal actions. A license to use an existing copyright for advertising is obtained through negotiations directly with the copyright owner or his representative, such as a Mechanical Rights Agency. Active music publishers commonly solicit ad agencies to interest them in using their copyrights in advertisements.

A license to use an existing copyright in a radio or television commercial generally provides for payment of a flat fee to use it for a certain period of time—such as the customary 13-week cycle in broadcast advertising, with options for extended use—or on an annual basis.

Criteria used to determine the license fee for use of a preexisting copyright in a commercial include: popularity or prestige of the song, its importance to the campaign, budget of the campaign, market and competitive influences, the contract term, media to be used (i.e., radio and/or television), and whether the commercials are to be broadcast on a local or a national basis. A license usually provides for unlimited use of the copyright within the confines of the agreement during the license term.

License fees to use a song in a national media campaign vary widely. For example, radio jingle licenses that are one year in duration and provide for national airplay can range from $500 to $35,000 or more (for a local campaign, the fees are lower). Some copyrights have reportedly earned in excess of $100,000 for use in a one-year radio/television license.

Some musical compositions seem naturally to lend themselves to adaptation for advertising announcements. For example, hook lines (in original or adapted form) from the following songs have been used to promote the product or service indicated: "Ain't She Sweet"/ginger ale, "Anticipation"/catsup, "The Candy Man"/candy bar, "Feelings"/telephone service, and "Up, Up and Away"/airline.

See also RESIDUAL (TV AND RADIO COMMERCIALS AND PROGRAMS).

AFM. *See* AMERICAN FEDERATION OF MUSICIANS OF THE UNITED STATES AND CANADA.

AFTRA. *See* AMERICAN FEDERATION OF TELEVISION AND RADIO ARTISTS.

AGAC. *See* AMERICAN GUILD OF AUTHORS AND COMPOSERS.

AGMA. *See* AMERICAN GUILD OF MUSICAL ARTISTS.

AGVA. *See* AMERICAN GUILD OF VARIETY ARTISTS.

Agent. The artist's representative for employment. An agent, also referred to as a *booking, talent,* or *theatrical* agent, functions primarily in procuring performing engagements for his clients and setting up concert tours. The agent finds out when the artist is available to per-

Some Popular Jingles Through the Years

Hook Line	Product/Business Advertised
'When the values go up, up, up . . . and the prices go down, down, down"	clothing retailer
"N-E-S-T-L-É-S, Nestlé's makes the very best . . . chocolate"	powder mix
"Double your pleasure, double your fun, with double good, double good, Doublemint Gum"	chewing gum
"Chock Full o' Nuts is that heavenly coffee"	coffee
"Mmm, mmm, good . . . mmm, mmm, good . . . that's what Campbell's soups are, mmm, mmm, good"	soup
"Ask any mermaid you happen to see, What's the best tuna? Chicken of the Sea"	tuna fish
"Brylcreem . . . a little dab'll do ya"	hair cream
"Nothing goes with everything like Mueller's"	noodles
"Datsun . . . we are driven"	automobile
"Life Savers . . . a part of living"	mint

form and seeks bookings as well as considers proposals from purchasers of entertainment such as concert promoters and club talent buyers. He negotiates compensation and other contractual terms with the prospective employer, prepares engagement contracts, and arranges for payment. An agent who has exclusive representation also attempts to find employment for his client in other areas of the entertainment field. Agents often work for companies (agencies) that represent many music performers or have large rosters of clients from all areas of show business.

Agency Organization. Specialized music agencies are primarily concerned with obtaining concert engagements for music performers, while larger agencies deal actively in this and other areas of entertainment. The large, diversified talent agency° maintains several

° Examples are William Morris Agency and International Creative Management (ICM).

departments to accommodate all areas of client representation. These may include the following departments: film/motion pictures; television; commercials and merchandising; legitimate theater or "stage"; music: one-nighter department, variety department (location engagements); literary.

Agencies often attempt to obtain exclusive representation of a performer (i.e., representation in all areas of entertainment). In some large talent agencies, an agent who oversees a particular act is known as the *responsible agent*, or *RA*, for that act. The RA (who often has signed the artist) represents the artist by putting together tours for him, as well as representing the agency to the artist's personal manager. However, different agents in the same department might be responsible for the same act in different ways. For example, representation of an act to promoters, clubs, and colleges in different regions of the country may be under the auspices of different agents. But although these agents handle an assigned geographical area, they must still transfer offers to the responsible agent.

Interdepartmental communication and working together are important to operations in a large agency. For example, a music agent may not wish to limit the artist's employment to concert performances. He will communicate with agents in other departments, who may attempt to find employment or create opportunities for work in additional areas—on television, a talk show, variety show, series, or "special," or a film scoring assignment. Because a large agency may also represent television, motion picture, and stage producers, screenwriters, authors, and others, it is often in a position to get quicker and better results. Large talent agencies usually have offices in New York, Los Angeles, and a few other major U.S. and foreign cities.

Booking Concerts. The following summarizes a common concert booking procedure: An act decides to do a concert tour. The decision of which cities and venues an act will tour is usually made by the group, its personal manager, and its agent, and on many occasions, the record company (e.g., the artist development department). Factors to be considered include public demand for or drawing power of the act, the group's "market value," its experience, record sales, chart successes, current releases, what the act wants to accomplish, and the size of the venues and the markets.

In booking concert engagements at large venues, the agent deals with concert promoters (usually those with whom he has a prior working relationship). The agent contacts each concert promoter he hopes will produce a concert in a certain area, and if the promoter is interested, they have preliminary discussions regarding terms of the engagement, including the artist's guarantee and percentage, the promoter's percentage and estimated expenses, ticket prices, the venue where the act should perform, its seating capacity and stage size, and the date. The agent in turn brings the terms to the personal manager, who may approve or reject them. If the terms are acceptable, the promoter will then determine the availability of the hall for the particular night (if it is not available, he may book it for another date or try another suitable venue). Established promoters often have "deals" with particular halls, providing for priority in booking acts.

The agent will attempt to make a booking when and where it is advantageous for the artist, as well as obtain the highest pay rate the market will bear. He will be careful not to schedule a booking on the same night as an important sports event or a competing performance by another popular artist, or book, for instance, a rock act in a large hall in a "college town" during the summer months. Sometimes the agent will learn the agendas of the venues and have the promoters schedule the concert.

It is the agent's responsibility not only to know the basic mechanics of booking and promoting but also to be familiar with the various marketplaces and to oversee advertising, the structuring of ticket prices and sales. Most of the agent's "deal making" is done over the telephone.

Agencies have an "asking price" for an act, which the agent tries to obtain for concert performances. He will stress the value of the act to concert promoters in an effort to obtain that fee. The agency might also try to "package" acts from its roster. A lesser-known artist may thus become the opening or supporting act for a headliner.

Concert promoters generally remit a deposit to the agent of 10% to 50% (or more) of the stipulated guarantee or fee, which is held in escrow until the engagement. At the engagement, any balance due the artist is remitted directly to him or his representative (i.e., road manager or business manager). The agent's commission is subsequently remitted. (AFM regulations require the *musician* to receive payment for an engagement and then remit the commission to the agent.) When an artist is doing a concert tour, he may sometimes hold all the agent's commissions until completion of the tour. At that time the agency will draw up a statement indicating the money it has collected on the artist's behalf and what commissions above and beyond this amount are due it.

Union Franchises. Professional musicians and singers are normally members of one or more entertainment UNIONS. It is the policy of some of the unions to assist their members in securing the services of honest agents to protect them from unfair dealings (such as with respect to wage scales and commissions) and establish standards of performance for these representatives by preparing guidelines under which the agencies must operate. The business relations between performers and agencies are regulated by the "franchising" of agencies. A franchised agency signs a union agreement that establishes rules and regulations for the agency to abide by. While not all agencies operate as union franchises, the larger ones do. AFM, AFTRA, AGVA, and SAG all regulate the dealings of agents insofar as representation of their respective members is concerned. A union might restrict its members from engaging the services of an agency that is not franchised by the union and administer disciplinary action to those who do.

Commissions. Agents receive for their services commissions that normally range from 10% to 20% of the gross proceeds received. There are limits on these percentages set by the unions and these vary with each. Under the AFM Booking Agent Agreement, an agent may earn a maximum of 15% on all engagements whose duration is two or more consecutive days per week and 20% on single miscellaneous ("one-nighter") engagements; booking agents that have negotiated a Personal Management Agreement with members filed with and approved by the president's office may extract an additional 5% commission from the member for each engagement performed. AFTRA's agency contract sets a maximum commission of 10%, provided the performer receives a fee that is equivalent to at least scale *plus* 10%.

Agents of Serious Music Artists. The preceding discussion of agents pertains to those whose artists perform popular music. Performers of serious music are often represented by agents who may also act in the capacity of personal managers. A discussion of such representation is found in ARTIST MANAGEMENT AGENCY.

State Licensing of Agencies. The business operations of employment agencies in each state are regulated by law and theatrical, talent, and booking agencies are sometimes under the jurisdiction of state employment agency laws. States that regulate talent agency operations at this writing include California,

New York, Nevada, Michigan, Massachusetts, New Jersey, Pennsylvania, Maryland, Illinois, Ohio, Colorado, Delaware, and Arizona. Consequently, to operate legally in states with such laws, bona fide agencies must obtain a license and must comply with state law.

Airplay. There are various methods of promoting a record, but getting *airplay,* the broadcast of a recording by radio stations, is generally the most important. For a RECORD COMPANY, getting airplay is the responsibility of the promotion department.

In most cases, airplay is essential for sales of an artist's SINGLE and as a result the album in which it is contained (singles sell albums). However, because each year thousands of records are released, there is a highly competitive atmosphere in which promotion workers compete to get a record played by a station, added to its playlist, or rotated on a heavy basis. Many stations in primary markets will not even program a record until there is evidence that it is already a hit. Thus records are often "broken" in secondary and tertiary markets (*see* MARKET).

Airplay is especially vital in "breaking" a new artist, who will usually not attract large audiences at concerts until an identification has been established through exposure on the radio. Superstars and other established artists, however, may sell a large quantity of records without airplay, owing to a large devoted following and concert touring. In the long run, though, most artists cannot sustain their popularity and record sales without substantial airplay.

Airplay also results in performance royalties for songwriters and music publishers (*see* PERFORMING RIGHTS ORGANIZATION).

Album Cover. The graphic arts and the merchandising of records are inextricably bound to one another. Album covers function as artistic showpieces designed to attract consumer attention in the competitive arena that is the retail record store, so as to create favorable interest in albums and motivate purchases.

While other factors such as airplay, favorable regard for the artist, word of mouth, and record reviews, may be the chief determinants of people's deciding to purchase a specific product, it is hard to deny the influence of an attractive album cover. Modern techniques of packaging records, utilizing photographs and imaginative designs printed in full color on LP jackets which are covered with shrink wrap before being shipped, are a far cry from turn-of-the-century packaging, in which discs were merely inserted into kraft paper bags or envelopes. To comprehend the value of visual stimulation, one need only visit a record emporium and observe the attractive displays of full-color albums that line the aisles, causing them to be filled with browsers; or ask a consumer if the product he purchased was one that caught his eye or the one he intended to buy when he entered the store.

Record manufacturers have long recognized and utilized the merchandising power of record packaging and graphics to bring their product to the attention of consumers and boost their purchase. For the art, merchandising, and marketing departments of the label, album cover design is a creative art form, attended to with strategic planning. To sell their product, recording artists whose records do not receive adequate airplay or whose albums do not contain a hit single record have to depend on the album art and whatever promotional information it conveys. Of course, no album cover, regardless of how attractive it is, can substantially promote the sales of a poor recording.

Retail record merchants have likewise recognized that a record's aural appeal may not be enough to create sales and have arranged their floor plans, racks and bins, and point-of-purchase tools to attract consumers to as much product as possible and motivate them to purchase goods. The dealer desires to capitalize on "impulse buying."

As the record industry has developed new mediums and configurations for storing sound, graphic concepts, too, have evolved and kept pace. No matter what form, shape, or size sound-storing devices will take, one can be sure that they will be packaged creatively, aesthetically, and interestingly. For it is clear that sound and art combine to make the record industry the multibillion-dollar industry it is.

How an Album Cover Is Made. The general procedure for making an album cover is as follows:

1. A visual concept is decided on. This may be derived from or based upon the album title, the artist's name, the demographic target market, or such factors as whether the album is a CONCEPT ALBUM or a "live" album or whether the establishment of visual identification of the artist is being sought. It is also decided whether a photographic or an illustrative approach should be used, or a combination of both.

The concept may come from anywhere. Major recording artists and musical groups frequently create their own album concepts, with the help of friends, personal managers, professional free-lance designers they employ, and others. Lesser personages usually depend on the concept of the art director and/or record company designer (see 3 below). Often a graphic artist or an illustrator is given an idea from which to make a "thumbnail" sketch or layout.

2. Composite layouts are made. If an illustration is to be used, the illustrator will prepare a rough sketch of the concept. If a photograph is to be used, a few are selected and made into large, album-sized prints to indicate how the album design might look. At this point the lettering and type are decided on.

3. Approval is sought. Certain recording artists have contracts that provide for their right

of mutual approval of the album cover design. Lacking that, an artist is commonly extended the courtesy of approving the design. Should a conflict exist in such case, the final decision lies with the record company. Other artist contracts provide for a right of supplying art with mutual consent. Work on the album cover is usually done concurrently with the artist's recording sessions.

4. Artwork is completed. This might include retouching, lettering, and gathering of credits, courtesy approvals for guest artists, publishing information, etc.

5. Design is put into final mechanical form (camera-ready art).

6. Graphic material goes to a color separator (company that prepares color separations and proofs).

7. Negatives and proofs are transmitted to the jacketmaker (printer). He makes the four-color plates, and lithographs the jacket material in large flat sheets (covers are printed "several up" on each sheet).

8. The sheets are cut into individual jacket units, which are die cut, scored, folded, and glued, forming the jacket.

9. Finished jackets come off jacketmaking machines, are boxed, and are shipped to record pressing plants.

10. At plants, records are individually inspected, are put into sleeves and inserted in jackets, are shrink wrapped, and are then ready for distribution.

Four-color Separation. Most album covers are printed in four colors: red, yellow, blue (the primary colors), and black. Combined, they can produce virtually any color (or tint) in the rainbow. Albums are less frequently printed in black and white, although it is not uncommon for the album front to be printed in full color and the back in black and white.

Album Package. An album cover consists of artwork and/or photographs and printed information. Printed information may include titles of selections, credit lines, liner notes, and any of the information described in the Copy Worksheet for Albums.

The album cover is printed on either a "coated sulfate board" .018 to .022 inches thick, or a paper "slick" mounted to cardboard. Album jackets vary slightly in dimension according to manufacturer and origin (i.e., foreign), but are generally 12¼ by 12¼ inches (*see* ALBUM JACKET).

Liner Notes. Annotations appearing on the back cover of an album. Liner notes pertain to some aspect of the album (e.g., the composers). Liner notes are used infrequently today except on the back covers of classical music albums and some country, jazz, and blues albums.

Album Cover Information. Certain information normally appears on the covers of an album (front and back) and on its spine. "Copy worksheets" which indicate what information should appear, are commonly used by record company LP production departments in the preparation of album covers. A sample worksheet appears on the facing page.

See also COPYRIGHT NOTICE; COPYRIGHT REGISTRATION CLASSIFICATION SYSTEM; COPYRIGHT REGISTRATION OF A SOUND RECORDING; TRADEMARKS.

Album Cut. A "band" or a recorded selection contained in an album. A "cut" from an album may be subsequently released as a single if it is believed to have commercial potential. (In some cases, selections are issued as singles prior to the release of the album.) Albums of popular music commonly have from 6 to 12 cuts, or tracks. While many radio stations program only hit singles, cuts from various types of albums are played on stations with AOR (ALBUM-ORIENTED ROCK) and other formats.

Album Jacket. A storage container and protective device for disc recordings, an album jacket consists of front and back covers and a spine. The spine is printed with information which identifies the record when only the spine is visible, such as during shelf storage with other albums. Two-disc record sets are packaged in double-pocket gatefold albums.

American Arbitration Association. *See* ARBITRATION.

American Federation of Labor and Congress of Industrial Organizations (AFL-CIO). A voluntary federation of over 100 national and international labor unions in the United States. The 100-plus affiliated unions of AFL-CIO are made up of more than 60,000 local unions, which conduct the day-to-day relationships with their members' employers. Each AFL-CIO member union is autonomous and conducts its affairs as determined by its members, establishes its own economic policies, carries on its own contract negotiations, and sets its own dues. Local unions seek to improve wages and working conditions for workers, support legislation that will aid workers, establish relations between employees and employers through COLLECTIVE BARGAINING, and ensure compliance with contract terms by employees and employers.

The major AFL-CIO performer unions include Actors' Equity Association, American Federation of Television and Radio Artists, American Guild of Musical Artists, American Guild of Variety Artists, Hebrew Actors Union, Inc., Italian Actors Union, Screen Actors Guild, Screen Extras Guild—(all of which receive their jurisdictional charters from ASSOCIATED ACTORS AND ARTISTES OF AMERICA (FOUR A's)—and American Federation of Musicians of the United States and Canada.

AFL-CIO was established on December 5, 1955, by the merger of the American Federation of Labor and the Congress of Industrial Organizations.

American Federation of Musicians of the United States and Canada (AFM). Labor union that represents U.S. and Canadian in-

COPY WORKSHEET FOR ALBUMS

<u>FRONT COVER</u>

ARTIST NAME:

ALBUM TITLE:

CATALOGUE #:   COMPANY LOGO:

<u>SPINE</u>

CATALOGUE #:   COMPANY NAME:

ARTIST NAME:

ALBUM TITLE:

PRICE CODE:

<u>BACK COVER</u>

COPYRIGHT NOTICE: © ℗

ADDITIONAL LOGO: CATALOGUE #:

INTERNATIONAL NUMBER(S):
(50% of catalogue #)

Anti piracy line: 6 pt. ALL RIGHTS RESERVED. UNAUTHORIZED DUPLICATION JS A VIOLATION
                          OF APPLICABLE LAWS.

RIAA Seal and Copy: 6 pt. THIS RECORD HAS BEEN ENGINEERED AND MANUFACTURED IN ACCORDANCE
                            WITH STANDARDS DEVELOPED BY THE RECORDING INDUSTRY ASSOCIATION
                            OF AMERICA, INC., A NON-PROFIT ORGANIZATION DEDICATED TO THE
                            BETTERMENT OF RECORDED MUSIC AND LITERATURE.

Polydor logo

MANUFACTURED AND MARKETED BY POLYDOR INCORPORATED, 810 SEVENTH AVENUE, NEW YORK, NY 10019.
DISTRIBUTED BY POLYGRAM DISTRIBUTION, INC.

Printed in U.S.A.

ALSO AVAILABLE ON 8-TRACK (   ) AND CASSETTE(   )

strumentalists, orchestras, leaders, contractors, arrangers, orchestrators, copyists, and orchestra librarians in the following fields of work: club dates, lounge dates, and other casual engagements, recordings, jingles, radio, television, motion pictures, theater, and symphonic and concert presentations. Its jurisdiction extends throughout the United States, Canada, Guam, Puerto Rico, and the Virgin Islands.

Eligibility for Membership. Membership in AFM is open to musicians and other individuals as stated above who are citizens of the United States or Canada; aliens who have filed citizenship papers or are allowed by government decree to work in the U.S. or Canada; foreign faculty members and foreign students affiliated with or attending an accredited U.S. college or university who have received permission from the union's International Executive Board; and U.S. or Canadian residents who do not intend to become citizens of either country but have received permission from the International Executive Board.

Affiliation and Organization. AFM is affiliated with AFL-CIO. AFM's constitution and bylaws establish and define its organization.

AFM consists of local unions (there are several hundred) and an International Union, the latter comprised of elected representatives from the locals. A member's local union and the International Union both determine policy that plays an important part in his career.

Local Unions. A local union is a group of musicians that has been granted a charter to operate within a specified geographical area. Each local conducts its own local affairs, subject to the rules and standards of the parent international organization. Local unions have jurisdiction over wage scales and working conditions in local areas of employment such as cafés, clubs, hotels, and local (non-network) radio and TV stations. Thus UNION SCALE may vary in different localities for these areas of employment. A local's officers and governing

board are elected by its membership.

International Union. Normally, AFM holds a yearly international convention, at which elected delegates from locals enact new policies or change old ones, and also elect international officers and members of the International Executive Board. The officers and the Board are responsible for administering AFM, resolving interlocal conflicts, and negotiating labor agreements for the entire AFM membership in the following fields: phonograph records, electrical transcriptions, network radio and television, TV videotape, educational TV, commercial announcements; theatrical motion pictures, TV films and nontheatrical non-TV documentary and industrial films. Hence union scale in these areas is uniform everywhere throughout AFM's jurisdiction.

Fees and Dues. Members are required to pay an initiation fee to the local they join, a federation initiation fee to the national, and periodic dues as lawfully prescribed by their locals. Local chapters pay an initial charter fee plus Federation Per Capita Dues on a quarterly basis at a prescribed rate.

A local may require any traveling AFM member who is not a member of such local and performs within its jurisdiction to pay to it a percentage of his scale wage earned. This levy is known as "work dues."

Union Funds. AFM makes available to its members the following funds:

AFM-EPW Fund—Employers in fields of work where the International Union is the bargaining agent, such as phonograph records, motion pictures, and others (see above), make contributions into AFM's Employers Pension and Welfare Fund. This fund was established in 1959 and is administered by a Joint Industry-Union Board of Trustees.

Music Performance Trust Fund—Recording companies make semiannual payments to this fund, based on their record sales. These proceeds, which are administered by an independent trustee, are used exclusively to present admission-free public concerts in the U.S. and Canada at such places as parks, hospitals, and schools. This fund was created in 1948.

Phonograph Record Manufacturers' Special Payments Fund—Record companies make semiannual payments into this fund (based on the number of records sold each year), which is subsequently distributed to musicians based on their scale wages earned in the phonograph record industry. Each musician is credited on a calendar-year basis for 5 consecutive years.

Recording Session Agreements. The working relationship between AFM and its membership with individuals and companies in the recording field is established by the Phonograph Record Labor Agreement and the Special Payments Fund Agreement, which are periodically revised. *See* AMERICAN FEDERATION OF MUSICIANS PHONOGRAPH RECORD LABOR AGREEMENT/SPECIAL PAYMENTS FUND AGREEMENT.

History. The American Federation of Musicians was founded on October 19, 1896, when a trade union charter was drafted at a convention held in Indianapolis. Through the years AFM has continually negotiated for higher wages and more beneficial terms of employment for its members. For many years now it has been the largest entertainment union in the world. In 1980, AFM had 604 locals and 304,000 members.

See also UNIONS.

American Federation of Musicians Phonograph Record Labor Agreement/Special Payments Fund Agreement. In the recording industry, there are industry-wide agreements between bona fide companies which employ the services of performers and others for making sound recordings, and the unions representing these participants. These agreements are negotiated by COLLECTIVE BARGAINING and provide for minimum scale wages and other terms of employment for union members.

The agreement AFM has with the recording industry (i.e., record companies and production companies) is known as the Phonograph Record Labor Agreement/Special Payments Fund Agreement, and it contains the basic contractual terms under which its members make master recordings.° (It also applies to recording artists who are instrumentalists unless they have negotiated contracts with their labels containing more favorable terms.) The agreement contains three exhibits: Exhibit A (Minimum Wages and Other Working Conditions), Exhibit B (Pension Welfare Funds), and Exhibit C (Phonograph Record Manufacturers' Special Payments Fund Agreement). The agreement is periodically revised (generally every 2 years), primarily with respect to wage scales and allied financial benefits. This entry examines the basic terms of the labor agreement AFM has with the recording industry.

Basic Provisions

Obligation. The signatory promises "fully and faithfully to perform each and every term, condition, and covenant on its part" pursuant to the agreement.

Scope of Agreement. The agreement covers and relates to AFM members who perform or are employed as instrumental musicians, leaders, contractors, arrangers, orchestrators, or copyists, in the making of recordings in the United States or Canada or territory or possession of either.

Union Security. Any person employed by the company for the purpose of making sound recordings who is a member of the union in good standing or who is not a member on the execution date of the agreement between AFM and the company, must remain or become a member in good standing. Employees of the company hired on or after the signing of the agreement for the purpose of making recordings must within 30 days following the

---

° Record companies and production companies pay a fee in becoming signatories to the agreement.

beginning of employment, become or remain members in good standing.

Scale. The company must pay persons covered by the agreement the minimum union scale as provided in Exhibit A (see below).

Releases. Each month the company must advise AFM of all recordings it released during the previous month and their serial numbers. If it assigns, leases, or licenses any master record to another party, it must report this to the union.

Audits. AFM may periodically and during business hours have its duly authorized agents examine and audit the company's records and accounts concerning all transactions involving the company's sale of phonograph records.

Music Acquired or Licensed. A record company may not manufacture or distribute any records or tapes from masters acquired or taken by license from any other person, firm, or corporation unless the music was recorded under a Phonograph Record Labor Agreement and the musicians, leaders, contractors, copyists, and arrangers received wages not less than scale. The company may satisfy this union requirement by incorporating in such an acquisition or licensing agreement a representation and warranty by the sellor or licensor (which the company shall guarantee if the sellor or licensor was not a party to the Phonograph Record Labor Agreement with AFM at the time the recording was made) that such music does not come within the terms of the agreement or that the requirements of the agreement have been satisfied.

Exhibit A (Minimum Wages and Other Working Conditions). Exhibit A contains separate provisions for two collective groups: (1) instrumentalists, leaders, and contractors; and (2) arrangers, orchestrators, and copyists. Following are terms that apply to the first group with respect to making nonsymphonic and symphonic recordings.

Nonsymphonic Recordings: Basic Session. With respect to the making of nonsymphonic master recordings, there is a minimum call

Basic Regular Session of 3 hours, which entitles instrumentalists, leaders, and contractors to minimum wages as set forth in the agreement. There are overtime rates for Regular Sessions in half-hour or quarter-hour units. Premium rates for the basic session are as follows: 1½ times the basic session and overtime rates to be paid for all hours of recording between midnight and 8 A.M., and after 1 P.M. on Saturdays and Sundays; 2 times the basic session and overtime rates to be paid for all hours of recording in the United States on New Year's Day, Washington's Birthday, Memorial Day, Independence Day, Labor Day, Thanksgiving, and Christmas; in Canada, for New Year's Day, Good Friday, Easter Monday, Victoria Day, Dominion Day, Labour Day, Thanksgiving, and Christmas.

During a basic session, there may be produced not more than 15 minutes of finished recorded music. In a session where sweetening (instrumental performances added to music recorded at a previous session) is performed, not more than 4 single record sides or 4 segments of long- or extended-play records may be sweetened.

SPECIAL SESSION. There may be a special session of 1½ hours during which there may be recorded a maximum of 2 sides containing not more than 7½ minutes of recorded music. Musicians must be previously notified regarding the status of the special session, otherwise it shall be deemed a regular session.

CONTRIBUTION. The company is required to contribute to the Health and Welfare Fund of the AFM local a specified sum of money for each AFM member who performs on the session.

Symphonic Recordings: Basic Session. With respect to records recorded by symphonic orchestras, there is a Basic Regular Session of either 3 or 4 hours, during which the playing time may not exceed an average of 40 minutes for each hour (with an average rest period of 20 minutes for each hour). No more than an average of 7½ minutes of finished recorded music may be used from each half-hour segment of a recording session (including all overtime periods). There is a specified minimum scale per sideman for both a 3- and a 4-hour basic session; overtime rates are in half-hour and quarter-hour units. There are premium rates for recording during certain hours, days, and holidays, as stated above. Members of the symphony orchestra not called to the engagement must be paid for at least the first 2 hours of the basic session at a specified rate.

LEADERS AND CONTRACTORS. At each session (nonsymphonic or symphonic), one person is to be designated as a leader. For any session in which 12 or more sidemen are employed, there must be a contractor, who must be in attendance and who may or may not be one of the sidemen at the session. The leader and the contractor receive double the applicable sideman's scale.

DOUBLING. When a musician doubles, or plays more than one instrument, he receives an additional 20% of the applicable session and/or overtime rate for the first double (or different instrument) and an additional 15% of such rate for each double thereafter.

CANCELLATION. A session, once arranged, cannot be canceled, postponed, or otherwise rescheduled less than 7 days prior to the date of the session. In the event of an emergency, however, this may be done if the approval of the Federation president is obtained.

ROYALTY MUSICIANS. The Phonograph Record Labor Agreement provides that any "royalty artist" is to receive the basic session and overtime wages for the first session at which he performs. A "royalty artist" is a musician who either records pursuant to a recording contract which provides a minimum royalty of 3% of the suggested retail list price of records sold (less customary deductions) or is a member of (not a sideman with) a recognized self-contained group.

Exhibit B (Pension and Welfare Funds). Signatories of AFM's agreement are required to contribute an amount equal to 10% of the employees' scale wages paid under the agreement into a pension fund.

Exhibit C (Special Payments Fund Agreement). Record companies that are signatories to the contract are required to make semi-annual payments into the union's Special Payments Fund on the basis of the number of records sold each year. Payment is to be made within specified time periods to the Administrator of the Fund and is computed as follows: 0.6% of the manufacturer's retail list price of each record sold for those that don't exceed $3.79 in price; 0.58% for those that exceed $3.79 in price; and 0.5% of the manufacturer's suggested list price for wire or tape recordings. Addendum A of Exhibit C sets forth payment rates and provides for the deduction of certain "allowances" by record companies in calculating payments to the Administrator.

Allowances. The manufacturer pays on 100% of net sales, with certain allowances provided for: a packaging deduction of 15% of the suggested list price for disc records and 25% of the suggested retail list price for tapes and cartridges. There is also an allowance for "free" records, tapes, and cartridges actually distributed of up to 20% of the total sold. With respect to record/tape clubs, if any, the allowance for "free" and "bonus" records, tapes, and cartridges actually distributed may be up to 50% of the total distribution; as for records and tapes distributed by clubs in excess thereof, the company pays the full rate on 50% of the excess of such "free" and "bonus" records and tapes.

Length of Provision. Special payments for records and tapes made and sold pursuant to the agreement take place for a period of 10 years, terminating at the end of the 10th calendar year after which commercial records are first released for sale. For example, if phonograph records produced from a master record made pursuant to the Phonograph Record Labor Agreement (August 1980) were first released for sale in September 1980, payments are due for all sales of the record that take place during the calendar years 1980–89 inclusive.

Distribution of Phonograph Record Manufacturers' Special Payments Fund. The Administrator, after deducting administrative expenses, distributes this fund to all sidemen, leaders, contractors, and music preparation members who have participated in recording sessions, in proportion to scale wages earned in the industry per calendar year for the most recent 5-consecutive-year period.

There is a formula for allocating the distribution to each participant, which is illustrated by the following example: Suppose a musician employed in recording sessions earned scale wages of $10,000 each year from 1977 to 1981. The fraction of the distribution payable to that musician would be calculated as follows:

```
1981—$10,000 × 100% = $10,000
1980—$10,000 ×  80% = $ 8,000
1979—$10,000 ×  60% = $ 6,000
1978—$10,000 ×  40% = $ 4,000
1977—$10,000 ×  20% = $ 2,000
                       $30,000
```

This sum ($30,000 in the example) is referred to as the "extended scale wage." Now, suppose again that in 1981, $17 million was paid into the fund based on industry sales of records and tapes, and after expenses were deducted from the fund there remained $15 million. Also, assume the total "extended scale wages" earned by all participating musicians (from 1977 to 1981) was $93 million. The following formula will determine the "distribution percentage":

$$\frac{\text{Amount to be distributed after administrative expenses}}{\text{Total Extended Scale Wage}} \text{ or } \frac{\$15 \text{ million}}{\$93 \text{ million}} = 16.12903\%$$

This percentage (16.12903%) times the "extended scale wage" gives the participant his "royalty" or "musician's share of the fund." In accordance with the example, then, the musician would receive 16.12903% of $30,000, or $4,838.71.

American Federation of Television and Radio Artists (AFTRA).
Labor union that represents performers, other than exclusive instrumentalists, who work in the fields of radio, television (videotape), and phonograph recordings. With respect to phonograph recordings, AFTRA performers include actors, singers, announcers, sportscasters, narrators, and sound effects artists. The union's jurisdiction extends throughout the United States, its territories and possessions.

Affiliation. AFTRA is affiliated with AMERICAN FEDERATION OF LABOR AND CONGRESS OF INDUSTRIAL ORGANIZATIONS (AFL-CIO) and is a branch of ASSOCIATED ACTORS AND ARTISTES OF AMERICA (FOUR A's).

Fees and Dues. In order to join AFTRA and remain a member in good standing, a performer must pay an initiation fee and regular dues.

History. AFTRA was officially formed in September 1952 by the merger of two organizations—the American Federation of Radio Artists (AFRA), founded in 1937 by George Heller to represent radio artists, and the Television Authority (TVA). In 1980, AFTRA had 38 locals and approximately 40,000 members.

See also AMERICAN FEDERATION OF TELEVISION AND RADIO ARTISTS NATIONAL CODE OF FAIR PRACTICE FOR PHONOGRAPH RECORDINGS; UNIONS.

American Federation of Television and Radio Artists National Code of Fair Practice for Phonograph Recordings.
The agreement between AFTRA and the recording industry for making master recordings is known as the National Code of Fair Practice for Phonograph Recordings. This is a national, uniform agreement providing minimum scale and oth-

er terms of employment for AFTRA members (singers, narrators, etc.) who make sound recordings. It is renegotiated periodically (usually every 3 years), primarily with respect to session fees and allied financial benefits. AFTRA's code is determined by COLLECTIVE BARGAINING between representatives of AFTRA (usually the national executive secretary and the executive secretaries of the New York, Los Angeles, and Nashville locals) and representatives of the record companies (normally attorneys who are labor relations executives with the companies). This entry examines the basic provisions of the National Code of Fair Practice for Phonograph Recordings.

Basic Provisions

AFTRA Representation. The company recognizes AFTRA as the exclusive collective bargaining agency for all artists engaged by the company to make recordings who fall under AFTRA's jurisdiction.

Union Security. Artists who are employed by the company must be members of AFTRA or become members within 30 days of their first recording engagement.

Arbitration. All disputes and controversies between AFTRA and the record company or an AFTRA member and the employer as covered by the code may be submitted for ARBITRATION to be conducted under the Voluntary Labor Arbitration Rules of the American Arbitration Association.

Minimum Scale. An employer is obliged to pay AFTRA members minimum rates of compensation for their performing services on phonograph recordings as set forth in the agreement. Scales for soloists, duos, and group singers are specified fees per hour or per side, whichever is greater. (The scale diminishes as the size of the group increases.)

Compensation Deadline. Artists are to be paid in legal tender of the United States within 21 calendar days after their performance. There are penalties for late payments which accrue for each day's delinquency up to 30 days (excluding Saturday, Sundays, and designated holidays); thereafter, AFTRA or the member may, by registered mail, give written notice of nonpayment to the company. If full payment is not made within 10 working days thereafter, the penalty payment resumes on the 11th day and continues without limitation.

AFTRA Distribution. Companies are to render session payments with a statement specifying the name of the employer, the dates of performance, the amount of payment and of each deduction, and all other pertinent information that may be necessary for tax deduction. Checks are to be made payable in the performer's name and mailed to the local AFTRA office for distribution. AFTRA then mails these checks to members.

Contractors. An AFTRA contractor is required on all engagements of group singers consisting of 3 or more.

Reports. The contractor must furnish AFTRA and the company with a Phonograph Record Sessions Report (countersigned by an authorized agent of the company), for each individual recording session. This report is to give full and specific information sufficient to permit computation of the performer's fee with respect to the services rendered by the performer and the gross fee paid. The form shall be as set forth on AFTRA's Schedules A and B.

Artist Contracts. Companies that enter into contracts with artists are bound by all the terms and provisions of AFTRA's National Code of Fair Practice, and where there are any inconsistencies between the contract and the code, the code prevails, except where a contract provides more favorable terms, compensations, and conditions for the artist, in which case the contract prevails. The AFTRA code also requires the company to furnish, at least semiannually, royalty statements to artists regarding sales of units.

Purchased Master Recordings. AFTRA requires signatories to the code that purchase or lease master recordings to obtain from the sellor or lessor a warranty and representation that all artists whose performances are embodied on the recording have been paid the minimum rates specified in the code and that all due payments to the AFTRA Pension and Welfare Funds have been made. Proof of such warranty and representation when masters are purchased is to be supplied to AFTRA by the company on the union's Form D. In the absence of a warranty, the company may furnish Schedule A, listing performers and payment by the company. If the sellor or lessor was not a signatory to an AFTRA Phonograph Recording Code at the time the recording was made or when purchased or leased by the company, the company is then "obligated to make the minimum scale payment required together with any applicable contributions thereon, to the AFTRA Pension and Welfare Funds."

AFTRA Pension and Welfare Funds. Recording companies must make payment to the AFTRA Pension and Welfare Funds. Under the 1980–83 code, this payment is an amount equal to 8½% of the gross compensation actually paid to an artist by the company for services rendered. The term "gross compensation" includes, but is not limited to, salaries, earnings, royalties, fees, advances, guarantees, bonuses, profit participation, bonds, and shares of stock. The payment (8½%), however, is limited to the first $100,000 of gross compensation paid to the artist in any calendar year regardless of time or method of payment. Such funds or trust funds are administered under the AFTRA Pension and Wefare Funds Agreement and Declaration of Trust, dated November 16, 1954, as ratified. The welfare benefits include death, accidental death, dismemberment, hospitalization, surgical expense, medical expense, and temporary disability. The plan of pension benefits is subject to the approval of the Internal Revenue Service.

Live Performance Recordings. When an artist's live concert at such locations as concerts and nightclubs (but excluding festivals and original cast albums) is recorded, the artist is to be paid an amount equal to a minimum call of 2 hours for all performances recorded in a 24-hour period, whether or not any sides are released. If the recording is released, the artist is to receive the difference, if any, between the amount he received and the applicable minimum scale payment.

Contingent Scale Payments. Appendix A of the code provides that in addition to session wages, certain supplementary ("contingent scale") payments are due to artists who are not under royalty contracts to employers if the recordings in which they performed reach certain plateaus with respect to sales. Such payments expire 10 years after the date of the recording's first release, in any format. Contingent scale payments apply only to net sales of albums (LPs, cassette or cartridge tapes) or singles in the U.S. and in retail outlets, with an allowance for reasonable reserves for returns and excluding units distributed as "free" goods or promotional goods. Sales through record clubs, mail order, and premium are also excluded. For a recording released in an album to qualify, it must have not been previously released in an album format; for singles, the side must have not been previously released as part of a single.

Amount of Contingent Scale Payments. With respect to albums, qualifying artists are to receive a contingent scale payment equal to the product of the aggregate of the applicable minimum scale payable to such artist, multiplied by the applicable contingent scale factor (excluding hourly, premium, and multiple-tracking payment). The contingent scale factors under the 1980–83 AFTRA National Code of Fair Practice for Phonograph Recordings (subject to change at the expiration of this contract) are as follows:

Type	Unit sales	Factor
cast albums	320,000	40%
	460,000	30%
	600,000	30%
	740,000	30%
all other albums	157,000	50%
	275,000	50%
	400,000	50%
	525,000	50%
	675,000	50%
	1,000,000	50%
singles	500,000	33⅓%
	600,000	33⅓%
	750,000	33⅓%
	850,000	33⅓%
	1,000,000	33⅓%
	1,500,000	33⅓%

Example. A group singer who sings on 10 sides (earning a scale wage of $38 per side, or $380) put on an album selling up to 525,000 units would earn 200% of the total session fee, or $760. Sales of over 1,000,000 units would entitle each nonroyalty performer to an additional 100% of the minimum scale.

American Guild of Authors and Composers (AGAC).
A membership organization comprised of songwriters, AGAC serves to represent, protect, and strengthen the rights of composers and lyricists in their dealings with music publishers, and offers various services to its members with respect to their songs and catalogs.

The AGAC Contract. AGAC is noted for its Popular Songwriters Contract, which it provides and urges its members to use in signing music publishing contracts. This contract was written with the view of giving songwriters the basic minimum benefits and protection to which they are deemed entitled. The AGAC contract, first issued in 1933 and updated and revised a number of times since, was revised in 1978 to accommodate changes from the Copyright Act of 1976.

Services. AGAC offers its members various services, including the following:

Royalty Collection Service—AGAC collects a writer's royalties from all publishers with whom he has entered into contract, remits this income to him, and makes periodic investigations of those publishers' books. AGAC will send the member a year-end royalty report for tax purposes. The organization charges a commission of 5% for the first $20,000 collected and 0.5% on the next $80,000.

Copyright Renewal Service—With respect to pre-1978 compositions, AGAC can inform a writer when his copyrights are due for renewal at the Copyright Office. Notification takes place a year in advance of the renewal date, and for a small fee, AGAC will file the renewal application for the writer.

Catalog Administration Plan—For members who publish their own songs, AGAC can administer their catalogs. This administration service does not include any ownership participation in the catalog on behalf of AGAC or exploitation or promotion work. The service is also available for the catalogs of deceased members (Estates Administration Plan). AGAC performs this service on a commission basis.

Catalog Financial Evaluation—AGAC can provide a realistic idea of the worth of a song catalog (there is a fee for this). Financial estimates are often needed for estate evaluations, gift tax purposes, and renewal negotiations.

Other services include sponsoring weekly "Askapro" sessions, workshops, and scholarships programs.

Membership. There are three types of membership in AGAC—regular, estate, and associate. Associate membership is available to anyone who has not had a song published. There are annual dues for each category.

History. AGAC was founded in 1931 by three prominent songwriters—Edgar Leslie, Billy Rose, and George Meyer—who desired a standard contract for songwriters. This was not the first attempt to organize composers and lyricists (four others failed), but it became the first successful one. Joined by 50 other writers, they created the first basic minimum songwriters' contract in America, and within 6 months the Songwriters' Protective Association (SPA) was recognized as the official advocate for its members. The name was changed in 1958, and in subsequent years AGAC has continued to enforce the rights of writers with respect to music publishing contracts, copyright legislation, and other areas. By 1980 there were approximately 4,000 members in AGAC. AGAC has offices in New York and Hollywood.

See SONGWRITER/MUSIC PUBLISHER CONTRACT.

American Guild of Musical Artists (AGMA).

Labor union that represents concert and operatic vocal soloists, choristers, instrumental soloists, dancers, dance groups, actors, narrators, stage directors, and stage managers in the professional entertainment fields of grand opera, ballet, dance, concert, recital, and oratorio. AGMA's jurisdiction extends throughout the United States, its dependencies and possessions.

Eligibility for Membership. Any person who has performed, who performs, or intends to perform within the jurisdiction of AGMA is eligible for membership.

Dues. AGMA members are required to pay dues, which are scaled in accordance with income earned while working in a field under AGMA's jurisdiction. To ascertain their dues, members file a report with the union's national office, stating the gross income earned for employment under AGMA's jurisdiction during the previous calendar year. There is no initiation fee.

Affiliation. AGMA is a branch of ASSOCIATED ACTORS AND ARTISTES OF AMERICA (FOUR A's) and is affiliated with AFL-CIO.

Agreements. AGMA makes legally binding contracts with employers and managers (known as Basic Agreements) which: establish minimum compensations; limit rehearsal hours; limit the number of years a manager may sign an artist; provide for overtime compensation, sick leave, and comfortable travel accommodations; set up a maximum percentage that a manager may charge as a commission; stipulate that the manager guarantees the artist minimum earnings; provide that no commissions will reduce the artist's earnings below AGMA's minimum fee; entitle the concert artist to an accounting by the manager; and require the employer to post security deposits as a guarantee that he will abide by the terms of the Basic Agreement.

The Basic Agreement contains provisions which the individual members of each company (group of artists) decide upon before AGMA begins to bargain with the employer. Negotiations are carried on by AGMA, and before any final agreement is signed, the members must again approve the terms on which an agreement has been reached by AGMA with the employer or manager.

The agreements establish maximum percentages managers may charge as commissions for bookings in the various concert fields, provided that no commissions will reduce the artist's earnings below the AGMA minimum fee. Under the Basic Agreements, the maximum commission concert artists' managers may charge with regard to bookings of singers is as follows: 20% of earnings for concerts, 15% for organized-audience concerts (i.e., community and civic engagements), and 10% for services rendered in opera, ballet, and concert. These commission rates generally apply to engagements of AGMA instrumentalists also. Concert artists normally receive a flat fee for concert bookings, as opposed to earning a percentage of the box office receipts, as many popular musical artists do. Fees can vary widely, depending on the artist, and may range from $1,000 to $50,000 per performance (the highest fees are usually paid to large groups, such as symphony orchestras).

Most Basic Agreements with employers and managers are not national in scope. The minimum compensation AGMA members earn varies from city to city or employer to employer throughout the United States and is dependent upon the resources of each city, its cultural atmosphere, and the length of operation of a local organization. There is, however, one uniform situation:

Touring dance companies are normally competitors for the same job (an exception would be a resident dance company, such as the New York City Ballet). AGMA therefore has a uniform agreement with the North American Ballet Association, which represents the employers of touring dance companies, including the San Francisco, Pennsylvania, Boston, Houston, and Dallas ballets. In addition, there are agreements with major dance companies, including American Ballet Theatre, New York City Ballet, and the Joffrey Ballet.

History. AGMA was founded as an independent organization on March 11, 1936, in hope that it would eliminate unfair practices detrimental to musical artists. Its founding members included Jascha Heifetz, Deems Taylor, Eva Guathier, Alma Gluck, and Lawrence Tibbett. Other early members were George Gershwin, Fred Waring, Efrem Zimbalist, Paul Whiteman, and Lily Pons.

AGMA received its charter from Four A's on August 30, 1937, and was granted exclusive jurisdiction in the fields stated above. Initially, it was merged with the Grand Opera Artists Association, the organization that previously held the charter for the opera field, and in 1938, it absorbed the Grand Opera Choral Alliance, which had represented opera choristers under Four A's charter. Through the years it has made numerous gains in promoting the common aims and interests of these artists. In 1980, the union had approximately 4,500 members. AGMA's headquarters is in New York.

See also ARTIST MANAGEMENT AGENCY; UNIONS.

American Guild of Variety Artists (AGVA).

Labor union that represents singers, dancers, comedians, skaters, jugglers, magicians, and other variety performers who work in nightclubs, cabarets, music halls, stadiums, theaters (non-Broadway), at carnivals, fairs, private clubs, mountain and seashore resorts, banquets, on boats, and in similar venues where there is live entertainment. AGVA's jurisdiction extends throughout the United States and Canada.

Eligibility for Membership. Membership in AGVA is open to any person who is engaged as an artist in the variety entertainment field or who demonstrates to the union's executive board an intention to become engaged in such field or who has been employed by the union as a field representative for at least 24 consecutive months. There are two classes of membership—senior and junior—the latter being for those under 18 years of age (who are ineligible to run for office). There is also a category for honorary members, who have no voice or vote.

Fees and Dues. There is an initiation fee and periodic dues are payable by each AGVA member.

Affiliation. AGVA is a branch of ASSOCIATED ACTORS AND ARTISTES OF AMERICA (FOUR A's) and is affiliated with AFL-CIO.

Agreements. AGVA is the exclusive COLLECTIVE BARGAINING representative of its members for negotiating and contracting with employers, operators, agents, nightclub owners, managers, impresarios, producers, and packagers.

Funds and Plans. AGVA has established (as

separate legal entities) a Welfare Trust Fund and a Sick and Relief Fund (East and West). To be eligible to receive the benefits of the Welfare Trust Fund, a member must meet certain requirements. All members of AGVA, active or inactive, in need of assistance may receive benefits from the Sick and Relief Funds.

Awards Program. Since 1972, the union has sponsored the *AGVA Entertainer of the Year Award Show*, which is broadcast nationwide over network television.

History. AGVA was founded in 1939. In 1980, there were approximately 5,000 members. AGVA's headquarters is in New York and there are regional offices in certain major cities throughout the United States and Canada.

See also UNIONS.

American Society of Composers, Authors and Publishers (ASCAP).

A PERFORMING RIGHTS ORGANIZATION, ASCAP licenses on a nonexclusive basis to users of music the nondramatic public performance rights of the copyrighted works of its members and affiliated foreign performing rights societies.

ASCAP, formed in 1914, is a nonprofit unincorporated membership association owned and run by its members—composers, lyricists, and music publishers. All receipts, less its overhead, are distributed to its members and affiliated foreign societies. ASCAP policy is set by its board of directors, comprised of 12 writers and 12 publishers elected respectively by the society's writer and publisher members. The society's officers, all of whom are directors, except for counsel, are elected by the board.

As a performing rights organization, ASCAP distributes "performance royalties" to its members when their works are included in the ASCAP sample survey. ASCAP's Weighting Rules for awarding credits for performances and its formulas and rules for distributing royalties to writer and publisher members are set forth in a consent decree, which is under the jurisdiction of the U.S. District Court for the Southern District of New York, and are reviewed not only by the society's staff and outside experts, but by the Department of Justice and by court-appointed Special Distribution Advisers, who regularly report to the Federal Court and the Society's members.

The consent decree also provides a mechanism by which a music user who feels a license fee quoted by ASCAP is unreasonable can ask the court for the Southern District of New York to determine a reasonable fee.

A user may obtain a license from ASCAP merely by submitting a written application, upon which the society must then advise the applicant in writing of the license fee it believes reasonable. A mandatory 60-day negotiation period follows, during which either the user or ASCAP may ask the court to fix an interim license fee. That fee is subject to retroactive adjustment when a reasonable fee is determined.

If negotiations are unsuccessful, the user (but not ASCAP) may then apply to the court for the determination of a reasonable license fee. In any such proceeding, the burden of proof is on ASCAP to establish the reasonableness of the fee quoted. Once a reasonable fee is determined by the court, ASCAP must offer licenses at that fee to all other similarly situated users, but the court-determined fee does not affect licenses previously issued.

Following are discussions on the types of licenses ASCAP grants to music users, logging methods, systems for domestic and foreign distribution of income to members, and other pertinent information about this performing rights society.

Licenses and Fees. ASCAP's only sources of income are the fees it collects from music users it licenses, interest on investments, and royalties received from foreign societies for the licensing of the ASCAP repertory. It licenses on a bulk or blanket basis all types of music users and has separate agreements with each type (e.g., local radio stations, TV networks). A license permits the music user to perform any or all of the works in the ASCAP repertory, as frequently as desired, for the specified fee.

Among its most important licensees are local radio and television stations, and the television networks. The terms of these licenses are negotiated with committees appointed by the National Association of Broadcasters, in the case of radio and television stations, and with representatives of each of the networks. ASCAP licenses broadcasting stations either on a "blanket" or "per program" basis (at the station's option). Under the blanket agreement, the licensee is granted the right to broadcast nondramatic performances of any and all musical compositions in the ASCAP repertory for a fee based on its receipts from sponsors for all programs. Under the current local radio station blanket license, each station's fee is 1.725% of "net receipts from sponsors after deductions" plus a "sustaining fee." With the per program agreement, while the licensee still obtains a blanket license, the fee is a higher percentage of net receipts from sponsors, but only on those programs which carry AS-CAP-licensed music. The local television stations also pay fees based on a percentage of net receipts from sponsors after deductions and have the blanket or per program option. The networks pay the society flat fees (approximately $4 million per network, as of this writing). The agreements made between AS-CAP and its radio and television station licensees typically are for 5-year periods.

License fees for other types of music users are based on such objective factors as the number of nights per week music is performed, seating capacity, whether admission is charged. Concert presenter fees are paid on a graduated scale based on the price per seat and the seating capacity. In the serious music field, orchestras are classified as major, region-al, metropolitan, urban, or community, and pay fees based on either earned income or the total payroll for musicians and conductors. Representatives of ASCAP and a committee representing colleges and universities recently concluded a license agreement. Each college has the option of having its fee based solely on enrollment or on a combination of enrollment and the number of concerts where the artist is paid $1,300 or more and an admission is charged.

Any user objecting to the particular fee has the right to apply to the U.S. District Court for the Southern District of New York for the determination of a reasonable fee.

ASCAP Survey of Performances. There are tens of thousands of music users licensed by ASCAP, delivering millions of musical performances during any given period. ASCAP allocates its distributable revenue among its writer and publisher members, based primarily on a sample survey of performances. To monitor and log every music user at all times would be economically prohibitive. It is AS-CAP's Survey of Performances, designed and monitored by ASCAP's independent survey experts, that attempts to tally performances "fairly and scientifically and economically." The survey samples performances on radio and television (both local and network), on background music services, in colleges and universities, in symphony and concert halls, and on airlines. Noncommercial broadcasters are included in the survey, as are pay cable systems.

Broadcasters. Performances of musical compositions broadcast on *network television* are determined from program logs supplied by the three U.S. television networks, cue sheets and logs provided by the producers of the programs, and other sources. These specify the musical compositions performed and whether they were used as a feature, theme, or background. The society uses audio and video tapes of network broadcasts to check the accuracy of these reports. All network performances are credited. The society's survey of *local television* stations utilizes a combination of *TV Guide,* audio tapes, and cue sheets. Some 30,000 hours of local television are included in the society's sample of these uses.

To determine performances of works on the thousands of local *radio stations,* ASCAP tapes 60,000 hours of local radio each year. The stations to be surveyed are selected randomly by computer. The frequency with which a station is to be taped is related to the license fee it pays. For example, a station paying $40,000 in ASCAP license fees would be included in the survey, and taped twice as much as one paying $20,000. (This same principle is used in the local television survey.) Both AM and FM stations are included in the sample, which each year covers every category of stations. An outside research firm schedules the taping, based on computer selection, and instructs people around the country as to which stations to tape and when (ASCAP staff and the stations do not know). After completion of the recording, the tapes are sent to New York (ASCAP headquarters), where trained monitors identify the selections.

Background Music Services. Background music services, such as Muzak, supply ASCAP with program logs of compositions used—lists of their music libraries, showing titles, writers, and publishers sampled.

Symphony, Concert, and Educational Operations. Symphony orchestras, serious concert promoters, etc. supply concert programs from which the society surveys compositions performed. Such performances, with the exception of those in educational institutions, are counted on a complete or census basis. Performances in educational institutions are sampled.

Hotels, Clubs, Bars, and Other Licensees. Because of the prohibitive cost, no survey is taken of the performances of the 30,000-odd general licensees of the society. The survey experts have concluded that feature uses on radio and television are representative of performances in these diverse areas and the license fees are distributed on that basis.

Weighting Rules. The moneys ASCAP distributes to writers and publishers reflect the amount and types of performances their works receive. The society classifies music and types of performances in various ways. This section discusses some of the weighting rules used by ASCAP in determining the value of particular types of performances. These credits are ultimately assigned monetary values (the value depending on the amount of money available for distribution for a particular time period) and the applicable earnings are paid to members in quarterly distributions.

Each use of a composition reported by the ASCAP survey receives a performance credit or fraction thereof. Performances that appear in the survey are weighted; a "feature" performance, for example, earns more than a performance of a "theme" or of "background" music. A feature performance such as a visual instrumental or vocal performance is awarded one "use credit"; a fractional use credit will be awarded to a composition performed as a theme or jingle, as background, cue, or bridge music, or for performances of copyrighted arrangements of works in the public domain. ASCAP awards multiple use credits for performances of serious works 4 minutes or longer in duration. ASCAP defines a "performance credit" as "the unit of measure of the results of the survey, being derived by multiplying uses or fractional uses by the applicable sampling and economic multipliers."

Network Television Programs. Different amounts of credit are awarded for performances of works on television network programs based on the time of day. For television network programs broadcast Monday through Friday, those that begin between 2:00 A.M. and 12:59 P.M. receive 50% of the otherwise applicable credit; between 1:00 P.M. and 6:59

P.M., 75%; between 7:00 P.M. and 1:59 A.M., 100%. On Saturdays and Sundays, programs that begin between 2:00 A.M. and 12:59 P.M. receive 50% of the otherwise applicable credit; those that begin between 1:00 P.M. and 1:59 A.M., 100%. If a program is broadcast on New Year's Day, Memorial Day, Independence Day, Labor Day, Thanksgiving, or Christmas, performances are credited as if the program were broadcast on a Saturday or Sunday.

Jingles. For a work to qualify as a jingle in the ASCAP survey, it must be "an advertising, promotional, or public service announcement containing musical material (with or without lyrics) where: a) the musical material was originally written for advertising, promotional, or public service announcement purposes; or b) the performance is of a musical work, originally written for other purposes, with the lyrics changed for advertising, promotional, or public announcement purposes with the permission of the ASCAP member or members in interest."

Concert and Symphony Performances. Recognizing the different character of "serious" music, the society credits performances of such works on the basis of the length of the work, and in the case of live concert performances, the instrumentation (e.g., full orchestra, quartet). In determining the royalties available for distribution for performances of works in concert and symphony halls, ASCAP multiplies by 5 the license fees it receives from these users.

Copyrighted Arrangements of Public Domain Works. A copyrighted arrangement of a public domain work receives 10% of the otherwise applicable credit if it is separately published and copyrighted in the U.S.; or is included in a copyrighted collection of hymns or religious anthems which is offered for sale in a regular trade edition; or is primarily an instrumental work. Copyrighted arrangements of PD works retaining the same title but containing new lyrics may receive up to 35% of the otherwise applicable credit, depending upon the extent of new material, and up to 50% if there is an entirely new title and lyrics. If there are changes in the music, it may receive an additional 10% to 50% of the otherwise applicable credit. If the copyrighted arrangement is primarily an instrumental work, it may receive up to 35% of the otherwise applicable credit if there has been a transfer from one medium to another, and from 35% to 100% if the work "exhibits creative treatment and contains original musical characteristics and is identifiable as a set piece apart from the source material."

Specific Situations. ASCAP has weighting formula provisions for specific situations concerning performances on network and local television programs. Examples of performances (other than of jingles or themes) that would be credited as features include: a vocal or instrumental performance of a composition which is announced or specifically brought to the attention of the audience; a performance as part of a song or dance act; a performance in an audience-participation program where persons attempt to identify the composition being performed; and announced instrumentals at public events (such as football games).

On quiz games, a vocal or instrumental performance to introduce or accompany the description or presentation of prizes or the appearance or departure of participants or a change of scene or subject would not be credited as a feature performance under the weighting formula. Likewise, unannounced instrumental performances at public "spectator" events, a vocal or instrumental performance used as a bridge to or from a commercial announcement, and other situations specified in the weighting formula would not be credited as feature performances.

Domestic Distribution. Works that appear in the society's scientific sample generate performance credits (or fractions of such a credit), each credit having an economic value determined by the total revenues available for distribution. This available revenue comes from license receipts and interest from investments the society receives, less operating expenses and moneys paid to foreign societies, and is divided equally between publisher and writer members. The writers' and publishers' halves are distributed in accordance with separate formulas adopted by the writer and publisher members. ASCAP pays its members 6 times a year: 4 distributions cover U.S. performances and 2 cover foreign performances.

Writers may choose to receive their royalties by either the 100% Current Performance method or the Four Fund system. Under the first method, writers receive distributions based on the value of their credits within 4 quarters. The Four Fund basis allows the writer to average performances, and therefore earnings, over a number of years, thus receiving income during otherwise unfruitful years and relieving tax pressures during high earning periods. Each method will be examined in more detail.

Distribution Systems. The writer dollars available for distribution (i.e., half of all distributable revenue) are computed for each calendar quarter. To arrive at a credit value, this revenue is divided by the total number of writer credits in the 4 most recent quarters. The individual writer's royalties are then determined by multiplying his or her performance credits by the credit value. Special provisions apply to members who have more than approximately 48,000 performance credits.

The moneys available for distribution under the Four Fund system are those left over from the total writers' distributable income after all the Current Performance dollars have been deducted. Each of the component funds in the Four Funds method is allocated a certain share of its total distribution: the Average Performance Fund receives 40% of the total; the Current Performance Fund, the Recognized Works Performance Fund, and the Continuity

of Membership Fund each receive 20% of the total.

Distribution to each writer under the Average Performance Fund is based on the average performance credits of all works written by the member and licensed by ASCAP during the 5 latest fiscal survey years. Distributions to writers from the Current Performance Fund are based on credits in the most recent 4 quarters and are calculated in the same way as distribution to writers by the 100% Current Performance method. Distribution to each writer from the Recognized Works Performance Fund is based on a 5-year performance average of recognized works only. (A recognized work is one that enters the survey anytime 4 quarters after a performance of such work first had appeared in the society's survey.) Distribution to each writer from the Continuity of Membership Fund is based on the average of such writer's annual ratings for each of the preceding 10 fiscal survey years, taking into account the number of continuous quarters of the writer's membership in ASCAP, up to no more than 168 quarters.

New writer members in ASCAP may elect to collect royalties under the Four Fund method only after the first 3 or 4 full survey years of membership, at which time the performance credits recorded during the years in which the writers received payment on a Current Performance basis are used in computing their standing in the Four Fund system. Until that time they may receive distribution only under the 100% Current Performance method.

Publishers receive distributions only on the Current Performance basis, with quarterly payments. The quarterly distribution to a publisher is based on the ratio of its performance credits to the total performance credits of all publishers. The distribution on the Current Performance basis for publishers is different from that for writers. Quarterly distributions are made and adjusted in accordance with a publishers' Distribution Formula. Briefly, distributions to publisher members are made on an "on account" basis in the first 3 of the 4 distributions that comprise a fiscal distribution year. In the fourth and final distribution of the fiscal distribution year, a yearly credit value is determined and this credit value is the same for all publisher members of the society for that year.

Foreign Distribution. ASCAP has agreements with performing rights societies in foreign countries. It pays these societies when works of their members are performed in the U.S. and appear in ASCAP's survey, and it receives royalties from performances of its members' works in these countries. Survey methods and moneys transmitted between societies are in accordance with each society's rules.

With respect to income received from foreign societies, ASCAP distributes such revenue to its writer and publisher members on the Current Performance basis. Where the income from any source during a one-year period exceeds $200,000 and the foreign society remits payment in a form that allows the society to identify its members in interest, ASCAP distributes royalties to them based on information received. Otherwise it makes distribution based on the most reliable information it has as to foreign performances in general. In fact, the society seeks to distribute royalties in accordance with the reporting of the foreign society even in those instances where it recruits less than $200,000, as long as the foreign society identifies the ASCAP members in interest.

Special Awards. Most beginning writers encounter difficulties in the highly competitive world of music. As ASCAP is concerned with helping them, it makes available monetary prizes, called Panel Awards, whose major beneficiaries are these young writers. ASCAP's Writer's Distribution Formula provides that an amount not exceeding 5% may be deducted from writer members' distributable revenue for the purpose of making special awards

to writers whose works (1) "have a unique prestige value and for which adequate compensation would not otherwise be received" and (2) are "performed substantially in media not surveyed by the Society." The awards are in 2 categories, "popular" and "standard," and are determined by independent panels of experts appointed by the writer members of the board of directors.

Membership. Membership in ASCAP is available to qualified writers (composers and lyricists) and publishers. Writer membership is in 2 categories: full and associate. Full membership is available to any writer who has had at least one original musical composition commercially recorded, published, or performed by an ASCAP-licensed user. A full member receives royalties when performances of his or her works appear in the ASCAP Sample Survey. When a member's works appear in the survey, he or she is eligible to vote in the society's elections for the board of directors or board of review in the next year. ASCAP's writer membership agreement is effective for a period of 10 years, with members having the right to resign at the end of any year on giving 3 months advance written notice. Full members pay annual dues of $10; there is no initiation fee.

A writer who does not meet the requirements for full writer membership may join as an associate member, provided he or she has at least one musical composition copyrighted. No voting rights are accorded to an associate member, whose status will be changed to full member when he or she meets such requirements.

Publisher membership is available to any person or business whose copyrights have been commercially recorded, published, or regularly performed by an ASCAP-licensed user. The publisher agreement, and rules with respect to resignation, are the same as for writers. Publishers pay annual dues of $50; there is no initiation fee.

Deceased Writer Members. When an AS-CAP writer member dies, his or her heirs are eligible to be elected as successors to the deceased member and receive royalties based on performances of the musical works until the copyrights in the works expire.

Resigning Writers. A writer who resigns from ASCAP has the following options: the member with a co-writer or publisher remaining in ASCAP may leave the rights to all his or her ASCAP-licensed works with the society and place in the new performing rights organization only those works written after the new agreement first takes effect; or the writer can place the nondramatic performance rights to all works previously licensed through AS-CAP in the new organization. Rights to these works, however, cannot be taken from ASCAP and placed in a new performing rights organization until ASCAP's agreement with the category of music users expires and his co-writers and publishers agree the writer may withdraw the works from ASCAP. For example, a writer could not take rights for radio broadcasts of his compositions until that license expires. In addition, a writer who has any outstanding indebtedness to the society may not withdraw works until it is repaid.

American Symphony Orchestra League (ASOL).
Nonprofit educational organization that serves to assist symphony orchestras artistically and administratively by coordinating various activities.

Membership. Membership in the league is in two classes—voting and associate. Voting membership is available to U.S. orchestras of the following classifications: major, regional, metropolitan, urban, community, chamber, college, and youth. Associate membership may be held by individuals, symphony women's associations, state orchestra associations, educational institutions, organizations and firms interested in the symphony orchestra and its development.

Activities. Activities of ASOL include: conducting research in all facets of orchestral work and related musical and cultural developments, and publishing reports, studies, and analyses for distribution to its members; sponsoring training and study programs for conductors, instrumentalists, managers, and members of orchestra boards; exchanging data between its member orchestras; providing a counseling service for its member orchestras; monitoring legislative and government activity that affects symphony orchestras; sponsoring regional workshops, composer projects, and music critic projects; and presenting annual awards to its members in recognition of outstanding work in various phases of orchestra administration.

History. ASOL was founded in 1942 by Mrs. Leta Snow, manager of the Kalamazoo Symphony Orchestra. It was granted a charter by the Congress of the United States in 1962. In 1980, the league had 4,300 members.

See SYMPHONY ORCHESTRAS.

Amusement and Music Operators Association (AMOA).
Trade association that represents the coin-operated music and amusement industry.

Membership. Members of AMOA are jukebox operators, jukebox and amusement game manufacturers and distributors, one-stops, exhibitors, operators of coin-operated amusement games and vending machines, amusement centers, and all allied businesses. Any firm in these categories may become a member.

Programs and Activities. In addition to sponsoring general programs and activities as described in TRADE ASSOCIATIONS, AMOA sponsors training schools for coin machine mechanics, provides its members with tax and regulatory information; promulgates an annual membership directory; and sponsors an annual international trade show.

History. AMOA was founded as a 14-man

committee in 1948 to combat legislation then pending in Congress that it believed would be detrimental to the coin-operated music industry. Originally formed to represent jukebox operators (it was called the Music Operators of America), the organization successfully opposed the legislation, aimed at eliminating the so-called jukebox exemption (this exemption was eventually removed by the 1976 Copyright Act). In later years, as most jukebox operations included coin-operated amusement games and vending machines, MOA's name came to depict less than the association actually stood for, and in 1976 the organization was renamed. The Amusement and Music Operators Association had 1,382 company members in 1980. The association is based in Chicago.

See also Jukebox.

Angel. *See* Limited Partnerships (For Investments in Theatrical Productions).

Anonymous Work. Defined in the 1976 Copyright Act (Section 101) as "a work on the copies or phonorecords of which no natural person is identified as author." Under the act, the Copyright Duration of a work created on or after January 1, 1978, is different if the authorship is anonymous than if a natural person is identified as the author.

Rarely, a musical composition is published with anonymous authorship. One example, however, was the lyrics to "The Marine's Hymn" ("From the Halls of Montezuma to the shores of Tripoli"), written anonymously by a marine on duty in Mexico in 1847, to go with an old French melody. (Most printed editions of this work do not name an author of the words, and the few that have, differ in the credit.) The melody was later identified by John Philip Sousa as the Gendarme's song from Jacques Offenbach's opéra bouffe *Geneviève de Brabant*. The composition was copyrighted in 1919 by the United States Marine Corps.

See also Pseudonymous Work.

AOR (Album-Oriented Rock). Radio station format that plays album cuts from rock LPs and, on a limited basis, hit singles. As many as 5 or 6 cuts from a feature album may be programmed during a particular time period (some of these, however, may actually have been released as singles and become hits). Cuts broadcast are generally those deemed to be the best from a particular album.

AOR stations may vary considerably in their programming. For example, some program progressive rock music only, while others concentrate on the Top 40. Selections are determined by the program director, who makes his decision in accordance with the aims of the station.

DJs on AOR stations often provide background information on the records and their artists. AOR stations sometimes simulcast live concerts. The target audience of AOR stations is usually 18 to 34 years old.

Arbitration. Process by which a dispute is judged by one or more impartial persons chosen by the contestants, or appointed. (A decision is known as an "award.") Agreements of various unions and guilds in the music business, such as AFTRA and AGAC, stipulate that controversies arising out of or in connection with their contracts are to be submitted to arbitration under the prevailing rules of the American Arbitration Association.

Arbitron. The nation's leading Radio Ratings Service.

Arbitron measures the listening habits of radio audiences mainly by distributing diaries to persons in its randomly selected samples of all telephone households (the 1980 sample in the radio market of Los Angeles, for example, was 9,368; New York, 8,617; and Chicago, 8,841). It is from the information the listeners provide in the diaries that the ratings for a survey period are determined (*see* Diary).

An Arbitron representative calls the selected

household and asks if the resident will keep a radio diary. If the person consents (approximately 13% refuse), the caller determines the demographic composition of the household and has a diary sent to each eligible member (12 and older). Members are instructed to return the diary at the end of the survey period. The response rate is approximately 50%. Some of the returned diaries from the survey are rejected on the basis of incomprehensible information. However, a 50% response rate is considered to provide a statistically accurate sample.

Arbitron has found the rate of consent and response by mail from certain population groups to be inadequate to derive meaningful data because the groups don't respond to the standard diary technique in the same fashion as the general population. To acquire representative information from these groups, it uses a modified retrieval system. For instance, with black populations, a representative interviews listeners daily by telephone and records the results in the diary; with Spanish populations, it increases participation by personally placing, following up, and collecting bilingual diaries.

To include unlisted telephone numbers in its survey, Arbitron employs a procedure known as the Expanded Sample Frame. In a particular market, for instance, a study using a computer and a telephone directory will indicate all telephone exchanges containing residential phone listings. For this analysis, a telephone exchange is defined as the first 5 digits of the 7-digit telephone number (e.g., 627-12----). A computer identifies all 100 numbers in the 627-12---- exchange (627-1200 to 627-1299), from which all numbers listed in the telephone directory are deleted. From the remaining numbers, all of which are unlisted or unassigned (the unassigned numbers are deleted), a systematic random sample is then drawn from the unlisted numbers that can be dialed for the ESF metropolis area sample.

Arbitron Surveys. Arbitron measures radio audiences by conducting surveys (ranging from 10 to 12 weeks in length) up to 4 times per year. The quarterly measurement periods are winter, spring, summer, and fall. The results of a survey for a particular market during a particular survey period are printed in a "book" (i.e., a report of a market for one of the survey periods). There is no requirement that a station be a subscriber to Arbitron books to have its audience measured. Those stations in a particular market that meet Arbitron's minimum reporting standards are included in the market's book.

Ratings and Shares. The relative "popularity" of a station is expressed by Arbitron in *ratings* and *shares*. Arbitron's basic frame of reference is the average quarter hour—that is, the average number of persons in a demographic group listening to radio for at least 5 minutes during an average quarter hour in a given time period.

A rating is the percentage of all people within a demographic group in a survey area who listen to a specific station.

$$\frac{\text{Listeners}}{\text{Population}} = \text{Rating (\%)}$$

Example: In a particular market, there are 100,000 homes. At a given point in time (e.g., Monday through Friday, 8 A.M. to 9 A.M.), 10,000 of these homes are tuned into WAAA. WAAA therefore has a rating of 10 (10%). In those 100,000 homes, there are 54,000 men 18 years or older. Of the 10,000 homes tuned in (to WAAA), 6,000 are men 18+.

Therefore: $\frac{6,000}{54,000}$ = .11111% or WAAA has a rating of 11 for men 18+ during a particular survey period.

A rating of 1 equals 1% of that population.

A share is the percentage of all listeners in a demographic group who are tuned to a specific station.

$$\frac{\text{Average quarter-hour persons to a station}}{\text{Average quarter-hour persons to all stations}} = \text{share}$$

Example: If 10,000 people are listening to all stations in a particular geographic area, and WAAA gets 2,000 of those listeners, its share is

$$\frac{2,000}{10,000} = 0.20\% \text{ or } 2$$

Arbitron will occasionally "delist" a station from a book if it feels the station has engaged in rating distortion—any activity designed to cause diary-keepers to report more listening than they did. "Hypoing," on the other hand, is a broadcaster's attempt to improve a rating during a survey period for the purpose of obtaining a higher rating and share.

Arranger. One who prepares and adapts a previously written musical composition for presentation in other than its original form. An arrangement is characterized by melodic and rhythmic variation, reharmonization, and/or development of the composition.

Arrangements of songs are written for performance in various fields, including phonograph recordings, jingles, television, theatrical motion pictures, and nightclubs, and for print. The arranger's role may vary for the different mediums for which he prepares arrangements. In television and motion pictures, for example, he might score someone's theme to the film, sketching different parts and assigning instruments to play them (leaving the ORCHESTRATOR to write the actual voicings); in commercial recordings, he might write the complete "charts" for all the instruments and background voices or "sweeten" existing tracks with the creative use of strings and other instruments; and for print, he may write just the piano and vocal part for sheet music or the complete arrangement for band and orchestra editions. The arranger creates lines and approaches to the existing composition that best frame it for a particular performance or medium. Arranging requires compositional skill and creativity.

Commercial Recordings. Although an arranger's creative input to a commercial recording may contribute substantially to its success, arrangers normally work as employees for hire. Consequently they have no copyright status in the material they arrange, nor do they receive royalties on sales of such recordings. For their work, they receive a one-time fee. Arrangers are hired by the producer or record company, or in some cases, by the artist. Arrangers working in the recording field are members of AFM.

In preparing songs—pop, rock, R & B, country, etc.— for recording, the arranger often creates one or more background "hooks"—instrumental, vocal, or both—which serve to make the recording more interesting and commercial.

Occasionally recordings are made in which an arrangement is devised spontaneously by the performers, reading off lead sheets and experimenting, under the guidance of the producer, with various renditions. This is referred to as a "head arrangement."

Printed Editions. Some arrangers work for music publishers and print-music licensees. They are employed to write various kinds of arrangements for popular and educational editions (*see* PRINTED MUSIC). Such arrangers may be salaried staff employees or free-lance workers. As employees for hire, they have no copyright interest in the works they arrange but usually receive name credit on printed editions. In some cases, an arranger will receive a royalty based on sales of printed music; this depends upon his bargaining position.

Training. Arranging is a highly skilled profession. The trained arranger has studied woodwind, brass, string, and percussion instruments (particularly their range, sounds, and technical limitations), theory, composition, harmony, counterpoint, arranging, orchestration, and electronic music. He must be versatile, and able to write arrangements for most or all styles of music. He often progresses from the status of full-fledged arranger to full-fledged composer—arranging his *own* music. Most film composers and many concert composers started as arrangers after completing their studies.

See also DERIVATIVE WORK.

Artist. *See* RECORDING ARTIST.

Artist Development. *See* RECORD COMPANY.

Artist Management Agency. Specialized management agencies commonly represent individual and group "concert artists" in the following fields: musical, theater, opera, classical music, dance, recital, and choral. The term "concert artists" as used with respect to these fields is broad in meaning and includes vocalists, solo and group instrumentalists, orchestras, chamber orchestras, symphony orchestras, conductors, instrumental ensembles, dancers, dance companies, ballet groups, choral groups, touring theatrical groups, and opera companies.

The extent of representation of a client's career by a management agency may vary greatly, ranging from booking single engagements or tours to total career guidance encompassing concert bookings, recordings, motion pictures, television, and radio. Management agencies may also participate in the supervision of concert programs and advise their clients on such matters as what repertoire to perform, where and how often to perform, and how to expand their audience.

Professional concert artists who are singers, dancers, solo instrumentalists, and stage directors are members of the AMERICAN GUILD OF MUSICAL ARTISTS (AGMA). This union makes legally binding contracts with managers known as Basic Agreements, which regulate the contractual relationship between the artists and their managers. Some of its provisions are discussed in the AGMA entry.

U.S. artist management agencies may also represent foreign concert artists with respect to American concert bookings. In such cases, the managers may obtain the necessary documents to permit entry and work, make hotel reservations, get a piano accompanist (where necessary), and do anything else needed to fulfill the requirements of the engagement or tour.

Artist Tour. *See* TOUR, CONCERT.

ASCAP. *See* AMERICAN SOCIETY OF COMPOSERS, AUTHORS AND PUBLISHERS.

Associated Actors and Artistes of America (Four A's). The parent AFL-CIO international through which various entertainment unions derive their jurisdictional charters. Its major branches are Actors' Equity Association, American Federation of Television and Radio Artists, American Guild of Musical Artists, American Guild of Variety Artists, and Screen Actors Guild. Other affiliates include Hebrew Actors Union (HAU), Italian Actors Union (IAU), Screen Extras Guild (SEG), and Asociación Puertorriqueña de Artistas e Tecnicos del Espectaculo (APATE), a union representing Puerto Rican actors and actresses.

The affiliates of the Four A's are autonomous in their day-to-day operations. Their constitutions and bylaws are adopted by their respective memberships and are revised and amended from time to time, so long as such rules and regulations are not in conflict with those of the international body. In the event of jurisdictional disputes between unions over a particular field, the International Board of

Four A's may make a final determination.

Four A's is a voluntary association that was founded in 1919 to represent the performing arts in what was at that time the American Federation of Labor. Its headquarters is in New York.

See also AMERICAN FEDERATION OF LABOR AND CONGRESS OF INDUSTRIAL ORGANIZATIONS (AFL-CIO); UNIONS.

Associated Label. *See* RECORD COMPANY DEALS.

Association of Canadian Television and Radio Artists (ACTRA). *See* CANADA.

Attorney, Music Industry. The complex legal interests of participants in the music business usually require the services of skilled lawyers. Those who specialize in practices related to the music field are sometimes referred to as music industry attorneys or entertainment lawyers.

Clients. Within the music industry, attorneys are called upon to represent clients in two general categories: "talent" and business. "Talent" includes recording artists, record producers, songwriters, motion picture, television, and stage composers, arrangers, orchestrators, instrumentalists, vocalists, and air personalities. The business interests include record companies, music publishers, record/tape wholesalers and retailers, recording studios, personal managers, agents, unions, guilds, music rights licensing organizations, trade associations, professional organizations, and broadcasting stations.

Areas of "Music Business Law." The attorney who practices in the music industry must be prepared for a variety of matters. These may fall into any of the following areas: contracts, copyrights, general business and corporate practices, immigration law, libel/slander, privacy and publicity rights, taxes, and trademarks.

The music industry attorney should have a solid, thorough understanding of virtually every aspect of the music business. This includes knowing the basic functions of all industry participants (companies, unions, talent, etc.) and the structure and operations of record companies, music publishers, talent agencies, and other entities. International practices and laws applicable to the industry should also be known. Because of the constant revisions in tax and copyright laws, government regulations, union agreements, and "standard" industry contracts and licenses, the music industry attorney's education is continuous. The attorney must stay current with trends and developments (including new technologies) as well as be able to "see" ahead. Furthermore, the crossovers between the music industry and the motion picture, television, stage, and radio industries will often require that the attorney's skill and experience go far beyond the music industry itself.

Recording Artist Clients. Attorneys of recording artists may play an important role in their clients' careers. In negotiating recording contracts on their behalf, the attorney tries to acquire large advances, high royalty rates, overscale wages for recording sessions, large budgets for advertising and promotion of product, tour support, and other terms that are favorable to the artist and likely to encourage sales of his client's recordings. He may also try to retain the artist's merchandising rights. Attorneys sometimes negotiate for the eventual reversion of recording masters to the artist's control.

To negotiate recording contracts successfully, the attorney should know the terms of other recent artists' deals, the financial resources of each company, and what the market can bring. Attorneys who represent top-selling artists often are regarded as having "clout" and can deal with the chief executives of record companies. An ethical attorney, however, will not seek advantages for a new artist in return for concessions on the part of a "star" client.

Attorneys often represent their clients not just as artists but in personal and business matters unrelated to the entertainment business. For example, the attorney whose clients include performers may represent such persons' interests with respect to divorces, leases, house purchases, drug busts, paternity suits, palimony suits, automobile accidents, and property damage suits (e.g., damages in hotel rooms).

Fees. Attorneys commonly charge for their services based on time and results. With respect to recording artist clients and negotiating deals for them with record companies, some attorneys may be willing to work on a contingent fee basis—that is, they earn a percentage of the deal they obtain or negotiate for their client, typically 10% or more. A percentage participation in a record deal could represent either a profit or a loss to an attorney, depending upon the actual ascendency or fall of his client's career over an extended period of time.

Miscellaneous. The work of the music attorney may often supplement or overlap certain functions of other representatives involved in the career of the recording artist, such as the personal manager, the agent, and the accountant. (Like them, the attorney must advise, counsel, and represent his client.) He should therefore establish working relationships with these individuals. Some industry attorneys depart from the active professional practice of law to form their own music companies or to become executives of record labels, music publishing companies, and licensing organizations. Often they are recruited to key executive positions because of their experience, contacts, and skills, and their ability to keep an "overview" of the whole industry.

Audiophile Record. Disc that offers superior sound quality because of the relatively unconventional techniques used and extra care taken in its recording and manufacture. Audiophile records yield less distortion and less surface noise ("pops" and "clicks") than conventional discs and have better clarity and transient response, and much greater dynamic range.

Audiophile records represent a particular era's technological pursuit to obtain the highest quality of audio reproduction in the home. Consequently the techniques used to produce and manufacture an audiophile recording during one time period may be considered the conventional means in a later one. By the late 1970s, audiophile recordings fell into three major categories: DIRECT-TO-DISC RECORDING, DIGITAL RECORDING, and HIGH-PERFORMANCE ANALOG RECORDINGS.

Most audiophile records are manufactured from virgin vinyl. This is a clear vinyl that has never been used in record processing (most conventional discs are made from a reprocessed vinyl—see PHONOGRAPH RECORD).

Audiophile records for the most part and until recently have been produced and distributed by small specialty labels. The marketing procedures of these labels vary from those of the more commercial manufacturers. They sell through independent distributors or directly to retailers and consumers. These small companies generally lack the finances to engage in substantial merchandising and advertising programs. Because retailers often buy direct from manufacturers of audiophile records, their profit margin with respect to sales of these discs is generally greater. These labels, however, almost always have a no-return policy. Audiophile discs are often featured in the audio hardware section of retail stores.

Audiophile recordings, particularly direct-to-disc, are made not only in state-of-the-art recording studios but at concert halls and other locations, to which equipment is transported. Remote recording serves to capture the ambience, or acoustic environment, of the hall or other location.

Enthusiasts of these high-fidelity sound recordings are referred to as *audiophiles*. Audiophile records further serve to demonstrate the superiority of the audiophile's equipment.

Audiovisual Work. *See* MOTION PICTURE MUSIC.

Audit, Royalty. A royalty audit is a formal examination of the books and records of account of a company, corporation, organization, or other entity to verify the correctness of the statements rendered to an individual or firm that has a royalty contract or license with such entity. Royalty audits are a regular and important part of music business practices.

The right to audit is normally provided for in royalty contracts or licenses, with the restrictions that to perform an audit, reasonable notice be given in writing, that it must occur during normal business hours, and that the period of the right to perform it (if any) has not expired. Royalty audits are normally performed by a firm of certified public accountants on behalf of the client.

Types of Royalty Audits. There are many different types of royalty contracts and licenses in the music business; consequently there are various different types of royalty audits. These include audits of: (1) record companies on behalf of artists, record producers, production companies, joint venturers (such as associated labels), foreign licensors, and music publishers; (2) domestic and foreign licensees on behalf of record companies (a record company's licensees include record/tape clubs, record merchandisers, and foreign labels), or on behalf of artists as third-party beneficiaries to their record company's contract; (3) domestic and foreign licensees on behalf of music publishers (a publisher's licensees include print licensees, printed-music selling agents, and sub-publishers); (4) music publishers on behalf of songwriters, copublishers, and foreign licensors; and (5) merchandising companies on be-

half of artists who have licensed the right to use their name and likeness.

Audits of Record Companies on Behalf of Recording Artists. Many of the procedures used in auditing record companies on behalf of artists are basic to other types of royalty audits. Therefore, this type of royalty audit will be examined.

Planning the Audit. Before an audit is performed, it must be determined whether such a procedure is feasible. No artist or auditor considers spending a large sum of money for an audit without first making an inquiry into the return that can be expected. Audits may be very costly, and the prospect of a small financial recovery would make the idea of doing the audit impractical.

A feasibility study includes the following:
Review of the contract. The artist's representative will first review the artist's recording contract. Clauses that will be particularly examined are those relating to the royalty rates for different areas such as (1) sales of records and tapes by the company; (2) sales by company licensees; (3) "special" sales such as budget LPs, cutouts, premiums, exports, compilations; (4) "free" goods, promotional copies, etc.

It is observed whether royalties are based on the wholesale or the retail list price, if there are escalation clauses, and whether there are packaging deductions.

Review of the royalty statements. The artist's royalty statements will be examined to determine such things as: which selections are accounted for, what types of royalties have been reported, what deductions have been made, the total amount of royalties paid, and whether the artist is in a recouped or unrecouped position.

If the feasibility study indicates that an audit would be economically desirable, it will be performed. The CPA will be inclined to perform an audit if the artist's royalty earnings have been large and if the artist is not in an unrecouped position. In addition, if the CPA has had experience auditing record companies, reliance will be made on his knowledge of the field, of the accounting systems, and of the probability of errors. Comparing the royalty provisions of the agreement to the royalty statements, he may find obvious discrepancies.

If it has been determined that an audit is to be performed, the client will send written notice of his having retained the CPA in order to audit the record company. Before commencing his fieldwork, the CPA will thoroughly analyze the contract and royalty statements in order to thoroughly understand the audit before he arrives at the record company. The audit will be custom designed to follow the provisions of the contract (every artist's contract is different). If there are any questions of interpretation, the artist's legal or personal representative will be consulted in advance so that his interpretations may be applied in the audit.

The Audit. The fieldwork will be an inspection of those accounting records deemed pertinent by the auditor. It will begin with an analysis of the accounting system used by the manufacturer. This encompasses tracing units (records and tapes) from (1) production, (2) to inventory, (3) through the distribution system, (4) into the royalty system, and (5) into the royalty statement.

The basic areas of investigation in the royalty audit are:

1. Production, inventory, and sales of records and tapes. The number of records and tapes manufactured reduced by the number sold and given away should equal the inventory. The auditor will check to see if these amounts are all accounted for and balance out.

Data on giveaways, such as promotion copies, "sampler" records, or "free" goods given to accounts for buying product in volume, will be examined to ensure that the amount of giveaways did not exceed any contractual limitations. The books will also be checked to see if the record company held back any excess reserves for returns of records (assuming such reserves are contractually permitted) and if it recouped all advances properly. The auditor will compare information revealed from the audit with what was reported in the artist's statement. The auditor will be able to determine if there exist unreported units on the royalty statement.

2. Statements from domestic licensees. A common practice is for record companies to license masters of popular recordings to record/tape clubs, record merchandisers, program suppliers, and other companies that manufacture and distribute records and tapes embodying such masters, under terms prescribed by their licensing agreement. Income from these sources can be substantial, so it is important to verify what royalties (and advances, if any) have been derived therefrom. The auditor will examine statements received by the label from its domestic licensees to make sure that the information on these was accurately reported to the client and to determine if the provisions of the label/licensee contract are consistent with the label/artist contract.

3. Statements from foreign licensees. Foreign sales of the artist's product are either made through a foreign subsidiary of the record company or through an independent foreign company licensed to manufacture and distribute the product. Some successful artists do not grant worldwide rights to the record company, but make separate deals directly with foreign companies.

Where an artist's product is sold abroad via a foreign licensee arrangement with his domestic record company, the artist is normally paid either a specified royalty rate based on unit sales, or a percentage of such income by his label. Whatever the case, the auditor will examine the foreign licenses and statements to determine if they are consistent with the client's contract and that all royalties have been accounted for.

Systems Errors. A company will have a particular accounting system it uses to report royalties. It is possible that an artist's contract is so unique that the system was not flexible enough to account for special contractual provisions. Also, if the input to the system—as many are computerized—was incorrect or incomplete, the artist's royalty statement will consequently be incorrect.

Audits of bona fide record companies are performed not because of integrity but because of complexity. With artists selling millions of albums and company accounting systems not continually updated, there may be reasonable cause to believe a royalty statement could be inaccurate.

Audit Claims. After the audit has been completed, the auditor will prepare and submit a report to the client and his representatives. The report will indicate any discrepancies, and what royalties, if any, are due the artist. A final report will then be submitted to the record company for settlement of claims resulting from the audit.

Fees. Fees for royalty audits are generally charged on an hourly basis plus a per diem where travel is involved. The factor of an audit's complexity might also affect the price. Often, where a feasibility study performed by a reliable CPA indicates that an audit should be performed, the client's financial recovery will be far greater than the cost of the audit.

Author. As used in the Copyright Act, "author" is a term that refers to the creator of intellectual property, such as literary, musical, dramatic, choreographic, pictorial, graphic, and audiovisual works, or sound recordings. Under the statute, therefore, the term "author" may denote a composer, lyricist, record producer, choreographer, artist, photographer, writer, or other creator. The law also provides that under a WORK MADE FOR HIRE agreement, the employer or other person for whom the work was prepared is considered the author.

With respect to theatrical productions (musical shows and straight plays), the term "author" may refer to any creator of literary or musical material—the playwright, dramatist, adaptor of the play, composer, lyricist, or novelist.

See also BOOK; COPYRIGHT OWNER.

Awards. In music and its related industries, various entities present prizes of merit in recognition of outstanding achievements of one sort or another. These serve not only to honor deserving recipients but to enhance the stature of a particular field by attracting to it both industry-wide and public attention.

Awards are often presented at formal ceremonies broadcast over network television. Hence these are coveted prizes holding nation-

Celebrated Industry Awards

Field	Name of Award	Sponsor
Advertising (including jingles)	Clio	Clio Awards
Broadway	Tony	American Theatre Wing
Motion Pictures	Academy Award	Academy of Motion Picture Arts and Sciences
Off Broadway, Off-Off Broadway	Obie	The Village Voice (newspaper)
Records (Artistic)	Grammy	National Academy of Recording Arts and Sciences
Record (Sales)	Gold/ Platinum Record	Recording Industry Association of America
Television	Emmy	National Academy of Television Arts and Sciences

Awards

Many different types of awards are presented regularly in recognition of outstanding achievements. Recipients are given trophies, and above are pictured some of the most famous ones: (*clockwise*) Oscar, Grammy, Tony, Emmy, and Juno.

wide and even worldwide prestige. Entities that sponsor and present these awards include TRADE ASSOCIATIONS; PROFESSIONAL ASSOCIATIONS AND EDUCATIONAL ORGANIZATIONS; and UNIONS.

The table on page 43 gives the major or most well-known awards presented in the United States that recognize musical achievement in a particular field.

There are also awards presented to honor members of and achievements in a particular music field—such as the Country Music Awards and the Dove Awards (gospel)—or awards of a general nature—such as the AGVA Entertainer of the Year Awards and the American Music Awards. Other awards include the Golden Glove Awards (film), the New York Drama Critics' Circle Awards (theater), and the Pulitzer Prize (musical composition).

B

B Side. *See* SINGLE.

Background Music. "Background music" is used in various media of public entertainment. In general, it may be described as music performed in conjunction with other sounds and/or visual sequences, which is not meant to be the principal focus of audience attention and whose purpose is to produce a particular psychological or physiological effect on the viewer or listener. Background music performed in facilities (*see* BACKGROUND MUSIC SERVICE) is not performed in conjunction with any other sounds or visual sequences.

Background music is used in the following:

Radio and television—ASCAP and BMI, performing rights organizations, pay their writers and publishers for performances of background music on radio and television. Under ASCAP's weighting formula, "background music" means "mood, atmosphere or thematic music performed as background to some non-thematic subject matter being presented on radio or television program." BMI defines background music as "music used other than as feature or theme." In calculating performance royalties, both organizations give reduced credit values for performances of background music that are monitored or logged or otherwise determined.

Theatrical motion pictures—In theatrical motion pictures, background music generally is used to underscore the development of a theme, character, or passage. Ideally, background music in motion pictures manipulates the viewer's emotions without his being aware of it.

Legitimate theater.
Facilities.
See also PROGRAMMING SERVICES (RADIO).

Background Music Service. Company that transmits renditions of musical compositions to the premises of paying subscribers, most often facilities where people work or shop. Background music programming consists of songs performed by an orchestra (which may vary in size and instrumentation from selection to selection.) Unlike entertainment music, the idea behind programming background music is that it be heard but not consciously listened to. The music is considered to be functional in the sense that it makes people work better, feel better, or respond in a particular way.

The demands of users of functional music are specialized and it is difficult for any supplier to distribute music that is at one time all things to all people. The selection of the particular songs on a program and their order of appearance depend on the use of the material. Heavy industry, for example, would have a different program than business offices. Songs in a program are generally sequenced to go from the least to the most stimulating (while still not attracting attention). Consequently selections in a program may progress in tempo and rhythm and have larger instrumentations toward the end. The order of selections is important in achieving the music's intended effects. Less popular and, in some cases, unfamiliar songs may be employed to establish a mood or feeling rather than engage a person hearing the music in some level of active involvement.

Altogether, an operation may have a library of thousands of recorded selections. Frequently, arrangements used for functional music are produced expressly for this purpose. Many times, publishers will underwrite the costs of production for such recordings. Expenses may be recovered with the inclusion of these recorded works by the background music companies and additional revenue is derived from public performance royalty payments.

Background music is usually supplied on cartridges or reel-to-reel tapes; some large services may transmit it via telephone wire or FM sideband. It is anticipated that satellites will someday play an important role in the transmission of background music. At present, increasingly specialized demands by functional music users are stimulating the entry of additional companies into the business and causing other organizations continually to reevaluate their material in distribution.

Background Singers. In accompanying a featured singer or supporting the presentation of audio or audiovisual material, background singers work in virtually all fields of musical entertainment: recordings, jingles, television, motion pictures, legitimate theater, and concerts, plus other areas of live performance. Some background singers, particularly those who make jingles or sing backup in commercial recordings, have annual incomes that may surpass those of many successful recording artists. Yet while the sounds of these singers' voices may be firmly ensconced in the public's mind, their names are little known outside industry circles.

Skills Needed. Background singers must possess professional skills. With respect to jingles and recordings, a background singer must be able to sight-read, sing in tune, sing and improvise harmonies and background "ooh"s, "aah"s, and riffs, provide excellent articulation and diction (particularly for jingles, where it is imperative that every word be un-

derstood), and very importantly, blend well with others. Background singers are often required on recording dates to produce a particular "sound" or perform in a particular style and must therefore be versatile in their capabilities. Consequently they are almost always chosen to perform at jingle sessions and important recording sessions on the basis of their reputations.

Wages. Minimum pay rates to background singers depend upon the union that has jurisdiction over the particular field of performance. For phonograph recordings and radio jingles, AFTRA's agreement prevails; for television commercials, the AFTRA/SAG agreement prevails; for theatrical productions, Equity or AGMA's contract controls; and for nonclassical concert appearances, the background singers' wages are usually determined by negotiation with their employer or the concert promoter. (Further information can be found in the respective unions' entries.)

Background singers performing on phonograph recordings are usually nonroyalty participants. AFTRA's agreement with record companies, however, provides that AFTRA singers who perform on phonograph records that sell over certain quantities (for both singles and albums) are entitled to receive "contingent scale payments" (*see* AMERICAN FEDERATION OF TELEVISION AND RADIO ARTISTS NATIONAL CODE OF FAIR PRACTICE FOR PHONOGRAPH RECORDINGS).

AFTRA and SAG background singers who participate in the recording of radio and television commercials and shows may earn residuals in addition to their initial fees. With respect to television commercials and shows, the basic fees of background singers are based in part upon whether the singing is on or off camera and the number of singers in the group. Doubling, sweetening, or multi-tracking may earn additional payments for these singers, and when the jingle tracks on which they performed are used in other commercials for the product, additional scale payments are required.

Other Names. Background singers are sometimes referred to as backup singers, studio singers, jingle singers, chorus members, or nonroyalty singers.

Bar Coding. Industries that manufacture products sold through grocery, drug, and mass-merchandise outlets have used uniform product coding systems to assign unique identification to goods in all channels of distribution and to improve productivity, merchandising, and cost savings in retail stores. In 1977, a committee comprised of members of all echelons of the recording industry reviewed the advantages and disadvantages of a number of different product coding systems and concluded that use of a system would be advantageous to the industry; it was decided that the Universal Product Code (UPC) was most adaptable to the recording industry's needs.

Implementation of the UPC, as of other product coding systems, requires the printing of bar codes or symbols on consumer goods. A bar code is a machine-readable symbol consisting of bars, spaces, and numbers which identify the manufacturer, the specific product, and the configuration of that product.

Bar coding offers various benefits for the recording industry: product movement information; cost savings in inventory control and processing of returns; automatic resupply possibilities; checkstand productivity information, including customer count and per capita sales; store administrative information, including department and store reports; profitability data, including linear footage analysis; improved customer service; productivity improvement possibilities; and the means to reduce checkout errors and pilferage. Bar coding also offers benefits in warehousing and shipping.

The bar code used by the recording industry, a slight modification of the UPC code, consists of ten digits, the first five designating the manufacturer, the fifth and next four identifying the selection, and the last indicating the configuration (i.e., 7-inch single, LP, 8-track, cassette, other). UPC bar codes are usually placed on the upper-right-hand corner of the back cover of LPs and in truncated versions on the front of cassettes and cartridges.

The UPC symbol can be "read" by a variety of optical scanners, which, in a fraction of a second, translate the symbol into the code numbers and flash the number to a computer for processing. The computer "looks up" the item in its file, retrieves the name and price, and sends the information back to the checkstand, where item description and price are printed on the customer's tape and flashed on a small display screen for customer and cashier.

Any company in the recording industry may utilize the UPC or any other system of its choice or none at all, regardless of recommendations by the Industry Coding Committee. While the use of bar codes has met with opposition among some record companies, art directors, and designers (often because the bar code is seen as "unattractive" and clashes with album art), it is gaining acceptance. In 1978 it was first used by some small labels and in 1979 CBS became the first major U.S. label to adopt the system; other major labels, including MCA, Warner Bros., RCA, A & M and Capitol, followed, though on a limited basis. Bar coding for the new video recordings—cassettes and discs—is at the incipient stage, with the new RIAA/VIDEO division structuring guidelines for a voluntary system. RCA SelectaVision VideoDiscs was the first major U.S. video label to adopt the UPC system, with its first releases in March 1981.

Berne Union. *See* INTERNATIONAL COPYRIGHT RELATIONS.

Billboard. *See* CHARTS; TRADES.

BMI. *See* BROADCAST MUSIC, INC.

Bonus. A sum of money given in addition to what is required to be paid, and, as opposed to an ADVANCE, not recoupable from future royalties.

The practice of giving bonuses, in recognition of or as a result of commercial success, exists to a certain extent in the music business. Music publishers, performing rights organizations, and record manufacturers are some of the entities that give bonuses.

A music publisher, for example, may give a bonus to a songwriter as an incentive in a negotiation to acquire or retain the rights to a particular composition or a group of compositions. The amount of the bonus reflects the value of the composition(s) to the publisher. Some record companies give bonuses to staff producers who produce hit records for artists on their labels.

Book. This term has a few different meanings.

In theater, the term "book" refers to the script of a musical play. A book may be original or an adaptation of a preexisting work, such as a play or novel. It is generally believed that a "first-rate" book is necessary for a musical play to be successful, regardless of the virtues of the score and cast.

Usually, the writing of the book precedes the composing of the songs for a Broadway musical. A producer will either option the rights to a property and have someone adapt it for theatrical production by writing dialogue (the person who writes the book is called the *playwright* or author), or have a playwright write a book based upon an original idea. Sometimes the writing of the score is done concurrently with the writing of the book. A playwright may designate in the book where he thinks songs should be inserted.

Book in theater may also refer to a pamphlet containing the text to an opera or extended choral work.

In broadcasting, *book* refers to a radio station's ratings as determined by a radio ratings service's sampling system. The station's "book" is important because it gives demographic information about its audience and is the basis of its advertising rates. Advertisers and advertising agencies use radio stations' books to assist them in deciding where to place their advertising.

To *book* means to engage a performer for employment, such as to sing or play at a concert or a recording session.

Booking Agent. *See* AGENT.

Bootlegging (Records/Audio Tapes). Bootlegging refers to the practice of recording, without permission, an artist's live or broadcast performance, and making and selling phonograph records or audio tapes embodying such performance. Examples of bootlegged recordings include a concert taped without permission by a person in attendance or at home from a radio simulcast. A bootlegged recording is sometimes referred to as an "underground" or "white label" record or tape.

A "white label" record album consists of an album jacket that is blank and a mimeographed sheet, stating the name of the artist, the selections, and the place and date of performance, inserted between the jacket and the shrink wrap to identify the recording. Sometimes a picture of the artist is reproduced on the mimeographed sheet.

Bootleggers often go to festivals, concert halls, theaters, stadiums, arenas, and other such places to make or sell their unauthorized recordings. It is also not uncommon for these spurious recordings to be sold in small record stores, at flea markets and fairs, etc.

Protection. Bootlegging is a violation of various laws. Under the federal copyright law, the act of reproducing a musical composition, or publicly distributing records or tapes of one without authorization from the copyright owner or compliance with the law's compulsory license provision, constitutes a COPYRIGHT INFRINGEMENT.

Certain states, including New York, California, Florida, and Virginia, have specific anti-bootlegging statutes which make the recording of a live performance without permission from the performing artist illegal and punishable by prison term, fine, or both. In New York, the bringing of a recording device into a concert hall without permission is prohibited by law.

An artist may also be able to seek legal recourse from bootlegging under the Lanham Act (Trademark Act of 1946). This law protects registered TRADEMARKS (i.e., names) from being used commercially by others. An artist may also protect the rights to his name or performance under the doctrine of UNFAIR COMPETITION or common law.

See also COUNTERFEITING (RECORDS/AUDIO TAPES); PIRACY (RECORDS/AUDIO TAPES).

Broadcast Music, Inc. (BMI). A PERFORMING RIGHTS ORGANIZATION, BMI licenses on a nonexclusive basis to users of musical compositions the nondramatic public performance rights of the copyrighted musical works of its affiliated publishers and writers and foreign performance right societies. BMI is a nonprofit performing rights licensing body that was formed in 1940 by a group of broadcasters (these stockholders neither collect dividends nor receive special licensing rates).

Licenses and Fees. A music user must have a license from BMI to use the works legally in its repertory. The fees and terms of licensing agreements for broadcasters result from negotiations between BMI officials and industry committees. (These committees are comprised of owners and executive personnel of broadcasting stations across the U.S.) The fees are based upon a broadcasting station's annual income from advertising, less certain deductions.

In licensing other types of music users, BMI often negotiates license fees and terms with an established trade organization, association, or group representing the particular interest. Outside of broadcasters, license fees are based on certain criteria particular to the establishment. For example, hotel, motel, and café fees are based upon annual expenditures for musicians and entertainers, and concert hall fees are determined by their seating capacity. For other establishments, such as ballrooms, fees are computed as a percentage of gross annual income. Employees from BMI field offices across the U.S. answer queries of local music users about their need to comply with copyright laws and acquire a BMI license to perform works in the BMI repertoire.

Determination of Performances. It is BMI's objective to determine accurately in which media its affiliates' works are performed and how often, because it distributes license fees to affiliates based on these factors. For the different types of media where music is performed, BMI uses various methods to determine the frequency of performances of its affiliates' musical works.

Radio. To ascertain which songs are performed on radio and how often, BMI uses a sampling system method. On a quarterly basis, a representative number of stations from the thousands in the U.S. are asked to log by title, composer, and publisher the music they use hour by hour and day by day for one week and submit this to BMI. Sampling is done on a statistical basis; stations are scientifically chosen and represent a cross section of broadcasting activity and area. Communication with the stations providing logs each quarter is carried on by an independent accounting firm, and BMI personnel are not informed which stations are being monitored until the logging quarter is completed.

To determine the approximate total number of U.S. stations broadcasting a BMI work, a performance on a local station is multiplied by a statistical "factor" based on the ratio of stations logged to stations licensed in each station classification. For example, if BMI licenses 400 stations of a certain kind and 10 of them were logged during a particular period, every performance of a song listed would be multiplied by 40; the writer and publisher would thus receive credit for 40 performances every time the song appeared on the log.

Television. Producers of television programs supply BMI with cue sheets which list theme, cue, and all other music performed. BMI determines the number of performances of music in motion pictures, syndicated film series, and other types of television series with the aid of cue sheets and regional editions of *TV Guide.* For network performances, a single performance is multiplied by the number of interconnected stations carrying the broadcast.

Other Media. BMI determines from concert programs which of its works are performed in concert halls and similar venues. BMI does not monitor or log performances of works in nightclubs, discos, hotels, restaurants, bars, colleges, etc., its policy being that any such attempt would not be economically feasible. Although BMI collects license fees from these and similar types of music users, it distributes royalties on the basis of performances on radio and television stations and, for concert music, on the basis of live concert performances.

Distribution. BMI distributes all the license fees it collects to its affiliated writers and publishers, except for operating expenses and necessary reserves. Payments are divided between writers and publishers on an equal basis.

BMI allocates "base rates" for single performances of a popular song or concert work on radio and television. Different base rates are allocated to the different types of performances as categorized by BMI, and are set forth in a "payment schedule." For radio, a base rate is allocated to a composition depending upon whether it is used as a feature performance or radio theme and whether it is

performed on a station whose annual license fee is more (Group 1) or less (Group 2) than $4,000. FM as well as AM stations are categorized as Group 1 or Group 2, depending on the amount of the license fee paid to BMI. No payment is made for performances on radio as background or cue music, or for any partial performance of a composition.

The following is an example of a top 40 song's earnings as it would be computed under BMI's system: A work logs 40,000 performances on Group 1 radio stations and 20,000 on Group 2 radio stations for a given quarter. At a Group 1 rate of $.06 and a Group 2 rate of $.03, the work would earn base royalties of 40,000 × $.06 plus 20,000 × $.03, or $3,000 for that particular quarter.

Television performances are accorded different base rates depending upon whether the composition is deemed to be a feature performance, a television theme, or background music. Within each of these categories there are separate base rates for local and network performances. Rates for the latter category are further divided into Group A and Group B performances. A Group A performance, which has a higher monetary value, is any television program broadcast between the hours of 7 P.M. and 1 A.M.; all other programs are deemed broadcast in Group B time.

Bonuses. BMI pays bonuses for works that receive more than 25,000 logged U.S. feature performances as reflected by its records. BMI thereafter pays bonuses for such performances other than television network and public broadcasting station feature performances. Bonuses are accorded as follows: Plateau A: 25,000 to 49,999 performances (1½ times the base payment rate); Plateau B: 50,000 to 299,999 performances (2 times the base payment rate); Plateau C: 300,000 to 999,999 performances (2½ times the base payment rate); Plateau D: 1,000,000 performances and over (4 times the base payment rate).

U.S. network television and public broadcasting station feature performances are counted in computing the plateau of a work, but such performances themselves are not subject to bonuses. A work in the BMI repertoire on July 1, 1980, receives U.S. feature broadcast performances after that date based on its cumulative performances from and after January 1, 1960. U.S. feature performances of "show music" are automatically entitled to Plateau D status, and U.S. feature performances of "movie works," Plateau C status if the latter were cleared since 1980.

Definitions. With respect to the foregoing, BMI makes the following distinctions: A feature radio performance is "a performance of not less than 90 seconds duration which is the sole sound broadcast at the time of the performance and which therefore constitutes the sole focus of audience attention." A feature television performance is "a performance that constitutes the main focus of audience attention at the time of performance. The vocalists and/or instrumentalists, respectively, must be on camera except where the music is used as part of a choreographic routine which constitutes the main focus of attention." If the feature performance is between 15 and 45 seconds duration, it receives half feature credit. Feature performances of less than 15 seconds duration are credited at specified monetary rates for network and local usage. A television theme "is a theme that comprises both the opening and closing musical works performed on a program." Where a work is used as an opening or closing, it receives half payment only. The theme is credited at background rates when performed other than at the opening or closing.

BMI defines "background music" as "music used other than as feature or theme." With certain exceptions (as stated below), BMI makes payment to its affiliates for background music based on the use of music up to one half of the duration of the program. For uses in excess of one half of the duration of the program, a proportional reduction is made for the purpose of division among publishers and writers entitled to such payments, but payment will not exceed that which would have been made for a usage of one half of the program duration. With respect to programs broadcast more than three times a week, the rate for background music is one third the usual rate unless the music is performed on a single instrument, in which case it is computed at one fourth the usual rate.

Exceptions for the rate of payment of background music pertain to its use in motion pictures made for television (more than 90 minutes in duration), quiz and audience participation shows, debates, discussions, newscasts, lectures, commentaries and similar programs, and untimed background music used to mark entrances, exits, play-ons, play-offs, and changes of scene. For each of these, BMI prescribes a particular monetary value.

Other Crediting Rules. BMI promulgates the following rules with respect to performances of musical works: no payment is made for performance of a work as part of a promotional announcement but payment is made for commercial jingles that are not written for hire and run for at least 15 consecutive seconds as the main focus of audience attention; material contained on spoken-word records is not accepted for clearance or license; a work (other than a concert work) which exceeds 7 minutes as commercially recorded may be eligible for additional credit; lyric and instrumental performances of the same work are credited as the same work unless each version bears a different title; for performances of 45 rpm records embodying two or more works: (1) full logging credit is given if such recording contains no more than two musical works and the performances of each work consist of a full chorus or more, and (2) single logging credit is given if such recording contains more than two musical works. However, BMI will follow a directive from the publishers of the works specifying division of the single logging credit.

Foreign Performances. BMI has agreements with performing rights societies in foreign countries which render appropriate payments to BMI on a periodic basis when works in the BMI repertory are performed locally and monitored. BMI distributes performance royalties it receives from foreign performing rights organizations to its affiliates to whom they are due, after deducting 3% of the gross amount received for handling and administrative expenses.

Frequency of Distribution. BMI pays writer and publisher affiliates for U.S. broadcast performances 4 times per year. Distribution of royalties reflecting foreign performances is made semiannually and statements and payments related to live concert performances are rendered once a year.

Affiliation. Writer affiliation is open to anyone who has written, alone or in collaboration with others, a musical work that has been commercially published or recorded, or is otherwise likely to be performed. The BMI writer's contract endures for 2 years and is automatically renewed unless either the writer or BMI gives notice 60 days before termination of the contract. BMI publisher affiliation is available to applicants who have musical compositions being performed or likely to be performed by broadcasting stations or other public performance areas at the time of affiliation.

Broadway Musicals. The premier showcase for theatrical productions (musical and straight play) in the United States is the *Broadway* show. Broadway is an avenue in Manhattan (a borough of New York City) that is famous for its theatrical district. Actually, most of the so-called Broadway theaters are located on side streets near the intersection of Broadway from West 41st to West 53rd streets.

Sales and Activity. Sales and activity reports issued by the League of New York Theatres and Producers, Inc. (see below) indicate the drawing power of Broadway shows. For example, the league reported that during the 1969–70 season, attendance was 7.1 million and actual ticket sales were $53 million. Attendance a decade later (during the 1979–80 season) was 9.6 million, for actual ticket sales of $146 million. During the 1979–80 season there were 61 new productions on Broadway—38 straight plays, 17 musicals, 4 special attractions, and 2 revues. By the close of the season there were 31 productions running, 11 of which were carryovers from previous seasons. It was estimated that 14 million people throughout the United States attended touring Broadway shows that year, paying approximately $181 million in ticket sales. Revenues from touring companies are an important source of income for authors and producers; hence a "Broadway show" is not just limited to Broadway.

Broadway Season. Historically, "Broadway season" referred to September–June, because new shows opened during those months only. Technically, however, the Broadway season begins on the first Monday following June 1 and ends on the Sunday of the last week the following May.

"Life" of a Show. A figure of 500 consecutive performances is often used as a bench mark to indicate a hit show. A show that has had that many runs or more, however, is not necessarily a financial success; there are examples of perdurable musicals that have closed at a loss to their investors. In general, though, a show needs a long run to recoup its expenses and enjoy economic fruition. Following are the number of performances some of the most successful musicals have had (followed by the year of original Broadway production): *Grease,* 3,388 performances (1972); *Fiddler on the Roof,* 3,242 (1964); *Hello, Dolly!,* 2,844 (1964); *My Fair Lady,* 2,717 (1956); *Man of*

La Mancha, 2,329 (1965); *Oklahoma!,* 2,248 (1943); *South Pacific,* 1,925 (1949); *Hair,* 1,750 (1968); *Mame,* 1,508 (1966); *The Sound of Music,* 1,493 (1959).

Tickets. Tickets for a Broadway show may be purchased at the box office, by telephone (with a valid credit card), by mail, at TKTS (half-price tickets for day of performance only), at Ticketron outlets, through licensed ticket brokers, and through group sales agents. Theater box offices accept credit cards, personal checks, and cash for ticket purchases. In 1980, the range of ticket prices for a Broadway musical was $18 to $30; for a straight play, $9 to $25. The average paid admission inclusive of tickets purchased at TKTS and group sales discounts was approximately $17 (for all shows for all performances).

The League of New York Theatres and Producers, Inc. A professional trade association whose members consist of producers, theater owners, lessees, and operators, the league negotiates labor contracts with the theatrical trade unions, conducts marketing and economic research, promotes touring shows, develops urban environment programs, is a liaison with all levels of government, performs institutional public relations and promotion, and presents the American Theatre Wing's Tony Awards.

Critics. Critics are customarily not invited to review a show during an out-of-town *tryout* or a *preview* at a Broadway theater. Normally, critics review a Broadway show on its opening night performance, though sometimes there are a limited number of previews from which the producer offers a choice of performances to review.

Production Costs. There are many costs involved in mounting a theatrical production. Because these can altogether be substantial—Broadway musicals usually run well over a million dollars today—producers seek outside investors to raise the capital needed. Such money is normally amassed by producers un-der the form of business known as the LIMITED PARTNERSHIP. The capital raised goes to finance a variety of costs allocated in the following areas:

Fees and advances—author; director; set, costume, lighting, sound, and hair designers; assistant director; accountant, general manager; attorney, and casting director. Also, there are fees for orchestrations, vocal and dance arrangements, copying, and demo tapes.

Physical production—sets, props, costumes, lighting, and sound equipment.

Prerehearsal expenses—casting and auditions, scripts, transportation, audition space, and per diems.

Rehearsal expenses—salaries to cast (principals and chorus), stage manager, company manager, general manager, musical director, musicians, rehearsal pianist, and secretaries. Also, there are costs for rehearsal space and local transportation.

Administrative—office expenses, general manager's expenses, accounting, legal advertising, insurance, pension and welfare, vacation, payroll taxes, per diems, opening night expenses, utilities (telephone and electricity), and preliminary box office expenses.

Bonds and deposits—union bonds (AEA, AFM, ATPAM, IATSE, and TWAU) and theater deposit.

The sum of all the above is the production costs for presenting a Broadway musical. Production costs, then, are the total expenses, charges, and disbursements incurred in connection with the production of the show preliminary to its New York opening.

Running Expenses. Once a show is actually in progress, certain costs, fees, and percentages are deducted from the weekly box office gross before the net receipts are derived. These aru the show's *running expenses* (discussed in LIMITED PARTNERSHIPS). The running expenses include percentages payable to certain parties, customarily: composer, lyricist, and play-

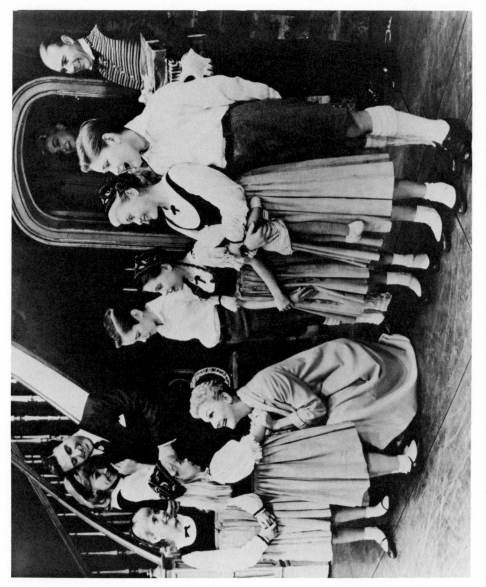

Broadway musicals are expensive to mount, but a "hit" may be extremely lucrative for its composer, lyricist, and bookwriter as well as the producer and any limited partners. This picture is a scene featuring Mary Martin in one of Broadway's greatest musicals, Rodgers and Hammerstein's *The Sound of Music*.

wright (6%–8%), theater management (25%), director (2%–2.5%), choreographer (2%), designers (2%). There may be percentages payable for the underlying rights to the property on which the play is based (1%) and for any contracts entered into with "star" performers. Also, general partners usually receive (in addition to 50% of the net profits of the play) a producer's management fee that runs to 1.5%–2% of the gross weekly box office receipts from all companies under the partnership's management or license. The percentages earned by such principals as the authors and the directors may increase after there has been a recoupment of production costs. In a limited partnership, the net profits are divided among the limited and general partners.

Theater Rental. To rent a Broadway theater, producers pay either a percentage of the show's weekly gross box office receipts (approximately 25%) or the cost of operating the theater plus a percentage of the show's weekly gross (such as 10%). In some instances, the theater is rented and theater operating expenses, including salaries, are paid by the producer.

Licenses. Musicals, such as those presented on Broadway, as well as other productions, including Off Broadway, stock, dinner theater, and amateur, are dramatico-musical works. Consequently any producer, theatrical company, amateur or other group wishing to perform such a work must obtain a license for the rights to performance. These rights are licensed by the copyright owner or his agent.

With the multitude of productions by regional, stock, and touring companies, and amateur, school, and other groups throughout the U.S. and other parts of the world, a musical that is originally a hit on Broadway may continue to generate much revenue for many years. Shows with several national companies have been known to gross over $1 million a week from such productions alone.

Publishers. A publisher normally obtains the rights to a show score by either having the composer and lyricist under contract or making a financial investment in the show. After the authors write all the songs and before the show is actually produced, they will play the score for the company's creative staff, who select the most commercial numbers, make demos, and "exploit" them.

A few hundred LPs containing the best selections, for example, may be pressed. The professional staff will audition these songs with record companies, producers, recording artists, and cabaret performers. If a single is released and becomes successful, the song may not only be covered by other artists and motivate people to buy the ORIGINAL CAST SHOW ALBUM, but generate interest in the show and help sell tickets. Publishers consequently often assist in obtaining airplay for the recorded material. The active publisher will continue to exploit the score even after the show closes.

Motion Pictures. Successful Broadway musicals are sometimes made into theatrical motion pictures. One of the first was Sigmund Romberg's *The Desert Song*, which became a Warner Brothers film in 1929. Because of the early successes of screen musicals, Hollywood has often turned to Broadway. Recently, film producers have been known to pay large sums of money for the motion picture rights to successful musicals. For example, Columbia purchased the film rights to *Annie* for $9.5 million.

See also ACTORS' EQUITY ASSOCIATION (AEA); OFF BROADWAY/OFF OFF BROADWAY THEATER; TONY AWARDS.

Budget Album. Record or tape that wholesales or retails at a price lower than current front-line products.

Budget albums are often older records and tapes that the manufacturer feels are marketable enough to be continued in its catalog but are no longer salable at their full (original) value. They may also be original recordings specifically produced to be sold at a lower list price than front-line products. Albums of the latter category are normally issued by the manufacturer on a separate LABEL, known as the *budget* or *economy line.*

Budget lines are often created to market recordings whose audience is generally not prone to buying albums at front-line prices (such as children's recordings) or buys records for a special occasion (for example, Christmas recordings). Budget lines also include issues of classical LPs, instrumental renditions of popular tunes, cover versions of movie and television sound tracks, and compilations of artists' greatest hits performed by an orchestra or a studio artist. Assuming the retail list price of front-line records are $7.98 to $8.98, budget LPs would range in price from $2.99 to $5.99.

See also CUT-OUT.

Buenos Aires Convention. *See* INTERNATIONAL COPYRIGHT RELATIONS.

Business Laws, Federal and State. Federal and state laws aimed at regulating business practices apply to the operations of record and tape manufacturers, wholesalers, retailers, and others in the record/music industries. These laws serve to prevent abusive business practices, such as price fixing, price discrimination, boycotts, tie-in sales, and unfair trade practices, in the record and music industries.

Federal Statutes. Following are some of the important federal statutes that regulate interstate business practices:

Sherman Antitrust Act (1890)—Makes illegal contracts, combinations, and conspiracies in restraint of trade.

Clayton Act (1914)—Prohibits certain practices that were not specifically enumerated in the Sherman Act, such as mergers, tie-in sales (forcing one to buy a second product in order to be able to purchase desired goods), and in-

terlocking directorates of corporations. The Clayton Act also provides for certain exemptions from the antitrust laws, such as labor union and insurance activities.

Federal Trade Commission Act (1914)—Prevents unfair or deceptive acts or practices in commerce. The FEDERAL TRADE COMMISSION (FTC) was created to administer the FTC Act.

Robinson-Patman Act (1936)—Amended the Clayton Act to prohibit price discrimination. The law requires sellers to sell goods of like grade and quality at the same price. Cost-justified discounts (e.g., volume discounts) are permitted.

Lanham Trade-Mark Act (1946)—Provides for the registration and use of trademarks.

Fair Packaging and Labeling Act (1966)—Prevents unfair or deceptive packaging or labeling of certain consumer commodities.

State Laws. Several states have laws that similarly regulate business practices. See, for example, the California Business Practices Code and New York General Business Law.

Business Manager. Person who handles the financial affairs related to the careers of recording artists, entertainers, and composers. Usually, only those whose incomes are substantial retain this representative.

The services provided by business managers are many and varied; each tailors services to the needs of the particular client. There are some basic areas, however, that business managers normally deal in.

Business managers collect the client's income from the various sources—such as recording, producing, songwriting, films, merchandising, tie-ins, and endorsements (seeing that it is remitted when due); check and pay the client's bills; keep systematic records of all transactions; and periodically submit financial statements to the client. This representative may administer normal business expenses such as paying the personal manager or public relations firm, or bills for wardrobe, travel, and related items.

The business manager is frequently involved in devising budgets for recording and concert touring. He may also accompany the artist on tour, as ticket revenues may be considerable and it would be best to have a competent financial representative deal with promoters and others in overseeing the calculation of percentages and the collection of receipts. He is available to assist in negotiating recording, merchandising, television, motion picture, and other contracts.

The business manager may also function to advise the client on making investments. In effect, the representative attempts to maximize the client's net worth during his high-income years so that the client can later enjoy the economic benefits of growth investment, the average "life" or high-income years of an entertainer being relatively brief. The business manager also attempts to minimize the output of income received.

With respect to taxes, the business manager advises the client of the tax consequences of business decisions and prepares returns. He functions to minimize taxes in high-earning years and spread them out during years when income earned is low.

The business manager may, on behalf of the client, conduct royalty AUDITS of companies with whom the client has a royalty contract as a recording artist, songwriter, or producer. Audits may also be performed on behalf of a publishing company owned by a client. Though many business managers are certified public accountants, often a manager will retain accountants expert at these special audits.

Business managers' fees may be charged as: (1) a percentage of the client's gross income, commonly ranging from 5% to 10% (where a client's income is so large, a limit on the commission may be fixed); (2) a flat rate per year or per month; (3) an hourly fee; or (4) a minimum fee against a percentage (commission). The method of billing varies from business manager to business manager and from client to client.

See also AUDITS, ROYALTY.

C

Cable Television. Cable television is of significance to copyright owners and creators of musical compositions because of the revenue they may earn from certain transmissions of their works by these systems. Their right to enjoy compensation from such transmissions was first provided for by the Copyright Act of 1976.

Description. Cable television, also known as CATV, is defined by the Federal Communications Commission as "a system by which television signals are collected at a central point and distributed by wire (cable) for a fee." Typically, a cable system consists of: (1) head end section, the point at which a signal is introduced to the system; (2) trunk line section, the part which carries the signal from the head end to the community; and (3) distribution system, which brings the signal from the trunk line to an individual subscriber's home.

CATV was developed in the late 1940s to service communities where terrain or distance from TV stations resulted in poor or no reception. Cable offers clearer pictures, particularly for color television, and a larger number of channels (an average currently of 10 per system, although some can offer 60 or more). Some systems originate their own programming, such as sports, movies, news, and specials, and charge additional fees for this service; others offer subscribers audio services as well, particularly classical music.

CATV and Copyright Law. The Copyright Act of 1976, which became fully effective on January 1, 1978, provides a compulsory license for cable television systems. Under this provision, cable systems pay compulsory license fees for "secondary transmissions" (i.e., programs originally broadcast by television and radio stations) of copyrighted works.

The compulsory license for transmitting copyrighted works is available to cable operators who are authorized by the Federal Communications Commission to carry a particular signal. Under the compulsory license, CATV operators are required to file with the Register of Copyrights the number of channels on which the cable system made secondary transmissions to its subscribers, the names and locations of all primary transmitters whose transmissions were further transmitted by the cable system, the number of subscribers, the gross receipts for the basic services of providing distant secondary transmissions, as well as other data as the Register of Copyrights may, after consultation with the Copyright Royalty Tribunal from time to time, prescribe by regulation, along with the royalty fee for the 6-month period covered. The total royalty fee for the period covered by the statement is computed on the basis of specified percentages of gross receipts from subscribers to the cable service during the period for the basic service under a formula prescribed by the law.

Fees are paid to the Register, who, after deducting reasonable costs incurred by the Copyright Office, deposits the balance in the Treasury of the United States (the Treasury is required to invest all funds in interest-bearing U.S. securities). Royalty fees are later distributed by the Tribunal. Any copyright owner is entitled to royalty fees whose works were included: (1) in a secondary transmission made by a cable system of a distant non-network television program in whole or part; (2) in a secondary transmission identified in a special statement of account; and (3) in distant non-network programming consisting exclusively of aural signals (radio).

Annually in July, each person claiming to be entitled to royalties must file a claim with the Copyright Royalty Tribunal. After August 1, the tribunal determines whether a controversy exists. If not, it deducts its administrative costs and distributes the fees to the copyright owners or their agents. If a controversy does exist, the tribunal must publish a notice of commencement of proceeding and render a final decision within 1 year from the date of publication of the notice.

The law provides for periodic review of the royalty rates, as described in the COPYRIGHT ROYALTY TRIBUNAL entry. The law also sets forth four exemptions to the compulsory license for cable TV.

Cable television systems, which grossed more than $1 billion in 1978, paid $12.5 million to the Copyright Office for that year. This sum (less the Register's administrative costs) was later divided among filmmakers, music copyright owners, sports producers, and broadcasters. The Copyright Royalty Tribunal determined music copyright owners should receive 4.5 percent of these compulsory license fees. The fees were allocated to the performing rights organizations as follows: ASCAP, 54%; BMI, 43%; and SESAC, 3%. If the growth of cable continues, then it appears it will serve as a rich source of income for these copyright owners. Some programming is exclusively relayed by satellite, a technology that promises to offer more selections as well as wider and improved communication.

Canada. Over the years, Canada has been a leader in the world market for selling records and prerecorded tapes. During the 1970s, its annual sales were consistently among the highest ten of countries throughout the world.

The Canadian market may be illustrated by

Canada's Record and Prerecorded Tape Sales by Market (1978)*

($ MM)

	% of Population	Record Sales	% of Canada	Pre-recorded Tape Sales	% of Canada
Atlantic Provinces†	9.4	11.6	6.3%	5.0	7.5%
Quebec	27.2	51.1	27.9%	11.9	17.8%
Ontario	35.9	68.5	37.3%	23.5	35.3%
Manitoba/ Saskatchewan	8.5	14.4	7.9%	8.9	13.3%
Alberta	8.0	16.2	8.9%	8.6	12.9%
British Columbia	11.0	21.5	11.7%	8.8	13.2%
Total Canada	100.0	$183.3	100.0%	$66.7	100.0%

Est. population January 1979: 23,597,600.‡

* Source: Canadian Recording Industry Association.
† Atlantic Provinces: Newfoundland, Prince Edward Island, Nova Scotia, New Brunswick.
‡ Source: *Canada Year Book 1978-79*, Statistics Canada.

the above table, which breaks down record and prerecorded tape sales in the various Canadian provinces and territories for 1978. That year, the total market for records and prerecorded tapes in the country exceeded $250 million in sales (representing an increase of 41% over the previous year).

While the current styles of music and popular recording artists in Canada may vary from those in other countries, Canada's music industry is comprised of the standard recording, publishing, and other music companies (whose operations are similar to those of companies in other countries), licensing, trade, and professional organizations, and unions. It has bilateral copyright relations with the United States and is a member of international copyright conventions.

Consequently this entry examines only organizations, unions, laws, and other matters particular to Canada (the general operations of record companies, music publishers, etc., are covered elsewhere in this book). The following are discussed here: AM and FM radio regulations; Canadian copyright law; employment of

Courtesy: *Billboard*

U.S. artists in Canada; imports and exports (phonograph records); mechanical rights and licensing; performing rights organizations; trade associations and professional organizations; trademarks; and unions.

AM and FM Radio Regulations. The policies set out in Canadian broadcast legislation call for a system of radio and television "using predominantly Canadian creative and other resources" which will "safeguard, enrich and strengthen the cultural, political [and] social . . . fabric of Canada." As a means of implementing these policies, the Canadian Radiotelevision and Telecommunications Commission (CRTC) established Canadian content requirements for AM and FM radio, which have come to be known in the industry as the "Cancon" regulations. CRTC established the regulations with the view that they could be changed or eliminated as they ceased to be necessary. While CRTC has not as yet done an assessment, there is every indication that the

regulations have had the significant indirect effect of contributing to a stronger Canadian recording industry.

The Canadian content regulations for AM radio, which have been in effect since January 18, 1971, are as follows:

1. At least 30% of the musical compositions broadcast by a station or network operator between the hours of 6 A.M. and midnight shall be by a Canadian and shall be scheduled in a reasonable manner throughout such period.

2. From January 18, 1971, to January 17, 1972, a musical composition shall be deemed to be by a Canadian if it fulfills at least one of the conditions set out in subsection 5.

3. After January 19, 1972, a musical composition shall be deemed to be by a Canadian if it fulfills at least two of the conditions set out in subsection 5.

4. After January 18, 1973, at least 5% of the musical compositions broadcast by a station or network operator between 6 A.M. and mid-

night shall fulfill the condition set out in either b or c of subsection 5.

5. The following are the conditions referred to in subsections 2, 3, and 4:

    a. The instrumentation or lyrics were principally performed by a Canadian.

    b. The music was composed by a Canadian.

    c. The lyrics were written by a Canadian.

    d. The live performance was wholly recorded in Canada, or was wholly performed and broadcast live in Canada.

6. A mechanical reproduction of a musical composition that is deemed at any time to be by a Canadian continues to be so deemed thereafter.

7. If a station operator is able to demonstrate to the satisfaction of the commission that the application of this section would result in a significant reduction in the quality and diversity of program service within the area normally served by the station, the commission may vary the application of this section.

8. For the purposes of this section, a person shall be deemed to be a Canadian if:

    a. he is a Canadian citizen;

    b. he is a landed immigrant as defined in the Immigration Act; or

    c. his ordinary place of residence was in Canada during the six months immediately preceding his contribution to the musical composition in question.

FM Canadian Content. The commission's FM policy calls for FM radio stations to generally achieve at least 30% Canadian content in their music programming. The specific requirement differs from station to station, depending on the programming mix, the locality, and the resources available to each station.

Canadian Copyright Law. Copyright law in Canada is under the exclusive jurisdiction of the federal government and set out in its Copyright Act. This law provides protection upon creation for every original musical, artistic, literary, or dramatic work. Protection also extends to contrivances that mechanically reproduce sound, such as records and prerecorded tapes.

The Copyright Act grants to the author of any such work certain exclusive rights (see below), provided: the author was a British subject or citizen of a country that adheres to the International Copyright Convention when he produced the work; and in the case of a published work, the work was first published within Her Majesty's Realms and Territories or in a Convention country.

The copyright term for a written work is for the life of the author plus 50 years; for sound recordings it is 50 years from the date of the making of the original plate.

Registration of a work is not a statutory requirement, but it does provide prima facie evidence of copyright ownership. Copyright applications are sent to the Commissioner of Patents, with the applicant's name, title of the work, and registration fee. Copies of the work being registered are not required and should not be submitted (there is a requirement, however, that 2 copies of the first printing of every book printed in Canada be sent to the National Library of Canada).

The Canadian Copyright Act grants to copyright owners the exclusive rights to reproduce; to perform in public; to publish; to adapt; to broadcast; and to authorize any of the foregoing.

International Copyright Law. Canada ratified the Universal Copyright Convention on August 19, 1962. The UCC provides automatic protection for unpublished works in UCC countries, including the United States. The UCC extends to original works first published in Canada automatic copyright protection in the U.S. and other Convention countries, provided that all copies bear the prescribed copyright notice (*see* INTERNATIONAL COPYRIGHT RELATIONS).

Employment of U.S. Artists in Canada.

Employment authorizations are required for all U.S. acts performing in Canada. Canadian Immigration makes two distinctions regarding documentation necessary for entry into Canada:

1. If an act is going to play at a facility such as a *club*, where food and alcohol are served, then the members of the group need:
   a. A Confirmation of Offer of Employment, or Form 2151. The employer in Canada must apply for Form 215l at a local Canada Employment Centre (CEC) on behalf of the act. The CEC then can mail the 2151 directly to the members of the act (if they are American citizens or permanent residents—i.e., green-card holders), or to the immigration section at a Canadian consulate in the U.S.
   b. An Employment Authorization, or Form 1102. Upon receipt of the 2151, if the members of the act are U.S. citizens or permanent residents (green-card holders), the members of the act may proceed to the Canadian border to obtain the Employment Authorization, which is the actual permission to work. Citizens of other countries must apply for Form 1102 at a Canadian consulate. These requirements are provided because the priority of the Canadian government is employment for its own citizens and permanent residents, rather than foreigners.
2. If the act is going to play in a concert hall, stadium, or other such venue, where the principal reason for the performance is the presentation of the art, then the members of the group need:
   a. A copy of the contract.
   b. An 1102, which may be obtained at the border on presentation of the contract and proof of American citizenship (birth certificate, passport, or voter registration card) or proof of resident alien status in the U.S. (green card); it may be obtained at a Canadian consulate by citizens of other countries.

Acts Performing in the Province of Quebec. Acts performing in a club-like facility in Quebec will also need a Quebec Certificate of Acceptance (Certificat d'Acceptation), which the CEC should arrange for on their behalf.

Foreign Acts Working in Canada. For any acts from outside the U.S. the same regulations apply, the difference being that *no* authorizations can be obtained at the port of entry. All authorizations must be obtained prior to entry into Canada through an immigration office of the Canadian embassy or consulate, preferably in the country of residence of the members of the act.

Employment authorizations are not transferable from one employer to another; thus, the above procedures must be followed for each club or concert date.

Imports and Exports (Phonograph Records). All phonograph records going into Canada are dutiable; there is also a federal tax imposed upon these goods. When goods are shipped into Canada, the customs office there advises the buyer or importer of the arrival of the merchandise. At the time the goods are picked up, duty and federal tax are payable, based on the higher of either the fair market value of the merchandise in the country of export or the actual selling price to the Canadian customer. (In 1980, duty was 15% and federal sales tax was 9%; these percentages are subject to change.) Duty policies are reviewed by Revenue Canada and the Department of Finance of Canada.

Exports to U.S. With respect to phonograph records mailed from Canada to the United States, if the shipment goes to an importer and its value is over $250, a formal entry is required. A notice of arrival of the mail shipment (CF 3509) is sent out by the Mail Branch of U.S. Customs, notifying the addressee that the shipment is being held for formal customs entry. The importer then sends his representative with the notice of arrival of mail shipment, invoice, and other pertinent documents, to make entry and pay the duty.

If the value of the goods sent to an importer is under $250, the customs mail specialist will assess duty on the mail entry (CF 3419) and affix it to the parcel, which is turned over to the post office for direct delivery to the addressee and collection of customs duty. When merchandise is sent to individuals the procedure is the same; if the merchandise is a gift, worth under $25, it can be entered free of duty.

Mechanical Rights and Licensing. Under Canadian copyright law, the owner of copyright has the exclusive right to make mechanical reproductions (discs, tapes, etc.) of a musical work. Once a first recording has been made, however, anyone may acquire the rights in the musical work necessary to make and distribute subsequent recordings by following procedures set forth in the "compulsory licensing" sections of the law (Canada, like many other countries, has a "compulsory license" provision in its copyright law). These procedures provide for the person or company making the recording to give the copyright owner or his agent notice of his/their intention to produce or sell a recording (each musical work to be included in the recording must be specified) and to pay royalties on each recording manufactured and sold, according to a prescribed method of payment (which is on a quarterly basis).

Canada's statutory royalty for recordings is currently $.02 for each playing surface. Manufacturers usually pay $.02 per selection for singles and $.015 to $.02 per selection included in each album or tape, with royalties calculated on each unit manufactured and sold. Virtually all mechanical licenses are issued under terms that vary from the statute's compulsory licensing provisions.

Mechanical licenses are often issued on the copyright owner's behalf by CMRRA (see below). If the copyright owner is not represented by CMRRA, licenses are issued directly by the copyright owner.

Canadian Musical Reproduction Rights Agency Limited (CMRRA). A MECHANICAL RIGHTS AGENCY. CMRRA administers the reproduction rights of music publishers by licensing and charging the applicable royalty fee for reproductions of its affiliates' music manufactured in Canada and sold in or outside Canada. Four main types of reproduction rights are administered by CMRRA—mechanical rights, synchronization rights, commercial use rights, and reprography rights. Reprography is the reproduction of sheet music or lyrics or other printed editions of music by any copying process.

Licenses for mechanical reproductions issued by CMRRA are normally at a rate of $.02 per title up to 5 minutes duration and $.005 per additional minute or fraction thereof (producers are free to negotiate lower rates with publisher affiliates, in which case CMRRA issues licenses according to the publisher's instructions).°

Synchronization licenses are issued where music is used in motion picture films, television productions, videocassettes, videograms, videodiscs, and synchronized slide presentations. CMRRA issues standard form licenses to producers, depending on the particular use, but takes the publishers' instructions regarding fees and terms.

Use of musical works for radio and television commercials, background music, and syndicated radio programs is also licensed by CMRRA. Fees are set by the publisher on a

---

° The Canadian government is presently revising the Copyright Act and it is expected that new rates in mechanical licenses will be included. New statutory rates will be carried through in the rates at which licenses are issued by CMRRA.

situation-by-situation basis. CMRRA is in addition a publisher's licensing agent for reprography rights.

CMRRA collects the agreed license fee from producers and accounts for and distributes the fees to copyright owners on a quarterly basis. It presently retains commissions of 5% for mechanical rights and 10% for the other reproduction rights. The agency controls and administers reproductions of its clients' works produced in Canada for the Canadian and world markets. It also has authority to license reproductions made outside Canada but intended for the Canadian market, and not copyright-cleared at the source. CMRRA has agreements with foreign mechanical rights agencies to ensure that CMRRA-administered Canadian works are accounted for abroad.

CMRRA was established by the Canadian Music Publishers Association and is incorporated under the Canada Business Corporations Act.

Performing Rights Organizations. The "performing right" as included in the Canadian Copyright Act grants the copyright owner the exclusive right to perform the work in public. Thus, in order for a radio or TV station, concert hall, club, or any other establishment or medium of public entertainment to legally use a copyrighted musical work, it must have permission from the owner of copyright.

Because of the quantity of copyrighted musical works in existence, obtaining a license from the copyright owner of each song a performer uses would be an expensive, if not impossible, task. The administration of performing rights on behalf of music publishers and composers and lyricists is handled by performing rights organizations (which administer nondramatic performing rights for all copyrights in their repertoires).

Canada has two performing rights organizations: the Composers, Authors and Publishers Association of Canada Limited (CAPAC) and the Performing Rights Organization of Canada Limited (P.R.O. Canada). These license copyrighted music in most fields of public performance, including radio, television, motion pictures, theatrical stage productions, and in such locations as concert halls, clubs, hotels, fairs, planes, and trains.

Composers, Authors and Publishers Association of Canada Limited (CAPAC). Founded in 1925 as the Canadian Performing Right Society Limited, CAPAC is a federally incorporated company. All its shares are held for its writer and publisher members by the Canada Permanent Trust Company under a trust agreement.

CAPAC licenses commercial users of music in Canada, collects fees from them, and after deducting operating expenses, distributes the revenue to its members—composers, lyricists, and publishers. Commercial music users obtain licenses by paying a fee based mainly on an annual blanket formula. This entitles, for example, private AM and FM broadcasting stations to perform any or all of the musical works in the CAPAC repertoire an unlimited number of times during the licensing period. The license fee for a broadcaster is based on a percentage of its total gross revenue for a year. This format is used to determine the license fees for other types of music users, but each has its own formula.

The license fees CAPAC may charge for use of its repertoire are established by a Canadian government tribunal, known as the Copyright Appeal Board. The board was established in 1937 by an amendment to Canada's Copyright Act. Each year, CAPAC must file with the board statements of fees, charges, or royalties it proposes to collect from music users; music users, in turn, have the opportunity to appear personally before the board and file objections regarding various types of usage.

After weighing arguments from each side, the board establishes rates which CAPAC may charge for the forthcoming year. In the absence of voluntary compliance, CAPAC may lawfully sue for collection of payment.

DISTRIBUTION. License fees collected from users of music are distributed to CAPAC members under rules and procedures established by CAPAC's board of directors (board members are voted into office by CAPAC's general membership body). Moneys are distributed in accordance with the number of performances that have been logged by CAPAC during a particular distribution period. All members whose works are logged share equally in the distribution, with variation in payment depending on the number of individual performances logged for each musical work.

Distribution is subdivided into the following categories: (1) broadcast, general, and concert hall (made twice a year); (2) television (made twice a year); (3) motion pictures (made once a year); and (4) foreign (made once a year). The 6-month distribution pool comprises those moneys collected in any given year from January 1 to June 30 and from July 1 to December 31. Statements and checks are sent separately to composer, lyricist, and publisher members.

Under CAPAC regulations, if a work has not been published and there are separate music and lyric writers, the composer and lyricist each collects 50% of the moneys earned; if the composition has been published, the distribution is 25% to the composer, 25% to the lyricist, and 50% to the publisher. For works subpublished outside Canada, the distribution is normally 25% each to the composer and lyric writer, and 25% each to the original publisher and foreign subpublisher. CAPAC has bilateral contracts with performing rights societies in most countries around the world. Under the bilateral contract, CAPAC administers the performing rights of copyrighted works of members of foreign societies, and foreign societies administer the performing rights of works of CAPAC members in their countries.

Membership as a composer or lyric writer in CAPAC is available to those whose work has been (1) published by a bona fide music publisher; or (2) recorded by a bona fide record company; or (3) performed in some area of public performance which CAPAC licenses.

Performing Rights Organization of Canada Limited (PRO Canada). PRO was formed by Broadcast Music, Inc. (BMI) of the United States in 1940 as BMI Canada Limited, to license in Canada works in BMI's repertoire. By 1947, vigorous efforts to work on behalf of Canadian composers, writers, and publishers were being made from Toronto, and in 1948 PRO Canada's Montreal office was opened. A second branch was opened in Vancouver in 1968. On July 15, 1977, BMI Canada was established as a wholly Canadian-owned not-for-profit organization, and its name changed.

PRO Canada licenses nondramatic performing rights on behalf of copyright proprietors of musical works for public performances. Writer and publisher affiliates are supplied with registration forms on which to provide all relevant information regarding their works. This is returned to the index department of PRO Canada, enabling identification of works for which the affiliate is entitled to receive payment.

PRO Canada monitors performances of works in its repertoire in the following way: Each quarter, it logs a scientifically chosen representative cross section of radio and television stations. Stations logged provide PRO Canada with complete information on all music performed during the logging period in that quarter. The logs (lists) are put through a computer system, which multiplies each performance by a "factor" that reflects the ratio of the number of stations logged to the number licensed and the region. Stations being logged in a given week are not notified in advance.

Television theme and background music compositions are logged by the information producers supply on "cue sheets" which list all music performed in a program. The number of performances of music in motion pictures, syndicated film series, and certain other types of programs appearing on television is determined with cue sheets and TV guides. PRO Canada ascertains actual performances of concert works composed by its affiliates by securing programs of symphony orchestras, concerts, bands, etc.

Publisher affiliation is available to applicants who have some musical composition being performed, or likely to be performed, by broadcasting stations or otherwise. PRO Canada requires that publishers register their company as a business enterprise. PRO Canada has reciprocal agreements with foreign performing rights organizations so that it can collect and pay royalties for foreign copyrights performed in Canada, and to its affiliates when their works are performed in foreign territories.

Writer affiliation is open to those who have written a musical composition, alone or in collaboration with other writers, that is either commercially published, recorded, or likely to be performed. The term of writer affiliation is 5 years.

Trade Associations and Professional Organizations

Canadian Academy of Recording Arts and Sciences (CARAS). An organization created to foster the development of the Canadian music and recording industries and to contribute toward higher artistic standards, CARAS is comprised of individuals working in all segments of the record industry. Members include record company employees and record producers, recording artists, personal managers, talent and booking agents, concert promoters, music publishers, composers, arrangers, album designers, record retailers, rack jobbers, distributors, engineers, and broadcasters.

JUNO AWARDS. Each year CARAS presents the Juno Awards, given in recognition of artistic achievement in the Canadian music industry (these are equivalent to America's GRAMMY AWARDS). There are various categories of awards, and members of CARAS vote for recipients. Award categories (which may change from year to year) have included Album/Single of the Year, International Album/Single, Male/Female Vocalist, Group, Country Male/Female Vocalist/Group, Most Promising Male/Female Vocalist/Group, Comedy/Children's/Classical and Jazz Recording, Producer/Engineer, and Best Album Graphics. The Hall of Fame Award is given annually to a Canadian recording artist for his/her contribution to the greater international recognition of Canadian artists and music. Past winners include Guy Lombardo (posthumously), Oscar Peterson, Hank Snow, and Paul Anka.

The Juno Awards evolved from an awards program established in 1964 by *RPM*, a Canadian trade magazine, and most of the country's major record companies. Renamed in 1969 after the Roman goddess, the Juno Awards also honored the long-standing contributions made by former CRTC chairman Pierre Juneau, who was a key figure in implementing the "Cancon" requirement in 1971 (see above).

Canadian Recording Industry Association (CRIA). A trade association representing the Canadian recording industry, CRIA offers membership to Canadian companies that manufacture and sell records and prerecorded tapes in Canada.

CRIA represents the industry on many levels, communicating with government, maintaining relationships with international organizations devoted to industry interests, conducting programs to control record and tape piracy, sponsoring a gold/platinum awards program, and compiling a national chart of best-selling recordings. A prime objective is also to develop and promote Canadian artists and music on a national and international level.

HISTORY. Canada's first association to represent the recording industry was created on April 9, 1963, with 10 charter members. Some of its priorities at that time included the "reclassification of truck rates on the movement of records" and an effort to reduce the postal rates for phonograph records.

In October 1966, it moved to have the Canadian who would be attending the Revision of the Berne Convention in 1967 represent its views on copyright in sound recordings. Other main concerns over the years have been proposed changes in the Canadian Copyright Act and controlling the illegal duplication of tapes and records. In 1980, CRIA's 46 members issued approximately 98% of all sound recordings manufactured and sold in Canada.

GOLD/PLATINUM AWARDS. CRIA issues gold and platinum awards for Canadian record/tape sales as follows:

	units
1 million Award (album)	1,000,000
Quintuple Platinum Album	500,000
Quadruple Platinum Album	400,000
Triple Platinum Album	300,000
Double Platinum Album	200,000
Platinum Album	100,000
Gold Album	50,000
Double Platinum Single	300,000
Platinum Single	150,000
Gold Single	75,000

Double albums count as one unit and all sales are verified by an independent accounting firm. Since the Canadian market is approximately one tenth the size of the U.S. market, the criteria for CRIA awards are accordingly lower. The certification program has been in effect since August 1975.

Canadian Music Publishers Association (CMPA). Trade association representing the Canadian music publishing industry. Its purpose is to advance the country's music publishing business by cooperative efforts; to encourage fair trade practices and maintain high standards of workmanship and service; to cooperate with trade associations representing other music industries and with organizations of an educational or cultural nature; and to advance the interests of the composer and publisher. To effect this latter purpose, CMPA has established the Canadian Musical Reproduction Rights Agency Limited, which administers the reproduction rights of music publishers whose works are recorded or copied in Canada. CMPA had 42 members in 1980.

Trademarks. In Canada, the continued right to a trademark is maintained by use, not registration. An application to register a trademark in Canada may be made prior to use, but the registration will not be issued until use of the trademark in Canada has actually begun. However, registration can be obtained in Canada in respect of trademarks that have been made known in Canada or registered and used in a foreign country that is a member of the International Convention for the Protection of Industrial and Intellectual Property. In the case of such registrations, the registrant must establish use of its trademark in Canada to avoid the registration's being challenged at a later date for nonuse.

Applications for trademark registrations are submitted to the Registrar of Trade Marks with a filing fee. After examination at the Trade Marks Office, registrable applications are advertised in the *Trade Marks Journal.*

Anyone who opposes the registration of the mark must institute proceedings within 1 month of the advertisement. Applications that are unopposed, or have any opposition rejected by the Registrar, are registered. The registration remains in force for 15 years and may be renewed for any number of additional 15-year periods. If use of the mark in Canada is discontinued, the Registrar may remove it from the register.

Unions. In Canada there exist certain labor unions to protect performers' rights in different working mediums. Performers working in the recording field are represented by ACTRA and AFM.

Association of Canadian Television and Radio Artists (ACTRA). A labor union that represents singers, announcers, actors, and disc jockeys who make audio programs and recordings, ACTRA also represents performers and writers working in television and feature films.

ACTRA enters into agreements with employers on behalf of its members who perform in the production of audio recordings. These agreements stipulate the terms, rates, and conditions of employment with regard to the production of audio recordings and programs (including audio discs, cassettes, cartridges, tapes, and similar devices used for reproducing sounds, local and syndicated radio programs, slide films, and audio training devices). Audio Codes are generally negotiated each year; employers sign a letter of adherence to the code, which constitues a binding obligation.

An employer is required to contribute a specified amount of the gross fees earned by each performer to ACTRA's insurance and retirement plans. Employers are also charged a percentage of the total talent fees paid to performers in all audio programs, for administration of the code.

The Audio Code provides for employers to render payments within particular time limits, with penalty fees for late payment. It establishes minimum rates of payment to singers who perform on audio recordings sold to the public, based on the following factors: whether the singer is a soloist or part of a group or 3 or more singers, the amount of time of services rendered, and the amount of finished recording time (there is a minimum 3-hour work session). The code provides payment to singers of demos at a rate equivalent to 50% of the rate established for commercial audio recordings. It also has fee structures for payment to performers engaged in the production of inflight entertainment tracks and radio and TV station IDs.

See also AMERICAN FEDERATION OF MUSICIANS OF THE UNITED STATES AND CANADA (AFM).

Canadian Academy of Recording Arts and Sciences. *See* CANADA.

Canadian Music Publishers Association (CMPA). *See* CANADA.

Canadian Musical Reproduction Rights Agency Limited (CMRRA). *See* CANADA.

Canadian Recording Industry Association (CRIA). *See* CANADA.

"Cancon" Regulations. *See* CANADA.

Cash Box. *See* CHARTS: TRADES.

Cassette Tape. Cassette tapes are popular high-fidelity mediums in which stereo sound recordings (albums) are reproduced and marketed. Since their commercial debut, they have undergone many technical improvements and have enjoyed increasing sales as prerecorded SOFTWARE items.

Cassette tapes first commercially appeared in 1964. (N.V. Philips, a giant electronics manufacturer, invented them and holds the fundamental patent.) Because of the narrow tape and narrow recording tracks used (which originally resulted in high noise and hiss levels), plus their low speed (1⅞ ips, which reduced high-frequency response), they were primarily intended to be used for dictation purposes and not for high-fidelity sound reproduction. However, though cassette tapes offered poorer sound reproduction than open-reel tapes or disc recordings, they had a major advantage—they were much more convenient to use. They were not bulky and they were simple to load. And unlike phonograph records, they did not suffer excessive audible wear from repeated playings.

Record manufacturers, realizing that consumers might sacrifice sound quality for convenience, began to offer them this opportunity. In subsequent years, continuous improvements in both cassettes and playback equipment have made this software item a rival of discs and other mediums and an important part of the home audio market.

Cassette systems, as a main stipulation in the N.V. Philips license, must conform to a standard. Cassettes use tape of approximately $\frac{1}{8}$-inch width and are played back on conventional tape decks at a speed of $1\frac{7}{8}$ inches per second. As better reproduction fidelity is obtained by increasing the speed at which tape is moved past the heads of a tape machine, a few decks, contrary to Philips's license stipulation, record and play back at $3\frac{3}{4}$ ips.

Cassette tapes come in standard playing-time lengths of 30, 45, 60, 90, 120, and 180 minutes (manufacturers designate playing time as C-30, C-45, C-60, etc.). A cassette tape has two programs in four tracks, which means there is uninterrupted recording and playback time per two-track side of 15, $22\frac{1}{2}$, 30, 45, 60, and 90 minutes, respectively. A tape plays half its four tracks by moving in one direction; the other half may be played by turning it over and inserting it into the playback unit so the remaining two tracks will be in the "playing" position. The longer the playing time, the thinner the tape and base material, or "backing."

Cassette tapes are commonly available in the following types (with the chemical symbol of their magnetic material indicated in parenthesis): ferric oxide (Fe_2O_3), chromium dioxide (CrO_2), and ferrichrome (FeCr). Metal tape, which uses particles of pure iron (conventional tape uses iron and chromium oxides), is also used; it offers the advantage of wider dynamic range and better signal-to-noise ration, albeit at an elevated price.

Many albums are simultaneously marketed in disc, cassette, and 8-track cartridge formats.

See also EIGHT-TRACK TAPE CARTRIDGE; OPEN-REEL TAPES.

Catalog. With respect to various industry participants, the term "catalog" has the following meanings:

Music publisher—All the copyrights (musical compositions) the company owns.

Songwriter—All the songs written by that writer.

Recording artist—All the recordings the artist has made (a written itemization of this is referred to as a *discography*).

Record company—Either the company's list of current and backlist titles of records and prerecorded tapes available for purchase by wholesalers and retailers, or all the master recordings it owns, whether or not records and tapes manufactured therefrom are available for purchase.

Wholesaler or retailer—The records and tapes it carries from many different record/tape manufacturers or all the titles it sells within a particular category of music, such as rock, country, or jazz.

The term "catalog" is most commonly used in reference to the collection of songs owned by a music publisher. Some larger music publishers have catalogs consisting of tens of thousands of copyrights. It is a common practice for small publishers to have larger ones administer their catalogs for a percentage of their receipts and have their catalogs represented in foreign territories by "subpublishers."

Catalog, Acquisition of a Music Publisher's. The acquisition of a music publisher's CATALOG is in many ways a unique form of investment; musical compositions are intangible assets, as are songwriting contracts, which may be included with the sale of such catalog or business. Musical compositions are also a unique product in that they may be continually rearranged, exploited, and promoted during their statutory term of copyright. A single new recording of a song that becomes successful can generate enough royalties in various areas to bring a substantial return on the purchaser's investment. Yet not only is the market highly competitive but songs are subject to the fickleness of the times and public taste, and that is why a decision whether or not to acquire a publisher's catalog requires scrutiny of the material and prudence, ingenuity, and foresight on behalf of the prospective buyer.

Catalog Analysis. In deciding whether or not to purchase a catalog, consideration will be given to the prospective buyer's present catalog (if there is one) and the catalog being offered for sale. If the purchaser is not presently in the music publishing business, it must first be determined if the purchase of such catalog will provide a solid base from which the investor can enter and expand in the business.

Where the prospective buyer already owns music copyrights, certain criteria in his present catalog and operation must be evaluated: what are the weak spots in the catalog; are there voids in certain kinds of music; how will the catalog being offered for sale fill the company's needs and fit into its operations; is the company's staff able to handle additional copyrights from both creative and administrative standpoints?

In analyzing the catalog being offered for sale, some of the important criteria that should be examined are:

1. The age of the catalog. For each pre-1978 song (i.e., published or registered for copyright prior to 1978), what is the number of years remaining before renewal registration; who owns the renewal rights, or if it is in its renewal term, what is the number of years re-maining in such term before it enters its 19-year extension; and for songs written after 1977, what is the period remaining before rights revert to the author?

2. The number of earning copyrights in the catalog.

3. Past activity of the catalog. This is evaluated in terms of past earnings, recent recordings of copyrights, whether there were any hits or chart successes, which artists recorded the songs originally and in cover versions, and whether there are any "standards" or compositions with standard capability.

4. Creative exploitation activities. Prior to their being offered for sale, for which artists, producers, labels, etc., were the songs auditioned and what were the results; are there any potential recordings or uses in advertising, motion pictures, television films, or other areas?

5. Administrative management of the catalog. Are the company's files, books, and records of account maintained orderly or will it require substantial costs and efforts to integrate the catalog's paperwork with the buyer's present one? Will additional personnel be necessary to administer the new catalog?

6. Potential financial benefits. What are the long-range and immediate financial benefits that may be obtained from acquisition of the catalog?

7. Creative supplementation. How will the songs in the catalog being offered for sale fill any voids in the present catalog and/or enhance it?

8. Writer aspects. Will purchase of the catalog "acquire" any new writers for the buyer? Are existing exclusive contracts the company has with its writers due to expire shortly? Are they assignable? Do they contain "key man" clauses that enable the writer to terminate if certain persons are no longer working with his material?

9. Subpublishing agreements. What are the terms of existing contracts with subpublishers?

(Subpublishers may have the rights to specific copyrights in certain territories under various different agreements.) What advances have been paid, and have they been recouped? What advances are due? What foreign covers have been obtained or is the subpublisher obligated to obtain? When do the contracts expire, do they have option-to-renew clauses, and may they be terminated by the purchaser for any other reason?

10. Ownership of compositions written on a WORK MADE FOR HIRE basis.

The prospective buyer should take ample time to make a detailed evaluation of all records and should retain an outside specialist if needed. A realistic determination of the expected return on the investment should be made, as well as a consideration of problems that may be encountered in the future. The buyer's creative staff should also fully evaluate the new catalog in terms of exploitation potential of individual compositions. When the prospective buyer does not own a catalog or when he is seeking to enhance an existing catalog, a determination should be made whether to invest the purchase price in new songwriting talent to create new copyrights, as opposed to purchasing existing copyrights and contracts. As a practical matter, the primary criterion in analyzing a proposed acquisition is often the income the catalog has generated in the past 3 to 5 years.

Determining the Value of a Catalog. There are several formulas used to assess the financial value of a music publishing catalog. Three common ways are:

1. Determining the catalog's average annual income received from a performing rights organization over a period of years and multiplying the result by a specific figure (which can range from 5 to 10, the multiple becoming less with the fewer years remaining in the copyrights). This method is more often used with respect to older catalogs.

2. Adding the net income of a catalog year by year for a period of years (usually the last 5 years) and using the total as a purchase price. This method is more commonly used where a substantial number of years in the life of the copyrights remain.

3. Multiplying the average net income of the catalog in the past 3 to 5 years by a particular figure (this varies from situation to situation, but is never too far from 5).

Often, however, because of the unique circumstances of a catalog, no particular formula can be used. Annual earnings may be erratic, a particular artist or group may have recorded the copyrights during a particular time, a limited number of copyrights may account for the bulk of the earnings of the catalog, earnings may be heavily imbalanced between mechanical income as opposed to performance income, and potential foreign income may be subject to large unearned advances.

Other factors to be considered in determining a formula for a purchase price are the tax advantages (a copyright is a depreciating asset because it has a limited life) and whether the purchase price is to be paid out over a period of years from income earned or in one lump-sum payment.

Assimilation of a Purchased Catalog. After a catalog is purchased, its copyrights may be integrated with the ASCAP, BMI, or SESAC catalog of the purchaser's existing company, or the purchaser may wish to keep the catalog intact and use its original name (unless this is contractually forbidden). It is common for new owners to retain the catalog's name where it is prestigious or recognizable. In other instances, the copyrights may be gradually assimilated into the new owner's existing catalog.

Charts. The relative success of currently popular records is measured in the music industry by the charts. A *chart* is a numerical ranking of the most popular singles or albums in a given time period. Charts are compiled by the TRADES, according to their own particular research and methodology. In general, records are included on the charts and sequenced on the basis of sales, radio airplay, or both, and reflect a record's success on a national basis.

The industry trades, *Billboard, Cash Box*, and *Record World*, compile charts for singles and albums in their weekly issues. Charts are prepared in various categories of popular music, as well as other areas. The most important charts (reflecting the largest cross section of music and national popularity) cover "pop" singles and albums. These include hit product of not only mainstream pop but also rock, rock fusion, and crossovers from other genres, such as R & B and country. In essence, the "pop" charts rank those records that are the most widely programmed and/or the biggest sellers throughout the country.

Each trade has different names for its various charts, as is indicated in the following lists of the singles and album charts compiled by *Billboard, Cash Box*, and *Record World*.° Also included are any other charts that may be compiled by the trades. Radio charts, for example, denote records that have been added to radio station playlists, have the greatest upward movement on stations' playlists, are receiving the most airplay, etc. Radio charts may include the names of particular radio stations and their location.

Billboard Charts
  HOT 100®†
  TOP LPs & TAPE®†(1-200)
  Hot Soul Singles (1-100)
  Soul LPs (75)
  Hot Country Singles (100)
  Hot Country LPs (75)
  Bubbling Under the Top LPs (201-210)/Hot 101-110
  Top 50 Adult Contemporary

_____
° Lists current as of 1981.
†Registered trademarks of Billboard Publications, Inc.

Disco Top 100 (National)
Jazz LPs (50)
Latin LPs (25 Pop and Salsa)
Hits of the World (12 countries weekly)
Spiritual LPs (35)
Videocassette Top 40
Singles Radio Action Chart (National plus 8 regions)
Album Radio Action Chart (National plus 5 regions)
Inspirational LPs (35)
Classical (40)
Box Office Chart (stadiums, auditoriums, arenas)
Rock Albums (50)
Top Tracks (60)
Top Adds (Rock Albums) (10)

Cash Box Charts
Top 100 Singles
Top 100 Albums
Top Albums/101 to 200
Top 100 Country
Country Albums (Top 75)
Top 100 Black Contemporary
Black Contemporary Albums (Top 75)
Jazz Albums (Top 40)
Radio Chart (Top 100 Singles)
Rap Report (Rock Album Programmer)
The Juke Box Programmer
    Top New Pop Singles
    Top New Country Singles
    Top New R & B Singles
    Top New Dance Singles
International Bestsellers

Record World Charts
  Singles
  Singles 101-150
  Albums
  Albums 101-150
  Albums 151-200
  Country Singles
  Country Albums
  A/C Chart
  Disco File Top 50
  Black Oriented Singles
  Black Oriented Album Chart
  The Jazz LP Chart
  Classical Retail Report
  Radio Marketplace
  Album Airplay
  Retail Report
  Latin American Hit Parade
  International

The charts are numerical rankings of the most successful records during a given time period. They also contain much other useful information. This is *Billboard*'s Hot 100.®

What a Record Chart Listing Tells. The singles and album "pop" charts in *Billboard, Cash Box,* and *Record World* reflect the widest cross section of national popularity of records (as stated above) and are consequently regarded as the most important charts. A listing in these charts provides a variety of information. The following paragraphs contain the information included in both singles and album pop charts by these trades and additional information particular to just the singles or album chart.

"Pop" singles and albums charts information°—name of record; record's current numerical ranking; record's numerical ranking for the previous week; length of time (in weeks) the record has been on the chart; upward mobility (if substantial), based on increase in sales indicated by bullet or star† (a record can have upward mobility yet not get a bullet or star); name of label; name of distributor (if different from the label); record's catalog number; whether record has been certified "gold" or "platinum" by RIAA (*Billboard* only).

"Pop" singles chart additional information—name of publisher;‡ performing rights organization of publisher;‡ name of producer;‡ name of writer(s) (*Billboard* only); name of sheet music supplier, if any (*Billboard* and *Cash Box* only).

"Pop" album charts additional information—retail list price of LP; retail list price of 8-track and cassette tapes (*Billboard* only); crossover positions of country and soul LPs (*Billboard* only).

In general, the position (including a bullet or star, if any) indicates how a record is doing in comparison with others over a particular time period re sales and/or airplay, under methodology used by the compiling trade publication. To some degree, this may indicate the marketing efforts of record companies and the current commercial success of artists, producers, and writers. The charts may also be viewed as barometers of the most current musical tastes of the public.

Using the Charts. The charts are important tools for various interests in the music business, as follows:

Radio Stations—The charts are often used as a guide in radio programming, as they enable program directors to see which records are currently successful or are progressing weekly. This information combined with local research and sales reports may help determine which records they add to, keep on, or drop from their playlists. *Jukebox operators* use chart information similarly in buying product.

Retailers, rack jobbers, one-stops—Chart positions are used by retailers and subdistributors in determining which new records they should add to their inventory or stock in even greater quantity. Some large wholesalers compile charts based on their own local sales for distribution to their accounts and to customers of these accounts.

Record manufacturers—Since chart activity influences radio programming decisions and wholesale and retail buying decisions, charts consequently affect the manufacturer's sales. They may also measure (to some degree) the performance of the company's marketing and promotion staffs; consequently they may induce a label to change its marketing and promotional strategies.

A company that consistently has records on the charts holds much prestige, and this can enhance its ability to attract and sign new artists and those signed to other labels, as well as renew contracts of those on its roster at expiration. Chart positions also influence foreign record licensees seeking new associations.

Charts are used by label promotion repre-

° Current as of 1981.
† *Billboard* awards superstars to those products showing greatest upward movement on the current week's chart.
‡ *Record World* contains this information in a separate alphabetical listing.

sentatives as tools in convincing program directors to add records to their stations' playlists or to increase airplay on records already on the playlist. Manufacturers sometimes publicize high chart rankings in trade advertisements directed to radio stations, record retailers, and wholesalers.

Recording artists—As chartmaking records enhance an artist's reputation, such listings can be used as a bargaining ploy in obtaining more favorable terms when renegotiating recording contracts. A chart ranking may also induce a record company to provide tour support for an artist and it may facilitate more bookings (and in larger venues and under better financial terms), bring more media exposure, and attract top record producers to work with the artist.

Personal managers—Personal managers of chartmaking artists can use such listings to acquire for their clients the representation of top booking agents and concert promoters. Chart rankings may be a reflection of their services to their clients.

Booking agents, concert promoters—Since these entrepreneurs are interested in filling venues with the talent they book or promote, they must work with hit acts or up-and-coming ones. They study the charts to gauge such information and check for new artists entering the charts.

Music publishers—As the charts indicate which artists and producers are "hot," music publishers will study the listings and "cast" and submit appropriate material. A publisher may solicit chartmaking writers to sign with it or induce them to make copublishing deals. A chart listing may also influence a subpublisher to represent the composition in its territory, or if it already represents it, increase its efforts. Having songs on the charts holds great prestige for music publishers.

Songwriters—Songwriters with chart success can use this as a bargaining ploy in negotiating a staff job with a publisher, in acquiring a

percentage of the publishing rights to their compositions, or in making copublishing deals.

Performing rights organizations—It is prestigious for a performing rights organization to have songs in its repertory on the charts. These organizations publicize such achievements in the trades, which may serve to attract new writers and publishers to their folds. Chart activity and positions also influence the license fees the organization can command from music users. The performance royalties SESAC pays to its affiliated music publishers and writers are to a large degree based on the chart positions of their songs in *Billboard*, *Cash Box*, and *Record World*.

Consumers—Retailers post trade charts on their walls and these may serve to remind consumers which records they like or were interested in purchasing. The charts may also assist the customer in finding a selection when he or she remembers only the name of the artist and not the song title. *Billboard* has a highly successful feature called "Traffic Center," a pull-out section containing huge blowups of some weekly charts. These are designed to be hung in retail and one-stop outlets and in discos.

How the Trades Compile Their Charts. *Billboard*, *Cash Box*, and *Record World* use individual research procedures to determine which records should be on the charts and in what order, and which should be awarded bullets, stars, or superstars to indicate exceptional airplay and/or sales activity. These methodologies may undergo minor revision periodically, but basically they remain the same, being compiled on the basis of sales information as reported by rack jobbers, one-stops, and retailers, and airplay information as reported by radio stations in primary, secondary, and some tertiary markets.

In some instances, either sales or airplay information is the sole factor in determining a record's position, many album charts being compiled on the basis of sales alone. The following is a general overview of how *Billboard*,

Cash Box, and *Record World* compile their charts.

1. *Billboard* compiles its HOT 100 (pop singles) chart using both sales and radio reports. Singles are assigned points based on sales and radio information that is gathered and their position on the chart depends largely on their total point value (subjective elements are also considered, as explained below). Singles can enter the charts by achieving sales points, radio points, or both. Radio activity is a criterion for positions from the bottom to the top of the chart.

Each week, *Billboard* makes up Sales Check Sheets, containing the titles of an average of 180 singles arranged in alphabetical order. These are sent to one-stops and rack jobbers (hereinafter called subdistributors) and to dealers. On Friday and Monday of each week, members of *Billboard*'s chart department call these dealers and subdistributors to determine how the products listed on the check sheets are selling (the majority of calls are made on Monday, to include sales during the weekend, usually the most brisk selling period). The Sales Check Sheets serve the purpose of reminding dealers and subdistributors to note sales information on these records in advance of the calls.

Billboard accumulates sales data on a *qualitative* basis. Dealers and subdistributors are asked to report on product selling Very Good, Good, and Fair, and to name their top 15 selling items. Singles reported to be selling Very Good, Good, and Fair are assigned point values of 20, 10, and 5, respectively. The top 15 singles are given points inversely, the number 1 best-selling single getting 15 points, the number 15 item receiving 1 point. All sales information is recorded on data processing sheets for subsequent input to a computer.

Radio stations are called every day (stations vary as to when they update their weekly playlists), the cutoff time for each week's chart being Tuesday evening. Each week, chart personnel contact over 150 pop radio stations to find out what records are on their current week's playlist, which are hit-bound, day parts, night parts, LP cuts, new music extras played, etc. (in determining album positions on the LP charts, airplay received by cuts is taken into account). Radio stations are weighted 1, 2, 4, and 6, depending on their importance in the market. Radio information is likewise recorded on data processing input sheets.

After both sales and radio reports have been completed, data is fed into a computer and a HOT 100 worksheet is printed (material is entered again for verification). The worksheet contains a suggested position for each single for that week, each record's previous week's chart position, and various other information, including plus or minus changes in the total product points for the current week (these are based on sales, Top 15 points, and radio points). The singles are then positioned by hand, also taking into account key add-ons on all the top radio stations for the current week, summaries of product receiving airplay that is not yet being tracked, and reports of late add-ons.

To be charted, a record must be commercially released, and in most cases *Billboard* does not check any product unless it is moving over 30,000 pieces nationally on a reorder basis (although strong radio activity reported in advance of obtaining sales information may qualify it for charting). In determining which retailers and subdistributors to contact for sales information, *Billboard* considers recommendations made by the sales departments of record companies, to come up with over 400 dealers, including chains, one-stops, and rack jobbers. This actually fans out to over 11,000 locations. Chart personnel use recommendations made by the promotion departments of labels and retailers in one-stops determining which radio stations to contact. Stations are qualified as to format, importance in the market, etc. Chart personnel meet each week with label promotion representatives, who also inform them of new product releases for possible inclusion in the Sales Check Sheets.

Billboard's TOP LPs & TAPE chart is compiled by an identical methodology, except that radio is not used as an input factor and the LP Sales Check Sheet lists approximately 280 LPs. The computer printout contains the information as described above, including the current week's suggested position. LPs are again positioned by hand, but certain other factors are considered in determining their final positions, such as whether a single has been released from the album and whether the radio calls indicate that a cut from the album is getting significant airplay.

The country LP and soul singles and soul LP charts are determined by substantially similar means, but since many radio stations with country formats have playlists with many more selections than their pop and soul counterparts, *Billboard* limits a country station's total report to 60 items. In addition, playlist ranges are weighted as follows: a number 1 record gets 5 points; numbers 2 through 10, 4 points; numbers 11 through 20, 3 points; numbers 21 through 40, 2 points; and 1 point for any record over 40 or in limited rotation. Playlist points are multiplied by the station weighting factor to give the record its total points. Airplay data is fed into a computer with sales information, to produce a summary sheet. The summary sheet together with the subjective elements described above are used by the staff to determine the position of records on the country singles charts.

2. *Cash Box* compiles its pop, R & B, and country singles charts using a combination of airplay and over-the-counter sales reports. Its album charts in these areas as well as its jazz and classical charts are based on sales reports only.

Airplay information is gathered from calls made to stations in various markets. The sales reports, which are qualitative (i.e., *Cash Box*

asks for the top 30 best-sellers), are obtained from a number of wholesalers and retailers, in the ratio of 60% from retailers and one-stops, and 40% from rack jobbers (the approximate ratio of their business establishments in the United States). Reports from these stations, subdistributors, and retailers are taken each week and the lists of these entities are updated twice per year.

For the singles charts, the ranking of new records or those positioned near the bottom is based almost exclusively on airplay. Airplay, however, plays less of a role for a record's ranking as it moves up the charts; positions at the top are based almost exclusively on sales reports.

3. *Record World.* This trade compiles its singles chart based on a combination of both airplay and over-the-counter retail sales reports. The sales reports predominate in the determination of the order of records at the top of the chart, airplay prevails for the lower portion.

Record World uses quantitative rather than qualitative research in compiling its sales reports. In obtaining a sales report from a dealer or subdistributor, it requests a piece count of merchandise sold rather than a subjective report on sales such as very good, good, and fair.

Record World weighs airplay activity heavily at the bottom of the charts, as new releases do not usually sell well immediately. Airplay generally precedes and causes sales, and reports of such activity are used to get a record started on the charts.

Records played by radio stations are weighted under a point system. A certain number of points enables a record to get on the chart. To move up, a single needs to increase its spread of airplay by picking up more of the stations in the point system. After a certain amount of time, it must begin to exhibit sales activity. Sales are researched weekly in the manner mentioned above. Airplay and sales data are combined and used to arrive at the chart numbers each week. A record's movement depends on these two factors, with sales becoming the bottom line as a record moves to the top. Chart rankings are based on the results of the information compiled.

The position of an LP on *Record World*'s albums chart is determined strictly by over-the-counter retail sales (as opposed to shipping figures). This represents sales of units actually purchased by consumers. Sales information is based on reports from thousands of retail outlets around the country. (It should be noted that a report from a single retail chain could cover up to a few hundred units.) One-stops are also contacted to gauge a record's reorder pattern from retailers. *Record World*'s country singles chart is based exclusively on airplay. The publication compiles its black-oriented singles chart on a combination of airplay and sales reports. The stations used in the compilation of these charts are given specific point values. Sales data is accumulated from *retail* sales.

How a Record Breaks Onto and Moves Up the Charts. The following is an example of how a record might break onto and move up on the pop singles chart of a trade publication: As a result of promotion efforts by the label, a record receives airplay in various tertiary and some secondary markets. This is reported in the trade's survey and the record receives enough points to be added to the bottom of its pop singles chart or a position below the top 100. Program directors from stations in other secondary markets analyze the chart and information from additional sources and add the record to their playlists or give it more frequent airplay. The record continues to move up as it receives more airplay from an increasing number of stations, including those in primary markets. As it reaches the upper portion of the chart, sales reports will for the most part determine what position it receives and whether or not it gets a bullet, star, or super-star. Some stations in major markets play new records (particularly those of superstar artists) upon release without waiting to see if they first become successful in other markets. The

combination of primary market radio airplay with that of secondary and tertiary radio market airplay and some sales activity will enable a record to enter the singles chart at a higher position.

Criticisms of Charts. The charts are often criticized for not accurately representing a record's relative popularity. Manufacturers, for example, sometimes stress this by comparing chart rankings with in-house sales reports. It should be noted, however, that house sales reports indicate only shipments to dealers, one-stops, and rack jobbers, and not net sales as reported to the trades by retailers and wholesalers (hence chart information should be more accurate, whether compiled by qualitative or quantitative research).

It is also claimed that accounts, under pressure from manufacturers and distributors, make exaggerated sales reports for certain product; that shipments of free merchandise to dealers, one-stops, and rack jobbers can influence their sales reports; and that advertisements placed by manufacturers can influence a trade's ranking of a record. Another criticism is that "payoffs" to radio station employees can influence the reporting to the trades of radio airplay. While there may be some validity to these claims, at best such activities would be isolated incidents and have only a small influence upon the rankings. The charts themselves are compiled under systems that are relatively free from human tampering and are all credible, respected, and important to the industry.

Classes PA, RE, SR, TX, VA. *See* COPYRIGHT REGISTRATION CLASSIFICATION SYSTEM.

Clayton Act. *See* BUSINESS LAWS, FEDERAL AND STATE.

Clearance. Authorization obtained to perform a copyrighted musical work over radio or television.

Radio and television stations or networks

The writing of songs is very much a collaborative process for certain professionals. Traditionally, songs written for stage and motion pictures particularly have been written in collaboration. Pictured here is one famous partnership, Richard Rodgers (*right*) and Oscar Hammerstein II, who have written the scores to such musicals as *Oklahoma!*, *Carousel*, *South Pacific*, and *The King and I*.

may lawfully broadcast copyrighted musical compositions only with the authorization of the owners of the copyrights. In commercial practice, permission to perform a nondramatic musical composition is in the form of a license granted by a PERFORMING RIGHTS ORGANIZATION on behalf of the copyright owner (a license permits the music user to perform any or all of the compositions in the organization's repertory). A network is indemnified against any infringement claims made for performances of "cleared" works in the performing rights organization from which it obtains a license. Nondramatic performances of compositions are logged and reported by the networks.

Coin-Operated Record Player. *See* JUKEBOX.

Collaborator. Person who writes songs with one or more other persons. Collaboration most commonly involves two partners—one of whom writes the music, the other the lyrics. In some collaborations, the partners contribute creatively to both words and music.

  Dividing Song Rights. Rights to a song (and consequently income generated by it) may be divided between collaborators in any way they choose. Commonly, where there are two collaborators, the writer's share in the song is divided equally between them (i.e., 50/50). Where more than two collaborators are involved, the division of income is usually in accordance with 50% to the composer(s) and 50% to the lyricist(s). For example, a composer and two lyricists of a song might split the writer's income as follows: 50% for the composer and 25% for each of the two lyricists.

  As stated above, some collaborators contribute creatively to both the words and music. The following is an example of how the earnings of a song written by several writers, some of whom contributed to both words and music, would be divided: A, B, and C write the music. B, C, and D write the lyrics. Since 50% of the songwriter's income goes to the compos-

ers and the other half to the lyricists, the three composers (A, B, and C) get 16⅔% each and the three lyricists (B, C, and D) get 16⅔% each. Thus the songwriters' earnings would be divided as follows: A—16⅔%; B—33⅓%; C—33⅓%; D—16⅔%.

  Who Collaborates? Members of a musical group often collaborate, as do artists and producers, artists and songwriters, and composers and lyricists who are not performers.

  Why Collaborate? Collaboration between songwriters is often necessary because there are very few who can consistently write both words and music successfully. A poor lyric wedded to a great melody, or vice versa, can destroy appreciation for the song; hence many writers seek out competent partners.

  Renowned Collaborators. Notable collaborations in popular songwriting include the following: W. S. Gilbert and Arthur Sullivan; George and Ira Gershwin; Lew Brown, B. G. DeSylva, and Ray Henderson; Richard Rodgers and Lorenz Hart; Richard Rodgers and Oscar Hammerstein II; Burt Bacharach and Hal David; John Lennon and Paul McCartney; Elton John and Bernie Taupin; and Barry, Robin, and Maurice Gibb.

  Finding a Collaborator. Collaborators may be found in various ways: through music publishers, producers, musicians, and others working in the music industry; by means of ads placed in music magazines or signs posted in music stores, schools, recording studios, and local music unions; or by visiting local clubs and seeking out talent.

Collective Bargaining. The major function of the various performer labor UNIONS. Through collective bargaining, union representatives negotiate with their members' employers, settle issues (e.g., minimum wages), and complete a labor contract. Thus AFM and AFTRA representatives negotiate with those from record companies, AEA with theatrical producers, SAG with theatrical motion picture producers, etc. If, in negotiating, the terms are not agreeable to the union members, they could threaten or implement a strike.

See also NATIONAL LABOR RELATIONS BOARD.

Color Disc. Vinyl phonograph record with a color tint. The usual colors in which these discs are manufactured are white, red, blue, and yellow, or clear in different shades of these colors. Other colors, such as orange and green, may be specially ordered. Color discs can have the same reproduction qualities as standard-color (black) discs.

The manufacturing process for color discs is the same as that for standard-color discs, except that the desired pigmentation is mixed with clear vinyl (clear vinyl contains no carbon black). For light-colored discs, such as white, yellow, and certain light shades of red (pinkish in hue), extra care is required, to eliminate any impurities that may contaminate the desired color or show as foreign matter in the finished record.

Color discs are usually "feature" items for a record company or recording artist. Stickers are often added to album covers to promote the color disc, or the record company may use album jackets with die-cut holes in the center to display the vinyl's color. Color discs cost approximately $.15 more per 12-inch record and about $.08 more per 7-inch disc to manufacture than a black record of the same size.

See PICTURE DISC.

Commercial. A "commercial" may be a short advertising, promotional, or public service announcement intended for broadcast over radio or television. Commercial messages may include narration, dialogue, songs, jingles, or other matter that depict or mention the advertiser's or sponsor's name, product, or service. In radio, commercials are inserted between songs, patter, news reports, and other announcements. In television, they appear at the opening and closing of a program and between scenes. Some commercials made as motion pictures are exhibited at movie theaters before the start of the feature film or between features.

"Commercial" also refers to that which is directed to popular consumption (as opposed to individuals with discriminating tastes) or to that which has proven mass appeal. The term is commonly used in reference to a recording, musical composition, recording artist, or idea.

It is the aim of certain participants in the music business—songwriters, music publishers, recording artists, producers, and labels—to create or exploit commercial works. Such participants have financial gain, success, immediate results—and usually artistic excellence—as their primary objectives. Commercial product, however, is often construed to be artistically inferior, second-rate, or untasteful.

What makes one recording commercial and another not? This is difficult to answer, as music is often an emotional experience and personal taste is a subjective matter and defies definition. But this question may be considered by examining the constituent elements of a recording. First there's the song. What style of music is it? Pop, rock, country, and R & B songs are in general of a commercial nature, while classical, folk, ethnic, and certain forms of jazz are not (actually, what's currently in vogue in the general marketplace is the determinant as far as style goes). Do the lyrics have the potential for mass appeal? Is the melody catchy? Is there a HOOK?

The artist's performance is another important factor. Is it strong enough? Does the singer have an identifiable style or does he sound too similar to other artists? Does his voice have "top 40" appeal or lend itself to airplay on contemporary radio stations, or is it too stylized, as in the tradition of a musical show singer?

Finally, the "sound" of the record is a major factor. Is it contemporary as well as unique?

Have the instruments and voices been recorded satisfactorily or are there flaws? Is the length of the recording not too long and not too short? Is it mixed well? The "time" of release also has important consequences. These are some of the factors that collectively determine whether a recording has the potential to appeal to a large portion of the record-buying public.

Common Law Copyright Protection. Common law is a system of laws of a community, state, or country that are generally unwritten (as opposed to codified written laws) but which are based on traditional usage and upheld by court decisions. Under certain circumstances, a literary, musical, dramatic, or artistic work may be protected from copying by others by common law. In the United States, most works are now protected by common law only if they are not "fixed"—fixed works are protected under the federal statute.

Common Law Copyright Protection Prior to 1978. Under the Copyright Act of 1909, effective for the most part through December 31, 1977, there existed a dual system of copyright protection: common law and statutory. A work would be under common law protection from the moment it was created until it was published or registered for copyright. Common law varied from jurisdiction to jurisdiction, but provided protection indefinitely if a work was never published or registered. Under the 1909 act, not all unpublished works could be registered and protection for such unregistrable works before publication was under common law. While both the statutory and common laws provided protection for original works, they differed in terms of providing dates of creation and in remedies allowed for damages, statutory remedies for an infringed copyright owner being more beneficial.

A popular practice among songwriters to secure greater protection under common law was to mail to themselves songs they wrote and leave the envelopes unopened after receipt. (It was their contention that the date on the postmark would establish a date of creation for the work.) However, this method, sometimes referred to as "poor man's copyright," usually proved to be unsatisfactory or to have no significance in litigation.

Effect of the Copyright Act of 1976. The 1976 act, which became fully effective January 1, 1978, established a single national system of statutory protection for all COPYRIGHTABLE WORKS, published or unpublished, that are "fixed" in a tangible form of expression. The act of creating and fixing a work in a copy or phonorecord now *automatically* secures a copyright under federal protection, whether or not the work has been published or registered for copyright. Thus common law protection no longer applies to a work once that work is written or recorded.

A work not fixed, however, such as an instrumental improvisation, would still be under common law protection until such time as it is fixed (written or recorded).

Works under common law protection prior to 1978 are now protected by the federal copyright statute. For certain unpublished (and unregistered) works created long ago, the law provides that no such copyright will expire before December 31, 2002.

Communications Act of 1934. Law passed by Congress that establishes the basis for the regulation of commercial broadcasting.

The 1934 act is the law under which the FEDERAL COMMUNICATIONS COMMISSION (FCC) operates and which it enforces. While it forbids the government or its regulatory agency, the FCC, to censor programs, it requires broadcasters to serve the public interest. Various FCC rules and policies exist to provide for radio and television regulation in accordance with the objectives of the act.

The Communications Act was signed on

June 19, 1934. Prior to its enactment, jurisdiction over interstate and foreign wire and broadcast communications was at various times held by the Department of Commerce, the Post Office Department, the Interstate Commerce Commission, and the Federal Radio Commission. The act unified the regulatory powers of these various federal agencies and broadened the scope of such regulation under the authority of a single, independent agency, the FCC. Several of the provisions of this law were taken from the Radio Act of 1927, whose chief purposes were to allocate frequency bands and various services, assign specific frequencies to individual stations, and control station power.

A major objective of the 1934 act is "to make available, so far as possible, to all the people of the United States a rapid, efficient, nation-wide and world-wide wire and radio communication service."

Compilation Album. Album that is a thematic collection of several previously released recordings, most or all of which have been "hits." The tracks on a compilation album may have been recorded by one artist or many and likewise have been released by one label or many.

The binding element of a compilation album is the theme. For example, one type of compilation album is the "greatest hits" genre. These are basically of two types: (1) an individual artist's "greatest hits" performed by the artist (as opposed to the "greatest hits" of an individual artist by another performer, such as an orchestra or pianist, which would be an example of a cover album or "sound-alike" recording) and (2) "original hits by the original artists." Variations of the latter might include such theme-oriented packages as "Greatest Hits of the '70s" or "Rock 'n' Roll's Greatest Hits."

Another example of a compilation album would be "Songs for Lovers," containing several previously released popular recordings of romantic ballads. An album of an individual orchestra's rendition of "Best Songs from Broadway" or "Christmas Favorites," however, whose tracks have not been previously released, again would be an example of a cover recording.

Compilation albums are commonly marketed by record merchandisers, who license the preexisting masters from the owners (record companies). The albums are normally available either by direct mail (from television or mail order advertisements) or at certain "key" retail outlets.

See also Copyright Notice; Record Merchandising Company.

Composer. *See* Songwriter.

Composers, Authors and Publishers Association of Canada Limited (CAPAC). *See* Canada.

Compulsory Licenses (General). Ordinarily, anyone who wishes to use a copyrighted work for commercial purposes must negotiate a license with the owner of copyright, or his authorized agent, and pay a royalty under the terms set forth in the license. In a few special cases, however, the copyright law enables the user to obtain a "compulsory license," whereby the copyrighted work can be used in certain ways without permission from the copyright owner, as long as the user complies with statutory procedures and pays established royalty fees at designated intervals.

There are four categories of compulsory licenses provided by law: music recordings, Jukeboxes, Cable Television, and noncommercial Public Broadcasting. Compulsory licenses in these categories respectively establish rates and procedures for: the manufacture and distribution of phonorecords embodying nondramatic musical compositions, jukebox performances of musical works, retransmissions by cable television systems of programs originally broadcast by television stations, and performances of published nondramatic musical works by noncommercial public broadcasters. Other types of works (i.e., pictorial, graphic, sculptural, audiovisual) may also be affected by the compulsory licenses in some of these categories.

Compulsory licenses for jukeboxes, cable television, and public broadcasting were first provided for by the 1976 Copyright Act. Prior to the enactment of this law, owners of musical copyrights were not compensated for performances of their works on these devices or over these systems.

Compulsory licenses are not written instruments per se. Rather, they are statutory grants of permission for works to be used in certain ways provided certain conditions are met.

See also Compulsory/Mechanical Licenses (Phonorecords); Copyright Royalty Tribunal.

Compulsory/Mechanical Licenses (Phonorecords).

One "limitation"° on the exclusive rights of a Copyright Owner given by the U.S. copyright law is the "compulsory license for making and distributing phonorecords" embodying nondramatic musical compositions. This compulsory license provides that once a copyright owner has made or authorized a recording of a nondramatic musical work for reproduction in Phonorecords, anyone else may make and distribute phonorecords embodying the work to the public for private use without permission from the copyright owner, by following a procedure set forth in the statute and paying established royalty rates at stated intervals.

In commercial practice, however, the provisions of the compulsory license are regarded as too stringent to follow by the record manufacturing community and the compulsory license for making and distributing phonorecords is almost never used without some variation. Rather, licenses containing modifications from the statutory compulsory license requirements, referred to as *mechanical* or *record* licenses, are used by virtually all parties wishing to make and distribute phonorecords embodying the work.

It is this compulsory license provision of the law, however, that creates the legal basis for anyone to make and distribute phonorecords without permission from the copyright owner and thus prevents a monopoly copyright owners might have in authorizing the making and distribution of records and tapes containing the copyrights they own. Furthermore, it is within the framework of terms prescribed by the compulsory license that the terms of mechanical licenses are established. For this reason, the terms of the compulsory license for making and distributing phonorecords as prescribed by law will be examined.

The Compulsory License for Music Recordings. As stated above, the statute provides that once phonorecords of a nondramatic musical composition have been made and distributed to the public in the U.S. under authorization of the copyright owner, the copyrighted work becomes subject to the compulsory license provisions of the copyright law. In order to obtain the benefits of such, the user must comply with the following provisions of the compulsory license:

1. The primary purpose in making phonorecords is to distribute them to the public for private (home) use.

2. The user has the privilege of making a musical arrangement of the work to the extent necessary to conform it to the style and manner of interpretation of the performance involved, but the new arrangement cannot change the basic melody or fundamental character of the work.† (The new arrangement is not subject to copyright as a Derivative

---

°The U.S. copyright law does not specifically refer to the compulsory license for music recordings as a "limitation," but many regard it as such.

†The music may not be "perverted, distorted or travestied" (House Report 94–1476).

WORK unless express consent is given by the copyright owner.)

3. To obtain the compulsory license, a notice of intention must be sent by the prospective licensee to the copyright owner. It must be served before or within 30 days after making, and before distributing, any phonorecords of the work. The notice must comply with the form, content, and manner of service required by the regulations of the Copyright Office. If the registration or other public records of the Copyright Office do not identify the copyright owner and his address, the notice is to be filed with the Copyright Office, accompanied by the required fee. Failure to serve or file the required notice of intention forecloses the possibility of a compulsory license, and in the absence of a negotiated license, the user is subject to the applicable remedies for infringement.

4. For every phonorecord made and distributed, the compulsory licensee is to pay to the copyright owner either $.04, or $.0075 per minute of playing time or fraction thereof, whichever amount is larger.° The copyright law considers a phonorecord "distributed" if "the person exercising the compulsory license

has voluntarily and permanently parted with its possession."†

5. Royalty payments are to be made on or before the 20th day of each month. Each monthly payment must be made under oath and must comply with the requirements of regulations prescribed by the Copyright Office.

6. A detailed cumulative annual statement of account certified by a certified public accountant must also be filed for every compulsory license. The monthly and annual statements of account must conform to the form, content, and manner of certification with respect to the number of records made‡ and the number of records distributed, as prescribed by Copyright Office regulations.

Responsibilities of the Copyright Owner. To be entitled to receive royalties under a compulsory license, the copyright owner must be identified in the registration or other public records of the Copyright Office; he cannot recover any royalties for phonorecords previously made and distributed. Early registration is therefore advisable for copyright owners. Copyright registration of a musical composition is effected by the filing of Form PA. If the ownership of a copyright has changed hands since registration, or if the owner of the recording right is different from the "copyright claimant" identified in the copyright registration, a document of conveyance should be recorded in the public record in the Copyright Office. The requirement under the Copyright Act of 1909, for the copyright own-

---

°Under the Copyright Act of 1909, the statutory rate was $.02. The 1976 Copyright Act, effective January 1, 1978, changed the rate to $.0275 or $.005 per minute of playing time or fraction thereof, whichever amount was greater. The current rate is the result of the Copyright Royalty Tribunal's ruling on December 19, 1980, effective as of July 1, 1981. Both music copyright owners and record companies, the two opposing interests in the rate issue, appealed the CRT's ruling.

On June 23, 1981 a United States Court of Appeals upheld the tribunal's increase in the mechanical rate to $.04. The Court of Appeals, however, held that the tribunal "exceeded its authority" in deciding that the rate is to be adjusted on January 1, 1982 and on an annual basis until 1987 when the Copyright Royalty Tribunal may, pursuant to the copyright law, hold adjustment hearings on the mechanical rate. The annual adjustment beginning in 1982 was to be based on the change, if any, in the average retail list price of albums, such price to be determined by the tribunal from surveys and/or studies. The Court of Appeals ruled that the tribunal could adjust the mechanical rate for inflation as determined by the Consumer Price Index or some other barometer to insure the fairness of the rate until 1987.

---

†Record companies have interpreted this to mean, in record licenses, that they are only obliged to pay the copyright owner of the song "mechanical" royalties on phonorecords sold at the retail level; that is, they are not obliged to do so on promotions or returns.

‡A House Report notes a distinction between "made" as used in the language of the law, and "manufactured." "Made" has a meaning broader than "manufactured." It is meant to include within its scope every manufacturing or other process capable of reproducing a sound recording in phonorecords.

er to file a notice of use on Form U in the Copyright Office as a condition of receiving royalties from anyone who recorded that work without an express license, was eliminated by the 1976 act.

If monthly payments and the monthly and annual statements of account are not received by the copyright owner when due, the owner may give written notice to the licensee that if the default is not remedied within 30 days from the date of the notice, the compulsory license will be automatically terminated. Termination renders the making or distribution, or both, of phonorecords for which no royalty has been paid actionable as acts of infringement.

Mechanical Licenses. In the music industry, virtually all record manufacturers obtain licenses to make and distribute records and tapes embodying musical compositions under terms that vary from the compulsory license provisions of the statute (as just described). These are referred to as *mechanical* licenses and they serve to ease the burden of making payments and statements of account as prescribed by the compulsory license provision.

Typically, a mechanical license will vary from the statute's compulsory license by stipulating that the licensee (record manufacturer) shall account to the copyright owner (music publisher) for records and tapes manufactured and sold on a quarterly basis and nullify the need by the licensee to serve or file notice as required by the copyright law. A mechanical license may be limited to the United States, its territories and possessions, and Canada.

Mechanical licenses customarily provide for payment by the record company to the music publisher of the full statutory royalty rate for each phonorecord manufactured and sold (see 4 above). These agreements are generally standard licenses maintained by music publishers or their agents (*see* MECHANICAL RIGHTS AGENCY) and are issued to record companies when they request a license to use a music

publisher's copyright. SESAC, a performing rights organization that handles mechanical licensing rights for its affiliated publishers, titles its agreement "Phonorecord/Tape Recording License."

Record companies sometimes request and negotiate a royalty rate lower than that provided for by the statute. For example, royalty rates paid by record clubs are frequently less than statutory; a music publisher having several compositions on an album might accept a lesser rate for one or more songs. Compositions on budget albums are also commonly licensed at lesser royalty rates.

Reserve Funds for Record Returns. The Copyright Office permits a compulsory licensee to maintain a reserve fund of mechanical royalties against returns of phonorecords, since licensees are only accountable to pay royalties on records "permanently parted with." Pursuant to the 1976 act the Register of Copyrights implemented regulations providing a time period of nine months after shipment that companies can hold in reserve royalties payable under the compulsory music license. These regulations are subject to revision by the Register of Copyrights.

Concept Album. Album with a central theme. The songs on a concept album may be linked lyrically or musically—for example, by a story line, character, motif, or beat. The theme, if lyrical, is usually stated in the title of the album or the first cut (which is often the title song).

Because each song on a concept album interacts with the others to form a unifying whole, the writer of the songs is able to develop the underlying themes and use literary devices such as allegory, allusion, satire, and irony. These elements were cleverly used in the Beatles' Grammy Award–winning "album of the year" *Sgt. Pepper's Lonely Hearts Club Band* (Capitol).

Concept albums are generally regarded as

not being very commercial. This is because the emphasis is more on the essential theme than on commercial "singles" that might be culled from it. Airplay is essentially obtained on AOR stations, though a hit single will of course enjoy airplay on top 40 and contemporary radio stations.

A concept album may have a lyrical theme such as life in the city, a person's search to find himself, the world of the future, or a religious movement. Other concept albums that have been best-sellers include the rock operas *Jesus Christ Superstar* (which became a Broadway musical and a motion picture), *Tommy* (which also was made into a theatrical film), and Pink Floyd's *The Wall*.

Concert. For fans and artist alike, there is nothing—not recordings, television shows, or motion picture musicals—that can re-create the excitement of an artist's performance as a "live" concert. It is not unusual to find, at exciting rock concerts, fans dancing in the aisles, standing on their seats and swaying to the music, converging to the stage to get a better view, and applauding each number with loud screams, whistles, and occasional hysteria. Concerts of course serve to stimulate record sales, but more important, they put artist and fans in touch with one another. They are "events." In addition, the publicity associated with the concert can serve to create an awareness of the artist, attract new fans, and develop or enhance the artist's image and career, as well as reach segments of the public that are not necessarily consumers of his recorded product.

There is, too, the financial opportunity. Financial participants in addition to the artist include his personal manager, his booking agent, the concert promoter, and the proprietor of the venue where the performance is presented. Record companies may benefit from the sale of product resulting from the "promotion" of the artist's music, and music publishers and songwriters earn performance royalties. Other beneficiaries may include concessionaires, accountants, public relations firms, advertising firms, sound and lighting technicians, travel agencies (there are specialized concert tour agencies), and government agencies that derive tax revenues.

Over the years concerts have become increasingly more expensive to produce, what with artists demanding large shares of the box office receipts and mounting costs in several other areas. But despite the fact that promoters can take great losses (as well as earn great profits), the public demand to see and hear live performances of their favorite artists will probably always be great and there will always be entrepreneurs ready to fill that need.

Venues. Concerts are presented at many types of facilities, or venues. These include concert halls, theaters, auditoriums, convention halls, civic centers, sports arenas, stadiums, coliseums, amphitheaters, gymnasiums, racetracks, ballrooms, clubs, discotheques, restaurants, cabarets, and amusement parks. Public parks are also utilized.

Attendance. Attendance at concerts is based on a variety of factors. These include popularity, image, and drawing power of the artist, size, location, and type of the venue, advance publicity, advertisement, word of mouth, whether other concerts are being given on or around the same date, the economy, weather, season, demographics of the artist's audience, ticket prices, number of ticket sellers or outlets, the amount of advance time for the ticket sale, what performers are in the show besides the headliner, whether the artist has current releases and the commercial success of these.

Security. Concerts presented at large halls always have security teams working. These may be provided by the concert promoter, the venue, or both. Security problems and concerns at concerts range from minor to major and may include: the use of alcohol, marijuana, drugs, fireworks, or weapons, disturbances created while the artist is performing, sexual molestation, rape, fighting, throwing of objects, littering, pickpocketing, stealing, arson, crowd hysteria, dancing in the aisles, rushing onto the stage, disrupting of barriers, fences, or gates, entering the backstage area without permission, the unauthorized making of recordings and films, the selling of bootleg items, crowd entry and exit, parking and traffic jams.

Concert promoters and managers of venues must take care not to violate any local ordinances and regulations relating to such as overcrowding and fire hazards. Medical personnel and facilities should always be provided at concerts where large attendances are anticipated. In all types of venues, insurance is required and must be obtained by the promoter to cover all aspects of liability at the concert date.

Venue Rental/Expenses. Venues rent space, labor, and services to promoters in any of the following ways: flat fee, percentage of the gross box office receipts, or flat fee plus percentage. Some charge the higher of either a specified flat fee or a percentage of gross box office receipts. For example, for rental of space, a large arena may charge $8,500 or 17.5% of the gross, whichever is greater. Others charge a flat fee and a percentage of all gross receipts over a certain sum. A deposit is normally required to be paid upon signing of the contract (usually half in the case of flat fees), with the remainder to be paid before the show.

It is generally the responsibility of the promoter to pay for all labor and services, which include ushers, ticket takers, box office, security, porters and matrons, stagehands, electricians, and cleanup crew, and also for music licensing fees (ASCAP, BMI). Large facilities often require promoters to pay for first-aid services (physician and minimum of one nurse). Expenses for a one-night concert could run between $18,000 and $25,000 or more.

The artist or his representative may arrange for the sale of artist-related merchandise at concessions. Many arenas and stadiums contract their concessions to an outside firm. For example, Harry M. Stevens Corp. is the concessionaire at Shea Stadium, Nassau Coliseum, the Meadowlands, the Orange Bowl, and Madison Square Garden. Canteen Corp. does Yankee Stadium, Ogden Foods the Superdome in New Orleans. The concessionaire usually pays the venue a percentage of its gross income for the right to operate. All deals for merchandise are then conducted through the concessionaire. (A list of various types of merchandising items appears in MERCHANDISING TIE-INS.) Venues, or their concessionaires, normally participate in such revenues on a commission basis.

Visual Effects. Special visual effects are often used at concerts to enhance the show. These may range from simple to elaborate and include slides projected on a wall or screen, lasers, holograms, light shows, smoke and mist illusions, animals, clowns, vehicles, and other paraphernalia. Many shows are also choreographed, with both artist and backup singers performing dance routines.

Licenses. If a concert is held outdoors at a public park or on a street, a permit issued by the local government is almost always needed. In local areas, applications are often filed with the town clerk, who has the legal authority to issue permits for outdoor concerts either on his own accord or with the consent of the town council. In cities (and certain local areas), permits are generally obtained from the parks and recreation department. In municipally owned and run arenas, a permit is usually required to transact business. The management works closely with local government agencies, so they are aware of upcoming events. In privately owned and operated arenas, a permit is not necessary.

Union Aspects. Various types of workers

employed at venues where musical concerts are held are members of the International Alliance of Theatrical Stage Employees and Moving Picture Machine Operators of the U.S. and Canada (IATSE), which is affiliated with AFL-CIO. Members of IATSE include stagehands, ushers, ticket sellers, box office treasurers, and employees working in other crafts. IATSE has over 800 local unions, each of which is governed autonomously as long as it does not infringe upon the bylaws of the international constitution and alliance.

Ancillary Rights. Substantial revenues may be earned from ancillary rights related to live performances. These include the right to make and release sound recordings, videotapes, videodiscs, television films, and theatrical motion pictures based on the performance. Such rights are commonly reserved by the artist (particularly in the case of superstars) in the contract rider.

Advertising/Promotion. Advertising is handled by the concert promoter or the facility where the performance is to be held (in the latter case, a fee is usually charged for such services). For radio and television, advertising time is sometimes bought by trading concert tickets for an equal value of airtime or by both cash payment and ticket trade. For example, $1,000 in advertising time may be bought with a $500 cash payment plus an equal value of tickets. Stations give tickets to employees and business contacts or use them for contests or drawings held to increase the station's audience and boost its ratings. Newspaper advertising space is usually bought on a cash basis only; ticket exchanges occur less frequently, if at all, in this medium.

See also RECORD COMPANY; TOUR, CONCERT.

Concert Edition. *See* PRINTED MUSIC.

Concert Promoter. A concert promoter, or talent promoter, is in the business of engaging musical acts to perform at concert shows he produces. The promoter usually deals with agents in securing the services of artists and negotiating contracts. The promoter of course hopes to recoup the expenses he invested in producing the show and realize a profit, as large as possible.

Booking Concerts. A concert booking may be initiated by either the promoter, who contacts the agent of the act he wishes to engage, or the act's agent, who contacts the promoter. A description of how a concert may be booked appears in the AGENT entry.

Operations. In general, established concert promoters have certain markets within which they promote concerts. It is desirable for the promoter to negotiate for exclusive representation of the artist in these cities. Sometimes a promoter will handle an artist's tour on a national basis. In such cases, he will sometimes present concerts in association with promoters in local areas and split the receipts.

Before making an offer to book an act, the concert promoter will consider the act's live performance history in terms of experience, drawing power, and the quality of its show, its recording history and the status of its current releases, and the demographics of its audience. He may also inquire as to how the act will cooperate in publicity (e.g., local in-store autograph signings, radio interviews). Promoters take great risks; they may earn considerable profits, but also stand to lose much money.

Division of Concert Receipts. There are various ways in which artists and promoters split concert receipts. Most commonly, the artist receives a flat fee (guarantee) plus a percentage of the box office receipts—gross or net, depending upon individual negotiations.

In a gross deal, the promoter's profit (a percentage of the gross receipts) is added in as an expense and the act gets all moneys above and beyond. In a net deal, the expenses are deducted from the gross and the act and the promoter each gets a percentage of this. The artist's percentage normally ranges from 60% to 90%, the concert promoter earning the difference. For star attractions, the most common artist/promoter splits are (in terms of percentages) 80/20, 85/15, and 90/10.

Example: A concert promoter books an artist to perform one show at a local hall. Their contract provides for the artist to receive a $30,000 guarantee against 80% of the net box office receipts. The performance grosses $100,000 and expenses run to $50,000. All costs (guarantee and expenses) are deducted off the gross, leaving $20,000. The promoter receives 20% of this sum, or $4,000, and the artist receives 80%, or an additional $16,000. The artist's total earnings would be $46,000. From this sum, commissions, various salaries (e.g., road crew), and expenses would have to be deducted before the artist's profit can be determined.

Expenses. There are numerous expenses encountered in promoting a concert. These are normally deducted from the gross box office receipts (along with the artist's guarantee) before the artist and promoter divide the remaining receipts (if on a net deal). Expenses incurred in running and promoting a concert may include the following:

> rent
> ticket commissions (e.g., Ticketron)
> box office (of the venue)
> ticket outlets (e.g., record stores)
> staff (e.g., ushers)
> stagehands
> stage managers
> security and police
> insurance
> cleanup
> ticket printing
> miscellaneous
> runners
> ASCAP, BMI, and/or SESAC
> refreshments
> advertising
> limousines
> stage barricade and sound wings
> spotlights
> forklift
> firemen
> chairs
> medical
> electricians
> sound and lights
> tuner
> organ and piano rentals
> support talent

Performer/Concert Promoter Agreements. The performer/concert promoter agreement sets forth the general terms and conditions of the concert "date" and is a form which may be utilized by the concert promoter and the many artists he engages. The terms of such agreement are basic and generally include the name of the employer, engagement location and dates, compensation, seating capacities, and force majeure and breach considerations.

The *contract rider* to a performer/concert promoter agreement is a very personal statement of additional terms required by said artist incidental to the main agreement but necessary to the physical, mental, and financial well-being of the artist. Contract riders are common supplements to performer/concert promoter agreements, particularly those involving major acts. Following are some terms that may appear in a contract rider:

Billing—The star act is to receive 100% exclusive billing in any and all advertising, displays, marquees, programs, and publicity (also specified may be the precise manner in which the artist's name is to appear).

Ticket manifest—The promoter shall supply a ticket manifest showing the number, color, and price of all tickets for the performance. The manifest must be printed by a bonded printer and notarized.

Counterfeit tickets—The promoter is liable for any and all counterfeit tickets; under no circumstance shall the artist assume loss on any such tickets.

Complimentary tickets—The promoter shall limit all complimentary tickets to 1% of the total manifest.

Payments—All guaranteed payments shall be made in the form of cash, certified check, or money order, and all overage shall be made in the form of cash.

Stage manager—The promoter shall supply the services of a stage manager, who is completely responsible for stagehands, unloading and loading of trucks, and any technical difficulties that occur before, during, and after the performance. The stage manager shall have the facility ready for load-in (8 hours) prior to the start of the performance.

Power—The promoter must furnish a qualified electrician to assist the act's road crew from stage call through completion of the performance. Power of specified amperage must be available within a certain (specified) length from the stage.

Stagehands and forklift—The promoter shall provide a certain minimum number of stagehands to assist in the unloading and loading of the artist's sound, lighting, and other equipment, plus a forklift capable of loading and unloading equipment and placing it on stage.

Security—No uniformed police are allowed in the dressing room or backstage area; uniformed security guards shall be present at all times at the mixing platform to prevent unauthorized persons from entering the area in which the mixing equipment is located.

Dressing rooms—Clean and private dressings rooms capable of being locked with a key shall be provided for the artist, road crew, and authorized guests, with adequate security provided (but no uniformed police).

Refreshments and food—As specified by the artist; for star acts this often includes assorted deli, fresh fruit and cheese trays, sandwiches, hot meals, candy, miscellaneous

snacks, spring or distilled water, juices, soft drinks, alcoholic beverages, coffee, cups, plates, napkins, silverware, ice, and towels. These must arrive as specified (e.g., no later than 2 hours prior to showtime).

Backstage personnel—Only working personnel, performers, and authorized guests are permitted backstage or in the artist's dressing rooms before, during, and after the performance. During the performance, only employees and authorized guests of the artist are to be allowed on stage.

Lights—The promoter shall arrange for all lights not specifically required by local safety ordinances to be turned off during the performance (e.g., clocks, scoreboards, advertising billboards, and concessions in halls). All doorways to lighted hallways shall be curtained.

Ancillary rights—During the performance, vending is not permitted in the audience; the promoter guarantees not to commit the artist to any personal appearances or interviews; and no portion of the engagement may be recorded on film, videotape, or otherwise, or be reproduced photographically or by any sight or sound device by the purchaser, or any other person. The artist expressly reserves such rights for himself and his licensee(s) and designee(s).

Transportation—The promoter shall supply limousines to the artist for each engagement (sometimes at the promoter's expense).

Expenses incurred in any of the above areas are normally assumed by the artist. Promoters sometimes have their own rider they make part of a contract, qualifying specific information for the specific hall (i.e., curfews, opening-doors time, etc.).

Licenses. There are no state requirements for a person or company to engage in the business of concert promotion. In booking shows, however, city or local laws may require a permit or license to be obtained (i.e., to sponsor a public gathering). The venue where the concert is being held often obtains the license on behalf of the promoter charging him the cost. Promoters must be particularly careful when presenting an outdoor concert (at a park, for example) to obtain the proper permit(s). (*See* CONCERTS.) It may be the promoter's responsibility to obtain a performance license from ASCAP, BMI, and/or SESAC.

Getting Started. It is often difficult for one wishing to break into concert promotion to do so, as a relatively small number of established promoters in the United States dominate the field. Booking agents try to get the best work available for their clients for the most money, and the experienced promoter is most likely to fulfill these requirements. Also, agents are more inclined to work with those who are established, have a fine reputation and good track record, and with whom they have developed a personal working relationship.

Budding promoters often get started and establish a reputation by booking "baby" or developing acts into clubs, theaters, and other venues in a particular city, gradually booking them into larger facilities. By doing this, they may help build such acts into headliners. When an act achieves such status, it will usually request to continue working with the same promoters. Agents are more likely to provide headliner talent to those promoters who have "proved" themselves and such promoters are likewise better able to negotiate larger percentages for themselves.

Advertising/Publicity. Promoters often advertise an event 3 to 4 days before tickets are first placed on sale. Promoters advertise or provide pertinent information via newspapers, magazines, radio, television, billboards, posters, handbills, direct mail, telephone, and in-store fliers. The promoter initially assumes the cost of advertising, which is normally recouped as part of "expenses." "Star" acts often provide the copy they wish to appear in advertisements.

See also ADVERTISING; RECORD COMPANY; TOUR, CONCERT.

Concert Tour. *See* TOUR, CONCERT.

Consumer (Records and Tapes). The ultimate objective of companies involved in the DISTRIBUTION OF RECORDS AND TAPES is of course the purchase of these goods by consumers. Various different types of entities are involved in the distribution system, but the record/tape manufacturer is perhaps most concerned with bringing products to the attention of as many people as possible. As the consumer audience for records and tapes is vast and most recordings appeal only to particular segments of the public (though these may be large), the marketing, merchandising, advertising, promotion, and publicity campaigns of manufacturers are aimed at specific target audiences. Consumer research has proved a valuable tool in determining these.

Research. Manufacturers, trade associations, research firms, and other entities conduct research to discover who's buying what—why, where, when, and how much—and the demographics of these consumers. Research—into buying habits, what media and other forms of influence are most effective, musical tastes, and even psychological desires—is conducted through interviews, questionnaires, testing, surveys, and many other means. As a result, record manufacturers are able to analyze the musical tastes and buying habits of consumers and release appropriate commercial products (*see* DEMOGRAPHIC SURVEYS).

Information about New Recordings. After a company determines its target audience for a recording, it is faced with the task of reaching this market. In some cases it can inform a market easily, and in others it can't. Consumers learn about new recordings in various ways and from various sources, including the following:

Performances—radio; television; concerts; motion pictures; clubs, discos, etc.; background music sources; jukeboxes; hearing recordings at friends' houses, parties, etc.

Advertisements—newspaper; magazine; radio; television; billboards; etc. (*see* ADVERTISING).

Artist interviews—newspaper; magazine; radio; television.

Record reviews, articles, and commentaries—newspaper; magazine; radio; television.

Retail—point-of-purchase displays; in-store advertising; cross-merchandising.

Word of mouth.

Contractor. Person who secures (contracts) the services of musicians and/or singers for performing at a musical event. A contractor thus puts together orchestras or choruses or combinations of these for a particular occasion. Many contractors "specialize" and handle particular areas, such as recording sessions, jingle sessions, motion picture recording sessions, television shows, stage musicals, or rock, jazz, and classical music concerts.

The contractor selects performers known to him who have demonstrated an ability to perform accurately and work efficiently and who can enhance a musical event (he learns and keeps in mind the strengths and weaknesses of each person). A contractor's reputation usually rests on the quality of musicians or singers he provides. He usually deals with a pool of the best available performers (often free-lancers) in his locality.

Contractors themselves are hired by various types of employers, depending upon the nature of the musical event. Such employers include record companies, record producers, jingle producers, motion picture producers, theatrical producers, and impresarios, as well as conductors, arrangers, and recording artists. Contractors are hired when any of these need musicians or singers for a specific event (employers generally do not have the time or expertise to assemble such groups). Frequently, contractors are performers themselves; some

are inactive players who have turned to contracting; others are business people.

With respect to recording sessions, contractors and the performers they hire are usually union members. Consequently the employers they deal with are generally signatories to union agreements which establish minimum session fees and other terms of employment. Contractors who hire instrumentalists are members of AFM; AFTRA contractors hire vocalists.

A contractor has many responsibilities. These commonly include: supplying performers with all the proper information, making sure they arrive on time (and with respect to musicians, that they bring their assigned instruments), being able to get last-minute replacements, ensuring that all rented musical equipment arrives on time, making sure that the performers are given the proper rest periods (as per the union's agreement), advising the employer of remaining time and overtime costs, computing all session fees (including additional wages for doubling on other instruments as well as his own fee), submitting the appropriate union forms to the employer and copies with the union office, administering union paperwork (for pension and welfare funds, etc.), and overseeing the timely compensation to the performers (as per the union agreement).

Contracts. The music business is, so to speak, a "paper" business; it depends upon "rights" and services, deals, permissions, and promises, all set down on the essential contracts between the parties. A variety of contracts are used in the music business and only a few of them are "forms." For the most part, they have to be tailored to complex individual arrangements.

A *contract* is a promissory agreement between two or more parties to do or to refrain from doing a particular thing (transfer ownership of a copyright, record an album, manage an artist, etc.). To be enforceable by law, a contract must be entered into willfully by each party and there must be an exchange between the parties (called a *consideration*). This is something of value (such as payment of money) given or done in exchange for something of value (such as performance of a service or transfer of a property). Inducing a party into a contract by misrepresentation or fraud is grounds for the deceived party to avoid obligation thereof. If the deceived party acts within a reasonable period of time after discovering the truth, the contract cannot be enforced. Furthermore, there are special laws governing the rights of MINORS.

A *license* in the music business is a specialized contract generally dealing with "rights" granted by a copyright owner or his agent. A license gives permission or authorization to use a right or rights in a particular way or ways for a specified period of time in a defined territory in return for some kind of compensation. The license may be exclusive or nonexclusive. The *licensor* is the party who gives or grants the license and the *licensee* is the party to whom the license is granted. There are various types of licenses issued by the owner of a copyright or his agent (*see* MUSIC PUBLISHER).

Following are listings of the contracts and licenses, and also copyright forms commonly used by various individuals and entities in the music business. These are limited, of course, to matters directly related to the music business.

Songwriter
Songwriter/music publisher agreement (individual composition)
Exclusive songwriter/music publisher agreement
AGAC popular songwriters contract
Assignment of copyright contract
Application for Copyright Registration for a Work of the Performing Arts (Form PA)
Application for Renewal Registration (Form RE)
Songwriter/performing rights organization agreement (ASCAP, BMI, or SESAC)
Collaboration agreement
Songwriter/theatrical producer agreement

Dramatists Guild Inc. Dramatico-Musical Production Contract
Composer/theatrical motion picture agreement

Music Publisher
Songwriter/music publisher agreement (individual composition)
Exclusive songwriter/music publisher agreement
AGAC popular songwriters contract
Assignment of copyright contract
Application for Copyright Registration for a Work of the Performing Arts (Form PA)
Application for Renewal Registration (Form RE)
Music publisher/performing rights organization agreement
Mechanical license agreement
Music publisher/mechanical rights agency agreement
Synchronization license (television film or videotape)
Motion picture synchronization and theatrical performance license
Print license for sheet music, folio, etc. (licensee/distributor or selling agent)
Printed matter agreement
Dramatic performing rights license (grand rights license)
Jingle license
Background music transcription license
Music box agreement
Videocassette/videodisc agreement
Publisher/lyricist agreement
Miscellaneous licenses based on copyright (posters, greeting cards, etc.)
Administration agreement (with other publisher)
Copublishing agreement (participation agreement)
International subpublishing agreements
International administration agreements (collection agreements)

Recording Artist and/or *Musician*
Recording artist/record company agreement
Recording artist/record producer agreement
Recording artist/personal manager agreement
Recording artist/booking agent agreement
Recording artist/business manager agreement
Recording artist/public relations firm agreement
Recording artist/motion picture company agreement
Union membership agreement(s)
AFTRA Exclusive Agency contract (singers)
AFM Exclusive Agent—Musician Agreement (musicians)

Group partnership agreement
Merchandising licenses (posters, T-shirts, etc.)
AFM Performance Contracts
    C-1 Live Performance
    CP-1 Live Performance subject to pension
    B-4 Phonograph Records
    B-5 Demonstration Recording
    B-6 Commercial Announcements and Electrical Transcriptions
    B-7 Films (TV and Theatrical)
    B-8 TV Videotape

Record Company
Recording artist/record company agreement
Record producer/record company agreement
Production company/record company agreement
Master record purchase agreement
Master lease agreement
Arranger/work-for-hire agreement
Application for Copyright Registration for a Sound Recording (Form SR)
Application for Renewal Registration (Form RE)
Record company/tape manufacturer license
Distribution agreement with other record company
Custom label agreement
Phonograph Record Labor Agreement and Special Payments Fund Agreement (AFM)
National Code of Fair Practice for Phonograph Recording (AFTRA)
Mechanical reproduction license (with music publisher)
Sale or license of master record (between record companies)
Merchandising licenses
Record company/record promoter contract (with rider)
Motion picture company/record company contract (licensing of label's master)
Motion picture company/record company soundtrack album agreement
Videocassette or videodisc license
Theatrical producer/record company cast album agreement
Licenses of master recording to record club, record merchandising or mail order company
International master licensing agreements

Record Producer/Production Company
Recording artist/record producer agreement
Record producer/record company agreement
Production company/record company agreement

Master record purchase agreement (with record company)
Coproducer agreement
Foreign sublicensing agreement
Application for Copyright Registration for a Sound Recording (Form SR)
Application for Renewal Registration (Form RE)

Booking Agent
Booking agent/artist agreement
AFM Exclusive Agent–Musician Agreement
AFTRA Exclusive Agency Contract
AGVA Agreement
Concert promoter/agent agreement

Personal Manager
Recording artist/personal manager agreement

Concert Promoter
Concert promoter/agent agreement
Concert promoter/facility contract
Performing rights organization license

Performing Rights Organization
Songwriter/performing rights organization agreement
Music publisher/performing rights organization agreement
Music user licenses (including):
    Radio station license agreement (blanket or per program)
    Television station license agreement (blanket or per program)
    Colleges and universities
    Theme park license
    Theaters—live talent
    Symphony—major
    Symphony—metropolitan
    Symphony—urban and community
    Skating rinks
    Private club license
    Motion picture theaters—recorded intermission music
    Ice skating shows
    Hotels and motels
    General license agreements: restaurants, taverns, nightclubs, etc.
    Dancing schools
    Circus
    Background music license
    Amusement park license

See also DRAMATISTS GUILD INC. DRAMATICO-MUSICAL PRODUCTION CONTRACT; INTERNATIONAL MASTER RECORDING LICENSING AGREEMENT; IN-

TERNATIONAL SUBPUBLISHING AGREEMENT; RECORD AND TAPE CLUB; RECORDING ARTIST/RECORD COMPANY CONTRACTS; SONGWRITER/MUSIC PUBLISHER CONTRACT.

Copies. Term used in the federal copyright statute. A COPYRIGHT OWNER has the exclusive right to reproduce and publish a work in copies with certain exceptions.

Definition. "Copies" is defined in the 1976 Copyright Act (Section 101) as "material objects, other than phonorecords, in which a work is fixed by any method now known or later developed, and from which the work can be perceived, reproduced, or otherwise communicated, either directly or with the aid of a machine or device. The term 'copies' includes the material object in which the work is first fixed."

Examples. Examples of "copies" include sheet music, songbooks, lead sheets, manuscripts, books, films, videotapes, and videodiscs.

Copublishing Agreements. A common practice in the music business is for two or more music publishers to own the rights to the same musical composition (copyright). Such an arrangement is generically referred to as *copublishing*. There are various types of copublishing agreements, with differentiations made as to the administering publisher—i.e., in a *joint* publishing agreement each publisher will administer its own share; in a *copublishing* or *participation* agreement, either the original or the participating publisher would be the administrator.

Participants in copublishing agreements involve all types of music publishers: independent, record company–affiliated, and those owned by recording artists, producers, songwriters, and managers. Copublishing agreements arise under various circumstances, such as co-writers of a song each assigning half of the publishing rights to their respective publishing companies; an artist or a producer obtaining a "piece" of a copyright from the writer or publisher for recording it; a record company publisher obtaining a portion of the rights to musical compositions written and/or recorded by artists on the label's roster; or a manager and an artist "splitting" the rights to all songs written and/or recorded by that artist (the manager having had the bargaining position to demand this).

It is particularly common for writer/publishers to enter into copublishing agreements with large publishers, as such an arrangement is often beneficial to each. Many large publishers seek copublishing deals with established writers who have many hits to their credit, or in some cases, with promising new writers, as this enables them to obtain ownership rights to the new songs of talented writers, which they would not otherwise acquire. Publishers, to be competitive, generally need new and fresh songs with commercial potential.

For successful writers, copublishing agreements are attractive for their cash flow benefits, as they are often able to negotiate large advances. In addition, large companies are usually better equipped to exploit songs and maximize their income, an inviting prospect. Some publishers also offer free office space, telephone service, use of office equipment and supplies, and other resources. The writer of a copublished song or catalog generally receives one half of the gross earnings less direct expenses other than administration fees. In some cases, the larger publisher will waive its commission for administering the writer/publisher's catalog.

Example of Copublishing/Administration Agreement. A singer/songwriter with a few hits to his credit as both a writer and a recording artist signs a recording contract with a large record company. He has a music publishing firm and makes an agreement with his label's publishing affiliate to copublish all the songs he writes for the length of his recording contract with the label, each publishing company to own 50% of the copyrights. The copublishing agreement states that the label's publishing arm will administer the copyrights for a fee of 10% of the gross income.

Foreseeing the possible advantage to the label in reducing the statutory mechanical royalty rate for each record or tape sold, the singer/songwriter's copublishing agreement stipulates that for all the songs they copublish, the mechanical royalty will be the full statutory rate.

The following is an example of how mechanical royalties for a particular royalty period would be divided: The record royalties of the copublished catalog for a particular royalty period amount to $25,000. From this income the administrator/copublisher deducts its 10% commission, or $2,500, leaving a balance of $22,500. It then forwards a check to the writer for one half of the gross royalties,° or $12,500, leaving a balance of $10,000. The $10,000 balance is then divided equally between the two copublishers. In conclusion, the administrator/copublisher's gross earnings are $2,500 plus $5,000, or $7,500. The writer/copublisher's earnings are $12,500 plus $5,000, or $17,500.

The copublished songs might of course have earnings in other areas for that particular royalty period, such as from public performances or print sales. It should be noted, however, that writers receive their performance royalties directly from their performing rights organizations (see below) and most songwriter/music publisher agreements provide for a print royalty to the songwriter at a rate that is

---

° The writer's royalties are one half of the gross received, less expenses such as for demos and lead sheets that the writer was contractually obligated to assume a share of, or unrecouped advances, but as far as this example goes, any such moneys are not deducted.

less than that receivable by the publisher.

Copyright Registration and Notices. In a copublishing agreement, a copyright application for registration of a musical work, containing the name and address of each copyright owner, is filed at the U.S. Copyright Office by the administering publisher. If a song was registered before the agreement took effect, the administrator/copublisher would record the transfer in part of copyright ownership in the Copyright Office. In printed publications of the mutually owned works, the copyright notice will contain the names of both publishers, with reference normally but not necessarily made to the administrator of the copyright.

Performing Rights Organizations. ASCAP, BMI, and SESAC, in recognizing the practice of sharing in the ownership of copyrights, make separate performance royalty payments to publishers and writers of songs with co-ownership interests after receiving instructions to that effect. For all three organizations, writers receive their performance royalties directly from their organization and not from their publisher.

Mechanical Rights Agencies. A MECHANICAL RIGHTS AGENCY, such as The Harry Fox Agency or the American Mechanical Rights Association, will, after receiving instructions, make separate payments to publisher co-owners in a copyright for record royalties and synchronization and transcription fees it collects on behalf of its affiliated publishers. Mechanical rights agencies in the U.S. do not pay writers their share of earnings directly. Writers receive such income from their publishers. In a copublishing agreement where each publisher administers its own portion of the copyright and one is affiliated with a mechanical rights agency and the other is not, instructions are given to record companies on how to make payments—either through a mechanical rights agency or directly to the publisher.

Copyist, Music. Person who reproduces the individual parts from a musical score onto manuscript paper. (A musical score is prepared by a composer, an arranger, or an orchestrator.) From these pages, the members of a band, an orchestra, or another ensemble perform their parts.

The music copyist's aim is to afford the musician or vocalist ease in reading the written musical part. He lays out the page so that the person can concentrate his efforts on performing the music without having to be distracted by illegible notations or irregular spacing.

Music copying is a field populated by various types of professionals. Besides the full-time music copyists, there are arrangers, orchestrators, and composers who supplement their income by working in this capacity. Many professional copyists have extensive musical training, particularly in music theory, harmony, composition, orchestration, and notation. Such training is vital, as their work often, for example, requires them to transpose parts, correct compositional or orchestral errors, or write lead sheets of a song from hearing it performed live or on tape.

Equipment. The equipment used by the music copyist in his profession includes music writing pens (which are able to draw thick and thin lines, depending upon the stroke used), rulers and straightedges (preferably with beveled edges to prevent ink from sliding underneath), an electric eraser, a blotter, an emery cloth (to smooth and adjust the pen points), ink (generally black, waterproof, and opaque), a liquid pen cleaner, manuscript paper, transparencies (for reproductions), and stencils and rubber stamp sets (for titles).

Union Aspects. Professional music copyists are members of the AMERICAN FEDERATION OF MUSICIANS OF THE UNITED STATES AND CANADA (AFM). AFM establishes national minimum wage scales for music copying in various categories, as phonograph records, commercial announcements (jingles), TV films, theatrical motion pictures. For certain other categories, AFM locals establish minimum wage scales for music copying done in their jurisdiction (e.g., Local 802 in New York sets minimum scale for copying for Broadway shows).

Copyists get paid by the copied page, not the score page. Wages are computed on page and half-page rates. Regular union scale applies to work performed in an 8-hour period from 9 A.M. to 6 P.M. Monday through Friday. There are overtime wages for copying done beyond the 8-hour period and premium rates for copying done on weekends and holidays.

Related Career Aspects. Some music copyists are also autographers and engravers; others move on to becoming music editors for music publishers and librarians for symphony orchestras.

Copyright. Term that refers to the exclusive rights granted by laws of countries to owners of musical, literary, dramatic, pictorial, audiovisual, and certain other types of works. In the United States, the Copyright Act of 1976 grants to an owner of copyright the exclusive rights to reproduce, adapt, publish, perform, and display the work, or authorize others to do so. Anyone who uses these exclusive rights without permission from the copyright owner, except as provided by law, is subject to the penalties of infringement. The terms of copyright protection, which may vary, are discussed in COPYRIGHT DURATION.

Under the U.S. law, a work is immediately protected by the federal statute when it is "fixed" in any tangible medium of expression from which it can be perceived, reproduced, or otherwise communicated for a period of more than transitory duration. Both unpublished and published works may secure a federal copyright, but a work may satisfy certain requirements to be copyrightable. A work protected by federal law is referred to as a *statu-*

tory copyright; one not protected under the federal statute is a *common law copyright.*

Music Copyrights. Commonly, when reference is made to a "copyright" in the music business, it refers to a musical composition. A music copyright may be any type of musical work—a pop, rock, country, gospel, or jazz song, a symphony, or some other type of musical composition. A music copyright particularly includes the rights of performance, mechanical reproduction, print reproduction, adaptation, arrangement, and synchronization.

See also COPYRIGHTABLE WORKS.

Copyright Act of 1976. *See* COPYRIGHT LAW OF THE UNITED STATES.

Copyright Deposit and Registration. Under the U.S. copyright law, *deposit* and *registration* are regarded as two closely related, albeit separate, acts.° The Copyright Act establishes a mandatory deposit requirement for works published in the U.S. Copyright registration is, in general, a legal formality aimed at placing on public record the basic facts of a registration. It is thus voluntary (although advantageous). Special provision is made in the Copyright Act with respect to works published in the U.S. for a single deposit to satisfy both the deposit requirements for the Library of Congress and the registration requirements. In order to have this dual effect, the copies or phonorecords must be "accompanied by the prescribed application and fee" for registration.

Deposit for the Library of Congress. The 1976 Copyright Act makes it mandatory for works published with the notice of copyright in the United States to be deposited in the Copyright Office, generally by the copyright owner or the owner of the right of first publi-

cation. The statute requires that a deposit of two complete copies of the "best edition" of the work,† or in the case of sound recordings, two "complete" phonorecords together with "any printed or visually perceptible material" published with such phonorecords,‡ be made in the Copyright Office within 3 months after the work has been published with notice for the use or disposition of the Library of Congress.

If compliance with this provision is not made by the owner of copyright or of the exclusive right of publication, the Register of Copyrights may demand deposit. If the required copies or phonorecords are not deposited within 3 months after the demand is made, the copyright would not be invalidated but the owner would be liable to the following: a fine of not more than $250 for each work; and payment into the Library's specially designated fund of the total retail price of the copies or phonorecords demanded; and an additional fine of $2,500 if the person willfully or repeatedly fails or refuses to comply with such a demand.

Regulations of the Copyright Office [Section 202.19(c)(4)] provide that musical works published only as embodied in phonorecords are exempt from the mandatory deposit requirements of Section 407(a) of the U.S. Copyright Law. This does not exempt, however, the SOUND RECORDING from mandatory deposit.

Copyright Registration. Registration of a claim to copyright for both published and unpublished works can be made at any time during the copyright term by the owner of copyright or of any exclusive right in the work. The claim may be registered by depositing

---

°The 1909 Copyright Act combined deposit and registration into a single requirement.

†The edition published in the United States before the date of deposit that the Library of Congress determines most suitable for its purposes, regardless of any other U.S. editions published before the date of deposit.
‡This includes textual or pictorial matter appearing on record sleeves or album covers.

copies or phonorecords of the work together with the proper application and fee.°

In general, the material to be deposited for an unpublished work is one complete copy or phonorecord of the work, and for a published work, two complete copies or phonorecords of the "best edition." For works published in the United States, the statute provides that a single deposit may satisfy both the deposit requirements for the Library and the deposit provisions of registration.† Deposit for the Library can be combined with registration if the deposit of copies or phonorecords is accompanied by the prescribed application and fee and any additional identifying material the Register may require by regulation. Registration of a published musical composition is more beneficial to the copyright owner than merely complying with the deposit requirements.

Copyright registration of published and unpublished works is voluntary; it is not a condition of copyright protection,‡ but a prerequisite to the institution of an infringement suit and of certain remedies. A copyright owner who has not registered his claim can have a valid cause of action against someone who has infringed his copyright, but no action or proceeding against the infringer may be instituted in the courts until he has registered his claim.

The 1976 Copyright Act offers an incentive for prompt or early registration of a claim to a work by tying certain remedies for an in-fringement to the effective date of registration of the work. If an infringement occurs before the effective date of registration,§ the copyright owner would be entitled to the ordinary remedies of injunction (i.e., to restrain further publication of the work) and actual damages. If the infringement commenced after registration, however, the copyright owner would be entitled to remedies of statutory damages and attorney's fees. The statute provides a 3-month grace period after publication to effect registration. This means that if an infringement occurs between first publication and the effective date of registration, the latter being not more than 3 months after first publication, the copyright owner is entitled to full remedies.

In one particular case, copyright registration is a means to secure statutory protection of a work. This applies to works previously published without a notice of copyright or with a notice omitting the name and date. The statute provides that an omission does not invalidate the copyright (1) if the notice has been omitted from "no more than a relatively small number" of copies or phonorecords publicly distributed; or (2) if registration for the work has been previously made or is made within 5 years after publication without notice and "a reasonable effort" is made to add the notice to all copies or phonorecords publicly distributed in the United States after the omission has been discovered; or (3) the notice has been omitted in violation of an express written agreement. These provisions also apply to foreign works seeking U.S. copyright protection where publication occurs with an omission in the copyright notice.

°For registering musical compositions, the Copyright Office accepts phonorecords in place of printed or written notated copies to satisfy the deposit requirement.

†For purposes of copyright registration of published works, the "best edition" containing such works is the same as for deposit with the Library of Congress. For copyright registration of an unpublished work, what must be deposited is a complete copy or phonorecord representing the entire copyrightable content of the work for which registration is sought.

‡Except where registration is made to preserve a copyright that might be invalidated due to an omission of the copyright notice.

---

§The effective date of a copyright registration is the day on which the Copyright Office receives an application, deposit, and fee (which are later determined by the Register of Copyrights or by a competent court of jurisdiction to be acceptable for registration); if the items are received separately, the date of receipt of the last item controls.

The compulsory license provision of the copyright law regarding phonorecords provides yet another incentive for prompt registration under this provision: a copyright owner must be identified in the registration or other public records of the Copyright Office to be entitled to receive royalties under a compulsory license. The owner is entitled to receive royalties for mechanical reproductions made and distributed after being so identified, but not for those made and distributed previous to his identification.

The 1976 statute requires the Register of Copyrights to register a claim and issue a certificate of registration under the seal of the Copyright Office to the claimant when the material deposited "constitutes copyrightable subject matter" and other formal requirements have been met. The certificate constitutes prima facie evidence of the validity of the copyright in any judicial proceedings made before or within 5 years after publication of the work. For registrations made thereafter, the court is given discretion to decide what evidentiary weight the registration certificate shall have.

Supplementary Copyright Registration. In general, only one basic copyright registration can be made for the same version of a work. Such registration in the Copyright Office ordinarily stands as the fundamental copyright record on which subsequent records relating to the particular work can be built.

There are two exceptions to this general rule, however: if a work has been registered in unpublished form, a second registration to cover the published edition, even if substantially similar, may be made (this is not required, however); or where in the earlier registration the copyright claimant is not the author, the author may make a basic registration in his or her name.

A supplementary registration (Form CA) can be made to either "correct" errors or "amplify" information given in a basic registration. Examples of an incorrect basic registration include incorrect identification of the author of the work, or a work registered as published when publication had not actually occurred. Examples of "amplification" would be to give the name of a coauthor whose name was omitted in the basic registration, or to register individual titles of selections from an album that was originally registered on Form SR.

There is a fee for a supplementary registration.

See COPYRIGHT REGISTRATION OF A MUSICAL WORK; COPYRIGHT REGISTRATION OF A SOUND RECORDING.

Copyright Duration. The Copyright Act of 1976 grants terms of copyright protection to original works created on or after January 1, 1978, as explained below. The law also extends the renewal term of works published or registered for copyright prior to 1978 that were not in the public domain on January 1, 1978. This entry examines the length of protection all copyrights receive under the federal law.

Works Created on or after January 1, 1978. For published or unpublished works (such as musical compositions or sound recordings) that are created ("fixed" in a tangible form for the first time) on or after January 1, 1978, the act provides durations of copyright protection for works of various types of authorship as follows:

General term—The period of protection is for the AUTHOR's life plus an additional period of 50 years after the author's death.

Joint works—For a work prepared by two or more authors, the term is for the life of the last surviving coauthor plus an additional period of 50 years after that author's death.

Anonymous works, pseudonymous works, and works made for hire—The duration of copyright for these works is for a period of 75 years from first publication or 100 years from creation, whichever is shorter. In the case of anonymous and pseudonymous works, if the identity of the author (or in the case of a joint work, the coauthor) is revealed in the Copyright Office records before the copyright expires, the copyright endures for the life of the identified author plus 50 years. If after a period of 75 years from first publication or 100 years after creation of a work, whichever expires earlier, the Copyright Office records do not indicate whether a particular author is living or the date of his death, a certified report authorizes one to presume that the author has been dead for at least 50 years. Reliance in good faith in this presumption is a complete defense in an infringement action (an author should, therefore, notify the Copyright Office of his existence if he is still living in one of the above-stated intervals). There is no renewal term for any work created on or after January 1, 1978.

Works in Existence but Not Published or Copyrighted Before January 1, 1978. A work that was created before January 1, 1978, but neither published nor registered for copyright, was generally under common law protection. Such works are automatically brought under the statute and receive federal copyright protection for the same life—plus-50 or 75/100-year terms provided for works created on or after January 1, 1978. The statute guarantees a minimum of 25 years of statutory protection for all works in this category, however, by specifying that in no case shall a work expire before December 31, 2002, and if the work is published before that date, the term is extended for another 25 years, until December 31, 2027.

Works Under Statutory Protection Before 1978. Under the copyright law that was in effect before 1978, statutory protection began for a work of any type of ownership on the date it was published, or for an unpublished

work, on the date a registration was made for it in the Copyright Office. In either case, the copyright was granted a first term of 28 years of protection from the date it was secured. If the copyright was renewed during the last year of the first term, it was extended a second term of 28 years. If not renewed during the last year of the first term, the copyright fell into the public domain.

The 1976 act retains the first term of copyright of 28 years, but provides for a renewal term of 47 years. Thus a copyright subsisting before 1978 may have a total term of copyright protection lasting 75 years. For copyrights in their first term on January 1, 1978, renewal registration is necessary to obtain the second term, which is a 47-year term, or a total of 75 years. Claims to renewal copyrights (for works originally published or registered between January 1, 1950, and December 31, 1977) should be submitted with Form RE.

Copyrights already in their renewal term on January 1, 1978, automatically had their renewal terms extended for an additional 19 years, or a total of 75 years. Works that would have expired between September 19, 1962, and December 31, 1976, were extended by congressional enactments through December 31, 1976. The 1976 act provides for these copyrights to endure for a period of 75 years from the end of the year in which the copyright was originally secured.

Expiration Date of Copyright Terms. The 1976 act provides for all terms of copyright to run to the last day of the calendar year in which they would otherwise expire. Hence the last day of statutory protection for a work is December 31 of that copyright's last year. For works in their first copyright term on January 1, 1978 (i.e., those originally copyrighted between 1950 and 1977), the time for renewal registration will run from December 31 of the 27th year to December 31 of the following year.

Practical Examples of Copyright Duration

Example: A song is written on March 3, 1982, and is registered in unpublished form on June 10, 1982. The writer of the composition dies on January 11, 2004. When does the copyright expire?

Since the composition was created after January 1, 1978, the copyright term is for the life of the author plus 50 years, with the copyright to endure through the end of the calendar year in the last year of protection. Thus the copyright would fall into the public domain after December 31, 2054.

Example: A sound recording made under a work for hire agreement was copyrighted on June 18, 1975. When must a renewal application be filed and to what date will proper renewal extend copyright?

A renewal application must be received in the Copyright Office between December 31, 2002, and December 31, 2003 (applications received before or after will not be accepted). Proper renewal will extend copyright protection until December 31, 2050.

Example: A song was first published on October 25, 1925, and a renewal registration was made between October 25, 1952, and October 25, 1953. When is the last day of the work's copyright protection?

Copyrights in their renewal term on January 1, 1978, were automatically extended for an additional 19 years of protection, for a total renewal term of 47 years. Thus the work would enjoy statutory protection until December 31, 2000.

Example: A song was created on April 11, 1969, but was neither published nor registered for copyright. The author died the following year. The composition was later rediscovered, registered, and then published on August 2, 1980. Till when does the song enjoy copyright protection?

The law provides that in no case shall a work in existence but not published or copyrighted before January 1, 1978, fall into the public domain before December 31, 2002. Any work published on or before this date has its term extended for another 25 years, till the end of 2027.

Example: A recording is made under a work for hire agreement on November 9, 1984, and released the following year (1985). When does the copyright expire?

Seventy-five years from first publication, or after December 31, 2060.

See also COPYRIGHT GRANTS, TERMINATIONS OF; COPYRIGHT RENEWAL REGISTRATION.

Copyright Entries, Catalog of. A publication of the Copyright Office containing essential facts concerning registrations and renewals of works with the Office, the *Catalog of Copyright Entries* is divided into parts according to the classes of works registered, each part issued regularly in book form and covering all registrations and renewals made for that class during a particular period.

The *Catalog* is often used in investigating the copyright status of a work or to obtain certain information about it. The publication, however, does not include entries for assignments or other recorded documents and cannot be used for searches involving the ownership or rights. Information on older registrations can be found by consulting past editions. The *Catalog* was first published in book form in 1891.

The Fourth Series of the *Catalog of Copyright Entries* reflects changes made as a result of the 1976 Copyright Act. It is divided into eight parts: Part 1, *Nondramatic Literary Works* (all material registered in Class TX except serials and periodicals); Part 2, *Serials and Periodicals;* Part 3, *Performing Arts* (all material registered in Class PA except motion pictures and filmstrips); Part 4, *Motion Pictures and Filmstrips;* Part 5, *Visual Arts* (all material registered in Class VA except maps); Part 6, *Maps;* Part 7, *Sound Recordings;* and Part 8, *Renewals.*

The different parts of the *Catalog* are printed and issued periodically (e.g., quarterly or semiannually), and are available at major libraries or by purchase from the Copyright Office.

Copyright Grants, Termination of. The U.S. copyright law permits authors who have transferred or assigned away rights to their works to recapture such rights at a later time. Termination of transfers and licenses granted by an author may be made during certain time periods if there is compliance with the regulations set forth by the law. These rules, which are somewhat complicated, are discussed below; but to better understand and appreciate this statutory provision, it might first be helpful to see why it was written into the Copyright Act of 1976.

Background. Under the law in effect prior to the 1976 act, there existed a feature known as the renewal system. This system provided that after a first term of 28 years, an author or specified beneficiaries may renew a copyright for a second consecutive term of 28 years. In commercial practice, however, where rights to a work were assigned to third parties, most assignees would insist on an inclusion in the original grant of renewal rights to the work from the author. If the author lived till the renewal period, he was bound by the assignment of the renewal term. If he did not, however, his beneficiaries, as the courts have held, were able to recapture the rights to his work and renew the copyright in their names. In this sense, therefore, it was beneficial to an author's family if he died before the renewal term, because that was the only way they could reclaim the renewal copyright.

It was with a view toward eliminating this and other pitfalls of the renewal system—which also mandated that failure to renew a work during the last year of its first statutory term would invalidate the copyright—that certain provisions of the 1976 act were writ-

ten. Moreover, the act aimed to solve a problem referred to as "protection of authors against unremunerative transfers"*—that is, to aid authors who, at the time of transferring rights to works to another party or grantee (such as a publisher), were in a poor bargaining position and/or have received an unreasonable financial return from their assigned works. One such substitution in the 1976 act, for the old renewal system, is Section 203, "Termination of transfers and licenses granted by the author." This section provides that an author or certain beneficiaries may terminate any grant or license he or she made for a work within certain times during the copyright's subsistence. The statute provides this termination right for works copyrighted both before and after 1978 (the effective date of the 1976 act), with different time limits according to whether the work was copyrighted under the old or the new law. As termination and reversion of rights is not automatic, however, careful planning and understanding of this provision is necessary in order for an author or specified beneficiaries to terminate within the proper time limits any grant or license made and recapture the rights to that work.

Termination of Transfers and Licenses Made on or after January 1, 1978. The statute provides that with the exception of a work made for hire, any transfer of exclusive or nonexclusive rights to a work made by an author on or after January 1, 1978, may be terminated. The grant may be terminated at any time during a 5-year period that begins at the end of 35 years from the date of execution of the grant; or, if the grant covers the right of publication, the 5-year period begins 35 years from the date of publication. But if that date is more than 40 years from the date of execution of the grant, the period begins at 40 years

---

*Register of Copyrights, Copyright Law Revision, Pt. 6, Supplementary Report on the General Revision of the U.S. Copyright Law: 1965 Revision Bill 71, 89th Cong., 1st Sess.

from the date of transfer. Termination is effected by the serving of a written notice upon the grantee no less than 2 or more than 10 years before termination is to take effect. The notice must comply with Copyright Office regulations and a copy of it must be recorded in the Office before the effective date of termination, as a condition of its taking effect.

Who May Terminate

1. Where a grant is made by one author only, the grant may be terminated by that author. If the author is dead, the termination interest may be exercised, unless otherwise provided by will, by a widow or widower and children or grandchildren, with the provision that in cases of conflict, those who own a total of more than one half of the author's termination interest may exercise the termination right. Where an author is dead, termination rights may be executed by survivors as follows:

    a. The widow or widower owns the entire termination interest where there are no children or grandchildren.
    b. The author's child or children, or children of any dead child of the author, own the author's termination interest where there is no surviving widow or widower.
    c. Where both a widow or widower and a child or children survive, the widow or widower owns 50% of the termination interest and the child or children own 50%. The statute provides that the rights of the author's children and grandchildren "are in all cases divided among them and exercised on a *per stirpes* basis° . . . [and] the share of the children of a dead child in a termination interest can be exercised only by the action of a majority of them."[†]

For example, if a deceased author leaves a widow, two children, and three grandchildren of a dead third child, the widow owns 50% of

---

°A *per stirpes* basis is where descendants of a parent take and share that portion of interest the parent would have acquired if living.
[†] Title 17 U.S.C., Section 203(a)(2)(c).

the termination interest and the remaining 50% is divided equally among the children. Since one child is dead, the two surviving children get 16⅔% each and the three grandchildren get 16⅔% together, or about 5½% each. The widow, of course, is a necessary party to obtain the majority needed to exercise the termination right. To effectuate termination, she may be joined by either child or both grandchildren. Even if she was joined by one grandchild, giving a 55½% interest, such parties could not effect a termination since the grandchildren must act together in order to count for the share of the dead child. The widow would have to be joined by one of the children or one other grandchild to effect a termination or make another transfer of the reverted rights.

2. In the case of a joint work, termination of a grant may be effected by a majority of the authors who executed the transfer. Where an author is dead, that author's termination interest may be exercised as a unit by the person or persons above, who own and are entitled to exercise a total of more than one half of that author's interest.

Effect and Limitations of Termination. All rights originally granted by an author or authors revert, with one exception, to those with a right to terminate on the effective date of termination. The exception is for any derivative works prepared under authority of the grant before termination, which may continue to be utilized under the terms of the original grant after its termination.

The rights that revert upon termination revert to everyone who owned termination rights on the date the advance notice was served to the grantee, whether or not they joined in signing it. If in the interim a beneficiary dies, that person's heirs or legal representatives inherit such shares of reverted rights.

A further grant or agreement is valid only if it is signed by the same number and proportion of owners in whom the termination right was vested. Also, such further grant or agreement is valid only if it is made after the effective date of the termination, except that a new transfer to the original grantee or his successor may be made after the notice of termination is served. This in effect gives the grantee or his successor a right of first refusal and a preference over others, since either such party may have a 2-to-10-year lead time in dealing for the rights. The author, of course, may not accept competitive offers by contract until the effective date of termination.

Example of Termination of Transfer. A person writes a song and grants all rights to it to a music publisher on August 4, 1982. The song is published on February 11, 1990. Depending upon the nature of the contract, either of the following could happen:

1. If the grant did not cover the right of publication, termination of the grant could be made to take effect between August 4, 2017 (35 years from execution), and August 4, 2022 (end of 5-year termination period). If the songwriter decides to effect termination on August 4, 2017, the advance notice would have to be filed between August 4, 2007 (the 10-year maximum), and August 4, 2015 (the 2-year minimum).

2. If the grant did cover the right of publication, the 5-year termination period would begin 40 years from the date of the grant (rather than 35 years from date of publication) and would therefore commence on August 4, 2022 (rather than August 4, 2017—35 years from execution; or August 4, 2025—35 years from publication). If the songwriter decides to effect the termination on August 4, 2022, the advance notice would have to be filed between August 4, 2012, and August 4, 2020.

Termination of Transfer and Licenses Covering Extended Renewal Term. The 1976 Copyright Act extended by 19 years the second term of protection for works already under statutory protection on January 1, 1978.

Thus, instead of a renewal term of 28 years, the second term was extended to a total of 47 years if renewal was properly made. To give an author the benefit of this extended term, the law provides that the creator may terminate a transfer to recapture the 19 years of protection such copyrights are accorded.

Termination of a grant may be effected at any time during a 5-year period which begins at the end of 56 years from the date the copyright was originally secured, or beginning on January 1, 1978, whichever is later. The author may effect termination, or his family may, with termination interests appropriated as above. To effect termination, a notice must be served upon the grantee or the grantee's successor in title and must be signed by the author, or by those who executed the grant or their duly authorized agents. Such notice must comply with Copyright Office regulations, with a copy of the notice recorded in the Office before the effective date of termination.

All rights contained in the original grant revert to those with the right to terminate on the effective date of termination, except for derivative works prepared before termination. These may continue to be utilized under the terms of the original grant. There are also no termination rights whatsoever in works made for hire.

Copyright Infringement. A copyright infringement occurs whenever any of the exclusive rights granted by the copyright law to a COPYRIGHT OWNER are violated.° Remedies for infringements are set forth in the Copyright Act of 1976 and may be granted by a federal court of law where it determines such a right has been violated. Under the statute, a copyright infringement may also occur when copies of phonorecords are imported in viola-

---

°The copyright law places certain limitations on these exclusive rights (see COPYRIGHT OWNERS, LIMITATIONS ON EXCLUSIVE RIGHTS OF).

tion of certain provisions (see below).

Examples of Infringements of Exclusive Rights. There are many ways the exclusive rights of a copyright owner may be violated. With respect to these exclusive rights, the following would constitute infringements under law if permission from the owner of the right was *not* obtained to use the copyrighted work as stated:

- Reproducing a sound recording onto tapes and discs and selling them (this is commonly referred to as "piracy").
- Performing music in public for commercial advantage (such as over the air by a broadcasting station or at a concert by a performer) other than in religious services.
- Performing a musical comedy on the legitimate stage.
- Using a musical composition in conjunction with a motion picture.
- Printing sheet music and offering it for sale.
- Photocopying sheet music or printed music from songbooks and folios outside the bounds of FAIR USE or other than certain reproduction by libraries and archives.
- Putting an advertising message to the melody of a song and performing it as a jingle.
- Translating the lyrics of a song.
- Copying a substantial portion of a copyrighted musical composition.

Infringement Arrived at by Copying of Musical Compositions. The United States copyright law provides protection for "original works of authorship fixed in any tangible medium of expression." Questions of infringement are determined in a United States federal court. In an infringement suit, the plaintiff bears the burden of proving that the work is validly copyrighted (there is prima facie evidence of validity if the author registers his work and publishes it with proper notice) and that such work has been copied. To prove actionable copying, the plaintiff must demonstrate that the defendant had "access" to the previously written work and that there is "substantial similarity" between the two compositions.

The plaintiff will try to show access by establishing that the defendant came in "contact" with the work through direct evidence or by demonstrating that the work was so widely performed or distributed that a court could reasonably infer that the alleged infringer had access. In cases involving unpublished works, access might be more difficult to prove since there would be no inference of access resulting from wide performance or distribution. In general, the greater the evidence of substantial similarity, the lesser the burden of showing access, and vice versa.

Substantial similarity in infringement cases is shown by a musical analysis of the two compositions, often given in court by musicologists or other expert witnesses. The belief that a particular number (e.g., four) of similar or duplicate bars constitutes an automatic infringement is erroneous. The law sets forth no mechanical rules as to the amount that can be copied. In some musical compositions the theme may be contained in a lesser number of bars and in others a greater number. Consequently the duplication of only a few notes may constitute an infringement in a particular circumstance, and the duplication of a series of notes in several measures in another circumstance may not. Rhythm and harmony are also considerations in an infringement case where copying is an issue; however, they are rarely the sole basis for an infringement award.

Registering a musical work with the COPYRIGHT OFFICE and receiving a certificate for such registration does not conclusively establish that the work is original; however, registration constitutes prima facie evidence of the validity of the copyright and of the facts stated in the certificate. In other words, the plaintiff will not be forced to prove the validity of the copyright unless the defendant, by effectively challenging it, shifts the burden of proof to the plaintiff. Moreover, registration is a prerequisite to the initiation of an infringement suit and to the award of statutory damages and attorney's fees.

As the statute establishes the principle of divisibility of copyrights, it provides for "the legal or beneficial owner of an exclusive right . . . to institute an action for any infringement of that particular right committed while he or she is the owner of it."° The beneficial owner of a copyright would be anyone who assigned away his legal title in a right of the copyright to receive royalties from sales or license fees.

Remedies. Under the copyright law, remedies for an infringement action fall into the following areas:

Injunctions. The law empowers courts having jurisdiction in a civil action arising under the statute to grant temporary and final injunctions to prevent or restrain subsequent infringements.

Damages and Profits. The law provides that a "copyright owner is entitled to recover actual damages suffered by him or her as a result of the infringement plus any profits of the infringer"† or statutory damages.

A copyright owner may elect to recover statutory damages at any time before a final judgment is rendered. A court is obliged if it finds infringement to make an award of statutory damages of not less than $250 or more than $10,000, whatever it considers just. Any one infringer of a single work is liable for a single amount no matter how many acts of infringement were involved. If a single infringer is liable for more than one work, statutory damages must be awarded for each work. Statutory damages may be multipled if separately liable infringers and separate works are involved in the action.

Where the court finds willful infringement, it may raise the award of statutory damages to a maximum of $50,000. If the court, in its discretion, finds the infringer "was not aware and had no reason to believe his or her acts constituted an act of infringement,"‡ it may reduce the statutory award to $100. The statute precludes the courts from awarding any statutory damages where the infringer was a teacher, librarian, archivist, or nonprofit public broadcaster who was acting in the honest belief that his or her actions would fall under the FAIR USE provisions of the law.

Cost and Attorney's Fees. The court may award full costs to any party in an action except the U.S. or its officers. The prevailing party in a suit may recover attorney's fees. The amount of this is left to the court's discretion.

Impounding and Disposition of Infringing Articles. Courts are empowered to order the impounding of allegedly infringing articles at any time while an action is pending. Such articles include "all copies or phonorecords" and "all plates, molds, matrices, masters, tapes, film negatives, or other articles by means of which such copies or phonorecords may be reproduced."§ If the court finds the articles to be infringing, it may order the destruction or other disposition of them.

Criminal Offenses. Under the statute, the following are criminal offenses:

1. Criminal infringement. This applies to "any person who infringes a copyright willfully and for purposes of commercial advantage or private gain."‡‡

2. Fraudulent placement of copyright notice. That is, where a person with fraudulent intent places a notice of copyright that such person knows to be false on any article or publicly distributes or imports any article containing such notice.

3. Fraudulent removal of copyright notice. That is, where a person with fraudulent intent removes or alters a copyright notice on a work.

°17 U.S.C., Section 501(b).
†17 U.S.C., Section 504(b).

‡17 U.S.C., Section 504(c)(2).
§17 U.S.C., Section 503(a).
‡‡17 U.S.C., Section 506(2).

4. False representation. This applies to any person who knowingly makes a false representation on an application for copyright registration.

Under the statute, a criminal offense is punishable by fines, imprisonment, or both. Where a criminal infringement has occurred with respect to sound recordings and motion pictures, the statute specifically provides for a fine of not more than $25,000 or imprisonment of not more than one year, or both, for a first offense. Each subsequent offense is punishable by a fine of not more than $50,000 or imprisonment for not more than two years or both.

Statute of Limitations. The copyright law establishes a three-year statute of limitations on criminal and civil actions. A criminal proceeding must begin "within three years after the cause of action arose."* A civil action must commence "within three years after the claim accrued."†

Infringing Importation of Copies or Phonorecords. Under the copyright law, two separate situations regarding the importation of foreign articles are infringements: (1) the importation into the United States of copies or phonorecords made without the copyright owner's authorization (e.g., pirated songbooks, LPs, and tapes); and (2) the unauthorized importing of lawfully made copies or phonorecords of a work.

There are three exceptions to unauthorized importation. The importation of copies or phonorecords is permitted under the authority or for the use of a federal, state, or local government; a single copy or phonorecord may be imported if for the private use of the importer and not for distribution; and an organization operated for scholarly, educational, or religious purposes and not for financial gain may import no more than one copy of any audiovi-

sual work and a maximum of five copies or phonorecords of any other work where it will be used for certain library lending or archival purposes.

The U.S. Customs Service is given the authority to bar the importation of copies and phonorecords unlawfully produced abroad but not to prevent the importation of such articles lawfully made. The statute gives authorization to the Secretary of the Treasury to prescribe a procedure under which any person claiming an interest in the copyright in a particular work will be entitled, upon payment of a specified fee, to notification by the Customs Service of the importation of articles that appear to be copies or phonorecords of the work.

Copyright Law Manufacturing Requirement. A requirement under the 1976 Copyright Act that, with certain exceptions, copies of works consisting "preponderantly" of nondramatic literary material in the English language that are created by U.S. authors must be manufactured in the United States or Canada prior to July 1, 1982. The law provides for the elimination of this requirement as of that date.

The manufacturing requirement does not apply to musical, dramatic, pictorial, graphic, or public domain works. Thus sheet music, songbooks, music folios, or album covers (consisting of liner notes, artwork, and/or photographs) are not covered by the requirement (the preponderant product in each of these cases is either music or the sound recording and not a nondramatic literary work). A book of lyrics, however, would be subject to the requirement, and if by a U.S. author would have to be manufactured in the U.S. or Canada prior to July 1, 1982.

History. A manufacturing requirement was originally provided for by the Copyright Act of March 3, 1891 (commonly known as the "International Copyright Act"). This law provided statutory protection for the works of foreign authors (which theretofore had no such

---

*17 U.S.C., Section 507(a).
†17 U.S.C., Section 507(b).

protection and were consequently pirated in the United States), but it was limited. Manufacturers and labor unions in the U.S. printing trade feared that lower-cost foreign manufacturing of foreign works would cause employment problems. To alleviate their fears, the act required books and certain other works in the English language to be manufactured in the U.S. A manufacturing clause was continued in the next general revision of the statute, the Copyright Act of 1909. As a result of these laws, the statement "Made in U.S.A." or a similar one commonly appears on printed copies of such works.

Copyright Law of the United States. The basis for the United States Copyright Law is given in the U.S. Constitution (Article I, Section 8, Clause 8), which empowers Congress "To promote the progress of science and useful arts, by securing for limited times to authors and inventors the exclusive right to their respective writing and discoveries." With this authority, Congress enacted the first federal copyright statute in the U.S. in 1790. The statute has undergone various changes since then and a fourth general revision, known as the Copyright Act of 1976, is the law upon which the American copyright system is now based. The 1976 act not only is a product on ideologies that modernize U.S. copyright practice and make it applicable to contemporary and future technological utilizations of copyrighted works, but is also the culmination of the series of copyright statutes and amendments that have long prevailed in America, and whose own origins are often based on laws that antecede the nation's founding.

History. Prior to America's declared independence from Great Britain in 1776, the British government applied its legal system of the Statute of Anne of 1709 and English Common Law to the American colonies. Thus an author or copyright owner had the exclusive right to print, reprint, publish, copy, and vend his work or authorize others to do so.

Upon independence, the colonies set up governments of their own, many of which adopted the provisions of their colonial charters. It wasn't until January 1783, however, that the states began ratifying local copyright statutes (Connecticut was first, followed by Massachusetts, Maryland, New Jersey, and New Hampshire). By April 1786, all of the 13 original states except Delaware had enacted copyright laws under the Articles of Confederation, and these were patterned after the English Statute of Anne. The laws generally varied from state to state, with the exception of a couple of provisions: most laws extended copyright protection only to citizens or residents of the United States, and registration by the author or copyright proprietor was mandatory. In the early enactments of state laws, many states would not extend copyright protection to authors living in states that had not yet passed similar protective legislation.

A single system of copyright law for all states was realized on May 31, 1790, when America's first federal copyright law was enacted under the U.S. Constitution (this law, too, was based upon the Statute of Anne of 1709). It gave protection to books, maps, and charts for a term of 14 years, with the privilege for renewal for another 14 years. Copyright registration was made in the U.S. district court where the author or proprietor lived. Statutory protection was available only for copyrighted works of U.S. citizens or residents and protection for unpublished works relied mainly on the common laws of the states; hence a dual system of copyright protection began, a bifurcation that was to endure until its abrogation by a single national system that entered into force 188 years later.

On February 3, 1831, came the first general revision of the U.S. copyright statute, and among other changes, it provided protection for musical works and extended the first term of copyright to 28 years (while retaining the right of renewal for 14 years). This law repealed the acts of 1790 and 1802, the latter being the first amendment of the law.

A second general revision was effected on July 8, 1870. It centralized deposit, registration, and other copyright activities in the Library of Congress (it wasn't until 1897, however, that the Copyright Office was established as a separate department of the Library and the position of Register of Copyrights created). Under the Chace Act, the works of non-resident foreigners became eligible for copyright protection on March 3, 1891, but only on the condition that their countries accorded similar protection to the works of American authors. This provision was further limited in scope by the manufacturing requirement of the law.

On January 6, 1897, a bill was enacted that granted to copyright owners the exclusive right of public performance in musical compositions; hence copyrighted music was protected from unauthorized public performance for profit. Compliance with this statutory mandate was minimal if at all existent, however, and copyright owners received virtually no income from this right. The situation persisted until 1914 despite a third general revision of the statute, the 1909 act, which limited the performance right for copyright owners of musical works to public performance of non-dramatic musical compositions "for profit."

The Copyright Act of March 4, 1909, which became effective on July 1, 1909, was an important revision for copyright owners of musical works because of certain innovations. It provided for a "compulsory license" to make mechanical reproductions of nondramatic musical works once a copyright proprietor had authorized the commercial recording of a specific work (the statutory royalty under a compulsory license for recording music was $.02 per mechanical reproduction); it allowed for copyright registration of certain classes of unpublished works (including musical composi-

tions); it provided for the measurement of statutory protection from the date of publication rather than the date of recordation of the title of the work; and it increased the renewal term to a period of 28 years.

On July 13, 1914, the U.S. became a member of the Buenos Aires Copyright Convention of 1910 and thereby established copyright protection for its authors in certain Latin American countries. The copyright statute, as amended, was codified into positive law on July 30, 1947, as Title 17 of the U.S. Code, entitled "Copyrights." On September 16, 1955, the United States joined the Universal Copyright Convention, which extended protection of certain works of U.S. authors in various foreign countries throughout the world.

A copyright in sound recordings was created by an amendment that was enacted on October 15, 1971, and effective as of February 15, 1972. The Sound Recording Amendment extended statutory protection against the unauthorized duplication of sound recordings "fixed" (i.e., recorded) and first published on or after this date (at this writing, all states except Vermont have "antipiracy" statutes to protect certain recordings made and publicly distributed before February 15, 1972). Protection in certain foreign countries against unauthorized duplications of phonograph records and tapes was accorded copyright proprietors beginning March 10, 1974, the effective date of United States membership in the Geneva Phonogram Convention of 1971.

Copyright Act of 1976. The fourth general revision of the copyright law was approved by Congress and signed by the President on October 19, 1976, although most of its provisions did not enter into force until January 1, 1978. This statute became Public Law 94-553, also referred to as the Copyright Act of 1976, the Copyright Revision Act, or Title 17 of the United States Code. It had taken 21 years to be approved, as Congress first funded a program for the research and study of a copyright law revision by the Copyright Office in 1955.

The 1976 Copyright Act is perhaps more a completely new copyright statute than a general revision. It makes several fundamental changes in the American copyright system and keeps pace with modern technology and new developments in communication. Principally, it establishes one national system of copyright protection, it increases the duration of copyright protection, it extends copyright owners' rights to modern communication techniques, and it relaxes formalities regarding deposit, registration, and copyright notice. These and other provisions bring U.S. copyright law closer to international practice.

The provisions of the 1976 act, as they directly relate to creators, copyright owners, and other participants in the music business, are covered in the following entries:

Anonymous Work
Author
Cable Television
Compulsory License (General)
Compulsory/Mechanical Licenses (Phonorecords)
Copies
Copyright
Copyright Deposit and Registration
Copyright Duration
Copyright Grants, Termination of
Copyright Infringement
Copyright Law, Manufacturing Requirement
Copyright Notice
Copyright Office
Copyright Office Fees
Copyright Owner
Copyright Owners, Limitation on Exclusive Rights of
Copyright Ownership, Transfer of
Copyright Protection and National Origin
Copyright Registration Application Forms
Copyright Registration Classification System
Copyright Registration of a Musical Work
Copyright Registration of a Sound Recording
Copyright Renewal Registration
Copyright Royalty Tribunal
Copyrightable Works
Derivative Work
Fair Use

Joint Work
Jukebox
Phonorecords
Pseudonymous Work
Public Broadcasting
Public Domain
Sound Recording
Work
Work Made for Hire

Copyright Notice. The United States copyright law requires that when a work is published under the authority of the copyright owner, a *notice of copyright* be placed on all publicly distributed copies and on all publicly distributed phonorecords of sound recordings. This entry examines the statutory provisions of copyright notice and includes common examples of notices of copyright placed on copies and phonorecords according to industry practice.

Visually Perceptible Copies. The Copyright Act of 1976 requires that whenever a work is published in the United States or elsewhere by authority of the copyright owner, a notice of copyright is to be placed "on all publicly distributed copies from which the work can be visually perceived, either directly or with the aid of a machine or device." Errors in, or omissions of, the notice are not fatal, however, and the law enables corrections to be made within certain time limits before copyright protection is completely lost (see below).

Applicable Works. Examples of works that are embodied in visually perceptible copies include musical compositions (in sheet music, songbooks, music folios, and other printed editions), and liner notes, artwork, illustrations, and photographs contained on album covers. Each of these works is protected if accompanied by the copyright notice as prescribed by law.

Form of Notice. The statute specifies the form of notice that is to appear on copies embodying a work. The copyright notice consists of the following three elements:

1. *The symbol* © (the letter C in a circle), or the word "Copyright," or the abbreviation "copr."

2. *The year of first publication* of the work (in the case of compilations or derivative works incorporating previously published material, the year date of first publication of the compilation or derivative work is sufficient).

3. *The name of the owner of copyright* in the work, or an abbreviation by which the name can be recognized, or a generally known alternative designation of the owner.

Example: © 1981 Mary Evans

Position of Notice. The law provides for the notice to be affixed to the copies "in such manner and location as to give reasonable notice of the claim of copyright."

Non-necessity of © Notice on Phonorecords. Public distribution of a sound recording via phonorecords constitutes "publication" of an embodied musical composition. However, there is no requirement that the copyright notice for musical works be placed on phonorecords in which they are embodied and publicly distributed. As stated above, the copyright law requires the notice to appear on "copies from which the work can be visually perceived." (A musical composition cannot be visually perceived on a phonorecord.)

Phonorecords of Sound Recordings. The Copyright Act requires that whenever a sound recording is published in the United States or elsewhere by authority of the copyright owner, a notice of copyright is to be "placed on all publicly distributed phonorecords of the sound recording." Errors in, or omissions of, the notice are not fatal and may be corrected within certain time limits (see below).

Form of Notice. The statute specifies the form of notice that is to appear on phonorecords. The copyright notice consists of the following three elements:

1. *the symbol* ℗ (the letter P in a circle); and

2. *the year of first publication* of the sound recording; and

3. *the name of the owner of copyright* in the sound recording, or an abbreviation by which the name can be recognized, or a generally known alternative designation of the owner.

Example: ℗ 1981 Clip Record Co.

Position of Notice. The law provides for the notice to be placed "on the surface of the phonorecord, or on the phonorecord label or container, in such manner and location as to give reasonable notice of the claim of copyright."

Presumption of Producer on Notice. If no name appears in conjunction with the copyright notice, the producer's name, if given on the phonorecord labels or containers, shall be considered a part of the notice.

Omission of Notice. The 1976 Copyright Act provides that the omission of the copyright notice from copies or phonorecords does not invalidate the work if either of the following conditions is met: (1) no more than a relatively small number of copies or phonorecords have been publicly distributed without notice; or (2) registration for the work has been previously made, or is made within 5 years after the publication without notice, and a reasonable effort is made to add notice to all copies or phonorecords publicly distributed in the U.S. after the omission has been discovered.

Therefore, a work does not fall into the PUBLIC DOMAIN if the copyright notice is omitted from a relatively small number of copies or phonorecords. If the copyright notice is omitted from a larger number of copies or phonorecords, it does not *immediately* fall into the public domain. However, a reasonable effort must be made to add the notice and the work must be registered, if not already, within 5 years of publication without notice.

Copyright protection is also not lost if the notice has been omitted in violation of an express written agreement requiring that as a condition of the copyright owner's authorization, publicly distributed copies or phonorecords bear the prescribed copyright notice.

Under the statute, any person who innocently infringes a copyright, by acting in reliance upon an authorized copy or phonorecord from which the copyright notice has been omitted, incurs no liability for actual or statutory damages for infringement acts committed before receiving actual notice that registration for the work has been made, if such person can prove he or she was misled by the omission.

Error in Name or Date. With respect to errors in the name or date in the copyright notice on copies or phonorecords publicly distributed by the authority of the copyright owner, the 1976 act provides for their correction and not immediate forfeiture of the copyright.

Wrong Name. Where a person's name not that of the owner of copyright has been given in the notice, the validity and ownership of the copyright are not affected. However, prior to a registration of the work in the copyright owner's name, or a correction of the error made in the Copyright Office, an innocent infringer misled by the notice would have a complete defense to any action for such infringement.

Wrong Date. Where the year date in the notice is earlier than the year of first publication, any statutory term is computed from the year appearing on the notice. If the year date given is more than one year later than the year of first publication, then the work is considered to have been published without any notice and the cure must be made accordingly.

Omission of Name or Date. Where either a name or a date has been omitted from the notice, the work is considered to have been published without any notice and the procedure for correcting the omission applies.

New Versions. Generally, the copyright notice is required to include the year of first publication of the work. However, for "new versions" of previously published or copyrighted works (such as musical arrangements or adaptations), the notice is not usually re-quired to include more than the year of first publication of the new version itself. New versions are independently copyrightable as "new works," with the copyright in the new version not affecting or extending the protection, if any, for the underlying work.

Commercial Applications of Notice and Other Information. It is a common practice for copyright owners in the music industry to include other information with the prescribed copyright notice on published copies of their works. The following are examples based on actual published copies (such as sheet music or songbooks), with explanations.

> *Example:* Copyright © 1980 by Jim Johnson Music, 1650 Broadway, New York, New York 10019
> International Copyright Secured.   All Rights Reserved

Explanation: The copyright notice contains both the word "Copyright" and the symbol ©. Either one would suffice, but the use of the symbol © with the date of publication and the copyright owner's name secures protection under the Universal Copyright Convention if the work is by a U.S. citizen. The copyright owner's address is given to indicate to parties wishing to license the work where he may be contacted. The use of "International Copyright Secured" is not required but is an indication to the public that the work is protected in certain foreign countries, including those adhering to the Berne Convention if a "simultaneous" publication is made. The phrase "All Rights Reserved" grants the copyright owner protection under the Buenos Aires Convention.

> *Example:* Copyright © 1980 by Smith Music and Jones Music and Chuck Music. All rights administered by Alex Music Co.

Explanation: This example indicates that the publishing rights are owned by three companies and that another company administers the copyright.

Example: Copyright © 1978, 1980 by Charles Jones Music Co.

Explanation: This notice probably indicates that the composition was originally registered with the Copyright Office in 1978 as an unpublished work and was published with new matter in 1980. If no new matter was included, it would be sufficient to use the year date of registration of the unpublished version in the copyright notice affixed to published copies.

Example: Copyright © 1970 by Light Music Co.
This arrangement Copyright © 1980 by Light Music Co.

Explanation: This notice provides protection for a new arrangement made of a previously registered or published work. The copyright protection in the "new matter" would continue to subsist after the portion of the underlying work originally registered entered the public domain.

Example: Copyright © 1980 Dark Music Co. Used by permission

Explanation: In a fakebook or music folio containing several songs owned by different music publishers, the print licensee (or "publisher" of the songbook) customarily prints the phrase "Used by permission" under the copyright notice of each song to indicate that the use of the song in the particular copy is with the copyright owner's authorization.

Album Compilations. Some companies license hit recordings owned by several different manufacturers and issue them on a single album. The date and name in the copyright notice for such a compilation need only be the year date of first publication of the collective work and the author of the collective work as a whole. Separate notices are not required for the individual selections.

Where there has been substantial remixing, alteration of sounds, or other changes made to an individual selection to qualify it as a derivative work, its new publication entitles it to protection as a new work. The copyright owner, in exercising his exclusive right to have another party reproduce his work in a compilation for public distribution, is not transferring the entire copyright to such party unless such transfer is expressly made.

See also ADMINISTRATION OF A MUSIC PUBLISHER'S CATALOG; COPYRIGHT RENEWAL REGISTRATION; DERIVATIVE WORK; INTERNATIONAL COPYRIGHT RELATIONS; PUBLICATION.

Copyright Office. Office whose responsibility is to perform the administrative functions of the United States copyright law—Title 17 of the U.S. Code.

Administrative Functions and Duties. The Office distributes applications for copyright registrations, examines claims to copyrights, registers claims that satisfy statutory requirements, issues certificates of registration to copyright claimants, catalogs all registrations, and maintains documents dealing with copyright ownership, including records of assignments and exclusive licenses. The Office also conducts correspondence regarding claims; supplies general information concerning copyright law, practices and operations of the office, and procedures for making registrations; and reports on facts found in its public records.

The Copyright Office does not "grant" copyrights. It merely registers claims to copyrights and issues certificates of registration. The registration, however, puts others on notice that a claim to ownership of a work has been made and establishes a date of the claim.

Services Not Provided. The Copyright Office does not do any of the following: offer legal advice and opinions on copyright matters; compare for similarities copies or phonorecords deposited for registration; give opinions on the validity of claims; give advice on questions of possible copyright infringement; recommend particular publishers, agents, or lawyers; interpret or enforce contracts; or assist in getting a work published, recorded, or performed.

Searches of Copyright Office Records. The official records of all copyright registrations, recordations, and other written instruments relating to copyright are open to public inspection. Individuals wishing such information who are unable to inspect the Office records personally may consult the *Catalog of Copyright Entries* or have the Copyright Office make the search and furnish a report.

The procedure for an official search is as follows: An interested party provides the Office with as much information as possible regarding a particular work or works. The Office sends back an estimate of its fee to conduct the search. The party may then remit the fee to have the search conducted. The Office proceeds with the search and returns a typewritten report, together with any refund of overpayment.

Location and Mailing Address. The Copyright Office is located in the James Madison Building, 101 Independence Ave., S.E., Washington, D.C. 20559. Mail to the Office, including copyright registrations, should be addressed to: Register of Copyrights, Library of Congress, Washington, D.C. 20559.

Register of Copyrights. All administrative functions and duties that come under the Copyright Office's jurisdiction are the responsibility of the Register of Copyrights as director of the Copyright Office of the Library of Congress. The Register of Copyrights as well as other officers and employees of the Copyright Office are appointed by the Librarian of Congress.

History of Copyright Registration and the Copyright Office. There are four basic time periods of U.S. copyright registration history: (1) From 1790 to 1870, claims to copyright were made at the federal district court where the author or proprietor resided (these entries were made in sequential order, however, and no statistics were kept by type of work). (2) From 1870 to 1909: On July 8, 1870, Congress centralized all deposits, registrations, and other copyright activities in the Library of Congress. (The various laws in effect from 1870 to 1909 imply that only published works were subject to registration.) On February 19, 1897, the Copyright Office was established as a separate department of the Library of Congress and the position of Register of Copyrights was created. (3) From 1909 to 1977, published works and certain unpublished works (including musical compositions) were registered with the Library of Congress. (4) In 1978, a new classification system for copyright registration was implemented. A computer system, SCORPIO, permits quick retrieval of registration information. File access points for SCORPIO include author, claimant, title, and registration number. Another system, COINS, allows Copyright Office staff to track correspondence about claims.

Copyright Office Fees. The copyright law establishes fees for registrations, recordations, and other services performed in the Copyright Office. The Office recommends that all remittances be sent in the form of a check, money order, or bank draft, payable to: Register of Copyrights. The Office does not assume any responsibility for loss of currency. Material submitted outside the United States should be accompanied by remittances payable immediately in U.S. dollars. An International Money Order or bank draft is acceptable; a check drawn on a foreign bank is not. Copyright fees are as follows:°

Registration of copyright claims (including a certificate bearing the Copyright Office seal)
Basic registration for a published or unpublished work in Class TX, PA, VA, or SR $10

°Current as of 1981.

Supplementary registration with Form CA or
   GR/CP 10
Renewal registration in Class RE 6
*Recordation of statements (including
certifications)*
Basic fee 10
(for recordation of a statement revealing the
author of an anonymous or pseudonymous
work, or for the recordation of a statement relating to the death of an author, where either
statement is 6 pages or less and covers 1 title)
Additional pages or title 1
(for each page over 6 and each title over 1)
*Recordation of documents (including
certification)*
Basic fee 10
(for recordation of a transfer of copyright
ownership or other document of 6 pages or less
covering 1 title)
Additional pages or title .... .50
(for each page over 6 and each title over 1)
Certifications
Additional certificate 4
(certified copy of a record of registration)
Other certifications 4
(including certifications of photocopies of
Copyright Office records)
*Filing notice of intention to make phono-
records under compulsory license*
Fee 6
Import statements
Fee for issuance of an import statement re-
quested with Form IS 3
Receipt for deposits
Fee for issuance of a receipt for a deposit 2
Search fees
Hourly fee 10
(for each hour or fraction spent by the staff of
the Copyright Office in searching the official
records and for the making and reporting of a
search; searches are not made to determine
whether a similar work has already been copyrighted)

Copyright Owner. The U.S. Copyright Act
grants certain exclusive rights to the owner of
a copyright. These exclusive rights are:

1. To reproduce the copyrighted work in
copies or phonorecords.
2. To prepare derivative works based upon
the copyrighted work.

3. To distribute copies or phonorecords of
the copyrighted work to the public by sale or
transfer of ownership, or by rental, lease, or
lending.
4. To perform certain works publicly.
5. To display certain works publicly.°

Under the law, ownership of a copyright
may be transferred in whole or in part. A
copyright owner, therefore, is the owner of
any one or more of the exclusive rights comprised in a copyright.

The First Owner of Copyright. With one
exception, the first ownership of all the exclusive rights comprised in a work vests in the
AUTHOR, or in the case of a joint work, the
coauthors. The exception is a WORK MADE FOR
HIRE, in which case the employer or other
person for whom the work was prepared is
considered the author of the work and the initial owner of all rights comprised in the copyright. Commercial sound recordings and motion pictures are commonly created by producers under work made for hire agreements
and consequently record manufacturers and
motion picture companies are often copyright
owners.

In the case of contributions to collective
works, where each separate contribution is distinct from copyright in the collective work as
a whole, the copyright vests initially in the author of that contribution.

**Copyright Owners of Musical Composi-
tion.** In signing a publishing contract, a songwriter normally transfers all rights in a work
to a music publisher. The music publisher
then becomes the copyright owner of the work
for the term of the assignment. Provided all
rights are transferred, the transferee may also
be referred to as a copyright *proprietor*. Proprietors of musical copyrights commonly license certain rights, such as for print reproductions, but these are usually nonexclusive li-

---

°17 U.S.C., Section 106.

censes, which do not constitute a transfer of ownership, but only a right of usage. An exclusive licensee is given *copyright* status. Since "the owner of a particular exclusive right is entitled, to the extent of that right, to all of the protection and remedies accorded to the copyright owner"° an exclusive licensee may sue to protect its interest.

As stated above, one of the exclusive rights of a copyright owner is to authorize reproduction of a copyrighted work in phonorecords. There is a special provision in the copyright law, however, which subjects the exclusive rights in nondramatic musical works to compulsory licensing. Under this provision, anyone may make and distribute phonorecords embodying the musical work without permission of the copyright owner by complying with conditions established by the law, once phonorecords of the work have been publicly distributed in the U.S. under the authority of the copyright owner.

Copyright owners have the exclusive right to publicly perform or authorize the public performance of their works. In commercial practice, they almost always grant the right to license nondramatic public performances of their works to a PERFORMING RIGHTS ORGANIZATION. Anyone who violates the exclusive right of a public performance of a copyright owner (i.e., performs the work in public without permission from the copyright owner or his agent) is an infringer of copyright and is subject to civil actions by a court of law. The performance need not be for profit, as was the requirement under the copyright law in effect before 1978. Exceptions to the exclusive right of public performance are for particular uses of works under Section 110 of the law and uses that constitute FAIR USE.

Copyright Registration. If a work is filed for copyright registration, the author (including, in the case of a work made for hire, the employer or other person for whom the work was prepared) is the claimant if he has not transferred his rights to the work. If ownership of a copyright, which initially belongs to an author, is obtained by a person or organization, such person or organization becomes the claimant. The basic application for copyright registration, in accordance with the statute, requests a copyright claimant, if other than the author, to give a brief statement summarizing how the claimant obtained ownership of the copyright.

See also COMPULSORY/ MECHANICAL LICENSES (PHONORECORDS); COPYRIGHT OWNERSHIP, TRANSFER OF.

Copyright Owners, Limitation on Exclusive Rights of. The Copyright Act of 1976 grants to the owner of a copyright the exclusive rights of reproduction, adaptation, publication, performance, and display. Certain limitations are placed on these exclusive rights, however, which enable others to use a work in specific ways or circumstances without the consent of the copyright owner. This entry is concerned with the statutory limitations on these exclusive rights for musical works and sound recordings.

Musical Works

Reproduction. See FAIR USE.

Adaptation. A work created from a preexisting work is referred to in the statute as a "derivative work." Copyright owners enjoy the right to prepare or authorize the preparation of derivative musical works with two general exceptions—certain print and recording arrangements.

The Music Guidelines that amplify the FAIR USE section of the statute permit purchased copies of printed music to be edited or simplified, provided that the fundamental character of the work is not distorted and existing lyrics are not altered in any way nor are lyrics added if none exist.

The making of a new musical arrangement

°17 U.S.C., Section 201(d)(2).

of a popular song for a sound recording does not normally require the permission of the copyright owner. The copyright law recognizes the practical need to make new arrangements under the compulsory license provision for making and distributing phonorecords, and grants to any person "the privilege of making a musical arrangement of a work to the extent necessary to conform it to the style or manner of interpretation of the performance involved, but the arrangement shall not change the basic melody or fundamental character of the work."

Even though the compulsory license is rarely used in commercial practice and mechanical licenses are issued instead, these do not indicate any grant of copyright ownership in an arrangement. Moreover, if the fundamental character of the original work has been changed, the copyright owner may refuse to grant a license and the transformed work would not be subject to the compulsory license provision. No copyright in a new arrangement could subsist unless the copyright owner gave his express consent. An unauthorized arrangement could not be copyrighted.

Publication. There is only one exception to the exclusive right of the copyright owner to publish his work in its entirety. This is the statutory grant for making and distributing phonorecords of nondramatic musical works, under the compulsory license. The compulsory license provides that once the copyright owner has authorized the first recording of a work, any other person may make and distribute phonorecords of the work by complying with procedures set out in the statute. Although, as described above, the compulsory license is rarely used, it nevertheless provides the authority for this practice to exist under negotiated terms.

Public Performance and Displays. The statute exempts specific types of unauthorized public performances and displays from copyright liability. The following uses are not infringements:

1. Performance or display of a work by instructors or pupils in the course of face-to-face teaching activities in a classroom or similar place devoted to instruction.

2. Performance or display of a musical (or nondramatic literary) work in the course of transmission (i.e., via closed-circuit TV), provided three conditions are met: the transmission must be part of the systematic instructional activities of a nonprofit institution; the performance is directly related and of material assistance to the teaching content of the program; the transmission is made "primarily" to other classrooms, to persons whose disabilities prevent their attendance in classrooms, or to government employees as part of official duties or employment.

3. Performance or display of a nondramatic musical work or dramatico-musical work of a religious nature, in the course of services at a place of worship or other religious assembly.

4. Performance or display of a nondramatic musical work at a public concert if: there is no purpose of direct or indirect commercial advantage; no payment of any fee or other compensation is made to the performers, promoters, or organizers; there is no admission charge, or if there is, the net proceeds are to be used only for educational, charitable, or religious purposes. However, if the copyright owner serves a written notice "at least seven days before the date of the performance," it may not take place.

5. Public reception of a performance or display caused by someone who merely turns on a radio or television.

6. Performance or display of a nondramatic musical work by a governmental body or at an annual agricultural or horticultural fair or exhibition.

7. Performance of a nondramatic musical work at retail establishments (such as record stores), provided the purpose of the performance is to promote sales and the performance is not transmitted beyond the place where the establishment is located and is within the im-

mediate area where the sale is occurring.

Sound Recordings. Under law, the exclusive right in a sound recording is limited to the rights of reproduction, adaptation, and publication. It does not include any right of performance (at this writing).

The exclusive right of reproduction is limited to the right to duplicate the sound recording in the form of phonorecords, or of copies of motion pictures and other audiovisual works, that directly or indirectly recapture the actual sounds fixed in the recording.

The exclusive right of adaptation is limited to the right to prepare a derivative work in which the sounds are remixed, rearranged, or otherwise altered in sequence or quality.

Another limitation on the exclusive rights in a sound recording is that authorization from the owner of copyright is not needed to use sound recordings in educational television and radio programs, distributed or transmitted by or through public broadcasting entities, provided that phonorecords of such programs are not commercially distributed by or through such entities to the general public.

The exclusive rights in sound recordings are also limited by the FAIR USE section of the law.

Copyright Ownership, Transfer of. It is common practice for songwriters to assign to music publishers the rights to songs they have written or for music publishers to transfer copyrights or catalogs they own to other music publishers (usually by virtue of a "sale"). Copyright proprietors also transfer particular exclusive rights (usually by the grant of an exclusive license). There is a statutory basis for such transfers.

The copyright law provides that the ownership of a copyright may be transferred in its entirety or in part by any form or assignment or conveyance or by operation of law. This would include a mortgage, an exclusive license, and any alienation or hypothecation of a copyright, or of any of the exclusive rights comprised in a copyright. (The granting of a nonexclusive license, however, would not constitute a transfer of ownership; it is, rather, only a right of usage.) Ownership may also be bequeathed by will or pass as personal property by the laws of intestate succession.

Execution of Transfers. A transfer of copyright ownership, other than by operations of law, must be made by an instrument in writing, signed by either the owner of the rights conveyed or such owner's authorized agent. Although a certificate of acknowledgment is not required for the validity of the transfer, such certificate issued by a person authorized to administer oaths (such as a notary public) is for transfers executed in the U.S. prima facie evidence of the execution of the transfer; for transfers in foreign countries, the certificate must be issued by a diplomatic or consular office of the U.S. or other authorized person.

Any assignment or transfer of copyright ownership of a musical composition should include the following information: name and address of assignee (or transferee), title of the composition, name(s) of the writer(s), Copyright Office Registration Number, date of assignment (or transfer), name and address of assignor or transferor, and "words of present conveyance," such as "hereby assign," or "do grant."

Recordation of Transfers. Any transfer in whole or in part of copyright ownership may be recorded in the Copyright Office. There are no forms issued by the Office for conveying transfers; rather, any document pertaining to the transfer may be filed for recordation in the Office if it is signed by the person who executed it; a copy of the original, signed document may be filed for recordation if accompanied by a sworn official certification stating that it is a true copy. There are COPYRIGHT OFFICE FEES for a recordation of a transfer of copyright ownership—a basic fee for a statement of 6 pages or less covering one title, and an additional fee for additional fee or title.

Remittances must accompany each document sent for recordation. Upon receipt of these, the Copyright Office will record the document and return it with a certificate of recordation.

The recordation of a document in the Copyright Office gives all persons constructive notice (i.e., a conclusion of law that cannot be contradicted) of the facts only if (1) the document specifically identifies the work so that after it is indexed by the Office, it would be revealed by a "reasonable search" under the title or registration number; and (2) registration for the work has been made.

A transferee cannot bring an infringement action against anyone until an instrument of transfer is recorded. However, a suit may be instituted after recordation and cover infringements made prior to the recordation. All recorded transfers, assignments, and other instruments relating to copyright are maintained in the Copyright Office, where they are open to public inspection. Upon request, together with a proper fee, the Office can search its indexes covering records of assignments (and other recorded documents covering copyright ownership) and furnish facts regarding the recorded document as shown in its index. The Office will not make any legal interpretation of the content, however.

Conflicting Transfers. In the case of a conflicting transfer, the one first executed prevails if properly recorded within 1 month of its execution in the U.S. or within 2 months after its execution outside the U.S. or at any time before proper recordation of the later transfer.

Where a conflict exists between a nonexclusive license and a transfer of ownership, the former prevails, whether recorded or not, if signed by the owner of the rights licensed or his authorized agent, and if (1) the license was taken before the transfer was executed, or (2) the license was taken "in good faith" before, and without notice of, the recordation of transfer.

Recordation of Transfers of Publishers'

Catalogs. When a music publisher sells its catalog, the new copyright owner will normally record the transfer in the Copyright Office. For recordations of transfers of large catalogs (some publishers have tens of thousands of copyrights in their catalogs), the question arises as to whether each copyright in the transfer should be listed in the document filed for recordation. This is not required by law, but there are advantages. As stated above, the law provides that if the work is identified in the Copyright Office, that document will serve as "constructive notice" to others. This may be interpreted to mean that everyone is assumed to know that the transfer has taken place and ignorance of the transfer will be no defense. The document of recordation of transfer must identify the work by title or registration number. The disadvantage of recording each copyright in the transfer is that it can be costly, in terms of both copyright fees ($10 for recording and $.50 for each title over one in the document) and administrative expenses.

Copyright Notice. The copyright owner's name that appears in the copyright notice of works transferred should be the name of the owner of copyright. If all rights are assigned, the assignor is no longer the owner. In commercial practice, the prior owner's name often continues to be used if it has prestigious value, even if the company has been merged with another and assumes a new identity. Usually, however, there is a gradual integration of such copyrights under the new owner's identification.

Example of a Copyright Transfer by a Songwriter. A songwriter transfers his ownership of a song to a music publisher. The publisher, depending upon whether the composition has been registered, would do one of the following:

1. If the writer registered his song in unpublished form with the Copyright Office, the publisher would take possession of the writer's copyright certificate and would record the doc-

ument of transfer in the Copyright Office.

2. If the song was never registered, the publisher would register the song in its name after the transfer but before publication.

3. If the song was never registered, the publisher could wait until publication to register the work. Even then, it would not be required to register it, although it would have to comply with deposit requirements if the work was first published in print form with notice of copyright for the composition. The publisher does not have to deposit the musical work if it is only published in phonorecord form (although the owner of copyright in the sound recording does).

See also CATALOG, ACQUISITION OF A MUSIC PUBLISHER'S; COPYRIGHT DEPOSIT AND REGISTRATION.

Copyright Protection and National Origin. The 1976 Copyright Act (Section 104) provides that *unpublished* works are subject to statutory protection without regard to the nationality or domicile of the author. For copyright protection to subsist in *published* works, however, one of four conditions must be met:

1. On the date of first PUBLICATION, one or more of the authors must be a national or domiciliary of the United States, or a national, domiciliary, or sovereign authority of a nation that is a party to a copyright treaty of which the U.S. is also a party, or is a stateless person, wherever that person may be domiciled.

2. The work must be first published in the U.S. or in a foreign nation that, on the date of first publication, is a party to the Universal Copyright Convention.

3. The work must be first published by the United Nations or any of its specialized agencies, or by the Organization of American States (this is in compliance with a treaty obligation of the U.S. from the Second Protocol of the UCC).

4. The work must come within the scope of a Presidential proclamation. Alien authors whose countries are "proclaimed" to extend copyright protection to works of authors who are U.S. citizens or domiciliaries, or to works first published in the U.S. on substantially the same basis as they grant their own citizens, may enjoy copyright protection for their works in the United States.

Copyright Registration. *See* COPYRIGHT DEPOSIT AND REGISTRATION.

Copyright Registration Application Forms. Most applications for copyright registration will be submitted on one of the following five basic forms: TX, PA, VA, SR, and RE. Three other forms, CA, GR/CP, and IS, are used in special situations. To comply with the requirements of the federal copyright statute (Title 17 U.S.C., Section 409), each of these applications requires copyright claimants to provide certain information regarding the works they are registering.

Applications for copyright registration must be submitted only on those forms printed and issued by the Copyright Office; photocopied submissions are not acceptable. All application forms for copyright registration are supplied free of charge, and may be requested in writing from: Copyright Office, Library of Congress, Washington, D.C. 20559.

Copyright Registration Classification System. A claim to copyright for an original work of authorship may be made by registering the work in a "class." Under the classification system for copyright registrations there are five classes: TX, PA, VA, SR, and RE. Registration in each class is made by filing a form corresponding to the class and submitting other materials as required to the Copyright Office.

Class TX: Nondramatic Literary Works. Class TX consists of all published and unpublished works expressed in words (or other verbal or numerical symbols) except for dramatic works and certain kinds of audiovisual works.

Examples of "nondramatic literary works" include fiction and nonfiction, textbooks, reference works, directories, catalogs, advertising copy, and compilations of information. Song lyrics without music (which may be considered as poetry), collections of lyrics, and any liner notes or text printed on the back of a record album that is not accompanied by photographs or artwork may be registered in this class. A registration in Class TX is made on Form TX ("Application for Copyright Registration for a Nondramatic Literary Work").

Class PA: Works of the Performing Arts. Class PA covers published and unpublished works prepared for the purpose of being "performed" directly before an audience or indirectly "by means of any device or process." Works of the performing arts include musical works such as popular songs (including any accompanying words); musical arrangements; adaptations; songbooks, music folios, and other collections of printed music; serious musical compositions (such as symphonic, chamber, and choral works); musical scores to plays; operas; pantomimes and choreographic works; and motion pictures. Song lyrics without music may be registered in Class PA (or also Class TX, as specified above). A registration in Class PA is made on Form PA ("Application for Copyright Registration for a Work of the Performing Arts").

Class VA: Works of the Visual Arts. Class VA comprises published and unpublished pictorial, graphic, and sculptured works, including two- and three-dimensional works of fine, graphic, and applied art, photographs, prints, art reproductions, charts, technical drawings, and diagrams. Also within this class are pictorial or graphic labels and advertisements and "works of artistic craftsmanship." Photographs, artwork, and printed designs that appear on album covers may be registered in this class. If liner notes or text accompany said artwork or photographs, they may all be copyrighted together as one work under class VA. A registration in Class VA is made on Form VA ("Application for Copyright Registration for a Work of the Visual Arts").

Class SR: Sound Recordings. Class SR is used to register published and unpublished (1) sound recordings and (2) sound recordings including the musical composition or other work embodied in the sound recording. The term "sound recording" refers to works resulting from the fixation of musical, spoken, or other sounds (hence fixed vocal and/or instrumental performances), but not the sounds or audio portions that accompany motion pictures or other audiovisual works. These are considered an integral part of the audiovisual work as a whole and are registrable in Class PA. Recorded selections on singles and albums should be registered in Class SR, as well as sound effects and nondramatic spoken material including narration, interviews, panel discussions, and training material.

As long as the claim on the sound recording itself is included, all authorship contained in the sound recording unit can be registered on the SR if the ownership in all the elements is the same. A registration in Class SR is made on Form SR ("Application for Copyright Registration for a Sound Recording").

Class RE: Renewal Registrations. Class RE covers claims to renewal copyright in works that were in their first 28-year term on January 1, 1978, regardless of the class in which the original registration was made under the previous copyright law. Class RE is appropriate, then, to renew those works originally copyrighted between January 1, 1950, and December 31, 1977. Renewal registration can be made only during the last year of the first 28-year copyright term, and it has the effect of extending copyright protection for an additional 47 years. (Works in their second term on January 1, 1978, were automatically extended to a total second term of 47 years.) A renewal registration is made on Form RE ("Application for Renewal Registration").

Forms for Use in Special Cases. There are three forms that may be used in special cases:

CA, GR/CP, and IS. Form CA ("Application for Supplementary Copyright Registration") should be used for supplementary registration in order to correct an error or amplify information given in a previous copyright registration. (The information in a supplementary registration augments but does not supersede that contained in an earlier registration.) Form GR/CP ("Adjunct Application for Copyright Registration for a Group of Contributions to Periodicals") should be used when one submits a basic application on Form TX, Form PA, or Form VA for registration of a group of contributions to a work that qualifies for a single registration. Form IS ("Request for Issuance of an Import Statement") is used to request an import statement under the manufacturing provisions of the copyright law.

Copyright Registration Numbering System. Works registered in Classes TX, PA, VA, and SR are assigned numbers with letter prefixes that represent the respective classes. Unpublished works' numbers are marked with a "u" following the class prefix. Examples: "PA 4423"; "SRu 6235." Class RE constitutes a separate numbering series, with no published or unpublished status indicated. Example: "RE 3821."

See COPYRIGHT REGISTRATION APPLICATION FORMS; COPYRIGHTABLE WORKS.

Copyright Registration of a Musical Work. Copyright registration of a musical work, published or unpublished, is made in *Class PA: Works of the Performing Arts.* This covers all types of musical compositions, including popular songs, symphonies, operas, and other works of the performing arts, as specified in COPYRIGHT REGISTRATION CLASSIFICATION SYSTEM. The appropriate application to use for copyright registration of both published and unpublished works in this class is Form PA ("Application for Copyright Registration for a Work of the Performing Arts").

Registration of a Musical Work. A claim to copyright for a musical work may be regis-

tered by sending the following three elements to the Copyright Office:

1. Form PA, properly completed and signed.
2. A deposit representing the entire work as follows:
   a. For an *unpublished* work, one complete copy or phonorecord.
   b. For a *published* work, two complete copies or phonorecords of the best edition.
   c. For a *work first published outside the U.S.,* one complete copy or phonorecord of the first foreign edition.
   d. For a *contribution to a collective work,* one complete copy or phonorecord of the best edition of the collective work.

3. Registration fee of $10 (for instructions on remittances, *see* COPYRIGHT OFFICE FEES).

The application, deposit, and fee should be sent in the same envelope or package to: Register of Copyrights, Library of Congress, Washington, D.C. 20559.

Supplementary Registration. If a musical composition (or other work) has been registered for copyright as an unpublished work, it is not required of the owner of copyright to file again after the work has been published; this is optional. It may be advisable for a basic registration to be filed again, however, if the published version is substantially different from the unpublished work. (This registration is only to cover the new material in the published version.)

Registration of a Musical Composition in Class SR. In certain cases, published and unpublished musical works may be registered in *Class SR: Sound Recordings.* Where the same copyright claimant is seeking to register not only the sound recording but also the musical work embodied in the sound recording, Form SR may be used to file a claim to copyright for both works.

Unpublished "Collections." The Copyright Office permits registrations of unpublished "collections." A registration of an unpublished "collection" is a simultaneous registration of two or more unpublished works made with one application and one fee. A registration of an unpublished collection may be made under the following conditions: the elements of the collection are assembled in an orderly form; the combined elements bear a single title, identifying the collection as a whole; the copyright claimant in all the elements and in the collection as a whole is the same; and all the elements are by the same author, or if they are by different authors, at least one of the authors has contributed copyrightable authorship to each element. Registration of songs as unpublished collections may be beneficial for those songwriters who write songs expeditiously and wish to register them for copyright but don't have the finances to copyright each one separately.

An unpublished collection is indexed in the Copyright Office only under its collective title. At a later date, a copyright claimant may desire to make a separate registration or have an individual title card prepared for an individual selection previously registered as part of an unpublished collection. The claimant may file Form CA after registering the "collection," or if new material has been added, file a basic registration for each such new version. If an individual work has been published, a basic registration may be filed for the published version.

See also PUBLICATION; APPENDIXES B, C, D.

Copyright Registration of a Sound Recording. A sound recording is registered for copyright in *Class SR: Sound Recordings.* This class is appropriate for registering published and unpublished works in two situations: (1) where the copyright claim is limited to the sound recording itself, or (2) where the same copyright claimant is seeking to register not only the sound recording but also the musical (or literary or dramatic) work embodied in the sound recording. The appropriate application to use for copyright registration of both published and unpublished sound recordings is Form SR ("Application for Copyright Registration for a Sound Recording").

Registration of a Sound Recording. A claim to copyright for a sound recording may be registered by submitting the following materials at the Copyright Office:

1. Form SR, properly completed and signed.
2. A deposit representing the entire work as follows:
   a. For an *unpublished* sound recording, one complete phonorecord.
   b. For a *published* sound recording, two complete phonorecords of the best edition together with "any printed or other visually perceptible material" published with the phonorecords.
   c. For a *work first published outside the U.S.,* one complete phonorecord of the work as first published.
   d. For a *contribution to a collective work,* one complete phonorecord of the best edition of the collective work.
3. Registration fee of $10 (for instructions on remittances, *see* COPYRIGHT OFFICE FEES).

The application, deposit, and fee should be sent in the same envelope or package to: Register of Copyrights, Library of Congress, Washington, D.C. 20559.

Supplementary Registration. *See* COPYRIGHT REGISTRATION OF A MUSICAL WORK.

Copyright Registration of an Album. A record album may consist of several different copyrightable works: the sound recordings (of which there are commonly 10 to 12 selections), the underlying musical compositions, any liner notes or text on the back cover, and photographs, artwork, graphics, or illustrations appearing on the covers. If there is the same copyright owner for all the different copyrightable works and all these works are published together as part of the album, then a single registration on Form SR with one fee would cover registration of each separate work.

With the exception of the musical compositions, a record company commonly owns all the works comprised in an album (i.e., the sound recording, liner notes, photographs, and artwork), as they are often created under WORK MADE FOR HIRE agreements. If any of the works were prepared under a work made for hire agreement, this would be noted on the form.

See also APPENDIXES E, F.

Copyright Renewal Registration. Under the copyright law in effect before January 1, 1978 (the effective date of the 1976 Copyright Act), a work could have two consecutive terms of copyright protection. In order to secure a second term of protection for a copyrighted work, however, a renewal registration was required to be filed within strict time limits by the copyright owner or other copyright claimant.

When the current copyright law went into effect, it dropped the renewal system feature except for works still in their first term of copyright protection on January 1, 1978. The statute retains a first term of copyright protection of 28 years for these works, whether published or unpublished, but provides the possibility for a renewal term of 47 years.

Renewal registration, then, is applicable only to works originally copyrighted between January 1, 1950, and December 31, 1977. These copyrights must be renewed to secure a second term of protection. Since the statute provides that all copyright terms run through the end of the year in which they would otherwise expire, all periods of renewal registration run from December 31 of the 27th year of the copyright and end on December 31 of the following year.

Renewal registration is possible only if an acceptable application and fee are received by the Copyright Office during the renewal period and before the renewal deadline. If not filed within these time limits, the work falls into the public domain and the copyright cannot be restored.

Registering a Renewal Claim. 1. When filing for renewal registration, the time limits for renewal must first be ascertained, by taking the date of original copyright for the work, and adding 28 years to the year the work was originally copyrighted. This answer will give the calendar year during which the copyright is eligible for renewal, and December 31 of that year is the deadline to make a renewal registration. The original date of copyright for a published work is the date of first publication; for a work originally registered in unpublished form, it is the date of registration which is indicated on the copyright certificate.

2. Complete and send Form RE ("Application for Renewal Registration") along with a check or money order for $6 (payable to: Register of Copyrights) to: Register of Copyrights, Library of Congress, Washington, D.C. 20559. Copies of phonorecords of the copyrighted work should not be sent with the renewal application.

Example: A song was copyrighted on May 10, 1965. Thus it is eligible for renewal between December 31, 1992, and December 31, 1993. If renewal registration is made between these deadlines, the copyright will be protected for a second term of 47 years, or until December 31, 2040. If renewal registration is not made at the proper time, however, copyright protection will permanently expire at the end of 1993.

Renewal Claimants. Renewal registration may be claimed only by certain persons or proprietors, as specified in the law. If the renewal right is the author's, he or she may claim renewal. If the author is dead, the author's widow, widower, child, or children may claim. When no such heirs have survived the author and the author left a will, the executor of the author's will may claim. In the event there are no surviving heirs as listed above and no will, the deceased author's next of kin may claim renewal registration.

Where renewal rights were assigned or transferred by written agreement or contract and the author is alive at renewal, the transferee becomes the beneficiary (but not the claimant) of the renewal.° A music publisher who has been assigned the renewal rights to a popular song, for example, would file the renewal application giving the author as the renewal claimant. For certain other works specified in the copyright statute—posthumous, periodical, cyclopedic or other composite works, and works made for hire, the owner of the copyright at the time of renewal registration may claim renewal.

New Arrangements. Copyright in a new arrangement of a musical composition covers only the additions or changes appearing for the first time in that version. A copyrighted musical arrangement that is a new version for that song is independent of any copyright protection secured in material published or copyrighted earlier. Only the "author" of this new material may be regarded as the "author" in a renewal registration for the new version, and the person who wrote the original version of the work may not be regarded as such unless he contributed to the new or revised matter.

Copyright Notice for Renewal Term. Under the copyright law, there is no requirement to indicate "Copyright renewed" on copies or phonorecords of a work after the copyright has been renewed; however, such information might be valuable. There are two forms of notice a copyright that has been renewed may have on copies or phonorecords of the work issued during the renewal term. These are either the original form of copyright notice or a notice that indicates the work has been renewed, which might be regarded as more informative. For example, a renewal notice for a copyright renewed by an author's widow might appear:

Copyright 1953 John Doe
Copyright renewed 1981 by Jane Doe

° In such cases, the statute provides that the last 19 years of the 47-year renewal term may be reclaimed by the author.

Works Not Eligible for Renewal Registration. There are two categories of works not eligible for renewal registration. These are works originally copyrighted before 1950 and renewed before 1978 (which have had their renewal terms automatically extended to a period of 47 years by the statute) and works originally copyrighted on or after January 1, 1978 (there is only a single copyright term for these works, although the author may terminate a grant in certain cases within a 5-year period either 35 years from the date of publication or 40 years from the date of grant of copyright).

See COPYRIGHT GRANTS, TERMINATION OF.

Copyright Royalty Tribunal. A governmental body created by the Copyright Act of 1976, whose purpose is to determine whether royalty rates for the four compulsory licenses (phonorecords, jukeboxes, cable television systems, and public broadcasting entities) are reasonable, and if not, to review and adjust the royalty rates. The statute provides that the tribunal review the reasonableness of the mechanical rate in 1980, 1987, and every ten years thereafter;† the jukebox royalty in 1980 and every ten years thereafter; the cable television royalty in 1980 and each subsequent fifth year; and the public broadcasting rates in 1982 and every five years thereafter. In making determinations concerning the adjustment of copyright royalty rates, the tribunal is to take into account monetary inflation and deflation.

The statute appoints the tribunal to distribute royalty fees deposited with the Register of Copyrights by jukebox operators and cable

---

† Periodic reviews by the tribunal would seem, for instance, to prevent a recurrence of the problem that arose prior to the 1976 act concerning the mechanical royalty rate. The 1909 act established a $.02 royalty rate, which remained the same until the current law went into effect on January 1, 1978. Proponents of a higher royalty rate claimed that inflation and other factors antiquated the 1909 rate long before the 1976 act went into effect.

television systems to the copyright owners whose works were used. The tribunal may also prescribe terms and rates of payments to be paid by public broadcasters to copyright owners when these parties do not reach a voluntary agreement.

The Copyright Royalty Tribunal is composed of five commissioners appointed by the President and confirmed by the Senate. The statute provides that every final determination of the tribunal is to be published in the Federal Register and may be appealed to the United States Court of Appeals by the aggrieved party within 30 days after the publication in the Federal Register.

Copyrightable Works. The United States Copyright Law provides protection for "original works of authorship." Under the 1976 Copyright Act [Section 102(a)] works of authorship include the following categories: (1) literary works; (2) musical works (including any accompanying words); (3) dramatic works (including any accompanying music); (4) pantomimes and choreographic works; (5) pictorial, graphic, and sculptural works; (6) motion pictures and other audiovisual works; and (7) sound recordings. A work in any of these categories may be copyrighted, provided it meets certain requirements.

Requirements. Court decisions have established that in order for a work to be copyrightable under the federal statute, it must (1) be original; (2) contain a certain minimum amount of creativity; and (3) be fixed in a tangible form.

What Cannot Be Copyrighted: titles of songs and other works, short phrases, expressions, mottoes, slogans, catch phrases, names of individuals and performing groups, products, services, businesses or organizations, pseudonyms, ideas, plans, procedures, concepts, principles, discoveries, methods, systems, blank forms, and inventions and works of the United States Government. Protection for some of these, however, may be obtained

through TRADEMARKS (names, expressions, slogans); patents (inventions); and the laws of UNFAIR COMPETITION (titles, names, phrases). Also, an author's description, explanation, or expression of an idea can be copyrighted, but the idea, method, plan, system, or procedure in itself cannot be.

Generally, copyright protection is also not available for obscene or libelous works. These works may be registered at the Copyright Office, but a litigation might result in the court's finding no valid copyright for the work. This is a matter of subjective determination.

Choreographic Works. The statute provides for copyright protection to subsist in "choreographic works," but doesn't define these works. This meaning, however, may be derived from legislative and Copyright Office reports: for copyright purposes, choreographic works are understood to mean dance works created for presentation to an audience (1961 Report of the Register) but not to include social dance steps and simple routines (House Report 94–1476).

Counterfeiting (Records/Audio Tapes). The illegal practice of dubbing the sounds from a legitimate recording onto tapes or discs without authorization, manufacturing packaging that closely simulates the real product, and selling the resultant product (counterfeits) as the legitimate records or tapes. Let us examine these elements separately:

Sound Recording. A sound recording comprises two types of copyrights—the sound recording itself and the underlying musical composition. In counterfeiting, the sounds from the legitimate recording are dubbed onto phonograph records and/or audio tapes without permission from any of the copyright owners.

Packaging. Counterfeiting involves the creation of packaging that closely simulates and frequently appears to be identical with that of the genuine tape or record album. This includes reproducing on the album cover or tape container the company name, trademark, logo, artwork, photographs, design, copyright notices, credits, liner notes, text or other printed information—all just as they appear on the legitimate product. This is done without permission, of course.

Differences. From a visual point of view, counterfeit product is difficult to distinguish from legitimate product. The following, however, are often indications of counterfeit product: blurred or smudged printing; poor reproduction of original colors in the jackets, slicks, and labels; poor alignment and affixation of labels and slicks; use of off-brand cartridges for tapes; and loose or poorly fitting shrink wraps. Sonically, a counterfeit recording offers inferior fidelity, as it is a few generations removed from the legitimate master.

Protection. There are various sources of legal protection from counterfeiting. All sound recordings "fixed" (recorded) and published on or after February 15, 1972, are protected under federal copyright law; those fixed prior to that date may be protected by a state antipiracy statute. Under the federal copyright law, the unauthorized reproduction of a copyrighted work such as a musical composition, photograph, or illustration constitutes an infringing act. A violation of federal law may be a criminal offense, punishable by imprisonment, fines, or both; a violation of state law is either a misdemeanor or a felony. A federal anticounterfeiting law passed in 1964 (and later amended to increase the penalties) makes illegal the interstate transportation or sale of sound recordings bearing counterfeit labels or packages. Penalties for a violation of this law are the same as those for willful COPYRIGHT INFRINGEMENT. Since counterfeit merchandise is sold with the intention to deceive or defraud the public, companies may also bring civil lawsuits charging UNFAIR COMPETITION against alleged infringers.

Counterfeiting of Other Merchandise. Counterfeiting in the music business is not limited to records and prerecorded audio

tapes. Other merchandise counterfeited includes blank tapes, prerecorded videocassettes, sheet music, concert tickets, posters, and T-shirts. The sale of any counterfeit item deprives many of income they would have otherwise earned.

See also BOOTLEGGING (RECORDS/AUDIO TAPES); PIRACY (RECORDS/AUDIO TAPES).

Country Music. *See* POPULAR MUSIC.

Country Music Association (CMA). An industry-wide professional association that serves to promote country music. From its inception in 1958, CMA has been a significant force in the growth of country music.

Membership. CMA has two basic types of membership—individual and organizational—both of which are open to persons or entities earning a portion of their income from country music.

Membership is divided into certain categories, including advertising agency, artist/musician, manager or agent, talent buyer or promoter, composer, disc jockey, international, publication, music publisher, radio-TV, record company, record merchandiser, and affiliated (persons or entities engaged in country music that do not fall within one of the primary categories, such as attorneys or performing rights organizations). There are annual dues for individuals and organizations; in the latter case, the dues are tiered according to whether the organization joins as a benefactor, patron, sponsor, donor, or contributor.

Programs and Activities. CMA sponsors various programs and activities to achieve its objective of promoting country music. These include the annual presentation of the CMA awards show on network television to honor top country artists and composers; an antipiracy campaign; production of generic country music promotional materials, such as slides or films, for presentation to advertisers and media buyers; the compilation and dissemination of information about the industry, such as lists of country music radio stations, music publishers, artists, producers, labels, agents, publications, and clubs; the presentation of live shows featuring country music for industry conventions and the public; the production of a broadcast handbook to aid country music stations or those that play country music; and the publicizing of country music in newspapers, magazines, and other media all over the world. The Country Music Hall of Fame and Museum in Nashville was established by CMA in 1961 to honor country music greats.

History. The Country Music Association was founded in 1958, born from an idea of several prominent figures in the music industry. Its objective was to promote country music to people everywhere throughout the world, to make it an attractive alternative for advertisers, and to provide unity of purpose for the country music industry. Its membership grew from 233 in 1958 to nearly 5,500 in 1980 (members are from all over the world). The Country Music Association is based in Nashville, Tennessee.

See PROFESSIONAL ASSOCIATIONS AND EDUCATIONAL ORGANIZATIONS.

Cover Record. An artist's rendition on tape or disc of a song that was previously recorded by another artist. The cover artist conforms the song to his style and manner of interpretation. Hit songs with catchy melodies and universal themes are most frequently "covered."

Songs are "covered" by artists whose musical styles differ from the original. For example, a country artist might cover a pop hit in a country-flavored arrangement, a symphony orchestra may record an instrumental rendition of a current hit, or a disco artist might cover a pop song in an arrangement that would enable people to dance to it. Covers such as these are directed at particular markets or segments that probably would not purchase the original artist's recording, as well as aim to exploit the popularity of the singer or band releasing the cover version.

Covers are sometimes made to compete directly with the original recording. A cover record issued shortly after the original version is released or "breaks" may become more popular and outsell it, as the result of such factors as the popularity of the artist, the performance, arrangement, and production, as well as promotional efforts and resources of the label.

For the music publisher, obtaining covers of songs in its catalog is one of the most important means by which it exploits compositions and maximizes their income. A successful cover can generate substantial performance and mechanical royalties. In addition, it may stimulate the sales of previously published sheet music, which is particularly advantageous to the publisher since the costs of printing have already been paid.

The term "cover" is often used to refer to an artist's rendition of a song released several years after the original recording of the song. Such newer versions may more accurately be referred to as *remakes* or *revivals*. A recording rereleased at a later time is called a *reissue*.

Critics. *See* MUSIC CRITICS AND REVIEWS.

Cross-Collateralization. Term that refers to the practice of a company deducting from any royalties otherwise payable to an artist, writer, group, singer/songwriter, or other company, any and all unrecouped advances or charges incurred by the company pursuant to any contracts between the parties. For example, a cross-collateralization clause contained in a contract of a singer/songwriter signed to a record company and its publishing affiliate would provide for unrecouped advances to be deducted from income received under either contract. The right for a company to cross-collateralize moneys received under any agreements between it and another party is negotiable and, when requested, signatories to royalty contracts usually strive in negotiations to prohibit it.

Crossover. A recording, song, or artist, strongly identified with a particular musical style, that extends into, or achieves widespread acceptance in, a market (or markets) where another style of music is predominantly popular. Most commonly, the term is used in reference to records.

A record that enjoys airplay on certain types of radio stations may extend in popularity and appeal to other markets and be programmed by stations of another format. A country or soul hit, for example, might "cross over" onto pop stations and become a hit in pop markets.

Crossovers occasionally happen by accident. More often, getting a record to cross over is a deliberate attempt by a record company to bring it to the attention of more people and increase its sales. A record that crosses over into the pop market, for example, can cause a local or regional hit to turn "gold" or "platinum" and bring national recognition to the artist.

It is common for R & B or country records to be promoted to pop radio stations even before they become hits in their respective marketplaces. That is why the pop mainstream is so hard to define, it being a hybrid of many musical genres. The musical formats of the so-called pop stations include pop and rock records as well as country and R & B crossovers.

The charts published by the trades are categorized into different musical styles. It is not uncommon, however, to see the same record on more than one chart. Records commonly cross over from pop to country, pop to R & B, R & B to country, gospel to country, gospel to pop, jazz to R & B, country to adult contemporary, and disco to pop, among others.

Crossovers have occurred more frequently in recent years. This may be attributed to a number of factors: changing demographics, greater exposure of artists through mass communication media other than radio (such as television, cable TV, and magazines), a hybridization of musical styles, a wider variety of material recorded by artists and the use of more commercial productions.

Custom Label. *See* RECORD COMPANY DEALS.

Cut. To record performances on a MASTER from which discs and/or tapes may subsequently be manufactured (to *cut* a record); derived from the process of "cutting" a lacquer or acetate. At one time, records and acetate demos were cut directly while the performance took place; hence the use of the word. The term also refers to a track or recorded selection on an album (an album *cut*).

Cut-out. Record or tape that wholesales or retails at a relatively low price because it has been dropped from a manufacturer's catalog. A recording is "cut out" when the manufacturer feels it no longer has mass appeal and is not salable enough to continue as a catalog item. A manufacturer will try to deplete its stock of discontinued LPs, singles, cassettes, and 8-track tapes by offering these to wholesalers at marginal rates. Consequently these are sold to consumers at relatively very low prices. A cut-out is also referred to as a *deletion*.

Retailers often use cut-outs as a merchandising tool to combat front-line prices and attract consumers' attention. They display cut-outs in the front of the store, or place them in marked bins; cut-out tapes are often put in a special tape section. Cut-outs may be records or tapes of any genre; rock, jazz, and country are known to sell particularly well at the retail level.

See BUDGET ALBUMS.

D

Defamation. The statutes and judicial decisions relating to *defamation* are of particular interest to entertainers, publishers, and music critics. It is the concern of the entertainer to maintain and enjoy a reputation that cannot be maimed by untrue tales or unfounded accusations. As entertainers are public figures and frequently the subject of stories and "gossip" in newspapers and magazines, their right to safeguard their reputation is very important to them. Publications and music critics simultaneously seek to enjoy literary indulgence in reviewing a concert or recording, even to the extent of ridicule.

Defamation is a false statement which injures one's reputation. Defamation may be either libel or slander. If it is in writing, printing, or pictures, it is libel; expressed orally, it is slander. For the defamation to be actionable, it is necessary to establish three points: (1) that there was damage to reputation; (2) that the defamation identified the individual; and (3) that the message was made public (to a third party). Since 1974, it has also been necessary in most cases to prove damages. In that year, the Supreme Court held unconstitutional the former rule that damages are presumed by law in libel and slander cases in which the message imputes the existence of a loathsome disease, charges one with having committed a serious crime, injures a person in his business, or imputes unchastity to a female. The Supreme Court held that damages may be presumed in such cases only if it is shown that the writer knew the published statement was false or acted with reckless disregard of whether it was false or not. If such a showing is not

made, the plaintiff must prove damages.

However, even if all these points are proved, the defendant may be protected by public policy under an "immunity." Statements made in the course of judicial or legislative proceedings or executive communications are said to be absolutely privileged—no libel suit may be based upon them whatever the circumstances. In addition, statements made under circumstances evincing an obligation—such as the obligation of a credit agency to provide financial reports concerning entertainers—cannot become the basis for a libel suit provided they are made without malice. One class of privileged statements of particular importance in the entertainment industry is the category known as "fair comment."

Fair comment is the right of anyone to make statements on a matter of public interest (such as a concert or recording) in the honest expression of the writer's real opinion, even though the statements may not be true in fact. Generally, the courts have held that the reviewer is within the bounds of fair comment by using touches of irony, wit, and exaggeration to make his article readable, so long as the statements are not motivated by ill will or malice toward the person. However, if a public figure can prove a defamation was made with actual malice—that is, with knowledge it was false or with a reckless disregard for the truth of the statement—a recovery for libel will be possible.

A celebrated libel case involved the Cherry Sisters, a musical act that appeared in an Iowa town in the early part of this century. The publication of the following review by Billy

Hamilton of the Odebolt *Chronicle* caused one of the sisters to bring legal action:

> Effie is an old jade of 50 summers, Jessie is a frisky filly of 40, and Addie, the flower of the family, a capering monstrosity of 35. Their long skinny arms, equipped with talons at the extremities, swung mechanically, and anon waved frantically at the suffering audience. The mouths of their rancid features opened like caverns, and sounds like the wailings of damned souls issued therefrom. They pranced around the stage with a motion that suggested a cross between the danse du ventre and fox trot,—strange creatures with painted faces and hideous mien. Effie is spavined, Addie is stringhalt, and Jessie, the only one who showed her stockings, has legs with calves as classic in their outlines as the curves of a broom handle.

The defendants pleaded that the Cherry Sisters had given public performances that were coarse and ridiculous, and that the article, written to expose the character of the entertainment, was written without malice or ill will toward the plaintiff or her sisters.

The court, after viewing the evidence and even witnessing the plaintiff repeat some of her stage performances, ruled that the review was *not* actionable as libel.°

Demo. A relatively inexpensively made recording of a song presented on tape or acetate, which can have any of the following purposes:

1. To show the potential of the song for the purpose of getting it published or commercially recorded. (This is the most common use of a demo.)

2. To audition a performer. For example, a group might audition its musical ability to a club owner with a demo to obtain employment. Likewise, the demo may be presented to record company personnel or producers in the hope of securing a recording contract.

3. To teach an artist a new song. Many art-

ists cannot read music and rely on a demo in learning a song. Those who can read music often prefer to learn the basic song via a demo (rather than a LEAD SHEET or personal instruction) and then adapt it to their own particular style for recording or performance.

4. To assist in the making of a musical arrangement for a master recording. Arrangers sometimes use the demo rather than a lead sheet as a guide in writing the charts for a song that is going to be recorded commercially.

5. To show the skills of a musician, arranger, or producer seeking studio work or employment with an act or a record company.

6. To audition a jingle for an advertising agency or sponsor, or the score to an original show for theatrical producers.

Types of Demos. In the publishing field, demos may be categorized into the types produced by writers and publishers. Writer-made demos (the most simple) may consist of a piano (or guitar) and voice, or range in elaborateness to a rhythm section (guitar, piano, bass, drums) and vocals. Publisher-made demos are generally of the latter nature: a rhythm section with a lead vocal and often a background vocal accompaniment. There are also demo masters—demos that can be converted into master (finished) recordings at any time by adding extra parts, such as strings or horns, at a later date.

Demos may be recorded on any number of tracks from mono to 24; demo masters are usually recorded on 16-track tape, with several tracks left open for the recording of extra parts. A simple writer-made demo (voice and piano or guitar) is often made on a home tape recorder in mono or 2-track stereo. In a mono recording, all the material (instruments and voices) has been recorded on one track, with the same signal coming out of both speakers.

The more elaborate recordings are made using the multi-track process offered in re-

---

° Cherry v. Des Moines *Leader*, et al. (Supreme Court of Iowa, May 28, 1901).

cording studios. When as many tracks as the situation warrants have been separately recorded with material or "programs," they are "mixed" down or blended into a final recording. A 2-track recording means there are 2 available tracks on which to record; thus, the performances of all instrumentalists and/or vocalists must be combined at the time of recording. This produces a stereo mix, which is generally the final product. In a 4-track recording, four different sources have been recorded onto four separate tracks of the tape and are later mixed together into a stereo recording. Regardless of how many tracks are used (e.g., 8, 16, 24), the final product is usually a 2-track mix.

Writers are often confused as to whether they should make a live stereo (2-track) or multi-track demo recording. The table below lists the advantages and disadvantages of each.

Demo Costs. Demos can range in cost from nominal to expensive, depenfing upon one's personal tastes and finances. The most inexpensive kind is a home recording made on a reel-to-reel or cassette tape recorder, or in a semiprofessionally equipped home-type studio. Here, the only cost incurred (assuming

Two-Track (Stereo) vs. Multi-Track Recordings

	Advantages	Disadvantages
Two-Track (Stereo) Recordings	More inexpensive type of recording to make. Doesn't have to be mixed. Also means saving on studio rental and material (tape) costs.	Locked into the mix of previously recorded sounds. (Recording cannot be remixed.) No overdubbing.
Multi-Track	Greater flexibility in recording. For example, if after a rhythm track is laid down and the vocalist is overdubbing, he can "punch" in wherever he makes an error. That is, if a singer records a song to satisfaction except for a particular chorus, he can go back and rerecord the chorus by "punching" in at that spot without erasing any other recorded part. The writer can come back to the studio anytime and record a different vocalist if he is unhappy with the original vocalist's recording. A writer unsatisfied with his mix can come back to the studio anytime and remix the recording.	Studio rate for multi-track recording is more expensive. Songwriters tend to over-produce. That is, they record more than they need to for a demo. These recordings must be mixed. The writer must be careful to get a good mix. Writer also incurs extra time and material (tape) costs.

there are no talent fees involved and not counting the purchase price of the hardware) is for tape.

Recording a demo in a professional studio will cost considerably more. A simple vocal/piano or vocal/guitar demo may be recorded on mono or two tracks (stereo). The costs incurred here are for studio time, which ranges from $40 to $80 per hour, and tape.

A more elaborate (and expensive) demo would be recorded on 4,8, or 16 tracks and utilize several musicians and singers. Recording time for such multi-track recording ranges from $40 to $200 per hour. Multi-track recordings have to be mixed and studio mixing time ranges in price from $40 to $200. Musicians and vocalists are paid a session fee ranging from $30 to $150 for recording demos. There are also costs for the master tape, tape for the MIXDOWN, plus copies (cassette or reel-to-reel).

Example: The cost of making a professional demo of one song that takes 4 hours to record and mix, using 4 musicians and/or vocalists, would be as follows:

Studio time and material costs

16-track recording ...3 hours @ $90/hour	=	$270
16-track mixing........1 hour @ $90/hour	=	90
Tape (2″ master)......1 reel @ $125	=	125
Tape (¼″ master).....1 reel @ $30	=	30
Copies ....1 cassette @ $6	=	6
1 reel-to-reel @ $8	=	8
		$529

Musicians

pianist/vocalist	$100
bass player	$ 75
drummer	$ 75
guitarist	$ 75
	$325

Total cost for making
the demo   ($529 + $325) = $854

Costs can run substantially more or less. To reduce the above sample costs, less time can be spent recording on fewer tracks and the talent costs could be trimmed. When it comes to "talent," price depends on the value people place on themselves. (Note: There are minimum AFM demo scale wages, although many musicians negotiate lesser fees.) There are additional costs for a producer, an arranger, and a copyist, if used.

Presentation. A demo may be presented on OPEN-REEL TAPE, CASSETTE TAPE, or an ACETATE (8-track cartridge tape is rarely used for demonstration purposes). Reel-to-reel tapes should be leadered (which means splicing plastic white leader tape between songs) to provide easy access to specific songs.

Information. The following information should be provided on demos:

• Name, address, and telephone number of the owner of the material.
• Name(s) of song(s) (in proper sequence).
• Speed at which the recording is to be played (i.e., 7½ ips for open-reel tapes and 33⅓ or 45 rpm for acetates; for cassette tapes, do not indicate the speed).
• For open-reel tape, how it was recorded (e.g., quarter-track stereo).

This information should be typed or printed on a label that can be affixed to open-reel and cassette tape boxes or to the center of an acetate.

Demographic Surveys. Population studies that obtain vital social and economic data from samples of individuals or households under investigation. Demographic studies are frequently conducted in the record and broadcasting industries to determine people's buying and listening habits. Information from these surveys is valuable in helping companies formulate, refine, and administer advertising, promotion, merchandising, and marketing plans.

Demographic studies have provided the following information for the prerecorded-music industry: record buying by age group; amount of record/tape purchasing by demographics; the types of outlets where records and tapes are purchased (i.e., full-line record-tape retailers, department, variety, discount stores, etc.); types of music purchased (pop, rock, soul, country, classical); where or how buyers find out about new records or tapes; and profiles of record buyers and nonbuyers. Studies have also determined buyer habits—listening to radio or records, reading, and concert going.

Survey information is usually gathered through interviews and/or questionnaires from a probability sample. Results are projected to a particular population. Sample size, design, and methodology are crucial in deriving accurate information on which to base forecasts, conclusions, and responsive actions.

Studies are conducted continuously by individual companies, trade associations, media, and broadcast rating services to keep pace with shifting population demographics. The following characteristics are typically included as part of various demographic studies: age, sex, race, education, family income, marital status, and geography.

Deposit of Copyrighted Works. *See* COPYRIGHT DEPOSIT AND REGISTRATION

Derivative Work. Subject to certain limitations, the copyright law grants to the owner of copyright the exclusive right to prepare, or authorize the preparation of, "derivative works." Because a musical composition is so adaptable to new kinds of arrangements and other transformations of commercial use, this is a valuable right enjoyed by copyright owners.

Definition. The 1976 Copyright Act defines (in Section 101) a "derivative work" as "a work based upon one or more preexisting works, such as a translation, musical arrangement, dramatization, fictionalization, motion picture version, sound recording, art reproduction, abridgment, condensation, or any other form in which a work may be recast, transformed or adapted." (Thus a derivative work is characterized by extensive rewriting or revi-

sion over the earlier version and has substantial originality.)

Commercial Examples. The following are examples of derivative works: a translation of a lyric, an adaptation of a lyric (such as for a jingle), a motion picture based on a song, a jazz arrangement of a popular song for print publication. To prepare such works, or to claim a copyright in each of these, permission is needed from the copyright owner.

Copyrightable Works. The law provides that a new version of a preexisting work is independently copyrightable as a "new work," but copyright in a new version does not affect or extend the protection, if any, for the underlying work. Copyright protects only the material added to the original work. The original author cannot be regarded as an "author" of the new version unless that person contributed to the new matter.

Public Domain Arrangements. Copyright extends to new or derivative versions of PUBLIC DOMAIN works. Substantial revision of or additions to the public domain work must occur, however, to make the new version an "original work of authorship." Whether such modifications constitute a new copyrightable work depends largely upon the judgment of the creator, and may ultimately depend upon the decision of a judge or jury. While the statute provides no precise guidelines for this, courts have held that for a work to be copyrightable, it must be fixed, creative, and original. An arrangement of a public domain tune for a symphony would, for example, be copyrightable.

Sound Recordings. Derivative SOUND RECORDINGS may be made and copyrighted. A new version of a preexisting sound recording where substantial changes have been made in the sequence of choruses, verses, and instrumental interludes or where there has been a remixing of existing sounds of the addition of a "sweetener" track would be copyrightable. However, the mere electronic rechanneling of a mono recording into stereo without any other alteration would not consitute a copyright in the rechanneled recording.

Copyright Duration. The term of copyright for the preexisting material upon which a derivative work is based is not affected by a new copyrightable arrangement. The copyright in the new version covers only the additions, changes, or other new material appearing for the first time.

Copyrighted new versions made on or after January 1, 1978, as a WORK MADE FOR HIRE endure for a term of 75 years from publication or 100 years from creation, whichever is shorter; the same term applies for pseudonymous and anonymous works where the author is not revealed in Copyright Office records. Where an independent arranger/composer receives consent from the copyright owner to copyright his arrangement, such copyrightable material generally endures for the life-plus-50-year term.

Renewal. For arrangements copyrighted before 1978 and still under the first term of statutory protection, renewal registration must be made to preserve the protection of the new material. Renewal in such cases should be made at the Copyright Office in the 28th year following registration of publication of the arrangement and not in the 28th year following the original registration or publication of the work on which it is based. A new arrangement is considered a separate, copyrightable work.

Copyright Notice. The copyright notice for a derivative work based upon preexisting copyrighted material may use the year date of first publication of the new version. It has been held by the courts that the notice on a new version ordinarily need not include the date pertaining to the earlier work incorporated in it.

The copyright notice for a derivative work may, however, contain a notice for both the preexisting work and the new version. Such notice in the latter case may appear as follows:

This arrangement Copyright © 1980 by Brant Music Co.

See also COPYRIGHT OWNERS, LIMITATION ON EXCLUSIVE RIGHTS OF.

Diary. Questionnaire distributed by a RADIO RATINGS SERVICE for research. Diaries are used primarily to determine the size and demographics of a station's or market's audience. Respondents are asked to keep a written record of their radio listening activity for a certain period of time, normally one week.

There are many different types of diaries used in broadcast research. ARBITRON instructs its diary-keepers to indicate the times when they start and stop listening (each time they listen), whether the station is on the AM or FM dial, the call letters of the station, and whether the listener is at home or away from home; listening activity is recorded for one week (Monday through Sunday, 6 A.M. to midnight).

Diaries may be distributed through the mail or given to the respondents by the interviewer. They may vary in length, the way the questions are phrased, the particular wording in the questions, and the order of the questions, all of which may influence respondents and responses.

Digital Recording. Digital recording refers to the technique of storing and processing sounds in the form of binary-encoded pulses. It is a recording process that represents the first departure from the analog method invented by Thomas Edison in 1877. A recording made by this process yields audio fidelity some consider superior to that heard on conventional analog recordings and phonograph records.

How a Digital Recording Is Made. Digital recording works in the following way: A recordist produces sound into a microphone. The sound travels through amplifiers to an encoder similar to a computer, which converts the audio signals into large groups of numbers—"bits" ("bytes")—which are stored on magnetic tape. The sound is numerically encoded through pulses by pitch and loudness; the binary systems uses only two values—zero and one (that is, off and on)—as opposed to our decimal system, which uses ten-digit values. When the recording is played back, the process is reversed and the decoder translates these pulses into musical signals.

Analog Recordings vs. Digital Recordings. In analog recording, after sound is emitted by the recordist, it is stored on magnetic tape in the form of small magnetic fields which "follow" the sound undulations in exact sequence and proportion; hence the name "analog," from the Greek *analogos*, "proportionate." Some distortion is inherent to all analog recordings regardless of precautions and care taken to minimize it.

In digital recording, types of distortion normally associated with analog recording are eliminated almost completely. Furthermore, digital recordings offer superior dynamic range and response. The best analog recordings (including direct-disc recordings) have a signal-to-noise ratio of 65 decibels; comparatively, S/N for digital recordings can be 90 db or better. The process is not susceptible to the problems of tape noise, print-through, and wow and flutter which are common in conventional magnetic recordings. Digital recordings are also referred to as *PCM* (pulse-code modulation).

Editing. The master tape that results from the digital recording process may be edited (a major advantage over the direct-disc master), although the process is generally more complex than the editing of conventional analog tapes. In one system, editing is done by a special computer, since there may be almost a million "bits" of information on one second of tape and finding a particular segment of bits to splice into by hand would be virtually impossible. Other editing systems functioning identically to analog are available also.

Commercial Availability. Various digitally recorded pop and classical albums have been released commercially, but by 1980 none of these were available as digitally encoded discs. Rather, digital recordings were commercially available only in hybrid form—conventional analog discs embodying sounds transferred from digital master tapes. True digital discs are encoded with digital-pulse etchings (instead of conventional grooves), which when scanned by a laser beam can be decoded to the recorded musical program. The hardware to play such discs has not yet been put on the market.

International Standards. At this writing, no international understanding regarding technical standards for digital recording or playback systems has been reached. A uniform format in each is necessary for digital recordings to reach mass acceptance by the professional recording industry as well as the home market. Uniform digital playback systems may result in a new category of consumer audio hardware.

See AUDIOPHILE RECORD; DIRECT-TO-DISC RECORDING; HIGH-PERFORMANCE ANALOG RECORDINGS.

Direct-to-Disc Recording. The recording process in which an original performance is cut directly onto the master lacquer; tape is not used. The direct-to-disc method produces a disc with a reproduction quality considered superior to that of conventional phonograph records. Direct-to-disc recordings were among the most sonically superior offered by the technologies of the 1970s and have been a popular staple among audiophiles.

The basic technology for making a recording by the direct-to-disc method actually dates back to the time Edison made his first recording. As a matter of fact, most commercially released records were made from directly cut masters until the late 1940s. Although research on magnetic tape recording had begun as early as the 1930s, it wasn't until after World War II that the quality and reliability of magnetic tape and tape recorders were good enough to justify the use of tape as a recording medium in the studio. When it was used, however, the advantages of splicing and editing tape virtually eliminated the direct-cutting method. Multi-track tape and mixing technology eventually made tape recording an even more favorable method. Direct-to-disc recording, however, offers better clarity of sound because the process avoids the signal degradation caused in the original magnetic recording and by the commonly used successive generations of tape copying, normally employed in the making of a record. An interest in the direct-to-disc cutting method by some small audiophile recording companies in the early 1970s led to a resurgence of the direct-mastered disc.

The direct-to-disc cutting method is essentially as follows: From the recordist's performance, the signals from the microphone go through the console and directly into the cutting lathe that etches the master lacquer. This master lacquer is then used to produce the stampers which press the actual playable discs.

There are disadvantages inherent to the direct-to-disc cutting method: there can be no retakes (a single mistake, even at the end of a selection, may necessitate rerecording the selection from the beginning—and this may cause considerable pressure on the performers); there can be no overdubbing; all the musicians and singers must be present at the studio at the same time (unlike multi-track recording, in which the different performers can "lay tracks" at different times and places); there can be no splicing, editing, or readjustment of dynamic levels; and only a limited quantity of discs can be made from this process, as the metal masters made from the original lacquers wear out and cannot be replaced. Because of the limited editions

pressed, some direct-to-disc albums are already regarded as collector's items and have premium prices.

As a consequence of the necessity for limited editions, the direct-to-disc cutting method has not been widely used by mass-selling artists. Most direct-cut product to date has been in the fields of classical music and jazz, and a few of these albums have been recorded from actual concert performances.

Disc Jockey. *See* RADIO STATION.

Disc Mastering. *See* RECORD MANUFACTURING.

Disco Music. *See* POPULAR MUSIC.

Discography. *See* CATALOG.

Discotheque. A nightclub featuring music for dancing and the listening pleasure of its patrons. The music is usually recorded (as opposed to live), is played on equipment operated by a person referred to as the *disco DJ*, and is heavily amplified. "Discotheque" is an adaptation of the French word *bibliothèque*, library.

Sound equipment found at a discotheque includes turntables, amplifiers, equalizers, mixers, and speakers. *Discos*, as they are commonly called, often have elaborate, expensive lighting systems.

Record companies have found discotheques to be a viable medium for "breaking" new records and generating record sales in local markets. Likewise, radio stations with disco formats often gauge audience reaction to new records in discotheques before adding them to their playlists.

Proprietors of discotheques must obtain performance licenses for the right to play copyrighted music on their premises. A license, which is granted for a fee, is normally ob-

tained from a PERFORMING RIGHTS ORGANIZA-
TION. A license from ASCAP, BMI, or SESAC
generally permits the licensee to use all the
music in that organization's repertory for a
particular period of time.

The discotheque is a genre of nightclub entertainment said to have originated in Europe
during the 1950s. The disco movement in
America, however, didn't begin till the early
or mid sixties—when the "twist" and other
dance crazes became nationally popular. The
discos of the sixties often featured go-go girls
wearing high boots and dancing in elevated
cages.

During the late 1960s and early 1970s, discos flourished in large cities but catered mainly to gay communities and black and Hispanic
groups. Disco music as we know it today was
not the music featured in these venues then;
rather, records classified as Latin, funk, and
hard rock were played. These were the seeds,
however, that eventually gave rise to a form of
music that swept the country. By the late
1970s, disco was a national craze and even
generated subcultures.

When disco music evolved into a separate
identity and first gained national prominence
in the mid seventies, discotheques sprouted
everywhere, small towns and large cities, often
in converted bars, theaters, restaurants, cafés,
etc. Owners of roller skating rinks found they
could draw larger crowds by replacing the traditional organ music with the intoxicating beat
of disco music.

The discotheque can actually be brought
anywhere—with the *mobile disco,* an entertainment service whose operators bring sound
equipment and various lighting and special effects equipment anyplace to recreate the ambience of an actual discotheque. Operators of
mobile discos are hired for many celebrations,
including parties, weddings, and reunions.

See also RECORD POOL.

Distribution Deal. *See* RECORD COMPANY
DEALS.

Distribution of Records and Tapes. Any
process by which goods travel from manufacturer to consumer is referred to as *distribution.* In the recording industry, there are
many ways in which records and tapes move
from producer to consumer, and the system of
distribution involves manufacturers and various types of distributors, wholesalers, retailers,
and licensees.

The distribution system has increased in
complexity over the decades since records
were first made commercially available. The
process of distribution was actually quite simple in the industry's very early days: retailers
would usually buy product directly from the
manufacturer (in the beginning there were basically only a few manufacturers). As retail
volume grew, record manufacturers began to
service retailers through regional distributors,
who could attend to dealers more promptly
and could provide, because of immediacy,
more personal service. Just after World War
II, one-stops began operating, followed in the
1950s by the rack jobber and the record club.
Many of the small independent labels that
formed in the fifties utilized their own independent distributors, and later, the distribution branches of the majors. Additionally, various types of licensees and merchandisers have
evolved, marketing product through special
channels. Today, a plethora of companies exist
which serve as source, "middleman," or final
link in the distribution of product to the consumer.

Entities. In examining the distribution system, one must first understand the types of
entities that comprise it, their classifications,
and their accounts serviced, or customers. This
is summarized in the following table.

Distribution. Distribution of records and
tapes commences after they are manufactured

Type of Company	Classification(s)	Accounts Serviced, or Customers
Record company	Manufacturer (major or independent)	Distributors and licensees
Branch distributor (record-company-owned)	Distributor, wholesaler	Subdistributors and retailers
Independent distributor	Distributor, wholesaler	Subdistributors and retailers
Rack jobber	Subdistributor, wholesaler	Retailers (department, variety, discount stores, etc.)
One-stop	Subdistributor, wholesaler	Retailers (single unit), jukebox operators, libraries, schools, booksellers
Exporter	Wholesaler	Foreign wholesalers and retailers
Importer	Wholesaler	Subdistributors and retailers
Cut-out specialist	Subdistributor, wholesaler	Retailers
Record merchandising company	Licensee (of manufacturer)	Retailers and consumers
Record/tape club	Licensee	Consumers
Mail order company	Licensee	Consumers
Record/tape outlets (all types)	Retailer	Consumers

and scheduled for RELEASE. "Major" record companies distribute product to subdistributors and retailers through their distribution branches. A distribution branch of a major record company is actually a sales office. Its main function is to take orders for records and tapes from local accounts and phone (or telex, wire, or mail) them into one of the company's pressing plants or depots, where the orders are then shipped directly to the accounts. Subdistributors (as noted in the above table) then sell the goods to various types of retail outlets (and in the case of one-stops, to jukebox operators and other nonretail establishments). Once in the retail outlet, records and tapes are of course available for purchase by consumers.

"Independent" record companies distribute product via independent distributors. These operate similarly to the majors' distribution branches but purchase the product of the various labels they represent, mark up the prices, and generally function as the wholesaler/warehouser/sales agent/shipper of these record companies. Some independent labels enter into agreement with a major manufacturer to have their product distributed by the major (see RECORD COMPANY DEALS).

Licensees of major and independent record companies—record/tape clubs, mail order companies, and record merchandisers—manufacture their own records and tapes under licenses from record companies and sell these directly to consumers. Some record merchandisers do not sell directly but via "key" retail outlets.

The distribution of records and tapes in the United States may be represented by the diagram on pages 144–145.

Distributor (Printed Music). *See* PRINTED MUSIC, LICENSING AND DISTRIBUTION OF.

Distributor (Records and Tapes). A distributor is a WHOLESALER that functions in getting product from the manufacturer to the retailer, either by selling to subdistributors (i.e., rack jobbers and one-stops), who in turn sell to retailers, or by selling directly to retailers themselves. In the record industry, distributors are of two types: *branch* and *independent*.

Distribution Branch. A distribution branch is a distributor owned by a "major" record manufacturer—a company in which there is common ownership of the label and the network of distribution branches. As of 1981, there were six: CBS; Capitol/EMI; MCA; Polygram; RCA; and Warner/Elektra/Asylum.

A distribution branch is basically a sales office with a territorial definition of its selling area. It functions to take orders from local accounts and also to promote, advertise, and market the company's product in its territory.

A distribution branch or field office does not actually fill record and tape orders but transmits them to destinations where they can be filled. These are either *depots* (physical distribution points) or *pressing plants*. Polygram, for example, fills its orders from depots, while CBS's pressing plants function as depots and ship product directly to its accounts. Majors have either a few depots or pressing plants located throughout the country.

Branch Organization. A major record manufacturer has distribution branches in different cities throughout the United States, each servicing wholesalers and retailers in a particular territory. For example, a Boston branch might service all the accounts in New England or a Miami branch might handle all of Florida. Record companies group distribution branches into particular regions, and regional vice-presidents oversee the activity of the branches in their territories.

Companies vary in their number and location of distribution branches, but majors commonly have anywhere from 12 to 20 or more branch offices throughout the United States. The following is an example of a 5-region, 19-city field sales and distribution organization:

Southeast	*Northeast*
Atlanta	Baltimore
Memphis	Boston
Miami	New York City
	Philadelphia
Southwest	
Dallas	*Midwest*
Denver	Chicago
Houston	Cincinnati
	Cleveland
West	Detroit
Los Angeles	Minneapolis
San Francisco	St. Louis
Seattle	

A major might have more or fewer distribution branches than set forth above, depending upon the size of its operation. Other cities where it might have branches, in addition to or instead of the above, include Charlotte, N.C., Hartford, Indianapolis, Nashville, New Orleans, Houston, and Honolulu.

Distribution of Other Labels. A branch office will represent all labels affiliated with its parent company. Major record companies enter into agreement with other labels to distribute their product on a percentage or flat rate basis (*see* RECORD COMPANY DEALS).

Personnel. A distribution branch employs various types of personnel. These vary from label to label, but may include a branch manager, sales manager, salespersons, promotion, advertising, and market coordinators, singles specialists, field merchandisers, inventory specialists and clerical personnel. The chart on page 146 shows a possible setup for a major label.

Branch Operations. As stated above, major

DISTRIBUTION OF RECORDS

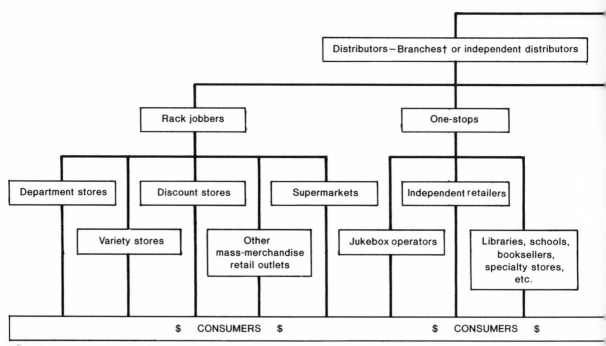

*A retail chain has buyers at a central warehouse or distribution center who purchase product on behalf of all the owned units.
†Orders taken by "major" record company branches are shipped from pressing plants or depots.

record manufacturers have either a few shipping depots or pressing plants located throughout the country and have distribution branches in various cities. Each branch represents the company and its associated labels for sales of their product in a particular territory. Salespersons from the branch are assigned specific accounts to take orders from and service on a periodic basis. This is how the sales and other branch personnel typically work:

1. The record manufacturer (headquarters) establishes a release date for new product. This is communicated to the branches; literature advertising new (and old) product is disseminated to salespersons.

2. Salespersons visit accounts, show buyers the company's catalog, and take orders

(branches normally have a quota for each new release). Discounts vary according to the classification of the account (e.g., rack jobber, one-stop, retailer) or its volume of business.

3. Salespersons call in orders to the nearest depot or pressing plant (depending on the manufacturer).

4. Depot or pressing plant fills and ships orders to accounts.

5. Accounts are billed (by depot or pressing plant, company headquarters, or the branch, depending on the manufacturer).

Salespersons will inform accounts of price structures, discounts, special deals, and all other information pertaining to buying product. (Salespersons may earn a commission in addition to a base salary.) Inventory specialists will

AND TAPES IN THE U.S.*

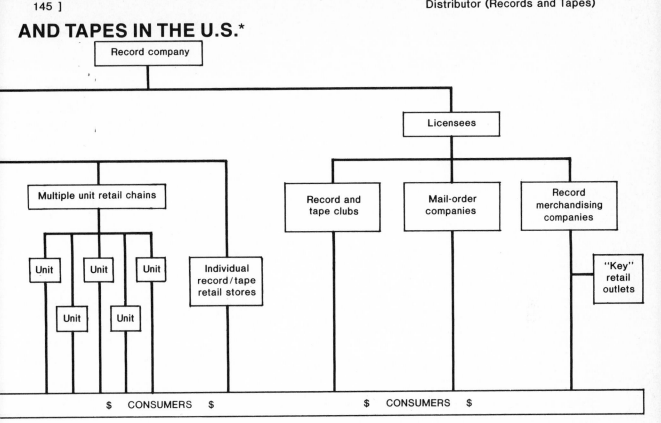

also regularly visit the branch's accounts to take inventory of their company's product, determine which recordings are good or steady sellers, and advise the accounts of what product to reorder. Field merchandisers will assist in setting up displays, merchandising aids, and special promotions.

Promotion coordinators promote records to local radio stations and retail outlets (for in-store airplay) and may arrange for autograph sessions in retail outlets when an artist is appearing locally. Advertising coordinators arrange for funds to be allocated to the branch's accounts for advertisements featuring the company's product.

Independent Distributor. An independent distributor ("indie") is a distributor not owned by a major record manufacturer. It distributes product for independent record companies and sometimes for majors if the manufacturers wish to supplement a market where a branch office operates.

Independent record distributors range from operations that distribute product in one local or regional territory to those that have branches in various cities and can distribute a label's product on a national basis. An independent record company therefore may arrange for national distribution by contracting with one, a few, or several independent distributors. Bona fide independent distributors may represent up to dozens of different labels in their territories.

The independent distributor purchases product from the labels it represents, marks up prices, and sells the merchandise to its ac-

DISTRIBUTION BRANCH*

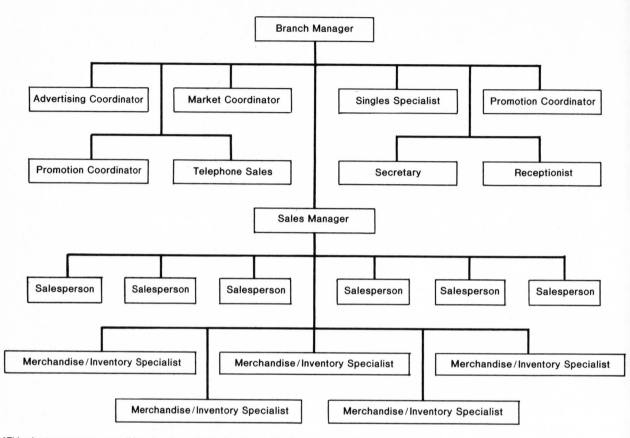

*This chart represents a possible set-up for a distribution branch. Positions, responsibilities, and number of employees vary with each company's distribution branches.

counts. The indie stocks records and tapes, takes orders, ships the product, and bills the customer. Some independent distributors are parts of operations that also comprise one-stops, rack jobbers, and retail outlets.

See also ADVERTISING; DISTRIBUTION OF RECORDS AND TAPES; RECORD COMPANY.

Doubling. Doubling refers to the recording of a vocal or instrumental part over an identical one that has already been recorded on a track. It serves to thicken, strengthen, and enhance that part and is a commonly used technique in recording.

Doubling may be accomplished mechanical-

ly, the performer overdubbing "live" (in sync) to the original track, or electronically, the already recorded part itself being overdubbed. Electronic doubling is done with a time delay so that the doubled part will be anywhere from 1 to 320 milliseconds behind (this gives the effect of two parts performed). The time delay may be (1) digital delay, where the delay is created with a small "computer," or (2) analog delay, where a tape machine or other device causes the delay of the sound.

Musicians who perform on more than one instrument at a recording session or "live" performing engagement are referred to as *doublers.* A woodwind musician, for example, may play two or more of any of the following instruments at a recording session: alto, tenor, baritone, or soprano saxophone, clarinet, bass clarinet, flute, piccolo, oboe, and English horn.

Dramatico-Musical Composition. A musical work whose performance relates a story both visually and audibly to an audience, is accompanied by dramatic action, costume, and scenery, and is written for presentation in the LEGITIMATE THEATER. Examples of a dramatico-musical composition may include any of the following: OPERA, operetta, ballet, musical comedy or play (such as a Broadway or Off Broadway show).

The right to perform dramatico-musical works on the legitimate stage or elsewhere is obtained directly from the copyright owner or his agent. The form used to grant stage performance rights to a dramatico-musical work is referred to as a *grand rights* license.

See also DRAMATISTS GUILD, INC., DRAMATICO-MUSICAL PRODUCTION CONTRACT; NONDRAMATIC MUSICAL WORK.

Dramatists Guild, Inc. An association that serves to represent, protect, and promote the professional interests of playwrights, composers, and lyricists whose plays and musical stage works are produced in the United States.

The guild negotiates periodically—as a changing theater and economy warrant—a Minimum Basic Production Contract which its members use for first-class and Off Broadway productions of their plays and musicals ("first-class," a technical business designation, generally refers to a production presented in a large city in a large theater and for an indefinite run and does not include stock, amateur, or resident theater productions). The guild also sponsors symposia and workshops and maintains an information service on grants, agents, and playwriting workshops.

The Dramatists Guild, Inc., with the Authors Guild, Inc., are corporate members of its parent organization, the Authors League of America, Inc. The Authors League handles matters that relate to both dramatists and authors, such as copyright and taxation, and matters such as contract terms and subsidiary rights, which fall within the jurisdiction of the respective guilds.

Membership. A member of either guild is automatically a member of the Authors League. There are three classes of membership in the Dramatists Guild: active, associate, and subscribing. Active membership is available to a playwright, composer, or lyricist who has had either a "first-class" production or an Off Broadway production since 1967. To qualify as an associate member, one must have completed a dramatic work (a one-act or full-length play or any component part of a musical—book, music, or lyrics), whether produced or not. Such associate member will automatically become an active member when his work is presented in a first-class or Off Broadway production. Subscribing membership is available to anyone engaged in a drama-related field and includes producers, directors, actors, agents, students, academicians, and patrons of the arts (playwrights are not eligible for membership in this category).

Active, associate, and subscribing members of the guild pay annual dues (different for each). Active members also pay 2% of their first-class royalties if the weekly amount is less than $3,000 ($4,000 for a dramatico-musical production), 3% if the royalty amount is greater than $3,000 ($4,000 for a dramatico-musical production). When motion picture rights in a member's play or musical are sold, members pay the Guild 2% of the proceeds received under such contracts.

See DRAMATISTS GUILD, INC., DRAMATICO-MUSICAL PRODUCTION CONTRACT.

Dramatists Guild, Inc., Dramatico-Musical Production Contract. The contract Dramatists Guild members use for first-class productions of their musicals.° An "author" (which hereinafter means a bookwriter, composer, or lyricist) will become a member of the guild, if he is not already a member, when his play is optioned for a first-class production.

The terms of the Dramatists Guild Contract are the minimum that the producer must give to an author. The author's representative (e.g., agent or attorney) is free to negotiate contract terms more favorable than the minimum terms and the producer may or may not comply with such demands, depending upon how badly he wants the option, the author's reputation, etc. The Minimum Basic Production Contract must be countersigned by the guild in order to be effective. The guild's legal staff first examines the contract to make sure that minimum terms have been complied with.

The Minimum Basic Production Contract consists of three parts: the basic contract (signed by parties to the agreement), a Schedule of Additional Production Terms, and an Appendix A to the Schedule of the Additional Production Terms, which contains the procedure to be followed by the film negotiator in the sale or lease of plays for motion picture production. The following highlights some of the Dramatico-Musical Production Contract's basic terms:

Scope of Agreement. The producer is granted the right to produce the author's play in the United States and Canada. If the producer satisfies certain terms of the contract, he acquires the right to share in proceeds as stipulated and is entitled to other benefits.

Option Payments. The producer may option the play (i.e., maintain his right to produce it) by making minimum payments in alternative ways: he may pay a minimum of $500 on signing for the first 3 months, followed by monthly payments of $100 for the

---

° The guild also has a separate minimum basic contract for dramatic productions, and contracts for revues, stock tryouts, and collaboration agreements.

next 3 months and by $200 per month for the next 6 months; or he may pay a fixed monthly compensation of $200 each to the bookwriter, composer, and lyricist for 12 consecutive months. These option payments constitute a nonreturnable advance against royalties (although not all option payments are considered recoupable advances). In practice, variations in making option payments may be used so long as the requirements for making minimum payments are followed.

Length of Option. The duration of the contract is for 1 year. The producer must present the play on the speaking stage in a first-class theater in a first-class manner on or before 1 year from the date of the contract or from the date the completed play is delivered to the purchaser, whichever first occurs (a completed musical play consists of at least 80 single-spaced pages and a score of music and lyrics for at least 12 songs). A producer may make provisions to extend the option to produce the play for an additional 6 months by providing in the contract for payment of an additional monthly fee, although the extension of such option must be predicated on certain circumstances which prevented the producer from presenting the play during the 1-year period (e.g., a particular star, theater, or director was unavailable).

Minimum Royalty Payments. The producer agrees to pay the authors a minimum royalty of 6% of the gross weekly box office receipts. This royalty may be divided in any way the authors—composer, lyricist, and bookwriter—choose. It is often divided equally—that is, 2% each—but sometimes the bookwriter will negotiate to receive half the royalty and the composer and lyricist will divide half.

Authors' Rights of Approval. The authors are granted the right of approval in selection of the cast, director, set designer, costume designer, conductor, and dance director.

Script Changes. Once the completed script

is delivered to the producer, no additions, omissions, or alterations may be made without the permission of the producer and the authors (bookwriter, composer, and lyricist). The producer may complain to the guild if he believes the authors are unreasonable and the guild may appoint a representative to prevail upon the authors to make changes, if they are deemed advisable, which the authors may or may not make.

Acquisition of Rights. The producer shares in certain rights (which could prove to be valuable) if the musical runs for a certain length of time as provided in the contract and the Schedule of Additional Production Terms. These rights accrue in the following manner: (1) if the production has played for a minimum of 21 consecutive performances in New York; or (2) if there have been at least 64 consecutive performances whether outside or in New York (outside New York, because of the necessities of travel, the 64 performances may be given within 80 days of the performance); or (3) if the producer has opened the play in New York, paying a $6,000 escrow payment for the royalties covering the first 3 weeks after the official New York opening to the guild on behalf of the authors (this last condition is rarely permitted by agents)—he is entitled to receive 40% of net subsidiary rights earnings for a period of 10 years after the last performance of the last first-class run of the play, 35% for the next succeeding 2 years, and for each of the next succeeding 2 years, 30%, 25%, and 20% respectively. Eighteen years after the play's last performance, the producer is not entitled to share in any subsidiary rights earnings.

The producer's percentage of subsidiary receipts are for motion pictures throughout the world and for the following rights disposed of in the continental United States and Canada: radio; television; second-class touring performances; foreign-language performances; condensed and tabloid versions; so-called concert tour versions; grand opera, stock, and amateur performances; and commercial uses, which may be any physical property representing a character in the play, or use of the name of a character or title of the play, or may be otherwise connected with the play or its title, and include toys, games, figures, dolls, and novelties.

The author alone owns and controls the play with respect to all subsidiary uses. However, the author agrees not to authorize or permit any outright sale (as distinguished from a lease, license, or other disposition) of any such rights prior to the first-class production of the play, except that an outright sale of motion picture rights prior to such first-class production may be permitted if made in accordance with certain terms set forth in the Schedule of Additional Production Terms.

British Subsidiary Rights. If the producer has produced the play in the British Isles (Great Britain and Ireland) in accordance with the contract terms, then he acquires the same financial interest in the net profits received by the author for the subsidiary uses when exploited in such territory. This provision is exclusive of motion picture rights.

Cast Album. The interests in the original cast show album will normally be divided in the proportion of 60% for the authors and 40% for the producer. The composer, lyricist, and bookwriter will negotiate how to divide the author's share and this is usually on an equal basis. The producer's acquisition of a percentage in the cast album is not predicated on his fulfilling the conditions set forth previously, since he furnishes the cast for his interest.

Publishing. Publication of the music and lyrics is controlled by the composer and lyricist alone. This includes the right of mechanical, print, and other types of reproduction. However, the composer and lyricist may not permit the publication or mechanical reproduction of the music prior to the initial first-class performance of the play without the producer's express written consent. For any publication of the musical works, copyrights are in the names of the composer and lyricist.

Arbitration. Any dispute between the author and producer arising in connection with the play is subject to arbitration. The Schedule of Additional Production Terms sets forth the conditions of arbitration.

Termination of Contract. The rights granted to the producer cease automatically under certain circumstances. These include the producer's failing to produce the play within the period of the option or extended option period, not making any option payment within 10 days after it is due, failing to pay the authors their royalties, and filing a petition of bankruptcy.

E

Easy Listening Music. *See* POPULAR MUSIC.

Eight-Track Tape Cartridge. A tape recording and playback medium in cartridge form. The popularity of eight-tracks in recent years has been significantly affected by the increasing preference for and the superior playback quality of present cassette tapes. Prerecorded eight-track tapes commonly contain four stereo "programs" on eight tracks, each set of stereo tracks containing up to a few selections.

Eight-track tapes are approximately ¼-inch wide and run at a speed of 3¾ ips. Eight-track tape cartridges were introduced commercially in 1962.

Electrical Transcription. A disc recording specifically made for radio broadcast. Electrical transcriptions were most commonly used during the 1930s and 1940s, before the advent of tape recording. They were originally made on 16-inch discs, playable at 33⅓ rpm,° were cut with a 3/1000-inch-wide groove, and usually contained 30-minute programs, 15 minutes on each side. Such programs might consist of commercials, radio plays, soap operas, comedy shows, songs, musical performances, or any combination of these.

The programs were recorded for two basic purposes: historical (they were stored in the radio station's archives) and rebroadcast or repeat use. With regard to the latter, the programs could be rebroadcast on the same station or, if duplicated or pressed in quantity,

---

° Commercial records at that time were usually made to play at 78 rpm.

distributed to other stations on that network. During radio's early years, most programming was "live" (stations employed staff musicians and singers, whose "live" performances were broadcast). A program broadcast nationally, however, would face the problem of being heard throughout the United States in completely different time slots, because of time zones. To remedy this problem, studios would broadcast programs "live" on the East Coast and at the same time directly record these programs onto acetate. Electrical transcription discs could be mailed to other radio stations for later broadcast, or the remote stations could receive the programs on telephone lines and record it directly onto acetates for playback and broadcast at a more desirable time. Alternatively, an originating station could play the transcription and, through a high-quality telephone line to the remote stations, provide the programming at the desired time. In this manner, "time shifting" was possible and the program could be broadcast on the same day and hour, in different time zones, as the original. This practice allowed stations in the central and western United States to transmit such programs at a preferred time or the same time slot as the East Coast original broadcast.

With the development of long-playing microgroove recording, transcriptions, albeit very rare at this point, are available on 10- and 12-inch vinyl discs (almost identical to a commercial phonograph record), for wide distribution of very specialized programming. The advent of the magnetic tape recording caused the demise of electrical transcriptions as the means to store and rebroadcast radio programs. Today, jingles, ads, and syndicated and automated programs that are produced exclusively for radio transmission are usually recorded and supplied on tape. Technically, a magnetic recording cannot be considered similar to an electrical transcription, the operation of which is mechanical.

Emmy Awards. Prizes of merit given annually in the United States by the National Academy of Television Arts and Sciences for outstanding achievements in the television industry. The Academy presents numerous awards in recognizing excellence in television, including some in music categories (these change from year to year). Over the years these categories have included Best Male Singer, Best Female Singer, Best Original Music Composer for Television, Best Music Series, Outstanding Music Program, and Individual Achievement in Music (Composers, Conductors, Arrangers, Music Routines, and Choral Direction). More recently, Emmy Awards have been given for Outstanding Classical Program in the Performing Arts, Outstanding Comedy-Variety or Music Program, and Outstanding Music Composition for a Series (Dramatic Underscore, Theme Song, or special material—with or without lyrics).

Suggestions for a symbol and name for these awards were requested in 1948 by Charles Brown, the president of the chapter that preceded the formation of the national organization in 1952. Television engineer Harry Lubcke (who had been president in 1949–50) suggested the name "Emmy," derived from the nickname for the image orthicon tube, "Immy." The symbol for the trophy was selected from a sketch submitted by designer Louis McManus, out of a pool of around 118. The first annual TV awards were first presented at the Hollywood Athletic Club on January 25, 1949.

See also AWARDS.

Employee for Hire. *See* WORK MADE FOR HIRE.

Endorsement. The public tends to be positively influenced by advertisements in which a product is endorsed by a celebrity. Consequently commercial sponsors have for a long time presented advertising messages with famous persons promoting their goods. Well-known *entertainers* have pitched everything from stereo equipment, blank cassette tapes, and musical instruments to deodorants, pimple creams, and beer. Commercials are generally attractive to artists for both the money they earn and the wide exposure they receive. However, celebrities should not necessarily endorse every product offered. There are certain factors to be considered in making endorsements:

Validity. The performance or effectiveness of the product and the accuracy of the manufacturer's claim are of utmost importance. A deceptive claim in U.S. media may not only cause disfavor with the public but may also risk action taken by the FEDERAL TRADE COMMISSION (FTC).

The FTC has adopted guidelines (effective January 18, 1980) on the use in advertising of endorsements and testimonials, which are treated identically in the context of the enforcement. The FTC defines an "endorsement" as "any advertising message (including verbal statements, demonstrations, or depictions of the name, signature, likeness or other identifying personal characteristics of an individual or the name or seal of an organization) which message consumers are likely to believe reflects the opinions, beliefs, findings, or experience of a party other than the sponsoring advertiser."

The FTC is concerned with ads for all products. The obligation to substantiate applies to all affirmative claims for products. Verification of the accuracy of a claim made about a product should therefore be made before its advertisement is presented on radio or television or in print. For certain products, it may be in the performer's best interest to order independent scientific tests before touting the product. Liability may be created where an endorser personally guarantees a product.

The guidelines require that endorsements reflect only the honest views of the endorser and not contain claims that would be deceptive or could not be supported if made directly by the advertiser. When the endorsement represents that the endorser actually used the product, he or she must, at the time the endorsement was given, have been a bona fide user of the product. An advertiser may use a celebrity or expert endorsement only so long as it has good reason to believe the endorser continues to subscribe to the views presented. The advertiser may satisfy this obligation by securing at reasonable intervals the endorser's views. Reasonableness is determined by such factors as new information on the performance or effectiveness of the product, a material alteration in the product, changes in the performance of competitors' products, and the advertiser's contract commitments.

Image. An identification is usually made between the individual and the product or service he or she endorses. Therefore, the effect the endorsement will have on the artist's image or career should be evaluated. While the celebrity serves to enhance the public's opinion of a particular commodity, the public may already have a preconceived view of the brand or associate the product in a certain way. For example, a reputable well-known product might enhance the image of the endorser while a woman's promoting, say, an underarm deodorant might create a public opinion that is unfavorable for her career. Much consideration should be given to the product the artist endorses and the long-range identification that may result between the two.

Compensation. Endorsements may be a lucrative source of income for celebrities. Contracts have been known to provide six-figure incomes for endorsers, and commercials repeated over a long period of time on radio and television may bring additional income in the form of residuals. The amount of compensation is a matter of negotiation between the parties involved. Of course, financial remuneration is not always a concern or not a criterion in deciding whether to make an endorsement, particularly in the case of endorsements of charities, political candidates, and various causes (e.g., environmental protection). There may also be payment in the form of other valuable consideration, such as merchandise. Manufacturers of stereo equipment or musical instruments may, for example, offer their product in exchange for an endorsement.

Engineer, Recording. The technician who controls and operates the electronic equipment during RECORDING. Engineers may be employed by a RECORDING STUDIO or work as free-lancers (e.g., an artist or a producer might hire one with whom he has a working relationship for a particular project).

With respect to recording sessions, the engineer's work falls into three basic areas:

1. Prerecording. The engineer sets up and prepares all the equipment needed for the session. His duties include preparing the recording area, setting up chairs, music stands, and sound baffles, selecting appropriate microphones and placing them as required, checking and adjusting headphones and the monitoring system, checking and setting individual microphone "line" levels, preparing recording track sheets, consulting with the clients and discussing with the producer his intentions, plans, and "desired sound." Some of the less technical duties may be performed by an assistant engineer.

2. Recording. The engineer operates the equipment in the control room and ensures that all sections are recorded to their best advantage and to achieve the desired result. He may use various electronic devices to enhance and/or modify the original signals picked up by the microphones. The engineer will properly mix the separate microphones (which may feed a single track), and the tracks being recorded (i.e., he gets the desired balance through the monitor speakers and in headphones for those performers who are using them). The engineer works with the recording track sheet and keeps careful records of desired takes, editing information, etc. These are stored with the master tape and may be referred to by the client for his use in editing the original tape, selecting desired takes, and getting a final mix.

3. Postrecording. The engineer works with the client to perform the MIXDOWN from the master tape. When all the mixing is complete, the tape is edited (spliced and reassembled) if desired.

Other Aspects. There are certain qualities a competent engineer should have. The engineer must be able to work efficiently and be able to improvise in case of difficulty with equipment or microphone operations, particularly in effecting quick repairs for minimum "down time."° The engineer must have a thorough knowledge of tape recorders and recording, special effects and mixing techniques, specialized recording and equalizing equipment, microphone characteristics and operation, all production equipment (mainly their theory of operation and potential), and the studio itself. It may be his responsibility also to maintain and repair all equipment in the studio. He must keep up with the latest tech-

niques, equipment, and developments in recording technology.

The engineer should be able to guide, inform, and advise clients where necessary (with respect to their options and costs in using certain techniques or equipment to enhance their recordings or achieve a desired final effect). He should be able to work compatibly with all individuals involved in the recording and maintain a relaxed atmosphere while ensuring that there are no lags, which will result in excessive studio-use costs. The engineer should have an understanding of all types of music that he records, and of sound, particularly with respect to the vogues and effects in current use. He must in the final analysis be able to obtain the ultimate "effects" desired by the client and/or musicians.

Engineers are often required to work long and "irregular" hours, sometimes from the early evening through the early morning hours, or on weekends and holidays. Some recording engineers also do mastering work, though this is often the area of other engineering specialists.

EP. An EP, or *extended play* record, is a 7-inch PHONOGRAPH RECORD containing two selections or one longer-than-standard selection on each side. EPs are manufactured to operate at speeds of 45 or 33⅓ revolutions per minute. The retail price of an EP is greater than a SINGLE's but lower than an LP's. EPs have been released in the United States on a limited basis only.

Equity. *See* ACTORS' EQUITY ASSOCIATION (AEA OR EQUITY).

Evergreen. *See* STANDARD.

Exclusive Songwriter's Agreement. *See* SONGWRITER/MUSIC PUBLISHER CONTRACT.

° "Down time" is the period of time when the studio is nonoperational—usually due to a technical breakdown—during a client's session.

Exporter (Records and Tapes). A WHOLE-SALER who sells records and tapes to retailers and wholesalers located outside the country. The company may represent the catalog of any or all domestic manufacturers. It generally resells products to foreign dealers at discounts ranging from 30% to 50% off the list price. Some exporters also sell record and tape accessories and audiovisual hardware and software. The company will ship by air or sea and the customer usually pays for the shipping costs and import duty.

See also IMPORTER (RECORDS AND TAPES).

F

Fair Packaging and Labeling Act. *See* BUSI-NESS LAWS, FEDERAL AND STATE.

Fair Use. The exclusive right of a COPYRIGHT OWNER to reproduce a work in COPIES or PHONORECORDS is limited by the statutory provision of "fair use." Preceding an explanation of the law's fair use section is a short discussion of how this provision evolved into federal law, which will perhaps help the reader better appreciate its inclusion in the statute.

The "Fair Use" Doctrine. The U.S. Constitution grants the legal authority for Congress to enact copyright laws, which, by granting exclusive rights to owners of copyrights, promote the progress of science and the useful arts for the public welfare. A history of court decisions has held, however, that in certain cases the unauthorized use of a copyrighted work could be to the benefit of the public without being to the detriment of the copyright owner, and was therefore lawful. Such limitations on the exclusive rights of copyright owners as developed by the courts came to be known as "fair use."

In granting a copyright owner exclusive rights, the Copyright Act of 1976 places certain limitations on these, some of which outline the concept of fair use (this is the first statutory recognition given to this doctrine). While the statute falls short of giving an exact definition, fair use may be regarded as the reasonable use of a work, without permission from or payment to the owner of copyright, under certain circumstances. The act legally clarifies the limitations on exclusive rights but permits judicial interpretation of the "fair use" doctrine based on the individual facts of each case.

"Fair Use" under the Copyright Law. The 1976 Copyright Act provides that the fair use of a copyrighted work is not an infringement of copyright and includes the following situations: reproduction of a work in copies or phonorecords for purposes such as criticism, comment, news reporting, teaching (including multiple copies for classroom use), scholarship, or research. The law also sets forth four factors to be considered, but not to be limited to, in determining whether a particular usage of a work constitutes a fair use. These are:

1. The purpose and character of the use, including whether its use is of a commercial nature or is for nonprofit educational purposes.

2. The nature of the copyrighted work.

3. The amount and substantiality of the portion used in relation to the copyrighted work as a whole.

4. The effect of the use upon the potential market for or value of the copyrighted work.

Music Guidelines. Clarification of these factors with respect to the educational fair use of copyrighted music materials was made in guidelines set forth by five professional music and educational associations in conjunction with the House Copyright Subcommittee. The purpose of the guidelines is to state the minimum and not the maximum standards of educational fair use under Section 107 of House Report 2223. It was agreed by the parties that the conditions determining the extent of permissible copying for educational purposes may change in the future; that certain types of copying permitted under these guidelines may not be permissible in the future; and conversely, that in the future other types of copying not permitted under these guidelines may be permissible under revised guidelines.

Moreover, the guidelines below are not intended to limit the types of copying permitted under the standards of fair use under judicial decision, which are stated in Section 107 of the Copyright Revision Bill. There may be instances in which copying that does not fall within the guidelines stated below may nonetheless be permitted under the criteria of fair use.

Guidelines with Respect to Copyrighted Music Material

A. PERMISSIBLE USES

1. Emergency copying to replace purchased copies which for any reason are not available for an imminent performance provided purchased replacement copies shall be substituted in due course.

2. For academic purposes other than performance, multiple copies of excerpts of works may be made, provided that the excerpts do not comprise a part of the whole which would constitute a performable unit such as a section, movement, or aria, but in no case more than 10% of the whole work. The number of copies shall not exceed one per pupil.

3. Printed copies which have been purchased may be edited or simplified, provided that the fundamental character of the work is not distorted or the lyrics, if any, altered or lyrics added if none exist.

4. A single copy of recordings of performances by students may be made for evaluation or rehearsal purposes and may be retained by the educational institution or individual teacher.

5. A single copy of a sound recording (such as a tape, disc, or cassette) of copyrighted music may be made from sound recordings owned by an educational institution or an individual teacher for the purpose of constructing aural exercises or examinations and may

be retained by the educational institution or individual teacher. (This pertains only to the copyright of the music itself and not to any copyright that may exist in the sound recording.)

B. PROHIBITIONS

1. Copying to create or replace or substitute for anthologies, compilations, or collective works.

2. Copying of or from works intended to be "consumable" in the course of study or teaching, such as workbooks, exercises, standard tests and answer sheets.

3. Copying for the purpose of performance, except as in A.1 above.

4. Copying for the purpose of substituting for the purchase of music, except as in A.1 and 2 above.

5. Copying without inclusion of the copyright notice which appears on the printed copy.

Fakebook. *See* PRINTED MUSIC.

Fan Club. Membership organization comprised of individuals who are zealous followers of a recording artist or an entertainer. A fan club is formed to bring together people with a common interest in the performers, and it may be run for commercial or noncommercial purposes.

For the recording artist, a fan club can be beneficial in several ways. It can promote his image and add to his prestige; boost his record/tape sales; increase mail order sales of his product; increase attendance and raise the spirit of enthusiasm at concerts (fan club members often make and display signs and posters); broaden his audience; draw greater attention to him (possibly resulting in greater media coverage); sustain his popularity; increase sales of his merchandising tie-in products; and increase his income.

For the artist's followers, the fan club unites those who share an enthusiasm, satiates their desire for information and products relating to their idol by offering news and selling merchandise, and may simply be a healthy hobby for the avid devotee. A fan club may also sponsor bus transportation to the artist's concert.

Members of most fan clubs are largely female preteens and teens. The objects of their affections are usually youth-oriented performers whose music may be classified as rock, pop, R & B, or country. There are also some fan clubs for older, middle-of-the-road artists who appeal strongly to housewives and middle-aged audiences.

Fan clubs may be started by individual fans with or without a commercial interest, by business enterprises (such as merchandising firms), individual profit seekers, or the artist's personal manager or label. Advertisements for fan clubs may appear in the form of fliers inserted into the artist's record albums, printed notices on the back of album covers, ads in certain publications (commonly teen magazines and comic books), or handbills passed out at concerts.

Membership in a fan club is typically by an initiation fee and/or dues. This may entitle the member to any of a variety of items (often a fan club *kit*), including a club membership card, membership scroll, photos of the artist (wallet size and 8 by 10), periodic newsletters and badges, bookmarks, calendars, and posters. Newsletters commonly provide such information as names of the artist's new recordings and dates of releases, upcoming concert schedules and tour itineraries, personal and professional data on the artist, and names and addresses of fan club members for correspondence.

Federal Communications Commission (FCC). Independent agency of the United States government responsible for regulating interstate and foreign communication by ra-

dio, television, wire, cable, and satellite. The commission was created by Congress—the legislative body to which it directly reports—by the adoption of the COMMUNICATIONS ACT OF 1934 and began operating on July 11, 1934. Its jurisdiction covers the 50 states, Guam, Puerto Rico, and the Virgin Islands.

Regulation of Broadcasting. One of the major functions of the FCC is the regulation of broadcasting. Its activities here fall into the following categories: (1) allocating space in the radio frequency spectrum to the broadcast services (and to many nonbroadcast services); (2) assigning to broadcasting stations in each service frequency, power, and call signs (the FCC considers applications to build new stations or sell existing ones and issues licenses to operate); and (3) regulating existing stations by inspecting to see that they operate in accordance with FCC rules and the technical provisions of their authorizations (the FCC processes applications for license renewals).

Broadcast stations in the United States are licensed to serve the public interest and it is the commission's responsibility to ensure that stations abide by the Communications Act as amended, and FCC rules and policies. FCC concerns include advertising "payola," lotteries, obscenity, fraud, and the "fairness doctrine" (the mandate of Congress that a station provide reasonable opportunity for the presentation of opposing viewpoints on a controversial public issue when that station has aired one viewpoint).

Administration. The FCC is administered by 7 commissioners, who are appointed by the President, with the approval of the Senate, for 7-year terms. One of the commissioners is designated by the President to serve as chairman. No commissioner may have a financial interest in any FCC-regulated business and no more than 4 may be members of the same political party. There are approximately 2,100 employees of the FCC.

Federal Trade Commission (FTC). Independent law-enforcement agency of the United States government responsible for promoting fair and free competition in interstate commerce by preventing unfair and deceptive business practices. Its regulatory actions may apply to the music industry in many ways. For example, the FTC has been concerned with record club monopoly practices, price fixing, "payola," celebrity endorsements and testimonials in advertisements, trade names of record labels that imitate names of other industry companies and mislead purchasers, "sound-alike" recordings that deceive consumers, and "hyping" by radio stations.

The FTC investigates corporate and business practices, and it also makes reports on various other matters to Congress and the public. By issuing cease and desist orders after an administrative hearing and by applying to the federal courts to issue injunctions, it can act against businesses and individuals whose practices restrict normal business competition or deceive consumers. While the FTC does not have the authority to fine or imprison, it may sue for civil penalties to obtain redress if one of its final cease and desist orders is violated.

To articulate the legal obligations of the business community and to inform consumers of their legal recourse when they recognize unfair or deceptive business practices, the FTC has authority to issue Trade Regulation Rules and Industry Guides, which define practices that violate the law. It also issues business advice (called Advisory Opinions) to corporations and individuals making such requests.

The FTC was created by the Federal Trade Commission Act on September 26, 1914. Of all U.S. government agencies, it has the broadest authority over domestic business practices.

The FTC is administered by 5 commissioners. They are appointed by the President, subject to the approval of the Senate. Not more than 3 commissioners may be members of the same political party.

See BUSINESS PRACTICES, REGULATION OF; PAYOLA; TRADEMARKS.

Federal Trade Commission Act. *See* BUSINESS LAWS, FEDERAL AND STATE.

Festival. Musical event of special character that endures for an extended period of time (some up to a few days) and is presented at a centralized location. Festivals are presented featuring musical performances in many areas of music, such as rock, jazz, folk, chamber music, and opera. At rock festivals, several groups—ranging from star to supporting-act status—will perform. Festivals are usually held outdoors and there is no reserved (assigned) seating.

Fixed Work. The U.S. copyright law requires a work to be "fixed" in any tangible medium of expression in order to be eligible for copyright protection under the statute. A work is "fixed" in a tangible medium of expression when "its embodiment in a copy or phonorecord by or under the authority of the author, is sufficiently permanent or stable to permit it to be perceived, reproduced, or otherwise communicated for a period of more than transitory duration."° Thus the law provides that a tangible fixation of a work is not limited to its being visibly perceptible. Sound recordings constitute another perception and copyright in a musical composition can be secured by its embodiment in a sound recording. The songwriter, then, who records his composition on a home tape recorder has "fixed" his work and it would be entitled to statutory protection as such. Without the work's fixation in a copy or phonorecord, however, it would not enjoy copyright protection under the federal statute.

° 17 U.S.C., Section 101.

Under the law, a work consisting of sounds, images, or both that is being transmitted is considered "fixed" if a fixation of the work is made simultaneously with its transmission.

See COPIES; PHONORECORDS.

Folios. *See* PRINTED MUSIC.

Folk Music. *See* POPULAR MUSIC.

Foreign Entertainer. *See* IMMIGRATION AND EMPLOYMENT OF FOREIGN ENTERTAINERS.

Foreign Income. The income sources available to owners of original U.S. recordings released, or U.S. musical compositions published, in foreign countries are generally the same as in the United States. U.S. record companies release masters in foreign countries through subsidiaries or via licensees and the U.S. labels as well as the artists and producers of such masters earn royalties when records or tapes made therefrom are sold abroad. Royalties from recordings may also be earned in foreign countries from the licensing of tracks such as for compilation albums or for record club editions. In some foreign countries, performance royalties are paid to artists whose performances are embodied on records that are broadcast on the radio.

For music publishers and songwriters, foreign income for the use of musical compositions is primarily derived as performance, mechanical, and print royalties. Many U.S. publishers are represented in foreign countries by subpublishers. U.S. copyright owners whose compositions are embodied in motion pictures may earn performance royalties from theatrical exhibitions of such films in certain countries (in the United States, motion picture theater operators are exempt from paying license fees for performances of musical compositions embodied in motion pictures exhibited in their theaters).

Foreign Mechanical Rights Agencies. *See* MECHANICAL RIGHTS SOCIETIES (FOREIGN).

Foreign Performing Rights Organizations. *See* PERFORMING RIGHTS ORGANIZATIONS (FOREIGN).

Formats, Radio Station. A format refers to the style and concept of a radio station's *programming*—the type of music the station plays (with the exception of all-news/talk formats), the size of its playlist (if it has one), the personalities of the disc jockeys or announcers, the kinds and styles of jingles, commercials, and station IDs it airs, the promotions it runs, and its manner and tempo of segues. These elements contribute to the station's image.

There are various types of formats used in radio, selection being based on research, the target demographic audience, ratings history of the station, competition in the market, financial resources, public interest, and personal tastes.

The format of a radio station is determined by the owner or general manager. In some cases, an independent programming consultant is hired to determine the most economically viable format [*see* PROGRAMMING SERVICES (RADIO)]. Although many different formats have achieved great success, a format that is successful in one market may of course not be successful in another (that is, attract a significant number of listeners). There has been a history of listener groups organized to combat proposed changes in formats if such a change threatens a community with the loss of a unique source of specialized radio programming (e.g., from classical to rock music).

The following table lists and briefly describes several of the more common types of formats used by U.S. radio stations. Actually, many formats defy clear-cut definitions. Programming is often classified as being one format or another, yet it may encompass various

Radio Station Formats

Format	Description (Music or Records Programmed)
Adult contemporary	Current mainstream pop hits plus crossovers but no hard rock; target audience is typically 25+
AOR (album-oriented rock)	Cuts from rock-oriented albums and, on a limited basis, hit singles
Beautiful music	Primarily instrumental arrangements of contemporary and past hits
Big band	See Nostalgia
Black	Music oriented for a black audience—plays soul, R & B, and disco records (also called black-oriented rock [BOR], or urban contemporary)
Classical	Classical, serious, concert, orchestral, chamber music
Contemporary hit radio	A contemporary term for the top 40 format
Country	Country music, including pop/rock/soul crossovers
Disco	Youth-oriented dance music
Easy listening	Predominantly instrumental with contemporary flavor, using original rather than cover artists for vocal content
Ethnic	Programming skewed toward local ethnic audiences—e.g., Greek, Jewish, Polish
Free-form	No set format, plays everything (e.g., rock, disco, country, jazz, etc.); individual DJ or PD sets programming toward his mood
Gospel	Gospel, contemporary Christian music
Jazz	All types of jazz
Mellow	Soft rock, some pop

Radio Station Formats (continued)

Format	Description (Music or Records Programmed)
MOR (middle-of-the road)	Obsolete term, no longer descriptive of a station's programming content; format replaced by Adult contemporary
New wave/punk	Self-explanatory; very few, if any, stations have this format full time
News	News, information, weather, sports, and time reports; stations use wire services and have foreign correspondents
Nostalgia	Basically music from 1920s, '30s, '40s
Oldies	Predominantly hits of the past, some contemporary hits as well
Pop adult	Adult contemporary with heavy emphasis on oldies, including more "middle-of-the road" type artists
Progressive rock	Combination of free form and AOR; stations with this format often do not have a playlist
Religious	Basically block programming (of half-hour and one-hour segments) featuring religious shows; more evangelical than gospel format
Rock	See AOR (album-oriented rock)
Spanish	Geared to Hispanic audiences; Spanish-speaking; plays Latin music; such a common format it is not classified as ethnic
Talk	Interviews, audience call-ins, information, sports, etc.
Top 40	High rotation of current hit singles, also recurrents and oldies; limited playlist

styles of music. Music is by its nature an emotional experience, to which labels cannot easily be attached. But stations have proliferated, fractionalizing the audience, and hence the attempt to categorize their programming styles.

Forms PA, RE, SR, TX, VA. *See* COPYRIGHT REGISTRATION CLASSIFICATION SYSTEM.

Freebie. A record or tape given free to accounts for ordering a certain quantity of the same merchandise. For example, a retailer may get one free album (freebie) for every ten it orders. This serves to encourage dealers to purchase large quantities of product without giving them a cash discount.

Fusion. Term that refers to the blending of elements from two or more distinct musical styles to form a musical composition or genre of music that is a combination of these elements. Hybrids are formed, for example, from the fusion of country and rock, jazz and rock, folk and rock, Latin and soul, country and pop, and pop/rock/disco.

G

Gold Record Awards. Since 1958, the RECORDING INDUSTRY ASSOCIATION OF AMERICA, INC. (RIAA) has sponsored Gold Record Awards for recordings that achieve certain minimum sales under criteria it sets forth. Awards are given for Gold Singles and Gold Albums, and the criteria for certification have undergone various changes since the original standards were set.

To qualify for a Gold Award, a *single* must achieve a minimum sale of 1 million copies and an *album* (discs and/or their counterparts on prerecorded tape) must amass a sale of 500,000 units° (multi-record or tape sets are considered as 1 unit). Certification is based on domestic sales of units shipped and results from a sales-figure audit conducted by RIAA through an independent accounting firm. For recordings released on or after January 4, 1980, sales audits may be requested and "gold" certifications issued only after a single or album has been in release for 60 days (this post-qualification delay allows the awards to reflect more realistically early net sales by minimizing instances of subsequent returns, netting sales below the minimum levels required for certification).

Any company in the recording industry—whether or not a member of RIAA—may apply for certification. Audits and award plaques are billed at virtual cost as an RIAA industry service. Recordings are certified "gold" on a year-round basis.

°Thus an album that sells 250,000 LPs, 125,000 8-track tapes, and 125,000 cassettes may qualify for Gold Award certification.

History. Originally (in 1958), Gold Record Awards for singles were based on 1 million units shipped, but for albums they were based on dollar sales figures, because the suggested retail list price of new albums at that time ranged from 99¢ to $4.98. The criterion for a Gold Record Award for an album was $1 million of the manufacturer's sales based on 50% of list price. For example, for a record that listed at $4, $2 would be 50% of the list price and therefore 500,000 units needed to be sold to attain the $1 million sales figure and qualify for a Gold Award.

With the boom in sales of prerecorded tapes in the late 1960s, the criterion for certification was changed. In 1968, the standard for albums (combined discs and tape counterparts) became $1 million based at 33⅓% of list price. RIAA's board of directors later decided to base Gold Record Awards on a unit count for all recordings released on or after January 1, 1975 (this is as stated above, except without the post-release qualification delay; the post-qualification delay was originally set as 120 days, effective July 1, 1979, and later changed as described above). For all albums/tapes released prior to 1975, RIAA certification is made under the old standards.

The concept of golden disc awards precedes the first certification by RIAA. It is believed that the first "gold record" award ever given by a bona fide record company in recognition of outstanding sales was that presented by RCA Victor to Glenn Miller on February 10, 1942, to commemorate the sales of 1.2 million achieved for his orchestra's recording of "Chattanooga Choo Choo" on RCA's Bluebird label. Miller receive a gold-lacquered stamper. Many recordings released previous to this were reportedly million sellers, though they were honored by the presentation of other ornaments or not at all.

Many record companies began presenting their own golden disc awards for exceptional sales—probably as a publicity/promotion tool—but they generally would not disclose the number of discs sold nor was there a system to verify their sales claims, and the actual amounts of such sales became the object of speculation. This situation seemed to get out of hand and there developed a need for a uniform industry-wide certification program.

This need was satisfied in 1958 when RIAA initiated its program, conferring Gold Record Awards on 4 singles and 1 album. Not all record companies would allow RIAA to audit their books in the early years of its program, and certain hits did not receive RIAA certification. Through the years, most record companies have acceded to the audit.

See also GOLD RECORD AWARDS; Appendix J.

Gospel Music. *See* POPULAR MUSIC.

Gospel Music Association (GMA). An industrywide professional association whose objective is to promote gospel music.

Membership. GMA has two types of membership—trade and associate. Trade membership is available to persons who derive a portion of their income from gospel music. This type of membership is divided into several categories, including artists, musicians, composers, talent agency/artist management, promoters, performing rights organizations, and trade press. Associate membership is open to anyone who is interested in and supports gospel music. There are annual dues for both types of membership.

Programs and Activities. To achieve its objective, GMA publicizes gospel music through several mediums, including television, radio, concerts, fairs, and trade and consumer press. Consequently it serves as the public spokesman for the gospel music industry.

GMA also honors top gospel artists, songwriters, and companies through its Dove Awards, which it has presented annually since 1969. Categories of awards include Gospel Song of the Year, Gospel Songwriter of the Year, and Male and Female Gospel Vocalist. GMA sponsors the Gospel Music Hall of Fame Research Library and Hall of Fame Museum, dedicated respectively to the documentation and growth of gospel music, and to its recognition. It publishes an annual directory that contains essential data on the top gospel publishers, record companies, and artists.

History. The Gospel Music Association was founded in 1964 for the purpose of providing gospel music industry participants with a common ground to discuss problems, ideas, and goals of gospel music. GMA is based in Nashville.

See PROFESSIONAL ASSOCIATIONS AND EDUCATIONAL ORGANIZATIONS.

Grammy Awards. Prizes of merit given annually in the United States by the NATIONAL ACADEMY OF RECORDING ARTS AND SCIENCES (NARAS, RECORDING ACADEMY) to honor the achievements of creative contributors in the recording field. Grammys are awarded in many different categories to recording artists, producers, composers and songwriters, arrangers, conductors, engineers, album cover art directors, album note writers, and others.

Only eligible active members of NARAS may vote—thus these are awards based on peer recognition. The only criterion members are urged to use in voting is artistic excellence; sales and other criteria are not to influence decisions. The Grammys, considered to be awards of great prestige, are presented at a ceremony which is nationally televised.

Voting Procedure. The Grammy Award voting procedure extends over several months. The process comprises basically three stages: entering, nominating, and final voting.

Entering. Each year members of NARAS and record companies are mailed entry forms on which to list recordings released during the awards eligibility year that they feel are worthy of being considered for a Grammy the following year. The Academy then screens entries to ensure that the recordings were released during the eligibility period and that each has been entered into its proper category.

Nominating. After this procedure, copies of the list (called the Pre-Nominations List) are sent to each voting member of the Academy for their first round of voting. The list may contain thousands of entries, placed in many different categories. Voting members are those who have been actively engaged in making creative contributions to recordings.

Members may cast their nomination votes in four general categories—Record of the Year, Album of the Year, Song of the Year, and Best New Artist—and in a limited number of specialized fields, such as Pop, Rock, R & B, Jazz, Country, Classical, etc. For certain categories, such as arranging, engineering, producing, album packaging, album notes, historical repackaging, and jazz, the nominations come from special committees of members who qualify for membership in those crafts and whose selection has been approved by their individual chapters and the national trustees.

Final Voting. Lists of final nominations in all categories are next sent to all active (voting) members of the Academy. Again, to induce members to concentrate on those fields with which they are most familiar and qualified to judge, they may vote only in a limited number of categories. All members, however, may vote in the four general categories (as stated above).

All voting from the Pre-Nominations List and in the second and final round is by secret ballot in mailings supervised by an independent accounting firm which tallies the votes secretly. Nominations are announced in press conferences several weeks prior to the Grammy Awards ceremony. Outside the accounting firm, no one knows the results of the final round of voting to select winners until the sealed envelopes are opened for the first time during the awards ceremony.

Awards Categories. The Grammys are awarded in several categories, which vary in both number and type from year to year (some are deleted and new ones added). A list of Grammy winners appears in Appendix B.

Grand Rights. *See* DRAMATICO-MUSICAL COMPOSITION.

H

Hardware. Any equipment or equipment system used to reproduce or otherwise communicate audio or audiovisual material contained in a program source.

Examples of hardware include turntables, amplifiers, speakers, tape decks, and videocassette players.

See SOFTWARE.

Harry Fox Agency, Inc., The (HFA). A MECHANICAL RIGHTS AGENCY, The Harry Fox Agency licenses to users of music the mechanical and synchronization rights of the musical compositions of its affiliated music publishers. HFA is the largest mechanical rights agency in the United States and is a wholly owned subsidiary of the NATIONAL MUSIC PUBLISHERS' ASSOCIATION (NMPA).

HFA represents music publishers in connection with the mechanical reproduction of their copyrights—i.e., in phonograph records and audio tapes—as well as their use in motion pictures. It issues licenses under customary industry terms or under a publisher's specific instructions when directed. The Fox Agency can also represent a publisher in certain foreign territories with respect to collecting mechanical royalties, provided such publisher has not previously entered into a subpublishing agreement with a local (foreign) publisher or has not become a direct adherent of a local society.

Commissions. For its services, HFA charges commissions from royalties and fees it collects on behalf of publishers. Its commissions for licensing a copyright are as follows: for mechanical reproduction (e.g., phonograph records and tapes), 3.5%; for recording for radio broadcast purposes (e.g., audio tapes for syndicated radio shows and commercials) and background music, 10%; for television films, 10%; for use in TV commercials, 10% with a ceiling of $2,000; for use in theatrical films, 10% with a ceiling of $150.°

Distribution of Mechanical Royalties. Under HFA's mechanical (phonorecord) license, royalties are due from record companies on a quarterly basis. These royalties are likewise distributed to copyright owners on a quarterly basis. HFA periodically audits the books of the record manufacturers to verify the accuracy of their quarterly accounting.

Record Licenses. The license HFA issues on behalf of music publishers to record companies for making and distributing commercial recordings for private use varies from the compulsory license as follows: Licensees account quarterly and pay royalties on the basis of records made and distributed, notices need not be served or filed as required by the law, and annual and monthly statements of account are not required. HFA's license provides for royalty payments at the full statutory rate (the standard voluntary mechanical license). A licensee, however, may negotiate this rate with the copyright owner [*see* COMPULSORY/ MECHANICAL LICENSES (PHONORECORDS)].

Foreign Affiliations. The Harry Fox Agency maintains working relationships with various foreign mechanical rights licensing societies. This provides representation for the li-

---

° These commissions are current as of 1981 and are subject to change as economic conditions dictate.

censing of mechanical rights in such countries for U.S. publishers who have not made sub-publishing agreements with foreign publishers. The mechanical royalties a publisher collects in this way are the gross earnings less the local society's fee and Fox's 3.5% commission.

Obtaining a Mechanical License from HFA. Record licenses are issued by The Harry Fox Agency on behalf of publishers upon request. To obtain a license to make and distribute for private (home) use commercial recordings embodying a musical composition owned by an HFA client, the following information should be submitted: the name and address of the person or company to whom the license is to be issued; the title, writer, and publisher of the composition; the record number; the performing artist; the playing time of the record (in minutes and seconds); and the release data of the record. HFA then issues a license that becomes effective upon signing by the licensee.

History. In recognizing the need for a clearinghouse that publishers could use in licensing music copyrights for mechanical reproduction and synchronization, NMPA established in 1927 what later became known as The Harry Fox Agency, named after the man under whose direction it began to operate in 1938. Over the years, it has grown as a mechanical rights agency, to license, by 1981, catalogs of approximately 70% of all bona fide U.S. music publishers.

High-Performance Analog Recordings. Recordings made on conventional tape recorders that produce better sound quality than regular records because of certain practices adopted in the recording and manufacturing processes. Great care is given to the production and equipment used to make them (microphone selection and placement, console, etc.) and the recorder may be run at a very high speed during recording. In the manufacturing process, master lacquers are cut at half speed to extend high-frequency response, superior vinyl is used, there is detailed inspection, and exceptional care is taken in pressing the discs.

See AUDIOPHILE RECORD.

Hook. A repetitive phrase in a song or recording that "grabs" the listener's attention. Most commonly, the hook is a line containing both melody and lyrics—the melody being the catchiest, most infectious part of the tune and the lyrics stating the point or message of the song (often being or incorporating the title).

The hook is usually the song's chorus, but it may also come in the form of a chord progression, instrumental line, riff, rhythmic idea, groove, or beat, and there may be two or more different hooks in the same song or recording. A hook repeats itself at various intervals throughout the song. It literally "hooks" the listener's attention and is the part one remembers most.

I

Images (Recording Artists). People tend to associate recording artists known to them with a particular image. An image may be perceived because of any of a number of factors (as stated below), but the point at hand is that whatever image the artist does project is important, as an image may serve the purpose of establishing or reinforcing a public identification for the artist and enhancing and sustaining his career. Some artists sell records successfully without media visibility and an image, but most of these find their careers short-lived. Because artists seek mass popularity and career longevity, and images are a factor in these, particularly with new and developing artists, images are often devised carefully and plans made and implemented to get people to view the artist in this light.

An artist will project a certain image based on the style of his music, the particular songs he performs, his age, sex, color, physical appearance, personality, his name and reputation, and his stage presence during concert and television appearances. Consequently these should be considered when creating an image for the artist. Other factors include the artist's career goal, personal life, education, tour plans, and target audience.

Images may be devised by any combination of the following: the artist, his personal manager, agent, record company (i.e., artist development and publicity departments), and public relations firm. Publicity departments and public relations firms function to support the artist's projection of an image by promoting it through the media. An established artist will already have a defined image and it may not

be necessary to further cultivate this. Some experienced artists, however, pursue a new direction in their career or desire a more contemporary image, and thus one must be created and projected accordingly.

Immigration and Employment of Foreign Entertainers. It is the desire of many foreign individuals whose occupations are in the arts to work in the United States. This prospect is inviting to foreign artists not only for the obvious financial benefits they may realize but also for the chance to broaden their scope of popularity, the prestige of being recognized in the world's largest entertainment market, and the opportunity for greater artistic opportunity or freedom, particularly in the case of nationals who suffer artistic oppression in their homelands. Foreign entertainers seek employment in America in virtually all fields in, or related to, the performing arts, including concerts, phonograph recordings, television, radio, motion pictures, legitimate theater, dance, conducting, composing, songwriting, producing, arranging, and orchestrating.

Persons who are not citizens or nationals of the United States (i.e., "aliens") will enter in immigration categories where there are either no numerical limitations on the number of persons who may enter or where there are annual numerical restrictions. Immigrants admitted to the United States without numerical limitations are (1) "immediate relatives," that is, the children, spouse and parents of a citizen of the United States and (2) "special immigrants" including immigrants lawfully admitted to the United States for permanent residence who are returning from a temporary visit abroad and immigrants who were citizens of the U.S. applying for reacquisition of citizenship.

There are annual numerical limitations for those seeking entry into the United States in other categories. For any fiscal year there is a limit of 20,000 natives of any foreign single state who may enter and a total limitation of 290,000 for all such immigrants (170,000 for aliens born in any foreign state of the Eastern Hemisphere and 120,000 for aliens born in the Western Hemisphere).

Those who wish to immigrate to the United States, and must enter in categories where there are annual numerical limitations, are classified into certain categories known as "preferences" or the nonpreference category. They are as follows:

1. *First Preference*—the unmarried sons or daughters of U.S. citizens (divorced or widowed aliens are considered as unmarried)

2. *Second Preference*—the spouses and unmarried sons or daughters of permanent resident aliens

3. *Third Preference*—professionals with exceptional ability in the arts and sciences who will "substantially benefit prospectively the national economy, cultural interests, or welfare of the United States and whose services in the professions, sciences, or arts are sought by an employer in the United States"

4. *Fourth Preference*—the married sons or daughters of citizens of the United States

5. *Fifth Preference*—the brothers or sisters of citizens of the United States

6. *Sixth Preference*—persons capable of performing specified skilled or unskilled labor, "not of a temporary or seasonal nature, for which a shortage of employable and willing persons exists in the United States"

7. *Non-Preference*— other immigrants such as aliens with labor certifications and investors who meet certain criteria.

With respect to the above the U.S. Immigration and Naturalization Service defines a "child" as "an unmarried person under 21 years of age who is a legitimate child, or a stepchild; provided the child has not reached the age of 18 years at the time the marriage creating the status of stepchild occurred. . . ." Also, if the contracting parties to a marriage ceremony are not physically in the presence of each other, the 'marriage' is not recognized, generally speaking, for immigration purposes, unless the marriage was consummated after the ceremony."

If a person seeking to immigrate to the United States does not have an immediate relative (as defined above) or does not fall into the first, second, fourth or fifth preference (also as described above) or is not a refugee, he will seek to enter as a third or sixth preference immigrant or as a non-preference immigrant. Responsibility is placed upon the intending immigrant to obtain a "Labor certification" from the U.S. Department of Labor before a visa may be issued. This certification establishes that (a) there are not sufficient workers who are able, willing, qualified (or equally qualified in the case of aliens who have exceptional ability in the arts or sciences or who are members of the teaching profession) and available where the alien is to work and (b) such employment will not adversely affect the wages and working conditions of workers similarly employed in the U.S.

To support a claim of exceptional ability in the arts or sciences documentary evidence supporting the claim should be submitted. The evidence "may testify to the universal acclaim and either national or international recognition accorded the alien, show that he has received a nationally or internationally recognized prize or award or won a nationally or internationally recognized competition for a specific product or performance or for outstanding achievement." For example, critical reviews and newspaper and trade journal acclaims or reports of concert and record sale earnings may be submitted.

Aliens who work in the music business may also attempt to obtain a Labor certification under the other regulations of the U.S. Department of Labor. The Department of Labor promulgates lists known as "schedules" of professions and occupations for which it will (or will not) issue labor certifications in advance of a job offer. There is a Group II of the Labor Department's Schedule A available to aliens (except those in the performing arts) in the sciences or arts who have been practicing their science or art for a minimum of one year prior to the application for labor certification who intend to practice their profession or job in the United States. This category may be used then, by songwriters, composers, record producers, arrangers, and orchestrators. Under Group II an alien must have international recognition. Having hits in two or more countries for example, may satisfy this requirement. Documentary evidence testifying to the international acclaim accorded the alien should be submitted.

Aliens who enter the United States in any of the categories described above obtain *immigrant* status, which means the alien is a "permanent resident" of the United States (permanent residents are issued the so-called "green card," which actually is no longer green).

Aliens may also enter and work in the United States by obtaining one of the non-immigrant (temporary) visa statuses. A non-immigrant work visa is available to an alien artist having a residence in a foreign country which he does not intend to abandon in what is known as H-1 and H-2 categories.

H-1 Petition. Aliens of distinguished merit and ability who desire to come to the United States temporarily to perform services of an exceptional nature may submit an H-1 petition. Allegations of exceptional ability should be supported by affidavits attesting to and describing the extent of the ability, executed by an appropriate officer of the firm or organization wherein the artist acquired or performed

such ability, such as a record company, an agency, etc., or by critics or other artists of renown.

H-2 Petition. Aliens coming temporarily to the United States to perform temporary services or labor may file an H-2 petition. Attached to the H-2 petition must be a certification from the Department of Labor indicating that qualified applicants in the United States are not available and that employment of the alien will not adversely affect wages and working conditions of U.S. workers similarly employed. A concert tour or series of nightclub engagements would be considered of a temporary nature and could be the basis of an H-2 application.

U.S. Laws and Government Agencies. The law that regulates the entry of aliens into the United States is the Immigration and Nationality Act and the federal agencies involved with immigration are the Immigration and Naturalization Service of the United States Department of Justice; the Department of State; and the Department of Labor.

Denied Admissions. There are certain restrictions that prohibit aliens from entering the U.S. These deal with deficiencies in moral, mental, and physical standards and include drug addicts and chronic alcoholics. Also, an alien's past criminal conviction may prevent his admission.

Filing Petitions. An alien abroad seeking admission to the U.S. as an immigrant to engage in permanent employment may file a petition at his nearest American consulate or Immigration and Naturalization Service office abroad. Officers there will administer the oath or affirmation, where necessary, and provide the address of the Immigration and Naturalization Service office to which the petition should be submitted. If the alien is in the U.S., he should take or mail the completed petition to the nearest office of the Immigration and Naturalization Service.

A third-preference petition may be filed by

the alien himself or by any person on his be-half. It does, however, require an accompany-ing offer of employment. A sixth-preference petition can be filed by the employer only. If the petition is executed in the U.S., the com-pleted petition may be taken or mailed to the office of the Immigration and Naturalization Service having jurisdiction over the intended place of residence of the third-preference alien or over the intended place of employ-ment of the sixth-preference alien.

Nonimmigrant (H-1 and H-2) petitions must be filed with the office of the Immigration and Naturalization Service having jurisdiction over the area in which at least part of the ser-vices will be performed (these petitions must be executed and filed in duplicate). The H-2 petitioner may apply for labor certification by placing a job order with the local office of the state employment service serving the area of proposed employment. There are Immigration and Naturalization Service offices in many American cities and in certain cities in foreign countries around the world.

Importer (Records and Tapes). A Whole-saler who brings into the country for resale records and tapes purchased from a foreign source. The company buys directly from for-eign manufacturers and wholesalers and re-sells the product to domestic retailers. Imports (with the exception of budget records and tapes) are customarily high-priced products in a retailer's catalog. Companies import records and tapes by air or sea and usually pay for the shipping costs and import duty.

See also Exporter (Records and Tapes).

Income, Sources of. Individuals and compa-nies in the music business may earn both do-mestic and foreign income from various sources that are directly or indirectly related to their main area of musical or business con-centration. For various participants this may be as follows:

Recording Artist
Direct: Record/tape sales (including sales by the record company's *licensees*—see *Record Company* below).
Other: Live performances, arranging, song-writing, music publishing, television appear-ances, acting, merchandising tie-ins, endorse-ments.

Record Producer
Direct: Producing (royalty basis on record and tape sales or flat fee, or both).
Other: Arranging, songwriting, music pub-lishing.

Arranger
Direct: Arranging, scoring.
Other: Producing, songwriting, music pub-lishing, copying.

Songwriter
Direct: Songwriting (a song has various sepa-rate sources of income—see *Music Publisher* below).
Other: Arranging, producing, music publish-ing.

Music Publisher
Direct: Music publishing income—perform-ance royalties, mechanical royalties, print roy-alties, synchronization fees, license fees for other uses of the copyright (jingles, posters, etc.); there may also be publishing income from foreign licensees (subpublishers).
Other: Producing.

Musician/Singer
Direct: Recording sessions (records, jingles, television, motion pictures), live engagements (club dates, concerts, etc.).
Other: Producing, arranging, songwriting, music publishing.

Record Company
Direct: Record/tape sales (to wholesalers and retailers), licensing of masters (to record/ tape clubs, record merchandising companies, film producers, foreign labels, etc.).
Other: Distribution of other labels' products, merchandising tie-ins, record/tape manufac-

turing, music publishing, owning recording studios, retail record/tape outlets, etc.

Income from a Hit Record. This entry will consider the income earned by the recording artist and songwriter and music publisher from hypothetical examples.

Recording Artist Income. As an example of what a recording artist would earn in a practical situation from sales of his records and tapes assume the following:

- artist's royalty rate for singles: 8%
- artist's royalty rate for LPs and prerecorded tapes: 8% on first 250,000 units sold, 9% on next 250,000, and 10% thereafter
- payment to artist based upon 90% of sales
- retail list price of singles: $1.49
- retail list price of LPs: $7.98
- retail list price of prerecorded tapes: $8.98
- sales of single: 250,000 units
- sales of LPs: 300,000 units
- sales of prerecorded tapes: 50,000 units
- packaging deduction for LPs: 10%
- packaging deduction for prerecorded tapes: 20%
- advance to artist: $20,000
- recording costs: $75,000

What is the artist's total earnings?

From the total royalty earned, the advance ($20,000) and the recording costs ($75,000) are recouped, leaving a net royalty of $113,980 for the artist. Of course, this royalty is received by the artist in different amounts over a period of time as sales occur over an extended period. Record companies typically render royalty statements and checks to artists on a semiannual basis. It is also customary for

labels not to remit the full amount due the artist at the close of the royalty period as contracts provide for the company to withhold a certain percentage of royalties due for "reserves" (for returns of seconds). For further explanation of artist royalties and other terms *see* RECORDING ARTIST/RECORD COMPANY CONTRACT.

Songwriter and Music Publisher Income. In the United States, songwriters and music publishers generally split all income earned from uses of a song equally (an exception might be with respect to print royalties). As an example of what a songwriter and music publisher could earn in a practical situation, the royalties from record sales will be considered.

Assume that a song is recorded and released as a single and in an LP and prerecorded tape. Also assume that the single sells 600,000 units, the LP 400,000 units, and the prerecorded tape 100,000 units. What is the mechanical royalty earned?

A musical composition is usually licensed to a record company by the copyright owner at the full statutory rate [*see* COMPULSORY/MECHANICAL LICENSES (PHONORECORDS)]. For this example it will be assumed that the record company licensed the song at a rate of $.04 per unit sold (the rate is generally the same for sales in all configurations—single, LP, or tape).

In accordance with this example, one million units total embodying the song are sold at a rate of $.04. Thus the total mechanical royalty is $40,000. This royalty is remitted by the

Configuration	Royalty rate	Retail list price	Packaging deduction	Balance after packaging deduction	Royalty per unit sold	90% of units sold	Total Royalty
singles	8%	$1.49	—	$1.49	$.119(8%×$1.49)	180,000	$ 21,420
LPs	8%	$7.98	10%	$7.182(7.98-.798)	$.575(8%×$7.182)	225,000	$129,375
LPs	9%	$7.98	10%	$7.182	$.646(9%×$7.182)	45,000	$ 29,070
prerecorded tapes	8%	$8.98	20%	$8.082(8.98-.898)	$.647(8%×$8.082)	45,000	$ 29,115
							$208,980

record company to the publisher which in turn remits to the songwriter his portion; thus each party would earn $20,000. If the publisher is affiliated with a MECHANICAL RIGHTS AGENCY, such representative would deduct its commission before remitting to the publisher its collections. With respect to this example, if the agency's fee is 3%, then it would deduct $1,200 and remit the balance, $38,800, to the publisher. The publisher and songwriter would earn $19,400. Of course, this royalty is received by the copyright owner over a period of time as sales occur over an extended period. Record companies typically render statements and mechanical royalties to copyright owners on a quarterly basis and withhold from earnings a certain portion for "reserves" for returns of records.

Independent Record Company. *See* RECORD COMPANY.

Independent Record Producer. *See* RECORD PRODUCER.

Infringement of Copyright. *See* COPYRIGHT INFRINGEMENT.

Instrument Folio. *See* PRINTED MUSIC.

International Alliance of Theatrical Stage Employees and Moving Picture Machine Operators of the U.S. and Canada (IATSE). *See* CONCERT.

International Confederation of Societies of Authors and Composers (CISAC). CISAC is an international association of performing rights organizations and music publishers which serves to establish principles for the collection and distribution of performance royalties by societies throughout the world, strengthen copyright protection on an international level, and protect the rights of compos-

ers, songwriters, and lyricists. ASCAP, BMI, and SESAC are members of CISAC; NMPA is an associate member.

The systems used by CISAC performing rights society members to determine the allocation of performance royalties to publishers and writers vary with each and are subject to change by the local societies.

CISAC adopted the following rule in 1978 in conjunction with BIEM: For a music publisher to be admitted as a member of CISAC, all its subpublication agreements, whether they relate to an entire catalog or a specific work, must be for a minimum of 3 years. The 3-year minimum is viewed as the least possible reasonable period for the economic operation of the societies and also for the subpublisher to demonstrate its ability to manage the agreement efficiently and profitably. Subpublishing agreements for less than 3 years will be treated by the societies as if they did not exist.

See INTERNATIONAL SUBPUBLISHING AGREEMENT.

International Copyright Relations. The right to secure statutory protection for intellectual and artistic properties in countries throughout the world has long been an issue involving legal, political, moral, and social aspects. The earliest copyright laws of most nations limited statutory protection to their own citizens. Denmark, in 1828, and England, in 1838, granted copyright protection for certain nonresident authors on a "reciprocal" basis,° but it wasn't until the first Berne Union in 1886 that a multinational convention permitted nationals of countries that were signatories to the treaty to enjoy reciprocal copyright protection in all other member countries.

°A reciprocal basis generally provides that a work first published in one nation receives the same protection and treatment as if first published in the other nation concerned.

Formal copyright relations between different nations may exist by virtue of bilateral arrangements, proclamations, and/or international copyright conventions to which many countries may belong. Not all countries with statutory copyright laws, however, belong to the various conventions that exist, as a convention may, for example, be an exponent of certain ideologies to which a particular country might not adhere, or may be geographically restricted.

The United States has copyright relations with many independent nations throughout the world via bilateral treaties, presidential proclamations, and common international copyright conventions. Hence American musical compositions, sound recordings, and other artistic works enjoy copyright protection in many foreign countries. In addition, there are some countries that have not established copyright relations with the United States but honor obligations acquired under formal political status.°

This entry examines the major international copyright conventions and other arrangements that affect the status of U.S. copyrights in foreign nations.

Berne Union. The Berne Union† was formed in 1886 for the purpose of protecting literary and artistic works of authors. Since its inception, it has undergone several revisions to keep its provisions modern. Adherents to the convention may be a party to the texts of one or more of these revisions; countries with pre-existing memberships are not compelled to sign further revisions and new members are not obligated to adhere to earlier texts. Despite its various revisions, there is only one convention under the Berne Union and new members can adhere only to the last revised

text. Berne members include all the European nations except the Soviet Union and include also a large number of African, Asian, and Latin American states.

Conventions are commonly referred to by the name of the city where the revision occurred. The cities and year dates of these are Berlin (1908), Rome (1928), Brussels (1948), Stockholm (1967), and Paris (1971).

Despite the many revised provisions, there are certain basic features of the Berne Convention. Principally, these are that each country which belongs to the convention shall provide copyright protection to authors of other member countries on the same terms it grants its own citizens and that nationals of countries not belonging to the convention shall secure the same rights granted to authors of member countries when their works are published first or "simultaneously" in a member country ("Simultaneously" under the Rome text means publication must occur on the same day in both the nonmember nation and a convention nation; under the Brussels text and also under the last revised text, "simultaneous" publication may consist of an interval of 30 days between publication in the nonmember nation and in the convention nation.)

Other features of the Berne Union include the non-necessity for formalities regarding copyright notice and registration (i.e., lack of notice or registration will not invalidate the copyright); a general minimum term of copyright protection in member countries for life of the author plus 50 years (except for anonymous and pseudonymous works, for which the term is 50 years after the work has been lawfully made available to the public); and the exclusive right of creators of musical compositions to authorize recordings and arrangements of their works and the public performance of such recordings.

The United States is not a member of the Berne Convention—certain provisions of the

° An example, at this writing, is Thailand, which appears to have had a bilateral agreement since 1921.
† Its official name is International Union for the Protection of Literary and Artistic Works.

U.S. law's requirement to comply with formalities to secure copyright seem to be contrary to areas of the convention. Differences include copyright notice and the concept of "moral rights of authors" under the convention. The moral right of an author includes his right to be identified with his work regardless of contractual provisions and the right to object to any distortion, mutilation, or other modification of the work which would be damaging to his reputation. The U.S. statute does not recognize these moral rights, although they are frequently the subject of litigation on noncopyright bases—i.e., right of publicity, unfair competition, etc.

U.S. works, including musical compositions, are often published "simultaneously" in the United States and Canada (an adherent to the Rome text of the Berne Convention) and consequently enjoy copyright protection in convention countries (such a procedure is sometimes called the "back door to protection"). In such an instance there would probably be an indication of compliance with the Berne Convention requirement by the printing on the work of the statement: "Published simultaneously in Canada."

Membership in the Berne Convention is acquired by a nonmember's presenting written notice of adherence to procedural requirements of the convention to the director general of the World Intellectual Property Organization, which administers the convention. Membership is automatic and does not require the approval of member countries. Membership may be terminated by notification to the director general.

Conventions of the Western Hemisphere. There are various international copyright conventions limited to nations of the Western Hemisphere. These are the Montevideo Copyright Convention (1889), Mexico City Treaty (1902), Rio de Janeiro Convention (1906), Buenos Aires Convention (1910), Havana Convention (1928), and Pan-American Union in Washington (1946).

Of most significance to the United States is the Buenos Aires Convention of 1910. This has been signed by 18 countries of the western hemisphere, including the United States. This treaty provides that authors of any contracting country who have secured copyright in their own country will enjoy in any other contracting country the rights it accords its own works, provided a statement indicating the reservation of property rights appears on published copies. To comply with this requirement, publishers print the statement "All Rights Reserved" or "Derechos Reservados" on copyrighted works (the status of unpublished works under the BAC is unclear).

There are no formality requirements under the BAC except as required by the country where the work is first published. It also prescribes no minimum period of protection. Although the treaty provides protection for the reproduction rights of authors, past court decisions have held that where mechanical reproduction rights of musical compositions are concerned, such right is not secured by virtue of being a member of this convention, but only where a specific presidential proclamation has been given in the country concerned.

Where conflict exists between provisions of the Universal Copyright Convention and the Buenos Aires Convention, UCC terms normally prevail.

Universal Copyright Convention. In 1952, the Universal Copyright Convention, sponsored by the United Nations Educational, Scientific and Cultural Organization (UNESCO), was signed at Geneva; it became effective on September 16, 1955. Created for the purpose of establishing international copyright relations on a different level than the Berne Union, it differs in two fundamental respects: compliance with certain, limited formalities for copyright protection is permitted by UCC members, and the minimum exclusive rights a member country accords to foreign authors need not be greater than the rights in grants to its own citizens, so long as protection is "adequate and effective."

Basic features of the UCC include the following: a participating country is required to extend the same copyright protection to foreign works that meet convention requirements as it accords its own domestic works (unpublished works are granted protection on the same basis); copyright formalities° in all member countries, if any, are satisfied by a notice consisting of the symbol ©, the copyright owner's name, and the year of first publication, placed on all copies published under authorization of the copyright owner (each contracting nation may, however, have different formalities its own nationals are required to satisfy for works published in its own territory or for works of nationals published elsewhere); the minimum term of copyright in participating nations must be the life of the author plus 25 years or 25 years from the date of first publication.

The United States has ratified the 1952 Geneva Convention, which entered into force with respect to the U.S. on September 16, 1955, and the 1971 Paris revision, which likewise became effective on July 10, 1974.

Phonogram Convention. Just after the last revisions of the Berne Convention and the UCC in Paris in 1971, a new convention was drafted in Geneva to provide international copyright protection for phonograms, or sound recordings. This treaty was called the Convention for the Protection of Producers of Phonograms Against Unauthorized Duplication of Their Phonograms, Geneva, 1971, and its purpose basically is to protect against "piracy."

°"Formalities" are procedural requirements established by the statute that must be satisfied by a copyright owner in order to maintain full copyright protection of the work.

If the domestic laws of a contracting state to the Phonograms Convention require compliance with formalities as a condition of copyright protection, these requirements are considered satisfied if there appears on all authorized duplicates of the publicly distributed phonograms (or their containers) a notice consisting of: the symbol ℗; the year date of first publication (placed in such manner as to give reasonable notice of claim to protection); and the name, trademark, or designation of the producer (i.e., person or legal entity), his successor in title, or the exclusive licensee, if such identification does not appear on the duplicates or their containers.

A participating country is required to provide protection against the unauthorized duplication or importation of phonograms by offering protection through one or more of the following: a grant of copyright or other specified right, as the so-called neighboring rights; the laws of unfair competition; or penal sanctions.

Bilateral Copyright Arrangements and National Law. Bilateral copyright relations exist between the United States and many foreign countries, some of which are not signatories to either the Universal or the Buenos Aires convention. In the United States, Presidential proclamation may accord to foreign nationals

International Copyright Relations*

Country	Convention(s) Country Is a Party To				
	Berne	BAC	Phonogram	UCC	Bilateral†
Algeria				—	
Andorra				—	
Argentina	—	—	—	—	—
Australia	—		—	—	—
Austria	—			—	—
Bahamas	—			—	
Bangladesh				—	
Belgium	—			—	—
Benin	—				
Bolivia		—			
Brazil	—	—	—	—	—

International Copyright Relations* (cont'd)

Country	Berne	BAC	Phonogram	UCC	Bilateral†
Bulgaria	—			—	
Cameroon	—			—	
Canada	—			—	—
Central African Republic	—				
Chad	—				
Chile	—	—	—	—	—
China					—
Colombia		—			
Congo	—				
Costa Rica	—	—		—	—
Cuba				—	—
Cyprus	—				
Czechoslovakia	—		—	—	
Denmark	—		—	—	—
Dominican Republic		—			
Ecuador	—	—		—	
Egypt	—		—		
El Salvador			—		—
Fiji	—		—	—	
Finland	—		—	—	—
France	—		—	—	—
Gabon	—				
German Democratic Republic (GDR)	—			—	
Germany, Federal Republic of (FRG)	—		—	—	—
Ghana				—	
Greece	—			—	
Guatemala		—		—	
Haiti		—		—	
Honduras		—			
Hungary	—		—	—	—
Iceland	—			—	
India	—		—	—	—
Ireland	—			—	—
Israel	—		—	—	—
Italy	—		—	—	—
Ivory Coast	—				
Japan	—		—	—	
Kampuchia (Cambodia)				—	
Kenya			—	—	
Khmer Republic				—	
Laos				—	
Lebanon	—			—	
Liberia				—	
Libyan Arab Jamahiriya	—				
Liechtenstein	—			—	
Luxembourg	—		—	—	
Madagascar	—				
Malawi				—	
Mali	—				
Malta	—			—	
Mauritania	—				
Mauritius				—	
Mexico	—	—	—	—	—
Monaco	—		—	—	—
Morocco	—			—	
Netherlands	—		—	—	
New Zealand	—		—	—	
Nicaragua		—			
Niger	—				
Norway	—		—	—	
Pakistan	—			—	
Panama		—	—	—	
Paraguay	—			—	
Peru	—			—	
Philippines	—			—*	—
Poland	—			—	—
Portugal	—			—	
Romania	—			—	
Senegal	—			—	
South Africa	—				
Soviet Union				—	
Spain	—		—	—	—
Sri Lanka	—				
Sweden	—		—	—	—
Switzerland	—		—	—	—
Thailand	—				—
Togo	—				
Tunisia	—			—	
Turkey	—				
United Kingdom	—		—‡	—	—
United States		—	—	—	
Upper Volta	—				
Uruguay	—	—			
Vatican City (Holy See)	—		—	—	
Venezuela				—	
Yugoslavia	—			—	
Zaire	—		—		
Zambia				—	

*UCC status undetermined by UNESCO. U.S. Copyright Office considers that UCC relations do not exist.

†This column indicates those countries which have bilateral copyright relations with the United States by virtue of a proclamation or treaty.

‡Includes its territories: Bermuda, Cayman Islands, Gibraltar, Hong Kong, Isle of Man, Montserrat, the Seychelles, St. Lucia, and the Virgin Islands.

the rights granted to U.S. citizens if their respective countries grant American authors the same protection they allow their own citizens.

Before the United States joined the UCC in 1955, bilateral arrangements were commonly made to protect U.S. authors in certain countries. Such arrangements may take precedence over UCC provisions both countries might have adhered to later.

Some countries that have no formal copyright relations with the United States grant protection to U.S. works under the provisions of their domestic laws. Where U.S. works are protected under bilateral arrangements or national laws, the extent and terms of protection vary from country to country.

International Federation of Producers of Phonograms and Videograms (IFPI).

Represents the sound and audiovisual recording industry throughout the world. Founded in 1933 in Rome, IFPI is concerned with noncommercial matters affecting the recording industry, primarily copyright protection and negotiating internationally with authors, composers, publishers, performers, broadcasting organizations, film producers, film distributors, and others.

Funded by its members, IFPI is noncommercial and nonprofitmaking. It has formed national groups in 29 countries and has nearly 600 member companies in 67 countries around the world. Three organizations—Recording Industry Association of America (RIAA), Federación Latinoamericana de Productores de Fonogramas y Videogramas (FLAPF), and Australian Record Industry Association (ARIA)—are affiliated to IFPI.

IFPI has consultative status with UNESCO, the World Intellectual Property Organization, and the Council of Europe, and an IFPI Common Market Association has consultative status with the EEC. This enables IFPI to promote the rights of phonogram and videogram producers, nationally and internationally.

IFPI's activities include persuading governments to adopt effective copyright legislation in countries where it does not exist or is inadequate. It is leading and coordinating the recording industry's attack on piracy and private copying of records, tapes, and videograms, and is pressing for international acceptance of the principle that a royalty should be paid on the sale of recording equipment and blank tape.

IFPI establishes guidelines for negotiations of standard contracts with copyright owners and performers, and works to increase the income collected from users of recordings for broadcasting and public performance (at this writing the United States does not have a performance right in sound recordings). IFPI also persuades governments to reduce sales taxes and custom duties on phonograms and videograms to facilitate free circulation between nations of what is recognized formally by UNESCO as cultural material.

International Master Recording Licensing Agreement.

It is in the interest of U.S. record companies to have their recordings released in foreign countries. Not all foreign countries are suitable markets for American product, but substantial profits may be earned from the major markets where American recordings are released with strategic planning and proper exploitation.

While international companies° have subsidiaries in many foreign territories, most record companies' operations are limited to a domestic basis. These smaller companies therefore *license* their catalogs or specific product for release abroad, either through a single *worldwide* (or *overall*) *deal* with an international (multinational) company, or on a

---

°Examples include CBS, EMI, MCA, Polygram, RCA, and WEA.

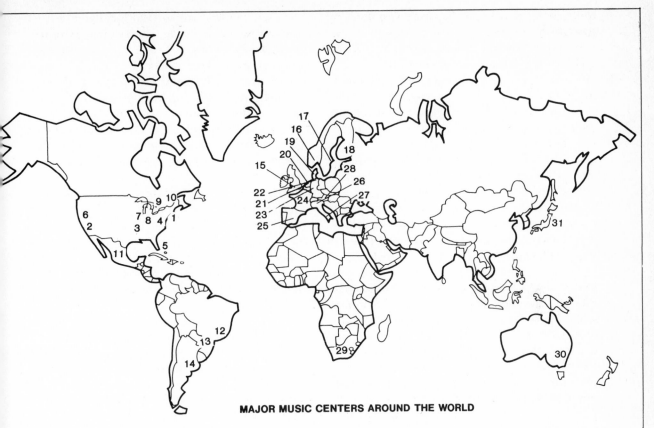

MAJOR MUSIC CENTERS AROUND THE WORLD

Key:
1. New York, U.S.A.
2. Los Angeles, U.S.A.
3. Nashville, U.S.A.
4. Philadelphia, U.S.A.
5. Miami, U.S.A.
6. San Francisco, U.S.A.
7. Chicago, U.S.A.
8. Detroit, U.S.A.
9. Toronto, Canada
10. Montreal, Canada
11. Mexico City, Mexico
12. Rio de Janeiro, Brazil
13. São Paulo, Brazil
14. Buenos Aires, Argentina
15. London, United Kingdom
16. Oslo, Norway
17. Stockholm, Sweden
18. Helsinki, Finland
19. Copenhagen, Denmark
20. Hilversum, Netherlands
21. Brussels, Belgium
22. Hamburg, West Germany
23. Munich, West Germany
24. Paris, France
25. Madrid, Spain
26. Milan, Italy
27. Rome, Italy
28. Vienna, Austria
29. Johannesburg, South Africa
30. Sydney, Australia
31. Tokyo, Japan

territory-by-territory basis with various local (foreign) companies.

Worldwide vs. Territory-by-Territory Deals. Worldwide deals (outside the country of origin) are made with international companies. These companies, with subsidiaries in important foreign record markets, obtain licensing rights to manufacture, advertise, distribute, and sell American labels' products in countries throughout the world. In countries where they do not have subsidiaries, distribution may occur via their own local licensees.

The advantages for a small record company to make a *worldwide deal* include the following: it is less costly to enter into one international agreement than to negotiate several sublicensing agreements; administration is simpler with a single liaison than with many separate licensees around the world; the licensor may enjoy the local resources and reputation associated with the international licensee; and the label of the licensor may be utilized on a worldwide basis. In general, the subsidiaries of international companies are powerful and can work a catalog effectively.

Disadvantages of a worldwide deal include these: there is a personal lack of contact with each of the sublicensees in the individual territories since the licensor essentially deals with the American headquarters of the international (consequently a licensor should, in making a worldwide deal, contractually provide for direct contact with subsidiaries and sublicensees); an international company might have an excellent branch in one country and a not so capable one in another; and advances may be cross-collateralized between territories.

In a *territory-by-territory deal,* the American licensor enters into individual licensing agreements with companies representing particular countries or territories. A local company may represent its own country or, in addition to its own, one or more nearby countries. The various foreign countries or territories (more than one country) commonly licensed for representing a record manufacturer's catalog are listed under INTERNATIONAL SUBPUBLISHING AGREEMENTS.

The advantages of this type of deal include the following: the licensor may maintain a closer working relationship with each foreign licensee; its total advances from all its licensees may be larger than a single one by an international company; it may obtain better representation and exploitation of its catalog since these individual companies may need the product more than the multinationals (which have sufficient amounts of their own product to deal with).

Disadvantages of a territory-by-territory deal are that it requires scrupulous investigation by the potential licensor to determine which company in each territory would best represent its product; it is somewhat more costly (i.e., additional legal fees, servicing each licensee with masters, artwork, information, etc.); and it is more inconvenient to deal with several licensees.

A common practice is for an "independent" American label to enter into a distribution agreement with a "major" record company to have its catalog distributed in the United States. It may be in the best interests for such a label to reserve the right to make its own licensing deals for countries outside the United States. New companies or those without substantial track records, however, may find that they have to give up worldwide rights to their product in entering into a distribution or label deal with an international company.

License Terms. Whether a deal is made on a worldwide or a territory-by-territory basis, there are certain basic terms that are included in the contract. Among these are the following:

Description of Product. The agreement should clearly define what product is included in the license. Does it include the entire catalog of all the artists on the label? If there are several labels within the company, does it include the catalogs of all? Does the licensee acquire the right to any new product the licensor acquires during the term of agreement? Licensors may provide that the acquisition of new catalog product is not included in the deal and make that the basis of a separate negotiation.

Rights Granted. The agreement should specify exactly what rights the licensor grants to the licensee. These normally include the rights to do the following in the territory covered by the agreement: manufacture, distribute, and sell records and tapes; publicly perform and advertise the product; use the name, biography, likeness, or other information regarding the artists involved (there may be warranties required that the licensor has the right to grant this on behalf of each artist); and license the product to local record clubs. Points of negotiation may include the rights of "coupling" (i.e., whether the licensee may include the licensor's masters on a COMPILATION ALBUM, a sampler album, etc.), whether the licensee has the right to sell product at budget or economy-line prices or for premium purposes, tour support for particular artists in the territory of release, as well as other provisions not included in the above.

A licensor may contractually stipulate that a licensee must sell front-line catalog product at its top-line price, and not at a lower one without its consent. Some licenses provide that the local company must withhold from issuing product at budget prices for a specified period of time (normally ranging from 1 to 3 years) after the release of the original product. Of course, it is in the interest of the licensee to recoup its advance (see below) and where it has been unable to obtain any "mileage" from a product at the full-line price, a contractual restriction may prevent it from profitably marketing a budget-line recording. Such restriction may be beneficial to the licensor if the licensor believes it can enter into another agreement for its catalog, so that such artists' new recordings will not have to compete with budget-line recordings of the same artist on a different label in the territory.

Duration of Agreement. The duration of a licensing agreement is negotiable and varies from contract to contract. While the general rule of thumb is for 3 years, some licensors seek shorter terms. Some licensors have granted, for example, an initial term of 1 year with options, or 15 months the first year. This grants 3 extra months to the licensee who may feel that it needs that extra time to better acquaint itself with the product, prepare artwork, advertising, and promotional materials, and make other preparations to market the catalog effectively.

A licensee may also request an additional minimum amount of time to exploit those products (masters) that it receives near the end of the agreement term—e.g., the last 6 or 9 months of the term. The licensee may therefore request a period of, say, 18 months from the time the masters are delivered to it, to exploit such product, even though the licensing period may have expired.

Sell-off Rights. A term granting the licensee the right to "sell off" those records and tapes that have been manufactured but remain unsold at the end of the term is included in foreign licensing agreements. This sell-off period commonly ranges from 6 months to 1 year. It may be prudent for the licensor to require a certification from an officer of the company (licensee), in either affidavit form or some form of sworn statement, stating how much inventory the company has and that no more manufacturing will be done.

As a measure of further caution, the licensor may contractually provide that if such inventory is sold during the sell-off period, its price must bear that of the regular retail list price.

This is to prevent "dumping" on the market for two reasons. First, it is quite possible that the licensor has already made a deal with a new licensee that includes the right to manufacture and distribute those very items; if the previous licensee still has the nonexclusive right to sell off inventory at reduced prices, this would interfere with the new licensee's selling efforts. Second, "dumping" may hurt the artist.

Royalty Rates. Royalties payable by foreign licencees are for sales of product times the royalty rate for the particular configuration less, in most instances, certain deductions. There may be deductions for packaging and tariffs, and royalties may be payable on sales of product ranging from 90% to 100% (*see* RE-CORDING ARTIST/RECORD COMPANY CONTRACT).

Royalty rates for sales of product by foreign licencees in their territories range from 7% to 18% of the suggested retail list price. The packaging deduction ranges from 10% to 20% of the retail list price (in Europe an amount is set by the international "mechanical rights" organization known as BIEM which companies may use). A packaging deduction of 5% of the retail sales price for singles is generally charged in foreign countries to cover two-color single covers. Royalties are usually paid on a semiannual or quarterly basis.

Consideration must also be given to whether the royalty the licensor receives (assuming it is from an American recording) includes the amount that has to be paid to the American Federation of Musicians' Phonograph Record Manufacturers Special Payments Fund and Music Performance Trust Fund, an amount based on the number of records sold. If contractual provision is not made for the licensee to pay the two AFM fund royalties, then the American licensor may be required to pay them from the income it receives from the foreign licensee. For example, if a licensor is receiving a 15% royalty rate on sales by its licensee in England, and the agreement does not specify the licensee is responsible for the AFM payments, the American licensor may, from the royalty received, have to pay the artist as well as make the necessary contribution to the AFM.

Advances. In making a territory-by-territory licensing agreement, the domestic label normally receives an advance from each licensee. These advances may vary considerably from territory to territory and the amounts are a matter of negotiation. In a worldwide agreement, advances are usually not allocated on a territory-by-territory basis by the international company. Rather, they are cross-collateralized, so that even with success of its catalog in one or more territories, the licensor will not see royalties above the advances received until the entire advance given by the licensee for all its territories is recouped. As stated above, this is a disadvantage for a licensor in entering into a worldwide agreement but in some cases licensors have been able to contractually prohibit such cross-collateralization of royalties.

In a worldwide deal with an international company, the licensor may negotiate separate advances from the different territories. For example, if the total foreign advance is $100,000, it might allocate $50,000 for the German-speaking countries, $20,000 for England, $20,000 for France, Belgium, and Holland, and $10,000 for Japan. Thus, if England is allocated $20,000 and $30,000 is earned, the licensor will receive an additional $10,000 and not have that extra money recouped from another territory's advance. In this way, the international licensee is forced to press each of its local companies to exploit the catalog. In a sense, this arrangement with a worldwide company is a territory-by-territory deal.

Advances are recoupable by the licensee from royalties earned, but in negotiating a licensing agreement, consideration should be given to whether, as in the case of a 3-year term, the advance is for all 3 years or on a yearly basis. Where there is a 1-year contract with options, the licensor will normally ask for additional advances beyond the first-year advance to exercise the options, which is the right of the licensee. A licensor may protect itself from the options clause not only by providing for a larger advance but by tying in the right to exercise the option with some success achieved by sales in the territory during the previous year.

If the advance is on a year-by-year basis, the contract should state whether the advances are recoupable from all royalties or from those earned on a yearly basis. It is in the interest of the licensor to have advances recouped from royalties earned within a stipulated period only so as to avoid for example, the following situation: A 3-year contract provides for a licensor to receive a $100,000 advance at the start of each year. At the end of the first year it is due an additional $25,000 royalty for that year. However, before the $25,000 is payable, the licensor receives its next $100,000 advance. When the statement of account finally arrives and shows first-year royalties of $125,000 and thus $25,000 due, there is not included the payment of $25,000 since the contract states that all advances are recoupable from all royalties. Hence the $25,000 is recoupable from the second $100,000 advance. The cautious licensor should then contractually stipulate that royalties are payable as of the date they are earned and cannot be offset by any advance paid in between.

Licensees normally protect themselves with regard to advances by including a provision in the contract that the licensor guarantee a certain amount of product to be delivered over the year or term of the agreement. Such a provision might state that if the masters are not delivered, the next advance is reduced on a prorated basis or that the contract may be terminated or that the term is extended until the minimum product is delivered.

Release Requirements. Licensors attempt to get a contractual guarantee from the licensee that it will release a particular percentage of the product licensed. This is less of a problem in English-speaking countries, or those where English-language records have nevertheless sold well (such as West Germany). However, in countries such as France, Italy, and Japan, the local licensees will desire the autonomy to determine which records should be released.

To protect itself from the possibility of a small number of records being released, there are certain formulas the American licensor can negotiate to determine a record's release in a territory. If, say, a record reaches a certain chart position in a U.S.. trade publication's chart (such as top 30 of the singles charts and top 40 of the LP charts), or if the artist hits the charts twice, or if a certain amount of the label's product hits the charts in particular areas, then the licensee must release those records or a percentage of that product in its territory.

Of course, it is in the interest of the licensee to release products to recoup its advances, but there may be an obligation the licensor has to an artist, particularly a superstar artist. In such case, the licensor may contractually provide for guaranteed releases of that artist's product. If the licensee demurs, the licensor may provide that if one or two records of a particular artist are not released, a reversionary right will free the licensor to make a deal with another company for that artist's product.

Such a reversionary right may be particularly important to the licensor and artist in foreign countries that are important record markets. The licensee may not be able to do an adequate job, as it handles lots of product, while there might be other companies in the territory that want and need the product.

Contracts may provide for foreign release of product simultaneously with that of the American release or within a couple of weeks of it, or even after a longer period, such as 18 months. This latter provision enables the foreign licensee to fully evaluate the record's success in American and estimate local expectations.

Manufacturing Materials. The licensee will audition American-manufactured recordings to determine which product it desires to manufacture and release in its territory. The American licensor then forwards the desired master tapes so that the foreign licensee may make the necessary parts to manufacture the records, or the very parts themselves, usually at actual cost. The licensee may also import negatives of the original album graphic materials. All manufacturing costs, shipping costs, and import duties are assumed by the licensee. Sometimes the foreign licensee will import large quantities of American-manufactured recordings for local distribution, though high tariff duties may tend to discourage such practice.

Limits on Free Records. It is customary for manufacturers in certain foreign countries to give away records to wholesalers and retailers who buy minimum quantities of goods from them. Since licensees do not pay royalties to licensors on free records, the American licensor may limit such distribution. This can be determined on a percentage basis or by a formula, such as 1 free record for every 5 sold.

Rights of Termination. Foreign master licensing agreements typically contain a clause providing for the American licensor to terminate such agreement if the licensee defaults in certain of its contractual obligations. For example, foreign licensing contracts commonly provide for semiannual payments and accountings to licensors, within certain time periods following June 30 and December 31 of each year. The licensor may desire a clause

providing it with the right to terminate a contract if the licensee is late in paying the royalties, when a bank or foreign currency conversion problem is not the cause. The prudent licensor may contractually provide for the foreign licensee to show evidence that it has sent to its bank the money to be transmitted to the American licensor. Another right of termination may relate to failure of the licensee to release a minimum number of records as contractually provided.

Other clauses may relate to bankruptcy and financial problems of the licensee. The licensor may agree, in consideration of the licensee's interests, to a clause that requires it to notify the licensee of any default and provides a period for the licensee to "cure" (remedy) such default. Provisions should be made as to whether an American or a local foreign court of law will be the forum for any controversies that arise from the contract. Naturally, each side will argue in favor of local jurisdiction and such point is a matter of negotiation.

Performance Right in Sound Recordings. In many countries throughout the world there exists a performance right in sound recordings. Under this practice, recording artists and record companies are compensated for the broadcast of recordings embodying their performances or masters. American licensors strive in negotiations to obtain a share of such receipts for airplay of their masters but foreign licensees may balk at sharing such local performance fees, since this practice does not exist in the United States (there have been efforts made in the U.S. to pass a bill that would create a performance right in sound recordings, but it has not, at this writing, been passed).

Logo. It should be predetermined on whose logo, or trademark, records will be released. The American licensor may simply desire a credit line. However, it is in the licensor's interest to have its logo, trademark, or name printed on the territorial records, not only for the prestige but to create an identity in case it ever decides to establish a local branch. The licensor's name and logo then should be registered for trademark and the licensor may seek to have the licensee pay for this. Often the label credits on a record include the name and logo of both licensee and licensor.

Copyright. The licensor should make sure their agreement provides for the licensee to put an appropriate copyright notice on the label to conform to the applicable local law providing copyright protection to the sound recording (as differentiated from the musical compositions contained on the recording).

Income Tax. Very often the licensee will ask for the right to deduct from the licensor's royalties certain income taxes that have to be withheld in the foreign country. The licensor may desire, therefore, to insert in the agreement a clause enabling the licensor to file a tax exemption form whereby the tax need not be withheld in that country as far as the licensor is concerned. Provision should be made for the licensee to process that tax exemption certificate and have it filed with the appropriate authorities so the licensor will not be subject to the tax withholding in the country. Alternatively, the U.S. licensor should obtain a foreign tax credit with the Internal Revenue Service in the event taxes are withheld.

Other Terms. Other contractual clauses normally relate to granting the licensor or its representative the right to audit the licensee's books and restraining the licensee from releasing local "cover" records of the same musical composition in its territory.

International Subpublishing Agreement.
Music is an art form that is universal. Thus it is not surprising for a song to enjoy simultaneous popularity in countries throughout the world, although lyrics often need to be translated. Indeed, songs have traditionally achieved success outside their country of origin, even long before developments in modern communication and technology. The market for popular music increased tremendously in scope, however, as the phonograph record became an international commodity, and the market continues to grow with the westernization of foreign cultures and standardization of tastes.

U.S. music publishers for a long time have exploited their wares in foreign countries, either via subsidiaries or through licensing arrangements with international or locally based companies. Today, a substantial portion of a music publisher's total income may be earned from foreign exploitation of its catalog. Of course, not all songs are adaptable to the various foreign markets, but those that have become particularly successful in the United States may be expected to be marketable in many countries. As may be observed, songs that achieve tremendous popularity in the United States are usually heard around the world. Additionally and also very important for U.S. publishers is the possibility that songs that have gone virtually unrecognized in America may enjoy tremendous success in foreign markets.

Aside from some very large companies,° most American music publishers do not have subsidiaries in foreign countries. Therefore, when a U.S. publisher without foreign subsidiaries wishes to have one or more copyrights from its catalog promoted and exploited abroad and have the moneys earned from uses of such songs collected in its behalf, it may enter into an agreement with a company that can provide these "services." Such an agreement is referred to as a *subpublishing agreement*, entered into by the licensor (originating publisher, copyright owner, or administering

---

°U.S. music publishers with foreign subsidiaries include April/Blackwood Music, Chappell Music, United Artists Music, and Warner Bros. Music.

publisher) and the licensee (subpublisher), which may be a local (foreign) publisher or an international publishing group.

Types of Subpublishing Agreements. Subpublishing agreements are generally of two types: (1) a *worldwide* deal (outside the country of origin), with an international company having branches in important music markets throughout the world; and (2) *territory-by-territory* deals with independent foreign music publishers in territories throughout the world. Such foreign publishers represent the U.S. copyrights in their own country or in a few countries comprising a particular "territory" (see below). Subpublishers may even, if contractually permitted, license the works to other publishers in countries included in the licensed territory (these latter publishers are called sub-subpublishers).

The subpublication agreement is akin to the INTERNATIONAL MASTER RECORD LICENSING AGREEMENT. Advantages and disadvantages of a worldwide vs. a territory-by-territory deal for licensing masters are discussed in that entry and these may be related to musical compositions and catalogs.

License Terms. Important terms of a subpublication contract, whether on a worldwide or a territory-by-territory basis, are usually the following:

Description of Copyrights. The agreement should clearly define what composition(s) or catalog is included in the license. In the case of a territorial deal, the licensor might divide up its catalog and license portions of it to subpublishers in various ways. For example, a publisher with a diverse catalog may license the country songs and jazz compositions to separate music publishers within the same territory. This is a matter of negotiation and is often used as a bargaining point in such negotiations.

Duration of Agreement. The duration (or "retention period") of subpublication contracts normally runs from 1 to 5 years, with 3 years as a common term. It is in the subpublisher's interest, of course, to have as long a term as possible and it will strive for this in negotiations (terms were once commonly negotiated to endure for the life of the copyright). It is the policy of some foreign performing rights societies to render payment (performance royalties) on material only where the assignment to the subpublisher is for a minimum period of time (*see* INTERNATIONAL CONFEDERATION OF SOCIETIES OF AUTHORS AND COMPOSERS).

The subpublication agreement should describe the local subpublisher's rights with respect to collecting and sharing in those royalties and license fees which accrue during the term but are not received until after the subpublication agreement expires. If a cutoff date is not established, a conflict could arise after an agreement has been signed with a new subpublisher who claims the right to collect all income.

Advances. An advance is normally paid by the foreign subpublisher to the licensor to represent the catalog in its territory. If a publisher enters into territory-by-territory agreements, then each licensee may pay a separate advance (these amounts will of course vary from territory to territory). If the deal is made with one large company on a worldwide basis, the overall advance may in rare instance be allocated for recoupment purposes on a territory-by-territory basis. Where the duration of a contract is on a multi-year term, consideration should be given as to whether the advance, which is recoupable against future royalties, is for all the years combined or on a year-by-year basis. Publishers view an advance from the licensee as an incentive to exploit the catalog harder so it can earn its "investment" back. The amount of the advance is also a method of "bidding" for the catalog if several subpublishers want representation.

Division of Income. The main types of income for a musical composition or catalog in a foreign territory are performance, mechanical, and print royalties. Income is usually split 75/25° between the licensor and the subpublisher for royalties generated by the composition in an American record, and in other proportions for recordings caused by the subpublisher. For example, an agreement may provide for the subpublisher to earn 50% of the mechanical royalties on cover records it obtains and 25% for compositions embodied in American recordings that are released in its territory. Also, with respect to sheet music and other printed editions, subpublishers normally pay licensors a percentage of the moneys collected from licenses (e.g., 75%) or a flat royalty based on the wholesale or retail selling price of the printed edition.

Translations. See TRANSLATIONS.

Licensing Territories. A publisher that subpublishes its catalog on a territory-by-territory basis will enter into agreements with foreign publishers in various territories. A "territory" may consist of one or more countries. The various territories commonly licensed on a territory-by-territory basis and listed in general order of importance are as follows: United Kingdom (including Eire); Germany, Austria, Switzerland (this territory is sometimes referred to as *GAS*); France; Benelux (Belgium, Netherlands, Luxembourg); Japan; Australia (with or without New Zealand); Italy; Scandinavia (Sweden, Denmark, Norway, Finland); Spain (with or without Portugal); Mexico; South Africa; Brazil; Venezuela; Argentina; Greece; and Central America. The remaining countries may be licensed separately but on an overall basis account for a very small portion of foreign revenues. Some United States music publishers subpublish in Canada while others reserve the Canadian rights for themselves.

°This is the common split at this writing; historically, it was 50/50 with respect to mechanical and performance income.

(The preceding territories are also those commonly licensed in territory-by-territory agreements for master recordings.)

Synchronization Rights. While it is in the subpublisher's interest to obtain the right to license copyrights for theatrical motion picture and television synchronization, such grant may be to the disadvantage of the licensor. For example, if the synchronization right was granted to a subpublisher, a situation could arise where the licensee is collecting synchronization income worldwide because it originally licensed the synchronization right. It is prudent for the licensor to reserve the synchronization right or require the licensee to obtain its approval before granting such right, or limit the synchronization right to films made in the foreign territory for *local* exploitation.

New and Unspecified Uses. The licensor should provide in the agreement that it shall earn a percentage of all revenues generated by the work or catalog in the territory of license from sources that are new or unspecified in the agreement. The particular percentage is negotiable and is usually 75%. Often all rights not granted are reserved.

Copyright Notice. The licensor should require the subpublisher to insert the copyright notice and other statements that relate to copyright protection (e.g., "All rights reserved") on recordings and printed copies of the work that are produced in its territory.

Rights of Termination. Foreign subpublishing agreements commonly provide for semiannual accountings and payments to the licensor, to be rendered within certain time limits after the close of the period (e.g., within 60 days following June 30 and December 31). The licensor may negotiate for the right to terminate the contract if the licensee is late in paying royalties, provided the delay is not caused by a bank problem or a foreign currency exchange problem. Rights of termination may also relate to other areas, such as where the subpublisher fails to comply with the terms of the agreement (e.g., failure to use the proper copyright notice) or goes into bankruptcy or fails to account accurately.

Negotiation Strategies: Incentive and Penalties. Two parties enter into any contract negotiation seeking terms that are favorable to each. Licensors often negotiate terms that in effect reward and penalize the subpublisher to the extent that it generates income. For example, the licensor may grant the local publisher a larger share in mechanical royalties from local cover records it obtains. This incentive may additionally be enhanced by granting the subpublisher a larger share of performance royalties on such covers. A formula may be devised for royalties the subpublisher can earn on cover and noncover records, such as 50% for covers and 25% for noncovers. On the other hand, some licensors negotiate for the rights to a particular song to be forfeited, the subpublisher's share reduced, or the term abbreviated if the subpublisher fails to obtain cover recordings.

Subpublisher Operations. The primary responsibilities of a subpublisher are to exploit the copyrights included in the license and to maximize and collect all income from uses of the works. The best and most effective subpublishers commonly work in the following way to obtain local recordings or covers:

1. After songs in the catalog are received from the licensor (in the form of masters and demos), the subpublisher has a meeting, during which its creative staff listens to and evaluates the material.

2. A determination is made as to which songs in the catalog have commercial potential in its territory and who are the most likely local artists to record those songs.

3. The material is then auditioned for these artists personally or via the mail. Auditions are continued until the songs get recorded.

4. After a song has been recorded, the publisher contacts the record company to find out the release plans—when the scheduled date is, or if there is none, why. In the latter case, the subpublisher will attempt to have the manufacturer schedule a release date.

5. Some foreign music publishers have promotion departments, which promote releases from both the company's catalog and those it represents.

6. The subpublisher sends information to the licensor regarding the activity of its songs in the territory—what songs have been recorded, scheduled release dates, status of previous releases, and sales data. If a record makes the charts, it will send photocopies of the listing.

7. The subpublisher tries to obtain additional cover records for those songs that get recorded, particularly chartmakers. The foreign publisher thereafter promotes and exploits the copyrights in other areas. (The subpublisher may also attempt to get U.S. recordings of copyrights included in the agreement released in its territory.)

Every foreign subpublisher, whether or not it actively seeks cover recordings, performs administrative functions relating to the copyrights. It registers each copyright with its local performing rights organization and takes all steps necessary to protect the copyright within its territory. It collects income, retains its percentage, and remits the balance to the licensors on a timely basis.

How the Licensor May Assist the Subpublisher. The U.S. publisher should assist the subpublisher in every way possible. It should provide the licensee with such materials as photocopies of U.S. chart listings of songs in the catalog, press materials from magazines and newspapers pertaining to the songs or the artists who recorded them, photos of the artists, promotion stickers, and other merchandising materials. These may assist the subpublisher in getting the songs recorded in its territory and in obtaining and/or expediting releases from the local record companies.

When an original U.S. recording becomes a hit in a foreign territory, a local tour by the artist may further enhance sales of the recording and popularize the song, thus resulting in various uses of it and of course generating more income. The management of the artist should be made aware (if it is not already) of the success of the recording in that territory and urged to have the artist make a concert tour there. The copyright owner will usually consult with management for such purposes, as will the artist's record company.

If a tour by the artist is not feasible, the licensor can still assist the subpublisher in promoting the song by providing film or videotape of the artist to be shown on television or in retail stores. It may also arrange for the artist to be interviewed by telephone with foreign radio stations and press.

Deciding Commercial Potential. Deciding the commercial potential of songs in the licensor's catalog in the local market is often a difficult task. It is widely, albeit erroneously, believed that unless a song becomes a hit in the United States, it is not worthwhile to exploit in foreign countries. Many smash U.S. hits never catch on abroad, while subpublishers have hits with copyrights that had little or no impact in the U.S. or other markets. The licensor should submit master recordings of all releases in its catalog as well as demos of unpublished musical works. It is usually best for the subpublisher to decide the commercial potential of a song in its market.

Finding a Competent Subpublisher. The qualities a licensor should look for in a subpublisher are, basically, honesty and competency. Such qualities may be determined by various means: investigating the publisher's success as subpublisher for other foreign catalogs, evaluating its success as a domestic publisher, finding out which top writers it publishes and which of its songs have been successful in territories outside its own country, as well as seeking recommendations from other publishers.

Is Subpublication Necessary? When recordings embodying compositions owned by U.S. music publishers are released in foreign countries, such publishers often ask if it is necessary to enter into subpublication agreements or should they attempt to collect income directly from the territories without using a subpublisher (or "middleman") and consequently not have to pay commissions. There are pros and cons regarding engaging subpublishers, and here are some of them:

Pros. The primary obligations of a subpublisher are to collect income and promote and exploit the music copyrights it represents. A capable foreign music publisher will be able to collect income generated by the copyrights it licenses more quickly (and perhaps more accurately) than the original publisher. Furthermore, this income may be increased by promotion and exploitation efforts by those subpublishers who have promotion departments capable of assisting record company promoters in areas such as radio, television, and the press. Such efforts may be crucial in achieving a hit in the territory.

A subpublisher also functions to obtain cover records. Its knowledge of its local markets will enable it to be more effective than the U.S. publisher, who often can do little more than mail recordings of songs overseas to artists, producers, and record companies. In addition, a licensee may cause a song, once it is popular, to be printed and distributed in sheet music or to be translated for promotion in the territory.

Other benefits of engaging subpublishers include the following: they acquaint their territories with the licensor's catalog; they monitor the distribution of royalties by licensing organizations, record companies, and other sources; their efforts may enhance the original composers' and lyricists' reputations outside the United States; and many have production companies and can get songs recorded in this way.

It may actually be imperative for a licensor to engage a subpublisher if it is the policy of the performing and mechanical rights societies in a country to make royalty payments only to companies based locally or owned by citizens of the country.

Cons. When an American recording of a U.S. publisher's song is released in a foreign country and it is anticipated that the bulk of activity (performances and record/tape sales) will be from the original recording, the full services of a publisher may not be needed, or may not justify the larger division of income. The recording (and hence the song) may be adequately promoted by the record company and promotional assistance from the subpublisher may not be needed. Furthermore, some songs are not very likely to be recorded by other artists, as the success of their original recording is largely based on the arrangement, production, and "sound" of the group. Investigating which subpublishers to engage and negotiating contracts may also be very time-consuming and expensive. For these and other reasons, some original publishers enter into "collection agent" agreements with local foreign publishers.

"Collection Agent" Agreement. For reasons just stated, a licensor may wish to engage the services of a foreign music publisher only as a "collection agent." Under a "collection deal," the foreign publisher will collect moneys earned from the original publisher's work(s) in the particular territory and remit this income to the original publisher after deducting its commission; exploitation, promotion, and other publisher services are usually not performed.

The commission earned by foreign publishers under a "collection deal" ranges from 15%

to 25% of the gross collections in their territory and is commonly 15% (such a split is typically referred to as "85/15"). Sometimes the percentage may vary for the different types of royalties (i.e., performance, mechanical, etc.). Licensors sometimes negotiate an advance from the subpublisher in a "collection deal." The licensor may view the advance as an exchange for the cash flow benefits to the subpublisher of such a relationship.

A licensor makes collection agreements when it wishes to collect quickly and efficiently moneys earned by its compositions in particular territories. (Payments coming directly from foreign performing and mechanical rights societies and record company licenses may take over 2 years to be received if they are transmitted to the licensor through its domestic performing rights society or mechanical rights agency.) A disadvantage for the licensor that makes a collection agreement undesirable is of course the lack of exploitation and promotion for its catalog in the territory.

The U.S. Publisher as Subpublisher. The subpublication of foreign catalogs in the U.S. works basically the same as described above. With certain exceptions, however, most of the material submitted to American music publishers from non-English-speaking countries requires a great deal of effort for exploitation in the U.S. and other English-speaking countries. Foreign lyrics, for example, usually have to be adapted, not just translated, into the vernacular of the American market.

Where American music publishers enter into contracts whereby they function as subpublisher, they should carefully investigate the policies of their licensor's performing rights society. Some foreign societies have rules that prohibit subpublishers from collecting more than a certain share of the subpublishing performance royalties. An American publisher, for example, might pay an advance for the right to collect 100% of a foreign catalog's earnings from all sources in the United States, then find the original (foreign) publisher did not have the right to grant that, as its local performing rights society has some contrary or conflicting arrangement with its U.S. equivalent to collect a part of those earnings.

In the Can. Trade jargon. Refers to a recording (single or album) that has been completed (i.e., a master) but not as yet put on the market by the record company (the record is *in the can*). Such masters may be scheduled for release at a future date or may never be released.

J

Jazz. *See* POPULAR MUSIC.

Joint Work. It is common for an original work, such as a musical composition, to be created by individuals who write in collaboration with one another. The copyright law contains specific provisions relating to the ownership and COPYRIGHT DURATION of a work jointly created.

The 1976 Copyright Act (Section 101) defines a "joint work" as "a work prepared by two or more authors with the intention that their contributions be merged into inseparable or interdependent parts of a unitary whole." A popular song written by a separate composer and lyricist would probably be an example of a "joint work," as would a sound recording "produced" by an artist and a record producer under a "coauthorship" agreement. Ownership of copyright in a joint work belongs to the coauthors unless transferred.

Jukebox. A coin-operated phonograph, or jukebox as it is commonly known, provides inexpensive musical entertainment for the patrons of the establishment in which it is placed—diners, restaurants, bars, and college coffeehouses among others. In addition, it is a promoter as well as a consumer of records. Jukeboxes establish a multimillion-dollar industry whose financial beneficiaries include jukebox manufacturers and operators, nightclubs, restaurants, and other establishments, record manufacturers, one-stops, recording artists, music publishers, and songwriters.

Description. A jukebox is an automatic player of phonograph records encased in a cabinet, which plays one or more records upon deposit of a coin in a slot, with push buttons for selection of records. The record capacities of jukeboxes commonly range from 50 records (100 selections) to 100 records (200 selections).

The Jukebox Operator. The person or business that owns and services jukeboxes is referred to as an *operator*. An operator buys jukeboxes from a *distributor* (usually a factory franchise) and puts into these records purchased from a ONE-STOP.

Jukeboxes are placed in *locations*, or establishments where the operator does business (proprietors of locations normally do not own their own machines, either because of the restrictive costs or their inability to service them). Operators "program" their jukeboxes carefully—that is, they study the patronage of a location and select and change records according to the preferences of the clientele. This requires a determination of what particular styles of music (rock, country, soul, etc.) and which particular records and artists will attract the most business.

Most jukebox operators today also own coin-operated amusement games, and in some cases, vending machines. That is why these businesses are collectively referred to as the *coin-operated music and amusement industry*. The trade association for individuals and companies associated with this industry is the AMUSEMENT AND MUSIC OPERATORS ASSOCIATION (AMOA).

History. The forerunner of the modern jukebox was a battery-powered phonograph encased in a cabinet, with multiple sets of ear-plugs attached. The deposit of a coin in one of its slots activated the mechanism and opened up one set. The insertion of additional coins opened up the others; one machine could receive several coins per play. This application of the phonograph player was the conception of Louis Glass, who installed such converted units in the Palais Royal saloon in San Francisco in November of 1889. Although these devices offered brief periods of listening and poor reproductions of sound, they enjoyed widespread popularity. "Phonograph parlors," equipped with several machines at one location, sprouted throughout the country and gave birth to a new entertainment industry. The word "juke" is believed to have its origin in the African word "jook," meaning disorderly or wicked. "Jukebox," however, is said to have been coined in England around 1910, where coin-operated phonographs were seen in "juke joints," or barroom–dance halls.

The first electric coin-operated multiselection record players were manufactured in 1927 by the Automatic Music Company of Grand Rapids, Michigan. Other important manufacturers in subsequent years have been Wurlitzer, Seeburg, and Rock-ola. Jukeboxes are believed to have rescued the record industry when sales plummeted to a low in 1933 of $5.5 million, down from $75 million in 1927.

It has been reported that in 1934 there were 25,000 jukeboxes in operation in the U.S. and that in 1939 one-quarter-million machines accounted for sales of at least 19 million records. AMOA reported that in 1979 there were approximately 5,000 operators and 300,000 jukeboxes in the U.S.

On the average, an operator owns about 70 machines; some own as many as 400. Jukeboxes ranged in price in 1980 from $1,700 to $2,500, the most expensive units containing digital integrated circuits. A new dimension to this entertainment medium is the videodisc jukebox, which debuted in the U.S. in 1979.

Copyright Law on Jukebox Performances. Under the Copyright Act of 1976, the owner of copyright in a nondramatic musical composition embodied in a PHONORECORD is given the exclusive right to publicly perform the work by means of a "coin-operated phonorecord player" (this term in the law refers to the jukebox). Hence jukebox operators are required to obtain licenses for the use of the songs embodied in discs.°

The 1976 act sets a limitation on this exclusive right by establishing a system of compulsory licenses covering jukebox performances. Under this system, operators need not negotiate licenses with copyright owners, but must comply with statutory procedures and pay an annual royalty fee.

Compulsory Licenses. To obtain a compulsory license for jukebox performances, an operator must do the following: (1) file an application on Form JB, identifying each jukebox to be covered; (2) pay to the Copyright Office a royalty fee for each jukebox identified on the application; and (3) affix to each licensed jukebox a certificate issued by the Copyright Office. Applications must be filed within 1 month after a machine is placed in use (if filed for the first time after July 1 of any year, the fee is reduced).

Revewal must be made during the month of January in each succeeding year. Two computer printout forms of the information the operator provided in the previous year and renewal application Form JB/R are mailed to

---

° This is as opposed to the law in effect before 1978, in which jukebox owners were not required to pay a public performance fee. The so-called jukebox exemption arose because under the Copyright Act of 1909, public performances by coin-operated machines in "penny parlors"—their principal locus at that time, and with no admission charged—were not deemed to be "for profit." When these machines were replaced by the modern jukebox, the language of the penny parlor exemption was applied.

Jukeboxes provide musical entertainment for the patrons of restaurants, nightclubs, bars, and other establishments, as well as promote records to the public. These coin-operated record players have changed in style and design through the years as shown by the various models above: (*clockwise from top left*) 1937, 1946, 1964, 1970, 1976, and 1981.

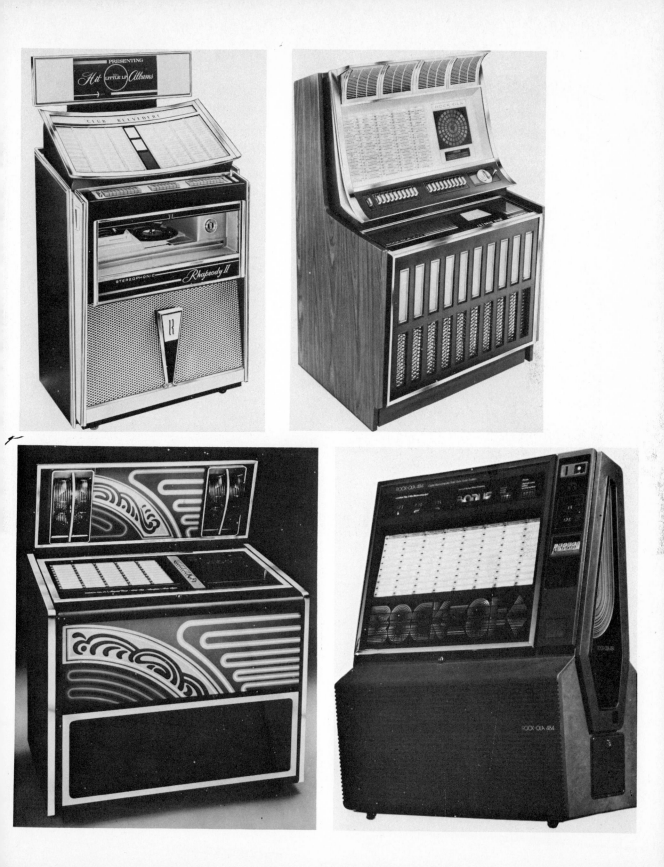

A view of one of the phonograph parlors which helped popularize recordings during the 1890s. These machines were the forerunners of the home phonograph and of the jukebox.

the operator by the Copyright Office. To receive renewal certificates, the operator must complete and send the application with the appropriate attachments and fee to the Office within the prescribed time limits.

Failure by a jukebox operator to comply with the compulsory licensing requirements with respect to a particular jukebox renders every unauthorized public performance of a copyrighted musical composition on that machine a separate act of copyright infringement under the law. Copyright owners could therefore bring civil, or in some cases criminal, actions for damage and other remedies against an operator in the federal courts.

Distribution to Copyright Owners. The royalty fees collected by the Copyright Office are deposited in the U.S. Treasury after the Office deducts reasonable administrative costs. These fees are invested in interest-bearing securities and are later distributed with interest by the COPYRIGHT ROYALTY TRIBUNAL. The statute provides for the tribunal to review the established royalty fee in 1980 and every 10 years thereafter, and make adjustments where appropriate.

Each January, every person claiming to be entitled to a portion of the jukebox royalty fees must file a claim with the tribunal (in accordance with regulations it prescribes). The claim shall include an agreement to accept as final the determination of the Copyright Royalty Tribunal in any controversy concerning the distribution of royalty fees. The final decision of the tribunal, however, is subject to judicial review as provided for by Section 810 of the law. After the first of October, the tribunal distributes the fees, after deducting reasonable administrative costs. If a controversy exists, the tribunal must conduct a hearing to determine the royalty distribution.

The statute provides for the tribunal to distribute the fees on a pro rata basis to copyright owners not affiliated with a PERFORMING RIGHTS ORGANIZATION, with the remainder to go to the organizations, either in accordance with an agreement among them or on a determination made by the tribunal. The fees collected by the organizations are subsequently distributed to their writer and publisher members or affiliates.

If there is any proceeding with respect to this compulsory license, the Copyright Royalty Tribunal is instructed to withhold from distribution an amount sufficient to satisfy the claims made in accordance with the controversy. It may at its discretion, however, "proceed to distribution any amounts that are not in controversy."

Juno Awards. *See* CANADA.

L

Label. The term *label* refers to either a record company or the "brand name" it puts on recordings it issues. With respect to names, some record companies use one label, others several, to designate price category (e.g., budget line, front line) or area of repertoire (e.g., classical, pop) of its product. An independent record company that enters into a "label deal" (*see* RECORD COMPANY DEALS) with a major is often referred to as an *associated* or *custom label*.

Label Deal. *See* RECORD COMPANY DEALS.

Label Information (Phonograph Records and Tapes). Print labels are affixed to the center of each side of a disc recording (single or LP) and on tape cartridges and containers to provide a place for information. Such information serves various purposes, besides the obvious one of identifying selections, artists, and songwriters.

For example, the display of a copyright notice protects the embodied sound recordings; stating the length of a recording aids radio station program directors and disc jockeys in their programming; and naming the performing rights organization affiliation of the publisher informs radio stations (which must obtain a license in order to broadcast copyrighted songs in the repertoire of a performing rights organization) whether or not they are legally permitted to broadcast the song.

In practice, labels vary in the amount of information they contain. Labels on discs and tapes released by bona fide record companies normally contain all or most of the following information: title of the song; name of the recording artist; name of the composer and lyricist; COPYRIGHT NOTICE for a sound recording; name of the publisher and its performing rights organization affiliation; length of the selection; whether the recording is stereo or mono; name of the producer; name of the arranger; record manufacturer's master (or catalog) number of the recording; name and logo of the label; side of the recording (usually designated as "A" and "B" for singles, and "1" and "2" for LPs and tapes); name and address of manufacturer/distributor.

Lanham Act. *See* BUSINESS LAWS, FEDERAL AND STATE; TRADEMARKS.

Latin Music. *See* POPULAR MUSIC.

Lead Sheet. A manuscript copy of a musical composition, containing a musical notation of the melody, the chord symbols, and the lyrics, if any.

A lead sheet is primarily used to promote or audition a song in its prepublication state, in conjunction with a DEMO. An arranger may use a lead sheet when writing the charts for a commercial recording, a songwriter to teach musicians the song when making a demo.

Lead sheets are used less commonly today than in the late 19th and early 20th century (music publishing's early Tin Pan Alley days). In that era, it was from the lead sheet that a publisher would play and audition his song for a performer. Since the advent of tape recording, the demo has been the primary means for auditioning a song and the lead sheet has taken a secondary role. Sometimes a lyric sheet is used in place of a lead sheet, so a person can read or follow the words to the song when listening to the demo.

Information Contained on a Lead Sheet. At the top of the first page of the lead sheet, the title is written. Under or adjacent to it, the name of the composer and lyricist, and the address and telephone number of either one, may be given. The style or tempo of the song is indicated above the first bar. Songwriters commonly put a COPYRIGHT NOTICE at the bottom of the first page of their lead sheets. Depending on the length of the song, a lead sheet may be one or a few pages long.

Lead Sheet Writers. As writers often cannot notate a song's melody (and the proper chord symbols), they seek the assistance of certain professionals, most often music copyists, music stenographers, arrangers, or musicians. By singing and/or playing the song on an instrument, the writer can convey the melody. Professionals may be found in the classified telephone directory under "Music Copyists," "Music Arrangers," or "Music Teachers." Lead sheet writers charge by the song, page, measure, and/or time. The cost of having a lead sheet of one song made by a professional may range from $10 to $80 or more. AFM sets forth minimum rates for copying.

See also COPYIST, MUSIC.

League of New York Theatres and Producers, Inc. *See* BROADWAY MUSICALS.

Legitimate Theater. Refers to plays or other artistic works performed on a stage by living professional actors and actresses (as distinguished from other media or forms of entertainment, such as theatrical motion pictures or television). The legitimate theater encompasses musicals, comedies, dramas, and other productions performed on Broadway, Off Broadway, and in regional, stock, dinner, and children's theater. *See* ACTORS' EQUITY ASSOCIATION (AEA OR EQUITY).

Libel. *See* DEFAMATION.

Licensees (Printed Music). *See* PRINTED MUSIC, LICENSING AND DISTRIBUTION OF.

Licenses. *See* CONTRACTS.

Licensing Masters. *See* INTERNATIONAL MASTER RECORDING LICENSING AGREEMENT; RECORD AND TAPE CLUB; RECORD MERCHANDISING COMPANY.

Limited Partnerships (for Investments in Theatrical Productions). Almost invariably, the form of business organization utilized to produce theatrical productions is the *limited partnership.* A creature of statutory law, it incorporates aspects of a corporation and a partnership. A limited partner's liability is only to the extent of the investment made, unlike the unlimited liability of a partner in a general partnership. The analogous position of a limited partner is the insulation afforded a stockholder in a corporation. Even though the limited partner has corporate-stockholder-type protection, he or she has the advantages under the tax laws of a partner—i.e., the right to deduct losses against ordinary income without limitation—while the loss of a corporate stockholder would be circumscribed by the applicable Internal Revenue Code limitations.

A limited partnership consists of one or more general partners—ordinarily being or including the producer(s)—and one or more limited partners—the investor(s). When financing a show, the producer will estimate total production expenses, the amount of money needed to open a show plus a reserve (capitalization). The capitalization is divided into units (expressed as percentages both of the capitalization and the share in profits), which the prospective limited partners buy. The acquired interest of an investor (also colloquially referred to as an *angel*) is considered a security under both federal and state law. The implication of deeming such interests to be securities necessitates careful solicitation by the producer offering participations in theatrical ventures (see below).

In a limited partnership formed for the purpose of producing a play, the risk of loss is especially high in contrast to the prospects for profits. Thus such securities should not be purchased unless the investor is prepared for the possibility of total loss. While no accurate industry statistics are available, it is claimed that most shows produced on Broadway result in total losses for their investors. However, because there *are* hit shows, because a successful one *can* garner for its investors enormous profits, and because a limited partner's liability is limited to the amount of his investment, angels can be found. (The glamour and excitement connected with a Broadway production may also be an impetus.)

Angels may be individual persons or corporations. Record companies sometimes invest in musicals in order to obtain the rights to the original cast show album. Likewise, motion picture companies make investments, not only to realize a profit but to obtain film rights.

In a public financing, producers will initially solicit potential angels through mass mailings, word of mouth, and sometimes newspaper advertisements. Those who inquire are typically invited to attend *backers' auditions*— sessions where the show's score is performed live (usually by the composer, the lyricist, and a few professional singers) and its book is reviewed. Many such auditions may be needed to raise the required capital. The commitment of a star to the show, a famous director, or even a "hot producer" may facilitate the raising of necessary capital. Once the capital is raised, the producer can begin mounting the production.

Through the limited partnership, business is conducted and controlled by the general partner, who, although he does not necessarily make an investment, assumes all liability over and above the capitalization. Limited partners cannot take part in the conduct of the business, hence they have no control over the production of the show, either creative or financial.

Net profits from the show are normally split 50/50 between the producer(s) and limited partners after all the capitalization is returned to the limited partners. Each limited partner receives that proportion of 50% of the net profits as the amount of his contribution bears to the original capital. The general partners receive the other 50% of the net profits.

The "net profits" split between producer and investors is the excess of gross receipts over all production expenses, running expenses, and "other" expenses. "Gross" is defined as all sums derived by the partnership from the presentation of the play and from exploitation of any or all of the rights in the play which the partnership possesses.

Production expenses are expenses incurred by the partnership in connection with the play preliminary to its opening, including the fees of the general manager, director, designer, company manager, and production assistants, as well as the costs of designing and constructing sets, costumes, and lights, securing an orchestra, properties, furnishings, electrical equipment, bonds and guarantees, insurance premiums, rehearsal charges, legal and auditing costs, publicity, theater costs, advertising, advance royalties, taxes, and any and all other expenses included in producing the play.

Running expenses are expenses, charges, and disbursements related to the run of the play, including percentages payable to the composer, lyricist, playwright, theater management, director, choreographer; salaries for the business managers, production associates and assistants, cast, and orchestra; costs for transportation, advertising, theater and other rentals; office facilities supplied by the producer; legal and auditing services; insurance; and all other expenses and losses incurred in connection with the operation of the play.

"Other" expenses incurred in connection with the operation of the business of the partnership include commissions paid to agents and moneys paid or payable in connection with claims for plagiarism, libel, and negligence.

The Uniform Limited Partnership Act (which has been adopted by most states, with variations) governs a limited partnership operation. A limited partnership agreement will include: the name of the partnership; the kind of business to be conducted; the location of the principal place of business; the duration of the partnership from the date of commencement; name and status of the partners; the investment by each partner; the additional contributions ("overall"), if any, to be made by each limited partner; share of profits which each limited partner shall receive as a result of his contribution; the right, if given, that a limited partner has to substitute an assignee of his interest and the terms of such substitution; the right of a limited partner to demand property other than cash in return for his contributions; and the right of the remaining general partner(s) to continue the business on the death, retirement, or insanity of a general partner.

A certificate of limited partnership, signed and sworn to by the general partner(s) individually and as attorney(s) in fact for the limited partners, and containing the above information, must be filed with the county clerk or court in the county where the partnership has its principal place of business, as provided by the particular state's statutes.

A limited partner or his representative has the right to inspect and examine the firm's books upon reasonable notice. In a theatrical production, the general partner will make available for inspection box office statements received from the theater or theaters at which

the play produced by the partnership is presented. After the formation of the partnership, the limited partners are furnished with financial statements, as required by state law. The general partner will also deliver to each limited partner information necessary to enable him to prepare federal and state income tax returns.

Net profits are distributed in the following manner: after the partnership has recouped and paid back to the limited partners their full investment, has a cash reserve in the amount stipulated in the partnership agreement, and has paid or made reasonable provision for the payment of all debts, liabilities, taxes, and contingent liabilities, all cash in excess of the reserve is periodically distributed to the limited partners in the pro rata shares described above.

Upon the dissolution of the limited partnership, the profits or assets of the firm are distributed according to priorities prescribed by law and as provided in the limited partnership agreement. Under usual statutory requirements, the order of distribution is creditors, limited partners, and then general partners.

The solicitation of investors for a limited partnership by a producer can be subject to regulation by federal and state authorities. The Securities and Exchange Commission (SEC) is charged with enforcing the federal law, while state law is dependent upon enforcement by various local authorities. Federal jurisdiction is applicable when a solicitation involves interstate transactions. Various states will assert their jurisdiction when a resident of the state is solicited. It is a rare situation in which an offering for a theatrical venture does not involve both federal and state regulation.

If an offeror—that is, a producer—is not in compliance with governing law, a plethora of sanctions is available to the government. Perhaps the most effective sanction is to require a producer to return the original investment and rescind agreements between the investor and producer. With the prospect of having to pay back investors their full participation in the event of a flop, it is the cavalier, if not unknowledgeable, producer who would accept funds without being in compliance with security laws and regulations. The thorny area of security regulation is best dealt with by consultation with legal counsel.

Liner Notes. *See* ALBUM COVER; COPYRIGHT REGISTRATION CLASSIFICATION SYSTEM.

Logo. A design, which usually includes letters, that may serve as a unique identification and a trademark or service mark.

Logos are placed on phonograph records, prerecorded tapes, and videodiscs, as well as on album covers and any other graphic materials, to identify the company issuing the product. A logo is most often comprised of the name (or symbol) of the company and a graphic representation (i.e., a photograph or illustration). A logo on an LP or single is printed on the center labels. A company's logo will also appear in company advertisements, on stationery, business cards, forms, merchandising pieces, etc.

Artist Logos. A logo may also be used as a graphic identification of a recording act. This usually consists of the act's name in a distinctive style of typography or lettering. Such a logo would be used on the act's recording product, merchandise related to the act, such as T-shirts and posters, and in advertisements.

Protection. Legal protection for a logo is most commonly obtained under the federal trademark law (*see* TRADEMARKS). Protection for a logo may also be derived from the laws of UNFAIR COMPETITION.

A logo may be copyrightable to a certain extent under Class VA. A picture appearing in the logo could receive copyright protection, but a name or standard symbol, such as a square, circle, or other design that does not have any original artistic authorship, would not be copyrightable (*see* COPYRIGHT REGISTRATION CLASSIFICATION SYSTEM; COPYRIGHTABLE WORKS).

Examples of Record Company Logos. One of the most famous record company logos is an RCA trademark: RCA's name appearing with a picture of a fox terrier dog (called Nipper) gazing into the horn of a phonograph. This picture is actually a scaled-down reproduction of the painting created by British artist Francis Barraud in the 1890s called "His Master's Voice." This was used as a trademark on phonographs and records beginning in 1901 by the Victor Talking Machine Co. When RCA purchased Victor in 1929, it acquired the American rights to the trademark. In 1968, RCA replaced the logo with a modernized trademark formed by the letters "RCA" enclosed in a circle. However, the Nipper logo was restored in 1977.

Artistic portions of other record company logos include or have included A & M's trumpet, RSO's pink cow, and Electra's butterfly.

LP. An LP (long-playing record) is a PHONOGRAPH RECORD 12 inches in diameter that is pressed with microgrooves and played at a speed of 33⅓ rpm. LPs of popular music commonly contain 4 to 6 or more selections on each side.

History. In June 1948, Columbia Records introduced a long-playing microgroove record (i.e., with grooves only 1/1000 inch wide) that operated at a speed of 33⅓ rpm. Columbia's LP was to become the first such commercially successful phonograph disc.

Columbia's LP wasn't the first, however. In 1931, RCA Victor issued special 12-inch 33⅓ rpm discs with playing times of approximately 15 minutes per side. Unlike Columbia's, however, these had grooves 3/1000 inch wide—the groove width of 78 rpm records. RCA's LPs didn't catch on with the public, because of the general unavailability and high cost of their players. They were subsequently used for

To dramatize the superiority of the long-playing record introduced by Columbia in 1948, Dr. Peter C. Goldmark, who helped develop the new discs, stands alongside a huge pile of 78-rpm records, holding the equivalent recorded repertoire in a handful of LPs.

radio (commonly called transcriptions) and in synchronization with motion picture films. During World War II, 33⅓ rpm 16-inch discs with wide grooves were commonly used in the broadcast transcription field.

It was realized that a single long-playing phonograph record with superior audio fidelity would be a marked improvement over the configuration to that day—78 rpm, fragile shellac records which in a package of several discs comprised an "album." A long-playing record's advantages could include uninterrupted playing, economic savings, nonbreakability, easier storage, and better fidelity.

There were various technological challenges to overcome in order to produce a 33⅓ rpm, 12-inch long-playing record. It was necessary to develop a microgroove cutting technique, a lighter-weight pickup arm, a finer stylus (or needle) to accommodate the narrower grooves, a way to reduce distortion as the stylus moved toward the disc's center, and strong plastic materials for the thin walls between grooves that would yield up to 30 minutes playing per side.

A team of CBS Laboratories' engineers headed by Peter Goldmark and William Bachman, using original work by René Snepvangers, another CBS Labs engineer, eventually developed the LP as it exists. Columbia demonstrated its narrow-grooved long-playing recording on June 21, 1948, in New York City. Columbia's technique of microgroove recording not only resulted in improved fidelity of sound reproduction, but reduced distortion and offered a disc that would play longer and be less susceptible to breakage than the 78 shellacs. (For a period of about 8 years, some LPs were issued in a 10-inch format, but this was eventually discontinued because it was not economically feasible.)

In early 1949, RCA Victor marketed a 7-inch fine-grooved disc that operated at 45 rpm and was incompatible with the LP hardware. Both Columbia and RCA realized that the new microgroove technology would phase out the 78 rpm shellac records, but each company wanted the recording industry to settle on its design as the main software medium. A struggle between the LP and the 45 ensued and became known as the "Battle of the Speeds."

This conflict initially brought much confusion to industry and public. Distributors and retailers often stocked the same recording in 33⅓, 45, and even 78 rpm speeds, and the two disc manufacturers besieged the public with advertising, each claiming a superior product.

While the evolution of a standard with respect to either of the two speeds seemed questionable at the time, the industry and the public were eventually to accept both speeds. LPs were the logical choice to market classical music, show scores, and compilations of selections recorded by an individual artist. The 45s appropriately embodied individual pop tunes and became the main vehicle for "singles." Production of 78 rpm records ceased in the late 1950s and in 1968 RIAA deleted all technical references to the 78 in its bulletins of home phonograph records, rendering that configuration as officially obsolete. LPs and 45s were virtually the only sources of recorded home entertainment until the advent of cassettes and 8-track tapes. With the development of video software, the long-term future of audio as a home entertainment medium may be questionable.

Lyricist. *See* SONGWRITER.

Lyrics. The words of a song. Lyrics, with or without music, may be copyrighted (*see* COPYRIGHT REGISTRATION CLASSIFICATION SYSTEM).

Changing or Adding Lyrics to Existing Musical Compositions. The express consent of the owner of copyright is needed by anyone who wishes to make changes in an existing musical composition except as provided by the compulsory license of the copyright law. Permission is needed, for example, to add lyrics to an instrumental or to rewrite or adapt the lyrics of an existing musical composition. These may have the effect of creating a DERIVATIVE WORK. The compulsory license for making phonorecords does not grant the privilege of writing new lyrics or of making any changes other than that as specified [see COMPULSORY/MECHANICAL LICENSES (PHONORECORDS)].

Usually, where a lyric is added to an existing instrumental work it is done by commission of the publisher. In such a case, the publisher and the original writer will contractually provide that the new lyricist will not participate in any of the royalties earned by the composition in its original form. A publisher may even engage a lyricist to write lyrics under a WORK MADE FOR HIRE arrangement and not convey any copyright status in the work to him. In this case, provision is normally made for the lyricist to share in the income from the song. Any writer is of course free to change or add lyrics to PUBLIC DOMAIN works. However, copyright in the work will extend only to the new material.

Controversial Lyrics. Some songwriters or recording artists write songs whose lyrics might be considered controversial. These might contain obscene words, graphically describe sexual acts, glamorize the use of illegal drugs, make racial or ethnic slurs, slander a person, or refer to religion, politics, or physical handicaps. Because such lyrics might meet with disfavor by radio station program directors, the FCC, and various public organizations (who might boycott the recordings), record companies may attempt to expurgate these songs. Where such action is contemplated, it is prudent for the label to seek legal advice to determine whether the action may subject the company to litigation by the writer or artist. The FCC issued a Public Notice pertaining to song lyrics on March 5, 1971 (see RADIO STATION).

Some songs that have been banned by certain radio stations because their lyrics were deemed objectionable include "Eve of Destruction," "My Girl Bill," and "Short People."

See also COLLABORATOR; TRANSLATIONS.

M

Mailing a Song. *See* SONGWRITER.

Manager. *See* BUSINESS MANAGER; PERSONAL MANAGER.

Manufacturing Requirement. *See* COPYRIGHT LAW MANUFACTURING REQUIREMENT.

Market. Term that refers to a population center (city); it may also refer to a category of buyers classified according to their musical preference (the *pop* market, the *country* market, etc.).

Radio stations are often categorized by the market that is primarily in the station's transmitting area. In the United States there are three basic markets (each based on population): *primary*, *secondary*, and *tertiary*. Primary (or *major*) markets are those with high population densities; secondary markets are medium population centers, and tertiary markets are those with relatively smaller populations.

The market a station is in—regarding both population and musical preference—has consequences with respect to RECORD COMPANY marketing campaigns. New releases will normally be first programmed (and hence promoted) in "breakout" markets before being picked up by or promoted to stations in other markets. Breakout markets are usually those with lesser populations—secondary and tertiary markets. Choice of breakout areas in which the records are promoted depends on the buying habits of consumers in that city or region. After a record achieves considerable airplay and sales in breakout areas, it will be promoted to other secondary markets, and if the response is favorable, to major markets. (In some cases, records are first promoted to stations in major markets, such as for a new release by a popular artist.) Merchandising, advertising, and other marketing activities are also geared to the markets in which records are promoted.

The following ranking lists primary, secondary, and tertiary U.S. standard radio markets.° Primary markets are those in the top 50, secondary markets are those from number 51 through 100, and all above 100 are tertiary markets.

1. New York
2. Los Angeles
3. Chicago
4. San Francisco
5. Philadelphia
6. Detroit
7. Boston
8. Washington, D.C.
9. Houston-Galveston
10. Nassau-Suffolk (Long Island, N.Y.)
11. Dallas-Fort Worth
12. St. Louis
13. Pittsburgh
14. Baltimore
15. Minneapolis-St. Paul
16. Cleveland
17. Seattle-Everett-Tacoma
18. Anaheim-Santa Ana-Garden Grove (Orange County, Cal.)
19. Atlanta
20. San Diego
21. Milwaukee
22. Denver-Boulder
23. Miami

°Source: Market Survey Schedule and Population Rankings 1980, Arbitron Radio.

24. Tampa-St. Petersburg
25. Providence-Warwick-Pawtucket
26. Cincinnati
27. Phoenix
28. Kansas City
29. Buffalo
30. San Jose
31. Norfolk-Portsmouth-Newport News-Hampton
32. Portland, Ore.
33. Indianapolis
34. New Orleans
35. Riverside-San Bernardino-Ontario
36. Columbus, Ohio
37. San Antonio
38. Sacramento
39. Rochester, N.Y.
40. Fort Lauderdale-Hollywood
41. Memphis
42. Louisville
43. Hartford-New Britain
44. Dayton
45. Birmingham
46. Nashville-Davidson
47. Greensboro-Winston Salem-High Point
48. Albany-Schenectady-Troy
49. Salt Lake City-Ogden
50. Oklahoma City
51. Toledo
52. Honolulu
53. Jacksonville
54. Wilkes Barre-Scranton (Northeast Pa.)
55. Akron
56. Allentown-Bethlehem-Easton
57. Syracuse
58. Richmond
59. Tulsa
60. Orlando
61. Charlotte-Gastonia
62. Springfield-Chicopee-Holyoke
63. Burlington-Plattsburgh
64. Omaha-Council Bluffs
65. Grand Rapids
66. Greenville-Spartanburg, S.C.
67. Youngstown-Warren
68. West Palm Beach-Boca Raton
69. Wilmington, Del.
70. Raleigh-Durham
71. Flint
72. Austin, Tex.
73. Fresno
74. Tucson
75. New Bedford-Fall River, Mass.
76. Knoxville
77. Lansing-East Lansing

78. New Haven-West Haven
79. Harrisburg
80. Baton Rouge
81. Bridgeport
82. Mobile
83. Johnson City-Kingsport-Bristol
84. Chattanooga
85. Albuquerque
86. El Paso
87. Canton
88. Wichita, Kan.
89. Worcester
90. Columbia, S.C.
91. McAllen-Brownsville
92. Las Vegas
93. Charleston-North Charleston, S.C.
94. Little Rock-North Little Rock
95. Davenport-Rock Island-Moline (Quad-Cities)
96. Beaumont-Port Arthur-Orange
97. Peoria
98. Bakersfield
99. Fort Wayne
100. York
101. Shreveport
102. Lancaster
103. Des Moines
104. Sarasota-Bradenton
105. Madison
106. Spokane
107. Stockton
198. Utica-Rome
109. Reading
110. Lexington-Fayette
111. Binghamton
112. Huntington-Ashland
113. Jackson, Miss.
114. Appleton-Oshkosh
115. Huntsville, Ala.
116. Evansville
117. Corpus Christi
118. Colorado Springs
119. Lakeland-Winter Haven, Fla.
120. Salinas-Seaside-Monterey
121. Augusta, Ga.
122. South Bend
123. Pensacola
124. Johnstown, Pa.
125. Kalamazoo-Portage
126. Duluth-Superior
127. Greenville-New Bern-Washington
128. Rockford
129. Erie
130. Eugene-Springfield
131. Charleston, W.V.

132. Melbourne-Titusville-Coco, Fla.
133. Montgomery
134. Modesto
135. Macon
136. Roanoke
137. Daytona Beach
138. Boise
139. Columbus, Ga.
140. Fayetteville, N.C.
141. Saginaw
142. Savannah
143. Portland, Me.
144. Springfield, Mo.
145. Lubbock
146. Topeka
147. Lincoln
148. Atlantic City
149. Wheeling
150. Terre Haute
151. Anchorage
152. Asheville
153. Green Bay
154. Reno
155. Cedar Rapids
156. Steubenville-Weirton
157. Waco
158. Amarillo
159. Manchester, N.H.
160. Lynchburg, Va.
161. Yakima
162. Tallahassee
163. Fargo-Moorhead
164. Waterloo-Cedar Falls
165. Altoona
166. Wilmington, N.C.
167. Lafayette, La.
168. Wichita Falls, Tex.
169. Medford-Ashland
170. Bloomington, Ill.
171. Pueblo
172. Tri-Cities (Richland-Kennewick-Pasco)
173. Sioux Falls, S.D.
174. Billings
175. Great Falls
176. Casper, Wyo.

Master. There are several different meanings of this term. A master may be any of the following: (1) a multi-track tape (2″ wide) containing recorded performances; (2) a "master mix" tape (¼″ wide) derived from the multi-track tape in its final form—i.e., mixed, edit-ed, sequenced, timed, head and tail leadered, containing test tones, and used to make the master lacquer and all other copies; (3) a "master lacquer" cut from the master mix (*see* RECORD MANUFACTURING); (4) a "running master" made from the master mix that is shipped to remote facilities, and from which either cassette or 8-track cartridge copies will be made; (5) a "safety" tape copy; (6) an original cut disc of a direct-to-disc recording—i.e., the disc cut directly in response to the "live" performance; and (7) any original tape or disc recording.

Mastering. *See* RECORD MANUFACTURING.

Mechanical License. *See* COMPULSORY/MECHANICAL LICENSES (PHONORECORDS).

Mechanical Right. A *mechanical* (or *recording*) *right* is, in essence, the exclusive right that may be granted in a copyright law to the owner of a musical work to authorize (license) his or her work for reproduction in records, tapes, and other audio devises.

Copyright Law. The basis for the mechanical right in the U.S. copyright law (Title 17) is given in Section 106, which states: ". . . the owner of copyright . . . has the exclusive right . . . to reproduce the copyrighted work in . . . phonorecords" (*see* COPYRIGHT OWNER).

Compulsory License for Music Recordings. The U.S. law provides that in the case of non-dramatic musical works, the exclusive right of copyright owners to make and distribute phonorecords of such works is subject to compulsory licensing under conditions set forth by law [*see* COMPULSORY/MECHANICAL LICENSES (PHONORECORDS)]. This provision specifies that a person may obtain a compulsory license only if his purpose in making phonorecords is to distribute them to the public for private use. In commercial practice, however, a copyright owner will issue a negotiated or modified *mechanical* (or *recording*) *license*. This is an agreement issued in lieu of the publisher's requiring the user to comply with the compulsory license provisions of the copyright law. The copyright owner's exclusive rights are not subject to compulsory licensing for a musical composition in phonorecords not distributed for private use—that is, recordings for radio programs or for transmissions by wire.

Mechanical Rights Agency. Many music publishers engage the services of a special representative for the purpose of licensing their compositions to be used by record companies, film producers, and others who reproduce copyrighted musical works in mechanical and audiovisual devices. Such a representative is referred to as a *mechanical rights agency.*

Representation by a mechanical rights agency is voluntary, and some publishers license their copyrights for reproduction in the so-called devices independently (though virtually all copyright owners affiliate with a performing rights organization for the licensing of nondramatic public performance rights and the collection of public performance revenue).

Publishers generally find it advantageous to engage the services of a mechanical rights agency. For example, for an active music publisher to issue mechanical licenses to record companies each time a song in its catalog is recorded and scheduled for release would create a burdensome and costly administrative task. Mechanical rights agencies serve to ease this burden and simplify the clearing of rights.

Definition. A mechanical rights agency is an organization that licenses music copyrights on behalf of music publishers for reproduction in phonograph records, tapes, and other mechanical and audiovisual devices. (Thus the mechanical rights agency actually licenses both the mechanical right and the synchronization right of music copyrights.) It issues a license to anyone who wants to record the composition in a particular device under specific terms (negotiating under the instruction of the music publisher). It collects royalties or fees from licensees and distributes these to the publishers after deducting its commission.

Licensing Music Copyrights for Reproduction. Specifically, the mechanical rights agency may license a publisher's musical composition for reproduction in:

1. Commercial recordings for private use. The licensing of copyrights for reproduction and distribution in *phonograph records* and *audio tapes* for home use is virtually always accomplished under terms that vary with the compulsory license provision of the copyright law. A mechanical rights agency will issue mechanical (or recording) licenses to record companies on behalf of a publisher under customary industry terms or under terms specified by the publisher.

2. Motion pictures. Since the compulsory license does not apply to recording music in synchronization with motion pictures, producers must obtain a license from a copyright owner to use his composition in motion picture films. This right is licensed to motion picture producers by mechanical rights agencies on behalf of publishers or by publishers acting independently. Musical compositions are licensed for television and theatrical motion picture synchronization.

3. Radio and television commercials. The right to use a music copyright in any form of advertising including a *commercial* broadcast over radio or television vests in the copyright owner. To use a composition in advertising, a license must be obtained, and this right is administered by mechanical rights agencies on behalf of publishers under their instructions.

4. Recordings for nonprivate transmissions. The use of music for transmission other than private use is subject to licensing. A mechanical rights agency licenses the recording of music for reproduction in *audio tapes* that are used by syndicated radio services, background music services, in-flight (airline) music programmers, etc.

5. Video tapes/discs. The compulsory license provisions of the Copyright Act do not apply to reproducing a musical composition in a video device and a license must be obtained from the copyright owner. Mechanical rights agencies represent publishers with respect to licensing compositions for embodiment in video devices.

Commissions. A mechanical rights agency normally operates on a commission basis: it charges a music publisher a particular percentage of the collections it makes on behalf of the publisher (music users render payment to the mechanical rights agency, which in turn pays the publisher after deducting its commission). The commission usually varies with respect to the medium in which the copyright is used—that is, phonograph records, motion pictures, etc.

Commissions for licensing musical compositions vary from agency to agency and some may provide other administrative services for the music publisher, such as filing copyright registration forms; preparing songwriter, co-publisher, and subpublisher agreements; and maintaining the publisher's books. The HARRY FOX AGENCY, INC. (HFA), SESAC INC., and AMERICAN GUILD OF AUTHORS AND COMPOSERS are among the American organizations that license mechanical rights.

Time of Payment. A mechanical rights agency will usually account to the music publisher shortly after receipt of royalty payments or fees. For example, it is customary for record companies to account to publishers for record/tape sales quarterly, usually three-month periods ending March 31, June 30, September 30, and December 31. There is a 45-day period after each quarter allowed for the accounting procedures, during which record companies prepare their statements. Royalties, then, would actually start coming into the agency on May 15, August 15, November 15, and February 15. After the statements are checked out, the agency sends the royalties to the publisher.

Mechanical Rights Societies (Foreign). The mechanical right of a music copyright is one recognized by copyright laws of most countries throughout the world. In these countries the owner of a protected musical work has the exclusive right, usually subject to certain limitations, to reproduce the work in a device that mechanically reproduces sound or to grant to others the right to do so.

The mechanical royalty rate varies in different countries. In many countries the mechanical royalty rate is based on a percentage of the retail selling price of the mechanical reproduction (as opposed to a fixed rate) and commonly ranges from 6.25% to 8%.

In various foreign countries (as in the United States) there are *mechanical rights societies* that license copyrights for mechanical reproduction and motion picture synchronization. Some countries have organizations that license mechanical, synchronization, and *performance* rights.

A list of foreign societies that license mechanical, synchronization, and/or performance rights appears on pages 248–251.

Mechanical Royalties. *Mechanical* (or *recording*) *royalties* are earned by music publishers and songwriters from sales of "mechanical" devices (such as phonograph records and audio tapes) embodying their musical compositions.

Virtually each mechanical reproduction of a copyrighted musical work is licensed by the publisher or its agent (*see* MECHANICAL RIGHTS AGENCY) to the record manufacturer at a certain unit charge, or rate, known as the *mechanical rate*. A manufacturer that produces records and/or tapes embodying a copyrighted musical composition pays periodically to the owner of the copyright a mechanical royalty equal to the total number of records and tapes embodying such composition made and distributed during a particular period, times the mechanical rate for each unit.° Writers and publishers normally divide equally the mechanical royalties earned by a composition. In commercial practice, the mechanical rate is usually the same as the statutory rate (see page 86).

Royalty rates that vary from the statutory rate. Anyone is free to negotiate a royalty rate that is lower than the one provided in the statute to make and distribute records and tapes embodying a musical composition. With the exception of granting licenses in certain circumstances however, a music publisher will usually not agree to a lower rate. The exceptions are as follows:

Cut-outs, Overruns, Budget Albums. It is a common practice for record companies to request a mechanical royalty rate lower than the statutory rate for records and tapes sold to wholesalers and retailers at a cost much lower than normal, and which might retail at substantially reduced prices. Examples of such recordings include cut-outs, overruns, and budget albums.

Mechanical reproduction licenses customarily do not provide for a reduction in the mechanical royalty rate for recordings that are "cut out," or deleted, from the label's catalog at a later date. When the situation arises, record companies usually negotiate with the publisher to pay a lesser royalty rate for records sold.

Record and Tape Club Editions. An industry practice has arisen among record and tape clubs with regard to paying mechanical royalties. Record/tape clubs normally pay 75% of the rate the recording was originally licensed

at, but not less than 75% of statutory.

Public Domain Compositions. Record companies are not required to pay royalties on records and tapes that embody public domain compositions. However, manufacturers are required to pay royalties on copyrighted arrangements of PD songs, although they may request and receive permission to pay a lower rate.

The following table lists the customary industry royalty rates for reproduction of musical compositions in various classifications of records and tapes:

Mechanical Royalty Rates

Classification	Customary industry royalty rate/composition/unit made and distributed
Records (singles, LPs) and prerecorded tapes	Full statutory rate
Cut-outs, overruns, budget LPs, premiums	Subject to negotiation
Record and tape club editions	75% of the licensed rate but not less than 75% of statutory
Records and tapes embodying PD compositions	No royalty paid except for copyrighted arrangements of PD compositions, in which case the rate may range to the full statutory rate
Audio tapes for broadcast and background music purposes	Subject to negotiation

Review of Statutory Royalty Rate. The copyright law provides for the COPYRIGHT ROYALTY TRIBUNAL to review the statutory royalty rate for making and distributing phonorecords in 1980, 1987, and every 10 years thereafter, and to adjust it to a reasonable rate if necessary.

°There is an industry practice of record/tape manufacturers withholding a certain portion of mechanical royalties otherwise due, as "reserves" for returns of records and tapes.

Merchandising Tie-ins. Royalties derived from the licensing of merchandising rights associated with an artist may provide an important adjunct to the income of rights owners (recording artists and record companies). The appearance of a famous artist's name, trademark, logo, picture, or likeness on various types of products can substantially boost their sale. Consequently "tying in" merchandise with popular recording artists is desirable for both licensees and rights owners. Such merchandise can be lawfully manufactured and distributed by a company only if it has obtained a license for such purpose from the owner of merchandising rights of the artist whose name, picture, or other likeness appears on the product.

Types of Merchandise. Many products, with a little creativity and ingenuity, can be "tied in" with an artist. Merchandise bearing the likenesses of recording artists that have previously been licensed for manufacture and distribution include the following:

belt buckles	mugs
bumper stickers	notebooks
buttons	pajamas
caps	patches
colognes	pen and pencil sets
coloring books	posters
disco visors	souvenir books
dolls	sweaters
games	sweatshirts
heat transfers	T-shirts
jackets	tote bags
jigsaw puzzles	toys
jogging outfits	trading (bubble gum) cards
lampshades	wastebaskets
lunch boxes	wines
mirrors	wristwatches

Licenses. Licensing deals for merchandising tie-ins are usually made between the merchandise manufacturer and the party that owns the artist's merchandising rights. The owner of an artist's merchandising rights may be the record company to which the artist is signed or the artist himself. Some rights owners enter into agreements with specialized companies for representation of merchandising rights to manufacturers. Licenses for merchandising tie-ins are sometimes referred to as "personality" licenses. Important terms of such a license pertain to the exclusivity, territory, and length of the term of the license. Licensing deals are normally on a royalty and advance basis. Terms are of course negotiable; there is no standard licensing agreement for any merchandise tie-in.

Artist Tie-ins. Merchandise is sometimes manufactured and distributed to coincide with an artist's concert tour or record release. If the product is to be vended at concerts at which the artist performs, arrangements should be made between the artist's representatives and the concert promoters, hall managers, and/or concessionaires. Authorized seller-licensees may even accompany the artist on tour to vend the products at his concerts. Unlicensed hawkers are subject to prosecution in some cities.

See also ENDORSEMENT; PRIVACY AND PUBLICITY, RIGHTS OF.

Method Book. *See* PRINTED MUSIC.

Minor. The nature of the music business is such that much of its creative resources—namely, talent in the form of recording and performing groups, songwriters, and producers—is young. This is due in part to the tremendous appeal of music to youth, which may be explained by aesthetics and emotions, among other reasons. The industry, as most of us have observed, has a history of minors enjoying successful and lucrative careers.

A minor is a person who is under legal age. (This varies from state to state. In some states it is 21 for both males and females, in others, 21 for males and 18 for females; it may further vary in others.) Those who have not yet attained the age set as majority are referred to as "infants."

Infants have the right to enter into contracts with record companies, personal managers, booking agents, music publishers, and other companies, but such businesses usually do so at their own risk. The law permits an infant to void a contract at his option, as it considers young persons likely to be too immature or inexperienced to be legally responsible for their contracts and in need of protection from adults who might exploit them during their tender years.° Only the infant may disaffirm the contract; the adult's obligation to the terms of the agreement is binding. After the infant reaches majority, he has a reasonable time to repudiate the contract he made as a minor. After such time passes, he is deemed to have ratified the contract and it is enforceable.

A parent is not liable for a contract made by a minor unless the parent joins the minor in making the contract. Many companies require a parent to become a signatory to the contract as a prerequisite for making a contractual agreement. Under such circumstances, where a minor has repudiated the contract, the parent may be held liable for damages incurred by the minor's failure to fulfill his contractual obligations.

Where a minor misrepresents his age under contract, he may still void the contract before reaching majority. Furthermore, he may not be held liable for not fulfilling the contractual obligations. It is at an adult's peril that he makes a contract with a minor, whether or not the minor misrepresents his age. The minor, on the other hand, may use his infancy as both a sword and a shield.

The jurisdiction for disputes over contracts is at the state (as opposed to the federal) level, and each state has its own statute. There are various states with laws that provide a procedure whereby persons dealing with minors can

ask for court approval and may provide that minors may not disaffirm those contracts entered into with such court approval.

Mixdown. The process of combining (mixing) the recorded tracks of a multi-track MASTER to a more condensed format, such as 2 tracks for stereo. The process of mixing allows the engineer to enhance the sound of each separate track by using effects such as equalization, reverb, and delay to achieve a final recording having the desired overall sound.

Mixing is done after the recording process is complete (i.e., after all the tracks have been "laid down"). After recording, there is a tape containing 4, 8, 16, 24, or whatever number of tracks have been used. It is necessary to transfer the sound on all these separate tracks onto a "master-mix" tape—usually a half-track stereo quarter-inch tape—that is used for lacquer or subsequent tape mastering (*see* RECORD MANUFACTURING). Mixing can be a complex and time-consuming process, depending upon the personal tastes of the mixer and producer and the degree to which they feel it is necessary. Some original recordings, primarily classical, are mixed down live at the session, the result being a finished 2-track stereo original master which requires no further mixdown.

Mixed Folio. *See* PRINTED MUSIC.

Monaural Recording. All phonograph records released prior to 1958 (when stereophonic records were commercially introduced to the public) were monophonic or monaural. Sales of monaural records became substantially reduced as stereophonic records enjoyed increasing popularity. Some major record companies, while still simultaneously releasing records in both mono and stereo, raised the retail price for mono pop albums to that for stereo around the mid 1960s, further contributing to their demise, and by the end of the decade monaural records were all but completely phased

---

° Infants may be liable, however, for contracts involving "necessaries"—food, shelter, medicine, clothing. Usually they must be 16 years old even for this rule to apply.

out. Various older recordings have been re-issued in "simulated stereo," in which the sounds originally recorded in mono on the masters have been reprocessed using one or more of several techniques to give a stereo *effect* when played on the proper equipment.

A monaural recording (disc or tape) has all the musical information stored and reproduced on one channel even though the inputs for such a recording could come from multiple sources. When a monophonic disc is cut, both walls of the groove are inscribed with the identical sound information. (On stereo records, the left and right channels are cut into the two groove walls.) Monophonic records may be played on stereo phonographs.

Today, "demos" are commonly recorded in mono. Also, record labels commonly give radio stations promotion copies of singles containing one side in mono, the other in stereo.

Motion Picture Music. Music has almost always played a vital role in motion pictures. Even before the development of a motion picture sound track in 1927, films (and viewers) enjoyed musical accompaniment; pianists and orchestras provided such fare for silent films. Much of the music pianists played was incidental and improvised spontaneously to underscore dramatic or other action on the screen. Background music eventually became more sophisticated, with the creation of full original musical scores. Later, symphonic orchestras replaced piano players in some theaters, and title and theme songs were used for movies. (These songs were largely supplied by "Tin Pan Alley" publishers in New York.) A popular title song could promote a movie and a successful movie could in turn encourage sales of the song's sheet music and recordings. The same holds true today.

The use of music in conjunction with motion pictures does not come within the scope of any compulsory license of the copyright law. To legally use a preexisting copyrighted musical work in a theatrical motion picture, a producer will seek from the copyright owner or its representative, such as a MECHANICAL RIGHTS AGENCY, the right to use a recording of the composition on the soundtrack of the film. Since the film is intended or likely to be exhibited in the United States, the producer must also obtain from the copyright owner the right to perform it publicly. In the United States it has been ruled that theatrical motion picture exhibitors are not required to obtain a performance license to show films containing copyrighted music (in contrast to the practice in many foreign countries where motion picture theater operators must take out a performance license); thus, publishers license the public performance right to the motion picture producer. Such rights are commonly granted on a single license. Producers often negotiate worldwide synchronization rights and U.S. public performance rights for the life of the copyright. License fees range from a small amount of money to substantial sums.

Determination of License Fees. As stated above, when music is used in a film a license fee is negotiated. Various criteria are considered in measuring the value of the composition to the movie. Among them are the following: the budget of the film, the cast (i.e., stars), the producer (i.e., a major motion picture company), the popularity of the song, the type of use of the music (i.e., whether it is vocal/visual, backgound vocal, visual/instrumental), the size of the orchestra, the length of the film, the timing of the music, the importance of the song to the film, the singer, the number of times the song is used, the territory or territories for which rights are being sought, and whether the producer is seeking the rights to use the film on television (free, pay, cable) or for purposes of selling videocassettes and videodiscs embodying it.

Copyright Aspects. Under the copyright law, motion pictures are considered "audiovisual works," defined in the 1976 Copyright

Act (Section 101) as "works that consist of a series of related images which are intrinsically intended to be shown by the use of machines or devices such as projectors, viewers, or electronic equipment, together with accompanying sounds, if any, regardless of the nature of the material objects, such as films or tapes, in which the works are embodied." Motion pictures, including sound tracks, may be filed for copyright registration in Class PA.

See SOUND TRACK.

Music Box. A box, case, or other object containing a mechanism that plays a tune.

Mechanism. Musical sounds result from the vibrations produced when pins projecting from a revolving cylinder or disc "pluck" tuned teeth cut in a comblike metal plate, at intervals corresponding to the rhythm of the melody. The sound vibrations of the tuned teeth are generally amplified by a "sounding board," much like that in a piano, to a reasonably audible volume level. The cylinder or disc's revolving motion is produced by the winding of a spring-driven mechanism and the revolution rate is controlled by a fly regulator.

Licensing of Tunes. Under the copyright law, music boxes are considered to be PHONORECORDS. Hence the compulsory license for making and distributing phonorecords embodying nondramatical musical works applies to music boxes. In commercial practice, however, mechanical licenses with terms that vary from the compulsory licenses are almost always used (these licenses are sometimes titled "Music Box Movement"). Musical compositions, though rarely appearing in their entirety in music boxes, are usually licensed at the full statutory rate.

Description. Music boxes are often artistically designed. The mechanism that plays the tune might be part of a jewel box or be embodied in an object such as a figurine or a small replica of a piano, gramophone, or bird cage. Music boxes may range in price from a few dollars, to a few hundred dollars or more for an elaborately decorated one. The songs that music box manufacturers reproduce are usually standards.

Music Critics and Reviews. Music criticism is a somewhat unique genre in the field of reviewing, as it is so diversified. Music critics review recorded performances, live concert performances (ranging from rock to symphonic concerts), musical shows presented in the legitimate theater, and operas. Reviews may of course have the positive effect of promoting record sales, stimulating ticket sales to concerts and theatrical productions, and enhancing a performer's career. On the other hand, they may have the opposite effect in each of these areas. The music critic, as any other reviewer, assumes the responsibility of entertaining, informing, and guiding with the public interest in mind.

Reviews of Recordings. In reviewing recorded performances, the critic states certain basic information: the name of the artist, album, or single, and the record label. Depending on the particular publication (and audience) he is reviewing for, the critic may also include any of the following: the name of the producer and arranger, the recording's catalog number, the distributor (if different from the label), the retail prices, and the configurations the product is available in—LP, cassette tape, 8-track tape cartridge, and/or reel-to-reel tape. If the selections were recorded in a special way, such as direct-to-disc, this would also be noted.

As most reviews normally run 100 to 350 words in length, it is important for the critic to get to the point quickly, but not dryly. The review may make reference to any of the following: the genre of music (rock, jazz, classical, etc.), the distinctive style and "sound" of the performer (if any), the performer's musical interpretation, the number of cuts, the best (and worst) cuts, the lyrics (short lyric extracts are often revealing), whether the songs are best suited for the artist and if the artist wrote any of them, if there is any chance the songs might be recorded by other artists, the chart potential of any of the cuts or whether success may be predicted on the package as a whole, the commerciality of the album, the production and arrangement in terms of suitability to the artist and material, how the album compares to previous releases by the artist, the quality of performances by other instrumentalists, vocalists, and artists, and their names if noteworthy, the album cover artwork, photographs, or liner notes, and for audiophile recordings, the quality of reproduction. A picture of the artist or album cover may accompany the review of new releases.

Reviews of Live Performances. Reviews of popular-music concerts in arenas, stadiums, concert halls, nightclubs, cabarets, etc., will contain some or all of the following basic information: the name of the performer, the venue and, depending on the publication, city where the artist performed, the date and time of the performance, the price range of tickets, the number of seats in the facility and the approximate percentage that were filled, and the audience response.

The review may evaluate the artist's performing ability, style, "sound," interpretation of songs, and stage presence, as well as the songs performed (indicating which ones got the best response), the arrangements, the overall musicianship (and vocal accompaniment), the conductor (where appropriate), the acoustics, and the quality of the sound system. It may also give the names of any backup musicians and vocalists, specify the opening and closing numbers, and mention whether the artist has a current recording available. Reviews of live performances are more commonly found in daily newspapers and weekly trades. A photograph of the performer may accompany the review.

Classical musical concerts run the gamut from debut piano recitals to important premieres of symphonic works. The reviewer of such concerts may comment on the performer's technique, interpretation, experience, and education as well as the composer of the work. The classical music reviewer has usually studied the works of important composers, music history, composition, and related courses including musical journalism on at least a college level.

Reviews of Musical Shows. Reviews of musical shows are of a different breed. Here, the critic must additionally focus on the book and the cast, and evaluate the integration of the book and the musical numbers. The reviewer may note if there are any "showstoppers," mention the ticket prices, and recommend seeing the show or not.

Reviews of musical shows may be very influential. Damaging reviews have been known to close expensive Broadway musical productions in as little as one night. On the other hand, a single enthusiastic review by a respected critic might persuade a producer to bring a show to Broadway. A Broadway show is usually reviewed on its official opening night performance, though critics are sometimes invited to review a Broadway or an Off Broadway show at an earlier performance.

Specialization of Critics. Critics working for magazines and large newspapers usually cover specific areas only. Typically, separate critics might write about popular music, classical music, and theater.

Qualities of the Critic. The qualities any competent critic should have include good judgment, high standards, objectivity, veracity, literacy, diligence, a crisp writing style, a sense of what the public will like, and the ability to write under deadline pressure.

Music Director. *See* RADIO STATION.

Music Jobber. Company that buys PRINTED

Music directly from music publishers or their print licensees, and sells this to retailers. A jobber handles such printed editions as sheet music, personality folios, mixed folios, method books, instrumental folios, and choral, orchestral, and band arrangements. A music jobber, also referred to as a *wholesale distributor*, *one-stop*, or *rack jobber*, usually offers retailers who buy music in small quantities faster service and greater savings in postage than the publisher or its representative.

Music jobbers vary in size and accounts serviced. A "full-line" music jobber, whose accounts include music stores, record stores, and booksellers, maintains a substantial inventory of printed music issued by all publishers. A rack jobber specializes—it maintains an inventory only on items that are fast movers, such as the top 25 personality folios. Music rack jobbers often service department stores and have programs for providing inventory and exchanging unsold merchandise.

Discounts. Music jobbers buy product from publishers, selling agents, and licensees at various discounts—generally ranging between 50% and 55% off the marked retail selling price. Jobbers, in turn, offer discounts to retailers normally ranging from 25% to 40%.

Music Publisher. Music publishers are the proprietors of a unique and special kind of property—*songs*. A song, which is intangible within itself, can be reproduced in many different objects and be communicated by various media to millions of people throughout the world. Furthermore, it is an artistic product that is not necessarily subject to antiquation. Many themes are timeless; moreover, music can continually be arranged to conform to the latest vogues. In view of the creativity of the music business and the volatility of public taste, a song can be a source of income for its life in the publisher's catalog, particularly if it becomes a STANDARD.

The music publishing industry has its basis in the *copyright law*. This law grants exclusive rights to copyright owners which enable them to authorize uses of their compositions for a limited time and collect fees for such uses.

Definition. A music publisher° is a company that seeks musical compositions with commercial potential from songwriters, negotiates and obtains the rights to them for a particular time period, and "manages" these songs with the objective of causing them to realize their full commercial potential. "Management" of a musical composition (as used in this definition) includes:

- Administering the copyright (*see* ADMINISTRATION OF A MUSIC PUBLISHER'S CATALOG).
- Causing the song to be recorded by popular and new recording artists with the intention that such recordings be subsequently released in records and tapes by bona fide record companies.
- Causing the song to be reproduced or used—usually after it has achieved substantial popularity in a recording—in: sheet music, songbooks, and other printed editions; theatrical motion pictures; television motion pictures and programs; videodiscs and videocassettes; advertising announcements; stage productions; syndicated radio programs; and "other" areas (see *ancillary revenues* below).
- Promoting and publicizing uses of the copyright in its various forms.
- Protecting the copyright from all types of infringements.

Period of "Ownership." As stated above, music publishers obtain rights to musical compositions for limited time periods. This is qualified by the following:

1. The copyright statute provides that for a work created on or after January 1, 1978, and assigned or transferred by the author to another proprietor (e.g., a publisher), such grant may be terminated within certain time limits

---

°There are various "types" of music publishers (as explained below), but this definition is applicable to bona fide publishers whose full-time operation is the "publishing" of songs. Also, this definition refers to publishers of "popular" (as opposed to "standard") music.

The Many Worlds of a Music Copyright. A music copyright may be used in many different ways and thus have various sources of income. Some of the ways a song may be used are in: radio, records and tapes, motion pictures, advertising, posters, music boxes, sheet music, songbooks, and other printed editions, other areas of reproduction such as this shower curtain.

at a later date (*see* COPYRIGHT GRANTS, TER-MINATION OF).°

2. Rights to a work created and assigned to a publisher before January 1, 1978, may be revested in the author or his heir for the renewal term, if the rights to the work in such term contractually revert to the author and renewal registration is properly made; where renewal rights for a work have been assigned to the publisher and the publisher makes proper renewal, the author of that work may reclaim ownership for the last 19 years of the 47-year renewal term of copyright protection.

3. Ownership of works made for hire becomes permanently vested in the employer (unless otherwise assigned or transferred by the employer) and authors may not recapture the renewal rights (for pre-1978 songs) under "work made for hire" or "employee for hire" arrangements.

4. Publisher (and author) no longer control and own the rights to a work when the period of copyright protection expires (*see* PUBLIC DOMAIN).

Types of Music Publishers. In the United States and other countries throughout the world, music publishers are diversified in both their size and the types of music they publish. Publishers range in size from one-person operations to considerable divisions of large companies.† Publishers' catalogs may comprise all types of popular music compositions or they may specialize in works that are primarily written for a particular medium or are of a particular style—show, film, gospel, religious, educational, or serious music.

Though all music publishers share the common goal of maximizing income from their catalogs, one may classify these entities into several different types, based upon the ownership of the operation. There are "independent" music publishers whose only business is publishing and exploiting songs. These companies have no ownership affiliation with a record or motion picture company.

There are also music publishing companies which are owned by or are affiliated with the various individuals and companies who create or acquire rights in musical compositions, such as songwriters, recording artists, record producers, managers, record companies, motion picture companies, and advertising agencies.

It should be noted that those publishing firms established by artists, producers, songwriters, and personal managers often do not perform copyright and business administrations, but enter into administration agreements with other companies or entities.

Many publishing companies deal with songs of several genres of popular musical. Most of these companies, however, do not publish educational or serious music. This entry will center on the full-functioning publisher of popular songs.

Sources of Income. A music publishing company derives its income solely from "uses" of its copyrights. A song may be used in many ways and the publisher serves to get the song used in these ways to maximize its earnings. Copyrights are almost always used by *licensees* (an exception would be the publisher that handles its own printing and distribution of sheet music).

The different types of income for a music copyright include:

1. Performance royalties (*See* PERFORMING RIGHTS ORGANIZATION).

°"Reversion" clauses in songwriter/music publisher agreements provide for the publisher to reassign the copyright to the writer if it fails to cause a commercial sound recording of the composition within a certain time period (usually 1 year from assignment) or pay a stipulated sum for an additional term in which to cause the song to be recorded.

†Examples of the latter include, at this writing: April/Blackwood Music Inc. (CBS), Chappell Music Co. (Poly-Gram Corp.), and Warner Bros. Music (Warner Bros. Inc.).

2. MECHANICAL ROYALTIES.

3. Synchronization fees. To use music in conjunction with motion pictures, a film producer must obtain a synchronization license from the copyright proprietor. A license fee is negotiated between the film producer and the publisher (or its agent) and is determined by several criteria (*see* MOTION PICTURE MUSIC). Synchronization fees are paid to use a copyright in theatrical motion pictures, television films, industrial films, and other types of motion pictures.

4. Print royalties. Songs are published in many types of printed editions, including sheet music, songbooks, folios, anthologies, and choral, band, and orchestral arrangements. Publication of printed copies is handled by the music publisher either directly or through selling agents or licensees.

5. Ancillary revenues. Copyrights can earn income from uses in other areas, including advertising (jingles), music boxes, magazines, posters, and greeting cards (lyrics), and items based on the copyright, such as toys, games, puzzles, calendars, greeting cards, sweat shirts, bath towels, umbrellas, and gift wrap.

Foreign Earnings. The administration, exploitation, and management of the copyright is performed in foreign territories by subsidiaries of the U.S. publisher or by subpublishers it licenses. Where American commercial records are not released abroad, the foreign publisher's function is usually to stimulate recordings and releases of the copyright in its territory and, in a non-English-speaking country, have a native translation of the lyric made. A foreign publisher collects all revenue earned by the copyright in its territory and transmits it to the U.S. publisher after making deductions for its negotiated share. Considerable amounts of money may be earned on U.S. copyrights published overseas, even on songs that aren't very successful in America.

Structure. Bona fide music publishing companies have several different departments to handle the multiform supervision of copyrights. Following is a general examination of the departments of a "major" music publisher. The reader should consider, however, that no two music publishing companies are structured alike or operate the same way, and different publishers may use different names for departments or titles for positions.

Copyright Department. This department deals with copyright and writer contract administration. It prepares copyright applications and documents conveying transfer of copyright ownership and files these in the U.S. Copyright Office, secures international copyright protection, logs songwriter contracts, files copyright renewals, and registers songs with the company's performing rights organization.

Licensing Department. Prepares and issues mechanical licenses for recordings and licenses for uses of the copyrights in other areas, including folios and songbooks, advertising, theatrical motion pictures, television shows, music boxes, and magazines. If the publisher is represented by an agent for licensing copyrights in mechanical reproductions, this department will instruct the agent with respect to license terms.

Accounting Department. This department administers the company's finances. It handles the books of account, collects royalties and license fees, and disburses overhead expenses and writers' advances and royalties. It regularly prepares internal statements of income (and loss) and balance sheets (statements of assets, liabilities, and net worth). It might also prepare and analyze budgets. The activities of the accounting department are supervised by the finance officer.

Royalty Department. Assembles and records information regarding royalties and fees received from performing and mechanical rights licensing organizations, print distributors, and other licensees, and prepares royalty statements for writers, copublishers, and publishers whose catalogs the company administers, in accordance with the terms of the contracts. Much of this work is done with the assistance of computers. In some cases, this department is combined with the accounting department.

Business Affairs Department. Negotiates songwriting, copublishing, administration, and subpublication agreements.

Legal Department. Drafts contracts with respect to the above and also handles claims, copyright infringements, and other matters dealing with the legality of a contract or copyright.

Creative Department. See below.

Large publishing companies, depending on their size, may also have any of the following departments:

Publicity Department. Prepares press releases and sends them to the trade and consumer press to promote the company's copy-

THE ROLE OF THE MUSIC PUBLISHER

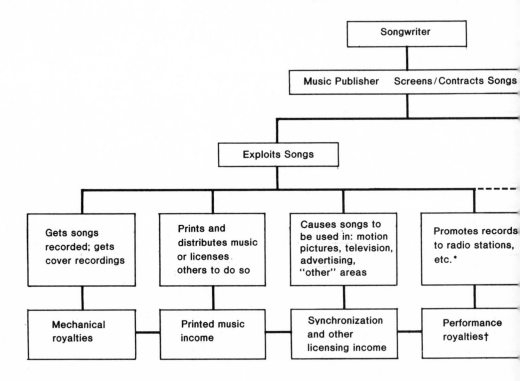

*The promotion of records to radio stations and other areas of public performance is not necessarily a function of a music publisher.

†The practice of performing rights organizations is to pay writers and publishers performance royalties separately.

**If the company copublishes songs with another music publisher, administers another publisher's catalog, or subpublishes a foreign company's catalog, it would remit revenues to such entity as per the agreement.

rights and maintain an industry and public awareness of its activities and achievements. It may also function to create copy for trade advertisements.

Promotion Department. Contacts radio stations to obtain airplay for releases containing compositions owned by the company. This department is sometimes combined with the publicity department.

Print Department. Oversees the publication of printed editions containing the company's copyrights, such as sheet music, songbooks, and folios. It employs or hires editors, arrangers, and proofreaders, whose functions are to prepare various compositions for print in the consumer and educational fields. Only a few of the very largest music publishers have print (or publication) departments. Publishers more commonly license print rights to their copyrights to other companies (*see* PRINTED MUSIC, LICENSING AND DISTRIBUTION OF). In such a case, the publisher may license songs for reproduction in sheet music and folios to one print distributor and for reproduction in edu-

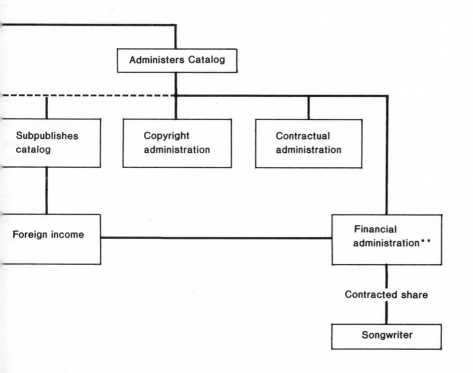

cational publications (including band, orchestral, and choral) to another.

Sales Department. Concerned with selling the company's printed products to distributors, wholesalers, jobbers, and retailers. Again, only a few publishers have such a department and it is sometimes combined with the print department. Personnel in the sales area include salespersons and shipping and inventory clerks.

Creative Department. Most music publishing companies, large or small, maintain a creative department. This department plays a very important role in the publisher's overall activities. Basically, it functions to acquire musical compositions with commercial potential and to get these and other copyrights in the catalog recorded and used in other media.

The creative department is staffed by one or more *professional managers.* The responsibilities of the professional manager fall into the following areas:

Scouts Songs and Talent. The professional manager seeks to acquire songs with hit potential for the company. He screens songs in the office from writers who submit demos by mail or play them at personal appointments. His search takes him outside the office, where he listens to the material of writers and singer/songwriters who perform at clubs, cabarets, coffeehouses, theaters, concert halls, and showcases. When interested in signing songs, he initiates contract negotiations by putting the writers in touch with the business affairs department.

Nurtures Talent. The professional manager works with songwriters signed to the company and with outsiders who show promising ability. He criticizes, edits, and restructures songs and develops commercial songwriting skills.

Makes Demos and Lead Sheets. In attempting to get songs in the company's catalog recorded, the professional manager auditions them with artists, producers, and others (see below), mostly via demos. If the writer does

not have an acceptable demo for a new song that the company acquires, the professional manager goes into the recording studio and makes one. An assistant professional manager oversees the making of tape and acetate demo copies so that songs may be submitted to numerous artists, producers, labels, and others. Lead sheets or lyric sheets are also prepared for songs the professional manager auditions.

"Casts" songs. In attempting to get a song in the catalog recorded, the professional manager will often first "cast" it. Casting involves determining which artists record "outside" songs, and of those, which ones the song would be suitable for or in the style of.

Casting may be done in various ways. For example, at meetings ("brainstorming" sessions), the creative staff may play songs in the company's catalog and decide which ones to present to particular artists. The professional manager studies the CHARTS to determine which artists are currently "hot."

Some professional managers maintain files indicating which artists seek outside material, their performing style and history of recording successes, the type of material they are looking for, any new musical direction or image they are seeking, and past contacts with them. The professional manager's own knowledge of and experience in the music business is of course invaluable in casting songs.

Auditions Songs. A song must be *exposed* in order to get recorded. The professional manager auditions the song (in demo form) with recording artists, record producers, record company employees (A & R coordinators, label executives, promotion representatives, etc.), arrangers, personal and business managers, booking agents, members of artists' bands—anyone who might be able to get it recorded.

He makes appointments and plays the demos at personal meetings or submits them by mail with a cover letter (e.g., "Dear Producer: Enclosed is a song I feel would be excellent for . . ."). He keeps records of all activities and follows up on submissions. Addresses and telephone numbers of individuals and companies he contacts may be published in the trades or in various directories. In some companies, each professional manager will have a list of producers he is responsible for servicing.

Gets Cover Records. After the song is initially recorded and the recording is released, it is the responsibility of the creative department to obtain "cover" records of it. In obtaining covers, the original artist's master is often sent out as the "demo." Songs that have been recorded previously are periodically "reworked" in this way.

In attempting to expose catalog material, publishing companies with a substantial number of hits in their catalogs sometimes press several hundred LPs containing a group of them or identifying excerpts from several and send them to producers, artists, labels, etc. In the case of a publisher promoting the talents of a particular writer who has had much chart activity, it will accompany the promotional LP or "sample album" containing his hits with a writer's "press kit," which includes a biography, a discography, and photos.

Other Areas of Exploitation. The professional manager will try to get the copyright used in other areas that can generate income, such as folios and songbooks printed and distributed by other companies, advertising announcements, theatrical motion pictures, television shows, stage productions, transcriptions, posters, greeting cards, etc. Such uses of the copyright may produce substantial earnings. If the company lacks a promotion department, the professional manager may also assist the record company in convincing radio station music or program directors to add the recording of the company's song to their station's playlist.

Miscellaneous Creative Duties. If the company has entered into subpublication agreements, the professional manager may be involved with these foreign publishers—recommending and submitting songs for them to work with in their local territories as well as trying to obtain covers on foreign songs that the company has rights to. He may also be involved with record production and publicity. If the music publisher is affiliated with a motion picture company, he screens the films it produces and plugs individual songs from the movies.

Other Aspects of Music Publishing

Obtaining Contracts with Labels for Artist- and Producer-Writers. Some music publishers seek to obtain recording and production contracts with record companies for those artists and producers who write their own material. The publisher of course signs these writers to contracts and owns or shares the rights to compositions they create under the term of agreement. Some publishers even produce finished masters containing songs they own and sell or license these masters to record companies.

Agreements with Other Publishers. Music publishers commonly enter into agreements with other music publishers. There are:

Copublishing agreements—Agreements in which publishers share in the ownership of a copyright or catalog.

Administration agreements—These involve a publisher's administering the catalog of another for a share of its receipts. This type of agreement is subject to termination at the expiration of the contract.

Foreign subpublishing agreements—These may be on a "collection" basis only or the full services of the foreign publisher may be engaged (i.e., exploitation, promotion, etc.).

Audits. In issuing licenses, music publishers normally reserve the right to audit the licensee. Music publishers either audit record companies and other licensees directly or have this function performed on their behalf by an agent, such as a MECHANICAL RIGHTS AGENCY. Music publishers might also be subject to audits by songwriters with whom they have entered into agreements.

International Subsidiaries. Large music publishers may have subsidiaries in one or more important music markets throughout the world. Important foreign markets include Australia, Belgium, Canada, England, France, Germany, Italy, Japan, the Netherlands, New Zealand, South Africa, Spain, Sweden, and Switzerland. Subsidiaries function as regular publisjing companies in their markets and exploit and promote copyrights owned by the company, including those that come from offices in other countries. Companies that do not have subsidiaries in foreign countries enter commonly into subpublication agreements (*see* INTERNATIONAL SUBPUBLISHING AGREEMENTS).

The table on the facing page indicates the main types of licenses a copyright owner (music publisher) or its representative issues.

Musical Theater. The musical theater encompasses various kinds of live theatrical entertainment utilizing music. In the 20th century, the American musical theater has been primarily associated with the musical comedy and the musical play. Both are similar in that dialogue and plot are closely integrated with songs and dances, they are collaborative efforts, and are guided by commercial considerations. In musical comedy, however, the plot is lighter, there are more jokes, and the characters are more overstated. Musical plays may deal with more serious matters, be more dramatic, possess a stronger book, and have tighter integration of story and music.

Examples of musical comedies are *My Fair Lady, Gypsy, Bye Bye Birdie,* and *Grease;* examples of musical plays are *South Pacific, West Side Story, The Sound of Music,* and *A Chorus Line.* Musical comedies and plays are presented on Broadway and throughout the United States by touring, stock, and regional companies and by amateur groups.

Theatrical productions in the United States are as old as the country itself (they actually predate its founding). At the time of the Revolutionary War there existed a form of musical theater consisting of plays with songs interpolated. The minstrel show, one of the few indigenous forms of American musical theater, began in the 1840s. It was characterized by a company of blackface performers giving a comic variety show of songs, dances, and routines.

The minstrel show was followed by other forms of musical theater, including variety, extravaganza, burlesque, pantomime, farce comedy, revues, and comic operas. European operas and operettas influenced the development of American musical comedies and plays.

Today's American musical theater is an industry in itself. It utilizes the talents of composers, lyricists, playwrights, singers, actors, musicians, choreographers, directors, producers, set designers, lighting and sound technicians, and others. Sheet music, printed scores, recordings, and motion pictures are some of its by-products.

See BROADWAY MUSICAL; OFF BROADWAY THEATER.

Musician. Music is more than just a popular form of entertainment. It is a pervasive aspect of our everyday life. Indeed it is all around us—at home or at the office, in a car or on a plane, at a restaurant or in a supermarket, at church or in school. The performers of music—*musicians*—consequently play a significant role in society's cultural development as well as comprise an important, albeit relatively small, segment of the work force.

Performance Fields of Employment. There are various fields of employment for performing musicians, including the following:

concerts and live performances
phonograph records
commercial announcements (jingles)

Licenses Issued for Uses of Music Copyrights

Use	Type of License Needed	Licensor	Licensee(s)
To make and distribute records and tapes of a song (under terms that vary from the compulsory music license provision of the copyright law)	Mechanical (recording) license	Copyright owner (or mechanical rights agency representing it)	Record company, record producer, tape manufacturer, record/tape club, record merchandising company
To publicly perform a song (e.g., over radio or television or at concert halls, clubs, hotels)	Nondramatic performance license	Performing rights organization representing copyright owner	Broadcasters, business proprietors, concert promoters, etc.
To publicly perform a dramatic musical work such as a musical comedy, play, light opera, or ballet	Grand rights license	Copyright owner	Theatrical producer; repertory, touring, regional or stock company; amateur or school group; etc.
To use a musical composition in conjunction with film for U.S. theatrical exhibition or on a television program, series or film	Synchronization and performance license*	Copyright owner (or mechanical rights agency representing it)	Motion picture producer, television producer
To reproduce and publish a musical composition in sheet music, folios, songbooks, and other printed editions	Print license	Copyright owner	Print licensee (if not printed and distributed by the publisher)
To share ownership or control of a copyright	Copublishing agreement	Copyright owner	Copublisher
To handle the administrative functions of a copyright or catalog on behalf of the copyright owner	Administration agreement	Copyright owner	Administrator
To represent and license a song in a foreign country	Subpublishing agreement	Copyright owner	Subpublisher

*For theatrical motion pictures, the producer will obtain the performance license from the copyright owner (or its representative); for television broadcasting, the producer will usually not have to acquire a performance license directly from the copyright owner, as the blanket license granted by a performing rights organization covers performance rights on all TV stations which hold such a license.

network radio and television
TV films
TV videotape
cable and educational TV
theatrical motion pictures
industrial films
electrical transcriptions
legitimate theater

Employers. Employers of musicians include orchestras (major, regional, metropolitan, urban, community, college, youth); motion picture, television, theatrical, and industrial show producers; record manufacturers; record producers; advertisers (sponsors and agencies); concert promoters; proprietors of concert halls, theaters, nightclubs, discos, cafés, and other venues where music is performed live; hotels, catering establishments; bandleaders; private citizens (for private music lessons, parties, etc.); and educational and religious institutions.

Job Opportunities. Employment opportunities for musicians vary. Some fields, particularly those involving recording and concert performance, have traditionally been overcrowded and highly competitive. The number of positions available for employment in phonograph, jingle, motion picture, and television recording or in symphony orchestras, for example, has long been exceeded by the number of qualified job seekers. Despite the situation as it exists in these competitive areas, however, there is always a need for outstanding musicians.

Other areas, such as teaching (in school or privately) or nightclub engagements, have offered reasonable opportunities for employment. Positions as teachers in public schools normally require state certification in addition to college or advanced degrees.

Unions. Professional musicians working in the fields of recording and live performance belong to unions, which make agreements with employers providing for minimum wages (scale) and other conditions of employment for their members. Most belong to the AMERICAN FEDERATION OF MUSICIANS OF THE UNITED STATES AND CANADA (AFM), which

has jurisdiction over most areas. Instrumental concert soloists are members of the AMERICAN GUILD OF MUSICAL ARTISTS (AGMA).

Musician's Glossary

Ax—a musical instrument

Bread—salary for a performing engagement

Chops—lips (term used in reference to brass instrument players)

Chord changes—harmonic modulations

Clinker—a mistake made while performing on a musical instrument

Date—a recording session

Gig—a recording session or a job where the musician or singer performs for a fee

Groove—the rhythm, beat, sound, or "feel" of a song

Horn—any wind instrument, particularly a brass one

Lick—a brief, improvised passage interpolated into a song by a musician

Platter—a phonograph record

Scale—minimum wage for an engagement as provided by the performer's union

Sideman—a musician at a recording session or performing engagement

Stick—a woodwind instrument

Studio—a recording studio; place where songs are recorded

Wax—to record; a phonograph record

See also SIDEMAN.

N

Names of Recording Artists. As recording artists are in the limelight, their personal or group *names* are of special concern. While success is of course based largely upon quality of performance and other factors, a distinctive name can enhance public identification and awareness of the artist. Consequently the artist desires a name that blends with and projects a certain IMAGE.

Names and Images. Often a name is intentionally devised by an artist, personal manager, or record company to create a particular image. For example, a name with "rose" in it, such as Rosewater or Rosebud, creates the feeling that the artist's music is of a soft rock or adult contemporary vein; a name with "sweet" implies the artist's music is melodic. On the other hand, a name with "blood," "fire," or "rock" in it connotes a group with a harder, more aggressive sound.

A comparison of the chartmakers on the pop, country, and soul charts reveals a preponderance of artists with simple or common names. However, a study of these charts indicates that the most simple names are often in country and the most inventive names in pop; soul lies somewhere in the middle.

Types of Names. The names of recording artists and performers generally fit into certain basic categories. These include the following (with examples used to illustrate the category):

Individual names (real or pseudonyms)—Elvis Presley, Engelbert Humperdinck, Carole King, Stevie Wonder, Dolly Parton

Individuals using one name (first or last) alone or with another word—Donovan, Tiny Tim, Mama Cass, Liberace, Montovani

Group names—Beatles; Lovin' Spoonful; Kiss; Blondie; Oak Ridge Boys; Styx; Manhattan Transfer; REO Speedwagon

Group names bearing the name of the featured performer, leader, or other person—Diana Ross and the Supremes, Dave Clark Five, Gladys Knight and the Pips, Tony Orlando and Dawn, Sly and the Family Stone

Group names indicating the number of members—Three Degrees, Four Seasons, Four Tops, Classics Four, Fifth Dimension

Names indicating a duet, trio, quartet, etc.—Simon and Garfunkel; Emerson, Lake and Palmer; Peter, Paul and Mary; Crosby, Stills, Nash and Young

Names indicating kinship or implying kinship—Allman Brothers, Ike and Tina Turner, Partridge Family, The Jacksons, Hager Twins

Name Changes. Entertainers may adopt a pseudonym with or without formally and legally changing their names. Anyone may change his or her name at any time, provided the change is not intended to deceive the public or defraud some creditor.

Name changes may be effected in either of two ways: by the mere adoption of a new name or through a petition made in a court of law. The former process is instantaneous, but without any kind of legal document the artist may have difficulty in trying to establish credit, obtain loans, travel, or collect income, and may be forced to continue his or her old name for particular purposes.

If the use of the new name or pseudonym is to be permanent, the best way to effect a name change is through a relatively simple procedure in a court of law (a legal change is normally made through a court of law). Each jurisdiction may have its own regulations with regard to name changes and a person should consult the local court of the county in which he resides. In New York, for example, a petition to assume another name is usually made by a resident of the state to the county court or the supreme court of the county in which he resides. If the person resides in New York City, he may make a petition either to the supreme court or to any branch of the civil court of the city of New York, in any county of the city of New York.

A court may require a valid reason for a name change and has the authority to refuse such requests. If the change will result in fraud as determined by the court (such as to escape creditors), it may deny such a request. Courts normally recognize the commercial value of a name change for performers and generally permit such change so long as it does not conflict with the name of an established performer. When a name has been changed, the person should contact a social security office to request a new card bearing the changed name.

Legal Protection of Names. The name of an entertainer, an act, or a company may be protected under the federal trademark law by registration of the name as a trademark or service mark. The application for registration must be filed with the Patent and Trademark Office and in the name of the owner of the mark. A competent specialist in the laws of patents and trademarks is essential.

Names of recording artists or performers may be registered if the name identifies a service. The name of a recording artist or performer is registrable as a *service mark* since it is considered that such a person (or group) is rendering an entertainment service. The requirement for federal registration of an entertainer's name is that the party have previously performed in at least two states using the name he seeks to register. Once service mark rights in a name are acquired, no one else can use it for the same or similar service. Even simple names may be registered in appropriate instances and for particular uses, though others might subsequently claim use of the name. Examiners at the Patent and Trademark Office use their experience and individual judgment as to whether the public is likely to be confused by the conflicting marks (*see* TRADEMARKS).

National Academy of Recording Arts and Sciences (NARAS, Recording Academy).

Organization that represents creative people in the recording field. It serves to recognize, encourage, and reward artistic achievement within the recording field and to advance its standards.

Membership. The Recording Academy's membership is comprised of individuals (but not companies) actively engaged in the recording field: singers, musicians, composers and songwriters, conductors, arrangers, engineers, record producers, graphic artists, photographers, art directors, and album note writers. Those creative contributors who meet prescribed qualifications may join as active (voting) members and thereby may participate in chapter and national activities, including voting for the GRAMMY AWARDS. Associate membership (nonvoting) is available to those in the recording field who are not eligible to join as active members but wish to support the objectives of the academy. Associate members include record company and music publishing executives, publicity and advertising personnel, managers, agents, promoters, and disc jockeys.

To qualify as an active member, an individual must have contributed creatively to at least six recorded sides or one half of an album in any of the following membership categories: vocalists and singers; leaders and conductors; producers; songwriters and composers; engineers; instrumentalists and musicians; arrangers; art directors, photographers, graphic artists, designers, album note writers; and creative contributors to spoken word documentary, educational, comedy, and children's recordings.

Recording Academy members belong to any one of seven chapters located in recording centers around the U.S.: Los Angeles, New York, Nashville, Chicago, Atlanta, San Francisco, and Memphis. Each chapter has a board of governors, which administers all local activities. Activities and policies of a national nature are regulated by national officers and a national board of trustees.

Programs and Activities. The Recording Academy seeks to publicly recognize and reward creativity in the recording field in various ways, including informative public relations through consumer and trade press, television, and radio. However, the Recording Academy is probably best known for its Grammy Awards, which it presents annually on network television. Other activities include granting scholarships to academic institutions and sponsoring university courses in the recording arts and sciences. Local chapters regularly hold meetings featuring noted panelists, speakers, and experts in various phases of recording.

History. The National Academy of Recording Arts and Sciences was founded in Los Angeles in 1957. It developed as a result of a program sponsored by the Hollywood Chamber of Commerce to honor talent in different entertainment fields by imprinting designs of stars containing their names in the sidewalks of the Hollywood and Vine area. The chamber asked five record company executives on the West Coast to provide names of recording artists, which they did. But their discussions revealed the need for an organization of creators in the recording field that could give proper recognition to the many deserving

achievements in recording. These executives subsequently formed the Recording Academy, which by 1980 had over 5,000 members.

See also PROFESSIONAL ASSOCIATIONS AND EDUCATIONAL ORGANIZATIONS.

National Academy of Television Arts and Sciences. *See* EMMY AWARDS.

National Association of Broadcasters (NAB). Trade association representing the U.S. radio and television broadcast industry.

Membership. Membership in NAB is of two types—regular and associate. Regular membership is available to commercial, noncommercial, and educational radio and television broadcast stations that hold an FCC license or construction permit. Associate membership is open to companies that do business with broadcasters, such as equipment manufacturers and news services.

Programs and Activities. In addition to sponsoring programs and activities of a general nature as described in TRADE ASSOCIATIONS, NAB: establishes radio and TV "codes" governing programming and advertising (these are for the guidance of member stations and compliance is voluntary); provides legal information to its member stations on such everyday broadcasting concerns as FCC rules and regulations (including license renewals, contests, promotions, logging, and the Fairness Doctrine) and copyright laws; and provides management, engineering research, and sales information and services.

Policy. NAB policy and decisions on industry-wide matters are made by a board of directors elected or appointed from the regular membership. The board is divided into a radio and a television board, each with its own chairman and vice-chairman. NAB has several committees which study industry problems and make recommendations to the board of directors for appropriate action.

History. The National Association of Broadcasters was founded in 1922 "to foster and promote the development of the arts of aural and visual broadcasting in all its forms; to protect its members in every lawful and proper manner from injustices and unjust exactions; to do all things necessary and proper to encourage and promote customs and practices which will strengthen and maintain the broadcasting industry to the end that it may best serve the public." Its membership grew from 13 in its founding year to approximately 6,100 in 1980. NAB is based in Washington, D.C., with additional offices in New York and Hollywood.

National Association of Music Merchants (NAMM). Trade association representing retailers and manufacturers of musical instruments and creative audio/sound products.

Membership. Membership is open to all firms actively engaged in the retailing, distributing, or manufacturing of musical instruments, audio/sound products, and related software and accessories. NAMM members are from not only the U.S. but also many foreign countries.

Programs and Activities. In addition to sponsoring programs and activities of a general nature as described in TRADE ASSOCIATIONS, NAMM: conducts management training, sales development, and market education seminars regularly throughout the United States; offers its members educational cassettes, manuals, and books to aid in retail music management; publishes a guide to federal advertising regulations and rules that relate to the music industry; provides a freight bill auditing service for the members; offers merchandising aids and slide presentations designed to increase sales in its members stores; and sponsors conventions that showcase new and established lines of musical merchandise (the convention attracts manufacturers and music dealers from all over the world).

History. The National Association of Music Merchants was founded in 1901 to provide assistance to music dealers through various programs, to deal with the common management problems of operating a music store, to foster equity in business dealings, and to represent the industry to the public, the government, and other industries and organizations. Its membership has grown from less than 200 in its founding years to more than 1,400 store and 750 manufacturer members in 1980. NAMM is based in Chicago.

National Association of Recording Merchandisers (NARM). Trade association representing the recorded music industry.

Membership. NARM membership is of two types—regular and associate. Regular membership is open to merchandisers of recorded music such as record and tape stores, multiproduct retail stores that sell prerecorded music, rack jobbers, one-stops, and independent record/tape distributors. Associate membership is available to all other entities working in the prerecorded music industry. While manufacturers of records and tapes constitute the greatest number of associate members, membership includes suppliers of record and tape accessories, T-shirts, posters, and other types of products sold in retail record outlets; manufacturers of display fixtures; album fabricators; advertising agencies; printers; trade press; and other organizations working in the recorded music business. In 1980, because of the growth of the prerecorded videocassette and disc business, in which many of NARM's regular and associate members were becoming involved, the organization expanded interpretation of its name to encompass all recorded entertainment (audio and video).

Programs and Activities. In addition to sponsoring programs and activities of a general nature as described in TRADE ASSOCIATIONS, NARM: holds a major annual convention; presents a series of regional meetings and conferences for its members; conducts a Retail Management Certification Program; sponsors an industry internship program; works against pirated and counterfeit product; presents industry awards; supervises a national Bank Card Program whereby its members benefit from lower discount rates; supports the NARM Scholarship Foundation for the benefit of employees of its member companies, their children and spouses; and gathers, publishes, and maintains statistical data.

History. NARM was founded in 1958 for the purpose of bringing together the small but growing number of specialty wholesalers of phonograph records known as rack jobbers, which were placing records into nonmusic stores, such as supermarkets, novelty stores, and discount stores. As these companies expanded their operations, many of them became retailers, independent distributors, and one-stops of records and tapes, and these additional categories were added to the regular membership over the next decade, resulting in NARM's growth as the trade association representing all aspects of recorded music merchandisers.

Record manufacturers were NARM's earliest associate members. Other types of music-affiliated businesses were admitted as the scope and importance of the association developed.

Its membership grew from 10 in its founding year to approximately 500 in 1980. NARM is based in Cherry Hill, New Jersey.

National Labor Relations Board (NLRB). An independent federal agency established in 1935 to administer the National Labor Relations Act, the principal labor relations law of the United States. The National Labor Relations Act defines and protects the rights of employees and employers, encourages collective bargaining, and seeks to reduce interruptions in commerce caused by labor disputes. NLRB functions to prevent unfair labor practices by either employers or unions and con-

ducts secret-ballot elections among employees to determine whether they wish to be represented by a union or not. This latter function is sometimes exercised when there is interest by members of performing groups, such as dance companies, to gain union representation. If a group unionizes, then such labor organization becomes its representative for COL-LECTIVE BARGAINING.

National Music Publishers' Association (NMPA). Trade association representing the U.S. music publishing industry.

Membership. Membership in NMPA is open to any person or firm that has been actively engaged in the business of publishing music in the United States for at least one year, whose musical compositions have been commercially published or used, or who assumes the normal financial risks involved in publishing musical works.

Programs and Activities. NMPA sponsors programs and activities of a general nature as described in TRADE ASSOCIATIONS. However, because music publishing is a unique industry in that its existence is fundamentally based on the copyright law, NMPA is particularly involved in representing the industry to the federal government on issues and legislation that affect it. It also studies technological developments and their impact on its industry. NMPA owns the HARRY FOX AGENCY, INC., which licenses music copyrights for certain uses on behalf of publishers.

History. NMPA was founded by 24 music publishers in 1917 as the Music Publishers' Protective Association. Its objectives were to "maintain high standards of commercial honor and integrity among its members, to promote and inculcate just and equitable principles of trade and business, and to foster and encourage the art of music and songwriting." These have continued to remain the association's objectives over the years. In 1966, the organization's name was changed to the National Music Publishers' Association. In 1980, there were over 200 members in the association. NMPA is based in New York City.

Noise Reduction. Any electronic system or procedure designed to reduce the noise, mostly in the form of hiss, that is caused by the analog recording of music signals, or any other material, onto magnetic tape. Although the noise in an original recording is not of such magnitude that it is problematical, subsequent copies of an original tape (generally called *generations*—that is, the original tape is *first* generation, a copy from it becomes *second* generation, etc.) add their own noise until the cumulative effect becomes noticeable to the point of annoyance, and the noise begins to mask some of the subtleties of the music signals, particularly in the softer passages. Increase in noise is also experienced when mixing multi-track tapes down to a 2-track stereo master. Each track adds its noise into the final master, and depending on any number of factors, not the least of which is the dynamics of the performance, a final mix can contain an unacceptable background noise level.

Some engineers have achieved a reduction of noise through the use of "compressors." A compressor is an electronic device that "limits," or holds down, the level of the loudest portions of the music signals. Since tape has a finite capacity to accept loud signals, the "volume" level of the loudest signals has to be held down in order to permit raising the level of the softest signals. The net result of this procedure, however, is that the dynamics of the original performance suffer. That is, the audible differences between very loud and very soft musical passages are reduced, sometimes substantially, upon playback of the compressed recording. Any material recorded using a compressor inherits a certain sonic quality which is immediately identifiable; sometimes, specifically in the recording of piano or percussive instruments, a certain

"breathing" sound accompanies the instrumental sounds. Generally speaking, the more the compressor "works," the more noticeable this breathing effect. At present, however, compressors are used mainly as vehicles to make the apparent level of music constantly loud (by reducing dynamic range) rather than to reduce noise.

In 1967, Dr. Ray Dolby introduced a noise reduction system (the professional Type A system) that was to become the standard for all the world. While up to that time all professional noise reduction systems limited the loudest portions of the sound to permit the overall level of the music to be raised sufficiently to minimize noise, the Dolby™ system employed a unique concept. Instead of limiting the loudest levels of the sound, it increased the volume or level of the softest sounds on record and restored them to the original level on playback while lowering the intrinsic tape noise. The Dolby system is a reciprocal system in that sound is processed and encoded on recording and reprocessed and decoded on playback, thus returning the music to its original state. The advantage of the Dolby system is that its operation is inaudible, without breathing or deleterious side effects—mainly because it works upon low-level signals, where any changes to the signal are not perceptible. The Dolby system offers other advantages, the main one being that "print-through" is reduced substantially. (Print-through is a phenomenon in which sound on one layer of the tape lying on another while wound on a reel prints through onto adjacent layers.) Print-through tends to cloud complex instrumental and vocal passages and is sometimes the cause of pre- and post-echo in recordings.

There are other noise reduction systems which are in present use in the professional recording industry, the most widely used being dbx.

Some of the professional noise reduction systems have worked their way into the nonprofessional home recording field, although in much simplified form. It was the Dolby B home noise reduction system (a simplified version of the more elaborate professional Type A system) that spurred the incredibly fast acceptance of the cassette as a high-quality home recording medium and in large part made possible the improvement of the hardware to its present point.

Nondramatic Musical Work. Term that refers to a popular or serious musical work. For example, a nondramatic musical work could be a popular song, such as a rock, country, jazz, or gospel musical composition; or the term could denote a symphony, concerto, or piano sonata (sometimes referred to as "nondramatic serious music").

A nondramatic musical performance is the performance of a musical composition without costume, scenery, and dramatic action. Copyright owners grant to performing rights organizations the nonexclusive right to license the nondramatic performing rights, or *small* rights, of their musical works. Consequently ASCAP and BMI are known as *small performing rights organizations* (SESAC licenses both nondramatic and dramatic performing rights).

See COMPULSORY/MECHANICAL LICENSES (PHONORECORDS); DRAMATICO-MUSICAL COMPOSITION; PERFORMING RIGHTS ORGANIZATION.

Notice of Copyright. *See* COPYRIGHT NOTICE.

Novelty Record. A record (particularly a SINGLE) that is considered unconventional in that it may be distinguished from those that conform to the pop mainstream, although it is directed to the pop market. A novelty record is usually characterized by a lyric or theme that is considered weird, comic, or zany. The artist's performance usually complements this and there may be use of special sound effects. Also, the structure of the composition may differ from those of other genres of popular songs (for example, a recording containing excerpts of several previously successful songs). Examples of novelty records over the years are "Witch Doctor," "The Chipmunk Song," and "Disco Duck." Novelty records occasionally make the charts and become commercially successful. If a single becomes popular enough, a novelty album may be recorded and released.

O

Obies. Prizes of merit presented annually to honor creative achievement in the Off Broadway and Off Off Broadway Theater. The Obies are sponsored by *The Village Voice*, a New York City weekly newspaper.

For many years the judges consisted of the *Village Voice* theater editor plus two guest critics (usually from the New York press); more recently the committee has been expanded to include the entire *Voice* reviewing staff in addition to the two usual guest critics. There are no rules or specific categories for awards—each year the judges make up their own rules and categories. Consequently, in some years there may be awards given in musical categories and in other years none.

Basically, the judges give awards to what they consider meritorious and create categories "after the fact." The criterion for an award is actually what the judges would consider "artistic achievement."

The Obies, founded in 1956, are considered the most prestigious Off/Off Off Broadway Theater awards. Past award winners in musical categories include *A Party with Betty Comden and Adolph Green* (1958–59 season), *Fly Blackbird* (1961–62), *The Boys from Syracuse* (1962–63), *What Happened* (1963–64), *The Cradle Will Rock* (1964–65), *The Last Sweet Days of Isaac* and *The Me Nobody Knows* (Tie, 1969–70), *A Chorus Line* (Special Citation, 1975–76), and *Ain't Misbehavin'* (Special Citation, 1977–78).

Off Broadway/Off Off Broadway Theater.

There are various forms of legitimate theater in New York City, including Broadway, Off Broadway, and Off Off Broadway. The expenses incurred in producing an Off Broadway or Off Off Broadway musical are considerably less than those of Broadway.

Shows presented Off Broadway sometimes become popular attractions and are moved to Broadway to accommodate larger audiences. Consequently these theaters may be spawning grounds for writers, performers, and shows. Successful musicals that began on the Off Broadway stage include *Hair, Godspell, Ain't Misbehavin'*, and *The Best Little Whorehouse in Texas*.

Most Off Broadway productions employ professional performers and stage managers who are members of ACTORS' EQUITY ASSOCIATION (AEA OR EQUITY). Equity requires that all productions in which its members are involved employ only Equity actors and stage managers. This includes understudies. Managers and producers of Off Broadway theaters and productions enter into the Equity agreement with actors entitled Minimum Contract for Off-Broadway Productions, whose provisions are based upon the Equity document Agreement Governing Employment Off Broadway. The Agreement, whose terms are negotiated between Equity and the League of Off-Broadway Theaters, sets forth various stipulations and provisions, including an actor's minimum weekly salary. Minimum Equity salaries for performers and stage managers are based on the seating capacity of the Off Broadway theater as well as on actual gross box office weekly receipts.

Equity regulations make the Off Broadway contract applicable to productions in the borough of Manhattan but prohibit its use in those presented in any theater located in an area bounded by Fifth and Ninth Avenues from 34th Street to 56th Street and by Fifth Avenue and the Hudson River from 56th Street to 72nd Street. The contract is also not applicable in any theater having a seating capacity of more than 499.

On a smaller scale than Off Broadway—in terms of prestige, ticket prices, working conditions, and pay scale to performers—is Off Off Broadway, where "showcase" productions are mounted in theaters of 99 seats or less. Equity codes govern minimum conditions under which members may perform Off Off Broadway; these vary according to income and funding the theater receives and number of performances given. It is less costly for a show to be produced at an Off Off Broadway theater than at one Off Broadway. Off Off Broadway has been a stimulus for much creativity and has provided a forum for writers, musicians, and performers to demonstrate their skills.

See also BROADWAY MUSICALS; OBIES.

Oldies. "Oldies" may be discussed in terms of retail trade and radio broadcasting.

In *retail trade*, an "oldie" is generally considered a single or album that is no longer on the charts. Insofar as albums are concerned, although this definition may appear to account for cut-outs and older record company catalog merchandise, oldies may be distinguished by their premium prices and their unavailability from cut-out vendors. Oldie albums are also usually not included in a manufacturer's catalog.

Oldie singles are available in two forms: the original 45 rpm disc and a *reissue* oldie, which contains a prior hit on each side—usually by the same artist—with center labels different from those on the original discs. Many retailers charge premium prices of $3 to $5 for hard-to-get original-label oldies, while rare

originals fetch up to $200 or more from collectors. Reissues retail at the same or at a somewhat higher cost than current single releases.

Oldies may serve as a traffic item for some dealers, a completely specialized form of business for others, particularly "mom and pop" retailers and mail order concerns. Dealers purchase oldies from wholesalers, manufacturers, jukebox operators, and collectors. Oldies may also be found at flea markets, auctions, and manufacturers' or retailers' closeouts. A major problem in the oldies market has been the infiltration of illegitimate product by pirates, bootleggers, and counterfeiters.

Wholesalers and retailers carrying oldies are diverse with respect to the number of different titles they carry. Wholesalers may carry 1,000 to 50,000 or more different titles; retailers, 100 to 10,000 or more, dependings on size of operation (those that carry the most are usually specialized dealers). Oldies that have achieved substantial initial success are sometimes marketed by manufacturers and retailers as "oldies but goodies."

In *radio,* "oldies" refers to a use by a radio station of records that have made and dropped from the charts. An "oldies" format programs these on a high-rotation basis or exclusively (an "oldies station"). Stations with contemporary formats may also play oldies, though only occasionally. For these stations, an oldie is generally regarded as a single that has been off the charts for at least 6 months. This is because contemporary radio stations broadcast current releases, recurrents and oldies. *Recurrents* are those records that have recently gone off the charts but are still programmed to a considerable extent because there is a demand for them and they are considered too new to actually be oldies.

The age of an oldie is another factor in a station's decision to program it. If the station is trying to reach an audience of 18-to-24-year-olds, oldies programmed might be from 1 to 10 years old; if the target audience is 35-to-55-

year-olds, records might be played that were originally released as long as 20 or more years ago.

One-Stop. A Subdistributor or Wholesaler that buys the records and tapes of a variety of manufacturers as well as related merchandise and resells these goods to small retail stores and jukebox operators. A one-stop may carry such other merchandise as prerecorded video-cassettes, blank tapes, record and tape care accessories, record and tape carrying cases, tape storage units, music books and related accessories. A one-stop offers the advantage, particularly with regard to records and tapes, of being able to buy all products from one source. Libraries, schools, booksellers, specialty stores, and dealers such as "head shops" and gas stations may also obtain merchandise from one-stops.

In furnishing merchandise to independent record/tape retailers, some one-stops also function to train or develop new firms. They may explain retail business practices (including ordering, inventory control, return privileges, credit terms, bookkeeping), develop advertising and promotion programs, assist the retailer in ordering an initial inventory, and guide its growth.

These subdistributors may be single-outlet businesses or parts of operations that have branches in various cities throughout the country. One-stops sometimes do business on a walk-in basis and through telephone sales and trade advertisements, but the majority of their business today is by methods similar to other wholesalers'.

History. One-stops began operating just after World War II. In their early years they functioned as specialized subdistributors that sold to jukebox operators. An operator with 200 jukeboxes, for example, would find it burdensome and time-consuming to obtain product from many different sources. One-stops solved this problem; through one wholesaler, jukebox operators could purchase records issued by all labels.

The convenience of transacting all business under one roof made one-stops attractive entities to do business with and small retailers began to buy records from them. Eventually, the trade of one-stops expanded as they went from selling primarily singles to albums and other products. Independent retailers pay a slightly higher price for goods purchased from one-stops than they would from local distributors, but for those who cannot get credit from such sources, one-stops are a welcome wholesale supplier.

Open-Reel Tape. An open-reel, or reel-to-reel, tape is commonly used by songwriters, music publishers, producers, recording artists, and others to demonstrate a song or a finished recording. It is often favored over acetates and cassette tapes because of its superior sound reproduction. To a small extent, albums, mostly classical, are commercially released in this configuration.

Prerecorded reel-to-reel tapes were introduced on the commercial audio market in the early 1950s. During their early years they were available only in a monaural sound reproduction format. They had two tracks: after the entire length of tape passed through the playback head, the user turned the reel over and played it in the other direction. Prerecorded tapes with stereophonic programming became commercially available in the mid 1950s and preceded stereo discs by a few years.

Although it was generally recognized that prerecorded open-reel tapes were superior to discs in terms of quality of sound reproduction and durability, public acceptance of them was limited. The task of having to thread the tape past the recording head and onto a take-up reel, the limited repertoire of open-reel software and availability of hardware, plus their relatively high prices, discouraged most consumers. Consequently prerecorded open-reel tapes became and remain a product for the audiophile.

Many songwriters and musicians own tape decks which they use for home recording. With open-reel tape, they can edit and splice recordings they make. Professional-quality recordings are obtainable on the sophisticated multi-track consumer tape decks.

Home tape decks commonly provide for recording and playing back open-reel tapes at speeds of 1⅞, 3¾, and 7½ inches per second, though most prerecorded tapes are made to operate at 7½ ips—a speed four times faster than the conventional cassette playback (1⅞ ips). Speed has more to do with the relationship between possible high-frequency response and signal-to-noise ratio than anything else. In addition, open-reel tapes have at least twice the track width of cassette tapes. The wider the track width, the higher the output, and the higher the output, the better the ultimate signal-to-noise ratio. Wider tracks are also less sensitive to dropouts and have stronger magnetic fields. All these factors account for the potentially superior sound reproduction of both prerecorded and home-recorded open-reel tapes.

Opera. A dramatic work, either tragic or comic, that is set to music. An opera has action, is performed with costumes and scenery, and may include dance. The words of an opera are wholly or mostly sung to orchestral accompaniment. An opera has vocal pieces (e.g., arias, recitatives, choruses, duets) and instrumental pieces (e.g., dances, interludes). The various kinds of operatic compositions include grand opera, opéra bouffe, opéra comique, and operetta.

Authorization is needed to perform an opera on the legitimate stage. Since an opera is a Dramatico-Musical Composition, ASCAP and BMI do not license the performance rights therein; these are normally licensed directly by the owner of copyright. Of course, operas in the Public Domain may be used in any way without permission from or payment to any party.

Public domain operas include *Aïda* (Giuseppe Verdi), *The Barber of Seville* (Gioacchino Rossini), *Carmen* (George Bizet), *Don Giovanni* (Wolfgang Amadeus Mozart), *La Bohème* (Giacomo Puccini), *La Traviata* (Verdi), *Madama Butterfly* (Puccini), *The Marriage of Figaro* (Mozart), *Romeo and Juliet* (Charles Gounod), and *Tristan und Isolde* (Richard Wagner).

Orchestrator. One who takes an arranger's sketch and scores the various voices and/or instruments, without changing or adding to the melodies, countermelodies, harmonies, and rhythms. In the field of popular music, orchestrators are employed with respect to commercial recordings, stage productions, television, and motion pictures.

Original Cast Show Album. Album containing the songs (and sometimes to a limited extent, the dialogue) of a musical show, recorded by the members of the original cast. An original cast album is recorded and normally released shortly after the show officially opens. Most often, original cast albums are made for Broadway musicals. In some cases they are made for Off Broadway or other productions.

See American Federation of Television and Radio Artists National Code of Fair Practice for Phonograph Recordings; Broadway Musicals; Dramatists Guild, Inc. Dramatico-Musical Production Contract.

Oscar. *See* Academy Awards.

Overdubbing. Term that refers to the process in multi-track tape recording of adding new audio tracks (instrumental or vocal) in synchronization with tracks previously recorded.

Multi-track tape recording permits overdubbing without loss of fidelity as new tracks are added. It is common for the basic (rhythm) tracks to be "laid down" at one session and additional parts to be recorded on "open" (unrecorded or unused) tracks at other sessions. With mixing, the finished master sounds as if all the parts were recorded together at a single session.

Overruns. Records and prerecorded tapes that have been overproduced because the manufacturer anticipated greater demand for the product than there was. Overruns are current items in the manufacturer's catalog and are usually accorded special deals or discounts; sometimes they are sold on the same basis as cut-outs. Overruns are also referred to as *overstock*. A *closeout* is a final sale with special discounts by a manufacturer who has too much stock of a certain product.

Overscale Artist. Artist who earns wages for a recording session, radio or television commercial or program, stage or other performance, over and above the minimum payment (scale) set forth in the prevailing union's agreement with the employer. The amount of an overscale payment is determined by negotiation and is usually secured only by "name" or established artists. For example, a well-known singer performing on a network television program would typically receive a fee substantially above the minimum scale provided for such a performance in his or her union's agreement. In theatrical productions, the managers, agents, or attorneys of famous artists sometimes negotiate overscale salaries for their clients plus a percentage of the gross box office receipts. Overscale artists are also referred to as "star" or "featured" artists.

The difference between an overscale and a *premium* payment should be noted. A premium payment is made to a performer on a recording session who earns a multiple of the basic session rate (usually 1½ to 2 times greater) by virtue of the fact that he is performing during late hours, or on a Saturday or Sunday, or on certain holidays.

P

Payola. Term that refers to the giving of some type of "payment" (see below) to get AIRPLAY for a recording in which the payer or his employer has a financial interest.

"Payola" is a universal term, however, and may refer to any form of exchange of goods for promotion or activity that is dishonest, unethical, anticompetitive, secret, disguised, or against the public interest. Thus payola exists in various forms and may also refer to such exchanges between music publishers and record producers to get songs recorded, record companies and music critics for favorable reviews in publications, or record companies and trade publications to get records positioned on the charts.

With respect to payola for getting radio station personnel to expose records on the air, such practice may result in the addition to the station's playlist of a record which then gets played several times per day. It is airplay that guides the record-buying habits of the public and can substantially increase sales, resulting in enormous profits for the record company.

Payola is of course not limited to the music business. It exists in various forms in many other industries. The practices as they exist in the music business, however, garner much attention from the media because of the glamorous and highly publicized nature of the industry.

Types of "Payments." Payola is a form of bribery that wears many hats. It includes such "payments" as cash, albums, stereo equipment, concert tickets, company stock, automobiles, gifts, merchandise, services, loan of credit cards, expense accounts, airline tickets, paid vacations, sharing of royalties, percentages of ownership rights in copyrights, prostitutes, and drugs. (When it involves the dispensation of drugs—such as for airplay—the practice is sometimes referred to as "drugola.") Payola has also come in the guise of payments to disc jockeys as "consultant's fees."

"Plugola." This is a kind of hybrid form of payola that involves a broadcast station owner or employee benefiting indirectly from the promotion ("plug") of a product or service on the air by virtue of his ownership or financial interest in it.

Origin of the Term "Payola." It is generally believed that "payola" was coined in the 1920s, when vaudeville was the predominant form of popular entertainment. As "pig Latin" was commonly used in show business then (i.e., changing a word by adding a suffix such as "ola"), the term may have been devised thus to describe the practice of song pluggers "paying" entertainers in musical comedies, revues, and other productions to introduce or use a song in their performance. Another school of thought is that the term was merely derived by copying other "ola" phrases popular in the early 1900s, such as "Pianola" or "Victrola."

Payola Scandal of 1959 and Resulting Legislation. In the 1950s, there was considerable reporting in the media of the widespread existence of payola in the music business: record companies buying the "favors" of disc jockeys. Rumors and confessions by some DJs touched off a scandal that by 1959 led to a federal investigation into the situation.

In 1960, the House Committee on Legislative Oversight, a congressional committee (whose chairman was Oren Harris of Arkansas), held open hearings on payola and the alleged "fixing" of network television quiz shows. The committee's investigation revealed that in a one-year period, over one-quarter million dollars in record company payola payments was received by disc jockeys and other radio station personnel in a number of U.S. cities for the purpose of playing certain records (it was reported that this information resulted from a limited "mail survey" and that the actual figures were much higher).

The investigation also focused on the activities of some prominent disc jockeys, most notably Dick Clark and Alan Freed. Clark maintained his innocence throughout the hearings and emerged clean from any charges, although he was forced to relinquish his interests in his music companies where there might be a conflict of interest with his employment as a DJ. Freed admitted that he had accepted payola and was indicted but given a suspended sentence.

The House committee concluded in its official report, "Payola and Other Deceptive Practices in the Broadcasting Field," that the broadcasting community needed stricter regulation and that the FCC should give closer scrutiny to its practices. The payola investigation consequently led in 1960 to amendments to the Federal Communications Act of 1934. These require: (1) any radio station employee who accepts money or other valuable consideration to disclose it to the ownership; and (2) a station to make an announcement when money or other valuable consideration is received for the purpose of exposing broadcast material (i.e., playing records).

Commercial bribery laws in some states have also been used to deter the payola practice.

Radio Stations. The payola scandal in the 1950s pertained mostly to DJs and other employees of top 40 or rock 'n' roll radio stations.

Under these formats, there is a high rotation of a relatively small number of records.

In more recent years, the practice of payola (while not to deny its existence) would seem less likely to exist, at least in its previous proportions. Reasons for this include tough federal laws and close concern with such practices by the FCC, FTC, and various trade organizations. Also, program directors (who determine which records get put on the playlist) are less likely to accept money or other goods and put their jobs on the line for a record that is a dud in an era when radio ratings are omnipotent.

Indeed playlists are so small in many top markets that PDs will often not program a record unless it is already a hit. Promotion workers from record companies often bear the burden of showing statistics and data of a record's previous or current success in other markets or on competitive stations to convince the PD to play it. If a station continually programs an unpopular record, it will "tune out" its audience and its ratings will diminish. At some stations independent program consultants are hired and they determine the station's playlists; at smaller stations the DJs may have a say in which records get programmed.

Music Publishers (Early "Payola"). The practice of compensating someone for a "favor" or service in the music business predates the development of radio. In the mid/late 1800s, some songwriters, to get their compositions performed, would pay entertainers, share royalties with them, or give them writing credit in those songs that they performed. In the early 1900s, it was not uncommon for song pluggers working for music publishers to pay singers to perform the company's songs in their acts or shows. The inclusion of a song in a show could boost sheet music sales tremendously, particularly if it was performed often enough and became popular (sheet music sales at that time were the most important source of income for music publishers and songwriters; several songs then sold over 1 million sheet music copies and some sold in excess of 5 million).

This illicit practice was getting out of hand and some important publishers united to protect their interests and forbid such payments in their industry. In the May 14, 1917, issue of *Variety,* there appeared an advertisement announcing the organization of the Music Publishers' Protective Association (later to be renamed the National Music Publishers' Association). Part of the ad read: "The general objectives of the Association shall be to maintain high standards of commercial honor and integrity among its members, to promote and inculcate just and equitable principles of trade and business, and to foster and encourage the art of music and songwriting." The MPPA's membership grew and for the most part abided by the association's objective—for a while at least.

The so-called big-band era of the 1930s once again witnessed the emergence of payola on a large scale. Bandleaders and featured soloists were frequently "cut in" on the income from a song by being made co-writers, in exchange for performing the song in personal appearances or on network radio. The FTC looked into this situation, but it was becoming clear that radio was evolving as a powerful medium to popularize records. Indeed it would not be too long before payola would flourish and the payola scandal of the late 1950s would surface, to great public attention.

RIAA Guidelines. In 1973, the RECORDING INDUSTRY ASSOCIATION OF AMERICA, INC. (RIAA) adopted an Action Program to safeguard sound legal and moral principles in the recording industry. RIAA established Standards of Conduct that provide guidelines for record companies and their employees (see below); recommended that each association member conduct intracompany investigations for any illegal practices, with discharge or appropriate disciplinary action for any employee found guilty of payola; advised that all record-

ing and music publishing industry personnel who contact radio station employees be required by their employers to sign "no payola" affidavits; and urged the music publishing, broadcasting, and other segments of the recording industry to adopt similar standards and practices.

The objectives of RIAA's Standards of Conduct are "to reaffirm lawful and ethical standards of business conduct" in the recording industry and to affirm to the public and government the commitment by RIAA and its members to adhere to these standards. Under the Standards of Conduct, recording companies and their employees shall not: "engage in payola practices of any kind, as defined and prohibited in the federal payola statutes; ask for or receive kickbacks from artists, producers, or others; provide illegal drugs to any person, or cause them to be provided; or attempt to influence in any illegal or unethical manner trade media chart ratings or reviews."

To ensure the credibility and authenticity of "popularity" charts in the trade media, the RIAA Action Program encourages the industry trades to develop standards of compilation. It also recommends that whatever action is necessary be taken to ensure that the purchase of advertising space or other consideration by a company does not artificially influence charts, reviews, or editorial coverage in the trades and "tip sheets."

Performance Royalties. *See* PERFORMING RIGHTS ORGANIZATION.

Performing Right. A *performing right* is, in essence, the exclusive right that may be granted in a copyright law to the owner of a musical work to authorize (license) his or her work for *public performance.*

Copyright Law. The basis for the performing right in the U.S. copyright law (Title 17) is given in Section 106, which states: "the owner of copyright . . . has the exclusive right . . .

to perform the copyrighted work publicly" (*see* COPYRIGHT OWNER). The public performance right also extends to literary, dramatic, and choreographic works, pantomimes, and motion pictures and other audiovisual works.

Under the law (Section 101), "to 'perform' a work means to recite, render, play, dance, or act it, either directly or by means of any device or process or, in the case of a motion picture or other audiovisual work, to show its images in any sequence or to make the sounds accompanying it audible." Also, under the law, to perform a work "publicly" means "(1) to perform . . . it at a place open to the public or at any place where a substantial number of persons outside of a normal circle of a family and its social acquaintances is gathered; or (2) to transmit or otherwise communicate a performance . . . of the work to a place specified by clause (1) or to the public, by means of any device or process, whether the members of the public capable of receiving the performance . . . receive it in the same place or in separate places and at the same time or at different times."

Clearly, a rendition of a work at a concert hall, club, theater, or similar venue—either live, through recordings, from retransmission by loudspeakers, or by broadcasting—would constitute a public performance of the work. A list of various types of "music users" appears in PERFORMING RIGHTS ORGANIZATION.

Limitations on the Performing Right. Under the copyright law, there are limitations on the exclusive right of public performance—the law specifically exempts certain "nonprofit" public performances of musical compositions from requiring authorization to be performed and grants compulsory licenses for particular performances. These exemptions are discussed in COPYRIGHT OWNERS, LIMITATION ON EXCLUSIVE RIGHTS OF.

Unauthorized Performances. Except for specified limitations, a public performance of a copyrighted musical work without authori-

zation from the owner of copyright is unlawful. Any person, business, or entity which publicly performs a copyrighted musical composition without permission or exemption is an infringer of copyright and may be sued in federal court.

Performing Rights Organization. Virtually all songwriters and music publishers have an agent for licensing the nondramatic PERFORMING RIGHTS of their musical works to users of music. Such an "agent" is referred to as a *performing rights organization*. In the United States, there are three performing rights organizations: AMERICAN SOCIETY OF COMPOSERS, AUTHORS AND PUBLISHERS (ASCAP); BROADCAST MUSIC, INC. (BMI); and SESAC INC.

Definition. A performing rights organization is an entity that: (1) is granted by copyright owners the nonexclusive right to license nondramatic public performances of their musical works;° (2) enters into licensing agreements with music users granting them the authorization to publicly perform nondramatic renditions of the musical compositions in its repertory (music users pay license fees); (3) monitors, logs, or otherwise determines the number of public performances works in its repertory receive from music users; and (4) distributes the license fees (after deducting operating expenses) to writer and publisher members or affiliates in an equitable manner.† These moneys received by the writers and publishers of the publicly performed works are known as *performance royalties*.

Why Have Performing Rights Organiza-

°Members or affiliates of performing rights organizations retain the right to license users of music directly.

†There are a few exceptions to this definition with regard to SESAC Inc., the smallest U.S. performing rights organization. SESAC is granted by copyright owners—and licenses to music users—both the nondramatic *and* the dramatic performing rights of musical works. Distribution of payments to affiliates is based largely on trade chart activity. Detailed information regarding this is found in the SESAC entry.

tions? The clearance of rights by performing rights organizations is the only practical way musical compositions can be licensed. There are, scattered throughout the world, millions of music copyrights and hundreds of thousands of users, many of whom perform thousands of different compositions annually. It would be virtually impossible for most music users to find and contact each copyright owner, and negotiate a separate license to publicly perform his work. Likewise, it would be extremely difficult and economically unfeasible for each copyright owner to negotiate separate licenses with music users and to monitor their public performances.

To ease the burden of direct licensing (which is still available to copyright owners if they so choose) and simplify the clearance of rights, it is necessary, then, to have organizations that serve as central clearinghouses. These are the performing rights organizations, which are essentially bulk licensors of music performing rights.

Practices. Members or affiliates of performing rights organizations are creators and owners of musical works. Joining or affiliating with a performing rights organization is voluntary. However, for the reasons above, virtually all professional writers and bona fide music publishers are members or affiliates of a performing rights organization. ASCAP is a membership organization and its writers and publishers are referred to as *members;* writers and publishers in BMI or SESAC are *affiliates.* BMI is owned by radio and television stations; SESAC is privately owned.

In practice, a writer may join or affiliate with only one organization, but a publisher may join or affiliate with all three through separate corporate entities or by using a combination of corporate and other legal arrangements. This permits publishers to accept and publish works created by writers who are members or affiliates of any organization.

A writer and a publisher must be members

or affiliates of the same performing rights organization to be eligible to receive royalties. Collaboration between writers who are members or affiliates of different organizations is allowed, but each writer must assign the ownership of his performing right to a publisher that is a member or affiliate of the writer's organization (of course, the writer may be the owner of the publishing company). ASCAP, BMI, and SESAC pay royalties to writer and publisher members or affiliates by separate check.

ASCAP, BMI, and SESAC have reciprocal agreements with foreign performing rights organizations that enable them to collect royalties for members or affiliates whose works are performed in foreign territories [*see* PERFORMING RIGHTS ORGANIZATIONS (FOREIGN)]. Normally, a member or an affiliate of a U.S. performing rights organization may not "join" a foreign society while still connected with the U.S. body. However, an organization may give permission to do so in a special circumstance, such as where a writer temporarily moves to another country and anticipates substantial performances of his works there.

ASCAP, BMI, and SESAC have individual methods of determining public performances of their members' or affiliates' works and procedures for distributing royalty payments. These are discussed in their respective entries. ASCAP and BMI each operate under a government "consent decree," which regulates certain of their practices.

Music Users. A music user is any person, business, institution, or other entity that publicly performs copyrighted music. A music user is required by law to obtain authorization to perform each such work from the owner of copyright. In commercial practice, such rights are obtained in the form of a license issued by a performing rights organization, which entitles the user to use any or all of the works in the organization's repertory. A music user publicly performs music by live nondramatic performance—including concerts, stage shows, variety shows, symphonies, and recitals (engaging the services of "live" musicians and/or singers)—or by transmission or retransmission of recorded music via broadcasting, telecasting, etc.

There are various types of music users, and the performing rights organizations generally have separate licenses for different categories. License fees paid by users differ, depending on such criteria as advertising income and wattage (for broadcasting entities), and seating capacity and frequency of operation (for clubs).

License fees for music users are negotiated between the user and the performing rights organization. In certain cases, the interests of a group of users are represented collectively for bargaining by a trade organization or association. For example, radio broadcasters are represented by the All-Industry Radio Music License Committee; hotel and motel owners by the American Hotel and Motel Association; certain orchestras by the American Symphony Orchestra League; and ballroom owners by the National Ballroom Operators Association. If there is no trade group or association for users in a particular field, the performing rights organization may negotiate licenses with major representatives of the field or with the users themselves.

In certain cases or situations, music users do not need a license to perform musical works. No license is needed to perform public domain compositions or protected works in a manner specifically exempted by the copyright law, such as religious works in the course of religious services. A television producer generally would not have to obtain a performance license to use copyrighted music in his show, as the network or local station broadcasting the show normally obtains a license that covers its performance. Motion picture theaters do not have to obtain a separate license to perform the copyrighted musical

works embodied in the sound tracks of motion pictures they exhibit. Movie theaters that play music from speakers before and after exhibition of a motion picture, however, must obtain licenses to use the works.

ASCAP, BMI, and SESAC vary in the number and types of establishments and media of public entertainment they license, and a music user may find it necessary to obtain a license from only a particular organization, although most obtain licenses from all three. In any case, the following types of music users may be licensed by a performing rights organization:

radio stations and networks
television stations and networks
public broadcasting entities
cable and pay TV operators
jukebox operators
concert halls
theaters
concert promoters
nightclubs
discotheques
taverns and bars
cabarets
restaurants
cafés
hotels and motels
stadiums
ball parks
amusement parks
theme parks
circuses
fairs and expositions
educational institutions
fraternal and veterans' organizations
country clubs
skating rinks
ice skating shows
rodeos
arenas
trade shows
dancing schools

ballrooms
movie theaters (indoor and drive-in)
banks
background music services
soundtrack libraries
steamships and ocean liners
airlines
certain retail stores
bandstands
symphony orchestras

Performing Rights Organization (Foreign).

The performing right of a music copyright is recognized by copyright laws of most countries throughout the world. In these countries, the owner of a protected musical work has the exclusive right, usually subject to certain limitations, to perform such work publicly or grant to others the right to do so.

Most developed countries have performing rights societies that administer, on behalf of composers, lyricists, and publishers, licenses for public performances of copyrighted musical works.° These societies grant the music user a license to use the works in their repertoires for fees and, after deducting operating expenses, distribute such moneys to their members in a proportion that reflects the number of performances of their works. Each society has its own methods for determining performances and distributing license fees to members, and many are regulated by government or are nonprofit societies.

Because works written and published by domiciliaries of one country are often performed in others, performing rights organizations enter into agreements with each other to enable writers and publishers to collect royalties. In these cases, a society will license the repertory of the foreign affiliate in its territory and vice versa. A society credits performances of foreign works and renders payments to for-

eign affiliates in accordance with its own rules.

In general, it could take publishers a long time to collect performance royalties earned in foreign countries. Performing rights organizations typically account to foreign affiliates once per year. In some cases, it has taken U.S. publishers up to two years or longer to collect such revenues. That is one reason why publishers enter into subpublishing agreements with foreign publishers throughout the world.

Subpublishers collect the original publishers' full share† of performance royalties (or a part thereof) at intervals of normal domestic distribution in the foreign country. When subpublishers collect the full share, they remit these earnings in accordance with their agreements (i.e., after taking out their specified commissions). This may considerably hasten the process by which the original publisher collects these moneys. Since societies pay writers performance royalties directly, the writers may not enjoy the benefits of a subpublisher for these collections and must wait until the transmission between societies has been completed and payment distributed by the local organization.

As stated above, performing rights societies around the world have reciprocal agreements. In 1980, ASCAP had agreements with some 40 foreign societies; BMI, 39; and SESAC, 17. (SESAC agreements may cover both performance and mechanical rights.)

Following is a table of the foreign performing rights societies. Because of the unfamiliar pronunciation of many of their names, they are commonly referred to by acronyms, which have been included. It should be noted that some of the societies also represent publishers

---

° China is an example of a country that, at this writing, does not have a performing rights society.

---

† Some foreign societies restrict their publisher members from granting a subpublisher the right to collect the full publishers' share in its territories. American subpublishers should consult with their American performing rights licensing organizations to determine these rules for individual countries.

Performing and Mechanical Rights Societies Around the World

Country	Name of Society	Acronym	Headquarters	Rights Covered
Argentina	Sociedad Argentina de Autores y Compositores de Musica	SADAIC	Buenos Aires	performance, mechanical
Australia	Australasian Performing Right Association, Ltd.	APRA	Sydney	performance
	Australasian Mechanical Copyright Owners Society Ltd.	AMCOS	Sydney	mecjanical, synchronization
Austria	Staatlich Genehmigte Gesellschaft der Autoren Komponisten und Musikverleger	AKM	Vienna	performance
	Gesellschaft zur Verwaltung & Auswertung Mechanisch Musikalischer Urheberrechte	Austro-Mechana GmbH	Vienna	mechanical, synchronization
Belgium	Société Belge des Auteurs, Compositeurs et Editeurs	SABAM	Brussels	performance, mechanical, synchronization
Bolivia	Sociedad Boliviana de Autores & Compositores & Escritores de Musica	SOBODAYCOM	La Paz	performance, mechanical, synchronization
Brazil	Sociedade Brasileira de Autores, Compositores & Escritores de Musica	SBACEM	Rio de Janeiro	performance
	Sociedade Brasileira de Autores Teatrais	SBAT	Rio de Janeiro	performance, mechanical, synchronization
	Sociedade Independente de Compositores & Autores Musicais	SICAM	São Paulo	performance
	Uniao Brasileira de Compositores	UBC	Rio de Janeiro	performance
Canada	Composers, Authors and Publishers Association of Canada, Ltd.	CAPAC	Toronto	performance
	Performing Rights Organization of Canada, Limited	PRO Canada	Ontario	performance
	Canadian Musical Reproduction Rights Agency Limited	CMRRA	Toronto	mechanical, synchronization
Chile	Departamento del Derecho de Autor	DAIC	Santiago	performance
Colombia	Sociedad de Autores y Compositores de Colombia	SAYCO	Bogotá	performance, mechanical, synchronization
Czechoslovakia	Ochranny Svaz Autorsky Slovensky Orchranny	OSA	Prague	performance, mechanical
	Zväz Autorsky	SOZA	Bratislava	performance

Performing and Mechanical Rights Societies Around the World *(cont'd)*

Country	Name of Society	Acronym	Headquarters	Rights Covered
Denmark	Selskabet til Forvaltning af Internationale Komponistrettigheder I Denmark	KODA	Copenhagen	performance
	Nordisk Copyright Bureau*	NCB	Copenhagen	mechanical, synchronization
England	The Performing Right Society Limited	PRS	London	performance
	Mechanical-Copyright Protection Society	MCPS	London	mechanical, synchronization
Federal Republic of Germany	Gesellschaft für Musikalische Aufführungs-und Mechanische Vervielfältigungsrechte†	GEMA	Berlin and Munich	performance, mechanical, synchronization
Finland	Säveltäjäin Tekijänoikeustomimisto	TEOSTO	Helsinki	performance
France	Société des Auteurs, Compositeurs et Editeurs de Musique‡	SACEM	Paris	performance, mechanical, synchronization
German Democratic Republic	Anstalt zur Wahrung der Aufführungsrechte auf dem Gebiete der Musik	AWA	Berlin	performance, mechanical
Greece	Société Anon. Hellenique pour la Protection de la Propriété Intellectuelle	AEPI	Athens	performance, mechanical
Hong Kong	Composers and Authors Society of Hong Kong, Ltd.	CASH	Hong Kong	performance, mechanical
Hungary	Bureau Hongrois pour la Protection des Droits d'Auteur	ARTISJUS	Budapest	performance, mechanical
Iceland	Samband Tónskálda og Eigenda Flutningsréttar	STEF	Reykjavik	performance
India	The Indian Performing Right Society Ltd.	IPRS	Bombay	performance
	Mechanical-Copyright Protection Society	MCPS	London	mechanical, synchronization
Israel	Société d'Auteurs, Compositeurs et Editeurs de Musique en Israel	ACUM	Tel Aviv	performance, mechanical
Italy	Societa Italiana degli Autori ed Editori §	SIAE	Rome	performance, mechanical
Japan	Japanese Society for Rights of Authors, Composers and Publishers	JASRAC	Tokyo	performance, mechanical, synchronization
Mexico, D.F.	Sociedad de Autores y Compositores de Musica	SACM	Mexico City	performance, mechanical

Performing and Mechanical Rights Societies Around the World *(cont'd)*

Country	Name of Society	Acronym	Headquarters	Rights Covered
Netherlands	Bureau voor Muziek-Auteursrecht	BUMA	Amsterdam	performance
	Stichting tot Expiotatie van Mechanische Reproductierechten der Auteurs	STEMRA	Amsterdam	mechanical, synchronization
Norway	Norsk Komponistforenings Internasjonale Musikkbyra	TONO	Oslo	performance
Paraguay	Autores Paraguayos Asociados	APA	Asunción	performance
Peru	Asociación Peruana de Autores y Compositores	APDAYC	Lima	performance
Philippines	Filipino Society of Composers, Authors and Publishers	FILSCAP	Manila	performance
Poland	Stowarzyszenie Autorow	ZAIKS	Warsaw	performance, mechanical
Portugal	Sociedade Portuguesa de Autores	SPA	Lisbon	performance, mechanical, synchronization
Puerto Rico	Sociedad Puertorriqueña de Autores, Compositores y Editores de Musica	SPACEM	Santurce	performance
South Africa	South African Music Rights Organisation Limited‖	SAMRO	Johannesburg	performance
	South African Recording Rights Association, Ltd.	SARRAL	Johannesburg	mechanical, synchronization
Spain	Sociedad General de Autores de España	SGAE	Madrid	performance, mechanical, synchronization
Sweden	Société Suedoise des Compositeurs, Auteurs et Editeurs de Musique	STIM	Stockholm	performance
Switzerland	Société Suisse des Auteurs et Editeurs#	SUISA	Zurich	performance
	Mechanlizenz		Zurich	mechanical, synchronization
United States	American Society of Composers, Authors and Publishers	ASCAP	New York	performance
	Broadcast Music, Inc.	BMI	New York	performance
	SESAC Inc.	SESAC	New York	performance, mechanical, synchronization
Uruguay	Asociación General de Autores del Uruguay	AGADU	Montevideo	performance, mechanical, synchronization

Performing and Mechanical Rights Societies Around the World *(cont'd)*

Country	Name of Society	Acronym	Headquarters	Rights Covered
U.S.S.R.	Vsesojuznoje Agentstvo po Avtorskim Pravam	VAAP	Moscow	performance, mechanical
Venezuela	Sociedad de Autores y Compositores de Venezuela	SACVEN	Caracas	performance, mechanical, synchronization
Yugoslavia	Savez Organizacija Kompozitora Jugoslavije	SOKOJ	Belgrade	performance, mechanical

* NCB also licenses mechanical and synchronization rights in Finland, Iceland, Norway, and Sweden.

† GEMA also licenses performance, mechanical and synchronization rights in West Berlin, Bulgaria, Rumania, and the Republic of China (Taiwan).

‡ SACEM also licenses performance, mechanical, and synchronization rights in the following territories: Algeria, Tunisia, Morocco, Andorra, Luxembourg, Monaco, Egypt, Lebanon, Turkey, Greece, and the territories of French-speaking African Republics, namely: Ivory Coast, Gabon, Voltaic Republic, Senegal, Cameroon, Congo-Brazzaville, Guinea, Dahomey, Mali, Niger, Central African Republic, Mauritania, Chad, Togo, Madagascar.

§ SIAE also licenses performance and mechanical rights in Vatican City and Republic of San Marino.

‖ SAMRO also licenses performance rights in Southwest Africa, Botswana, Lesotho, Rhodesia, and Swaziland.

SUISA also licenses performance rights in Liechtenstein.

and writers with respect to the mechanical and synchronization rights of their compositions [*see* MECHANICAL RIGHTS SOCIETIES (FOREIGN)].

Performing Rights Organizations, History of U.S. A performing rights organization licenses music on behalf of copyright owners for public performance. Indeed, it plays an important role not only in the music world but in society generally. As bulk licensors of the vast repertoire of music, performing rights organizations enable radio stations, television stations and networks, concert halls, theaters, nightclubs, bars, cafés, restaurants, ball parks, arenas, hotels, airlines, and other establishments to acquire economically and efficiently the rights to use music, as well as provide a system by which copyright owners can license their music for public performance without administrative burden or the difficult, if not impossible, task of monitoring all users.

While the value of performing rights orga-

nizations is quite obvious, the two largest in the United States—ASCAP and BMI—evolved indirectly as vehicles to deal with other problems. The first performing rights organization in America wasn't even founded until the second decade of the twentieth century, some 63 years after the establishment of the initial such society in Europe.

The first European performing rights organization was Société des Auteurs, Compositeurs et Editeurs de Musique (SACEM), formed in France in 1851. By the end of the 19th century, similar societies had been established in other major European nations. The first German performing rights society, Genossenschaft Deutscher Tonsetzer (GDT), the antecedent of today's GEMA, was founded in Berlin in 1903 by Composer Richard Strauss. England's Performing Right Society Limited (PRS) did not form until 1915.

In 1897, the U.S. copyright law was amended to grant to copyright owners the exclusive right of public performance; that is, no one could publicly perform a musical work for profit without permission of the owner. This law was passed, of course, before the advent of radio and other forms of wired communication, but the performance of songs at restaurants, hotels, nightclubs, and other public facilities by bands and orchestras was common. Compliance with this statutory mandate, however, was virtually nonexistent.

Sheet music was the main source of income for music publishers and songwriters early in this century. A song would often come to the attention of the public through its performance by bands and orchestras in public facilities. It was the contention of the band and orchestra leaders, as well as the proprietors of the facilities, who would have to pay the license fees, that since they were promoting songs, which resulted in sales of sheet music for the copyright owners, they should not have to pay for the right to perform them. Most music publishers accepted this premise for fear of having their works boycotted by the musicians. On the other hand, music was a drawing attraction in the public establishments and was, at least in part, responsible for their success.

The U.S. copyright law had been revised in 1909 and continued to protect copyright owners from unauthorized public performances for profit of their works. The law provided that violators were subject to a minimum fine of $250 plus costs for each offense. Since the law had never been tested to determine what a performance for profit was and since publishers and writers believed their right of performance was being violated by others, a lawsuit was necessary to clarify the nature of this right.

Music users had formed trade associations, so it was known they would be formidable opponents in a lawsuit. The most effective way to challenge them was for composers and lyricists to similarly band together. The impetus

was indirectly prompted by an Italian composer. According to one account, Giacomo Puccini visited the United States in 1910 for the premiere of his opera *La Fanciulla del West* (*The Girl of the Golden West*). He asked George Maxwell, the American representative of his publisher, how much money would be derived from performances of his compositions at restaurants and nightclubs, and was told that royalties were not paid for such renditions. This angered Puccini, who noted that in Europe, public performances of musical compositions yielded income. Shortly afterward, Maxwell, with composer Raymond Hubbell, approached copyright attorney Nathan Burkan about starting an American performing rights organization. Burkan supported the idea.

In October 1913, at Lüchow's Restaurant in New York, it was proposed that an organization be formed for composers and lyricists to ensure compliance with the copyright law. Only 9 out of the 36 men invited to the meeting came, perhaps due to inclement weather or misunderstanding of the meeting's purpose; however, composer Victor Herbert remained undaunted, and his enthusiasm inspired the group to plan another meeting.

On February 13, 1914, over 100 persons attended a meeting at the Hotel Claridge and established the American Society of Composers, Authors and Publishers (ASCAP). Maxwell was elected president, Herbert vice-president (he declined the offer of the presidency), Glen MacDonough secretary, John Golden treasurer, Raymond Hubbell assistant treasurer, and Burkan was retained as counsel. This organization was modeled after SACEM, the French society.

ASCAP made known its objectives and some 85 hotels agreed to pay license fees. They paid an average of $8.23 per month, which barely paid for the society's operating expenses; thus members could not be compensated for performances of their works. Many other establishments did not take out a license. A legal ruling was obviously needed.

An ASCAP publisher sued the operators of the Vanderbilt Hotel, claiming John Philip Sousa's "From Maine to Oregon" had been performed in its dining room as an unauthorized performance for profit. The judge agreed, but a circuit court of appeals reversed the decision on the theory that the diners had come not to hear music but to eat.

Victor Herbert then sued Shanley's Restaurant in Times Square on April 1, 1915, charging the unauthorized performance of his waltz "Sweethearts." Judge Learned Hand of the U.S. District Court decided against ASCAP and his decision was upheld by the circuit court of appeals. The picture seemed bleak for music creators and publishers until the case was brought to the Supreme Court.

On January 22, 1917, the Court unanimously affirmed a copyright owner's right to license his work for public performance for profit, even if no admission was charged. Justice Oliver Wendell Holmes wrote in his decision: "If music did not pay, it would be given up. If it pays, it pays out of the public's pocket. Whether it pays or not, the purpose of employing it is profit, and that is enough." ASCAP's existence and the copyright owner's right of public performance were firmly established now, but it would not be until 1921 that the society's income exceeded its legal and operating costs so that it could pay royalties to its members.

Over the years ASCAP continued to enforce its members' legal rights, as new media, such as radio, developed. It grew as a performing rights organization from a charter membership of 170 composers and lyricists and 22 publishers in 1914 to 20,737 members and 7,746 publisher members at the close of 1980. Its gross collections in 1980 were in excess of $150 million. ASCAP members include or have included Irving Berlin, Aaron Copland, George Gershwin, Duke Ellington, Harold Arlen, Cole Porter, Johnny Mercer, Burt Bacharach, Stephen Sondheim, Neil Diamond, and Stevie Wonder.

In the late 1930s, three record companies released the bulk of recordings purchased by American consumers and some 800 radio stations were licensed to broadcast recorded music. The annual performing rights license fees from broadcasters totaled approximately $6 million, which was shared by less than 150 music publishers and over 1,000 songwriters. Distribution of the license fees to ASCAP members was on the basis of *live* performance on the four radio networks in the U.S. during evening hours only. Broadcast of *recorded* renditions of musical compositions and performances on independent radio stations did not result in performance revenues for their publishers and writers. Thus thousands of music publishers and songwriters could not share in this source of revenue. Some individuals saw the need for an alternative source of licensing. This was realized when Broadcast Music, Inc. (BMI) formed in 1940.

Other efforts to provide a competitive source of licensing preceded BMI's formation. Beginning in the 1920s, various songwriters and music publishers had made attempts, and in the mid thirties, the Warner Bros. music companies, which represented a considerable portion of American popular music, had offered separate licenses.

A group of some 600 radio broadcasters formed BMI in 1940 as a nonprofit organization. Pledging half their 1937 license payments to ASCAP for funding, they paid $300,000 for stock, and the remaining total of $1.2 million as initial license fees.

Since its founding, BMI has grown rapidly in size, and it is now the world's largest licensing organization in terms of number of affiliates. Near the end of 1980, there were 21,130 publishers and 37,346 writers affiliated with BMI; publisher affiliates increase at an average of 1,000 per year, writers at 2,500. At this writing, some 8,000 radio and television broadcasters and 25,000 general licensees pay about $80 million per year in license fees. Among the writers who have been or are affiliated with BMI are Roy Orbison, Hoagy Carmichael, Joni Mitchell, Neil Sedaka, Paul Simon, Felice and Boudleaux Bryant, Hank Williams, Kris Kristofferson, and Dolly Parton.

The smallest United States performing rights organization is SESAC Inc. This private, family-owned company was founded in February 1931 by Paul Heinecke as the Society of European Stage Authors and Composers or S.E.S.A.C. (its full name was later dropped).

At its inception, SESAC primarily represented the music copyrights of European publishers in the United States—works by such composers as Sibelius, Schoenberg, Busoni, and Delius. As the broadcasting industry developed, the organization expanded, representing the catalogs of many American publishers. Much of the SESAC repertory in its beginning was from the gospel and country music fields, but over the years it has come to represent works from the entire spectrum of popular and classical music. In 1980, there were approximately 1,000 composers and lyricists and 550 publishers affiliated with SESAC. SESAC affiliates over the years have also included C.W. McCall, Chip Davis, Ted Harris, William Dawson, Jerry Gillespie, Dallas Holm, Peggy Forman, and Shirley Caesar.

Performing Rights Organization of Canada Limited (PRO Canada). *See* CANADA.

Personal Manager. Representation of artists (or talent) has been a customary practice in the music business. While various types of professionals may act on the artist's behalf, the function of the *personal manager* is probably the most important for the overall development and sustenance of the artist's career. For it is the personal manager who oversees the artist's career not only by directly participating in the artist's affairs on a day by day basis but also by often selecting the other representatives of the artist—agent, attorney, business manager—and making sure that their efforts work to the client's maximum advantage.

Definition and Responsibilities. A personal manager is one who renders such services and guidance as the client may reasonably require to enhance and further his career and to develop new and different areas within which his artistic talents can be developed and exploited. The client's career might encompass any combination or all of the following: musician, vocalist, recording artist, entertainer, songwriter, arranger, producer, actor, and writer.

In serving his client, the personal manager performs many functions. These may include but are not limited to the following:

- Engaging, discharging, and/or consulting with agencies (talent, booking, theatrical, etc.) for the purpose of securing employment, engagements, or contracts for the artist. (Note: it is illegal for a personal manager to seek employment for a client without the proper license in certain states— e.g., California and New York. Often, however, the practice of a personal manager booking dates for his client exists on an informal basis where the artist is not represented by an agent.)
- Consulting with employers and prospective employers so as to assure the proper use and continued demand for the artist's services.
- Representing the artist and acting as his negotiator with regard to contracts in all areas of the entertainment field.
- Considering and screening offers for the disposition, use, or exploitation of the artist's services, talent, personality, name, or likeness (such as for endorsements, merchandising tie-ins, and charity performances) and conferring with the artist in making a final decision regarding these.
- Being available at reasonable times and places to

confer with the artist in connection with all matters concerning his career, business interests, employment, and publicity.

- Attempting to obtain, in its absence, a recording contract for the client with a bona fide label.
- Informing the record company of the artist's tour schedule and overseeing the coordination of record company publicity, merchandising, advertising, and promotion.
- Creating excitement about the artist on the part of labels, agencies, and concert promoters.
- Making sure the record company properly promotes the artist's releases and the agency adequately secures engagements for the artist at the right prices and venues and oversees the prices of tickets.
- Ensuring that all publicity and promotion is in the artist's best interests and helping to build an image for the artist, arranging for publicity in the absence of a hired specialist.
- Representing the artist to record companies, attorneys, business managers, accountants, public relations firms, merchandisers, and other parties.
- Acting on the artist's behalf in the case of any problems with a record company, agent, promoter, publicist, etc.
- Representing the artist in dealings with unions.
- Acquiring for the artist the services of a record producer, road manager, backup musicians, vocalists, and any other parties he may need.
- Attending rehearsals and performances and advising the artist how to improve his performance and overall show (with respect to delivery, repertoire, costume, sound, lighting, stage design, choreography, etc.).
- Traveling with the artist to engagements when possible and overseeing the events.
- Creating for the artist free time for artistic development, the writing of songs, etc.
- Arranging, if possible, for advances for the artist from his performing rights organization and publisher, if the artist writes songs.
- Finding or screening songs for the artist to perform or record (though this is not necessarily a function of the personal manager, many do this).
- Handling the artist's business affairs (where such responsibility has not been delegated to a business manager or accountant).
- Maintaining and/or overseeing the keeping of timely and accurate business and financial records of all transactions concerning the artist.
- Building and sustaining the artist's career.

Compensation. The personal manager is compensated for his services on a commission basis. Commissions range from 10% to 30% or more of the artist's gross earnings, but commonly are 15% or 20%. The manager's commissions are usually paid as and when income is received (such as upon an engagement). Some arrangements provide for commissions to be paid at the end of each calendar month during the term of agreement. Commissions are derived from salaries, advances, bonuses, royalties, interests, percentages, shares of profits, merchandise, shares in ventures, products, properties, or any other kind of income that is reasonably related to the artist's career in the entertainment, music, recording, motion picture, television, radio, literary, theatrical, and advertising fields, and all similar areas in which the artist's talents are developed and exploited.

Some personal managers receive commissions on a sliding scale basis. For example, they may increase from 15% to 25% as different plateaus are reached with regard to the artist's gross earnings or as his earnings from record royalties reach a certain level. As earnings from record sales, publishing, and performing rights organizations are remitted quarterly or semiannually, provisions are made for commissions from such incomes to be accounted for separately.

Commonly, all the artist's earnings as they relate to the contract are paid directly to the personal manager. The contract may provide that from such collections, the manager may reimburse himself for any fees and expenses for which the artist is contractually responsible and which the manager advanced or incurred (such as agency fees, union dues, publicity, wardrobe, and traveling expenses, etc.). A contract may also establish that if the artist receives earnings directly, he shall hold in trust for the manager that portion of earnings commensurate with the manager's compensation.

Some artists contractually prohibit the personal manager from sharing in certain income. Such restrictions, for example, may apply to income received from songwriting, publishing, and performing rights organizations. Personal managers do not normally participate in income received that is not related to the entertainment industry.

Term. There are many different terms for artist/personal manager contracts. For example, some run for a period of one, two, three, or more years, others for an initial term with unilateral options on behalf of the manager, e.g., an initial period of one year plus four one-year options.

Label Aspects. A primary objective of the personal manager is to secure a recording contract for the artist, if none exists, with a bona fide label. The manager should be as aware as possible of the policies, internal operations, and reputations of the various labels and direct his selling efforts to those companies prepared to assume the financial expenditures necessary to properly promote the artist's recordings, once made.

Recording contracts provide for the artist to record and deliver a stipulated number of master recordings per year and it is the personal manager's responsibility to see that his client fulfills this obligation. Thus the manager may set aside a certain amount of time in the artist's schedule for creativity.

The personal manager should have or should establish working relationships with various personnel in the record company to which his client is signed. He should get to know employees in the following departments: A & R, artist development, merchandising, marketing, sales, publicity, promotion, advertising, and business affairs. Generating excitement in the company, smoothing out any problems these personnel have, and overseeing their work with respect to the artist serves the client properly.

Engaging the Services of Others. The manager may engage the services of various professionals at different points in the artist's career. This may be as follows: when a recording contract is offered, an attorney; once it is signed, an agent; prior to the release of product and/or the scheduling of a concert tour, a public relations firm, a road manager, and a business manager. It is the personal manager's responsibility to select individuals who can most competently serve the artist.

Appearances and Employment Considerations. A popular artist may be asked to appear on, in, or in connection with television talk shows, variety shows, radio and television commercials, theatrical motion pictures, endorsements of products, services, political candidates and causes, benefits, charity functions, or stage shows. Each of these may have a resounding effect (either positive or negative) on the artist's career and it is the personal manager's responsibility to predetermine to the best of his ability and advise the artist whether such appearances will enhance his client's career or affect it negatively.

Qualifications and Qualities. No license is needed for one to become or perform the services of a personal manager. However, as stated above, if the personal manager performs the services of an agent, he may be required to obtain a license and meet certain qualifications as prescribed by state law governing employment agencies.

In selecting a personal manager, an artist should look for such qualities as honesty, competency, and a willingness to work hard on the artist's behalf. Also, the manager should be capable of developing, enhancing, and furthering the artist's career. One who has such a large number of clients that he and his staff will not be able to devote adequate attention to an individual artist should be avoided. And of course artist and manager should be compatible.

Personality Folio. *See* Printed Music.

Phonogram Convention. *See* INTERNATIONAL COPYRIGHT RELATIONS.

Phonograph Record. A grooved disc that stores sound and mechanically reproduces it. Present commercial phonograph records are usually in the form of either an LP (33⅓ rpm) or a SINGLE (45 rpm). Some are manufactured in the form of an EP.

Phonograph records are molded primarily from polyvinyl chloride (PVC). Lamp black or a similar dye added to the mix in the manufacturing process gives a record its black color (use of virgin vinyl creates a transparent disc). As PVC is a petroleum product, it tends to be costly. Many record manufacturers therefore use reprocessed vinyl—that is, new vinyl blended with nonvirgin ground vinyl. Ground vinyl may be obtained from the scrappings of returns, from the trimmings of records in the manufacturing process (called *flashing*), and from rejected pressed records. Conventional discs, by and large, blend approximately 40% ground vinyl and 60% virgin vinyl.

Up until the 1940s, commercial discs (mostly 78.26 rpm) were manufactured from shellac (a thermoplastic in combination with a finely ground filler such as clog). This was replaced by synthetic thermoplastic resins and later by PVC.

A major complaint against conventional phonograph records is the surface noise ("pops" and "clicks") they produce when being played. This is sometimes caused by the addition of improper materials, an insufficient percentage of new vinyl, insufficient time in the mold, or bubbles or other imperfections that are molded into the vinyl during the manufacturing process (scratches, fingerprints, static electricity, and dirt can also cause surface noise).

See also RECORD MANUFACTURING.

Phonorecords. Term used in the federal copyright statute. A COPYRIGHT OWNER has the exclusive right to reproduce and publish a work in phonorecords, with certain limitations.

Definition. "Phonorecords" is defined in the 1976 Copyright Act (Section 101) as "material objects in which sounds, other than those accompanying a motion picture or other audiovisual work, are fixed by any method now known or later developed, and from which the sounds can be perceived, reproduced or otherwise communicated, either directly or with the aid of a machine or device. The term 'phonorecords' includes the material object in which the sounds are first fixed."

Examples. Examples of "phonorecords" include phonograph records (such as 33⅓ rpm or 45 rpm discs) and prerecorded cassette, 8-track, and open-reel tapes. (Phonorecords do not include material objects in which sounds accompanying a motion picture or other audiovisual work are embodied; thus videocassettes and videodiscs are not examples under the law of phonorecords, but rather of COPIES.) Other examples of phonorecords include electrical transcriptions, audio tapes for broadcast and background music purposes, and piano rolls.

"Phonorecords" Distinguished from "Sound Recordings." As opposed to a phonorecord, a SOUND RECORDING, basically, is the total amount of "fixed" sounds produced from vocal and/or instrumental performances and is a work of authorship. A phonorecord is the material object, which may embody two types of works of authorship: (1) the sound recording and (2) the underlying musical, literary, or dramatic work.

See COMPULSORY/MECHANICAL LICENSES (PHONORECORDS).

Piano Roll. *See* PLAYER PIANO ROLL.

Pick. Term that refers to the prognostication by trade publications, tout "tip" sheets, and radio stations that a particular record will become a "hit."

As used in trade publications, a *pick* may be

The advent of the two-sided record around 1905 was promoted in this ad by the Columbia Phonograph Company.

Edison's original phonograph, patented in 1877, consisted of a piece of tinfoil wrapped around a rotating cylinder. The vibration of his voice as he spoke into a recording horn (not shown) caused a stylus to cut grooves into the tinfoil. The first sound recording made was Edison reciting "Mary Had a Little Lamb."

either a new single or an album that has been chosen from the week's releases to be reviewed, on the basis of predictions that it will become a chartmaker. In *Billboard*, for example, an LP in its "Top Album Picks" is deemed to place in the top half of the charts; a 45 reviewed in its "Top Single Picks" is predicted to be a top 30 chartmaker. A trade pick reflects only the opinion of the publication's review panel.

In radio broadcasting, a *pick* designates a new single received by the station and given airplay because of the potential it is thought to have. The pick has not been added to the station's regular playlist yet.

Picture Disc. Record on which an image–usually a photograph or part of the album graphics—is molded into the vinyl. Picture discs are used primarily as promotion tools and usually manufactured in limited editions or quantities. This is partly because of limited public acceptance: their retail price may be substantially higher than that of regular discs and they are said to produce more background noise (caused by the insertion of materials containing the graphics during the pressing). Another factor is that only relatively small amounts can be manufactured per day by the semimanual pressing process required. Hence picture discs are often regarded as collector's items.

The manufacturing process for picture discs is similar to that for regular discs except as follows: a photographic or other paper containing the printed matter (image) is placed at the bottom of a mold, the printed matter facing down, or outward. On top of that is placed a colored chemical compound, and on top of that, another sheet of printed matter, this one facing up and also outward (this is the reverse "picture" side of the record).

On each half of the mold are nickel stampers, having the negative shape of the grooves of the finished record. When the press closes, the vinyl compound is injected into the mold under pressure (or prior to the closing of the press, pancakelike vinyl "biscuits" are inserted) and the hot stampers mold the grooves into the vinyl and the compound. During the initial time the press is closed, the compound is heated with steam under pressure and then both the press and the finished record are cooled with water. When the press opens, the record is ready for final finishing operations, with the imprinted image visible on each side and the grooves molded into the vinyl. The rough edges of the record (flashing) are then trimmed and the record is ready for inspection and packaging.

It is also possible to mold a design into the record surface itself. However, this procedure is very complicated and must be carefully supervised to ensure that the grooves are not modified in any way, thus generating distortion, noise, etc.

See COLOR DISC; RECORD MANUFACTURING.

Picture Sleeve. A SLEEVE with a photograph (usually of the artist) printed on it. Picture sleeves are used essentially as a merchandising tool for *singles* at the retail level. They may bring extra attention and exposure to the discs and increase sales, particularly when displayed by the retailer at the point of purchase.

A picture sleeve may also be used as a cross-merchandising tool. The picture sleeve of a single can promote the artist's album by containing a scaled-down reproduction of the album's cover; it can also print-plug the album.

In addition, a picture sleeve may be used as part of an artist-image campaign. It can serve to create a visual identification for a new artist or increase appeal for a more established one. The cost of manufacturing a picture sleeve may run as high as $.05 or more than for a regular sleeve.

Piracy/Counterfeiting (Printed Music). The unauthorized reproduction and selling of copyrighted music in print form has long been a problem to the copyright owners of musical compositions. Infringement of printed music

Legitimate vs. Pirated: Three examples are shown here of legitimate 8-track prerecorded tape cartridges on the left and the pirated counterparts on the right. If an attempt had been made also to duplicate the logo and artwork of the legitimate product, they would be designated in industry terminology as "counterfeits" rather than pirated tapes.

has two basic modes: the counterfeiting of sheet music and the reproduction of hundreds of copyrighted musical compositions owned by many different music publishers in fakebooks, sold at relatively low costs. Compositions counterfeited or pirated in print form are the successful and well-known popular tunes of the moment or the recent past.

The NATIONAL MUSIC PUBLISHERS' ASSOCIATION (NMPA) has been instrumental in thwarting printed-music piracy through investigatory activity and assistance to its publisher members who undertake legal actions. It was particularly active in foiling the upsurge of unauthorized song sheets containing lyrics of popular songs in the 1930s and of illegal fakebooks in the 1960s.

Since the advent and widespread accessibility of photocopying machines, writers and publishers have been deprived of income by users who copy printed music. The FAIR USE provisions of the 1976 Copyright Act attempt to limit such activity by establishing criteria by which the user may determine whether photocopying in a particular situation constitutes COPYRIGHT INFRINGEMENT.

Piracy (Records/Audio Tapes). An ever-present problem in the recording industry has been the making and selling of illegal recordings. Illegal recordings serve to compete with and diminish sales of legitimate ones, robbing record companies, artists, composers, and others of rightful earnings. Three forms of such illicit trade exist—BOOTLEGGING, COUNTERFEITING, and piracy. The term "piracy" is sometimes generically used to connote production or sale of all illegal recording product.

Definition. *Piracy* or pirating (in the specific as distinguished from the generic sense) is the duplicating of sounds from a legitimate recording onto tapes or discs without authorization from the copyright or master-tape owner—and the selling of these duplications with packaging, artwork label, trademark, and logo different from that of the legitimate product while still identifying the album title, performers, and musical selections.

History. Industry concern against piracy is indicated as far back as the 1890s and early 1900s. At the turn of the century, the American Graphophone Co. (the antecedent of today's CBS Records) put its dealers on notice that if they were found to be duplicating the company's recordings without authorization they not only stood in danger of losing their franchise but were liable to be prosecuted to the fullest extent of the law; other companies, such as National Phonograph Co., issued similar warnings as well as prohibitions against sale of the legitimate product to unauthorized dealers, or resale by the original or any subsequent retail purchaser. At that time, those believed to be duplicating recordings without authorization could be brought to court for violating patented recording processes (these have since expired), or companies could act in a civil court charging unfair competition. Also, federal agencies such as the Federal Trade Commission could enjoin unfair competition of this type [see, e.g., FTC v. Orient Music Roll Co., 2 F.T.C. 176, 179 (1919)].

Piracy persisted as a concern but at unalarming rates until the 1960s. The advancement in tape recording technology then so greatly increased the manufacture and sale of illegitimate recordings that by 1972, the sale of spurious product reached a then all-time high [the RECORDING INDUSTRY ASSOCIATION OF AMERICA, INC. (RIAA) claimed that bootlegging, counterfeiting, and piracy collectively drained well over $350 million from the U.S. industry's annual income]. The industry that year witnessed the sale of one illegal prerecorded tape for every two legitimate ones. Various states, starting with New York in 1967, passed antipiracy statutes, but these offered only limited protection.

A federal law was passed in 1971 to provide protection for all sound recordings "fixed" on federal law are greater than under state law. Despite federal protection, piracy (in the generic sense) has continued in strong force. For example, in the late 1970s, the sound track to *Grease* was counterfeited at record-high levels.

The Pirate's Operation. Once a pirate obtains a legitimate disc or tape, it becomes his "master" and he need only mass-produce copies from it to start his business. The majority of his recordings will be in tape form. An album may be reproduced by the pirate in mass quantities as follows: The pirate places the "master" onto a tape deck ("master recorder") that electronically transmits the sounds embodied therein onto several large spools of tape ("pancakes") mounted on machines ("slaves") linked by wire to the tape deck (each pancake can receive many individual programs). After several duplicating processes have been completed, the pancakes are then placed on other machines ("winders") that cut the large tape into several small spools, each containing the sounds of an entire album, which are then ready for insertion into empty cassette and cartridge containers.

Pirates make and distribute illegal sound reproductions via 7- and 12-inch discs, 8-track cartridge tapes, and cassette tapes. They can sell their product to wholesalers—or directly to consumers—at a lower price, since they incur none of the creative expenses in producing the original recordings, make no promotion or advertising outlays, and pay no taxes on their earnings. Pirates focus on the hits—pop, rock, country, or whatever—generally striking at the height of a record's popularity and promotion campaign. Investigations reveal that pirates range from individuals to organized crime operations, from small home-basement setups to large factories.

Victims of Piracy. The staggering loss of revenue due to piracy takes its toll against all who make the record business tick, including legitimate record companies, pressing and tape duplicating plants, distributors, rack jobbers,

one-stops, retail outlets, record clubs, recording artists, producers, music publishers, songwriters, and session musicians and vocalists. Also affected are federal, state, and municipal governments (which are deprived of tax revenues) and the consumer, who invariably ends up with an inferior product. In addition, the musicians' union pension and welfare funds are deprived of substantial revenues, as is the Music Performance Trust Fund, which obtains revenue from the sale of legitimate recordings and uses it to give work to unemployed musicians, who put on concerts and performances in depressed and rural areas, veterans' hospitals, old age homes, and the like.

Legal Protection Against Piracy

State Protection. Piracy of records existed through the years but reached alarming rates beginning in the 1960s when the technology to reproduce sound recordings in cassette and eight-track became available, and pirates found it easier to reproduce albums in these forms than in disc. There existed a need for stronger laws to deter or punish pirates and a federal statute still seemed dubious at this point.

New York was the first state to enact an antipiracy statute; its law was enacted on September 1, 1967. Through the years all states (except, at this writing, Vermont) have enacted antipiracy statutes, some of which have been amended through the years, making piracy a felony instead of a misdemeanor. State laws provide protection for all recordings "fixed" before February 15, 1972; federal law protects sound recordings fixed on or after this date. The 1976 Copyright Act limits state protection for sound recordings fixed before February 15, 1972 until February 15, 2047. At that time, all such state-protected recordings will fall into the PUBLIC DOMAIN.

The right of a state to regulate and define as a criminal act the unauthorized duplication of sound recordings not protected by federal law was affirmed by a United States Supreme Court decision in *Goldstein et al v. Califor-*

nia, 412 U.S. 546 (1973). Other decisions upholding the validity of state antipiracy statutes followed and state laws today are used to prosecute those who pirate sound recordings fixed before February 15, 1972. A table of the various types of offenses and penalties imposed for these under state laws appears on pages 264–280.

Federal Protection. The 1909 Copyright Act was amended in 1971 to provide protection for all legitimate sound recordings fixed and published on or after February 15, 1972. The Sound Recording Amendment provided fines, imprisonment, or both for offenders found guilty of criminal infringements.

The Copyright Act of 1976 (which supersedes the 1909 act as amended) gives copyright protection to all sound recordings, published or unpublished, that are fixed. Under the 1976 act (effective as of January 1, 1978), any person who infringes the copyright in a sound recording (or motion picture) willfully and for purposes of commercial advantage is subject to the following: for a first offense, a fine of not more than $25,000 and/or imprisonment for not more than 1 year; for each subsequent offense, a fine of not more than $50,000 and/or imprisonment for not more than 2 years.

All published records and tapes made on or after February 15, 1972, are required to contain, in order to secure statutory protection, the Copyright Notice for sound recordings: the symbol ℗ with the year of publication and name of the copyright proprietor. This notice is absent in records and tapes made and distributed prior to this date. The date a sound recording is fixed determines whether federal or state jurisdiction applies.

Prosecution

Criminal Actions. When a prosecutor initiates a criminal action in a federal court charging criminal infringement (this type of action has the most powerful remedies), he must show the following:

1. Ownership (that is, that the infringed work is the property of copyright claimant and the work is protected by a valid copyright).

2. Willful infringement (that is, that no authorization was given by the copyright owner to the defendant to reproduce the sound recording).

3. That the defendant knew he was committing an infringing act under the copyright law (often difficult to prove).

4. That the infringer made money, or a profit, or received or obtained some pecuniary benefit from his actions.

Civil Actions. It may sometimes be desirable or necessary for plaintiffs to initiate civil actions, as these are frequently easier to prosecute than criminal actions (you don't have to prove willfulness) and the remedies are sometimes effective. If the defendant is found to be an infringer, law enforcement agencies bringing the civil suits, or civil litigants, can confiscate or destroy all of the infringer's unauthorized recordings and the duplicating equipment used to make them. Sometimes, in an appropriate case, these can be seized through the court prior to and as a commencement of the civil suit, with appropriate safeguards to the defendants.

Other Ways to Convict Pirates. There are laws, other than the copyright statute, that are used to prosecute copyright infringers. Pirates may be convicted of: mail fraud and wire fraud (i.e., violaters use the mail and telephone to do business and/or scheme); interstate transportation of stolen property (a copyrighted work copied without authorization from the owner is considered stolen property); tax evasion; or laws dealing with organized crime, such as the Racketeer-Influenced and Corrupt Organizations Act (RICO) (18 U.S.C., Section 1961 et seq.), which outlaws the acquisition of an "enterprise" with any income derived from "racketeering activity."

International Protection. *See* International Copyright Relations.

Identifying Pirated Records and Tapes.

Distinguishing between legitimate tapes and records and the spurious is not very difficult (except in the case of counterfeit recordings—*see* COUNTERFEITING). There are some detectable differences. The Anti-Piracy Intelligence Bureau of txe RECORDING INDUSTRY ASSOCIATION OF AMERICA, INC. (RIAA), in its *Handbook for Enforcement and Prosecution,* lists the following as indications of an illegitimate (pirate) product:

1. An unfamiliar company name or no identification of a record manufacturer. Legitimate records and tapes conspicuously bear the name, address, and trademark of the record manufacturer, but a pirated good will either have the pirate's own trade name or there will be no manufacturer identification on it.

2. Unprofessional-looking packaging. Legitimate record companies package their product with a tight shrink wrap; pirated product is often loosely wrapped or not wrapped at all. Legitimate albums and tapes are artistically designed, often with 4-color artwork and photographs or illustrations. Pirates usually do not use 4-color artwork and rarely print a photograph of the artist. Pirates frequently use the same artwork on albums of various artists or tapes of music.

3. Statements on the product such as "Fees and royalties paid" or "The Copyright Law has been complied with." Even if the pirate is paying royalties to a music publisher, he is still acting illegally by duplicating a recording without authorization from the owner of the original. He is not acting within the compulsory license provision of the law (as many have unsuccessfully contended in court), as this provision does not give the right to duplicate an existing sound recording without permission.

4. Tapes or albums with more than one name performer, artist, or musical group. Recording artists are almost always under exclusive contract to one record company. Legitimate recordings rarely contain major performances by more than one act; pirated ones often do. This is not to be confused, however, with legitimate COMPILATION ALBUMS.

5. Unusual distribution or retailing practices. Pirated goods are often sold on street corners, in flea markets, gas stations, auto supply stores, and drugstores, and outside concert halls or auditoriums where the artist is performing. Some of these situations are legitimate, but extra caution is advisable. Pirated products are also sold at some regular retail outlets.

See also SOUND-ALIKE ALBUM.

State Antipiracy Statutes*

State	Type of Offense	Penalties Imposed	Scope of Coverage
Alabama Criminal Code A-8-80 through 13 A-8-86	*Felony*—Manufacture and/or distribution *Misdemeanor*—Retail sales; improper labeling	*Felony—First offense:* Imprisonment not less than 1 year, nor more than 3 years, and/or fine not more than $25,000; *Second and subsequent offenses:* Imprisonment not less than 3 years nor more than 10 years, and/or fine not more than $100,000.	*Felony:* Unlawful to knowingly transfer or cause to be transferred, without the owner's consent, recorded sounds with the intent to sell same or use for profit through public performance. Unlawful to manufacture, distribute or wholesale any article with knowledge the sounds thereon are unlawfully transferred.

State Antipiracy Statutes* *(cont'd)*

State	Type of Offense	Penalties Imposed	Scope of Coverage
		Misdemeanor—Unclassified. *Confiscation*—Statute provides for confiscation of duplicating equipment and unlawful recordings. Confiscation statute applies to any nonconforming recording, regardless of lack of knowledge or intent on the part of the retail seller.	*Misdemeanor:* Unlawful to knowingly retail or possess for purposes of retailing any recording unlawfully produced, manufactured, distributed, or acquired at wholesale. *Misdemeanor: Improper labeling*—Unlawful to sell recording not bearing the name of the manufacturer of the recorded material.
Alaska A.S. 45.51. 010 thru 45. 51.020	*Misdemeanor*	*Misdemeanor:* Imprisonment for a period of not more than 1 year, and/or a fine of not more than $1,000. *Confiscation* of unlawful stock.	Unlawful to reproduce, sell, offer for sale, or knowingly advertise for sale any sound recording reproduced without the owner's written consent. *Improper labeling:* Unlawful to advertise, offer for sale, sell, or resell a recording not bearing the name and full address of the manufacturer and name of actual performer or group.
Arizona 13 A.R.S. 3705	*Misdemeanor*	*Misdemeanor:* Class I misdemeanor—Imprisonment up to 6 months and/or a fine up to $1,000.	Unlawful to knowingly transfer or cause to be transferred, or sell or cause to be sold recorded sounds without the owner's consent.
Arkansas 41 Ark. Stats. 2375 thru 2376	*Misdemeanor*	*First offense:* Class A Misdemeanor—Imprisonment not exceeding 1 year and/or (1) a fine not exceeding $1,000 or (2) in the court's discretion, up to double his pecuniary gain from said activity; *Second and subsequent offenses:* Class A Misdemeanor—Imprisonment not exceeding 1 year and/or (1) a fine not to exceed $5,000 or (2) in the court's discretion up to double his pecuniary gain from said activity. Person in business of selling recorded sounds is given 30 days to sell and dispose of illegal stock. *Corporations*—Fine of up to double (1) or (2).	Unlawful to knowingly transfer, cause to be transferred, sell, distribute, circulate, offer for such, possess for purpose of such any recorded sounds without the owner's consent. *Improper labeling*—Unlawful to sell, distribute, circulate, offer for sale, distribution, or circulation, or possess for such purpose any recording on which sounds have been transferred unless such recording bears the actual name and address of the transferrer of such sounds on the package.

State Antipiracy Statutes* *(cont'd)*

State	Type of Offense	Penalties Imposed	Scope of Coverage
California Penal Code 653 h; 653s	*Felony / Misdemeanor*	*Felony—First offense:* Fine of up to $25,000 and / or up to 1 year in county jail or up to 1 year and a day in state prison; *Second and subsequent offenses:* Fine up to $50,000 and / or imprisonment up to 2 years. *Misdemeanor*—Imprisonment in the county jail not exceeding 6 months and / or a fine not exceeding $5,000.	*Felony:* Unlawful to knowingly and willfully transfer or cause to be transferred without the owner's consent recorded sounds with intent to sell or cause to be sold same or use for profit through public performance. Unlawful to knowingly transfer such records within the state. *Misdemeanor:* Unlawful to knowingly sell or cause to be sold such illegal recordings. *Misdemeanor: Bootleg statute*—Unlawful to knowingly sell or cause to be sold, transported, or cause to be transported within the state any recorded sounds of a live performance without the owner's consent.
Colorado 18 Crim. Code 4-601 thru 4-605	*Felony*—Manufacture *Misdemeanor*	*Felony:* Class 5 felony—Fine of not less than $1,000 nor more than $15,000 and / or imprisonment of 1–5 years. *Misdemeanor:* Class 3 misdemeanor—Fine of not less than $50 nor more than $750 and / or up to 6 months' imprisonment.	*Felony:* Unlawful to knowingly transfer without the owner's consent recorded sound with the intent to sell same or use to promote sale of any product. *Misdemeanor:* Unlawful to knowingly or without reasonable grounds to know, advertise, offer or possess for sale, resale, or distribution any such sound recording. *Misdemeanor: Improper labeling*—Unlawful to advertise, offer, or possess for sale a recording not bearing the actual name and address of the manufacturer and name of the performer or group.
Connecticut Gen Stat. 53-142b thru d	*Misdemeanor*	*First offense*—Fine of not more than $1,000 and or imprisonment for not more than 1 year; *Second and subsequent offenses*—Fine of not more than $2,000 and / or imprisonment for not more than 1 year for each subsequent offense. *Improper labeling*—Fine of not more than $1,000 and / or imprisonment for not more than 1 year.	Unlawful to knowingly and willfully transfer or cause to be transferred without the owner's consent, recorded sounds with the intent to sell same or use for profit. Unlawful to knowingly sell, offer for sale, or advertise for sale such recordings. Unlawful to knowingly offer for a fee, or rent any equipment or machinery used to reproduce such llegal recordings.

State Antipiracy Statutes* *(cont'd)*

State	Type of Offense	Penalties Imposed	Scope of Coverage
			Improper labeling—Unlawful to manufacture or knowlingly sell, distribute, or advertise for sale recordings not bearing the actual name and address of the manufacturer and the actual name of the performer or group.
Delaware Del. Code Ann. Ch. 11 920 thru 924	*Felony:* Manufacture *Misdemeanor:* Retail sales, advertising, possession, improper labeling	*Class E Felony: Manufacture*—Fine of up to $10,000 and/or up to 7 years' imprisonment. *Corporate:* Fine of up to $75,000. *Class A misdemeanor: Retail sale, advertising, possession*—Fine of not more than $1,000 and/or up to 2 years' imprisonment. *Class C misdemeanor: Improper labeling*—Fine of not more than $500 and up to 3 months' imprisonment.	*Felony:* Unlawful to knowingly transfer or cause to be transferred without the owner's consent, recorded sounds with the intent to sell, cause to be sold, or used for profit through public performance or to promote the sale of any such product. *Misdemeanor:* Unlawful to knowingly or with reasonable grounds to know, advertise, sell, distribute, or possess for such purposes such illegal recordings. *Misdemeanor: Improper labeling*—Unlawful to advertise or offer for sale, resale, sell, resell, or possess for such purposes any recordings not bearing the actual name and address of the manufacturer and performers or group.
Florida F.S.A. 540.11	*Felony*—Manufacture *Misdemeanor*—Sale, improper labeling	*Third degree felony*—Fine of up to $5,000 and/or imprisonment for up to 5 years. *Second degree misdemeanor*—Fine of up to $500 and/or imprisonment for up to 6 months. *Forfeiture*—All articles and any equipment and components used in production are subject to seizure, forfeiture, and destruction. Possession of 5 or more duplicate copies or 20 or more individual copies creates *rebuttable presumption* that recordings were intended for sale or distribution.	*Felony:* Unlawful to knowingly and willfully transfer or cause to be transferred without the owner's consent, recorded sounds or live performances (bootleg statute) with the intent to sell same or cause same to be sold or used to promote the sale of any product. *Misdemeanor:* Unlawful to sell, offer for sale, or possess for such purposes any such recordings with the knowlege or with reasonable grounds to know of their illegality. *Misdemeanor: Improper labeling*—Unlawful to sell or possess for sale any recordings not bearing the actual name and address of the manufacturer and name of the performer or group.

State Antipiracy Statutes' *(cont'd)*

State	Type of Offense	Penalties Imposed	Scope of Coverage
Georgia Crim. Code of Georgia 26-9938a	*Felony*	*First offense*—Fine of not more than $25,000 and or imprisonment not less than 1 year nor more than 2 years; *Second and subsequent offenses*—Fine of not more than $100,000 and/or imprisonment for 1 to 3 years.	Unlawful to knowingly transfer or cause to be transferred without the owner's consent recorded sounds or to sell, distribute, offer for sale, distribution, or circulation or possess for such purposes any recordings knowing they have been made without the owner's consent. *Improper labeling*—Unlawful to sell, distribute, circulate, offer for sale, or possess for such purposes any recordings not bearing the actual name and address of the transferrer of the sounds.
Hawaii Chapter 482c	*Misdemeanor*	Imprisonment up to 1 year and/or a fine not exceeding $1,000 and not exceeding double the pecuniary gain derived from the defendant's offense.	Unlawful to transfer or cause to be transferred without the owner's consent, recorded sounds with the intent to sell same or cause same to be sold or used for profit through public performance. Unlawful to sell or rent or make available any equipment or machinery with the knowledge it will be used for illegal duplication.
Idaho I.C. 18-7601 thru 18-7608	*Felony*—Manufacture *Misdemeanor*—Retail and improper labeling	*Felony*—Fine of up to $10,000 and/or imprisonment for up to 4 years. *Misdemeanor*—Fine of up to $1,000 and/or imprisonment up to 6 months. *Confiscation* and destruction of equipment and recordings.	*Felony*—Unlawful to knowingly transfer or cause to be transferred without the owner's consent, recorded sounds with the intent to sell same or use to promote the sale of any product. *Misdemeanor*—Unlawful to knowingly or with reasonable grounds to know, advertise, sell, offer for sale, or possess for such purposes any such illegal recordings. *Improper labeling*—Unlawful to advertise, sell, or possess for sale any recordings not bearing the actual name and address of the manufacturer and actual name of the performer.
Illinois 38 Ill. Rev. Stat. 16-7; 16-8; 43-1 thru 43-2	*Felony*—Manufacture, sell, advertise, offer equipment *Misdemeanor*—Improper labeling	*Class 4 felony*—Fine of not more than $10,000 and/or 1 to 3 years' imprisonment. *Class B misdemeanor*—Fine of not more than $500 and/or imprisonment for up to 6 months.	*Felony*—Unlawful to knowingly, intentionally or recklessly sell, offer for sale, advertise for sale, transfer, or cause to be transferred or used for profit, recordings reproduced without the consent of the owner, or rent or make available equipment for such manufacture.

State Antipiracy Statutes' *(cont'd)*

State	Type of Offense	Penalties Imposed	Scope of Coverage
		Confiscation and destruction of illegal recordings and machinery.	*Misdemeanor: Improper labeling*—Unlawful to intentionally, knowingly, recklessly, or negligently for profit manufacture, sell, perform, lease, distribute, vend, circulate, or deal in *un*identified sound recordings not displaying actual name and address of the manufacturer and actual name of the performer.
Indiana 35-43-4-1 thru 35-43-4-5.	*Class D felony*	Imprisonment for a fixed term of 2 years with not more than 2 years added for aggravating circumstances and a fine of not more than $10,000 (but a court may reduce it to a Class A Misdemeanor—fixed term of not more than 1 year and a fine of not more than $5,000).	*Theft*—Unlawful to knowingly or intentionally transfer or reproduce recorded sounds, without the consent of the owner of the master recording, with the intent to distribute the reproductions for a profit. *Receiving stolen property*—Unlawful to knowingly or intentionally receive, retain, or dispose of the property of another person that has been the subject of theft.
Iowa Iowa Code 714.15	*Theft: Class C felony*—Theft of property valued over $5,000 *Class D felony*—Theft of property whose value is $500 or less by person with two prior theft convictions, or theft by any other person of property exceeding $500 but not exceeding $5,000 *Aggravated misdemeanor*—Theft of property exceeding $100 but not exceeding $500 *Serious misdemeanor*—Theft of property exceeding $50 but not exceeding $100 *Simple misdemeanor*—Theft of property not exceeding $50	*Class C felony*—If not a habitual offender (habitual: often imprisoned up to 15 years), imprisonment up to 10 years, and in addition may be fined no more than $5,000. *Class D felony*—If not a habitual offender, imprisonment up to 5 years, and in addition, may be fined no more than $1,000. *Aggravated misdemeanor*—Imprisonment not exceeding 2 years, and/or a fine not exceeding $5,000. *Serious misdemeanor*—Imprisonment not exceeding 1 year, and/or a fine not exceeding $1,000. *Simple misdemeanor*—Imprisonment not exceeding 30 days, or a fine not exceeding $100.	Unlawful to knowingly transfer, or cause to be transferred without the owner's consent, any recorded sounds or sell, distribute, offer for sale, distribution, or circulation, or possess for such sale or distribution such recordings. *Improper labeling*—Unlawful to sell, distribute, circulate, offer for sale or distribution any recordings not bearing the actual name and address of the transferrer of the sounds.

State Antipiracy Statutes* (cont'd)

State	Type of Offense	Penalties Imposed	Scope of Coverage
Kansas 21 Criminal Code 3748 thru 3751	*Felony*—Duplication, manufacture *Misdemeanor*—Dealing in pirated sounds, improper labeling	*Class E felony*—Fine of up to $5,000 and/or imprisonment for 1 to 5 years. *Class A misdemeanor*—Fine of up to $2,500 and/or imprisonment up to 1 year.	*Felony*—Unlawful to knowingly duplicate or cause to be duplicated without the consent of the owner, recorded sounds, with the intent to sell or cause to be sold or given away as part of a promotion for any product or service such recordings. *Misdemeanor*—Unlawful to knowingly, or with reasonable grounds to know, sell, offer for sale or distribution, or possess for such purposes any such sound recordings. *Misdemeanor: Improper labeling*—Unlawful to sell, offer for sale, or possess for such purposes, any recordings not bearing the actual name and address of the manufacturer and the name of the performer or group.
Kentucky KRS. 434.445	*Felony*—Manufacture *Misdemeanor*	*Class D felony:* Manufacture—Fine not to exceed $10,000 and/or, in the court's discretion, double defendant's pecuniary gain from the crime, and/or 1 to 5 years' imprisonment. *Bootleg penalty*—Fine of $500 to $3,000 and/or imprisonment in the penitentiary for 1 year to 5 years. *Sale*—Fine of not more than $500 and/or confinement of 90 days to 12 months. Possession of 5 or more duplicate copies or 20 or more individual copies of unlawful recordings creates a rebuttable presumption that such recordings are intended for unlawful sale or distribution. *Improper labeling*—Fine of not more than $500. *Confiscation*—Police may confiscate all recorded devices.	Unlawful to knowingly transfer or cause to be transferred, recorded sounds without the owner's consent. *Bootleg statute*—Unlawful to knowingly transfer to any record, tape, or film, any performance, whether live before an audience or transmitted by wire or by radio or television, with the intent to sell or cause to be sold such article without the performer's consent. Unlawful to knowingly, or with reasonable grounds to know, to advertise, sell, or offer for sale, distribute, or possess for such purposes any unlawful recording. *Improper labeling*—Unlawful to knowingly sell, distribute, offer, or possess for sale and distribution such recordings or any recordings not bearing the true name and address of the transferrer of the sounds.

State Antipiracy Statutes* *(cont'd)*

State	Type of Offense	Penalties Imposed	Scope of Coverage
Louisiana LRS14.223	*Misdemeanor*	*First offense*—Fine of up to $1,000; *Second and subsequent offenses*—Fine of up to $2,000.	Unlawful to knowingly transfer, sell, distribute, circulate, or cause to be transferred, sold, or distributed any recorded sounds without the owner's consent.
Maine 208 MRSA 1261 *Deceptive Trade Practices Act* 206 MRSA 1211 thru 1216	*Misdemeanor*	*Transfer*—Fine of $500 to $5,000. *Advertising and sale*—Fine of $50 to $500. *Deceptive trade practices*—Injunction.	*Transfer*—Unlawful to knowingly and willfully transfer or cause to be transferred, recorded sounds without the owner's consent with intent to sell or use for profit through public performance. *Advertising and sale*—Unlawful to advertise, offer for sale, or sell such recordings. Unlawful to pass off goods as those of another or cause likelihood of confusion or of misunderstanding as to the source, sponsorship, affiliation, or certification of goods. (See statute for more details.)
Maryland 27 Annotated Code of Maryland 467A	*Misdemeanor*—First offense *Felony*—Second and subsequent offenses	*Misdemeanor*—Imprisonment for up to 1 year and/or a fine of up to $2,500. *Felony*—Imprisonment for up to 3 years and/or a fine of up to $10,000. *Forfeiture*—Recordings produced in violation of this section and the equipment used to make them are subject to seizure and destruction.	Unlawful to knowingly transfer (a) recorded sounds without the consent of the owner; (b) live or broadcast performances without the consent of the performer (bootleg statute) with the intent to sell same or to use for promotion of any product. *Improper labeling*—Unlawful to knowingly, or with reasonable grounds to know, advertise, sell, or offer for sale any recording produced without the consent of the performer or any recording not bearing the name and address of the manufacturer and the name of the performer.
Massachusetts ALM266.143	*Misdemeanor*	Fine of up to $5,000 and/or imprisonment for up to 1 year.	Unlawful to knowingly transfer or cause to be transferred, recorded sounds without the owner's consent, with the intent to sell, cause to be sold or used for profit through public performance, or to sell such recordings.

State Antipiracy Statutes* *(cont'd)*

State	Type of Offense	Penalties Imposed	Scope of Coverage
Michigan Compiled Laws Ann. 752.781 thru 752.785	*Misdemeanor*	*Transfer*—Fine of up to $5,000 and/or imprisonment of up to 1 year. *Sale, possession*—Fine of up to $100.	Unlawful to knowingly transfer or cause to be transferred, recorded sounds without the owner's consent, with the intent to sell or use to promote the sale of any product. Unlawful to sell, offer for sale, or possess for sale such recordings with knowledge or reasonable grounds to know that no consent of owner was given.
Minnesota MSA325.841 thru 325.844	*Felony*	*First offense*—Fine of up to $25,000; *Second and subsequent offenses*—Fine of up to $100,000 and/or imprisonment for up to 3 years.	Unlawful to knowingly transfer recorded sounds without the consent of the owner or to sell, distribute, offer for sale or distribution or possess for such purposes any such recordings. *Improper labeling*—Unlawful to sell, distribute, circulate, offer, or possess recordings not bearing the actual name and address of the transferrer of the sounds.
Mississippi 97-23-87 thru 97-23-89	*Misdemeanor*	*First offense*—Fine of up to $100 and/or imprisonment for up to 30 days; *Second and subsequent offenses*—Fine of up to $500 and imprisonment of up to 6 months.	Unlawful to knowingly and willfully transfer or cause to be transferred, recorded sounds, without the owner's consent with the intent to sell or use for profit through public performance. Unlawful to advertise or offer for sale such recordings. Unlawful to offer or make available for rental or sale any equipment with the knowledge that it will be used to illegally reproduce sounds. *Improper labeling*—Unlawful to manufacture or knowingly sell, distribute, circulate, or cause to be sold, distributed, or circulated for profit any recording, not bearing the manufacturer's actual name and address, and the name of the actual performer or group.
Missouri Criminal Code 570.225 thru 570.255	*Misdemeanor*—First offense *Felony*—Second and subsequent offenses	*First offense*—Fine of not more than $1,000 and/or imprisonment in the county jail for up to 6 months;	Unlawful to knowingly transfer without the owner's consent, recorded sounds with the intent to sell or use to promote the sale of same.

State Antipiracy Statutes* *(cont'd)*

State	Type of Offense	Penalties Imposed	Scope of Coverage
		Second and subsequent offenses (of Manufacture)—Imprisonment for 2-5 years.	Unlawful to knowingly or with reasonable grounds to know, advertise, offer, or possess for sale or sell any such sound recozding.
			Improper labeling—Unlawful to sell recordings not bearing the name and address of the manufacturer and name of artist or group.
Montana Revised Code 85-601 thru 85-607	*Felony*—Manufacture *Misdemeanor*—Sale / improper labeling	*Felony*—Imprisonment for up to 10 years. *Misdemeanor*—Fine of up to $500 and imprisonment of up to 6 months.	Unlawful to knowingly transfer recorded or live sounds or performances (bootleg statute) without the owner's consent with the intent to sell same or profit through the promotion of any product.
			Improper labeling—Unlawful to knowingly or with reasonable grounds to know, sell, offer for sale or distribution, or possess for such purposes any such recordings or recordings not bearing the name and address of the manufacturer and the name of the performer or group.
Nebraska 28-1458 thru 28-1461	*Misdemeanor*	Fine of not more than $1,000 and / or imprisonment in the county jail for up to 6 months.	Unlawful to knowingly transfer or cause to be transferred, recorded sounds, without the owner's consent, or to sell, distribute, circulate, offer for sale, distribution or possess for such purposes any recordings.
			Improper labeling—Unlawful to sell, distribute, circulate, offer for sale, distribution, circulation, or possess for such purposes any recording not bearing the actual name and address of the transferrer of the sounds.
Nevada N.R.S. 205.217	*Felony*	*First offense*—Fine of not more than $5,000 and / or imprisonment in the state prison for 1-6 years; *Second and subsequent offenses*—Fine of not more than $10,000 and / or imprisonment in the state prison for 1 to 10 years.	Unlawful to knowingly transfer or cause to be transferred any recorded sounds without the owner's consent or to sell, distribute, offer for sale and distribution, or possess for such purposes, any such recordings.
			Improper labeling—Unlawful to sell, distribute, circulate, offer for such, possess for such purposes any recordings not bearing the actual name and address of the transferrer of the sounds.

State Antipiracy Statutes* *(cont'd)*

State	Type of Offense	Penalties Imposed	Scope of Coverage
New Hampshire N.H. Rev. Stat. Annotated 352–A	*Felony*—Transfer *Misdemeanor*—Sale, improper labeling	*Class B felony*—Fine of up to $2,000 and/or imprisonment for up to 7 years. *Misdemeanor*—Fine of up to $1,000 and/or imprisonment for up to 1 year. Confiscation of recordings and equipment.	*Felony:* Unlawful to knowingly transfer or cause to be transferred recorded sounds or live performances (bootleg statute) without the owner's consent. *Misdemeanor: Improper labeling*—Unlawful to advertise, sell, offer for sale at wholesale or retail, or possess for such purposes any such recordings or recordings not bearing the name and address of the manufacturer and the name of the actual performer.
New Jersey Crim. Code 2A:111–52 thru 2A:111–55	*Fourth degree crime*—Transfer or sale	*Transfer or sale*—Fine of up to $500 and/or imprisonment up to 18 months.	*Transfer*—Unlawful to knowingly transfer or cause to be transferred recorded sounds without the consent of the owner with the intent to sell such recordings or to promote the sale of any product. *Sale*—Unlawful to knowingly or with reasonable grounds to know that such recording has been made without the owner's consent advertise, sell, or offer for sale such recordings.
2C:20–1 thru 2C:20–4 2C:21–1 thru 2C:21–2	*Third degree crime*—Theft *Fourth degree crime*—Criminal simulation	*Theft*—Fine of up to $7,500 and/or imprisonment of up to 5 years. *Criminal simulation*—Fine of up to $500 and/or imprisonment of up to 18 months.	*Third degree crime*—Unlawful to purposely obtain property of another by deception. (Deception is the purposeful creation or reinforcement of a false impression of another.) *Fourth degree crime*—Unlawful to purposely defraud anyone, knowing that you are facilitating the fraud of another, by making any object so that it appears to have value because of rarity, source, or authorship which it does not possess.
New Mexico 30 N.M.S.A. 16–41 thru 16–45	*Felony*—Transfer *Misdemeanor*—Sale, improper labeling, or equipment rental	*Fourth degree felony*—Fine of up to $5,000 and/or imprisonment for 1 to 5 years. *Misdemeanor*—Fine of up to $1,000 and/or imprisonment for up to 1 year.	*Felony*—Unlawful to knowingly and willfully transfer or cause to be transferred, recorded sounds, without the owner's consent, with the intent to sell same or use for profit through public performance.

State Antipiracy Statutes* *(cont'd)*

State	Type of Offense	Penalties Imposed	Scope of Coverage
			Misdemeanor: Improper labelling—Unlawful to advertise, offer for sale, distribute, or sell such recordings or rerecordings not bearing the actual name of the manufacturer and the name of the performer.
			Unlawful to offer or make available for fee or rental, equipment or machinery with the knowledge it will be used for such unlawful transfers.
New York Penal Law 275.00 et seq. and 420.00 et seq.	*Class E felony*—Manufacture of unauthorized recording *Class A misdemeanor*—Sale of unauthorized or improperly labeled recording	*Felony*—Imprisonment for not less than 1 nor more than 3 years and/or a fine of up to $5,000. *Misdemeanor*—Imprisonment for up to 1 year and/or a fine of up to $1,000. *Forfeiture*—Police officers are directed to seize recordings manufactured in violation of this statute and the equipment used to make such recordings.	*Felony:* Unlawful to knowingly transfer (a) recorded sounds without the consent of the owner; (b) live or broadcast performances without the consent of the performer (bootleg statute) with the intent to sell same or to use for promotion of any product. *Misdemeanor:* Unlawful to knowingly advertise, sell, or offer for sale any recording produced without the consent of the owner or performer or any recording not bearing the name and address of the manufacturer and the name of the performer *(improper labeling)*.
North Carolina Chap. 14 Gen. Stats. Article 58 14-432 thru .4-437	*Misdemeanor*	Each and every violation constitutes a misdemeanor punishable by a fine of up to $500 and/or imprisonment of up to 6 months.	Unlawful to knowingly transfer, or cause to be transferred, recorded sounds or live performances (bootleg statute) without the owner's consent with the intent to sell same or use for profit through public performance. *Improper labeling*—Unlawful to manufacture, distribute wholesale or retail such recording with the knowledge that the owner does not consent thereto, or where any recordings, do not bear the true name of the manufacturer.

State Antipiracy Statutes* *(cont'd)*

State	Type of Offense	Penalties Imposed	Scope of Coverage
North Dakota 47–21 .1 et seq.	*Felony*—Transfer *Misdemeanor*—Sale, improper labeling	*Felony*—Fine of up to $5,000 and/or imprisonment for up to 5 years. *Misdemeanor*—Fine of up to $500 and/or imprisonment for up to 30 days.	Unlawful to knowingly transfer, or cause to be transferred, any recorded sounds or live performances (bootleg statute) without the owner's consent with the intent to sell same or to profit through promotion of any product. *Improper labeling*—Unlawful to knowingly or with reasonable grounds to know, advertise, offer for sale, sell, distribute, or possess for such purposes any such recordings not bearing the actual name and address of the manufacturer and the name of the performer.
Ohio 2913.32	*Felony 4th degree*—Criminal simulation *Misdemeanor 1st degree*—Transfer *Misdemeanor 2nd degree*—Sale, improper labeling	*Felony*—Fine of up to $2,500 and/or imprisonment for 6 months to 5 years. *Misdemeanor:* Transfer—Fine of up to $1,000 and/or imprisonment for up to 6 months. *Sale/Labeling*—Fine of up to $750 and/or imprisonment for up to 90 days.	*Misdemeanor*—Unlawful to purposely transcribe recorded sounds without the consent of the owner with intent to sell or use same for profit through public performance. *Improper labeling*—Unlawful to advertise, offer for sale, or sell any such recordings or recordings not bearing the name and address of the manufacturer. *Felony*—Unlawful to "knowingly practice deception . . . reproducing any . . . phonograph record, or recording tape." Also unlawful to utter or possess with purpose any recording deceptively simulated.
Oklahoma 21.O.S. Supp 1865 thru 1869	*Misdemeanor: Reproduction*—First offense; sale *Felony: Reproduction*—Second and subsequent offenses	*Reproduction: First—Misdemeanor*—Fine of up to $500; *Second and subsequent offenses—Felony*—Fine of up to $2,500 and/or imprisonment for up to 6 months. *Sale: Misdemeanor*—Fine of up to $500.	Unlawful to knowingly reproduce for sale a second recording without the owner's consent or to knowingly sell or offer such recordings for sale.
Oregon ORS 164.865	*Class B misdemeanor*	Fine of up to $500 and/or imprisonment for up to 6 months. *For corporations*—Fine of up to $2,500.	Unlawful to reproduce for sale any sound recording without the written consent of the owner or to knowingly sell, offer for sale, or advertise for sale of such recordings.

State Antipiracy Statutes* *(cont'd)*

State	Type of Offense	Penalties Imposed	Scope of Coverage
Pennsylvania 18SA4116	*Misdemeanor*	Each and every manufacture, distribution, sale, or transfer at wholesale constitutes a separate offense and misdemeanor in 1st degree. *Confiscation*—Police shall confiscate all recordings.	Unlawful to knowingly transfer or cause to be transferred recorded sounds without the owner's consent, with the intent to sell or use same for profit through public performance or to manufacture, distribute, or wholesale such recordings. *Improper labeling*—Unlawful to knowingly retail or possess for purpose of retailing such recordings or any recordings not bearing the name of the manufacturer.
Rhode Island GL. 6-13.1- 15	*Felony*	*First offense*—Fine of up to $5,000 and/or imprisonment for up to 6 years; *Second and subsequent offenses*—Fine of up to $5,000 and/or imprisonment for up to 10 years.	Unlawful to knowingly transfer or cause to be transferred and recorded sounds without the owner's consent or to sell, distribute, offer for sale or distribution, or possess for such purposes any such recordings. *Improper labeling*—Unlawful to sell, distribute, offer for sale any recordings not bearing the actual name and address of the transferrer of the sounds.
South Carolina Criminal Code 16-11-910 thru 16-11- 950	*Misdemeanor*	*Transfer: First offense*—Fine of up to $5,000 and/or imprisonment for from 6 months to 2 years. *Transfer: Second offense*—Fine of up to $10,000 and/or imprisonment for from 3 to 5 years. *Advertisement, offer, sale, equipment sale, and improper labeling*—Fine of up to $1,000 and/or imprisonment for up to 1 year. *Confiscation* of recordings by law enforcement officers at time of arrest.	Unlawful to knowingly and willfully transfer or cause to be transferred recorded sounds without the owner's consent with intent to sell or use same for profit through public performance. *Improper labeling*—Unlawful to advertise, offer for sale, or sell such recordings or any recordings not bearing the actual name and address of the manufacturer and the name of the performer. Unlawful to offer or make available for fee or rental, the machinery or equipment with the knowledge that it will be used by another to reproduce sounds illegally.

State Antipiracy Statutes* *(cont'd)*

State	Type of Offense	Penalties Imposed	Scope of Coverage
South Dakota Compiled Laws 43-43A1 et seq.	*Felony*—Wholesale and transfer *Misdemeanor*—Retail, improper labeling	*Felony*—Fine of up to $1,000 and/or imprisonment in state penitentiary for up to 3 years. *Class 1 misdemeanor*—Imprisonment up to 1 year in a county jail and/or fine up to $1,000.	Unlawful to knowingly transfer or cause to be transferred recorded sounds, without the owner's consent, with the intent to sell or use same for profit through public performance or to manufacture, distribute, advertise, or sell such recordings. *Improper labeling*—Unlawful to manufacture, distribute, circulate, advertise, sell or offer for sale, or possess for purposes of sale, recordings not bearing the actual name and address of the manufacturer.
Tennessee 7 Tenn. Ann. Code 39-4244, 39-4250	*Felony*—Transfer, manufacture, distribute, wholesale *Misdemeanor*—Retail, improper labeling	*Felony: First offense*—Fine of up to $25,000 and/or imprisonment for from 1 to 3 years; *Second and subsequent offenses*—Fine of up to $100,000 and/or imprisonment for from 3 to 10 years. *Confiscation* of all recordings.	Unlawful to knowingly transfer or cause to be transferred recorded sounds, without the owner's consent, with the intent to sell or use same for profit through public performance or to manufacture, distribute, or wholesale or retail such recordings knowingly. Unlawful to manufacture, distribute wholesale or retail, or possess for such purposes any recordings not bearing the true name of the manufacturer.
Texas Various Ann. Civ. Stat. Art. 9012, Art. 8309-1	*Misdemeanor*—First offense *Felony*—Second and subsequent offenses	*First offense: Misdemeanor*—Fine of not more than $2,000. *Second and subsequent offenses: Felony*—Fine of not more than $25,000 and/or imprisonment for up to 5 years.	Unlawful to knowingly reproduce for sale any sound recording without the consent of the owner or knowingly sell or offer for sale any such recordings.
Utah Unauthorized Recording Practices of 1973 13-10-1 thru 13-10-6	*Misdemeanor*	Fine of up to $299 and/or imprisonment for up to 6 months.	Unlawful to knowingly transfer or cause to be transferred any recorded sounds without the owner's consent or to sell, distribute, offer for sale, or possess for such purpose any such recordings. Unlawful to knowingly rent, make available, or permit use of equipment or machinery for the purpose of transferring recorded sounds without the owner's consent.

State Antipiracy Statutes *(cont'd)*

State	Type of Offense	Penalties Imposed	Scope of Coverage
Virginia 59.1 Code of Va. 41.1 thru 41.6	*Misdemeanor*	Fine of up to $1,000 and/or imprisonment for up to 1 year. *Confiscation* of all recordings.	Unlawful to knowingly transfer or cause to be transferred any recorded sounds or live performances (bootleg statute) without the owner's consent with the intent to sell or use same for profit through public performance. *Improper labeling*—Unlawful to knowingly sell, retail, or possess for such purposes any such recorded device or any recording not bearing the true name of the manufacturer.
Washington 19RCW 25.010 thru 25.900; 26.90 thru 26.020	*Misdemeanor*—Improper labeling *Gross misdemeanor*—Reproduction and sale of recordings	*Misdemeanor*—Fine of up to $100. *Gross misdemeanor*—Fine of up to $1,000 and imprisonment not to exceed 1 year and confiscation of illegal stock.	*Misdemeanor: Improper labeling*—Unlawful to sell any recording not bearing the actual name and address of the recorder. *Gross misdemeanor*—Unlawful to reproduce for sale any sound recording without the owner's written consent or to knowingly sell or offer for sale or advertise for sale any sound recording that has "been reproduced without the owner's written consent."
West Virginia W. Va. Code 61-3-50	*Misdemeanor*	Fine of not more than $1,000.	Unlawful to knowingly and willfully transfer or cause to be transferred any recorded sounds without the owner's consent or to knowingly sell or possess with intent to sell such recording or any recording not bearing the actual name and address of the manufacturer and the name of the performer (*improper labeling*).
Wisconsin Crim. Code 43.207	*Misdemeanor*	*Transfer: First offense Class B misdemeanor*—Fine not to exceed $1,000 and/or imprisonment up to 9 months. *Second and subsequent offenses: Class A misdemeanor*—Fine not to exceed $10,000 and/or imprisonment up to 9 months. *Sale: Class B misdemeanor*—Fine not to exceed $1,000 and/or imprisonment up to 9 months.	Unlawful to knowingly and willfully transfer or cause to be transferred recorded sounds without the owner's consent with the intent to sell same or knowingly advertise, offer for sale, or sell such recordings.

State Antipiracy Statutes[*] *(cont'd)*

State	Type of Offense	Penalties Imposed	Scope of Coverage
Wyoming W.S. 40-13-201 thru 40-13-206	*Felony*—Manufacture *Misdemeanor*—Sale	*Felony*—Imprisonment in state penitentiary for 1 to 2 years and/or a fine of up to $10,000. *Misdemeanor*—Imprisonment in the county jail for not more than 1 year and/or a fine of up to $10,000. *Forfeiture*—Unlawful recordings and equipment used to make them are subject to seizure and destruction. Possession of 5 or more duplicate copies or 20 or more individual copies of recordings produced without the owner's/performer's consent is prima facie evidence that the devices "are intended for unlawful sale or distribution."	Unlawful to knowingly transfer: (a) recorded sounds without the consent of the owner; (b) live or broadcast performances without the consent of the performer (bootleg statute) with the intent to sell same or to use for promotion of any product. Unlawful to knowingly or with reasonable grounds to know, advertise, sell, or offer for sale any recording produced without the consent of the owner or performer.

[*] Courtesy: RIAA Anti-Piracy Intelligence Bureau

Plating. *See* RECORD MANUFACTURING.

Platinum Record Awards. Awards presented by the RECORDING INDUSTRY OF AMERICA, INC. (RIAA) in recognition of singles and albums that achieve a certain minimum amount of sales under criteria it sets forth.

The certification criteria for Platinum Awards are a minimum sale of 2 million copies of a *single* and 1 million copies of an *album* (LPs and/or prerecorded tapes of identical program material). Certification is based on domestic sales of units shipped and results from a sales figure audit conducted by RIAA through an independent auditing firm. Any company in the record business may apply for certification. For recordings released on or after January 4, 1980, sales audits may be requested and Platinum certifications issued only after a single or album has been in release for at least 60 days.

History. As sales of recordings swelled to unprecedented levels in the 1970s, RIAA decided to add a new awards program to its existing GOLD RECORD AWARDS. This was the Platinum Record Awards, for which only singles or albums released on or after January 1, 1976, are eligible. When the Platinum Awards program was first implemented, the certification criteria were the same as above, without the postrelease qualification delay.

In 1976, RIAA certified as Platinum 4 singles and 37 albums; in 1977, 3 singles and 68 albums; in 1978, 10 singles and 102 albums; in 1979, 12 singles and 42 albums; and in 1980, 3 singles and 66 albums.

See also PLATINUM RECORD AWARDS, Appendix K.

Player Piano Roll. From the late 1800s to the late 1920s—the height of popularity of player pianos in America—millions of player piano *rolls* were sold annually. This happened despite a lack of standardization (or interchangeability) for rolls until around 1908. The popularity of player pianos and hence rolls, however, declined after 1926, owing to the growing appeal of the young radio industry.

Description. Player piano rolls are special perforated paper rolls manufactured in large quantity from a cardboard *master* roll. Traditionally, two different recording methods are used to produce the master roll:

1. In the original "Hand-Played" method, a pianist (or pianists) plays on a "Marking Piano," which produces a "marked" roll indicating graphically the sequence and duration of notes played. The markings are cut out by hand, and after editing, the roll is mechanically copied onto a cardboard master roll.

2. A cardboard master roll can be cut directly from the keyboard of a "Recording Piano." The pianist does not actually play the selection, but rather "programs" the recording note by note. The "Recording Piano" is equipped with devices that enable the pianist to program musical arrangements that would be impossible for a single human pianist to duplicate in performance. By far the more prevalent method, it requires 6 to 8 hours to cut a standard-length master roll.

Recently, a new method of piano roll recording has been developed, in which an electronic master tape is generated from the pianist's live performance on a special piano. The commercial value of such a system is questionable in view of the unique characteristics of the player piano. It should be pointed out that the player piano per se is not capable of reproducing the playing of a human pianist,

and the satisfactory adaptation of music for piano rolls requires an understanding of the instrument's limitations as well as its capabilities.

Repertoire. Manufacturers of player piano rolls reproduce all types of music, including pop songs, motion picture and show tunes, country, children's, holiday, sacred and classical music, foreign songs, marches, dance and ragtime music. Reproduction of copyrighted musical works in player piano rolls and the sale thereof is a source of income to the publishers and writers of the compositions.

Licensing of Musical Compositions. Under the copyright law, piano rolls are considered to be PHONORECORDS; hence the compulsory license for making and distributing phonorecords applies to roll reproductions embodying nondramatic musical works.

As in the phonograph record industry, a roll manufacturer rarely uses the compulsory license. In commercial practice, a mechanical license is used, sometimes referred to as a *music roll* license. A manufacturer negotiates such a license directly with the publisher or its agent. The license fee is payable on each roll made and distributed.

The standard license fee is the full statutory rate for the use of the music and an equal amount for reprinting the lyrics on the roll. This ROYALTY is usually divided equally between publisher and writers. Artists who record tunes for player roll reproduction normally receive a one-time flat fee for the recording session, with no future royalties payable (the fee is negotiated). As phonorecords, piano roll performances may be copyrighted.

Rolls are commercially available at special dealers and certain retail piano outlets. Suggested retail prices of rolls in 1980 generally ranged from $3 to $6.50, depending on the length and type of roll.

Although the market for player rolls has significantly declined since its heyday, a substantial number of rolls are sold annually. In the late 1970s, QRS Music Rolls Inc., the world's largest manufacturer of piano rolls, reportedly sold between 600,000 and 700,000 per year, accounting for approximately 95% of the market.

Plug. Commonly used term meaning to promote or publicize. The term is used at virtually all levels of the music business. For example, *personal managers* plug unsigned artists to labels; *recording artists* plug new singles or albums on television shows and at concerts; *agents* plug artists to promoters; *promoters* plug concerts to the public; and *labels* plug singles and albums to radio stations.

The term probably first came into widespread use in the music business during music publishing's original Tin Pan Alley days. Certain personnel from publishing companies would plug songs in their firm's catalog to vaudeville performers, in the hope that they would perform (and popularize) the tunes and consequently promote sheet music sales. Hence publishing personnel with this responsibility were referred to as *song pluggers*. With the advent of radio, song pluggers auditioned songs for the big-band leaders. A performance of a song on network radio at that time could make it an "overnight" hit.

Plugola. *see* PAYOLA.

Point-of-Purchase Merchandising. Directing the attention of consumers to specific product at retail outlets is of chief importance to record manufacturers. The record company works to get its product played on the air and into the stores. But once albums are stocked in the bins and racks, they compete with product of other companies and the manufacturer may have a problem getting consumers to buy its particular merchandise.

General recognition of a song or artist through airplay, concert performances, re-views, and publicity is often insufficient to prompt a consumer to buy a particular product. Buying decisions are often made on the spur of the moment ("impulse buying"). "Advertising," however, at the place of purchase can influence a person who enters the store with no choice in mind to buy a particular selection, as well as alter someone's predetermined choice.

It is these factors that induce record companies to create and display in stores merchandising tools that are designed to attract attention to a particular album, arouse interest in it, and motivate purchase. This is referred to as *point-of-purchase merchandising*.

Point-of-Purchase Materials. Various point-of-purchase merchandising tools bearing the artist's name, photograph, or likeness are placed or displayed in retail record/tape outlets. These hang from the ceiling, and are displayed in windows, on the walls, on shelves and racks, on the floor and the counter. Apparel and other specially made items that feature products can be worn by salespersons. The following are point-of-purchase tools:

audiovisual presentations
balloons
banners
belt buckles
bumper stickers
buttons
caps
divider cards (4-color)
iron-ons
LP jackets (empty)
mobiles
placards
pop-up pictures (displays)
postcards
posters
signs
stand-up displays (cardboard)
T-shirts

In-store Airplay. One of the most effective

means of promoting a record or tape at the point of purchase is through in-store airplay. This can immediately bring attention to the product and prompt a customer to purchase it. In some retail outlets, "time" on the stereo system is rented to labels.

Popular Music. Popular music may be considered the realm of musical styles outside of classical and certain other types of music that have mass appeal or are directed for appreciation by large audiences. The most prominent styles of popular music are easy listening, rock, country, rhythm and blues, jazz, Latin, disco, gospel, and folk. Most of these categories themselves comprise several subgenres.

There are certain characteristics common to popular songs. They generally range in length from two to five minutes (three is about the average), contain different musical sections, have lyrics (except for instrumentals, such as certain jazz tunes), and may be performed by vocalists with small musical accompaniment. Popular songs also have catchy tunes that are easy to remember and sing, tell a story or give a message of a universal theme (e.g., love), evoke an emotional response, and contain attractive harmonies.

Following are brief descriptions of the various categories of popular music, and their subgenres where applicable. Attempting to define any style of popular music is problematic as, first of all, it is often difficult to express in words, or improper to label, an art form that evokes an emotional response and is therefore highly subjective. Moreover, many songs particular to each category are actually hybrids of other styles, as opposed to being of the genre in the purest form. Finally, classification of the different styles of popular music cannot always be made by the songs. Songs are most frequently conveyed to the public through recordings, and so other elements, such as the artist's vocal style, the arrangement, and production, sometimes are factors. But there are

general differences and one interested in the music business should at least be familiar with the various idioms of its product and their distinguishing characteristics.

Country Music. This style, traditionally associated with the southern and western United States, has evolved from simple tunes written by banjo and guitar pickers in the rural South to the various contemporary pop/rock-flavored songs created by musicians who work in a number of southern and western multi-track recording studios.

Country encompasses the folk music that came out of the rural southern areas, such as hillbilly and mountain music, Tex-Mex, Western swing, bluegrass, and rockabilly. It also includes the commercialized pop-oriented (but basically country) music that country artists have recorded from the 1960s on. Hence the once commonly used term "country-and-western" became outdated, as it insufficiently described the modern form of this musical genre, and was replaced by the catchall description "country."

Hillbilly refers to the music produced by inhabitants of the backwoods or mountain regions of the rural South. These were basically simple tunes—their melodies were unsophisticated and their subject matter dealt with the everyday affairs of simple existence. In the early 20th century, the music of these people, like their existence, hadn't changed very much. It would not be long, however, before the "music of the hills" would gain national recognition and popularity.

On January 15, 1925, Ralph S. Peer, a director for the Okeh Recording Company, named a band that had recorded six songs for the label the "Hill Billies." The name was adopted by other groups to describe their music and soon afterward the term "hillbilly" was applied to the music created and sung by the white folk of the rural South. Record companies took this local southern music form and brought it to urban areas throughout the country, where it remained popular for many years.

Western swing (also called *country swing*) was a popular style of music in the Southwest, particularly in Texas, in the 1930s and early 1940s. A combination of traditional country, jazz, cajun, and other popular styles, this music is performed on steel guitars, fiddles, and horns.

Bluegrass is a by-product of hillbilly music, differentiated by its instrumentation and vocal styling. Bluegrass bands utilize a variety of string instruments—guitar, five-string banjo, mandolin, fiddle—and others such as the concertina, clarinet, and drums, but no electrical instruments. Its lyrics are concerned with a variety of themes, most notably love, family, and nature. It developed into its well-known style in the mid 1940s.

By the early 1950s, a new uptempo form of country and western music had taken root. This was known as *rockabilly*. It was rockabilly, in combination with rhythm and blues, from which rock 'n' roll evolved.

Since the mid 1950s, country music has had discernible elements of easy listening, rock, and rhythm and blues. This hybridization of traditional country music became increasingly pronounced in the sixties and seventies. Influences from various cities in the southeast and southwest United States created new centers for recording and performing country music. Nashville, Tennessee, still remains the country music capital of the world, but there has also been much activity in other cities, such as Macon, Georgia; Austin, Texas; Bakersfield, California; and Muscle Shoals, Alabama.

Disco. A form of music that is primarily intended to be danced to. Characterized by a relentless beat, throbbing rhythms, and gliding strings, it is a hybrid of various musical stylings: rhythm and blues, Latin, Afro-Cuban, and rock. The melody and lyrics of disco music are not as essential as its danceability.

The national attention achieved by disco music in 1974 lasted till the end of the decade.

The beats per minute or BPM (a measure of a recording's tempo) of disco records accelerated after its introduction, going from 112 to 150 or more (125 BPM was predominant in 1978).

The popularity of and profit potential from disco added a whole new dimension to the record and related industries. Major record companies, slow at first to pick up on the trend (or perhaps viewing it as a passing fancy), eventually got deeply involved with it, often creating separate disco labels or expensive marketing campaigns to capitalize on the genre's success (in the beginning, only relatively small labels were in on the disco bandwagon).

Easy Listening. Sometimes called middle-of-the-road (MOR) or mainstream *pop*, easy listening is a broad genre ranging from ballads to uptempo tunes. Songs in this category may be distinguished from others by their universal themes (they generally deal with romance or subjects not overly controversial) and their simple but appealing melodies. Recordings of these songs are light or bouncy, as the case may be. The song is the important element here and the vocalist's performance and the arrangement function to best showcase it. Hence, extemporaneous matter such as wailing guitar riffs or improvised keyboard renditions is usually not included in recordings of easy listening songs.

Folk music. A broad category in the spectrum of popular music, ranging from the traditional forms such as ballads, spirituals, chanteys, railroad songs, and mountain songs to the more contemporary forms of recent decades, whose subject matter is commonly concerned with protest, social change, and environmental issues. From the latter group, many songs have entered and become successful in the arena of commercial music. This happened particularly in the 1940s–1960s. Traditional folk songs sometimes also become revitalized in adapted forms.

A mainstay in the past few decades in the

folk music field has been the "hootenanny," an informal public gathering of folk singers and musicians who perform or sing in a festival-like atmosphere.

Gospel. Gospel music has traditionally been regarded as the religious music of blacks, in a blues style.(By the 1970s, gospel evolved into a modern form of musical expression utilizing sophisticated arrangements that encompassed various other styles of music, including pop, rock, jazz, and disco. Commercially speaking, the gospel recordings released by various labels since the early seventies have been on a par with sophisticated pop product. Some people make distinctions between the various styles of music put out under the gospel label, such as black gospel, white gospel, contemporary Christian, southern gospel, and soul gospel. In recent years, gospel music has been quite popular among white people, particularly in the southern religious belt.

Jazz. Jazz is a musical art form indigenous to the United States. It is believed to have originated in the late 19th century. There are various categories of jazz, many of which are characterized by their extemporaneousness; a performer plays any melody so long as it sounds right against the chord patterns played by the rhythm section.

Ragtime is essentially a dance music form that developed around 1890 and remained quite popular till 1920. It is characterized by syncopated rhythmic patterns in the melody and is written chiefly for the piano, but is often arranged for orchestra. Some ragtime pieces, such as "Maple Leaf Rag" (perhaps the most famous ragtime composition), have an AABBACCDD structure.

Blues is a jazz style that was particularly popular in the early 20th century. Blues songs are slow in tempo and characterized musically by common-time meters, flatted thirds and sevenths, and twelve-bar phrases. Blues songs are considered to be derived from "sorrow songs" and spirituals sung by Negroes at the end of the Civil War.

Dixieland originated in New Orleans around 1900 and became popular in other cities, particularly Chicago, around the time of World War I. It is characterized by a two- or four-beat rhythm and improvisation by members of the band. A typical Dixieland band will have piano, banjo, guitar, trumpet, trombone, clarinet, and drums.

Swing is a jazz style that became popular around 1932. This music was often presented by large groups known as "big bands," who would play from formal written arrangements though much room was left for musicians to improvise when playing solo passages. The mid thirties marked the beginning of the "swing era," which lasted until around 1942.

During the latter part of the 1930s, a jazz form, chiefly a piano style, became popular. This was known as *boogie-woogie*, and was characterized by a persistent bass rhythm and a melodic pattern in contrary motion to the bass.

Bob, bebop, or rebop is a jazz style that began around 1940 and continued to be played steadily for about a decade. This articulated music was played very fast and had complex rhythms and dissonant harmonies.

Cool jazz started in 1949 and continued into the middle of the next decade. It was a relaxed style of jazz, without the tenseness and excitement of bop. Other jazz styles are described as *progressive* and *free-form*. Jazz is also played with elements of other musical styles and such fusions are appropriately titled. For instance, jazz played with a rock rhythm is known as *jazz-rock*.

Latin Music. Various idioms of Latin music have been an important part of popular music during the 20th century and earlier. Melodic and rhythmic influences from Brazil, Cuba, the Dominican Republic, Mexico, Puerto Rico, and other Caribbean and South American nations can be heard in rock, pop, rhythm and blues, jazz, and country. Some forms exist as separate idioms themselves in the commercial music scene. They are basically dance forms whose widespread popularity has caused them to be considered subgenres of Latin music.

Latin music's first major impact in the United States popular music scene occurred in 1914, when the *tango* (syncopated dance music in 2/4 or 4/4 time, characterized by deliberate gliding and twisting steps and low dips) became widely popular.

In 1930, the *rumba*, another rhythmical ballroom dance, having its origin among Cuban Negroes, became popular. Latin "society" orchestras, complete with string, horn, woodwind, and percussion sections, flourished in the late 1930s. The record charts in the 1940s found many Latin tunes climbing to the top, helped in no small way by the motion picture industry's utilization of Latin themes. Big bands of the "swing" era also featured many Latin songs. From the mid 1940s to the early 1950s, the *mambo* enjoyed popularity. The late 1940s also marked the beginning of a Latin and jazz fusion style as a viable hybrid.

Various Latin music/dance styles subsequently enjoyed popularity in the U.S., including the *merengue, cha-cha-cha*, and *bomba* in the 1950s and *bossa nova* in the 1960s. A combination of Latin and black music, the *bugalú*, emerged in the middle sixties. *Salsa*, a pulsating Latin dance music which dates back to the early 1900s, influenced black and rock music in the 1970s, and most notably, disco.

Rhythm and Blues (R & B). This music, a product of black American heritage, evolved from black folk music, southern rural blues, and various forms of jazz. It encompasses a number of musical styles, each mostly vocal, with a driving beat.

The phrase "rhythm and blues" was coined by small record labels in the late 1940s as a substitute for the unsavory term "race music," hitherto used to describe various forms of black music. These record companies, including Atlantic, Chess, Imperial, Savoy, and King, operated on a small scale. A staff of only a few people would assume the normal business functions of a record company—scouting tal-

ent, signing artists, producing and promoting records, and overseeing the lineup of independent distributors. In addition, they carried on other business functions, such as operating music publishing companies and managing and booking their acts. The records these labels produced were mostly of rhythm and blues music intended for black audiences.

With the decline of big band music by the late 1940s, jazz's inability to gain popularity with mass audiences, and changing tastes, there existed a void in the popular-music field. This vacuum was filled to some extent by R & B, which later, in part, gave rise to rock 'n' roll. Many white rock 'n' roll artists, observing and wishing to capitalize on R & B's appeal, gained much success by covering R & B tunes. It was only a matter of time, however, until black artists and recordings would become part of the mainstream of the popular music kingdom. In the late 1950s, *doo-wop* emerged, a slow form of rhythm and blues music, sung a cappella and characterized by appealing vocal harmonies.

With the increasing homology of R & B and rock 'n' roll, people attempted to differentiate the two by referring to R & B in the 1960s as *soul* music—a term that represented what R & B music had evolved into by the mid to late 1960s, a form of black music with apparent gospel elements, sung with more of a gut feeling, and having increased tempos and more accentuated rhythms. In the late 1960s, soul gave way to what was called *funk*. This term denoted a form of R & B with a bluesy sound and moving rhythm. It is not as fast as disco.

Rock. "Rock" is an all-encompassing term for a variety of musical styles that are similar in certain respects, so that they may all fall under this heading as a genre of popular music. The two vital components of rock are the vocals and the rhythm (which is driving and forceful). It is played mainly (outside of percussion) with electrical instruments (e.g., guitar, keyboards).

There are many forms of rock music. Inevi-

CHRONOLOGY OF AMERICAN POPULAR MUSIC* (1890–1980)

Year	Folk	Country	Jazz	Latin†	Easy Listening/Pop	Rhythm and Blues	Rock	Disco
1980								
							Punk rock Progressive rock Glitter rock Heavy metal	Disco
1970	Folk rock	Country rock		Salsa Mozambique Bugalú Bossa nova	Bubblegum	Funk	Soft rock Hard rock Acid rock	
	Protest songs		Free-form		British pop Surf	Soul	Rock	
1960				Plena/bomba/merengue		Doo-wop		
		Rockabilly	Progressive	Cha cha chá			Rock 'n' roll	
1950			Cool					
		Bluegrass		Mambo		Rhythm and blues		
			Bop	Samba				
1940		Western swing	Boogie-woogie		Middle-of-the-road songs			
			Swing	Rumba	"Hollywood" songs			
1930		Hillbilly						
			Dixieland (Chicago)					
1920					Patriotic songs (World War I)			
				Tango		Blues		
1910			Dixieland (New Orleans)		"Broadway" songs			
1900	Traditional folk songs: ballads, chanteys, spirituals, etc.	Traditional country and western: cowboy songs, railroad songs, mountain songs, etc.						
1890			Ragtime		Tin Pan Alley songs	Traditional Negro songs		

*Listings represent the *approximate* time the style of music began or reached greatest popularity.

†Some of the listings under Latin are actually dance forms but are included here because they are identified as subgenres of Latin music.

tably, more will spring into existence, but some are as follows:

Rock 'n' roll. The first form to evolve, *rock 'n' roll* developed by 1954. It is a derivative of rhythm and blues, country and western (particularly rockabilly), and pop music. It is characterized by a common-time meter, a strong driving beat, simple chord progressions, such as I-V-I and I-IV-V-I, instrumentation consisting of piano, lead guitar, bass guitar, and drums, and background vocals. A strong vocal medium, it features lyrics that exemplify youthful protest against society's ills, rebellion from parents and the establishment, and most important, male/female relationships.

Rock. As rock 'n' roll continued into the 1960s, it became more sophisticated. In general, the music became softer, more melodic, and addressed itself more to the problems of youths growing up, while continuing with the universal themes of love and human relationships. More appealing productions and arrangements were used in recording it, with strings, horns, and various new electronic instruments. The music became, simply, "rock," and this term came to refer to the entire genre of music, not only in its mainstream form but in all its exponents, including the various styles that emerged from the late 1960s and on:

Hard, acid, psychedelic, or heavy metal rock. Music played by small rock groups at an extremely high decibel level, with melody and harmony not very important; characterized by screeching guitar riffs.

Soft rock. In the early 1970s, there was a return to a subtler, more melodic form of rock, given this appellation.

Glitter rock. A subgenre that evolved in the early 1970s in New York City, where performers drew attention visually through the use of makeup, wardrobe, and stage antics. Led to punk rock.

Punk rock. Both aurally and visually oriented, punk has a sound that is hard and driving, with little emphasis on melody; performers act out the protest of the lyric by behavior ranging from prancing around on stage to acting in an offensive manner—spitting at the audience, inducing regurgitation, sticking pins through their cheeks.

Spiritually, punk was begun in the 1950s by the legendary music and motion picture star rebels. It became more pronounced with some of the rock bands of the sixties that were considered "raunchy," such as the Rolling Stones. With the decline in popularity by 1969 of hard and glitter rock bands, it appeared there would be a void, at least temporarily, in this vein, but it was filled by another British invasion, young groups who played in English pubs. Punk rock spread with some success in America, though perhaps such success resulted more from curiosity and media attention. Punk rock began around the mid 1970s and peaked in popularity by the end of the decade.

The term "new wave" is often used synonymously with "punk rock." Many are inclined to equate the two, while others differentiate vehemently. New wave is sometimes considered more melodic, and while the performers are visually interesting, they are not engaged in crazy antics while performing. Others describe it as an arty descendant of punk rock.

Posters. The appearance of an artist's picture, name, or logo on a poster can serve various purposes. Not only can it be a valuable source of income for the owner of the rights, but it can increase the artist's popularity (by acting as a visual reinforcement), enhance his prestige, stimulate record/tape sales, and be used as an advertising (point-of-purchase) tool.

Almost exclusively a product purchased by youths and young adults, posters adorn the walls of bedrooms, playrooms, bathrooms, dormitories, panel trucks, gas stations, and various retail outlets. They may be purchased in discount and department stores, gift shops, novelty stores, "head shops," and record stores. Record stores, of course, often use posters as point-of-purchase tools to promote album sales.

To manufacture and distribute a poster bearing the picture, name, or logo of an artist, authorization is needed from the owner of the artist's merchandising rights (*see* MERCHANDISING TIE-INS). Often the owner may initiate discussions for poster licenses with manufacturers.

Royalty licenses normally provide for an advance (recoupable) against royalties. The royalty is usually either a percentage of the wholesale price of the poster (normally 5% to 10%) or a fixed price per poster sold (normally ranging from $.05 to $.15).

Poster licenses commonly range in duration for 1 to 2 years and provide for distribution in a designated geographical territory. This might be for the United States and its possessions, for North America, for one or more foreign countries, or on a worldwide basis.

It should be noted that while the above terms present general guidelines, there is no standard licensing agreement for posters. Rather, the license terms of any agreement are negotiable and may be designed to fit the needs of the artist. For example, it would be advantageous for a recording artist making a tour of certain foreign countries to have posters distributed in those territories prior to, during, and after his engagement. A license might be negotiated then, to provide for manufacture and distribution of posters to coincide with such tour. A poster company may work in conjunction with record companies regarding concert engagements, album releases, and promotions.

Posters may be blown-up reproductions of a concert, studio, or informal shot of the artist made by the manufacturer's photographer or someone else. Sometimes posters are reproductions of album or publicity/promotion photographs. Most posters are made with 4-color printing. Posters that sell 100,000 copies are usually regarded as being successful; some have reportedly sold millions of copies. Sometimes record companies make their own posters for promotional purposes and distribute these to wholesale and retail accounts but do not offer them for mass distribution.

Poster manufacturer/distributors normally require substantial popularity on behalf of an artist—several hit recordings and/or a large following—before negotiating a license and producing the posters. This practice is somewhat problematic for poster companies. If they produce posters of unknowns there will obviously be limited sales. Conversely, some well-known artists are not very interested in the additional exposure or the relatively small "front money." Consequently this situation often results in unlicensed posters with inferior-quality designs selling in small stores.

Lyrics of popular songs are also reproduced in posters (though to a much lesser degree), usually accompanied by artwork. Thus the licensing of song rights for poster manufacture/distribution may be an additional source of income for music publishers and songwriters. Terms of such licenses may be similar to those described above.

Copyright Aspects. Posters may be registered for copyright. If the material printed is artwork, then Class/Form VA would be used; if it is text (lyrics), then Class/Form TX is applicable. If there are both artwork and text, registration should be made in the class whose work predominates. Copyrighted posters commonly bear the copyright notice in the bottom left- or right-hand corner.

Prerecorded Tapes (Audio). Commercially marketed cassette or 8-track cartridge tapes with selections or programs previously recorded on them, ready for playing. Prerecorded tapes are generally released in conjunction with LPs and contain the same tracks, although their sequence may be different. Open-reel tapes also are available with prerecorded material, but the offerings are very limited in scope and variety.

Pressing. *See* RECORD MANUFACTURING.

Posters are not only a profit-making center within themselves but serve to bring attention to the artist and perhaps enhance his record sales and image.

Printed Music. Music is printed to meet the needs and tastes of musicians. There are many types of instruments and performing ensembles and their skills vary widely. Consequently there is a vast and ever expanding repertoire of popular and classical printed music. This entry examines printed music in its various forms.

Sheet music—Editions of musical compositions printed on unbound sheets of paper and containing the music and any lyrics, sheet music is published for both popular and classical music.

Sheet music of popular songs is usually published in piano/vocal/guitar arrangements containing three staves—one for the melody (the vocal part), with the corresponding lyrics printed under the notes, and the other two for the piano part (right and left hand). The chords corresponding to the melody are written on top of the vocal part and there is generally a musical introduction, with the tempo or style of the composition indicated at the beginning. The sheet music of a popular song often contains a cover photograph of the artist whose recording of it has become successful.

Normally, publishers of popular music issue sheet music of a song only if a commercial recording of it has achieved success. Songs that "translate" well into print—that is, "hold up" naked of the production and arrangement embodied in the recording—usually enjoy the most sales in print form. Melodic ballads with meaningful lyrics sell particularly well.

Because of the nature of classical music, sheet music of these works is usually instrumental only. Standard classical works, recital pieces, and compositions by famous composers usually sell best.

Personality folio—A personality folio is an anthology of songs written, recorded, or performed by the same artist, group, or composer. It is usually published in a soft-cover edition containing piano/vocal/guitar arrangements and photographs, artwork, and biographical or editorial notes. On the cover there often appears a picture or logo of the individual or group. A personality folio containing a collection of songs from an album is also referred to as a *companion* or *matching* folio.

Mixed folio—A mixed folio is a compilation of songs by various writers and recorded by an assortment of artists that usually has a common theme or link. For example, a mixed folio might be a collection of love songs; top hits of a year, decade, or era; songs of a particular musical style; vocal selections from a Broadway show or motion picture or the hits from several different ones; hits of various superstars; or a group of religious songs or hymns. A mixed folio, also referred to as a *songbook* or *song compilation*, is usually published in soft cover and contains piano/vocal/guitar arrangements with photographs, artwork, and editorial notes.

A mixed folio may also come in the form of a *fakebook*. A fakebook is an edition which typically contains hundreds of songs, in melody-line-only arrangements, with chords and corresponding lyrics; it is used by professional musicians to play many different types of "dates" or "gigs." Fakebooks provide a quick reference to songs the musician is not very familiar with or does not know; with the melody known, the pro can play, or "fake," the song. A fakebook is also an excellent format for amateur musicians attempting to learn songs. In one volume the player has access to a great many selections and these are usually diverse in musical style. They also offer the musician flexibility in playing the tunes and enable him to develop improvisational skills.

Instrument folio—An instrument folio is a collection of songs that are "arranged" for performance for a particular musical instrument. Instrument folios are often published in the following editions: accordion, autoharp, B flat instruments, bagpipe, banjo, bass, bass guitar, bassoon, C instruments, cello, clarinet, classical guitar, drums, dulcimer, E flat instruments, flamenco guitar, flute, folk guitar, French horn, harmonica, harp, mandolin, melodica, oboe, organ, piano, recorder, saxophone, trombone, trumpet, ukulele, viola, and violin.

Concert edition—A musical work may be arranged for concert performance for a group of voices or instruments. Concert editions are published for school and professional groups. Arrangements for school groups are commonly available in the following editions: choral, orchestra, stage band, marching band, jazz band, and combo (these editions are usually categorized in easy, intermediate, and advanced levels of difficulty). Professional editions include symphonic band and orchestra scores, opera scores, cantatas, oratorios, and chamber pieces.

Method book—Method or educational books are published for virtually all instruments. These contain instructions and exercises for developing and improving technique on a particular instrument or playing a particular musical style. Method books are categorized according to their level of difficulty—beginner, intermediate, and advanced, or in grades—and usually contain pieces (often public domain works) corresponding to the book's level. Beginning piano and organ method books are sometimes published in "easy method" or "play-by-number" series. It is anticipated that video software will enjoy an important role as tools for instruction.

Printed Music, Licensing and Distribution of.
Historically, the popular-music publisher was actually a print publisher. He functioned to acquire songs with commercial potential and to print, sell, and distribute copies of these songs in sheet music form. This main function began to change as the phonograph record, invented in 1877, became the major vehicle for publishers to exploit songs (by around World War II). Recordings of songs have become the basis for the two most important types of royalties for publishers and songwriters—mechanical and performance royalties.

The selling of sheet music and other printed editions of songs is still an important source of income for publishers and songwriters, but most music publishers' operations today are not set up to handle the printing, selling, and distribution of sheet music, songbooks, folios, and other editions. Rather, they enter into agreements with "specialized" companies which handle these functions. The most common form of agreement providing for the fulfillment of these functions is an arrangement where the publisher licenses the print rights to a particular song or to its CATALOG.

The companies engaged by publisher-copyright owners have no generic name in the music business but may be designated as "print licensee/distributors." Pursuant to a print license, the licensee/distributor acquires the right for a specified period of time to print, sell, and distribute, on a ROYALTY basis, printed editions of the copyright owner's composition(s).

It should be noted that sheet music of a new song will not normally be printed and distributed unless a recording of the song is receiving a certain minimum amount of airplay. Publishers and licensees vary as to when they consider a market exists for the song in printed form. Some will print and distribute sheet music when the record enters a trade publication's top 100; others wait until it climbs to the top 40 or higher.

Licensee distributors commonly obtain the print rights to catalogs owned by different publishers that include several hit songs. It is desirable in such a case to print and sell individual songbooks or fakebooks containing many of these hits.

The royalty for a publisher whose works are included in a songbook or fakebook is normally 10% to 12.5% of the retail selling price for each copy sold, based on the total number of works it controls within the book as a percentage of the total number of copyrighted songs in the book. For example, if a songbook contains 10 copyrighted songs and retails for $5, a publisher with a royalty rate of 10% that owns one song included in the songbook would receive 10% of one tenth of the selling price, or $.05 for each copy sold.

The licensee's earnings for each copy sold, with respect to the above example, is as follows: from the $5 retail price, the trade discount to wholesalers and retailers must be deducted as well as the publishers' royalties. Assuming an average discount of 50% (or $2.50) per copy plus $.50 per copy in publishers' royalties, the licensee would earn $2 per copy. Its margin of profit, however, could be determined only after the costs of arranging, engraving, printing, advertising, overhead, etc., are deducted from this income.

For songbooks containing the compositions of an individual writer/artist or group, such artist or group may earn a small royalty if their picture is on the cover of the songbook.

Accounts. Print licensees and selling agencies have 3 basic types of accounts: (1) wholesalers or music jobbers; (2) large retail printed-music dealers, and (3) educational dealers (these handle only certain educational-type editions, such as band, orchestra, or choral arrangements).

Printed-Music Retailer. Retailers selling printed music include print music stores, musical instrument stores, record outlets (including record departments of mass-merchandising stores), and other retailers, such as booksellers. Depending on the size and nature of the operation, a dealer will carry the various types of music as described in PRINTED MUSIC as well as related items such as manuscript paper, writing tools, and musical instrument accessories.

Buying Printed Music. Printed music is purchased by the retailer from MUSIC JOBBERS and publishers (as used in this entry, the term

"publisher" will mean the actual publisher of the work or its licensee). A retailer will buy from a music jobber when its orders for a particular publisher's product are not large enough to merit opening an account with that publisher. Most publishers require a minimum-volume order, so retailers ordering, say, a few copies of sheet music of several songs issued by different publishers would deal with a music jobber. Jobbers offer discounts ranging from 20% to as high as 40%, depending on the item.

A retailer will buy merchandise directly from the publisher when its volume is great enough to meet purchase requirements for that publisher and/or the product needed is not readily available from a jobber. Typically, only large-volume stores order directly from a publisher.

Publishers sell printed music to dealers in two ways:

1. The *stock order rate* is used for large-volume ordering and the discount varies from publisher to publisher. Dealers receive the highest discount under this form, particularly for public domain material as there are no composer royalties to be paid. A publisher requires a dealer to either purchase a large quantity of copies of a particular item (for example, a minimum of 500 books) or have a minimum-net (i.e., after discount) dollar-volume order. Stock orders are usually given dated billing, with the amount usually due within 90 days.

2. The *daily rate* is used to order small quantities. Discounts often vary according to the net volume of the retailer's purchases over the previous year. The daily rate is usually billed on a net 30 day basis.

One of the keys to a successful printed music retail operation lies in the *buying*—ordering what is in demand and getting the best possible discount for it. Printed music is sent by publishers and music jobbers by parcel post or UPS and this cost is almost always paid by the retailer.

Display. Proper display of merchandise is effective in attracting attention and making sales. Publishers may supply in-store display items such as banners and posters, as well as special cardboard racks or browser boxes. As many consumers buy on impulse, point-of-purchase merchandise might include manuscript paper, writing pens, guitar strings, tuning forks, pitch pipes, and music magazines.

Personnel. Personnel should of course be knowledgeable. A salesperson usually handles the particular area of music in which his expertise or interest lies (salespersons often are musicians). Personnel should have a thorough knowledge of the merchandise in their area and should know the music publishers, as customers often request a particular item (such as a method book or an instruction book) by its publisher.

Pilferage. Precautions should be taken to prevent shoplifting. It is easy for the determined pilferer to place music under a coat or in a bag, briefcase, or newspaper. For this reason, many retailers require customers to check personal items at the front of the store.

Sales Policy. Because music can be photocopied or copied by hand, it is a common policy of printed-music retailers to inform customers that all sales are final—there may be no refunds or exchanges. Of course, it is also policy to exchange damaged copies or sheet music with missing pages.

Privacy and Publicity, Rights of. Important to entertainers and other figures in the limelight are the rights to be free from unwarranted publicity as well as to benefit economically from the commercial exploitation of their name, picture, or likeness. These rights, whose bases are provided for not by the copyright law but by state laws and legal precedents set by court cases, are known as the "right of privacy" and the "right of publicity." In their absence, a performer's private life could be intruded upon unduly by the media or he could find his name or picture being used to promote a product without his authorization.

The *right of privacy* is the right to be let alone, to be free from unwarranted publicity or invasion of personal life except as by what is determined to meet the community's right to the free flow of truth. Almost all jurisdictions recognize this right in one form or another and prohibit by statute or prior court cases the unauthorized commercial use of a person's name, picture, or likeness. The right of privacy exists in all states except (at this writing) Rhode Island, Nebraska, Texas, and Wisconsin. In most states it has been created by judicial decision rather than by legislative act.

As a result of judicial decision, four different types of interests may be protected under the right of privacy: (1) appropriation of a person's name or likeness for commercial use without the person's consent; (2) intrusion by physical trespassing into a person's private life; (3) public disclosure of embarrassing facts; and (4) publication of information which places a person in a false light before the public.

The right of privacy protects one against intrusion, if the intrusion grossly violates fair play. Thus an unauthorized trespassing into one's residence, taking of one's personal documents, or use of electronic surveillance devices such as wiretaps may be deemed to be an invasion of privacy by a court of law.

The publication of information that places a person in a "false light" before the public may not be defamatory, yet it may be an invasion of privacy if it is untrue. Also, a person may be protected from the public disclosure of embarrassing facts. The extent to which protection is accorded depends both upon the degree of notoriety of the public figure and how newsworthy the disclosure is. A cause of action arising from an alleged invasion of privacy may only be asserted by the victim, who must be living and who cannot assign this right to anyone else. In proving an invasion of one's privacy in some states, the plaintiff need not prove special damages—this is presumed by law.

The *right of publicity*, a legal concept independent of the right of privacy, has since 1953 been given credence by some judicial decisions. The right is still developing as new cases are decided, and it is not yet clear which states will adopt it and in what form. The right gives a publicly known person the power to authorize or prohibit the commercial use of his name, picture, or likeness. For example, recording artists are protected from companies that may exploit for economic gain their pictures on merchandising products (*see* MERCHANDISING TIE-INS) without receiving their consent or offering compensation. It has been ruled, however, that the use of a public figure's name in connection with an advertisement or news article where such use is just incidental would not be a violation of the right to publicity.

In entering into agreements with recording artists, labels will require the right to use, and permit others to use, the artist's name, picture, biography, or likeness in connection with the sales of recordings produced under the terms of the contract for advertising and purposes of trade in the geographic territories covered by the agreement. Furthermore, the record company obtains the right to use the phrase "Exclusive Recording Artist" during the term of the artist's contract and the use of the artist's name on a nonexclusive basis thereafter. Many contracts contain provisions in which the artist assigns to his label the right to use his name and/or photograph in merchandising tie-ins. If there is no such clause, however, the artist may be able to prohibit the label from exploiting his name or picture on such products even though such use may increase record and tape sales. Sheet music publishers request the right to utilize an artist's name and likeness on their publications, and this must be separately and positively negotiated between the artist and the music publisher.

Producer. *See* RECORD PRODUCER.

Product. Term that refers to records and prerecorded tapes available for sale. The amount of product manufactured, ordered, or sold is measured quantitatively (in "units") and in terms of value (dollars). The terms "product," "goods," and "merchandise" are used interchangeably.

Production Deal. *See* RECORD COMPANY DEALS.

Professional Associations and Educational Organizations. There exist in the music business various professional associations and educational organizations that serve to support, strengthen, and encourage a particular area of music or creative or professional trade. These groups are comprised of individuals, businesses, and/or other organizations. Some of the activities these groups may be concerned with include research, information services, educational programs, financial support, scholarships, award programs, and public relations.

The difference between professional associations/educational organizations and other entities in the music business should be noted. UNIONS are primarily concerned with establishing and protecting the contractual rights of their members and TRADE ASSOCIATIONS are mainly concerned with advancing and protecting the business interests of an industry. In other respects all these entities share a community of interest and there is often an overlap in activity.

Professional Manager. *See* MUSIC PUBLISHER.

Program Director. *See* RADIO STATION.

Major U.S. Music Professional Associations and Educational Organizations

Name	Area, Trade, or Profession Supported
American Composers Alliance (ACA)	Serious music composers
American Guild of Authors and Composers (AGAC)	Composers and lyricists
American Music Conference (AMC)	Amateur music participation
American Symphony Orchestra League (ASOL)	Symphony orchestras
Black Music Association (BMA)	Black music
Central Opera Service (COS)	Opera companies
Conference of Personal Managers (COPM)	Personal managers
Country Music Association (CMA)	Country music
Dramatists Guild, Inc. (DG)	Playwrights, composers, lyricists
Gospel Music Association (GMA)	Gospel music
Music Critics Association (MCA)	Music critics
Music Educators National Conference (MENC)	Music teachers
Nashville Songwriters Association, International (NSAI)	Songwriters
National Academy of Popular Music (NAPM)	Popular music artists, composers, entertainers
National Academy of Recording Arts and Sciences (NARAS)	Creative people in recording
National Association of Schools of Music (NASM)	Institutions that teach music
National Music Council (NMC)	Various music associations
National Opera Association (NOA)	Opera

Programming Services (Radio). Many radio stations utilize program material produced and distributed by independent companies as well as seek advice for their programming from outside persons or firms, to reduce operating expenses, improve ratings, and/or derive other benefits. Such programming services generally fall into the following categories: (1) programming syndicators; (2) production companies; and (3) programming consultants.

To grasp fully the interrelationship of these various services, a brief historical review of radio station growth in the United States may be helpful. In 1950, 3,035 stations were authorized to operate. In 1980, 9,142 stations, both AM and FM, (including noncommercial educational), were authorized. Growth in the number of facilities has resulted in fragmentation of listening and much more specialized programming.

In the sixties, regulatory action by the Fed-

eral Communications Commission mandated that FM stations owned in common with an AM station in a given community must offer programming on a nonsimulcast broadcast basis. This created demand for operating systems referred to as automation equipment. By expanding the concept of systems used for background music (such as are utilized by Muzak), employing reel-to-reel tape decks for music and endless-loop tape cartridges for commercials (predecessors to the 8-track consumer configuration), switching systems controlled the sequence of events, so that stations had the ability to sound "live."

The availability and refinement of automated equipment gave rise to the creation and expansion of production companies offering programming to radio stations, as syndicated distribution is economically more viable than local production. Automated radio stations broadcast programming that is prerecorded, and in some instances, join a network for the presentation of news. Automation equipment enables a facility to be operated with reduced or minimal attention, thus utilizing personnel on a cost-efficient basis. Some stations have refined operating techniques to the extent that a listener would be unaware that they are totally automated. Typically, such operations have an individual who records relevant items of a topical nature for a "chatter track" that dovetails with the music and other production elements.

Some stations use automation systems to store and control the sequencing of broadcast elements and have an announcer or disc jockey present at all times. A microphone is activated at designated intervals under the control of the system, with manual override capability to allow for eventualities such as system failures or other emergencies. This technique is called "live assist." Hardware for an automated broadcast station consists typically of open-reel tape decks, cartridge playback equipment, and sequencing or switching controllers, sometimes referred to as the "brain" of the system.

Prerecorded program formats are produced for virtually every programming taste, including classical, top 40, ethnic, rock, country, adult contemporary, AOR, easy listening, and beautiful music. The music library is determined selectively by a programmer at the company that produces the material. There are two commonly used techniques for arranging the music inventory portion of the programming. In "matched flow" the programmer designs a sweep or flow of music ranging anywhere from 2 to 4 or 5 selections in duration. Thus, when the format is presented on the air, a tape starts and runs uninterrupted through that particular music configuration. In the other technique, "random select," music is structured by categories. A rock format, for example, might be configured by having 4 categories—soft rock, hard rock, recurrents,

and oldies. The switching configuration is then determined according to some formula or structure and the additional elements of programming are incorporated, including information such as the title of songs played or about to be heard, commercials, news, time, and weather reports.

Some stations produce their own program material on tape, but with the typically larger resources of a production company offering syndicated programming, music on tape tends to be less expensive to acquire than to produce locally. Resulting radio station programming tends to be more consistent, as production companies do not have personnel turnover rates that might be encountered at an individual radio station. Thus a station is able to operate with minimal cost and reduced personnel while providing a high-quality level of entertainment.

Programming syndicators produce and distribute programs for a radio station's daily broadcasting and individual programs for special airing. Thematic programs are commonly offered which may be oriented to a specific type of listener or attempt to zero in on the "life style" of a particular audience. Popular feature programs include countdowns of hit recordings. Other specials might be an anthology of events of the past year or decade, music of a particular style, or recordings featuring a certain artist or group. These programs may run anywhere from one to several hours in length. Syndicated programs may be offered on tape or disc and there is growing interest in network-type satellite program distribution (*see* SATELLITE COMMUNICATIONS).

Sometimes it is difficult to distinguish categories of production companies by identification of their particular expertise. In the late 1950s and the '60s, production companies offered a variety of operating aids, with particular emphasis on station identification jingles. Today some do nothing but jingles, others provide only specific types of programs, and some offer an extensive variety of services or a range of music inventories.

Fees or rates for the services offered vary substantially. Typically, fees reflect the size of the market and are sometimes based upon a station's advertising rate schedule. Thus the same service may be supplied to stations in two different markets at drastically different rates. Generally, contractual covenants stipulate the manner of use, detailing the number of times a program may be broadcast and establishing a license fee for same. Usually the program is supplied to a station on an exclusive basis—no other station in the market is authorized to run it.

Sometimes programs are produced and made available to stations at no charge in return for broadcast of the program. Costs of production and distribution are carried by a sponsoring agency or association, be it a nonprofit group, such as a church, or a commercial entity, such as a national advertiser seeking to reach a particular audience economically.

With the proliferation of the number of stations and program services available, tremendous growth in the area of audience research and program consultation has taken place. A program consultant may generally be described as a person or firm retained for a fee by a broadcasting operation for programming advice that seeks to make the station competitive in its market, increasing its audience. Basically, a program consultant determines the needs of a station or identifies programming opportunities or voids in a market and recommends material for use and how to present same. The consultant may implement a new musical format, select records, and decide where to insert news, sports, weather, time, and traffic reports. Promotional campaigns either on or off the air may be devised and the types of commercials to be run and the number per hour also fall in the province of such consultants. They may advise, too, on the

manner in which disc jockeys should make their presentation and how they can blend with the station's desired image. Consultants may recommend the hiring and firing of personnel.

Program consultants are usually retained in any of the following circumstances: (1) the ownership/management of a new station desires advice on what type of format to implement and how to structure the station; (2) the ownership/management of an existing station wishes to change its format or increase the size of its audience; or (3) there is a change in ownership/management of an existing station. In each case, program consultants are hired in the hope that their recommendations will result in attracting a larger or significant share of the market audience, giving the station high and competitive ratings so its number of advertisers and the rates they pay will increase.

Program consultants have typically worked for years with radio stations in many markets. Their advice is based on a combination of factors, including experience, knowledge, and research of the market. Because the nature of radio station programming is dependent substantially upon a mix of entertainment and information, it is largely perceptual. For this reason, market testing and research has become more prevalent and refined.

The goal of research is to help a station determine what material it can broadcast that will most appeal to its target audience. Research data is accumulated from record/tape store reports, telephone and street interviews with consumers, questionnaires given out on the street, and information/response cards attached to albums in stores. Profiles are computed on songs, artists, and consumer tastes.

Contracts between program consultants and radio stations normally run for a minimum length of time, with the option by the station to renew. Fees are commonly paid on a monthly basis. Of course, where the consultant's advice consistently fails to yield the intended result, the contract will eventually be terminated. The consequences of recommendations are reflected and measured in the publication of audience surveys offered by RADIO RATING SERVICES. Some consultants are hired simultaneously by stations in several different markets.

Promotion of Records. *See* RECORD COMPANY.

Pseudonymous Work. Defined in the 1976 Copyright Act (Section 101) as "a work on the copies or phonorecords of which the author is identified under a fictitious name." Under the 1976 act, the COPYRIGHT DURATION of a work created on or after January 1, 1978, is different if the authorship is pseudonymous than if the author is identified by real name.

Pseudonyms are more commonly used and notable in the literary field (e.g., Mark Twain for Samuel L. Clemens) than in music (e.g., Will Huff for Henry Fillmore).

See also ANONYMOUS WORK.

Public Broadcasting. "Public broadcasting" designates nonprofit television stations. These entities are supported by grants, contributions, and similar funding. Public broadcasting entities air preexisting material as well as originate their own programming.

Compulsory License. The U.S. copyright law provides a compulsory license for the use of certain works in noncommercial broadcasting. Such works may be performed or displayed in the course of a transmission by a noncommercial educational broadcast station without permission from the copyright owners if compliance is made with established terms and rates of royalty payments.

Subject to the public broadcasting compulsory license are published nondramatic musical compositions and published pictorial, graphic, and sculptural works. Excluded are certain works including nondramatic literary works, plays, operas, ballets, motion pictures, and television programs. Thus a public television station could broadcast its own program with a nondramatic musical work synchronized to it, but not a motion picture or television program, without specific permission from the copyright owner of the work. The law also specifies that unauthorized dramatizations of nondramatic musical works beyond the limits of FAIR USE do not apply.

Although the law establishes a compulsory license, it encourages voluntary agreements between copyright owners and public broadcasting entities. Such agreements become effective upon their being filed in the Copyright Office. Where voluntary agreements are not reached, terms and reasonable rates of royalty payments are left to the discretion of the COPYRIGHT ROYALTY TRIBUNAL.

With respect to negotiating the terms and rates of royalty payments, the interests of public broadcasters are commonly represented by the Public Broadcasting System and National Public Radio; for copyright owners and creators of musical compositions, it is commonly the PERFORMING RIGHTS ORGANIZATIONS—ASCAP, BMI, and SESAC.

Pursuant to the enactment of the 1976 Copyright Act on January 1, 1978, BMI and SESAC voluntarily agreed to initial fees of $250,000 and $50,000, respectively, for a 5-year noncommercial license. After the failure of public broadcasters and ASCAP to reach a voluntary agreement, the Copyright Royalty Tribunal held hearings in the spring of 1978 and determined a reasonable fee for ASCAP to be $1.25 million annually through 1982, with annual adjustments for inflation as determined by the Consumer Price Index. Rates are to be reviewed by the tribunal in 1982 and then every 5 years thereafter. Licensing agreements voluntarily negotiated at any time between copyright owners and public broadcasters take effect in lieu of any determination of terms and rates made by the tribunal provided that copies of the agreements are filed in the Copyright Office within 30 days of execution in accordance with regulations prescribed by the Register of Copyrights.

Public Domain. Term that refers to the status of a work of authorship having no copyright protection and therefore belonging to the world. Thus, when a work is said to be "in" or have "fallen into" the public domain, it is available for unrestricted use by anyone—it may be used for any purpose without permission or payment.

How Works Lose Copyright Protection under the Law. The Copyright Act of 1976, which fully entered into force on January 1, 1978, provides statutory protection for various types of published and unpublished works of authorship. Under the law, copyright protection may be permanently lost in certain basic ways, most commonly by: (1) the expiration of the term of copyright; (2) improper or no renewal registration made for certain pre-1978 works; or (3) a faulty copyright notice on published COPIES or PHONORECORDS which is not corrected in accordance with provisions in the statute. The 1976 act provides terms of COPYRIGHT DURATION for works created on or after January 1, 1978, depending on whether they were created by an individual author or coauthor identified in the Copyright Office records or were made for hire. In each case, when the term of copyright for such work expires, that work is in the public domain, or *PD*, as it is commonly called.

For a work in its first term of statutory protection on January 1, 1978, the copyright must be properly renewed to prevent the work from entering the public domain. Works in their second term on January 1, 1978, automatically had their copyright extended.

Under the 1976 act, a work may also become invalidated if any of the following errors are made with respect to the notice of copyright: (1) complete omission of the notice from copies or phonorecords; (2) omission of the name or year date; or (3) use of a date that is more than 1 year later than the year in which publication first occurred. However, such omissions or errors may be cured within a 5-year period by complying with procedures set forth in the statute (*see* COPYRIGHT NOTICE). The statute provides that the year date may be omitted in certain cases: where a pictorial, graphic, or sculptural work with accompanying text matter, if any, is reproduced in or on greeting cards, postcards, jewelry, dolls, toys, and useful articles.

Works in the Public Domain. Generally, a musical composition is in the public domain, if it was: (1) first published or copyrighted before September 19, 1906; or (2) first published or copyrighted between September 19, 1906, and December 31, 1949, but not renewed (in such case the copyright expired on the 28th anniversary of the date it was first secured). If a renewal registration is not made at the proper time for any work first copyrighted or published between January 1, 1950, and December 31, 1977, the copyright will expire at the end of its 28th calendar year.

Investigating the Copyright Status of a Work. To determine whether a work is in the public domain or the facts regarding its copyright protection, a person may examine a copy or phonorecord of the work, search the COPYRIGHT OFFICE records or consult its *Catalog of Copyright Entries*, have the Copyright Office make a search, make inquiries to performing and mechanical rights organizations, or contact the publisher listed for the work in a previous copy or phonorecord of it. The information derived from any of these sources cannot be regarded as conclusive in all cases, however, and it may be necessary to consult a copyright attorney before a final determination can be drawn.

For example, a work may be under federal copyright protection but there may not be any information on it in the Copyright Office records if it was: (1) unpublished; (2) copyrighted under a different title or as part of a larger work; (3) registered so recently that catalog cards have not yet been made available; or (4) a foreign work which has secured U.S. copyright through the Universal Copyright Convention (such works are exempt from registration and deposit in the U.S. Copyright Offices). Works that have lost copyright protection in the U.S. are not necessarily in the public domain in other nations. Nearly every country has its own laws regarding term and loss of copyright protection.

Absence of Notice for Pre-1978 Works. The complete absence of a copyright notice on a work first published before 1978 generally indicates that the work is in the public domain. However, there are certain exceptions to this, such as: (1) accidental omission of the notice from a "particular copy or copies" (the statute preserves copyright protection in such cases); (2) unauthorized publication of a work where the infringer deletes the notice; and (3) unpublished works reproduced and distributed.

Copyrighted Arrangements of Preexisting Works. In examining a work, the date in the copyright notice is not necessarily a means to determine when copyright in some or all of the work will expire. The work examined may be a new arrangement of a copyrighted work and the copyright would apply only to the new material; the copyright in another part may expire at a different time.

In a copyrighted arrangement of a public domain composition, the PD material may be used by anyone without infringing upon the rights of the owner in the copyrighted arrangement. The "new" material, however, would have copyright status by the owner of copyright in the "new version." It may be necessary for a person to compare both old and "new" editions to see exactly which parts are in the public domain. In other words, there can be a copyright noticg on a PD song,

but the copyright in such work will extend only to the "new matter." Ownership in the copyrightable material will be claimed by either the arranger/composer or, in a WORK MADE FOR HIRE situation, the employer. To use the copyrighted arrangement of a PD work, authorization is needed from the copyright owner. Copyrighted arrangements of PD works may earn performing and mechanical royalties and fees from other uses.

Sound Recordings. *See* PIRACY (RECORDS/ AUDIO TAPES).

Examples of Copyrighted Arrangements of PD Compositions. Examples of PD musical compositions that have gained popularity in copyrighted arrangements appear on the facing page.

Public Relations. It is the aim of participants in the music business who are in the public eye, or are attempting to be, to build and/or sustain a favorable public image—one that can enhance their careers. These participants, mainly recording artists but also composers, songwriters, producers, and record company executives, often retain *public relations firms*, which function to form, influence, or shape public opinion in their clients' behalf as they desire. Through campaigns that cover many forms of public exposure—national and local television; syndicated radio programming; national, daily, Sunday, and weekly newspapers; national and regional magazines, both music and nonmusic oriented; wire services; trade publications; and alternative and underground press—these firms work to achieve their clients' goals.

Public Relations Firms. Public relations firms representing *recording artist* clients typically provide two services—public relations and publicity.

Public relations, or *PR,* functions in projecting a multi-dimensional *image* of the client, one that will result in a favorable public attitude and in career growth. This is not neces-

Composer	PD Source	New Title
W. Fosdick- G. Poulton	"Aura Lee"	"Love Me Tender"
Debussy	"Clair de Lune"	"Moonlight Love"
J. Ivanovici	"Danube Waves"	"Anniversary Song"
Chopin	"Fantaisie Impromptu"	"I'm Always Chasing Rainbows"
Beethoven	Fifth Symphony (opening theme)	"A Fifth of Beethoven"
Brahms	Hungarian Dance No. 4	"As Years Go By"
Neapolitan Song	"O Solo Mio"	"It's Now or Never"; "There's No Tomorrow"
Rachmaninoff	Piano Concerto No. 2	"Full Moon and Empty Arms"
Alexander Borodin	"Polovetsian Dances" in *Prince Igor*	"Stranger in Paradise"
Debussy	"Reverie"	"My Reverie"
Tchaikovsky	Symphony No. 5 (second move- ment)	"Moon Love"

sarily intended to gain business, but rather to draw attention to a client's accomplishments or aggrandize his reputation. *Publicity* serves to put the client's name and product before the public in such a way that *sales* of records and tapes and tickets to concerts will increase.

It is the intention of both public relations and publicity to enlarge the audience of the client and to effect, however indirectly, new business offers for the client. Typically, each client has separate PR and publicity campaigns, though in most cases they run simultaneously.

Record Company Publicity Department vs. PR Firm. While record companies customarily have their own publicity departments, their primary concern is to sell the artist musically—that is, the artist's records and tapes, and to a lesser extent, his concert appearances (which serve to increase the sale of product).

The artist interested in developing a "personality" often engages a public relations firm, which functions as stated above. The PR firm will also get the artist media attention during stagnating periods, such as between records or during lulls in record/tape sales. A PR firm may be also retained to enhance a label's publicity activities during a special campaign on behalf of a particular artist.

Public Relations Program. In conducting a public relations program, a PR firm will determine the client's goals, evaluate his public image, if any, and then devise and implement a program. In determining the client's goals, the public relations counsel meets with the client or, as recording artists are often inaccessible, the artist's personal manager. The PR worker will ascertain various positive aspects of the client and establish how much money is available to spend on the program. A goal of every recording artist is of course to become and/or remain a highly successful performer and record seller. Therefore the artist's aims are discussed in these lights.

There is sometimes the "gold" or "platinum" selling artist who lacks a public image. In such a case, the public relations counsel would inquire about the artist's nonmusical interests and hobbies (fashion and photography, for example) and utilize them to various advantages. In getting the artist known through these vehicles, the PR firm can introduce the client in an unfamiliar light, create an image for him/her, and perhaps even create a new audience for the artist's records and concerts. As another example, the PR firm could arrange for a composer/artist's hit songs to be choreographed by a dance company or played by the marching band during a half-time show at a football game. While such promotions will probably not result in direct sales of the artist's product, they may serve to enhance his public image and broaden his audience. They create an awareness.

Execution of Program. The PR firm will utilize all appropriate media to achieve its client's goal. After it devises a public relations/publicity campaign (national and international exposure are the usual priorities), it launches it. The PR firm will contact music and entertainment editors of consumer and trade publications, and producers, talent coordinators, and/or hosts of television and syndicated and local radio programs. To create interest for a major feature or interview, the PR firm sends out a press kit (see below) or a press release and a record album. A publicist will contact a particular publication or show and suggest why it should run a profile or schedule an interview with the client. Points of interest may be the artist's latest release or chart action, interesting developments in his career or personal life, some of his special attributes, and how he may "work" for the publication or show. The publicist will also research planned television specials to see which ones might be suitable vehicles for the artist. The firm's work is done on the telephone, through the mail, and during personal meetings.

The PR firm may "cross-collateralize" its client roster. For example, a large firm that represents a manufacturer of clothes, or of skin or hair products, can have one of its music clients wearing or using the product at a public demonstration where there might be large media coverage. Thus both clients may benefit from the exposure.

Interaction with the Artist's Other Representatives. In achieving its goals, the public relations firm will develop working relationships with certain other representatives of the artist: personal manager, record company

(particularly the publicity, artist development, and promotion departments), booking agent, and advertising agency. The PR firm maintains regular contact with these representatives and sometimes gears its activities to enhancing their campaigns. This also serves to prevent duplication of one another's work.

Artist Tours. It is important for artists to receive considerable publicity and promotion when touring, and PR firms work to accomplish this. The company will obtain a tour itinerary listing venues, cities, dates of engagements, and concert promoters and their telephone numbers.

The firm will send a press kit to media in each city well in advance so there may be preconcert publicity. It will then follow up these mailings with phone calls to determine interest and coordinate coverage and interviews, or this might be handled by road publicists, who travel to cities in advance of concerts to arrange publicity. When the artist has finished performing in the city, media will be contacted again to gauge reaction and request press clippings. Reports are sent to the artist so the press and audience reaction in each city can be evaluated.

Press Kit. An important tool for any public relations/publicity campaign, the *press kit* is sent to various media and serves to interest people in interviewing the client for an article for print publication or for a radio or television show; articles are sometimes written from the material enclosed.

A press kit for a recording artist typically consists of a biography (1 to 5 typewritten pages); black-and-white photographs (1 to 4); reprints of magazine and newspaper interviews, feature stories, profiles, and record reviews; and a discography. There may also be a sheet containing complimentary press remarks received by the artist.

These materials are assembled and inserted in a cardboardlike folder. The cover may be a visual reproduction of the album cover. On the cover and/or on the materials assembled inside are printed the name, address, telephone number, and cable address or telex number of the artist's representative. The artist's latest record album will usually accompany any mailing of the press kit.

PR Fees. For its services, a public relations firm may be compensated on the basis of a monthly fee plus expenses (a minimum number of months is usually required) or by a flat fee based on time (the PR representative keeps a time sheet and bills time), plus expenses. Expenses include those for offset printing, reprinting photos, mailings, long-distance telephone calls, transportation, and essentially all other out-of-pocket expenses incurred on behalf of the client. The client usually places a ceiling on the expenses. Recording artists who hire PR firms generally pay for their services themselves or split the fee with the label. In certain cases, a label will foot the entire PR bill for an artist on its roster.

PR Firm Structure. A large music or entertainment public relations firm will usually have at least two offices: a West Coast office, which can be closely in contact with the Los Angeles–based record companies and the Hollywood television and motion picture industry, and an East Coast office, to deal effectively with New York City's concentration of record companies and magazine publishers.

Such a large public relations firm might have a vice-president of entertainment and music, who oversees all programs or campaigns and is a creative consultant for all employees; West and East Coast directors, who handle most of the direct contact with the artist or his representative on a day-to-day basis, help create and implement a specific campaign geared to the needs of the artist, oversee the work of personnel immediately under them, and are responsible for the daily operation of the department; and public relations

representatives, writers, and publicists (including tour publicists). The company might also have foreign offices located throughout Europe and Far East affiliates.

See ADVERTISING; RECORD COMPANY.

Publication. Defined in the 1976 Copyright Act (Section 101) as "the distribution of copies or phonorecords of a work to the public by sale or other transfer of ownership, or by rental, lease or lending. The offering to distribute copies or phonorecords to a group of persons for purposes of further distribution, public performance or display of the work does not of itself constitute publication."

Commercial Application of Definition. Under the copyright law, the sale of copies or phonorecords constitutes publication of the underlying work. Since a musical composition can be embodied in a variety of material objects, publication can be accomplished via distribution of sheet music, songbooks, records, tapes, films, videocassettes, and videodiscs. Musical compositions, particularly popular songs, are normally first published today (and have been for many years now) in the form of disc recordings, with publication of sheet music and other printed editions to follow if the work is commercially successful. A song is not "published" if it is performed at a club or concert or on television, no matter how many people are exposed to the work.

Formalities. The copyright law contains provisions regarding deposit and registration of published works. The statute requires that for a "work published with notice of copyright in the United States," copies or phonorecords of the best edition be deposited in the Copyright Office.

Usually, record manufacturers do not place the copyright notice for musical works (i.e., ©, year, owner) on the disc or tape recordings themselves. Where publication of a musical work occurs without such notice on a phonorecord, the owner of the exclusive right of publication in the work would not have to deposit phonorecords. The owner of copyright in the sound recording, for which there would be a copyright notice (i.e., ℗, year, owner), would be required by law to comply with the mandatory deposit requirements.

For copyright registration of a musical work published in the form of phonorecords, the deposit requirements may be satisfied by the submission of phonorecords if such musical work was published only in phonorecords. The preference is for copies, rather than phonorecords, where a musical work is published in both copies and phonorecords. Only phonorecords will suffice for registering sound recordings, of course.

Copyright registration of published works is voluntary. A work first published outside the U.S. may be registered in the Copyright Office. Unpublished works of foreign origin may be registered without restriction.

See also COPYRIGHT DEPOSIT AND REGISTRATION; COPYRIGHT NOTICE; COPYRIGHT PROTECTION AND NATIONAL ORIGIN.

Publisher. *See* MUSIC PUBLISHER.

Q

Quadraphonic Sound. A concept in the recording and reproduction of sound, in which four separate channels (as opposed to the two channels in stereo) are used to convey a performance to the listener. Introduced commercially in 1971, quadraphonic sound (commonly referred to as "quad") was originally developed for classical recordings, to further carry the ambience of the hall in which the performance took place via two speakers at the rear of the playback room. The first experiments in quad recording date back to 1968 and the first public demonstrations were given during live broadcasts of the Boston Symphony Orchestra over two separate FM stations, one (WCRB) carrying the two front channels, the other (WGBH) the two rear channels.

When quad was embraced commercially, certain of the basic premises of the technique were changed. Particularly in pop recording, the emphasis was placed on "surround sound." That is, sound was recorded in such a way that instruments were assigned to each channel in quad (for example, vocals on left front, sax and guitar on left rear, piano on right rear, drums and bass on right front). Curiously, many classical recordings proceeded with the original quad premise and recorded the ambience or reverberation into the rear channels.

Quad, four-channel, recordings were realized as commercial records using two methods: "discrete" and "matrixed." Both types of quad records are "compatible" with stereo playback equipment in that they can be played back and a normal stereo effect is achieved, although none of the quad effects

are possible. In discrete quad records (JVC and RCA), the information in all four channels is summed, or mixed, and engraved onto the two walls of the groove as in a stereo record. Also cut into the groove is a supersonic (inaudible) "carrier tone" which contains "difference information" (that is, sound information achieved when the sound of each of the rear channels is subtracted from that of the other and from the front channels). On playback through a special "decoder," circuits extract the difference information from the carrier tone, and through special mixing and cancellation processes restore the separate, original four channels, which are then sent through the amplifying system, separately, to their four corresponding speakers. Discrete records operate in very similar fashion to the standard "multiplexing" used for stereo FM broadcasts.

In matrixed records, the four channels are mixed together with their "phase" shifted (that is, slightly changed in time). Upon playback, a special decoder "senses" the "phase shift" and directs the individual channels to their respective speakers. It is commonly believed that matrixed quad records do not provide the exactitude of separation of the original four channels that discrete records do (matrix record decoders are less expensive and less problematical than discrete record decoders). There are two main systems used in quad matrixed records: SQ (CBS) and QS (Sansui). These differ only in method of matrixing rather than in principle and may be played interchangeably. However, separation of the channels will suffer and best results are obtained through their respective decoders.

Quad never made it in the marketplace. Many reasons for its failure to capture the public's interest have been advanced, among them: incompatibility of the different systems, difficulty in setting up the systems, difficulty and expense in converting existing stereo systems to quad, problems in placing four speakers in a listening room optimally and in a visually acceptable manner, lack of variety in quad software, excesses in the recording of quad material, etc. Whatever the case, quad faded from the marketplace by 1974. At present, however, two companies still issue compatible records matrix encoded for quad: EMI in the U.K. (SQ encoded) and VOX in the U.S.

(QS encoded). Both encode only the ambience information onto the rear channels.

There is a strong movement, in the U.S. primarily, in what is called "ambience restoration." In this procedure, normal stereo records are played over a standard stereo system. The stereo signal is also processed through a "delay system" (a component that delays the stereo signal, digitally or otherwise, for varying intervals) and is sent through another stereo amplifier to a set of speakers placed at the rear of the room. Essentially this type of system is a "reverberation synthesis" system in which a "pseudo ambience" is created. It can be said that ambience restoration has to all intents and purposes replaced quad.

R

Rack Jobber. A Subdistributor, or Wholesaler, that services record and tape departments of mass-merchandise outlets and other retailers not primarily in the record/tape retail business. A rack jobber supplies records and tapes as well as record and tape accessories and related merchandise.

Mass-merchandise outlets serviced by the rack jobber include department stores and variety and discount stores. A jobber may also rack record and tape installations in such establishments as electronics and automotive stores.

In servicing a record and tape department, the rack jobber: selects and orders merchandise for the outlet (particularly the latest and most popular products); organizes the display of records, tapes, and other merchandise; supervises the sales force (employed by the outlet); takes inventory; exchanges unsold or slow-moving goods; develops advertising and merchandising programs; and maintains an accounting system.

Because of the nature of its operation, the rack jobber assumes many of the risks incurred by actual retailers, though the outlet that provides the space pays the rent, salaries, and other overhead expenses. The rack jobber pays a percentage of the sales receipts to the outlet's proprietor.

History. The rack jobber formed as a specialty wholesaler of phonograph records in the 1950s, placing records into nonmusic stores, such as drugstores, supermarkets, and discount stores. Not primarily being in the record retail business, these outlets found it advantageous to utilize the rack jobber's services. The jobber possessed the expertise needed to efficiently order products with the potential to sell profitably. Furthermore, it was the rack jobber whose investment paid for the stock of records in their establishment. The merchandising of records in these outlets under the rack jobbers' programs proved to be successful and these subdistributors quickly grew in number, importance, and power in the record industry. Today, they continue to account for a substantial percentage of the industry's over-the-counter sales.

Radio. Radio is an important and powerful communications medium and music plays a vital role in its programming. A symbiotic relationship exists between the radio and record industries whereby radio benefits from attracting listeners (and hence advertisers) through the broadcast of recorded music and the record industry benefits via the exposure its product gets from airplay (airplay leads to record and tape sales). Radio is also financially beneficial to other music industry participants, such as songwriters and publishers, who earn royalties from performances of their works on radio, and musicians and singers, who earn session fees and in certain cases, residuals for performing on commercial announcements.

As the airwaves are part of the public domain, regulation of radio stations is a responsibility of the federal government, which licenses broadcasters to serve the public interest. Communication by radio, television, and wire in the United States is regulated by the Federal Communications Commission (FCC). In the U.S., a Radio Station must be assigned a frequency, power, and a call sign by the FCC to operate legally. The commission grants radio stations licenses, which must be renewed every three years.

Call Signs. With the multitude of stations sharing the radio spectrum throughout the world, call signs serve to identify individual stations and distinguish their transmissions. Most countries are signatories to treaties providing for international allocation of frequency bands, as international cooperation is imperative to avoid chaotic conditions in the radio spectrum. The system of call signs provides for the identification of the nationality of the station, the type of station, and the individual station. International agreement, since 1927, apportions the alphabet to provide for national identification of a station by the first letter or first two letters of its call signal.

The United States is assigned three prefix letters—K, N, and W—exclusively. The FCC assigns individual call signals beginning with one of these letters. Another initial letter used by the U.S., A—which it shares with some other countries—is assigned to the Army and Air Force (N is used by the Navy and Coast Guard).

The call signs of U.S. commercial radio stations begin with either K or W. Stations west of the Mississippi River (and in U.S. territories and possessions) are assigned call letters beginning with K and those to the east have call signs prefixed with W. There are some exceptions to this (such as station KDKA, Pittsburgh), whose call letters were allocated prior to the adoption of the present system. During radio's infancy, most stations were assigned three-letter call signs (a few continue to use these today, such as WBZ, Boston). The many radio stations operating by the mid twenties necessitated the addition of a fourth letter. Stations may request to change their call signs; applications are filed with the FCC.

Frequency Assignments. In the United States, the FCC assigns specific frequencies in the radio spectrum to individual radio stations. Because the radio channels are limited, consideration is given to the requirements of the many radio services so as to limit congestion.

The space occupied on the radio spectrum by services (e.g., AM and FM) is called a "band." Presently, the AM (medium-wave) band occupies the space between 535 and 1,605 kilohertz; the portion between 88 and 108 megahertz is the FM (VHF) broadcast band.° AM, or amplitude modulation, refers to those stations that transmit program material by varying the amplitude of the radio signal; FM, or frequency modulation, describes those stations that transmit program material by varying the frequency of the radio signal.

Radio Ratings Service. Media research firm that measures radio listening audiences in marketing areas throughout the country by conducting periodic surveys. The results of these surveys are of immediate consequence to radio stations, advertisers, and their agencies.

Stations employ the ratings reports in establishing advertising rates, selling on-air time, attracting new advertisers, and making programming decisions to boost their ratings. Advertisers and ad agencies use the ratings when they plan the cost and efficiency of their radio campaigns and decide where to spend their advertising dollars. A radio ratings service sells its reports to broadcasters and advertising agencies.

The greatest challenge that confronts a radio ratings service lies in employing research measurement techniques that will most accurately gather data on and reflect listening habits. Over the years, different survey techniques have been used by research firms, including personal interviews, telephone interviews,

---

° The AM commercial radio band may be expanded as determined by the World Radio Conference, thus permitting more radio stations to operate. Any such expansion must be approved in the U.S. before being implemented by the FCC.

questionnaires, diary-keeping, and variations of these methods.

Radio ratings services have operated in the United States since the early days of radio. Companies that have at one time or another provided influential radio ratings include Hooper, Pulse, Nielsen, and Conlan. Since the early 1970s, the ARBITRON Company has been the most widely used ratings service (Arbitron uses a DIARY method of measurement). A project known as the All Radio Audience Measurement Study (ARMS I), which was conducted by the Radio Advertising Bureau in conjunction with the NATIONAL ASSOCIATION OF BROADCASTERS (NAB) in 1966, analyzed eleven different methods of capturing radio listening and found that diaries gauge listening activity most accurately. Arbitron became the first service to measure FM listening when it began to conduct its radio surveys in 1966.

Radio programming is continually evolving. As new, specialized formats are implemented and the differences between previous ones become clouded, one fact remains clear in the minds of all broadcasting and advertising industry participants: continuous, dynamic, and modern survey techniques and methodology by market research companies are needed to yield accurate and credible station ratings.

Radio Station. A radio station is a facility that transmits program material within the radio frequency spectrum that is intended to be received by the public. Radio stations are run for commercial and for educational (or other nonprofit) purposes.

Commercial broadcast operations are profit-oriented businesses whose income is derived from advertisements aired by the station. A station's advertising fees are usually based on the size of its audience in its market (as determined by a radio ratings service). The stations use the advertising revenue to pay their operating and related expenses; moneys received above and beyond this are their net profits. A private radio station functions to serve the public, but its goal is the same as that of any other business—to be as financially successful as possible.

Structure. The number and type of personnel a station employs is directly related to its income and format. Typically, a nonautomated contemporary music radio station employs the following personnel: general manager, sales manager, program director, music director, traffic manager, salespersons, disc jockeys and announcers, news director, reporters, and engineers. There are of course the usual other business employees, such as accountants, bookkeepers, secretaries, and clerks.

The owner of a station selects the station's format (or directs others to decide), hires the general manager, and may be involved in setting general policy. The *general manager* is responsible for the station's day-to-day operations. He oversees administrative, sales, technical, promotional, and program activities, determines salaries (with the consent of owner), and is responsible for the station's profit or losses.

The *program director*, or *PD*, is responsible for the station's programming content and schedule—what records to air and what the tempo of the music should be, what types of commercials to broadcast and how many per hour. Although the music director and disc jockeys may have a say in which singles and albums to add to the station's playlist, the final decision is that of the program director. The PD may also oversee news and weather reports, contests, and hiring of disc jockeys. At some smaller stations, PDs function in other capacities, including any of the folowing: disc jockey, musical director, engineer, and news reporter. The PD's goal is to program the station in such a way as to attract the maximum potential audience so that the station can increase its advertising rates and acquire more advertisers.

The *music director* meets with representatives of record companies (promotion workers) to listen to, screen, and discusss new releases, and brings those he considers the best to the PD (who selects additions to the station's playlist). In helping the PD select records, the music director conducts research. He may call retail record/tape outlets in the local market to see what product is selling best; phone individuals to find out their favorite new records, sometimes playing excerpts from new releases for them and asking their opinion; attend concerts; and study the trade and local press. *Assistant* music directors (only the larger stations employ them) maintain the station's record/tape library (where records and tapes are filed for easy access), file new recordings, and retrieve specific selections requested by the PD or the disc jockeys. Sometimes these responsibilities fall to a station's *music librarian*.

The *disc jockey* ("DJ," "deejay," or "jock") is the radio announcer (air personality), who presents the recorded selections broadcast by the station and makes various announcements. He reads advertisements, makes promotional announcements, gives information on contests, and intersperses nonmusical comments (i.e., reports of local events, brief time and weather reports, and jokes) between the playing of records. His patter will depend on the format of the station and the program director's goals. The disc jockey usually tries to project a certain personality ("image") which will attract listeners to the station and to his particular program; he tries to be entertaining and informative. In some stations the DJ has other responsibilities, but generally, the larger the station, the fewer they are.

Contemporary music radio stations typically have 6 or 7 DJ shifts daily. These vary from station to station, but commonly are as follows (the nicknames for the shifts are in parentheses): 6 A.M. to 10 A.M. (morning drive); 10 A.M. to 3 P.M. (midday); 3 P.M. to 7 P.M. (afternoon drive); 7 P.M. to 10 P.M. (early evening); 10 P.M. to 2 A.M. (night); and 2 A.M. to 6 A.M.

(overnight or "graveyard"). *Drive* refers to shifts that are on the air when people travel to and from work.

The *engineer* operates the equipment that keeps the station on the air, takes meter readings of transmitting equipment every few hours, and does production work, which inc.cludes transferring recorded selections from phonograph records to tapes. These tapes are called "carts" and each cart is made to contain one selection. Recordings are usually broadcast by playing the cart (rather than the record).

Members of the sales department sell air time to advertising agencies and sponsors. Traffic managers prepare the daily advertising schedule and keep logs of the spots aired by the station.

The types of personnel and the hierarchy of positions vary from station to station, but may be generally represented as follows:

Music Programming. Radio stations with contemporary music FORMATS have playlists—lists of records the station has selected to broadcast regularly during a given time period (usually one week). A "tight" playlist is the result of a station's aim to reach a specific audience by programming what it believes will most attract that audience. As stated above, the playlist is determined by the program director with recommendations from the music director (who gets feedback from promotion reps and DJs).

A playlist is typically broken down into several categories: the "hottest" current records, recurrents (recent hits), up and coming hits, and new releases. Stations typically refer to these categories in terms such as "superpower," "power," "heavy," "light," "top 30," etc.

The records on the playlist are played on a rotating schedule. The hottest records get the heaviest airplay, the next hottest get somewhat lighter play, and so on. The PD often sets up a "clock" for this rotation. For example, let's assume that at a radio station one record is played every five minutes (i.e., between top

RADIO STATION

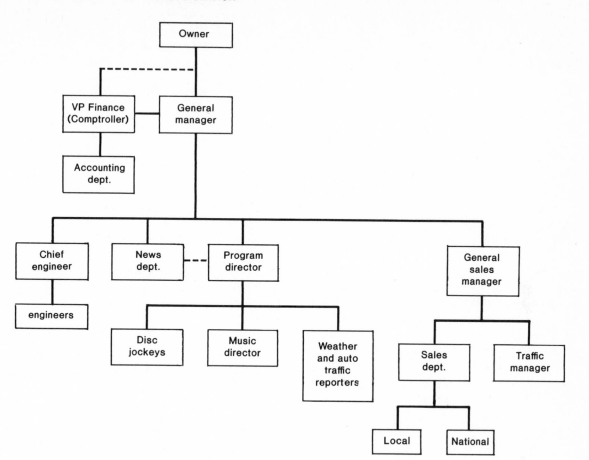

and bottom of the hour). There might be a clock in the control room filled in with different colors representing the different categories at five-minute intervals. For each colored interval (or category) there is a selection of records (commonly from five to six) from which the DJ may choose one to air. In addition to colors, stations denote programming categories with numbers, letters, etc. Computer routines for the sequencing of music are a new tool just coming on the scene at this writing. This is the start of what will probably be a growth area in the way music playlists are controlled.

Logs. Many stations keep logs in which all programming is accounted for (this is maintained by the traffic manager). This paperwork document is intended to show the commercial, promotional, and nonentertainment elements used by the station. A log will tell when commercials, promotions, news, sports and weather reports, and public service announcements were aired. Logs may be used in various ways—for example, by sponsors for proof that their commercials were broadcast or by inspectors from the FCC to check the station's programming. A list of records broadcast may be kept for the specific purpose of the BMI logging procedure.

Advertising. Radio stations usually set their advertising rates in relation to the audience rating they receive as measured by a RADIO RATINGS SERVICE. The higher a station's ratings, of course, the more advertisers it will attract and the higher the rates for advertising.

Song Lyrics. In response to complaints about song lyrics that glamorized the illegal use of dangerous drugs, the FCC issued a Public Notice on March 5, 1971, reminding broadcasters of their responsibility to be aware of the content of their programming. Without specifically prohibiting the broadcast of certain types of records, the notice informed licensees that the selection of records is a matter of their individual judgment.

Performing Rights Aspects. In order to broadcast a recording in which a copyrighted musical composition is embodied, a radio station needs permission from the copyright owner. Virtually all copyright owners affiliate with a PERFORMING RIGHTS ORGANIZATION (ASCAP, BMI, SESAC), which handles the licensing of nondramatic performing rights on its members' or affiliates' behalf. For a fee, performing rights organizations license music users (such as radio stations) to use the music in their repertoires for a certain time period.

See also RADIO.

Rating. *See* ARBITRON.

Record Charts. *See* CHARTS.

Record Club. *See* RECORD AND TAPE CLUB.

Record Company. Record companies are the producers, manufacturers, and purveyors of recorded sound performances. As technology has evolved over the past century, record companies have found that the devices which carry their product (recorded music) have changed remarkably. The industry's first commercial product came in the form of wax cylinders. Cylinders were eventually replaced by the more advantageous flat disc recordings. Wide-groove shellac records gave way to new disc materials and groove-size configurations in the late 1940s and 1950s (i.e., LPs and singles); and magnetic tape in an enclosed loop (i.e., the 8-track cartridge) and in cassette form (first commercially released in the 1960s) has subsequently enjoyed immense popularity as a playback medium. In addition, video software and compact digital discs promise to be other media in which record companies' wares will be mass-marketed.

The variety and development potential of devices to store and reproduce music serve not only to afford consumers a choice of the format they may use to reproduce an artist's performance but also to further the objective of record companies—bringing recorded entertainment to the public as creatively and as profitably as possible. While the term "record company" is not all-encompassing or completely descriptive of the merchandise of these companies, the name has become synonymous with such companies and is likely to remain firmly attached to them for many years.

Definition. A record company, also referred to as a record manufacturer° or LABEL, is a profit-oriented business enterprise responsible for the acquisition and development of recording artists and the manufacture, marketing, promotion, advertisement, and distribution of their recordings.

Consequently, the functions of a record company are to:

- Find and sign talent and maintain an artist roster.
- Nurture or develop the talent for recording, performing, and concert presentation.
- Produce the artist's recordings if he does not have a producer (this includes selecting material and preparing arrangements) or "match" him with an independent producer.
- Provide budgets for talent to record and supply master recordings.

° As distinguished from an actual record fabricator or pressing plant (which may or may not be owned by the record company).

- Manufacture or cause the manufacture of singles, LPs, prerecorded cassette and 8-track tapes, and other software.
- Distribute or cause the distribution of product to wholesalers and retailers.
- Develop merchandising aids that will stimulate the sale of product.
- Promote the recordings to radio stations and other entities.
- Secure publicity and reviews for artists and releases.
- Advertise the company's product.
- Create and sustain images for its artists.
- Remedy situations where an artist's recordings are not selling up to par.
- License master recordings for use by other companies (e.g., record/tape clubs).
- Pay artists and producers royalties earned.
- Handle the paperwork and administration of its business

Types of Record Companies. Record companies are classified as being either major or independent. A *major* record company is one that is fully equipped to handle its operation. It maintains various departments which manage its operations, has sales offices (distribution branches) throughout the country, generally owns manufacturing plants, and has foreign branches. In recent years, major record companies have been divisions of giant international corporations.

An *independent* record company is one that does not maintain distribution branches or own pressing plants. Independent record companies may be categorized into two types, one of which engages the services of private pressing plants and independent distributors for manufacture and dissemination of its product. Such a company may be a small specialty label, releasing records of a certain musical style (such as jazz, R & B, country, folk, classical, or foreign language), or be diversified in the types of recordings it releases and maintain a large artist roster.

The other type of independent is the company or supplier of recordings that enters into an agreement with a major, which then handles the manufacturing and distribution of its product, and in some cases provides certain other services (*see* Record Company Deals). Such an entity is usually independently owned, though there may be ownership participation (but not control) on behalf of the major. Independent record companies—of any type—are owned by artists, producers and managers, as well as by regular profit participants.

Sources of Income. A record company's primary source of income comes from selling records and tapes to wholesalers and retailers. It may also earn revenue by licensing its masters to record/tape clubs, record merchandisers, program suppliers (airline, radio, etc.), and foreign manufacturers. Income from these sources is normally in the form of advances and royalties. Additionally, sound recordings may be licensed to motion picture producers—theatrical or television—for synchronization with their films. It is anticipated that record companies will earn substantial revenues from the mass marketing of videodiscs and videocassettes.

There may be various other sources of income for the company. For example, most record manufacturers have publishing arms which derive income from uses of music copyrights they own and acquire. Companies may also negotiate contractually with artists to share in revenues earned from merchandising tie-ins.

Record companies may have additional sources of income by virtue of their ownership of other businesses, such as retail record/tape stores and wholesale record/tape merchandising companies. The manufacturing plants owned by major record companies manufacture product for other labels. A couple of large companies even own record/tape clubs. Majors also earn income from distributing other labels' product.

Viewed from a different perspective, all the revenue earned by a record company, particularly a major, may be only one source of income for the company that owns *it*. Other interests of large entertainment and leisure companies include motion picture producing, soft-cover and hard-cover book publishing, magazine publishing, and broadcasting.

Annual Sales of Records and Prerecorded Tapes*

Calendar Year	List price Value (millions of dollars)
1921	105.6
1922	92.4
1923	79.2
1924	68.2
1925	59,4
1926	70.4
1927	70.4
1928	72.6
1929	74.8
1930	46.2
1931	17.6
1932	11.0
1933	5.5
1934	6.6
1935	8.8
1936	11.0
1937	13.2
1938	26.4
1939	44.0
1940	48.4
1941	50.6
1942	55.0
1943	66.0
1944	66.0
1945	109.0
1946	218.0
1947	224.0
1948	189.0
1949	173.0
1950	189.0
1951	199.0
1952	214.0
1953	219.0
1954	213.0
1955	277.0
1956	377.0
1957	460.0
1958	511.0
1959	603.0
1960	600.0
1961	640.0
1962	687.0
1963	698.0

Annual Sales of Records and Prerecorded Tapes* *(cont'd)*

Calendar Year	List price Value (millions of dollars)
1964	758.0
1965	862.0
1966	959.0
1967	1,173.0
1968	1,358.0
1969	1,586.0
1970	1,660.0
1971	1,744.0
1972	1,924.0
1973	2,016.6
1974	2,200.2
1975	2,388.0
1976	2,737.0
1977	3,500.8
1978	4,131.4
1979	3,676.1
1980	3,682.0

*Figures from 1921 to 1966 are for records only; figures from 1967 on include total sales of phonograph records and prerecorded tapes. (Source: Recording Industry Association of America, Inc.)

Structure. To fulfill its ultimate objective of selling records and tapes in mass quantities, a record company is structured in such a way as to comprise various departments with separate responsibilities that interact as a unit under a coordinated plan. The sale of product is actually the result of various employees' functioning in different ways but working for a common goal.

Following is an examination of some of the departments of a record company—primarily a major. Independent labels may not have all these or they might consolidate the functions of some of them into departments whose responsibilities are broad. Of course, no two record companies—not even majors—are structured exactly alike and the responsibilities (and in some cases the titles) of the various departments may vary from company to company. But this discussion will focus on the general activities of the departments.

The departments that are examined are the

following: A & R, A & R administration, artist development, promotion, publicity, and sales.

A & R (Artists and Repertoire). The responsibilities of this record company department are broad but fall into two main areas: the "artist" area—finding talent and signing it (with executive approval) to the label—and the "repertoire" area—finding potential "hit" songs for the label's artists to record. These and other responsibilities of A & R are discussed in the general breakdown that follows:

1. *Scouting talent.* To find (or "discover") talent, the A & R coordinator (as certain employees of this department may be called) both seeks it out and auditions that which comes into the office by invitation and solicitation. In seeking out talent, the A & R coordinator will go to showcases, clubs, concerts, and other places where talent is performing (both in and out of town). Information regarding this comes from trade and consumer press, from personal recommendations, and by word of mouth.

Talent is also auditioned in the office by playing tapes and acetates brought in by producers, personal managers, agents, concert promoters, attorneys, and others who represent acts, or by the acts themselves. If there is interest, the A & R person will often observe the artist performing live.

The A & R department seeks both new and established talent. Where an established artist's contract with another label is about to expire, the A & R VP might attempt to induce that artist into signing with the company. As it is desirable that a new artist be well represented when signing to a label, the A & R coordinator might recommend personal managers, publicists, agents, and others where there is no such representation (this is also a function of the artist development department).

In signing talent, an A & R person must consider both pragmatic and creative aspects. He or she must know the reality of the market-place and conform to public tastes, but also strive for artistic excellence and uniqueness (what the public *might* enjoy) and be willing to shape that demand. In short, the A & R coordinator will seek talent that can grow in artistry, has mass appeal, and promises a long career. The A & R department will also consider the company's "sound" (if any) and the similarity of talent to artists already signed to the company, and will attempt to keep the label's roster at an appropriate level for the size of the company.

2. *Finding songs.* To find potential hit songs for artists signed to the label, the A & R coordinator auditions material submitted by and requested from music publishers and songwriters. Also, he will listen to album cuts of other artists to discover songs that might have hit possibilities if arranged and produced appropriately for an artist on the label. And the A & R coordinator will consider past and recent hits to determine if a remake or cover version by a label artist would have commercial potential.

3. *Preproduction functions.* Once an act is signed to the label, an A & R coordinator will be assigned to it. This person works closely with the act by providing creative input and direction (with the exception, usually, of star acts). If the act does not have a producer, the A & R coordinator may look for one who he believes is able to transform the artist's music into commercially palatable form, and attempt to pair them. When the act already has a producer, the A & R coordinator will develop a working relationship with that person. For artists who do not write their own music, the A & R coordinator will assist in finding songs capable of commercial success. In some cases the A & R coordinator might, in conjunction with the business affairs department, plan a recording budget for a project (this may also be done by the A & R administrator—see below).

4. *Production functions.* The A & R coor-

dinator will listen to the artist's recordings during the various stages of production and apprise A & R administration of the progress and anticipated date of completion so it can inform other departments.

5. *Postproduction functions.* After the finished masters are submitted, the A & R coordinator will listen closely to each track, checking to see that the production is on a professional level. In addition, he will determine if the tracks are satisfactory from an artistic viewpoint. He might recommend that certain tracks be remixed or remix them himself.

The A & R coordinator will assist in determining the sequence of selections on the album and which cuts to release as singles. He will also monitor the mastering and manufacturing of the record, attempting to find and eliminate any flaws that will affect the finished product. As the product gets ready for the marketplace, he will stress the value of the act to company personnel, getting them to support it, and will see that the efforts of the marketing, publicity, advertising, and promotion departments are interacting to serve the act.

6. *Other responsibilities.* An A & R coordinator will also audition masters that the company might license or buy and audition foreign talent, particularly artists signed to the label's foreign subsidiaries, to determine if their recordings would be marketable in the U.S. He may produce one or more of the artists signed to the label (in which case he may also be referred to as a *staff producer*). The A & R coordinator will see that the artist supplies the contracted amount of product and attempt to remedy situations where an artist's recordings are not selling up to par (see below).

DEPARTMENT STRUCTURE. A & R departments vary in size. They may range from one person in a small label to several in a major, where the head of the department, typically called the A & R VP, performs A & R functions as well as supervising the staff. A & R coordinators, assigned to work with specific acts on the label, may be given titles relative to the musical style of the artists they deal with—contemporary, pop, R & B, country, jazz, classical. Other titles for A & R positions are Creative Director and VP Talent Acquisition.

A & R REMEDIES. One important function of an A & R coordinator is to oversee the performer's artistic and commercial growth and longevity. His goal is to have the artist's recording career reach and sustain star status. Where record sales are below profitmaking levels, expected potential, or those of prior releases, the A & R coordinator determines and attempts to remedy the problem. The various ways of doing this include:

1. *Matching the artist with a new producer.* The producer the artist has been working with may not be "right" for him. Selection of a new producer, one compatible with the artist and able to obtain the proper "sound" in future recordings, may be necessary.

2. *Finding a new direction.* Cutting an artist in a different way, which will give new or broader market appeal, might enhance his record sales/popularity—for example, a country artist might record with more of a "pop" feel.

3. *Seeking outside material for self-contained artists.* Artists who record only the material they write may find themselves in need of a hit single. It is to their advantage if the A & R coordinator discovers a song with hit potential for them even though it was composed by a different writer.

4. *Devising strategies with marketing departments.* It is natural for an artist to sell records "off" his concert dates. Yet sometimes an artist who gives a strong concert performance draws small audiences. Therefore, recommen-

dations should be made (particularly to the artist development department) that will result in the artist's performing before large segments of the population (thus tending to increase record sales). Recommendations may include creating a new image for the artist or pairing him with a performer who will attract a different or wider audience.

The A & R coordinator may make suggestions to other departments under the marketing umbrella. To the merchandising department he might suggest new ways to bring the artist's product to the consumer's attention; to the art department, a new approach to the art and design on the artist's album covers; to the promotion department, other formats on which to obtain airplay that would broaden the artist's audience; and to the publicity department additional publications and life-style markets in which to publicize the artist or alternative approaches to getting the artist better known to the public.

5. *Making a "live" record.* Artists may give great concert performances and attract large audiences, but have record sales that never surpass a certain point. Since the excitement and spontaneity of a live performance sometimes cannot be captured in a studio recording, it may be beneficial to release recordings of his live concert performances.

A & R Administration. In a separate but related department, A & R administration handles the clerical aspects related to A & R and supervises various administrative activities. Chiefly, the responsibilities of the A & R administration department are the following:

1. *Planning and monitoring budgets.* At the time an artist is signed to a label, the company may or may not have planned a budget for each album or single to be recorded. Where no budget has been made, A & R administration may in conjunction with the producer devise a mutually agreed upon budget (subject to the approval of the business affairs

department). The A & R administrator will work with the producer in itemizing how the budget will be spent, with respect to studio time, talent costs, and other expenses, such as the artist's travel to the studio and lodging in a nearby hotel.

As the budget for a project is being exhausted, the A & R administrator will monitor (on a daily or weekly basis) the money being spent to see that the budget is adhered to or is not greatly exceeded. A & R administration may negotiate with recording studios to obtain discount rates on the basis of the volume of its bookings.

2. *Examining studio bills.* A & R administration approves studio purchase orders and later cross-checks them against the studio bills when they come in. The department also examines related bills to make sure they are in order. It submits bills to the accounting department for payments and tracks payments into log sheets under various headings.

3. *Examining union bills and overseeing timely payments.* All talent bills are submitted to A & R administration for examination. Information provided includes name of studio, dates and times of sessions, number of sides recorded, what instrument each person played, who performed as a "doubler," and the session fees earned by each performer. The scales designated by the contractor are cross-checked against those on the union contracts. If there is no problem, the A & R administrator promptly submits the bills to the accounting department so that the musicians and vocalists are paid within the time limits specified by AFM and AFTRA. Conflicts are immediately brought to the contractor's attention.

4. *Preparing studio reports.* As it monitors the budget for the recording while it is being made, the A & R administrator regularly prepares status reports indicating the project (name of artist and whether he is recording an album or a single), the planned budget and

money spent to date (for talent, studio, etc.), what point the artist is up to creatively, and the anticipated date of completion of the project. This last piece of information is necessary, as marketing, advertising, and promotion campaigns have to be planned well in advance.

5. *Ordering references and parts.* After the recording is completed, the A & R administrator orders reference dubs, to be heard by the A & R department. When the recording is approved for manufacture, the administrator then orders the metal parts for mastering, from which the pressings are made.

6. *Collecting information for label copy and packaging.* The A & R administrator gathers the information that will appear on the label and/or packaging: name of artist, title of album, sequence and lengths of selections, name of producer, stereo or mono designation, the recording's catalog number, and copyright owner of the sound recording. This information may come from various sources, including the producer (or executive producer), the artist, the artist's personal manager, and the A & R coordinator. The copy is proofread and sent to the departments that oversee printing.

Some recordings are released simultaneously in various configurations. Where the sequence of selections for a stereo 8-track cartridge is different from that in LPs and cassettes, the A & R administrator may work out a feasible sequence with the producer (*see* SEQUENCING).

7. *Deficiting tour support from royalties.* A record company may provide TOUR SUPPORT for an act signed to it. It may be the company's policy to recoup its tour support, or a portion of it, from the artist's recording royalties. If that is the case, the A & R administrator makes arrangements to deficit tour support money from the artist's recording royalties.

8. *Monitoring and reporting on contractual options.* A recording contract typically contains various options. The label may have the option of "overcall," for example, which entitles it to require the artist to supply additional product during the contract period. It is the A & R administrator's responsibility to keep track of all such contractual options and periodically issue pertinent reports to various label personnel.

For example, option reports might be issued monthly and contain on one page information regarding all options coming up for the following two months (stating the name of the artist, date option is due to be exercised, cost to manufacture album, sales data, and comments). The next few pages might be a "calendar spread sheet," indicating options and product commitment for each month of the following year. Option reports provide the company, particularly the president and the A & R and business affairs departments, with an overview of information regarding the artists and helps them to decide whether to renew an artist's contract or drop him from the label (in some companies option reports are prepared by the business affairs department).

9. *Copyrighting.* A & R administration is responsible for copyrighting those works in a single or album that are owned by the record company. These may include the sound recording, artwork, photographs, and liner notes. There may be a separate job title for the person who does the copyrighting, or in some companies, this function is performed by a copyright department. But in either case, such person or department usually reports to the A & R administrator.

10. *Obtaining mechanical licenses.* To use a copyrighted musical composition in a single or an album, a mechanical (record) license must be obtained from the copyright owner. The A & R administrator will request such a license from the publisher or its representative (usually a mechanical rights agency). Again, this function may be the responsibility of a differ-

ent job title or separate department—such as a mechanical licensing department—but either would usually report to the A & R administrator.

It is important for A & R administration to keep careful records and logs of its work and to make sure that references, label copy, and metal parts are all obtained by their scheduled due date. In summary, this department clerically tracks the making of an album from budget to completion and interacts with and reports to various other departments in the company.

Artist Development. The objective of this department is to oversee the overall *career growth* of artists signed to the label, giving whatever input is necessary for the artists to achieve and/or sustain commercial success so that they may enjoy a large and growing market for their records and tapes.

In working to achieve its objective, artist development activities fall into the following areas:

TOURING. A concert tour can substantially increase an artist's audience and record and tape sales, and is consequently a prime concern of artist development. To ensure proper touring, the department oversees the following elements of a tour:

1. *Timing.* It sees that the tour is timed in conjunction with product release and promotion activities. Both live performances and airplay can effectively increase sales, and the synchronization of the two is ideal. Artist development may work in conjunction with the sales department to see that retail outlets in the areas where the artist performs are stocked with his product.

2. *Markets.* It sees that the artist plays in the right markets under the proper circumstances. Artist development will determine from past experience with the artist, or from reports of radio airplay, which cities, regions, or portions of the country the artist should tour in.

3. *Venues.* Artist development recommends which auditoriums, halls, or clubs in the particular markets are most suitable for the artist to utilize.

4. *Packaging.* It may select other acts the artist could tour with that would most effectively increase his audience and promote his product. Artist development will explain to the artist's manager and/or agent why they should tour together and will help effectuate the packaging of the acts.

If an artist requires TOUR SUPPORT, artist development may attempt to acquire such funds from the record company. It will plan the tour economically, assess financial needs, prepare a report, and submit it to the appropriate label personnel.

In some major record companies, the artist development department may work with the distribution branches during an artist's tour. The branch offices across the country sell, market, and promote product in their respective locales. As a result of a properly scheduled tour, these distribution branches follow through by inviting key local radio, retail, and press representatives to the scheduled performances. This kind of professional execution is vital in the development of an attraction.

In a similar fashion, other departments in both the New York and the Los Angeles offices tie into the touring schedule of an attraction. These areas would include promotion, product management and merchandising, publicity, sales, and the college department. The artist development department, for example, will work closely with the promotion department, and lead the way in the structuring of radio station concerts, sponsored by key stations, in meaningful markets.

TELEVISION EXPOSURE. Proper television exposure can enlarge public awareness of the artist and enhance his image. Artist development will attempt to get artists booked on programs—whether broadcast on a network, syndicated to local outlets, or produced on cable television—whose formats are appropriate for them: e.g., music, variety, concert, dance, music award, and talk shows. Of course, not all acts are suitable for television performance, nor is it always the "right" time for those that are. Again, proper timing is vital.

LIVE PERFORMANCE. Professional presentation of concert and television performances by the artist is necessary. Artist development will attend live performances and work with the artist to improve all facets of his presentation. This may include advice on how to improve the following: stage presence; selection, arrangement, and sequence of songs; flow of performance; beginning and ending of the performance; wardrobe; set design, lighting, and sound (in these three areas, it may be necessary to hire special consultants). The goal is to have the artist project the desired image at appearances.

ARTIST REPRESENTATION. It is essential that the artist be represented by an able personal manager and agency. Where the artist lacks such representation, artist development will help him obtain it. Artist development will cultivate a relationship with the artist's representatives, work closely with them so that the artist enjoys the benefits of their coordinated efforts, and give such creative input as will help the artist attain and sustain star status.

Promotion. The basic function of the promotion department is to get AIRPLAY for the label's releases, both singles and albums.

The success of records is to a large extent predicated on the amount of airplay they receive. However, most contemporary-music radio stations are able to program only a few new records each week, as they have relatively small playlists. Some will play as few as 20 or 30 records per week, others not many more than 40. To attract the most listeners possible, contemporary-music stations are primarily interested in playing only hits—those of the moment, some of the past, and surefire up-and-coming ones. As hundreds of singles and albums are released each week, it is obvious that the competition among promotion workers to get their label's releases added to stations' playlists or played on a heavy rotation is fierce.

HOW RECORDS ARE PROMOTED. Singles are promoted with the intention of ultimately obtaining airplay on radio stations in all markets throughout the country, thus causing the record to become a national "hit" (hit singles are not only profitable in themselves but they promote albums featuring the artist). Singles are promoted by the promotion staff under a coordinated plan whose immediate goal is to "break" the single in certain markets. Airplay on stations in major markets will follow if the record is first successful in these markets. Album cuts are promoted to stations whose formats are receptive to playing such selections (e.g., AOR).

In deciding whether a particular radio station is "right" to take a release to, the promoter should be familiar with: (1) the station's format; (2) its market; (3) its demographic target audience; and (4) tastes of the music or program director. For each release, local promotion representatives determine which stations in their market they should promote the record to.

At meetings with music and program directors of stations in their area, branch and independent record promoters attempt to convince the directors that programming certain records will benefit their station. Promoters play a record, show reports and facts that support its commercial appeal and success to date, and stress its good points (their sales pitches are sometimes referred to as "hype").

The promoter uses trade publications, "tip sheets," and other tools. Thus he may show reviews of the record ("trade picks"), data indicating the success the record has had on stations in other cities, the record's demographic appeal (e.g., women 18 to 30 years old), which competition in the station's market is playing the record, and company sales figures. Other influential factors include the personal relationship between the promotion worker and the program or music director, the promoter's track record for bringing in hits (i.e., credibility), and special promotions sponsored by the label (for example, the coordinator may offer the station 50 LPs for a weekend album giveaway if the record is played). Timing is also an important factor. For example, when a female vocalist's record is going off the station's playlist, that may be a good time to promote another female vocalist's record.

Merchandising tools may promote enthusiasm in station personnel—jackets, T-shirts, and various gimmicks bearing the identity of the artist or his product. Likewise, a personal appearance by the artist at the station, the offering of tickets to his local concert, or inviting station personnel to meet the artist at a press party tend to reinforce admiration for the artist and influence airplay.

"BREAKING" A RECORD. A record is not just randomly promoted to radio stations in local areas. Rather, the label devises a strategy to obtain airplay, first in selected markets and later on a national basis if the record has been initially successful.

Records are first promoted to stations in "breakout" markets—cities or regions where radio stations play new, unproven releases. Therefore, it must be determined what areas of the country and what life-style markets would have stations most receptive to the record.

Certain cities or regions have traditionally been good breakout markets for different types of music: the southeastern United States, for example, for general pop releases, Cleveland for rock. Breakout stations are often in secondary and tertiary markets (*see* MARKET). If a record is successful in these markets, it will very likely be added to the playlists of stations in major markets. These stations usually

look for some indication that a record is a hit before adding it to their playlist.

For a rock record, promotion workers will try to "start a fire" by first getting airplay on FM stations. A record might be added for light rotation (i.e., played 1 to 2 times per day), with airplay gradually increased. After a record has been added to a station's playlist, promotion reps regularly call the station to get and give feedback on the record. There is also constant interaction between the station and local stores regarding sales of the record. If it is selling well, the rotation might be increased to 5 or 6 times per day and eventually the record might be picked up by AM and other FM stations. If the record receives enough airplay, the charts and tip sheets will pick up its progress. This will result in more stations' adding it to their playlists.

Promotion workers also promote records to independent radio station program consultants. The services of some consultants are widely used and their recommendations can result in a record's being programmed in several markets throughout the country.

OTHER RESPONSIBILITIES OF RECORD PROMOTERS. Promoters may also be involved in exposing the *artist* whose records they promote. They may arrange for radio station interviews, in-store appearances, visits to local wholesalers, and promotional appearances at shopping centers, hospitals, etc. Another responsibility may be to arrange for in-store airplay of the artist's record. Sometimes these functions are handled by branch artist development managers, field merchandisers, and other branch staff workers. A promotion worker may also promote records at discotheques or to disco DJs and disco pools.

It is important for the promotion representative to establish and cultivate relationships and credibility with local radio station music and program directors, disc jockeys, radio and television personalities, and writers. These people can make the public aware of new product and greatly contribute to a record's success.

MAILINGS. Promotion records (see below) are frequently mailed to radio stations that are not located near a local distribution branch and cannot be reached for personal servicing by the branch's promotion reps, or stations whose audiences are too small to warrant a personal visit. Album releases are sent, with suggestions on which cuts are most suitable for airplay.

INDEPENDENT PROMOTERS. Independent record companies often hire independent promoters to get airplay for their records. Independent promoters may also be engaged by a major record company to work on a special project or to supplement its staff in a particular market. For example, a major might hire an independent promoter to aid its staff when it is overburdened with a large amount of releases, to put a record "to bed" (i.e., ensure that an already successful record becomes a smash hit), or to get airplay in markets that the "indie" might be particularly strong in. Independent promoters are usually hired on the basis of a weekly salary and they may work for several labels (major or independent) at once.

PROMOTION RECORDS. In promoting records, labels give specially marked copies of the singles and albums they release to radio stations at no charge. These are called promotion or "promo" records. To prevent the sale of these records, record companies print a statement on them such as "For Promotion Only, Sale Unlawful." As a general rule, no royalties are paid to artists, producers, and copyright owners for complimentary records given for promotional purposes.

Publicity. The function of the publicity department is to bring press and other media attention to the artist which will, either directly or indirectly, aid in the sale of records and tapes. Inherent in this goal is overseeing the continual growth and development of the artist by maintaining his visibility in the marketplace.

The objectives of the publicity department are achieved by devising *publicity plans* (*see* samples on pages 325–27) and implementing them. On the basis of publicity "angles" and LP review strategies that are part of these plans, the department attempts to obtain publicity for the act in various media in conjunction with album releases and concert tours, and sends out albums for review to key publications. A published album review in a national or local publication might result in direct sales, while a local newspaper interview could aid in attracting a larger audience to a concert appearance, which may in turn bring greater record sales.

OPERATIONS. The following generally describes how a publicity department might achieve its aims and objectives:

1. *Publicist meets with artist and manager.* Topics of discussion include the performer's professional history, music, desired image, target audience, tour plans, personal interests, hobbies, and anecdotes. The publicist will try to learn about the artist as a person as well as get a feel for his music.

2. *Press angles are developed.* Based on the interview (particularly taking into account music, image, and personality characteristics), angles are developed that will create excitement and attract attention from writers and editors—on both national and local levels. Possible angles include any uncommon interests or past experiences of the artist, whether the artist writes original songs and if there have been any noteworthy covers of these, and what famous producer or musicians may be working or have worked on the artist's new album. Having many good angles is particularly important for "breaking" new acts. Where the band lacks an IMAGE, one may be created.

3. *Artist's bio is written,* taking into account angles and the label's marketing strategy for the artist and his product. A photo session is arranged, bearing in mind the desired image

(e.g., aimed for teen magazines). Finally, press kits containing the bio, photos, and other materials are assembled.

4. *Lines of communication are established* with other representatives of the artist—personal manager, agent, road manager, public relations firm, etc.

5. *Publicity plan is prepared* with the overall strategy in mind (each strategy is dependent upon the individual artist). Publicity is of course desired on a variety of levels. The plan is usually to establish a foundation of local press throughout the country and build upon this, with the eventual goal of obtaining feature articles in mass-circulation consumer magazines (reaching the maximum number of people).

6. *Publicity is obtained.* Various media are contacted, but approaches may differ, depending upon whether the artist is touring or not. If not, press kits and albums are mailed and followed up with phone calls. When the artist is touring, advance pieces and interviews are heavily pursued. Publicists aim to get stories printed with photos and, when possible, cover or feature articles. Larger publications are "fed" with local and road press to impress upon them the artist's importance and to obtain coverage.

It is important to know which writers, editors, and publications might be interested in and might react most favorably to each artist. This is often determined through "brainstorming" sessions with members of the department. "Angles," too, are thought up in this manner.

A publicist may coach an artist who is inexperienced in doing interviews. This may be approached by asking the artist: "What do you want people to know about you?" The publicist may tell him what points to bring up, how to mention a new album and single in case interviewers don't, how to get across what he wants to see in print, and basically how to "sell" himself.

7. *Report of tour publicity is prepared.* A report of press coverage obtained during the artist's tour is prepared, showing, on a city-by-city basis, the newspapers in which articles, concert reviews, and album reviews were printed. This enables the artist, his representatives, and the label to evaluate his weaknesses and strengths, and determine his popularity in each city, and offers the opportunity for improvements to be made.

8. *Visibility is maintained.* The publicity department continues to obtain media exposure for the artist, including coverage between album releases and concert tours. This serves not only to aid in record sales but to sustain the artist's career growth.

DAVID JOHANSEN: PUBLICITY PLAN

Ideal Image: The personification of a New York rock star, with the exception of probably being the only one with an intellectual twist—Johansen is the street kid with a sublime sense of aesthetics—his New York manners combine with a European ambience—he's literary, witty, and probably one of the greatest talkers in the world . . . has the aura of a foreign film star.

Tour: now doing warm-up dates in the Tri-State area; small clubs, will embark on nationwide tour later; playing huge (100,000 seater) date in Cleveland August 16.

LP Review Strategy and Goals: LP out 704. Met with Steve Paul several weeks ago and compiled list for him of about 35 NY press to send advance cassettes to. Plan is to hold off on interviews until there is substantial LP or single action— want a semi-success story this time as opposed to "here's another brilliant LP by the obscure David Johansen." DJ is a press darling and we expect the same rave reviews he garnered with his first LP.

Mailings: none planned at this time.

Press Angles: 1. This LP represents a natural progression in David's career from his Doll days to his first LP, which was still raw rock 'n' roll but evolving into this, the obvious next step, a more polished, more commercial musical statement but yet not selling out his rock roots. More radio accessible but maintaining the power, energy and emotion of first solo LP.

2. Once the LP gets going we will look to mags like *Oui, Playboy, People, Us, Interview, GQ,* and go for a human interest story in David's musical *and* physical progression—sort of "a Doll grows up" angle, showing his different stages.

3. Johansen was *the first* to have a "new wave," or "punk" type glitter band in the early 70's, *and* he's survived.

Challenges: to break this LP out of the cult circle of his first; to get a broader range of press exposure to introduce David to a new audience by way of non-music publications (see press angle #2).

Courtesy: CBS Records.

CHEAP TRICK PUBLICITY PLAN

Ideal Image: Young American rock 'n' rollers who combine sexy teen idol good looks with bizarre lunatic fringe appeal. Curious combination of youthful wholesomeness and exaggeration. Audiovisual impact is tremendous, appealing at once to R & R, New Wave, and Disco markets.

Tour: Begin US tour April 7 in LA (World Music Festival), Orlando April 14 (World Music Festival), May 24 and 25 Palladium.

LP Reviews—Strategy and goals: LP ships 503. We'll utilize momentum of "Budoken"'s success. Special advance mailings to rock press, teen press, on local, regional, and national levels. *Rolling Stone* piece on Japan tour will give added impact to "Dream Police" release.

Mailings: Special mailing of *Dream Police* sew-on badge. Special invitation to NYC gig.

Press Angles: 1. Cheap Trick's time has come. This is the year of mass recognition.

2. Super stardom in Japan as per *Rolling Stone* report.

3. *Dream Police* contains a disco-flavored cut, and Tom Petersson's first solo with the group.

4. LP sales figures and chart positions—without a hit.

5. Tom Werman as LP producer.

Our Challenge: Refresh all journalists with up-to-date facts and figures on *Dream Police.* The press on Cheap Trick has been remarkable, considering they've never had a hit. We cannot rest on laurels or expect past media praise to break this LP. We must work this LP as doggedly as we've worked earlier efforts.

Continued excitement and more press is the only way our momentum can work to break the group out with the *Dream Police* LP.

Courtesy: CBS Records.

Sales. This department is responsible for selling the company's product to wholesalers and retailers. It develops sales campaigns, determines policies for discounts, special deals and returns, takes orders for product and oversees sales activities on local levels, provides financial assistance to accounts for advertising, and oversees billing. The sales department of a major record company consists of members of the national sales department and senior executives, salespersons, and other employees of the branch distribution system.

The sales department functions on three levels: national, regional, and field. This is as follows:

1. *National.* National accounts are those accounts (such as rack jobbers, one-stops, and record store chains) that have offices in two or more territories that deal with two or more of the manufacturer's branches. With regard to national accounts, the sales department is concerned with the following:

a. Planning
   (1) merchandising
   (2) forecasting future needs
   (3) developing return policies
   (4) lining up special promotions nationwide rather than through local stores
   (5) providing label entertainment at conventions of national accounts, as well as audiovisual presentations (this can be especially helpful for breaking new artists)
b. Delivery of advertising dollars
c. Offering a forum for *national* accounts to expose them to new product and get them involved with campaigns.

The national director of sales coordinates all the label's sales campaigns. He helps develop campaigns and policies and channels this information to people in the field organization. The national sales director also oversees advertising and promotions for national accounts.

2. *Regional.* Major record companies have regional sales directors. Regions might be divided as follows: Northeast, Southeast, Northwest, Southwest, and West. A regional sales director (also called regional vice-president, regional director, or district manager) is responsible for all local branch activity in his region—sales, promotion, and merchandising campaigns. Each distribution branch (sales office) has a monthly sales quota based on a sales projection for one year. Thus each office is responsible for selling a certain amount of product for each release. The regional vice-president is responsible for each field office's reaching its sales quota.

3. *Field. See* Distributor (Records and Tapes).

exchanges and returns. Manufacturers have programs for their accounts to exchange or return unsold product. LPs, singles, and prerecorded tapes are generally sold on either of the following provisions:

Exchange allowance. An account may exchange a certain percentage of its purchases. This allowance may vary based on the type of account it is and the volume of its purchases. Front-line goods are usually sold on an exchange allowance.

100% return. An account is permitted to return any unsold goods for credit or exchange. Generally, only a small amount of product is sold on this basis (e.g., singles, albums of new or developing artists). There may be a call-back period for product sold on this basis (*see* Return Privilege).

billing. Accounts have a certain period in

ORGANIZATION PLAN FOR A RECORD COMPANY*

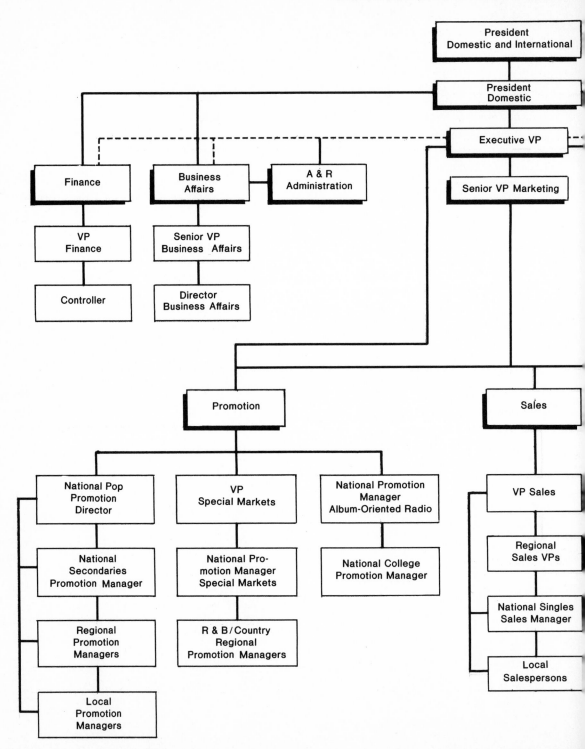

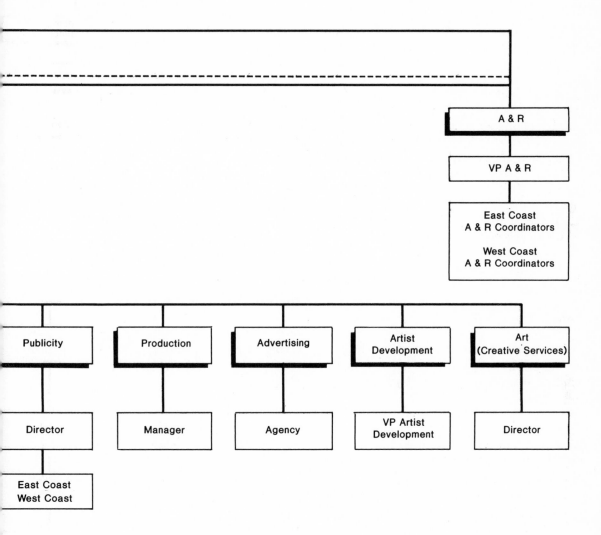

*No two record companies are structured alike. This plan represents a possible structure for a large record company.

which they are to pay for delivered product. This is usually 60 days but may be extended for certain releases (such as those by new artists) or for particular accounts (in which case the decision would be made by the credit department). When an account is overdue, it may be put on "hold," in which case the label will not ship any more product until it pays its bill.

FREE GOODS. *See* FREEBIE.

Foreign Subsidiaries. Large record companies have subsidiaries in foreign countries. A major international company may have subsidiaries in several important markets throughout the world, such as Australia, Austria, Belgium, Brazil, Canada, England, France, Germany, Greece, Hong Kong, Israel, Italy, Japan, the Netherlands, New Zealand, South Africa, and Switzerland.

A subsidiary functions as the domestic manufacturer—it signs, develops, and records local talent and manufactures, distributes, and markets product. The subsidiary also releases product of the foreign parent company and its licensees. In territories where an international record company has no subsidiaries, it may license its catalog for manufacture and distribution to local companies. It may, however, maintain offices in some of these countries that sign, develop, and record local talent.

Independent U.S. record companies license their catalog for foreign distribution through either a worldwide deal with an international company or through individual deals with local companies in various foreign territories (*see* INTERNATIONAL MASTER RECORD LICENSING AGREEMENT). Some independent labels have offices in one or a small number of foreign countries, such as Canada, England, and France.

Licensees. A record manufacturer may have various licensees. A licensee manufactures and distributes records in accordance with terms of a negotiated contract. The domestic licensees of a record manufacturer include record/tape clubs, record merchandising companies, and program suppliers (e.g., airline, radio).

See also ADVERTISING; ALBUM COVER; AUDIT, ROYALTY; DISTRIBUTION OF RECORDS AND TAPES.

Record Company Deals. There are various kinds of "deals" (i.e., contracts) that record companies enter into with suppliers and users of master recordings. *Major* record companies (manufacturer/distributors) commonly enter into "deals" with proven producers and smaller labels, which supply masters in exchange for financing, distribution, promotion, and/or other services. At their best, such deals can be mutually beneficial. The major acquires the ingenuity and expertise of others without being directly involved in financing and developing the artist, and can promote their product and try to realize handsome profits with a minimal investment. The other party gets the use of large record company staff, facilities, and distribution which it does not otherwise enjoy. Major labels also license their own masters to special marketing companies which sell records and tapes through other than regular retail outlets. *Independent* record companies make deals that provide for the distribution of their product with major labels or independent distributors. Like the majors, they license their masters to special marketing companies. Among the many kinds of "deals" record companies enter into are the following:

Production Deal. Agreement entered into between a record company and a record producer (or production company), in which the producer promises to supply a stipulated number of masters during the contract period. These may be recordings of artists of his own choosing or those designated by the record company, or both. The cost of making the recordings is financed by the record company. The producer, who is normally paid on an advance and royalty basis, devises a recording

Record Company Position/Department Summary

Title	Function
President (Domestic and International	Supervises and oversees operations of domestic company and all foreign subsidiaries; makes major decisions
President (Domestic)	Oversees all domestic label operations
A & R	Seeks talent for the label and finds songs for the artists
A & R Administration	Handles clerical aspects of A & R
Business Affairs	Negotiates contracts with artists wanted by A & R
Accounting Dept. (VP Finance)	Oversees financial affairs—disbursements for expenses, payroll, manufacturing payments, etc., and collection of bills
Royalty Dept.	Prepares royalty statements and oversees remittances to artists, producers, publishers, associated labels, etc.
Marketing VP	Supervises business activities that create public awareness of product and artists; oversees and coordinates work of all marketing departments
Advertising	Produces/designs advertisements (print ads or radio and TV spots); plans advertising space and/or time
Art (Creative Services)	Designs album covers
Artist Development	Oversees career growth of artist through touring, television, etc.
College	Handles promotion, sales, and merchandising at college level
Manufacturing (Production) or Inventory Control Dept.	Determines and orders quantities of records to be pressed; maintains inventory levels
Merchandising	Oversees making of point-of-purchase materials
Promotion (VP)	Plans promotion campaigns; oversees all promotion activities
Publicity	Promotes artist and product in media
Sales (VP)	Plans sales campaigns, determines policies, takes orders, and oversees local sales activity
Regional VPs	Coordinate activities of distribution branches in their territories
Distribution branch (field office)	
Advertising coordinator	Buys or pays for ads of local accounts featuring label product
Field merchandiser	Sets up in-store displays at local retail accounts
Inventory clerk	Takes inventory of label product at local accounts
Manager	Supervises branch activities, oversees campaigns
Promotion worker	Gets airplay for new releases on local level
Salesperson	Sells records and tapes to local accounts

budget with the label which includes his advance (this is recoupable against future royalties). Where the artist is signed to the producer, the royalties received from the record company will include both the producer's and the artist's royalties (referred to as the "all-inclusive" or "all-in" royalty). The producer in turn pays the artist whatever is called for by the terms of his recording contract with the artist.

In a production deal, the producer is given artistic control. The copyrights in the sound recordings are normally owned by the record company. Records and tapes are manufactured under the name and/or logo of the label, which provides the normal record company services, such as marketing, merchandising, advertising, sales, promotion, and distribution. (If the company is not a major label, these services may be provided by virtue of an agreement it may have with such a label.)

Record companies enter into production deals with independent record producers who have strong track records and are known to deliver commercial and competitive product.

Label Deal. Agreement entered into between a record manufacturer/distributor and a label (i.e., a smaller record company; labels that enter into such agreements are commonly called *associated, affiliated,* or *custom* labels), under which the label's operations (recording costs and operating expenses) may be partially or entirely financed by the major, which manufactures and distributes the label's product. The label decides which artists to sign, negotiates their recording contracts, and decides which product shall be released and when. The agreement provides for the label to receive an all-inclusive royalty on each unit sold, this rate normally ranging from 13% to 18% of the retail list price (the rate may be higher, depending upon the top range of royalties on recordings at the time), and is usually based on 100% of records sold. Moneys given to finance the label are considered advances and are recoupable from future royalties due the label.

A custom label usually has to have a modest staff of its own. It may coordinate marketing, promotion, merchandising, and publicity campaigns for product released, but often these are carried out by, or with substantial help from, the distributor. All records and tapes manufactured under a label agreement bear the logo of the label (though there is always a statement on such product naming the manufacturer/distributor). On occasion, the distributor's logo will also be displayed prominently on the label and packaging.

In terms of territory of distribution, label deals may relate to a particular area or to the entire world. Many smaller labels try to maximize their potential earnings by reserving the right to make separate distribution deals outside the U.S. and Canada. However, new or young companies or those without substantial track records may find they have no choice but to give up worldwide rights to their catalog to obtain the deal for the United States.

A typical key contractual term is who shall have the ownership of the sound recordings (masters) supplied by the label. A distributor

may believe that by financing the recording costs it should own them, and will therefore negotiate for their ownership. It is considered very desirable by small labels to arrive at a contract that provides for initial ownership by the distributor, with ownership reverting to the label after a certain number of years (usually ten).

Some labels are owned jointly (i.e., with the distributor). Under this type of deal, the major typically has worldwide distribution rights. The label and the distributor share equally in paying all expenses and divide the net profits, usually on a 50/50 basis.

Distribution Deal. In this type of deal entered into between a record manufacturer/distributor and a label, the distributor will manufacture and distribute records and tapes and remit a fixed price or royalty for each unit sold, retaining the balance for its manufacturing and distributing costs plus its profit. The label handles marketing, merchandising, promotion, advertising, and publicity for its releases. A distributor has no copyright ownership in the sound recordings and the label usually receives no financing from the distributor.

Licensing Deals. Record manufacturers license their masters to different kinds of users, including record and tape clubs, record merchandising companies, mail order merchandisers, and program suppliers and syndicators. These companies manufacture and distribute LPs and/or tapes embodying such masters, paying a royalty, a flat licensing fee, or a fixed fee per unit. Licensing agreements are limited in duration and are normally confined to a particular territory of distribution. An independent label without foreign subsidiaries or affiliates may license masters for manufacture and distribution abroad (*see* INTERNATIONAL MASTER RECORDING LICENSING AGREEMENT).

Independent Distribution. A record company without sales offices and without a distribution arrangement with a major record manufacturer will enter into agreements with independent distributors. There may be several of these, each representing the label's catalog in a particular territory, or one or a small number handling distribution on a national basis. The label assumes all the other responsibilities of a regular record company. The independent distributor buys product from the label at a price set by the independent manufacturer. The independent distributor then sells to the same retailers and subdistributors the distribution branches of the majors sell to. Labels that enter into this type of agreement are sometimes described as "independent record companies."

Record License. *See* COMPULSORY/MECHANICAL LICENSES (PHONORECORDS).

Record Manufacturing. Record manufacturing is the process through which the recording of a performance (usually stored on magnetic tape and made in a studio or concert location) is made into a relatively inexpensive record commercially pressed in large volume and sold in retail stores. This procedure involves three general steps: *mastering, plating,* and *pressing.* Each is a delicate operation which must be carefully attended to in order to ensure a final product of satisfactory quality. A simple mistake or carelessness at any stage can result in records that must be scrapped after pressing, or that exhibit ticks, pops, surface noise, and other types of noise that will render the final product unplayable in the home.

Mastering. Mastering is the process through which the material on a MASTER tape is engraved into the surface of a lacquer or master disc. It can be undertaken only in a special facility known as a disc cutting or record mastering studio. Very few recording studios have record cutting or mastering facilities. In addition, the process requires highly specialized disc cutting equipment and specially trained engineers.

The finished, 2-channel master tape is usually sent to the cutting facility "tails out" (in the "played" position). At the "head," or front, of the master tape, there is generally a section with reference tones which are used to align the tape recorder used in the cutting process to that on which the master tape was recorded. These alignment or reference tones are used throughout the entire tape recording process to ensure that the intrinsic octave-to-octave balance in the music is preserved and that no section of the audible spectrum is emphasized or deemphasized in the recording, dubbing, mixdown, and mastering processes. These tones are traceable to a "standard alignment tape" which is used to align the machines employed at the original recording session, ensuring conformity with recording industry standard levels, flat audio response, tape recording equalization, and flat frequency response. Once the playback machine in the cutting facility is adjusted to match the machine on which the master tape was made, the actual cutting process can proceed.

A blank lacquer disc is used as the medium into which the grooves will be cut. The blank lacquer is actually an aluminum disc very carefully coated on both sides with cellulose nitrate, or similar material, to an almost optically flat finish. The soft coating enables the cutting stylus, which is heated both to facilitate cutting and to produce clean and smooth groove walls, to form the grooves easily. The lacquer blank used to master 12-inch LPs is actually larger, measuring about 14 inches in diameter. The outer segment, or periphery, has a twofold purpose. Initially, it is used to adjust the cutting-stylus temperature, check the thickness of the coating (to determine maximum groove depth), and perhaps to test-cut some loud portion of the tape or even inscribe a test tone—all before the actual cutting begins. Subsequently, during pressing, it is this rim that secures the outer edge of the stamper in place in the record press.

The cutting turntable, or "lathe," is provided with a vacuum system used to hold the lacquer blank securely to the lathe platen in order to prevent slippage of the disc and to remove the fine thread of laquer that is cut away from the blank by the cutting stylus during the engraving of the groove into its surface. The vacuum system operates through a special tube attached to the cutting head itself.

The cutting head, which contains the cutting stylus (generally made from a synthetic ruby), is driven radially over the lacquer blank by a screw-type drive. The rate of turning and the pitch of the screw establish the distance, or "land," between grooves. The spacing of the grooves may be set manually through the screw drive, or automatically through a special "preview" head, which "plays" the tape into a small computer and senses the material before the standard playback head on the tape machine feeds it to the cutting head and its amplifier. Anticipating loud passages before they reach the cutting head, the preview head "orders" the drive screw to space out the grooves in order to accommodate the loud passages. It also senses the soft passages, and it instructs the cutting-head screw drive to constrict the grooves, which in turn permits longer playing time per side. Loud passages, particularly those with a great deal of bass or low-frequency energy, cause very wide and deep grooves to be cut into the lacquer. Great attention and constant visual inspection (most often with a microscope) are necessary to make certain that the absolute level selected for a particular recording is not so great that during the loudest passage the cutting stylus will literally lift off the lacquer (making the groove disappear) or cut so deeply that the stylus will pierce the lacquer coating and reach the aluminum core. If the mixing engineer was careful with levels, equalization, and compression during mixdown (with a view toward ultimately cutting and pressing a record), no surprises should be in store for the cutting engineer. However, it is not unusual for a cutting engineer to have to "compress" (using a compressor to limit the level of loudness of the loudest parts) in order to be able to cut the material on the tape onto a lacquer master. This and any other adjustments required in cutting a master tape are really not the job of the cutting engineer.

For these reasons, as well as others, a "reference" lacquer is sometimes cut before the final lacquer master, to permit the cutting engineer, producer, and artists to evaluate such factors as absolute level on the record, playback distortion during loud level passages, etc. Any such checking must occur prior to the cutting of the lacquer master to be used for plating. The groove walls cut into a lacquer are very soft and playback can damage the grooves and obliterate some of the high-frequency (treble) information engraved on the groove walls.

Lacquer blanks used for mastering are either 10 or 12 inches in diameter for 7-inch, 45-rpm singles, or 14 inches in diameter for 12-inch LPs (played at either 33⅓ or 45 rpm), for the reasons given previously. Reference lacquers are usually made with 12-inch blanks for LPs and with 8- or 10-inch blanks for singles.

Once the master lacquer is cut, it is imperative that it be plated as soon as possible. Due to the somewhat elastic quality of the lacquer, and other factors, such as oxidation, the groove walls and the sound modulations engraved thereon tend to change shape and become mechanically distorted. The longer the period between cutting and plating, the greater the deterioration of the groove walls will be.

Plating. At the plating plant, the master lacquer is electroplated in a process that ultimately yields the stampers used to press the actual records. Since the lacquer coating of the master disc is not a conductor of electricity (necessary for electroplating), it is first coated with a very thin layer of silver solution. Several solutions, including silver salts, are sprayed onto the rotating lacquer master (mounted on a special turntable). Chemical reaction generates the silver coating that is deposited on the surface of the lacquer. After cleaning, the silvered disc master is lowered into a "plating" bath, where nickel is electroplated onto the silvered surface of the master disc (some facilities rotate the silvered disc master while the electroplating is in process to ensure even nickel deposit) to a heavy thickness (the thickness of the nickel coating tends to vary from plating plant to plating plant). The temperature of the electroplating solution, the purity of the water, the concentration of the salts in the bath, and other factors will affect the quality of the electroplating and ultimately the quality of the record.

When the initial electroplating is over, the master disc is removed from the plating bath and the nickel coat is carefully peeled off the lacquer surface (sometimes the lacquer master is damaged during this operation). The nickel coat, called a "master," is a negative replicate of the lacquer disc; that is, the grooves protrude from the surface and have become "ridges." The nickel master is carefully cleaned and then mounted on a strong backing, usually made of a copper compound, and put into the plating bath once again for electroplating. This time the result is a coat that, when peeled off the nickel master, is the identical copy of the lacquer disc. It is called a metal "mother."

The mother is now mounted on a metal backing for support and dipped into the plating bath for another electroplating procedure, the coating of which yields another negative metal part, called a "stamper." The metal mother can be electroplated many times to produce stampers as may be required to produce the number of finished records ordered from the pressing plants. When records are to be produced in very large quantities, several metal mothers are produced to generate in turn the required number of stampers. In some cases, even several lacquer disc masters are cut to be able to generate the number of records to be pressed. The life of a stamper is finite. Depending on the specifics of the record pressing operation (temperatures, operator, raw vinyl materials, cycling time, etc.), a stamper can deteriorate after 500 to 750 operations, although it may be used for up to several thousand pressings, depending on the demand for the quality of the finished record. The life of other metal parts is limited as well (nickel master and mother), but usually they meet their demise through age or damage in one of the steps of replating rather than through wear.

Pressing. This is the process through which the actual vinyl record is formed, in large hydraulic presses. The stampers, one for each side of the record, are mounted on the press. The rim of each stamper is crimped and its edge "coined" to the press, and pins at its center secure it there (these pins ultimately form the center hole of the record). One stamper is secured to the upper side of the press (called the "head"), the reverse-side stamper to the bottom part of the press (called the "platen"). In most record presses, it is the platen that moves up to close the press during the pressing operation. The stampers are carefully centered on the press and with respect to each other so that the reverse impressions will match perfectly. In a typical operation, the operator places a preheated lower label on the bottom stamper first. Then he places a preheated, premeasured "biscuit," or "shot," dispensed by a special vinyl dispenser, at the center of the bottom stamper. The upper label is placed on top of the biscuit. The press is now closed with a pressure of about 110 to 120 tons/square inch and permitted to remain so for 20 to 30 seconds while steam under pressure (at about 130 pounds/square inch) is circulated through ducts to heat the press and the vinyl—sufficiently long to ensure that the vinyl biscuit has

Manufacturing finished records from a studio tape recording involves a series of steps. After the original tape recording is mixed, the "master mix" is sent to a mastering facility where a lacquer disc is cut. This disc is sent to a plating plant where stampers are ultimately derived, which are then used to press records. These photographs depict some of the major steps in the plating and pressing processes as well as through packaging. They are in the order shown: (*from top to bottom*) mastering, silver spraying, electroplating, separating the nickel coat from the master disc, crimping the stampers, visual inspection, sleeving, jacketing, shrink wrapping, and warehousing.

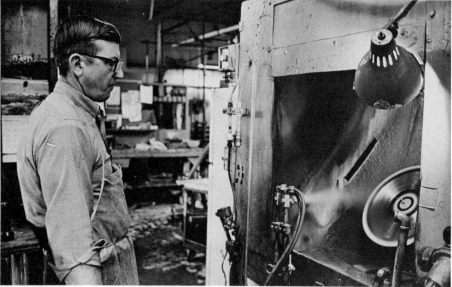

spread through and conformed to every nook and cranny, representing the groove and groove walls of the stamper.

After the press, the stampers, and what is now the vinyl record, are cooled by cold water running through ducts within the press (at a water pressure of some 160 pounds/square inch). The press is then opened and the record carefully removed. Upon its removal, excess vinyl "flashing" in the form of a ragged edge at the outside of the record must be trimmed off. At this point the record is warm and is quite pliable, so it must be handled very carefully and stored on a completely flat surface as it further cools, to prevent warping. The label, incidentally, is not glued on but is fused to the vinyl through the heat, pressure, and action of the hydraulic press. For temporary storage purposes prior to packaging, the freshly pressed discs are stacked on a spindle to cool, with separators stacked between every 10 to 12 records.

There are some pertinent factors concerning the actual record pressing. The vinyl biscuit which is automatically dispensed by a machine is not only heated (to about 310 degrees F.) but automatically weighed. Approximately 140 grams of the vinyl mixture are dispensed for a 12-inch LP. The exact weight depends on what the thickness of the record is to be after pressing. About 50 grams are normally used for a 7-inch single. The vinyl biscuit is not composed exclusively of pure PVC (polyvinyl chloride), but contains: lubricants to act as release agents, facilitating removal of the disc from the stampers without sticking or tearing of the grooves; carbon black or dyes to color the clear vinyl material and purportedly to distribute the heat more uniformly during the pressing process; plasticizers and stabilizers to keep the materials homogeneously blended during the pressing operation and to keep the vinyl from becoming brittle with time; and other types of vinyl, such as polyvinyl acetate to help the mixture conform to the very small high-frequency modulations of the stamper. The exact mixtures are proprietary and thus vary. Some advantages are claimed by individual companies for specific materials added to the biscuit.

The basic material used for records is not always virgin vinyl (that is, PVC which has never been used before), purchased from large chemical companies in the form of small pellets. Some records, usually but not always of the "budget" variety, are made with recycled vinyl—salvaged from the flashing trimmed off the finished record, from scrapped defective pressings, record store returns, etc. Although recycled vinyl is not necessarily inferior (low-grade vinyl produces a noisier or a defective record) the chances of impurities are many times greater than with virgin vinyl.

Record presses are manufactured in manual and automatic varieties. Whereas in a manual press the operator has to insert labels and biscuit, close and open the press, circulate both the heating steam and the cooling water, time and open the press, remove the pressed disc, trim the flashing off and carefully stack the record on the storage spindle, the fully automatic press performs all these functions without attention from an operator. There are semiautomatic presses, too, which perform some or most of these functions automatically, usually with the exception of inserting the labels and biscuits and removing the finished record and trimming off its flashing. On manual presses, the flashing is removed by placing the record on a rotating turntable while a stationary knife trims the excess vinyl. Automatic presses use different methods to trim the flashing but are essentially similar in operation to the manual method.

Some 45 rpm singles are "injection molded." In this method, the stampers are mounted on the press in a way similar to that in the pressing type of operation. The labels are affixed to the center of the upper and lower stampers and the press is closed, whereupon a liquefied plastic compound is injected under enormous pressure to fill the cavity and conform to the groove shapes. Its proponents claim that injection molding yields a better record, with greater fidelity to the mechanical shapes of the stampers. The opposition asserts that injection molding produces a record with poorer playing characteristics and a shorter life. In the past, some record manufacturers have used polystyrene rather than vinyl-based compounds. Injection molding for audio discs, at present, is not as prevalent as the compression pressing method.

Once the record is ready for packaging, it is first visually inspected. A random selection from each "batch" and each set of stampers may be subjected to a thorough visual and audio quality-control check. If the run is approved, the records are inserted, for dust protection, into their inner sleeves which in turn are put into outer jackets; these are shrink-wrapped and boxed in cartons of either 25 or 50 records and made ready for shipment from the factory. In most of the top record factories, all the procedures requiring handling are performed by operators wearing lintless cotton gloves to prevent fingerprints and body oils from contaminating the record grooves.

Playing a Record. As the record revolves on the turntable of a phonograph system and the tone arm and stylus, or needle, are brought onto the record, the stylus engages the "lead-in" groove and is brought to the beginning of the modulations in the groove walls. These modulations deflect the stylus in motions conforming to the shape of the undulations of the groove walls, which in turn conform to the original disturbances of the air created by the musical performance and transmitted to the groove walls via the microphones, tape recorders, cutting head and stylus, plating and pressing. The phonograph cartridge converts the mechanical motions of the playback stylus into electrical impulses, or signals, which are amplified by the audio amplifier of the pho-

nograph system and fed to the loudspeakers. The speakers accept the amplified electrical signals and convert them into disturbances of the air, thus creating "sound"—that is, producing air vibrations similar to those produced by the instruments during the original performances.

Record Merchandising Company. A company that licenses master recordings from one or more different record manufacturers, packages them in COMPILATION ALBUMS, and markets them through special distribution channels and promotion campaigns is referred to as a *record merchandising company* or a *record merchandiser*. Because these companies so often market such product on television, they are popularly referred to as "TV album marketers." Customers may purchase the product of these companies through the mail or at certain designated ("key") retail outlets.

It is not uncommon for a record merchandising company to spend a couple of hundred thousand dollars per national television advertising campaign or gross $10 million or more annually from such sales. Its method of operation as well as its product have proved to be popular with the public. Record merchandisers offer: an album that contains all hits (regular albums normally contain no more than a few), albums that sell at relatively low prices, the convenience of ordering in the home, and fast and reliable service. They are also able to reach people who ordinarily do not visit record stores.

On the other hand, advertising time is expensive, as are postage costs, and it is not always possible to predict public taste accurately. For these reasons, there has been a high mortality rate among these companies. Prominent record merchandising companies include or have included K-Tel, Ronco, Sessions, Vista Marketing, Tee Vee Records, Tele House, and Dynamic House.

Method of Operation. The following is a

general description of how a record merchandiser packages an album featuring the recent hits of numerous artists:

Selects singles—The merchandiser has a panel that reviews the top 100 singles CHARTS in the trades for the most recent few months and picks out the singles it is interested in (compilation albums may contain very recent hits, older hits, or combinations of these).

Contacts labels and negotiates licenses—The merchandiser then contacts the record companies that own the copyrights in these sound recordings. It may deal with the special products department, the company president, or the A & R VP. The merchandiser requests permission from the company to use the particular track for its purposes (sound recordings are *not* subject to compulsory licensing). If the company is interested, the two parties negotiate a royalty license. Royalty rates usually range from $.02 to $.05 per unit sold (merchandisers market product in LP, cassette, and 8-track tape configurations simultaneously). Occasionally, the record company (or "licensor") will insist on a higher royalty rate for cassette or cartridge tapes, as the retail prices for these are usually $1 higher than for LPs. For example, LPs might be licensed at a rate of $.03 per unit and tapes at $.035 per unit.

Advances are often paid by merchandisers to the master track owners and are recoupable against future royalties. An advance is based on a sales projection. Sales projections typically range from 10,000 to 1 million units. A royalty advance based on 10,000 units at $.03 each, for example, would be $300; for a million units, $30,000. In cases where the royalty rate is higher for tapes than for LPs, the advance is usually based on the royalty rate for LPs but held recoupable against royalties earned from unit sales of all configurations.

Contacts publishers and negotiates licenses—After approval is given by the record company and a royalty license is satisfactorily negotiated, the merchandiser contacts the copyright owner (music publisher) of the song in the recording to negotiate a mechanical license royalty rate (songs *are* subject to compulsory licensing). Merchandisers aim to pay a rate ranging from 50% to 75% of the statutory royalty rate (they rarely license a composition at the full statutory rate and in some cases are able to negotiate a rate lower than 50%). If a mutually satisfactory royalty rate cannot be negotiated between merchandiser and copyright owner, this could kill the deal, despite the fact that a license was successfully negotiated with the sound recording copyright owner. There are also publisher advances given in the same proportion as to the record company.

Compiles master tapes—Once licenses have been successfully negotiated with both the record company and the music publisher, each record company whose track will be used in the album sends the merchandiser a master recording (either 7½ ips quarter-track or 15 ips half-track).

Sequences the selections and manufactures product—After all the master tapes have been received, the merchandiser sends the tapes out (with sequencing instructions) to have the compilation album manufactured in LPs, 8-tracks, and cassettes. Manufactured product is shipped to the merchandiser's warehouse.

Markets the album—The merchandiser now advertises the product (typically on television and radio) and sells to consumers by direct response (i.e., mail order) or through certain "key" retail outlets it distributes to. Key retail outlets include variety stores, supermarkets, and certain other types of mass-merchandising stores (e.g., K-Mart, Woolco, J. C. Penney, and Sears). Merchandisers are normally prohibited in their agreements with the master track licensor from selling to regular retail record/tape stores, as their product might compete with sales of records and tapes issued by the record company.

FROM MASTER RECORDING TO PRESSED RECORDS

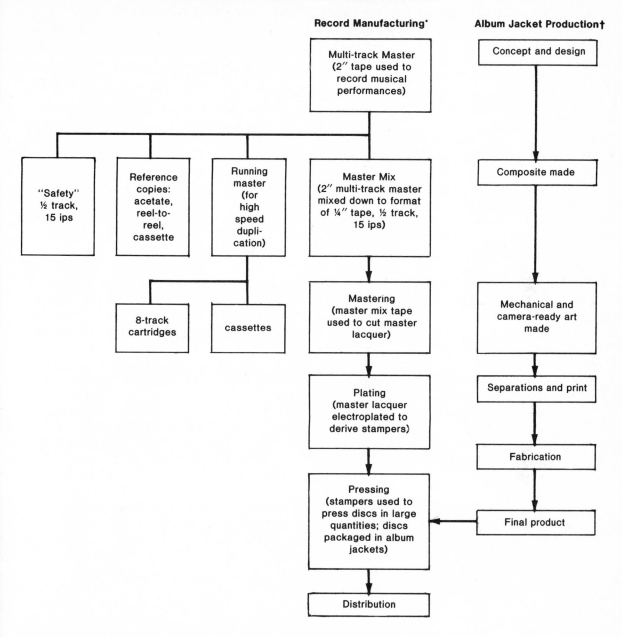

Record Manufacturing*

Album Jacket Production†

Multi-track Master
(2″ tape used to record musical performances)

"Safety"
½ track, 15 ips

Reference copies: acetate, reel-to-reel, cassette

Running master (for high speed duplication)

Master Mix
(2″ multi-track master mixed down to format of ¼″ tape, ½ track, 15 ips)

Concept and design

Composite made

8-track cartridges

cassettes

Mastering
(master mix tape used to cut master lacquer)

Mechanical and camera-ready art made

Plating
(master lacquer electroplated to derive stampers)

Separations and print

Fabrication

Pressing
(stampers used to press discs in large quantities; discs packaged in album jackets)

Final product

Distribution

*Recording and mixing are usually done at the same recording studio; mastering, plating, and pressing are generally done at separate facilities.

†Steps in album jacket production do not necessarily correspond in time to those of record manufacturing, as shown.

Record Pool. Service organization whose main function is to distribute to its members—disco DJs and discotheque operators—disco and dance records supplied by record companies, and in turn provide the record companies with feedback regarding their product.

The record, or disco, pool was born as a result of the proliferation of discotheques in the mid 1970s, to aid both record companies and disco DJs. For the record company it is a way of getting disco records played quickly, even before radio. The pool may be used to distribute unreleased product to disco DJs, who give feedback on the product based on audience response (this may be considered a form of "free" marketing analysis). Such response may guide the record company in its marketing campaign. For example, a poor response may induce the company to remix the record, have a small initial pressing, or not release it at all. A favorable response may result in a large pressing and a heavy promotion campaign.

Record pools require members to gauge public reaction from the records they play and put this information into feedback sheets, along with their personal reactions. Someone from the pool will compare the information given on the feedback sheets and evaluate the overall response.

The record pool is of service to disco DJs and discotheque operators because it is a central source from which they can acquire—promptly, continuously, and free of charge—the records they need. Otherwise they would have to devote much time to contacting each label to obtain new releases or buy them when they became available at the retail level.

Disco pools normally will not supply member disco DJs with product unless they are actually working in that capacity. The pool head will screen applicants and make periodic checks to verify members' employment status.

The record pool may also be of benefit to recording artists and, indirectly, to the public.

As the interests of recording artists parallel those of record companies, exposure from play of their records in the discos may result in increased record sales and consequently higher earnings. Disco patrons are exposed to records the DJ may not otherwise have known about or played.

A record pool may provide other services. It may teach new skills to disco DJs, act as a job placement service, provide trade publications and radio stations with charts of the top disco records in an area by compiling the information it receives from its members, promote artists by sponsoring guest appearances and autograph-signing parties, supply record company promotion workers with updated lists of active members and the clubs where they are employed, send informative newsletters to its members, record companies, record promoters, and other industry entities, and provide information to club owners that may result in better sound and lighting equipment in their establishments.

Record Producer. The record producer oversees all aspects in the making of an artist's recording. There are numerous creative and business responsibilities that are part of such supervision and these are summarized in the table on page 346.

Types of Record Producers. Record producers may be categorized into two basic types: *staff producers* and *independent producers*. Staff (or *in-house*) producers are employed exclusively by record companies to produce one or more artists signed to the label. They are salaried employees and many also have royalty contracts with their label. The independent producer produces artists or masters on a nonexclusive basis so that his services may be engaged by any label.

All record producers function to maximize an artist's talent on a recording and complete a technically (and often commercially) satisfactory product. The producer oversees the making of a MASTER from start to finish. The actual recording process itself may require several sessions. The artist may come into the studio to lay down his particular part only after the basic tracks have been recorded. Once the artist puts down his vocal he may not be involved in the recording process anymore, as the producer supervises subsequent sessions as well as postrecording chores such as mixing and editing. Clearly, the role of the producer is demanding and his efforts to a large degree guide the outcome of the recording.

The independent producer may be sought after by several record companies if he is known to work well with artists and to deliver strong commercial product. Some producers accept offers from a number of labels and arrange their schedule to produce the artists over a period of time. In this way, the producer will approach each artist's album as a project; when that album has been completed he will go on to the next artist.

There are "unproven" or "budding" record producers as well as established ones who can't get financing from a label who produce artists in the hope of making a deal with a record company. The prospect of large profits and the resultant reputation from having a "hit" record has induced many independent producers to invest their own money initially. It is also a way for unproven producers to demonstrate their ability or "break into" the business. It is in the interest of the producer who records an artist in anticipation of selling the masters to a label to have an agreement providing for the exclusive services of the artist, in connection with performing on master recordings, to be rendered to the producer for a certain period of time. A record company will usually require a guarantee that the artist will not record for another label and that future recordings by that artist over a specified peri-

od of time will be released on its label, usually for a period of 5 years from the date of the producer's agreement with the label. (*See* RECORD COMPANY DEALS.)

Executive Record Producer. Industry personnel make reference to an "executive" record producer. His role is essentially noncreative but such a person is involved in the making of a recording, as he is the superior or employer of a staff producer or an independent producer. For example, a staff producer may report to the A & R chief or other label executive who might have this title; likewise, the executive or proprietor of the production company that employs the independent producer might use this title.

The executive record producer works in various ways. He might match artist with producer, determine the recording budget, select the studio, and hire other people to complete the project. In some cases, he puts the whole package together. He may also be involved in the marketing, merchandising, advertising, and promotion of the recordings. Personal managers, investors, and other profit participants often act as executive producers.

Salaries, Advances, and Royalty Rates. Staff producers earn salaries from their record company employers and often have a royalty participation in the albums they produce. In such cases, royalty rates range from 1% to 4% of the retail list price and are frequently based on 90% of records sold.

Independent record producers usually work on an advance-against-royalties basis. Their royalty rates are higher than those of the staff producers. A producer with a production agreement in which the artist is signed to him receives from the record manufacturer a royalty that includes the artist's royalty (this is sometimes referred to as the "all-in" royalty). In such case, the producer's royalty rate may range from 10% to 18% of the retail list price. The producer in turn pays the artist his royalty in accordance with their negotiated agreement, commonly at a rate of 5% to 9%. Royalties paid to the producer again may be paid on 90% of sales. Of course, the record manufacturer recoups its advances paid from the independent record producer's royalty, who in turn recoups recording costs from the artist's royalty.

Production companies and other independent producers who produce artists signed to a label are paid on a royalty basis plus an advance or fee, and receive their royalties from the company independently of the artists. Royalty rates in this case normally range from 2% to 4% of the retail sales price and are frequently based on 90% of records sold.

Role of the Producer. A variety of responsibilities come under the heading of record producer. Producers, however, vary in the extent to which they get involved—both creatively and administratively—in producing a recording. Whether a producer is on the staff of a label or is independent also determines the degree and kind of involvement.

In general, the responsibilities of the *independent* record producer may be summarized by the table below.

Other Aspects. Much of the production work in the studio requires a considerable knowledge of recording techniques: the different types of equipment in the studio, how they work, their capabilities, the "sounds" that

The Record Producer's Role

Stage of Production	Creative Responsibilities	Business Responsibilities
Prerecording	Finds/signs talent (or is assigned by label) Establishes relationship or dialogue with artist Discusses with the label a direction for artist and recordings Reviews/selects material to be recorded Rehearses artist (works out right styling, phrasing, tempo, structure of songs, etc.)	Interests label in making a deal; negotiates production contract Anticipates budget and itemizes expenses Collects advance or fee Hires arranger, music copyist Hires contractor (who hires musicians and background vocalists; producer may select these participants) Selects studio, books time (makes arrangements for special instrument rentals)
Recording	Supervises sessions (guides the participants and technical aspects) Offers advice and ideas (maximizes the artist's talent on the recordings) Inspires momentum, confidence, and enthusiasm in the studio Creates the desired "sound" (decides which special effects to use) Monitors the recording into an artistic and/or commercial product	Monitors recording expenses (tries to keep within budget) Oversees union and studio paperwork
Postrecording	Mixes and edits tracks (or hires specialist) Oversees mastering Helps sequence tracks on album Helps select tracks to be released as "singles"	Delivers master tapes to label Informs record company of label credits (names of songs, writers, times, etc.) Sees that record company makes timely payments of bills (studio, talent, etc.) Suggests ideas for marketing, advertising, promotion Monitors progress of record/tape sales Collects royalties (pays artist his royalties if signed to producer)

can be achieved, options available, etc. This knowledge is usually obtained through much experience in the studio, a reason why record producing is a field into which engineers, recording artists, musicians, and arrangers gradually move—and why many producers contribute to the making of recordings in various other capacities. Many also own publishing companies and are involved in personal management.

Independent producers who earn substantial royalties frequently set up production companies for tax purposes. Under this arrangement, royalties are paid to the company rather than the individual, so that corporate expenses may be deducted and royalties are not taxable, as they are for an individual.

Historical Aspects. Traditionally, the record producer's role in making records has been essentially creative. In the early days of commercial recording, the producer was a salaried employee of a record company who would be assigned to produce artists on the label's roster. Finding the talent and the material to record was principally the job of the A & R men. The producer was sometimes a member of the A & R staff, and likewise, A & R men sometimes functioned as record producers.

Recording equipment and techniques used prior to the advent of singles, LPs, and stereo were relatively simple. There was no overdubbing or mixing, and masters would be completed in no more than a few sessions. After the producer made a master, his job ended with respect to that particular recording.

With the rise of rock 'n' roll in the 1950s, a practice developed whereby producers not employed by record companies would seek talent and record it, either with the prior approval of a label, which would finance the production, or out of their own pockets, in which case they had to "shop around" after completion of the masters and try to make a deal. These individuals became known as "independent" producers, or "indies."

This new breed of producers was more innovative than their counterparts in record companies, what with their appreciation for the music young people wanted to hear and their knowledge of developing tape recording techniques and use of them in the studio. Also during the 1950s, many small labels formed, and released the so-called race records, which the major companies were generally reluctant to issue. The proprietors of these small labels themselves often produced the artists signed to the companies. If such a label's release achieved local success, it would often be purchased by a major and promoted on a national basis.

By the late 1960s, other changes had been made or were beginning to be made in the production arena. The trend toward independent producing had boomed and the larger record companies were now employing only marginal staffs of producers. Artists frequently produced their own recordings, women actively entered the production field, and independent producers attained greater financial participation and artistic control than ever before, and even took a hand in guiding the destiny of their product. Producers formed companies that entered into production deals with record companies, and in some cases, label deals. Even staff producers were able to receive small royalties in addition to their salaries.

Consequently the producer's role today is much more diversified and increasingly complex. His job no longer ends after he submits his masters to the record company. Instead he has much input into such postproduction campaigns as marketing, merchandising, advertising, and promotion, and is involved in the overall career-building of the artist.

Record Promotion. *See* RECORD COMPANY.

Record Reviewers. *See* MUSIC CRITICS AND REVIEWS.

Record and Tape Club. A "membership" organization in which subscribers agree to purchase a minimum number of records or tapes (usually under a "negative option plan"—see below) within a given period of time. The incentive for a person to become a subscriber is from the club's initial offer of several records or tapes at no charge or at a very low cost to those who agree to the terms of membership as set forth in the advertisement.

Membership may be terminated at any time after the subscriber has ordered the minimum number of albums required, although written notification must be received by the club; otherwise the member will continue to receive the monthly announcements and response cards (see below). The customer assumes the cost of shipping and handling. Record and tape clubs attract customers through advertisements they place in magazines, newspapers, and other media, and by direct mail.

Record and tape clubs offer members hundreds of selections to choose from each month in many musical categories, including rock, soul, easy listening (instrumental and vocal), Broadway-Hollywood-TV, country jazz, and classical. Customers may be able to order albums in any of the following configurations: stereo records, 8-track cartridges, tape cassettes, and reel-to-reel tape. Record and tape clubs offer the convenience of buying merchandise in the home (particularly for those who are unable to or do not regularly shop at retail outlets), and the opportunity to select from a wide variety of product.

Negative Option Marketing. The major record and tape clubs (e.g., Columbia Record and Tape Club, RCA Music Service) market their merchandise via a *negative option plan*, or *prenotification plan*, as it is commonly known. This is a contractual arrangement under which a seller periodically sends to its members an announcement identifying merchandise it will ship and bill unless an enclosed response (negative option) card is re-

turned by a particular date, or within a specified period of time, with instructions to send no merchandise at all or an alternate selection described in the announcement.

Positive Option Plan. Some small specialized record and tape clubs may market their merchandise under a positive option system. Here, subscribers receive advance notice of the offerings but must affirmatively order the monthly selections.

Licensing Agreements. Record and tape clubs enter into licensing agreements with record companies to manufacture, advertise, distribute, and sell their product. Following is a discussion of some of the important provisions of record and tape club licensing agreements with record companies.

Manufacturing. Licensing agreements normally stipulate that product manufactured by the club must be identical in quality and appearance to the label's product (club-manufactured product, however, will normally contain a line stating it was manufactured by the club). The "licensor" (record company) will supply masters, film, and other parts for manufacture. Licensing agreements normally entitle the "licensee" (record and tape club) to manufacture records and tapes of all the product in the label's catalog. Some contracts have stipulated that the club may not market new releases before a specified period of time.

Geographic and Marketing Restrictions. Licensing agreements commonly grant to the licensee the nonexclusive right to manufacture, advertise, distribute, and sell records and tapes manufactured from master recordings supplied by the licensor in the United States. Canada is frequently included in the territory, except where the licensor has already assigned those rights to a retail licensee in Canada. Sale of product is also restricted to record club offerings; the licensee may not sell through other mail order plans or retail outlets.

Duration of Agreement and Sell-off Period. Licensing agreements are effective for a limited time period, commonly 2 or 3 years. At the expiration of such period and in the absence of a new or extended agreement, the licensee is contractually restricted from any further manufacturing of records and tapes duplicating the performances embodied in the licensor's master tape recordings. The licensee must also, at the licensor's request, either return or destroy the master recordings supplied by the licensor, as well as matrices, stampers, and other devices that may be used to reproduce the performances embodied in the masters. There normally follows a sell-off period, during which the licensee may advertise and sell any unsold merchandise manufactured prior to the expiration date.

Manufacturing Costs. The licensee normally assumes the responsibility and costs incurred for manufacturing records and tapes from the master tape recording supplied to it by the licensor and for the creation and production of album packagings such as jackets, sleeves, cartridges, shrink wrap, and other materials.

Copyright Notice. The licensee is required to affix the copyright notice for sound recordings on the album cover and/or labels of each phonograph record and tape manufactured and sold bearing the licensor's name if the sound recording was "fixed" (recorded) on or after February 15, 1972.

Advance/Royalties. Record and tape clubs typically pay an advance to a licensor for the right to manufacture, advertise, and sell recordings made from its master tape recordings. Such advances are normally nonreturnable and are recoupable from royalties payable to the licensor under the agreement.

In 1981, the royalty rate used by one major club for record and tape sales was 9.5% of the selling price less a packaging deduction, with royalties payable on 85% of net sales. For classical and sound track albums it used a royalty rate of 12% on the same basis. From such royalties received, the record company in turn pays the artist and/or producer their royalties in accordance with their recording agreements.

Record World. *See* CHARTS; TRADES.

Recording. Recording is the process of "storing" the performances of instrumentalists and vocalists on magnetic tape. Records and prerecorded tapes are ultimately made from a master tape which is derived from the original tapes made in a RECORDING STUDIO. Original tapes are almost always made in multi-track formats and the recording process involves various stages. This entry delineates how recordings are effected and a master is produced.

The making of a recording begins after all the preliminary steps are completed: preproduction planning, rehearsing, hiring, scheduling, etc. The first recording session, or "date," generally occurs after the A & R coordinator, the producer, and the artist have discussed and agreed to the orientation of and creative strategy for the recording, the material to be recorded has been selected and arranged, and has been adequately rehearsed by the artist. By this time, a contractor has been engaged to hire the necessary instrumentalists to complete the ensemble, plus any desired background vocalists. Once the budget for recording has been established and appropriated, a studio location is selected (or a number of different studios, if recording in different cities and times is required), recording time is booked, and all preproduction details are finalized.

In analog or conventional recording (certainly the most prevalent kind as of this writing), original tapes are made on multi-track recorders capable of producing tapes with 4, 8, 16, 24, or more individual or separate tracks. In some instances, two or more recorders with this type of capability are synchro-

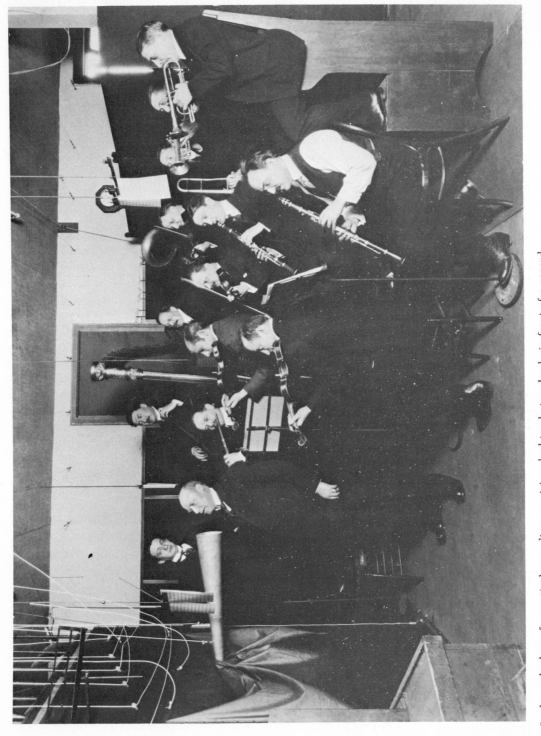

In the early days of acoustical recording, musicians had to cluster closely in front of a recording horn in order for the sounds of the instruments to be picked up.

nized to operate virtually as one machine via the use of a synchronizing device such as a SMPTE time code generator. Although one track per machine must be used as the synchronizing track to carry the time code, the net effect is greater flexibility in the recording through a number of individual tracks. For example, if 16-track and 24-track machines are used, the total number of usable tracks will be 38 (40 tracks total: 2 for time code and 38 open for recording); two 24-track machines synchronized offer 46 usable tracks (48 tracks total: 2 for time code and 46 open for recording). In very rare cases, three machines may be synchronized to achieve the required number of tracks for a recording. If, for example, only 8-track machines are available and more than 20 tracks are required, three 8-track machines may be synchronized to achieve 21 usable tracks (24 tracks total: 3 for time code and 21 open for recording).

The recording tracks occupy almost the full width of the tape—except for "guard bands" which serve to isolate adjacent tracks from each other—each track recording a separate and isolated input to the recorder itself. Original recordings, and the master tapes derived from them, usually run at speeds of 15 or 30 inches per second (ips); generally speaking, the higher the tape speed, the greater the dynamic range possible, the greater the "headroom" at high frequencies, and the lower the noise level on playback.

In multi-track recordings, different musical portions are recorded onto the different tracks in separate stages. While these stages vary somewhat from recording to recording, there appears to be one general rule: The *basic tracks* are recorded, or "laid down," first. The basic tracks generally consist of piano, rhythm guitar, bass, and drums. These instruments are sometimes assigned to separate or individual tracks. Depending upon the number of tracks available and the complexity of the recording, it may become necessary to record more than one instrument on one track (*see* pages 354–

55). However, when more than one instrument or voice or combination are recorded (or mixed) onto the same track, they cannot be separated later, during the MIXDOWN process, in order to vary the relative loudness of one instrument or voice. In such instances, the intrinsic balances, perspectives, timbres, etc., cannot be changed and are said to be "locked in."

The basic rhythm tracks are often recorded with a reference (or "scrap") vocal, which serves as a guide to the musicians while they're recording their tracks. The scrap vocal is never used in the final version, of course. The final lead vocal is generally dubbed over the scrap vocal through a process in which the scrap vocal is erased from its track at the same time that the lead vocal is recorded onto the same track.

After the basic rhythm tracks have been recorded, the overdubs are then laid down onto empty, available tracks. Subsequent sessions may consist, first, of the lead vocals, followed by background vocals, and additional sessions for the lead guitar, keyboards, and the various percussion instruments. A multi-track recording is said to be "sweetened" by the addition of string and horn parts. On those occasions where several of these instruments are to be recorded simultaneously at a single session, but on separate tracks, acoustical isolation between instruments is achieved by the use of acoustic "baffles," which absorb the sound energy from the individual instruments so that only that instrument's microphone(s) will receive the sound of the instrument, to record it onto its individual track. In this manner, if a particular instrument has to be rerecorded for any reason at a future session or dropped from the mix, it can be without affecting any other instrument or vocal recorded at the original session. In these cases, instrumentalists and vocalists who are laying down tracks at a session wear headphones which supply a "mix" of the sounds already on the tape plus those of any performers being recorded at that session, as a

HOW SOME "POP" RECORDINGS ARE MADE*

The first step in making a multi-track master recording is to "lay down" the basic (or rhythm) tracks. The drums, piano, bass guitar, and rhythm guitar are recorded on the first eight tracks or so. A reference ("scratch") vocal may guide the musicians in playing the song. The basic tracks are recorded first to lay the foundation on which the future overdubs will be built. When actually recording, the performers will be seated apart and perhaps acoustically isolated from one another with sound baffles.

Next, the lead singer records her part. Sometimes, the singer will record the part twice (known as *doubling*) to get a thicker, fuller sound.

The background singers then put down their part.

* Individual preferences of producers and availability of musicians and vocalists can affect the order in which the overdubs are recorded.

A string section (violins, violas, cellos) records on the next few tracks. The recording of these parts and those in the next picture is commonly referred to as *sweetening*.

Horn and woodwind players put down their parts on the next few tracks.

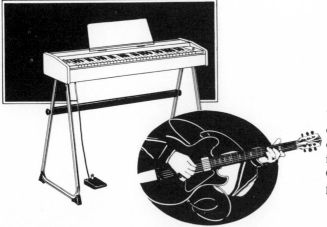

Various instruments will separately be recorded on the remaining open tracks to give the recording a particular sound, create special effects, or complete the arrangement of the song. Overdubbed most frequently are electronic and percussion instruments.

SOME COMMON TRACK ASSIGNMENTS OF INSTRUMENTS
AND VOCALS FOR MULTI-TRACK RECORDINGS'

Type of Recording	No. of Tracks →	1	2	3	4	5	6	7	8	9	10	11
2-Track (Demo)		piano (or guitar)	vocal									
4-Track (Demo)		drums	bass	piano (or guitar)	vocal							
8-Track (Demo)		drums	bass	piano	guitar	synthesizer (string sounds)	lead vocal	background vocals	tambourine (or percussion)			
16-Track (Master)		bass drum	snare drum	drum (left) ── (stereo)	drum (right)	bass	piano (left) ── (stereo)	piano (right)	rhythm guitar	lead guitar	lead vocal	background vocals
24-Track (Master)		bass drum	snare drum	hi-hat	drum (left) ──(stereo)── drum (right)	bass	piano (left) ──(stereo)── piano (right)	rhythm guitar	lead vocal	lead guitar	lead vocal

Track	Assignment (upper)	Assignment (lower)
12	background vocals	background vocals
13	violins	background vocals
14	cellos	violins
15	brass	violas cellos
16	percussion	violins (overdub)
17		violas cellos (overdub)
18		trumpets
19		trombones
20		saxophones
21		woodwinds (oboe, flute, French horn)
22		synthesizer
23		electric piano
24		percussion

*Many engineers and producers have individual preferences for track assignments, which may be different. Track layouts also differ with types of music being recorded. A rock layout, for example, would probably utilize additional tracks for drums, electric guitar, vocals, and electronic special effects. Many systems of computerized mixing also require two tracks for data storage. Tracks are designated "DATA A" and "DATA B."

The invention of the microphone and the development of electrical recording allowed the seating of musicians at a recording session to approximate a concert performance. The later use of multimicrophone recording techniques permitted even greater dispersion.

guide for their own performances. The headphones used are generally of the "circumaural" variety, which provide a good seal between the ear, the headphone elements, and the air, so that the microphone will not pick up the sound the headphones emit. It is for this reason that loudspeakers are not used in the studio itself, since any sound the speakers issue would be picked up by the microphones and rerecorded, along with the instruments being recorded at that session, onto the new tracks.

Multi-track recordings permit previously recorded tracks that are found to be unsatisfactory, or a performance part in error, to be rerecorded without erasing any other track. A particular performer, so long as he or she was recorded onto an individual track with no other instrument or vocal, may "punch in" at the spot to be rerecorded.

Once all the parts have been recorded to the satisfaction of producer and artists, the multitrack tape is ready to be mixed down (*see* MIXDOWN) to a 2-track master for mastering onto a record or tape. The actual mixdown is performed in the control room where specialized monitoring equipment (speakers of several varieties, high-powered amplifiers, etc.), echo-adding facilities, mixdown recorders, etc., are available.

Classical recording differs in philosophy and technique. Many classical recordings, particularly many of those made in Europe, are mixed down in "real time," at the session. The output of numerous microphones covering different sections of the orchestra are combined through a mixing console so that a 2-track original master is produced directly. However, even those classical recordings made on multitrack recorders (the present techniques make use of 8-track recorders, although in some instances, for recording large orchestral and choral compositions, 16-track machines have been used) do not permit rerecording of individual tracks, since there is generally no acoustical

isolation between orchestral choirs during the recording session. In fact, since most classical recordings are made in the hall in which the ensemble normally plays, there is an effort during recording to capture the natural reverberation and ambience of the location. Therefore, multi-track recording in these instances serves only to modify slightly, during mixdown, the balance between orchestral choirs. That is, the woodwind section, which is generally allotted two tracks of its own may be brought up or down in level with respect to the strings, brass, etc. Generally these are dictated by judgments in aesthetics and musical interpretation made by the producer and conductor. Even in cases where small ensembles are recorded, as in a string quartet, the effort is made to capture the ensemble sound, rather than provide the possibility of rerecording a single instrument at some future time. Editing many takes into a cohesive musical performance, however, is widely practiced in classical recording. It should also be noted that classical recording producers never use the common "enhancers" widely employed in multi-track recordings, such as flangers, phasers, harmonizers, etc. By and large, only small amounts of equalization and echo are used in classical recording.

Many discs are made using unconventional (non-analog) recording techniques—digital, direct-to-disc, and high-performance analog recordings. Discs employing these relatively esoteric methods, including special and careful plating and pressing techniques, generally offer superior audio fidelity.

See also DIGITAL RECORDING; DIRECT-TO-DISC RECORDING; ENGINEER, RECORDING; HIGH-PERFORMANCE ANALOG RECORDINGS; and RECORD MANUFACTURING.

Recording Artist. Individual or group° under

°As used here, "group" encompasses duos, trios, and assemblages of larger numbers of performers considered as one unit.

The Recording Artist's Professional Associations

Category	Professional Title	Function
Advisory (Business)	Personal Manager	Develops and guides artist's career
	Attorney	Represents legal interests of artist; negotiates contracts
	Agent	Obtains employment for artist in areas of live performance, film, television, theater, etc.
	Business Manager	Administers financial affairs related to artist's career
Creative Input (Recording)	Record Producer	Guides artist in making recordings; oversees all aspects
	Arranger	Writes instrumental and vocal charts for material artist records and performs
	Engineer	Technically embellishes recordings through skill in operating equipment
Image Builders	Publicity Dept. (Record Company)	Obtains publicity that can result in record sales
	Public Relations Firm	Publicizes and promotes artist; orientation toward developing and/or enhancing image and personality and stretching out career
Other	A & R Dept. (Record Company)	Signs artist; may match artist with producer; finds songs to record; stretches artist's career
	Artist Development Dept. (Record Company)	Oversees artist's career growth through touring, television, etc.
	Road Manager	Supervises various aspects in the touring of the artist
	Music Publisher	Exploits songs artist writes; administers copyrights; gives creative input with regard to songwriting
	Choreographer	Creates dance steps for stage performances

contract to a RECORD COMPANY or producer° to make master recordings from which copies in disc and/or tape form are manufactured and distributed for public sale. Most recording contracts provide for compensation to the artist, or act, on a royalty basis.

Recording is usually just one of several creative areas in which the artist participates. Others may include performing in concert, songwriting, producing, arranging, and scoring motion pictures. Commonly, the artist whose career is active and varied is profes-

_____

°Or production company.

sionally associated with many types of people and companies that serve to guide and influence his career, provide creative or artistic input, and handle other responsibilities in the line of work. This is summarized in the table above.

The artist is the focal point of attention for most of these participants. Of extreme importance are those the artist engages to handle his business affairs—the personal manager, attorney, agent, and business manager. An examination of industry practices reveals that many successful recording artists delegate the responsibilities that fall under each of these to separate individuals. In general, the key to proper advice and guidance for the artist is to engage experts in each area.

How a Recording Contract Is Obtained. A recording contract may be the stepping-stone to mass popularity. A contract, of course, is no guarantee of success—talent, good songs, arrangements, and productions, proper promotion, right timing, and other intangible factors are necessary. But the musical performer without a commercial recording (or a history of successful records) can generate only limited public awareness of himself and his scope as an entertainer.

There are various ways in which a recording contract is obtained. Interest in making a deal may be initiated by either the artist or his representative, or someone at the label, as follows:

1. A MASTER or DEMO made by the artist, plus other materials, such as photographs, a bio, and reviews, may be brought to the label by a representative, such as a producer, personal manager, attorney, agent, or music publisher, or by the artist himself.

2. The artist or his representative may invite an A & R coordinator or other label employee to a live performance (such as at a local club).

3. An artist who is already established (i.e., has records out) may have his personal manager or attorney contact a new label for the purpose of negotiating a contract that would take effect when the current one expires.

4. An artist whose contract is limited to particular territories (such as the United States and Canada) may negotiate contracts with foreign companies for representation in their territories based on the success of his domestic releases.

5. An artist whose record, released on his own label or a small label, is successful may be able to interest a large record company in "picking up" his contract, or such company may approach the artist.

6. A record company may approach the artist as a result of press reviews, recommendations, word of mouth, awareness of an artist's large local following, etc.

Other Considerations. In general, the material an unknown artist submits or performs for audition should be COMMERCIAL. Ideally, there should be one or more potential "hit" songs played at the audition. A record company often looks more favorably upon the artist who is represented by a competent personal manager and agent, though many artists without a recording contract are unable to obtain such representatives. In any case, professional presentation of the artist is vital.

Young performers who lack "contacts" should not be discouraged. While "contacts" may indeed be influential in getting the artist through certain doors, from a historical viewpoint it is apparent that the bottom line to success is *talent*—and without it, any artist will eventually fall by the wayside.

Recording Artist/Record Company Contract. A recording contract, in essence, represents an "investment" by both parties. The label will spend a large sum of money for recording, manufacturing, and advertising (in addition to normal overhead expenses for such areas as marketing, publicity, promotion, and artist development) in the hope that it will not only earn its money back, but realize a large profit. This decision is born out of the fact that even though a relatively modest investment can result in an enormous profit to the record company if the artist's product becomes successful, the majority of recordings do not even earn back their initial investment.° Further-

---

°The Recording Industry Association of America, Inc., commissioned an "Economic Study of the Recording Industry" by the Cambridge Research Institute, based on 1979 statistics. Presented to the Copyright Royalty Tribunal in April 1980, the study revealed that an average of 140,000 albums must be sold before an LP can recoup its costs. This figure is more than double the break-even point in 1972, when the total was 61,000 albums. In 1979, 84% failed to reach the break-even level, compared to 77% in 1972.

more, it typically requires a few years or 3 to 4 albums for a new artist to sell successfully. While established artists usually sell well, their advances have soared so high in recent years that record companies must devote great attention (sometimes to the detriment of lesser-known artists) to making their product profitable.

Likewise, signing with a label represents an "investment" by the artist, an investment not only of potential earnings but, perhaps more important, of career growth—or decline. To a large extent, the artist is putting his career in the hands of the record company. His best efforts may yield commercial product, but without the promotion and support of the label, much valuable time may be lost. Thus it is advisable for artists to seek the representation of a competent music attorney or personal manager before negotiating or signing a contract with a record company.

It is easy to see, then, just how important the terms of a recording contract are to each party. Such agreement will bind the parties together for a specified period of time, so the meaning of each term must be precisely clear, spelling out the obligations for each party and not leaving any item or area questionable.

It should be remembered that the terms of any contract are of course negotiable. There is no standard industry-wide recording agreement, but the artist or his representative should know the market conditions for artists. Beyond the terms of the contract, the artist and his representatives should believe in the record company before signing. Experienced professionals in the business will usually know the capabilities of a record company and the support the artist can expect to receive if the company makes a commitment. This entry will examine some of the more important terms of the recording artist/record company contract.

Recording Artist/Record Company Contracts: An Analysis of Terms

Term	Explanation	Basic Provisions	Comment
Duration	How long does the contract endure? Recording artist contracts usually provide for the artist's exclusive recording services to be engaged by the label for an initial term plus unilateral options exercisable by the company.	Terms vary, but a common one is for an initial period of one year plus four one-year options. Some contracts provide for an initial period of eighteen months so as to allow the record company enough time to make a realistic evaluation for its option period obligations.	If after a given number of releases the sale of the artist's product does not meet the level of expectation, the label may drop the artist at term expiration (i.e., not exercise its option). Contracts usually provide for a particular time (at least 30 days) prior to the commencement of the renewal period for the label to render written notice of its desire to exercise the option ("positive option"), but may provide, alternatively, for automatic option exercise unless the record company has sent notice to the artist of its decision not to renew the agreement ("negative option").

Recording Artist/Record Company Contracts: An Analysis of Terms *(cont'd)*

Term	Explanation	Basic Provisions	Comment
Territory of agreement	In what territories throughout the world does the record company have the right to manufacture, sell, distribute, and advertise the artist's recordings? Recording contracts grant the label such rights either on a worldwide basis or in a limited number of territories.	Most contracts grant the label worldwide rights; some successful artists are able to limit the territories, such as, for example, the United States and Canada.	If the artist grants rights only for the U.S. and Canada he may be able to make separate contracts for other territories throughout the world, negotiating collective advances that would be greater than those received by making a worldwide agreement with one company. But again, an artist without substantial bargaining clout will probably not be able to limit the territories.
Product obligation	What is the minimum number of masters the artist must record and deliver during the initial term of agreement and through the option periods?	Ranges from two masters (single sides) in the initial period to one or two albums or more during each option period.	This term sets the minimum number of masters the artist may record at the company's request, leaving the company free to request more. It is in the artist's interest to provide also for the maximum number he may record in any period.
Company direction of recording	There is often a term that grants the company the right to set the time and date of recording as well as select the studio, the producer, and musicians as well as the songs the artist may record.	Ranges from company having such right to artist having such right, or by right of mutual consent.	Established artists will seek to negotiate autonomy with respect to planning and making their recordings.
Company right of approval of masters	Does the label have the right to reject or not release masters delivered by artist if it deems such masters are not technically and commercially satisfactory?	A record company always reserves the right to determine whether a master is technically satisfactory and will often request and obtain the right to determine whether it is commercial enough for release.	The artist, depending on his track record, may be able to negotiate mutual consent with respect to the master being commercially satisfactory.
Master tape ownership	Who owns the masters recorded by the artist? (A master is a physical tape embodying recorded performances from which records and prerecorded tapes are ultimately derived.)	The company will usually own the master by virtue of its paying for the recording sessions in which they were made.	Artists with track records may be able to provide for ownership of the masters they make to be transferred to them after a certain time, such as ten years. Generally, however, the masters are permanently owned by the record company.

Recording Artist/Record Company Contracts: An Analysis of Terms *(cont'd)*

Term	Explanation	Basic Provisions	Comment
Sound recording ownership	Who owns the copyrights in the sound recordings made by the artist? (The sounds embodied in the artist's master are subject to copyright as a SOUND RECORDING.)	The company will usually be the copyright owner of the sound recording for the reason stated above. In such case, the artist or producer is deemed an "employee for hire."	Some very established recording artists are able to negotiate copyright ownership in the sound recordings they make although this is highly unusual.
Payment not to record	This term, sometimes referred to as the "pay or play clause," grants the record company the right to pay the artist a certain sum of money in the event the minimum number of masters as provided by the contract's requirement has not been requested by the record company nor recorded by the artist.	This is a contract term that record companies seek to include but artists attempt to negotiate out or place restrictions on. The payment is generally union scale or a percentage of union scale.	A record company may believe in a particular circumstance that it is in its interest to pay the artist a "relatively small" sum of money rather than incurring recording costs for masters it would likely not release, based on the artist's past recordings.
Royalty rates	The contract will provide royalty rates to the artist to accommodate the different configurations and special forms of distribution of the artist's recording both domestically and in foreign territories. Royalties are expressed as a percentage of either the retail list price or the wholesale price.	LPs and singles (U.S.): 5–20% ("regular royalty rate") of retail list price. Prerecorded tapes: 50–100% of regular royalty rate Domestic licensees (record clubs, record merchandising companies, etc.): 50–66⅔% of regular royalty rate based on the club or merchandised price,* or artist receives a negotiated percentage of royalties received by the record company Premiums and budget records: 50% of regular royalty rate based on the selling price of the premium or budget record Cutouts (deletions): no royalty Promotion records: no royalty to limitations placed on the number of "giveaways" Foreign licensees (foreign record manufacturer's editors, record clubs, etc.): 50–75% of regular royalty rates;† for subsidiary companies, artists receive 50–100% of the regular royalty rate.	The upper limits of royalty rates on the chart apply mostly to "superstar" artists, the lower limits to new artists. Contracts often provide for the royalty rate to escalate on a sliding scale based on sales or upon renewal of options.

Recording Artist/Record Company Contracts: An Analysis of Terms (cont'd)

Term	Explanation	Basic Provisions	Comment
Packaging deduction	Before royalties are calculated for sales in the various areas as set forth in the table above, it is customary for the label to deduct expenses it incurred for "packaging" costs such as for cardboard or plastic containers, paper sleeves, and graphic work.	"Packaging" deductions are typically as follows: 1) for single-fold LP jackets, 10% 2) for double-gate jackets, 12½% to 15% 3) for tape packaging, 20%. These deductions are based on the suggested retail list price and are for the U.S. only; foreign charges vary.	There is usually no packaging deduction in the United States for the sleeves that singles are inserted into (although labels commonly deduct for color sleeves); in foreign countries record companies include a singles deduction, usually of about 6% of the retail selling price.
Base payment rate	Royalties are not always payable on 100% of records sold; in many instances royalties are paid on 90% of records sold. The base is negotiable. Thus in calculating royalties for a particular period, the artist's royalty is determined by: (1) subtracting the packaging deduction from the retail list price of the record or tape; (2) multiplying this sum by the applicable royalty rate (this gives the royalty per recording); (3) multiplying this amount times the number of product sold in the particular configuration during the particular period (if royalties are payable on 90% of sales then the royalty per recording is multiplied by 90% of product sold in that configuration); and (4) adding royalties earned for all configurations. This gives the artist's total royalty due for the particular period. Of course, unrecouped advances, recording costs, and other expenses would be deducted from the total royalty before a check is remitted.	Royalties are usually payable on 100% of records sold for established artists and 90% for new or "unproven" artists and some established artists as well. This may depend on record company policy.	The 90% base which is still in practice today is a carry-over from the traditional practice of record companies calculating royalties due to an artist on 90% of records sold, the 10% difference attributed to a "breakage" allowance, where records would be returned due to breakage or defects. Records today are "unbreakable" but the 10% allowance still persists to a degree.

Recording Artist/Record Company Contracts: An Analysis of Terms *(cont'd)*

Term	Explanation	Basic Provisions	Comment
Advances	Record companies commonly pay an ADVANCE to artists. Advances and other charges incurred by the label shall be deducted from royalties otherwise payable to artist.	Advances may range from a few thousand dollars to a new artist for an initial term to several millions of dollars to a "superstar" for a multi-year term.	Artists may negotiate for advances to be payable upon the label exercising options. A BONUS paid to an artist based upon sales or option exercise is a payment which is nonrecoupable from royalties due to the artist.
Deduction of recording costs	Record companies normally finance an artist's recording of masters, and such expenses are deducted from royalties earned by and payable to the artist.	This is a standard stipulation in artists' contracts.	This provision is included in the contracts of both new and established artists.
Reserves	It is industry practice for record companies to allow their accounts to return unsold merchandise for exchange or credit, the percentage allowed varying from manufacturer to manufacturer. Since artists receive royalties on product sold (not shipped), manufacturers retain (reserve) a portion of the royalties otherwise payable to artists until a sufficient period of time has elapsed allowing for return, so that they would not be paying royalties on unsold (returned) merchandise.	The "reserve" clause is a standard stipulation in artists' contracts.	Artists commonly limit record companies to withhold reserves not longer than 18 months (3 accounting periods if paid on a semiannual basis) following the accounting period during which the recording has been shipped.
Use of artist's name, likeness, and biographical material in advertising and promotion	This term deals with the company's exclusive right to use the artist's name, likeness, and biographical material in advertising or trade related to the promotion and sale of the artist's recordings.	This is a standard stipulation in artists' contracts.	It is in both the company and artist's interest that promotion and publicity related to the sale of the artist's records be obtained, and obtaining these rights gives the company freedom to exploit the artist accordingly.
Use of artist's name, likeness, and photograph in merchandising tie-ins	Such a term grants to the company the right to exploit the artist's name, likeness, etc. in MERCHANDISING TIE-INS outside the record business.	Artists attempt to prevent the label from obtaining the merchandising rights related to their careers and, while many do, some new artists are not able to retain them.	Where artist cannot retain merchandising rights he might attempt to place certain restrictions on this, such as right of mutual consent.

Recording Artist/Record Company Contracts: An Analysis of Terms *(cont'd)*

Term	Explanation	Basic Provisions	Comment
Use of artist's recordings in audiovisual devices	Such a term provides for the company to have the right to authorize use of the artist's recordings in videocassettes, videodiscs, and other audiovisual devices.	Established artists are able to retain or restrict this right, while many new artists find they must relinquish it.	Where artist cannot retain audiovisual rights he might attempt to place certain restrictions on this. Royalty rates have not been determined for this type of use at this writing and many artists are negotiating for 50–50 splits with the record company for such income received.
Union membership	Such a term provides for the artist to be or become a member in good standing of AFM or AFTRA, depending on whether he is an instrumental musician or vocalist.	This is a standard stipulation in artists' contracts.	Label is required under its agreement with AFM or AFTRA to have its artist be or become a member in good standing of the applicable union under terms set forth by the agreement. AFM artist recording agreements should be registered with the union by the record company.
Assignment of contract	A contract provision will relate to the assignability of the artist's contract to a parent company, subsidiary, or a purchaser of all or a majority of the company's assets.	Artists attempt to put limitations on this term where the company may assign only the artist's contract by providing a reasonable right of approval on their behalf or that the assignee must fulfill the obligations of the recording contract for the remaining period of the agreement with primary liability remaining with both the assignor and assignee.	Some labels seek complete freedom to assign a contract to a third party. Because artists do not know ahead of time whether such assignment may be harmful (or beneficial) to their career, they attempt to negotiate restrictions in this.
Publishing clause	A contract may provide that all compositions written by the artist and recorded by the record company during the term of the agreement will be published by a company designated by the label.	The artist will be deemed to have executed a Songwriter Agreement as per an Exhibit attached to the recording contract with respect to each composition which is the subject of the agreement.	An unknown artist may be forced to sign away his publishing rights on compositions he has written; however, such artist may be able to retain at least one half of the publishing rights by use of negotiating skill and prowess.
Cross-collateralization	The contract may provide for the recoupment of recording costs from any moneys due to the artist "under this or any other agreement between the parties."	The record company may deduct unrecouped advances, expenses, and other charges it incurred pursuant to any contracts between the parties.	This clause may tie in two disparate agreements between the parties. The artist must fight the intent of the clause, although it is becoming increasingly prevalent.

Recording Artist/Record Company Contracts: An Analysis of Terms *(cont'd)*

Term	Explanation	Basic Provisions	Comment
Negative covenant "not to record"	Such a term is included to prevent the recording artist from rerecording his hit compositions as soon as his recording contract has terminated.	Covenants usually provide for the artist not to record the later of "five years from release of the recording" or "two years from date of termination or expiration of agreement."	Some companies attempt to tie-up the rerecording rights for a period of five years from the termination or expiration of the agreement.
Recording budgets	The budget is generally set by and within the purview of the record company.	A maximum recording budget for each album may be written into the contract with escalations in each option period.	The artist should be aware of the maximum recording budget set up for his album sessions; however, he should be aware, as well, that all such costs are chargeable against his royalties.
Controlled compositions	All compositions written and/ or owned in whole or part by the artist will receive a specified mechanical royalty rate from the record company.	The maximum mechanical royalty rate for a "controlled composition" on a single may be the statutory rate but is sometimes less. For albums, the maximum mechanical royalty is usually the number of controlled compositions thereon times the negotiated rate with a limit to the multiple (sometimes 10).	By this clause, the record company protects itself from mechanical royalty rate increases during the term of the artist's contract. Artist/writers should provide to extend the mechanical royalties accordingly for controlled compositions on albums comprising two or more discs.

° It is the practice of some record/tape clubs and other licensees to pay royalties based upon 85% of net sales.

† In many instances, for Canadian sales, U.S. artists will receive a domestic royalty rate.

Recording Industry Association of America, Inc. (RIAA). Trade association representing the U.S. recording manufacturing industry.

Membership. Members of RIAA are record companies; membership is available to any company engaged in the production and sale of recordings, under its own label, with its main office in the United States. Anyone engaged in the unauthorized duplication of recordings is ineligible for membership in RIAA.

Programs and Activities. In addition to sponsoring programs and activities of a general nature, as described in TRADE ASSOCIATIONS, RIAA: is actively involved in curtailing piracy, bootlegging, and counterfeiting (it maintains a national Anti-Piracy Intelligence Unit which collects information on illegal activities of this nature and disseminates it to record companies and federal, state, and local law enforcement agencies); promotes the achievements of participants in the sound-recording industry by auditing and certifying gold and platinum awards for best-selling recordings (*see* GOLD RECORD AWARDS, PLATINUM RECORD AWARDS); participates in industry labor negotiations; works for lower postal and freight rates with respect to shipments of phonograph and tape recordings; and devises and promulgates technical standards for phonograph records and prerecorded tapes to create compatibility with all listening equipment.

History. The record industry was a rapidly growing, though loosely organized, industry group prior to RIAA's founding in 1952. The excise tax imposed upon phonograph records at that time (many commodities, including books, had had that tax removed after World War II) provided just the impetus for the individual companies to band together and form an association to confront this and other issues. Leading record companies among the founders included Capitol, Columbia, Decca, Mercury, MGM, and RCA. Most major U.S. record companies have since become members of RIAA; by 1980, its more than 50 members issued approximately 90% of all recordings manufactured and shipped in the United States. In 1980, RIAA/VIDEO, a new division, was formed to serve manufacturers of prerecorded video products, some of them affiliates and/or divisions of regular RIAA member companies.

Recording Right. *See* MECHANICAL RIGHT.

Recording Studio. A facility designed and equipped to "store" audio performances on magnetic tape. A recording studio contains, in its most basic configuration, a room in which the performance to be recorded takes place (the "studio") and an area (the "control room") in which the recording equipment is placed and technical functions are undertaken. These two facilities are adjacent to each other, separated by a wall with a double soundproof glass window, thus permitting visual communication in either direction; or they may be physically separate, in which case closed-circuit video (TV) communication is generally installed. In both cases (indeed in any case), two-way audio communication is necessary to provide the required interchanges between producer, engineer, and artists.

A sound recording studio can range from as fundamental a facility as a room in an apart-

ment or a house containing the simplest of semiprofessional recording gear, to a large complex. Such a complex may have many types of rooms, each designed specially to meet the needs of the room's function. In addition to the control room and studio, there may be a separate mixing facility, a production or editing room, a mastering room (where master lacquers are cut), and a copy room (where audio and video tape copies can be made).

Facilities. The sections of a sound recording studio that are of main interest are the room, or *studio,* in which the actual performance will take place and the *control room,* in which all the recording and ancillary paraphernalia is located.

The recording room or studio can be made to differ depending on the type of recording being done. For classical recordings, the room will have a pleasant and comfortable acoustic atmosphere or ambience which will enhance the sound produced by the instruments and/or voices without undue emphasis of any part of the musical spectrum, but which will support and reinforce evenly the low registers of instruments. The room will also have reverberant characteristics that will add "air" to the instruments, permit good instrumental ensemble, and impart a "warmth" to the sound of the instruments (such characteristics have induced performers to describe a room as "warm"). There are many ways designers have attempted to create these qualities in studios: from the use of undulating wall surfaces (to generate random reflections of sound waves) through the alternating of areas on the walls that are reflective and absorptive (to prevent "hardness" and strong annoying echoes at midregisters) to varying room dimensions via sloping ceilings and angled walls (to ensure the minimizing of strong reflections that cause excessive reinforcement in specific music registers), or combinations of the above. In some instances, buildings endowed with the desired acoustics have been converted into recording studios. Alternatively, structures with the desirable acoustical characteristics have been "commandeered" temporarily as recording locations.

For contemporary or "pop" recording, all attempts are made to create a studio that is acoustically flexible. Instruments are commonly surrounded by acoustic baffles—heavy, movable, partitions, mounted on casters, which are meant to absorb the sound energy of the instrument in such a way that only its microphones receive the sound it generates. Some studios have special vocalists' recording booths which are adjacent to the main studio and control room in order to provide more isolation to the voice recording. The design philosophy for these recording studios varies, but essentially they are very similar in that great effort is taken to ensure that the intrinsic sound of an instrument is recorded exactly as the producer wants it, with no environmental interactions. Not only are very-close-microphone techniques employed, to minimize external effects, but the instruments themselves may be modified, as is the case with drum sets where the heads are "taped" and the resonating bottoms removed (highly specialized drums are manufactured specifically for recording studio use).

A great deal of care is sometimes given to the isolation of a recording room from the rest of the world—even from the building in which it is located. It is not uncommon to find double walls and doors in its construction, intended to exclude outside noise and vibration. Some construction even "floats" the recording room on a large pneumatic cushion, almost like a giant inner tube, in order to isolate it from sources of vibration.

The control room can vary in size depending on the amount of equipment in it and its ultimate functions. As great care is devoted to the acoustics of the control room as to those of the studio itself, since vital decisions which will affect the final sound of the recording are made based on the sound generated by the studio monitors and perceived by the producer, the engineer, and the artists in the control room.

The layout of the control room is standardized. The mixing console, which can have an almost infinite number of functions, is always placed squarely in front of the window, which is part of the common wall between recording and control rooms, to allow the operator of the console and the producer, who sits next to the operator (engineer), visual contact with the recording room (studio). If closed-circuit TV is used, the TV monitor(s) is generally placed above the window.

The console is the nucleus that controls the entire recording chain. Almost any function can be performed through the console. During the recording and mixing processes, various effects utilizing inboard as well as outboard equipment (outboard equipment is interfaced through the console's patch bay) can be introduced: equalizing, panning, reverb, digital delays, flanging, phasing, noise reduction, compressing, limiting, filtering—the list almost never ends and is constantly changing.

The monitor speakers are placed on either side of or above the window. Some studios monitor through two speakers (for stereo) regardless of the number of tracks being recorded, while others use more. In some cases, a control room will have pairs of different types and makes of speakers so that comparisons can be made before a decision is reached.

The tape recorders are most often placed out of the way, against a wall. The engineer can operate the tape recorder by remote control from the console itself, or sometimes an assistant engineer is assigned to operate the machine. The function of a tape operator is to cue the tape, punch in and out of the "record" mode, and gauge the amount of unrecorded tape left on the reel. The rest of the equipment in a control room may be wall or "rack" mounted in standard 19-inch racks to conserve space and facilitate convenient operation by the engineer.

Musical Instruments. Most recording studios have a compendium of instruments (and related equipment) for use by performers and for which, sometimes, a rental fee is charged. Generally, these are instruments and equipment that because of their size or complexity are not portable, as: a drum set, various guitar amplifiers and speakers, a piano and its variations and permutations (electric piano, honky-tonk pianos, harpsichords and clavichords), other keyboard instruments, organs, synthesizers, and percussion instruments.

Additional Functions. As mentioned earlier, recording studios may have facilities that can perform functions other than the actual recording.

Mixing Room. Most recording studios use the control room for both recording and mixing. Some facilities have separate "mixing rooms," which are, in essence, control rooms not attached to a studio. Many mixing consoles are computer-automated so that all adjustments made during the preliminary runthroughs in mixing are "remembered" by the computer and made automatically during the actual mixdown recording run.

Editing Room. A room equipped with tape recorders in various formats, some outboard equipment (i.e., equalizers and compressors), and a monitoring system. Sometimes the recording control room itself is used for editing. Editing is the function in which the original tape is "arranged" into a satisfactory performance or series of performances via "splicing" together sections of performances to achieve a correct and cohesive musical sequence. The editing function comprises cutting, rearranging, and reassembling the original tape into a different sequence, as well as removal of unwanted performances or portions of performances. During editing, "leadering" is performed, in which segments of leader tape (a plastic or paper tape without a magnetic coat-

ing) are placed between the different musical renditions to space properly in time the sequences of the renditions. Leader is also placed at the "head" (beginning) and "tail" (end) of the reel. Sometimes, once editing is finished, a copy of this completed original is made to be used as a "safety" (see below).

Copy Room. A section devoted primarily to making copies of masters for clients or licensees in other areas. Most copy rooms are used to make one-to-one copies in both open-reel and cassette configurations. Copies in identical format (same track configuration) to the master are made in case of damage to or loss of the master mix (these are known as "safeties"). Copy rooms do not perform the function of high-speed duplication plants, making mass quantities of commercial copies, such as cassettes. A copy room has the flexibility to provide copies in various formats, such as 15 ips half-track, 7½ ips half- or quarter-track, 15 or 7½ ips full-track, cassettes, 8-track cartridges, etc.

Video Recording. There are recording studios that can record performances in video as well as audio. Video recording, however, requires monumentally complex gear, not only for the actual recording of the video (in addition to the recording of the audio) but for the fulfillment of ancillary requirements, which include lighting, props, costumes, choreography, etc. Essentially, video recording equipment is much like that in audio recording and it is directly comparable to audio recording elements: video cameras (analogous to microphones), mixing and camera switching consoles, recorders, monitors, etc. Perhaps the only actual difference is that in video recording the original-performance tape usually contains the final image to be used. There are instances, however, in which two or three (or even more) recorders are used to capture different photographic angles during the performance and a selection is made later, during editing. In some cases, the audio portion is recorded onto the

A recording studio is a facility where the performances of musicians and vocalists are stored on tape.
All types of productions are recorded here such as
commercial recordings, jingles, and film scores. In
its basic configuration a recording studio consists
of the control room and the studio.

audio track of the video recorder directly. Normal operating procedure is to synchronize a multi-track audio recorder to the video recorder(s) and mix down at the time of final editing, when echo, special sound effects, equalization, etc., may be added. Major video studios, mainly because of investment costs, are primarily in the province of networks in Hollywood and other television production centers. Most of the video recording to date has been either for TV use and/or for the production of software material for VCRs and videodiscs. Because of the imminent growth of a lower-priced video market, there will probably be a proliferation of affordable equipment allowing inexpensive video recording. Essentially, video recording can be said to have supplanted (for most storage purposes) motion picture film, though filming using motion picture cameras (both 35mm in its various formats and 16mm) is sometimes undertaken. However, motion picture and video recording for entertainment via television is outside the scope of this section, since it has developed into an exact and very complex art form in which the performers are not necessarily, or always, the main ingredients in the final product—an amalgam of the talents of the performers, director, producer, cinematographer, recordists, editor, production designer, lighting director, costume designer, and the many others who are the backbone of a successful production.

Specialized Studios. Some studios are highly specialized facilities designed to perform recording functions very specific in nature. The foremost examples are: (1) studios mainly for production of ad-oriented material, including jingles and commercials in both audio and video; (2) studios for recording and synchronizing sound tracks to film and video tape; (3) duplicating studios where tapes in any format can be duplicated in the same format or into any other format (e.g., from 15 ips 2-track to 7½ ips quarter-track, or cassette, or 8-track); and (4) studios in which direct-disc recordings are made. Other examples are sound-effects studios and studios for mastering records (from tape master to lacquer master).

Studio Rates and Billing. Studio rates are equated with the complexity of the studio, its facilities, the services it offers, and its location. Generally, charges, which vary with the services required, are made by the use-hour or fractions of use-hours. In some studios, evening, weekend, and holiday rates are higher.

Rates for a session and all payment terms are established before sessions begin. Many studios print rate cards covering all services provided, though clients, particularly those who use the facilities frequently, are sometimes able to negotiate lower rates.

Performers affiliated with established record companies forgo rate negotiations, most specifically in those cases where the label contracts the recording studio to produce a recording. In general, the label (or producer) sets the dates and times for the recording sessions and prenegotiates the rates.

Studios require the establishment of credit prior to booking time for recording; in lieu of credit, a deposit or partial payment may be requested. Most studios have a policy of charging for scheduled time if notice of cancellation is not given by a stipulated date prior to the sessions (commonly, at least 48 hours in advance). Also, many studios may require full payment in cash or by certified check before the tape recorded during the sessions is delivered to the client.

Studio administrative procedures include the booking and tracking of studio time, invoicing, inventory control, ordering of supplies, setting up maintenance schedules, arranging for equipment repairs on the premises or elsewhere, amortization of equipment for tax purposes, all payroll functions, plus the standard accounting operations.

See ENGINEER, RECORDING.

Reel-to-Reel Tape. *See* OPEN-REEL TAPE.

Rehearsal Studio. Facility where rooms are available for rental to musicians for private rehearsal. Rehearsal studios provide groups with a place to prepare material for public performance, recording, or audition, and offer a location where acts can be showcased for record labels, personal managers, promoters, potential investors, press, and others.

Some rehearsal studios provide instruments such as pianos and drums without additional charge to the client; others rent such instruments, as well as sound and lighting equipment. Depending on the studio, it may have rehearsal rooms with adjustable acoustics, a reception room, storage lockers for equipment, and may furnish photography and videotape services.

Release. The "publication" or initial distribution of a record or tape (to *release* an album). A record company schedules a "release date," the date it will first ship a new record or tape to accounts, well in advance. This enables its internal machinery—marketing, merchandising, sales, advertising, promotion, and publicity departments—to develop strategies and campaigns designed to best expose the recording and promote sales.

Rentals (Musical Instruments and Equipment). There are companies that are in the business of renting musical instruments and equipment. These firms either deal exclusively in rentals or are retail musical instrument stores. The services of a rental company are commonly used by recording studios lacking particular instruments or pieces of equipment, touring acts whose members might need a certain instrument, and new acts whose members cannot yet afford to purchase their own instruments or equipment. Instruments and equipment commonly rented include electric pianos, organs, synthesizers, "tack" pianos, guitars, drums, sound systems, lighting equipment, and stages.

Residual (TV and Radio Commercials and TV Programs). A residual is a payment received, by a performer who participates in a radio or television commercial or TV program, for extended use of the commercial or for replay of the program.

TV and Radio Commercials. The UNIONS having jurisdiction over television commercials in which singers, dancers, announcers, and others perform are AFTRA and SAG. AFTRA and SAG collaboratively negotiate an agreement establishing minimum basic session fees and residuals for singers who perform on commercial advertising announcements used on television. AFTRA also negotiates minimum session fees and residuals for singers who perform on jingles made for radio broadcast only.

AFTRA's Radio Recorded Commercial Contract with advertising agencies provides for commercials on which AFTRA members perform to be broadcast for either an 8- or a 13-week period. Thus, after the commercial's first radio broadcast, it may be used on an unlimited basis without further payment to the AFTRA participant for either 8 or 13 weeks, depending on the option selected by the producer who buys the time in such cycles.

At the end of the period, if the jingle is to be used again, it may run for another cycle of the same total weekly period, for which the performers receive payments (residuals). AFTRA has a formula for determining the amount of residual payments based upon the number of cities in which the commercial is rebroadcast.

Television residual rates depend on whether the singing is done on or off camera and whether the commercial is used as a wild spot or a network spot. Wild spots are commercials broadcast on noninterconnected TV stations within a period of 13 weeks. Performers receive a session fee plus residuals for each 13 weeks of use, based on the number of cities in which the commercial is broadcast. For network spots, the performer earns a session fee plus a "per use" fee—every time the commercial is aired. However, there are fees for a guarantee of 13 uses within 13 consecutive weeks (television cycles run for 13-week periods). The maximum period commercials may be used for (except animated cartoon commercials) is 21 months after the commencement of the first fixed cycle.

As stated above, AFTRA and SAG conegotiate their contracts for TV commercials (until the mid 1960s, AFTRA and SAG had separate agreements with producers of television commercials). AFTRA's jurisdiction generally prevails in the case of videotaped TV commercials and SAG's for filmed TV commercials. Since jurisdictions sometimes overlap, the producer generally works through the union he has traditionally been signed with.

Television Programs. For reruns of television programs such as musical variety shows, chorus singers and other performers earn residuals (this is of course in addition to their initial session fees). Residuals earned by the performer for network replays under the AFTRA TV agreement are generally for the following percentages of the applicable basic minimum scale wage: first replay, 75%; second replay, 75%; third replay, 50%; fourth replay, 50%; fifth replay, 50%; sixth replay, 10%; seventh replay, 5%; eighth and each additional replay, 5%. Under SAG's schedule, the residual rate depends on when the vehicle was produced, where it is aired (e.g., network, local, cable, syndication), and what number run the TV program is having. "Name" singers normally work under negotiated terms that provide for higher rates of payment (*see* OVERSCALE ARTIST).

Retailer (Printed Music). *See* PRINTED-MUSIC RETAILER.

Retailer (Records and Tapes). The record industry, though controlled by generally accepted business practices, is unique in many areas, particularly retailing. Records and tapes are not items of necessity but rather entertainment products, whose sale is based upon personal taste. A multitude of records and tapes is constantly being released, and thus media exposure is essential to bring a recording to the public's attention. The bulk of retail sales are those recordings which are at the time receiving the most airplay (groups with large followings or those that do concert tours may not have to rely on airplay, and certain styles of music, such as jazz and classical, are not susceptible to ephemeral public acceptance). As airplay of records, even hits, endures for a relatively short time, the retailer needs to maximize sales of such product during their peak period of popularity. The retailer needs to be aware of current trends, industry practices, and conditions, and have a "feel" for artists, music, and public taste.

Basic Types of Retailers. Retail record and tape merchandisers are basically either full-line retailers or the music departments of mass-merchandising outlets. Full-line retailers may in themselves be distinguished by the size of their operations. There are single stores, or "mom and pop" operations, and chains comprising several retail units (a chain is usually considered as consisting of three or more units). Chains may be part of corporations having related interests—for example, rack jobbing and distributing.

Mass-merchandise outlets (which are serviced by rack jobbers) include department stores, discount stores, and variety stores. Records and tapes are also sold at supermarkets, drugstores, musical instrument stores, hi-fi dealers, electronic stores, booksellers, and toy stores, as well as through channels such as record/tape clubs and mail order companies.

Merchandise. Depending on the type and size of the outlet, record/tape retailers may carry any or all of the following types of merchandise:

Software—LPs, singles, prerecorded audio

In 1980 the Recording Industry Association of America, Inc. (RIAA) reported that sales, based on list price value, of records and prerecorded tapes were $3.682 billion. A record and tape outlet typically stocks merchandise in various departments: rock, pop, country, soul, jazz, classical, tapes, accessories, music books, etc.

tapes (cassette, 8-track), prerecorded video-tapes, videodiscs, and blank audio tapes and videotapes.

Record and tape accessories—needles and cartridges, record and tape care products (cloths, fluids, brushes, head cleaners), demagnetizers, leader, splicing tape, 45 rpm adapters, speaker wire, audio cables, record and tape carrying and storage cases, record/tape storage cabinets, empty LP jackets, batteries, earphones, headphones, cassette microphones.

Hardware—turntables, amplifiers, tape recorders, speakers, videocassette recorders, videodisc players, and other audio and audiovisual equipment.

Musical instruments and accessories—mainly guitars, but also organs and some band instruments. Accessories include guitar strings, picks, etc.

Printed music—sheet music, songbooks, folios, fakebooks, method books, educational books.

Alternative—concert tickets, T-shirts, heat transfers, jewelry (such as pins of rock stars), posters, greeting cards, belt buckles, mirrors, incense, pipes, cigarette paper and cases, lighters and other paraphernalia.

Fixtures. To stock and organize records and tapes, retailers use record and tape display racks, browser boxes and tables, bins, dumps, record and tape divider cards, placards and signs. Records are sometimes stacked on the floor and tapes are often locked in glass cases.

Organization of Record and Tape Departments. Retailers usually have diverse catalogs (in terms of number of titles and variety of musical categories and configuration of products). Records and tapes are organized and displayed in various categories in the retail outlets. These may include any combination of the following:

Africa
African
album specials
as advertised
ballet
band music
barbershop
belly dance music
best-sellers
big bands
blues
Broadway original cast albums
Broadway shows
budget
cassettes
chamber music
children's
choral groups
Christmas music
classical
classical guitar
classical organ
classical piano
classical violin
comedy
composers
concerto
contemporary
country (or country and western)
country female vocalist
country male vocalist
cut-outs
dance music
disco music
Dixieland
documentary
drama and poetry
easy listening
economy line
eight-track
electronic music
England
English
ethnic
female vocalists
folk music
foreign language
France

French
German
Germany
gospel music
Greece
Greek
groups
guitar
harpsichord
Hawaii
Hawaiian
hits
humor
Hungarian
Hungary
imports
India
Indian
instruction
instrumental groups
instrumentals
international
Ireland
Irish
Israel
Israeli
Italian
Italy
Japan
Japanese
jazz
language instruction
male vocalists
marches
Mexican
Mexico
Middle East
middle-of-the-road
miscellaneous
mood music
movies
movies and shows
new releases
new wave
Norway

Norwegian
nostalgia
oldies
old-time radio
opera
orchestra
organ
original casts
piano
piano-organ
Poland
Polish
polka music
pop
popular
Portugal
Portuguese
punk rock
quadraphonic
ragtime
reggae
religious
rhythm and blues
rock
rock and roll
rock and soul
Rumania
Rumanian
Russia
Russian
sacred
salsa
Scotland
Scottish
show music
soul music
sound effects
sound tracks
Spain
specials
spoken word
Sweden
Swedish
television
various artists

various countries
violin
vocal groups

Albums and tapes of popular music are normally shelved or racked into the various categories listed above, alphabetically (by artist's name or album title) or by chart position (for best-sellers). Retail outlets often stock and display crossover products in two different sections. For example, a country act whose records cross over onto the pop charts may have its albums placed in both the country and the rock sections. Classical records and tapes are usually in a separate section and arranged alphabetically by composer.

Size. Record/tape outlets commonly range in size from 1,500 to 3,000 square feet. There are some "superstores" that range from 5,000 to 20,000 or more square feet.

Floor Plans. The organization of the various departments of a retail outlet is an important aspect of business. Records and tapes are usually displayed with the intention of maximizing the amount of product that can be clearly seen in the space available and drawing as much attention to the records and tapes as possible. Floor plans for a full-line retailer and a racked department in a mass-merchandise outlet appear on the facing page.

Ordering and Inventory. Retailers order product on a regular basis. Chains usually have a central warehouse or distribution center where buying is done on behalf of all the chain's units. There may be specialized buyers, such as for LPs, singles, tapes, and accessories. Buying for an independent retailer or a small chain is generally made by the store's manager or buyer.

A large chain with a central warehouse or distribution center may have a catalog of all the product that it handles. Information on available inventory is transmitted to the individual stores, which order or reorder from the central location. Buyers for the chain will usu-

ally do the ordering for special product needs of the individual units. In some cases, a store manager may order new releases directly from manufacturers or distributors.

Every retail operation may have its own system for taking inventory. Often, sales slips indicating purchased product are collected at the end of each day and the information is put on a transmittal form. This is analyzed (in some chains by computer), and records and tapes that are "hot" or steady sellers will be reordered. Product that moves poorly or not at all may be deleted from the retailer's catalog. Of course, a retailer just doesn't simply buy product and stock it. The machinery of advertising, point-of-purchase merchandising, and promotion must go to work to increase the chance for a record's or tape's sale.

Dealer Promotions. In an effort to attract customers and stimulate sales, record/tape retailers often sponsor a variety of in-store or special promotions. These may include any of the following: running sales, operating 7 days a week, remaining open all night, offering "club" plans (e.g., buy 12 singles, get 1 free), giving discount coupons with purchases, sponsoring in-store personal appearances, distributing underground entertainment newspapers free of charge, and playing videocassettes or videodiscs to advertise artists' products. In-store play of music is often an effective promotional device and such play tends to create a particular atmosphere or image. A store may also have a bulletin board with information on upcoming concerts. Some retailers offer a special-order service on hard-to-find or out-of-stock items at no extra charge.

Records and tapes are sometimes offered for sale at prices substantially less than normal, or at cost or below cost, to draw customers into the store and promote sales of other material. Such product is known as *loss leader*.

Cross-merchandising. Many record/tape retailers find *cross-merchandising* an effective way to promote goods. In retail trade, this in-

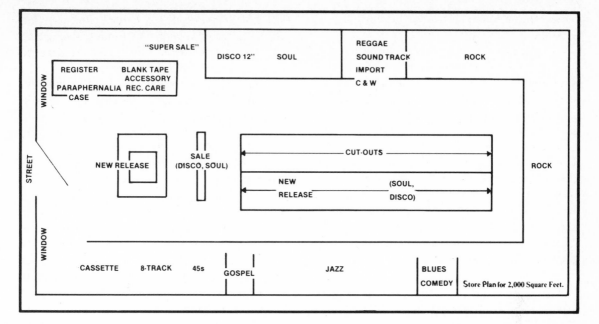

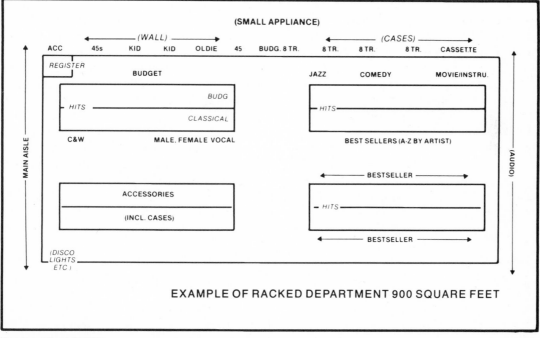

EXAMPLE OF RACKED DEPARTMENT 900 SQUARE FEET

Courtesy: *Music Retailer.*

volves two (or more) different businesses, each of which displays advertisements or cooperates in other types of promotions in an attempt to gain customers from the other's business (i.e., consumers who might not otherwise come in).

There are a variety of ways cross-merchandising could be employed by dealers (creativity, ingenuity, and relationships with other local entrepreneurs are the determinants). Record/tape retailers have used cross-merchandising effectively with concert promoters, audio hardware retailers, musical instrument stores, bookstores, fast-food chains, automobile dealers, clothing stores, toy stores, and movie theaters. A business may advertise the other's goods by displaying posters or cards or tempo-

rarily exchanging goods. For example, stereo equipment may be exchanged for albums where each vendor would display the other's goods as props with their own merchandise. Or each store might give away discount coupons redeemable on merchandise purchased at the other's store.

Personnel. The number and type of personnel a retail record/tape outlet employs depends on its size, products, and volume of business. It may employ any or all of the following: a manager (who is in charge of the store's operation), an assistant manager, clerks (whose combined duty it is to take care of customers, display the inventory, and guard against pilferage, and cashiers. If the retail

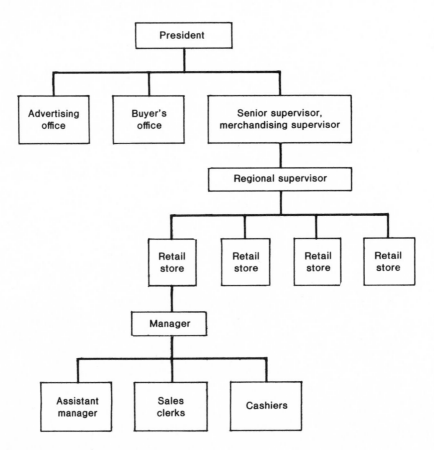

store is part of a multi-chain operation, there may also be a senior supervisor, who handles such matters as the payroll for all units, a merchandising supervisor, and regional supervisors, each of whom may be responsible for 4 to 6 stores in his territory.

The diagram on the facing page represents the types and hierarchy of personnel that may be found in a large retail chain.

See ADVERTISING; DISTRIBUTOR (RECORDS AND TAPES): NATIONAL ASSOCIATION OF RECORDING MERCHANDISERS (NARM); POINT-OF-PURCHASE MERCHANDISING; RETURN PRIVILEGE.

Return Privilege. In commercial practice, records and tapes are sold to wholesalers and retailers with the privilege of returning a certain percentage of unsold copies for credit or exchange. The *return privilege*, also referred to as *return authorization* or *RA*, allows a dealer to order more freely and take a chance with new and unproven products.

Manufacturers (which sell to wholesalers and retailers) vary in their return policies. These range from a full 100% return privilege down to 20% or less. The return allowance is adjustable by the manufacturer and generally reflects the company's or the industry's economic health.

The allowance is often based on customer classification (one-stop, rack jobber, etc.) and on a percentage of the customer's purchases from the company over a recent period (e.g., the last 4 months). A manufacturer may also have different RA policies for singles, LPs, and tapes. For example, it may allow 100% return for singles and limit LP and tape returns (thus a one-stop that buys $100 worth of albums and has a 20% RA may return $20 of such purchase). Manufacturers also have RA policies for defectives (often limited to 1% of purchases).

Manufacturers usually require their accounts to hold on to a product for a particular period of time—often a minimum of 60 or 90 days—before it is eligible for return. Some manufacturers permit a product to be returned until it is deleted from the company's catalog; others may limit the return period to a year or two or have a callback period for a particular album. Sometimes a record or tape is not credited at its full original value when returned.

Rhythm and Blues. *See* POPULAR MUSIC.

Road Manager and Road Crew. The concert tours made by bands to further their careers are usually attended by numerous duties that are time-consuming and complex. Most bands, particularly those with much equipment and extensive itineraries, hire road managers and road crews to tour with them and handle many of these affairs.

Factors to be considered in arranging and undertaking a concert tour include traveling, lodging, moving, setting up and packing of musical instruments and equipment, fulfillment of engagement contract terms by both artist and employer, safety of the artist, maximizing publicity for the artist during the tour, and compensation. It is in these areas that road managers, or "tour managers," and road crews work.

The function of the road manager is to oversee various aspects in the touring of the act. While responsibilities may vary from act to act, concert to concert, and tour to tour, road managers commonly coordinate certain basic aspects of a tour. The road manager: handles any problems that may arise when the band travels; arranges transportation and lodging for group members and entourage; discusses with the concert promoter prior to the performance various conditions related to the engagement and sees that the provisions of the contract rider are fulfilled; sees that the group fulfills its contractual commitments; may be the liaison for the band with record company publicists, branch or independent distributors, artist development coordinators, and local media; handles expenditures and incoming receipts, maintains records of all financial transactions, and accounts to the act or personal manager. Some acts retain business managers to accompany them on tour and handle their financial affairs.

The road crew may consist of set-up workers, carpenters, electricians, and sound and light technicians. Their main responsibilities are in setting up the equipment for each engagement. They unload, unpack, haul, assemble, and test the equipment before the group members arrive at the venue. The equipment, when there is much of it, may be systematically numbered for ease in handling and may be loaded and unloaded from the trucks with forklifts. Where the facility employs stagehands who are union (IATSE) members, the road crew's duties might be limited more to a supervisory capacity, as union regulations may require equipment to be unloaded by members (under prevailing wages). The road crew will arrive at the concert facility several hours or even a day or two prior to the engagement, in trucks, trailers, vans, or other vehicles containing the equipment. This will include sound and lighting systems, instruments, accessories, wardrobe, and for those acts whose shows are visually oriented, special effects equipment and materials. The road crew may also assist the house security team and will protect the equipment from theft or vandalism as the audience leaves.

The road manager and members of the road crew are usually compensated in the form of a weekly salary. Additionally, the road manager and crew are usually given a per diem while on the road. When the act is not touring, the road manager and the road crew's salaries may be reduced or temporarily discontinued.

Robinson-Patman Act. *See* BUSINESS LAWS, FEDERAL AND STATE.

Rock Music. *See* POPULAR MUSIC.

Royalty. Most commonly refers to: (1) a payment received by a recording artist or producer for sale of product in which the party contributed either performances or services, such payment being a percentage of the wholesale or retail selling price of the recording times the number of units sold over a particular period of time; or (2) the share of proceeds paid to a copyright owner and creator for sale of product embodying or based on the copyright or for performances and other uses of it.

An artist's or a producer's rate of royalty is determined by negotiation. An artist is usually represented by a manager or an attorney who negotiates a royalty contract on his behalf with the label. The royalty a copyright owner An artist's or a producer's rate of royalty is determined by negotiation. An artist is usually represented by a manager or an attorney who negotiates a royalty contract on his behalf with the label. The royalty a copyright owner is entitled to under the compulsory license provisions for making and distributing phonorecords (i.e., from sales of records and tapes) embodying his copyright is fixed by the law (except with respect to the first authorized recording). In practice, however, the statutory rate is sometimes negotiated to a lesser amount. The amount of performance royalties paid to a songwriter or publisher by ASCAP depends on the ratio of surveyed or logged performances of a work to the pool of money available for distribution. BMI pays performance royalties based on the amount indicated on its payment schedule for that performance times the number of performances logged (the payment schedule lists *minimum* amounts). SESAC's performance royalties are largely based on a song's average position in the trade charts.

There are actually several different types of royalties in the music business. This is partly because of the many ways in which a copyright can be used. An arrangement to pay a royalty is always in the form of a contract.

In the following table are the basic types of royalties in the music business and related information:

Royalties

Type	Basis of Royalty	Recipient(s) of Royalty	Payer(s) of Royalty
Artist royalties	Sales of phonograph records (singles and LPs) and pre-recorded tapes (cassette, 8-track, open-reel)	Recording artist	Record company
Producer royalties	Same as above	Record producer	Same as above
Mechanical (recording) royalties	Sales of records and tapes embodying the musical composition	Music publisher, songwriter	Record company or its licensees (this royalty may be transmitted to the copyright owner via a mechanical rights agency); also manufacturers of music boxes and player piano rolls
Performance royalties	Public performances of musical compositions on radio, television, wired music services, airlines, and jukeboxes, or at concert halls, clubs, colleges, universities, etc.	Music publisher, songwriter	Music user; for performances of nondramatic musical compositions, this money is almost always transmitted through a performing rights organization
Printed music royalties	Sales of sheet music, folios, fakebooks; band, orchestral, and choral arrangements; and other printed editions of the musical composition	Music publisher, songwriter	Licensee (printer/distributor) of music publisher; a few publishers handle print and distribution themselves
Miscellaneous royalties (for items using or based on a copyright)	Sales of products using the copyright (e.g., lyrics used in posters, greeting cards, etc.) or based on the copyright (games. drinks, etc.)	Music publisher, songwriter	Copyright user (different in each case)
Master recording license royalties	Sales of phonograph records and prerecorded tapes containing a licensed master track (e.g., record club editions or compilation albums)	Record company, recording artist, record producer	Licensee of the record company—record club, record merchandising company, mail order company

Royalties *(cont'd)*

Type	Basis of Royalty	Recipient(s) of Royalty	Payer(s) of Royalty
Foreign royalties	Same sources as all the above	Same as above in each individual category; in various cases, the royalty is shared with a foreign counterpart	Same type as all the above but from the foreign territory; in some foreign countries, one society represents both performing and mechanical rights

S

SAG. *See* SCREEN ACTORS GUILD, INC.

Satellite Communications. Satellite stations in space enable radio and television communication over long distances. Such communication is of interest to the music and broadcasting industries.

Satellite communication permits improved transmission quality of mono and stereo programs, that is, better than the best land systems (because the latter's carrier systems degrade the audio signal more than the satellite); satellites may be used as a central transmitting facility to broadcast music programs simultaneously (this is particularly advantageous to background music services, such as Muzak or 3M); audio signals can be transmitted instantaneously by satellite to cable TV systems throughout the country; satellites can be used to transmit live performances of artists in concert (rock, opera, etc.); and satellites can transmit programs to geographic locations that were previously inaccessible, as they were too expensive to service (another advantage for companies such as background music services). Consequently satellite communication promises new and wider audiences for the music industry and increased exposure of recording artists, possibly leading to greater record and tape sales. Also, such communication offers more programming variety, which provides additional creative outlets for authors and more revenue to the copyright owners and creators whose works are broadcast.

Communications satellites are placed in orbit approximately 22,300 miles above the earth's equator. At this distance, the speed of the satellite matches the rotation of the earth. Thus the satellite in this "geosynchronous" orbit appears to hang in the same spot above the earth.

The satellites contain from one to two dozen transponders—devices that receive a signal from an earth station (known as an "uplink"), amplify it after the long journey to the satellite, and transmit it back to earth (the "downlink"). The satellite earth stations are also used to relay telephone, television, telex, and facsimile messages.

History. Satellite communications experiments began in the late 1950s with the launch of the Army project Score satellite on December 18, 1959. Echo I, a giant aluminum-coated balloon, soon followed along with the Courier satellite, developed by the U.S. Army Signal Corps.

Telstar I was launched on July 10, 1962. This 170-pound satellite was used in the first transatlantic telecast on July 23, 1962, and later for the first color TV transmission across the Atlantic.

Later in 1962, on August 31, Congress passed the Communications Satellite Act, which states that "it is the policy of the United States to establish, in conjunction and in cooperation with other countries, as expeditiously as practicable a commercial communications satellite system. . . ."

The act also said that "United States participation in the global system shall be in the form of a private corporation." This private corporation, the Communications Satellite Corporation, or COMSAT as it is commonly known, came into being in 1963.

One year later, in August 1964, INTELSAT, the International Telecommunications Satellite Organization, was formed with 11 member nations, and COMSAT as the representative of the United States. As of early 1981 INTELSAT had 105 member nations and 134 countries using its satellites.

Late in 1980, INTELSAT launched the first of its new generation of communications satellites, INTELSAT V, to improve the global system. Each of these satellites has the capacity to carry 12,000 simultaneous phone calls and two channels of TV. This is a far cry from the first INTELSAT satellite (and the first commercial communications satellite), Early Bird, which could carry 240 phone calls *or* one channel of TV in 1965.

Scale. *See* UNION SCALE.

Screen Actors Guild, Inc. (SAG). Labor union that represents actors, including singers, announcers, narrators, specialty dancers, and specialty acts who work in theatrical, industrial, or educational motion pictures, filmed television programs, and/or filmed television commercials. Its jurisdiction extends throughout the United States, its commonwealths, territories, and possessions.

Eligibility for Membership. Membership in SAG is open to anyone who can supply a contract for a film engagement which states that the individual has worked as a principal (that is, anyone who has one, two, or more lines to say) in a theatrical, educational, or industrial film, a television film or commercial, or to anyone who has been a member of one of the affiliated unions (AEA, AFTRA, AGMA, AGVA, etc.) for one year or more.

Fees and Dues. There is an initiation fee for all SAG members and semiannual dues, the latter based upon earnings from employment within the union's jurisdiction.

Affiliation. SAG is a branch of ASSOCIATED ACTORS AND ARTISTES OF AMERICA (FOUR A's) and is affiliated with AFL-CIO.

Agreements. SAG has COLLECTIVE BARGAINING agreements in four separate but related types of motion pictures: (1) theatrical pictures; (2) filmed television programs; (3) television commercials; and (4) industrial and educational pictures. These contracts are renegotiated every 3 years. SAG members may only work as actors for producers or advertising agencies who are signatories to the guild contract. SAG has negotiated pension and welfare plans in its collective bargaining contracts which are available for qualifying members.

Minimum fees for SAG members singing in television commercials depend on such factors as the length of the employment, whether the performance is on or off camera, and whether the vocalist performs as a solo or duo, or in a group of 3 to 5, 6 to 8, or 9 or more. There are upgrading and use fees payable for doubling, dubbing, multiple tracking, and sweetening. Contractors are required on engagements using 3 or more singers.

Agents. Under the rules of SAG, no member may have as an agent in motion pictures any person or firm not franchised as an agent by the union. A contract between SAG and the Artists' Managers Guild, the agents' organization, establishes the business relations between actor and agent. The contract contains a set of rules and regulations to which the agent agrees to adhere.

History. Screen Actors Guild was officially founded on June 30, 1933, when articles of incorporation as a nonprofit corporation were filed at Sacramento, California. It formed to establish minimum wages for actors working in motion pictures and to improve working conditions. Its founders included Richard Tucker and Boris Karloff, and among the individuals who joined the guild in its first few months were Eddie Cantor, James Cagney, Groucho Marx, Gary Cooper, and Spencer Tracy. In 1935 the organization affiliated with AFL-CIO. Today, virtually all producers and advertising agencies of consequence in the United States have signed letters of adherence to the guild's Television Commercials Contract.

In 1980, there were approximately 50,000 members in the union. SAG's headquarters are in Hollywood, and it has several branches in major cities throughout the U.S.

Self-Contained Group. Term used to describe a performing group that does any of the following: accompanies itself instrumentally and/or vocally in "live" engagements and recording sessions; writes its own material; arranges its own material (for recordings or live performances); and produces its own recordings. In other words, the term is synonymous with "self-sufficiency" with respect to any of the foregoing.

Sequencing. Sequencing refers to the arranging of recorded tracks in the order in which they are to appear in manufactured LPs and tapes. There is no formula for choosing the order or rules for alternating selections. Some albums, for example, have several consecutive ballads and uptempo tunes. It is customary, however, for the first cut on side 1 to be the album's most commercial recording. This is not only to get the consumer "into" it right away but also because AOR radio stations generally play first and pay the most attention to the first cut on side 1 of an album.

The determination of the order of tracks on an album is made by any of the following or a combination thereof: a member of the record company's A & R staff, a label executive, the producer, the artist, the artist's personal manager. These individuals will listen carefully to the mixed tape recording of all the selections and make the decision or come to an agreement. After the sequence of selections is prepared, the master tape is sent to a mastering facility, where the lacquer is produced that is used to make the metal parts from which records can be pressed (*see* RECORD MANUFAC-TURING).

The sequence of selections on an LP may be different than on its counterpart 8-track tape cartridge. This is because an 8-track cartridge contains four different programs, each with a particular time limit, and programs must contain selections whose lengths fit into these time segments. LPs must balance material only for each side of the disc. Hence the lengths of selections are also a factor in determining their sequence in both tapes and records.

SESAC Inc. A full-service organization that represents publishers and writers with regard to performance, mechanical, and synchronization rights. SESAC, founded in 1931, is the second oldest and the smallest of the three U.S. PERFORMING RIGHTS ORGANIZATIONS. Unlike ASCAP and BMI, SESAC is not under a court consent order to have its system of determining performances and its formulas for distributing performance royalties to its publisher and writer affiliates reviewed. Also unlike the other music licensing organizations, SESAC licenses the dramatic music performing rights in its affiliates' works. The other two organizations do not represent mechanical and synchronization rights.

Performing Rights Aspects

Licenses and Fees. SESAC licenses the performing rights to the music in its repertory to all types of music users (agreements are generally effective for an initial period of 5 years). The annual fees paid by radio and television broadcasters (which comprise the major group of music users) are scaled according to the following factors:

1. For commercial AM and FM radio stations, the station's license fee is based upon the market classification (the population of the FCC city of license) and the station's highest 1-minute advertising rate as printed in *Standard Rates and Data*. (Commercial AM and FM stations each have 8 market classifications.)

2. For television stations, the license fee is also based upon the station's market classifica-

tion (population of the FCC city of license), and the station's highest 30-second spot advertising rate as it appears in *Television Rates and Data*.

Licenses for nonbroadcast music users are dependent on different sets of criteria. For instance, fees for hotels and nightclubs are based upon annual entertainment expenditures; for discos, the number of nights operating per week and room capacity; for auditoriums, theaters, and concert halls, seating capacity; for colleges and universities, total student enrollment.

Writer/Publisher Distribution. After deducting necessary administrative expenses, SESAC distributes royalties to its affiliated writers and publishers under SESAC's allocation system. In accordance with this system, credit is given to each affiliate for the following factors: total number of copyrights, their diversity, growth of the catalog, overall promotional activity, and most important, performances.

In the performance category, SESAC grants points to writers and publishers for single record releases, album cuts, trade picks, cover records, and the chart activity of each SESAC composition that appears in the three national trades, *Billboard, Cash Box,* and *Record World.* In addition, SESAC reviews and analyzes all national network logs and spot checks the programming of local radio and television stations. SESAC bases its performance royalties largely on trade chart activity. This is predicated on the fact that a record on the charts receives performances commensurate with its relative position on the chart, and that the trade charts are therefore reasonably accurate barometers of each song's performances. SESAC does not follow the other performing rights organizations in making payment to its writers and publishers simply on the basis of whether a work shows up on a survey of radio and television performances.

There are separate rate cards for the pop, country, and R & B singles charts. The top 100 compositions in each chart are divided into various sections, with a monetary value payable to writers and publishers. The payment is made based on the average of the highest chart position attained in each of the three charts. For instance: if the highest position a work achieves on the pop charts is number 4 in *Billboard,* number 7 in *Cash Box,* and number 11 in *Record World,* the average of the three positions is 7⅓, and the position to its highest, nearest whole number is 7. Therefore, the writer and publisher would each earn the rate corresponding to the number 7 position in SESAC's Pop Rate Card. If a work appears on two of the trade charts and not on the third, it is given the position of 101 for the third, which is used in the computation to arrive at the composition's average chart position.

SESAC also grants bonus payments. These are in recognition of a chart song's staying power and crossover activity. There are three types of bonuses: (1) a longevity bonus, which directly relates to the number of weeks that a composition has appeared on all three charts—for a minimum of 15 weeks, a 25% bonus, for 13 weeks, a 20% bonus, and if a record appears for a minimum of 11 weeks, a 10% bonus will be paid; (2) a crossover bonus of 50%, awarded for songs that cross over from one chart to another, for example, from R & B to pop; and (3) a carryover bonus, designed to compensate for performances that occur after a record has gone off the charts. To qualify for this third bonus, a song must have either (*a*) attained a top 10 average chart position or (*b*) been on the charts for a period of 15 weeks or more. The carryover bonus is for 10% of chart money paid over a 2-year period and an additional 5% of the chart money earned by the song paid in the third year.

With regard to record albums, SESAC grants money for the release of an album cut. There is also payment based on album chart activity. Additionally, "pick" money is available for album cuts. With the exception of the longevity and carryover bonuses, all payments begin in the first quarter in which a record is released and continue evenly over the following three quarters, so that payment in full is complete within the fourth quarter of the record's release. After the initial fourth quarter installment is paid, the longevity and carryover bonuses begin. The longevity bonus is paid over four consecutive calendar quarters.

SESAC makes payments to its affiliates for the performances of jingles. Payment is equally divided between writer and publisher and is based upon (1) medium (radio or television) and (2) whether it is performed on a national, regional, or local basis.

Mechanical/Synchronization Rights Aspects. SESAC represents music publishers with regard to the licensing of the mechanical and synchronization rights of their compositions. SESAC handles all negotiations with record companies and producers of syndicated programs. When musical works in the repertory of SESAC are used in motion pictures or television films, SESAC negotiates these licenses as well. SESAC's fee is on a sliding scale ranging from 3.5% to 10% based on volume (*see* MECHANICAL RIGHTS AGENCY).

Affiliation. Affiliation with SESAC is open to publishers whose compositions are distributed commercially, used in recording, and performed by the broadcast industry. Writer affiliation is available to those whose music is suitable for commercial recording.

Share. *See* ARBITRON.

Sheet Music. *See* PRINTED MUSIC.

Sheet Music, Printing of. Ordinarily, sheet music of pop songs will not be printed until the song has been recorded, records have been released by a bona fide label, and there is evidence that there is a market for sheet music of the song. Thus sheet music of most songs is not published until the recording enters the top 100 of the charts. In some cases, more caution is taken and sheet music won't be printed until the recording climbs to the top 40 or higher.

Some music publishers print and distribute sheet music, but most license print rights to a song or catalog to a printer-distributor (*see* PRINTED MUSIC, LICENSING AND DISTRIBUTION OF). When the licensee anticipates a demand for sheet music of a song and wishes to publish such a printed edition, it will request a lead sheet and a commercial recording of the song from the copyright owner–publisher. The licensee will then have a staff arranger prepare an arrangement (e.g., piano/vocal, "easy piano"). At the same time, it may contact the artist whose recording popularized the song, or his representative, to get authorization to use his picture, name, image, and/or likeness on the cover of copies and request photographs for such purpose.

After the musical arrangement is completed and proofread, the licensee will have its music engraving department make an engraving for the song. If it does not have in-house engraving capability, it will engage another company to handle this.

There are various ways to engrave a musical composition:

Music typewriter—The method most commonly used in the U.S., it is relatively inexpensive, but the quality of the musical symbols on many of these machines does not yield copies as good as from some of the other methods listed.

Plate engraving—In this process, the original art from which most modern methods evolved, notes are etched or hammered onto a soft metal plate. This method is very expensive and time consuming, but is generally conceded to yield the finest-quality work. This process is still in use in Europe, and a few master engravers can still be found in the U.S.

Photoengraving—A negative is made by placing the musical symbols on a slotted rectangular board containing staves. A photographic positive is then made. As with the music typewriter, the lyric is then typed and slurs, ties, and incidentals are added manually with a template and pen. The quality of musical characters compares favorably with plate engraving.

Autography—This is music engraving done manually with a special pen. Obviously there will be great variance in quality, depending on the skills of the individual practitioner.

Stamping—This method utilizes stamps containing musical symbols. They are inked and pressed onto paper containing predawn staff lines. This method is common in Europe and the Orient. Top-quality engravings are attainable from a few highly skilled artisans.

Computer—While the computer is still in its infancy as a music engraving device, a few are used for this purpose. Generally, much development is needed before it becomes a major source of engravings.

Sherman Antitrust Act. *See* Business Laws, Federal and State.

Showcase. A program or show for exhibiting or auditioning talent. Showcases are sponsored to spotlight recording artists, unsigned singers and musical acts, and songwriters. They are commonly held at clubs, theaters, halls, and rehearsal studios.

Recording artists in need of greater media and public exposure are often showcased at clubs (these are usually new and developing artists). Often a group's record company will support its engagement. For instance, the label may supplement the club's payment to the artist and invite critics, program directors, wholesalers, and retailers to the showcase, paying for their admission (with a guest) and even for their drinks. Record companies sometimes rent clubs to showcase groups for invited guests.

Club showcases for local talent, typically held under the banner of "amateur" or "talent" night, are often mutually beneficial for the proprietor and the budding musicians. Club owners typically pay no or little remuneration for groups that perform in showcases. The act, on the other hand, is given the opportunity to play before an audience, try out original material (if any), create new fans, expose itself to any music industry personnel in attendance, and possibly motivate the club owner to book the act in the future for a fee.

Showcases for exhibiting songwriting talent are also valuable. These are sponsored by music publishers, songwriting workshops, clubs or associations, and performing rights organizations. Their goal is to expose new songs and talented songwriters, and to initiate publishing contracts. Songwriting showcases may be attended by publishers, producers, artists, and others looking for new material.

Showcases are often advertised in the trade and consumer press or by posters, signs, handbills, and personal invitations.

Shrink Wrap. A transparent thermoplastic film wrapped around an Album Jacket or the container (Sleeve) of a prerecorded tape, which serves the dual purpose of protecting the package (from dust, moisture, and handling abuse) and serving as a merchandising aid by giving the package an attractive sheen and indicating to the consumer that it has not been previosusly used.

Sealing a cardboard album jacket or a tape container in shrinkable film is the last step in the manufacturing process before the product is packed and shipped. The film is thermosealed around the package, in a process that creates an airtight wrapping through exposure to a suitably controlled elevated temperature, which causes the film to contract (hence the name *shrink wrap*) and conform to, the shape of the product.

Sideman. A musician employed at a recording session whose playing supports a main artist. He is hired for the *date* (recording session) by a CONTRACTOR and is normally required to read manuscript charts prepared by the composer, arranger, or orchestrator. Sidemen earn minimum scale as stipulated by AFM's current agreement with employers. Top sidemen may negotiate overscale payments and those who act as *leaders* or play two or more instruments at the session earn extra payment, as provided by union regulations.

Prerequisites to being a successful sideman are to be able to sight-read well, play all styles of music and interpret them effectively, work in a studio environment with multi-track recording equipment (being able to overdub or sweeten preexisting tracks), work efficiently under the pressures that arise in recording sessions, get along well with others at the sessions, be prompt for sessions, and be reliable. Successful sidemen are among the highest-paid professional musicians.

A sideman is also known as a studio musician or session player, and the term may refer too, to a musician who is hired to back up a performer in concert or at clubs.

Singer-Songwriter. Singer who writes most, if not all, of the songs that he performs and records. The term was first widely used in the early 1970s, when the increasing number and success of singer-songwriters (mainly of the soft-rock genre) seemed to indicate a trend. Artists in the past who wrote the songs they performed and recorded were generally limited in number and often their biggest hits were written by others (there are of course notable exceptions to this).

The term "singer-songwriter" is used in reference to *individual* singers rather than groups (a band that performs and writes its own material is sometimes referred to as a SELF-CONTAINED GROUP). Singer-songwriters usually accompany themselves on guitar or piano and sometimes write their songs in collaboration with others.

Single. A single is a PHONOGRAPH RECORD 7 inches in diameter that contains one recorded selection of popular music on each side and is pressed with microgrooves and played at a speed of 45 rpm. The term may also refer to the recorded selection on the "A" side.

"A" and "B" Sides. A commercially released single has an "A" and a "B" side. The A side is the selection regarded by the label as having commercial, possibly "hit," potential. A record company promotes the A side to radio stations in the hope of getting it added to their playlists and generating enough airplay to induce people to purchase the single, or the LP or prerecorded tape in which it may also be released.

It is common practice for the singles that labels give to radio stations (called promotion, or "promo," copies) to contain the A side on both sides, one in stereo and the other in mono. If it contained the B, or *flip,* side of the commercially released single, that might be played by mistake or preference and interfere with coordinated promotion plans of the label.

Airplay. Constant AIRPLAY is necessary to "break" a single and cause it to eventually become a "hit." Many superstar artists automatically receive airplay just from the release of their singles, but the singles of lesser-known or new acts need proper promotion to get airplay.

Competition for airplay of singles is stiff. Most contemporary radio stations have playlists that are limited in number, with only a few slots open to new releases each week. In an average week, well over 100 new singles are released by bona fide record companies.

Some radio stations (particularly those in secondary and tertiary markets) have flexible programming and add several new singles to their playlists each week. Indeed these stations may be ultimately responsible for a record's success. Many new singles are reviewed each week in the TRADES.

Importance of Hit Singles to Artists. Having a *hit* single is usually vital to artists—at any career level. It can launch a new artist, sustain an established career, or revive that of an older artist. A hit single receives a tremendous amount of airplay throughout the country and exposes an artist to a mass audience. Hit singles establish or maintain an audience identification for an artist, and enough of them can lead to star or superstar status. They also serve to increase album sales—current as well as older catalog product.

Release. There is no particular procedure regarding the release of a single versus an album. A single may be produced before an album is recorded, with the album following only if the single is a commercial success; the album may be released first, with a single culled from it at a later date; or a single and an album may be released simultaneously.

When an album is recorded first and tracks from it are to be released as singles, the selections chosen are of course the strongest ones on the album. The choices are often made by any combination of the following: the artist, producer, A & R coordinator, promotion department, and the artist's personal manager. Labels sometimes release singles based on radio response to selections on the album.

Mechanical Royalties. Both the A and the B sides on commercially released singles are normally licensed by music publishers to record companies at the full statutory rate. This means that on sales of the single, the publisher and writer of the song that is embodied on the B side earn the same mechanical royalties as those of the A side. B sides, however, customarily earn little in the way of performance royalties, which may be the largest individual source of income for a song on a successful A side.

History. A 7-inch single, playable at a speed of 45 rpm with a maximum playing time of 8 minutes, was introduced in 1949 by RCA Victor. One factor that contributed to its introduction was competition: Columbia had introduced its long-playing record in 1948 and RCA needed a product that could compete with it. RCA believed that the 7-inch disc would be an excellent configuration to embody pop tunes, which were normally only a few minutes in duration, and that its relatively low price and small size would make it attractive to consumers. RCA marketed the product successfully and introduced hardware on which to play it. Over the years, the single has remained the configuration for marketing individual pop tunes. In the mid 1970s, some record companies marketed the so-called disco single, a 12-inch disc containing an extended selection (of disco music) on each side.

See also LP; PICK; SLEEPER; SLEEVE; TURNTABLE HIT.

Slander. *See* DEFAMATION.

Sleeper. A recording—particularly a single—that (1) is not an obvious candidate for becoming a "hit" but has the potential to be; or (2) achieves recognition and commercial success far exceeding the expectations the label had for it.

Sleeve. Open-end envelope, made of paper or high-density polyethylene film, used to protect a disc recording from dirt and surface damage. A 12-inch disc (LP) is inserted into a sleeve before being placed in an ALBUM JACKET and having SHRINK WRAP affixed; a 7-inch disc (single) is shipped and sold directly in its sleeve, without any other protective device. A sleeve may be unprinted, or printed in one color or multicolors. An album sleeve may contain lyrics to selections on the album, or a picture, or be used to present an advertising message (this is known as *cross-merchandising*).

An album sleeve is also called an "inner

sleeve" or "dust sleeve." In England it is commonly referred to as an "inner bag" and the jacket called a "sleeve."

The term "sleeve" may also refer to the cardboard container in which a prerecorded 8-track cartridge is sold.

See also PICTURE SLEEVE.

Small Rights. *See* NONDRAMATIC MUSICAL WORK.

Software. Any material object in or on which sounds or audiovisual programs can be or are stored and can be perceived, reproduced, or otherwise extracted with the aid of a machine or device.

Examples of software include phonograph records, prerecorded cassettes or 8-track tapes, videocassettes and videodiscs. Music programs on audio software may be monophonic, stereophonic, or quadraphonic.

See HARDWARE.

Song (Evolution and Pathway from Conception to Public Domain Status). Every recording offered for sale at the retail level has its unique history: the writer conceived of the lyric while strolling on a Caribbean beach late at night with his girl friend; the recording artist's uncle owns the label he is on; the disc jockey plugged the record his 8-year-old son liked. But while such uniqueness might be intrinsic to a particular stage of the process, the overall process is generally the same.

This entry traces, step by step, the "normal" route a song travels from its conception by a songwriter (one who is *not* an artist/writer), to its sale in retail outlets in the form of a sound recording, to its falling into the public domain.

1. Songwriter composes song, makes demo and lead sheet, and decides which music publishers to audition it for. He also copyrights the song.

2. Writer auditions and places song with a music publisher. He transfers copyright to publisher and signs a music publishing contract. Publisher records transfer of copyright ownership at the Copyright Office.

3. Professional manager at the publishing company makes a professional demo. He makes several tape copies of this and auditions the song for producers, A & R people, etc. A producer asks for a "hold" on the song.

4. Producer plays the song for a recording artist whom he produces. Artist likes the song and decides to record it in his upcoming album date.

5. A recording studio is selected and time is booked; an arrangement of the song is made, the artist rehearses the material, a contractor and a music copyist are hired, and musicians and background vocalists are engaged to perform at the sessions.

6. Artist records the song (along with the other album selections).

7. Master recordings of the songs on the album are submitted to the A & R coordinator of the artist's label. The decision is made as to which selections should be released as singles and in which order (our fictitious song is chosen to be released as the first single).

8. Record company copyrights the sound recordings at the Copyright Office; publishers of the songs embodied in the sound recordings issue the record company mechanical licenses.

9. LPs, singles, and prerecorded tapes are manufactured from the studio masters.

10. Marketing departments at the label—advertising, promotion, merchandising, etc.—plan campaigns; single is promoted to radio stations in certain markets. Distributors and subdistributors get records and tapes into retail outlets in these markets. After the single "breaks" regionally (and the record makes the charts), it is promoted in other markets and eventually on a national basis. Distribution of product parallels promotion efforts. Meanwhile, both single and album are advertised in trade and consumer press.

11. Artist tours to promote the album, and

the record climbs the national charts.

12. Music publisher arranges to have sheet music and other arrangements of the song printed and distributed. Publisher sends copies of the recording to other artists who may record the song, and also promotes the song to advertising agencies, TV and motion picture producers, etc. Song is licensed to various users.

13. Other artists record ("cover") the song. Publisher issues mechanical licenses and these artists' records are released.

14. Writer and publisher collect income from various sources (*see* ROYALTY). Royalties publisher collects on behalf of writer are remitted to writer in accordance with contract.

15. As the song was written and copyrighted after January 1, 1978, the writer sends a notice of termination to the publisher to recapture rights to the song, between 10 and 2 years before 35 years after the date of the song's "publication." When rights revert to the writer, he is free to negotiate a new agreement with the original publisher, transfer the rights to a different publisher, or publish the song himself. In any case, 50 years after the writer dies, the song falls into the public domain.

Song Shark. A company that: advertises for people to send in lyrics or poems they have written to see if these are suitable for completing into a song or if they have the potential for commercial success as a song; "accepts" virtually any such material submitted and agrees to set a melody to it for a fee, enclosing literature designed to excite the amateur about the "glamorous" career of songwriting and convince him to pay the fee; and attempts to lure the songwriter into paying for other "services" offered by the company (often at a later date), such as recording the song or making lead sheets of it. The operation of the song shark is considered unethical and is contrary to the business practices of legitimate companies in the music industry.

Target Customers. The song shark seeks to attract the business of people who will most easily fall prey to its "come-ons" (advertisements). These are songwriters who are usually beginning, inexperienced, or discouraged.

Finding Customers. Song sharks commonly solicit business through running advertisements in magazines. These advertisements feature such headings as: "Poems Wanted for Songs and Records"; "Songwriters—Your Songs Could Be Worth $$$"; or "Win Fame and Fortune Writing Songs." The song shark also reaches potential customers through direct mail, newspaper and radio advertisements, and other media. Writers are asked to send in their work for free appraisal, examination, or review.

Sales Pitch. Writers submit their material and invariably receive notification by return mail that it has been "approved." The company may suggest "necessary" revisions that it will make to improve the material, such as lengthening or shortening it or rewriting individual lines. In any case, writers are invited to remit a fee so one of the company's "professional" staff writers can set music to the lyrics. Literature will typically state that a lyric or poem "approved" can have music set to it in any style the customer wants and that the customer will have full ownership of the song—both the words he writes and the music written by the company's staff writer. The song shark may advertise then, or in a later mailing, that it can make a recording of the song, again for a fee. This, of course, is the most logical step after completing a song and the songwriter is tempted to have it done. To convince the writer to pay for this service, the company, in its literature, may promise to mail records to disc jockeys across the country, or guarantee that the recording will be broadcast on a particular radio program (announcing the song's title and its writer's name) and that each broadcast will be heralded to local music publishers and record companies. The song shark advertises that songs will be recorded by professional singers and musicians, that it may also copyright the song and make lead sheets of it (for additional fees), and that the writer will be given a royalty contract and paid for each record and sheet music copy sold. All these services may be offered in the first mailing under a "complete package plan."

Results. This all sounds good to the budding songwriter and many do pay for the "services" song sharks provide. However, all a writer receives in the end is a recording of a co-written song that has little or no commercial potential. He may have been bilked out of a few hundred dollars and may end up more discouraged than previously. A song shark's method may differ or vary from that described above, but the intended result is generally the same.

Investigating a Company. A writer may inquire about the reputation of a firm by writing to the Better Business Bureau, the U.S. Postmaster, or the chamber of commerce or consumer frauds agency of the city of the business in question. The performing rights organizations and the American Guild of Authors and Composers (AGAC) may also be able to provide information.

Songbooks. *See* PRINTED MUSIC.

Songwriter. Songwriters play a highly creative role in the music business. They conceive, construct, and shape together lyrics and music to create new songs, ones they hope will capture the public's liking. Many industry professionals feel that it is the song that is the key to a record's success and that a recording of a weak song, no matter how lavishly arranged, creatively produced, and dynamically performed, will not achieve popular success. '

Writing commercial songs requires talent, originality, and an understanding of the craft. Thus songwriting is a highly skilled profession and usually requires much dedication to suc-

ceed. Many do, however, as is evidenced by the number of professional writers who are members and affiliates of the performing rights organizations.

The term *songwriter*, meaning one who writes songs, may refer to the *lyricist* (writer of the words) or *composer* (writer of the music) or one who writes both the words and the music to a song.

Getting a Song Commercially Recorded. Songs today are normally first published in the form of *sound recordings* (sheet music and other printed editions follow only if the recording has created a demand for them). The following is the general means by which the songwriter (who is not a performer) gets his song recorded.

Make a Demo. Once a song is written, the means of getting it commercially recorded is to *expose* it to those who can record it or who can get it recorded. The vehicle for presenting a song is the DEMO. The songwriter, then, should make a demo that is an accurate rendition of the work.

Decide Whom to Send It to. The songwriter must next decide whom he is going to audition the song with. People or companies who are in a position to record the song or get it recorded include the artist, producer, any of the artist's personal representatives (personal manager, agent, attorney), the artist's record company, and music publishers.

Some songwriters first "cast" their songs. In doing this, a writer determines which recording artists the song would be "right" for. Creative judgment, a knowledge of the various artists, and "forecasting" are important. There may be artists who on first impression may not seem suitable candidates for the song but actually are. There may also be established artists changing direction or up-and-coming artists looking for potential "hit" material. The TRADES are excellent sources for finding out such information. After a song is cast, the writer may send the demo directly to the artist, his producer, his record company (to the attention of the A & R department), or his personal representatives.

The MUSIC PUBLISHER is perhaps the best route for the songwriter to go. The artist or his producer or representatives are often difficult to reach, while there are thousands of music publishers, many of whom are accessible. Professional managers of publishing companies are knowledgeable about the business and know whom to audition the song for and where to reach these persons. Their credibility, "contacts," and professional way of doing business will probably expose the song better than the songwriter could. Some publishers are associated only with a particular type or a few types of music. The writer may wish to classify his song and determine which publishers would be most receptive to it.

Send a Query Letter. Some publishers (as well as record companies, producers, and others) do not accept unsolicited material through the mail. To determine this, the songwriter can first send a typewritten query letter asking permission to submit his material. If the writer knows a publisher is listening to unsolicited material, a query letter is not necessary.

Audition the Song. The demo of the song may be auditioned with the writer present or, where the writer submitted the demo through the mail, at the listener's convenience.

Personal auditions are of course the best way to audition the song. The listener is likely to pay greater attention to the material, and even if it is rejected, the writer can find out why and also establish a rapport that will enable him to come back periodically and play more songs. The songwriter should provide the listener with a lyric sheet or lead sheet.

If submitting a song for audition by mail, the writer should assemble the various materials—the demo, the lyric or lead sheet, a brief typed cover letter introducing himself and providing any pertinent information, and a self-addressed stamped envelope—and place them in a strong box or envelope. (Actually, a demo may contain up to 3 or 4 songs; it is not advisable to send any more without specific permission.)

There are various ways to mail the package: first class is usually the best; a demo sent by registered or certified mail may be refused. When mailing a package to a company, it is best to send it to a particular person's attention. The songwriter should find out the name of the individual in charge of screening new material (for a music publisher, his title would be "professional manager"; for a record company, "A & R coordinator").

There are various sources that list publishing, record, management, and production companies and the names of personnel there. The weekly issues, annual supplements, or special directories of the trade publications provide this information. An artist's record company (usually cited on recording labels) might provide specific information for that artist. The classified telephone directory is another source.

Follow Up the Audition. If the songwriter does not receive a response to a demo he mailed within 3 to 4 weeks, a follow-up inquiry letter regarding the status of the submission would be justified. The writer should specify the name of the song, the configuration of the demo submitted (disc, cassette, or 8-track), the date it was sent, and his name, address, and telephone number.

Keep Records. The songwriter should keep orderly records—index cards and notebooks are handy to use—of all material sent out. Records should indicate the name of each song sent out, the name of the person (and company) to whom it was sent, the date it was sent, and the response (if any). This gives the writer an overview of whom he has sent his material to, the status of the submissions, and when to send follow-up letters. A study of these records might also result in the discovery of a person or company the writer forgot to submit a song to.

Other Considerations. Before auditioning the song, the writer has the option of copyrighting it (*see* COPYRIGHT REGISTRATION OF A MUSICAL WORK) or waiting for a contract and having the publisher make registration. The chances for "rip-offs" are slim if reputable companies and individuals are approached. A songwriter should never pay money to any company or individual to have a song published (*see* SONG SHARK).

Songwriters should be persistent and not easily discouraged. Rarely does a songwriter—even one who goes on to become successful—receive a publishing contract the first time he auditions a song. Rather, the process often takes years of constantly exposing songs, making contacts, writing new songs, auditioning them again, and *finally* playing the right song for the right person at the right time. But at all times throughout the songwriter's career, professional presentation of material and a professional attitude can only serve to expedite success.

The well-rounded songwriter understands various aspects of the music business, for such knowledge can create the confidence that makes the writer appear professional. He should (at the very least) be familiar with or knowledgeable about the following: the copyright law, the music publisher, performing and mechanical rights organizations, the trade publications, and royalties. The bottom line, of course, is talent.

Organizations. Professional songwriters are members or affiliates of the performing rights organizations—ASCAP, BMI, and SESAC. These organizations pay writers royalties for public performances of their works.

Other organizations comprised exclusively or partially of songwriters include AMERICAN GUILD OF AUTHORS AND COMPOSERS (AGAC),

Nashville Songwriters Association International, COUNTRY MUSIC ASSOCIATION (CMA), and NATIONAL ACADEMY OF RECORDING ARTS AND SCIENCES (NARAS).

See also CONTRACTS; SONGWRITER/MUSIC PUBLISHER CONTRACT.

Songwriter/Music Publisher Contract. The contract entered into by the songwriter and the music publisher sets forth the terms under which a musical composition is transferred, revenues earned by the composition are divided between the parties, and other conditions are carried through. Songwriter contracts vary from publisher to publisher, and even the same publisher may offer variable terms to two different writers. There is no bona fide "standard" songwriter/music publisher agreement in the industry, and the terms of any contract are negotiable. Criteria such as how badly a publisher wants a particular composition or the writer's track record will determine what terms the publisher will offer or how far it will go in conceding to the demands of the songwriter (or his representative). The writer should understand the basic provisions of songwriter/music publisher contracts in general, and the terms offered to him in particular, before signing or negotiating.

In entering into an agreement, the publishing company acquires a property it believes is a potential money-earner—the copyright—which it administers, exploits, promotes, and protects. It collects income from all uses of the copyright (except those exempt from payment under the copyright law) and shares this with the writer in accordance with the terms of the contract.° The writer in turn acquires the professional services of the publisher for his work.

There are numerous terms in songwriting

°Performing rights organizations pay writers and publishers directly and separately.

contracts and although these may be worded differently in each publisher's contract, they usually fall into various basic areas. The table that follows compares several publisher-orient-. ed terms found in songwriter/music publisher contracts with those contained in the agreement devised by the AMERICAN GUILD OF AUTHORS AND COMPOSERS (AGAC) for its members. AGAC's "Popular Songwriter's Contract" is considered the best in the industry for songwriters (its provisions contained in this text are those in the contract's revision made in accordance with the 1976 Copyright Act). The table should enable readers to observe contract terms as they range from common, unfavorable, and/or the minimum offered to what is considered optimum for a songwriter. Where an AGAC contract is not used, the writer should use the terms of the AGAC agreement as a guideline to what he (or his representative) should aim for during negotiation. In negotiation, it is always advisable for the songwriter to be represented by an attorney, preferably one who specializes in music or entertainment law.

Exclusive Songwriter Contract. Agreement entered into between a songwriter and a music publisher stipulating that the rights to all

Songwriter/Music Publisher Contracts: An Analysis of Terms by Comparing the AGAC Contract with a Publisher-Oriented Contract

Term	AGAC Contract	Publisher-Oriented Contract
Duration of transfer of copyright to the publisher	Negotiated number of years but not more than 40 years from date of contract or 35 years from first release of song in a commercial recording, whichever term ends earlier.	Rights granted to copyright for its entire term of statutory protection throughout the world. (Note: The 1976 Copyright Act provides for authors to terminate transfers despite contrary contractual terms—*see* COPYRIGHT GRANTS, TERMINATION OF.)
Scope of rights	All rights granted for the entire world.	All rights granted for the entire world.
Recapture rights	Publisher has maximum of 12 months from contract date to cause a commercial sound recording of the composition to be made and released, otherwise contract terminates. Publisher may retain rights, however, for an additional period of 6 months maximum by paying writer a minimum of $250.	No contractual provision; thus publisher retains rights to song whether or not it causes song to be released as a commercial recording.
Advance	Any advance is nonreturnable and may only be recouped from payments for the composition under contract.	Any advance may be recouped from payments made under any agreement between the parties (this is referred to as CROSS-COLLATERALIZATION).
Royalties: piano copies— U.S. and Canada	Negotiated percentage of the wholesale selling price but in no case less than: 1. 10% of the first 200,000 copies, plus 2. 12% of the next 300,000 copies, plus 3. 15% on copies in excess of 500,000.	A flat royalty ranging from $.03 to $.10 per copy (no sliding scale).

Songwriter/Music Publisher Contracts: An Analysis of Terms by Comparing the AGAC Contract with a Publisher-Oriented Contract   *(cont'd)*

Term	AGAC Contract	Publisher-Oriented Contract
Royalties: folios, song-books, etc.	For any publication issued by publisher containing 4 to 25 songs, writer's share is determined by dividing 10% of wholesale selling price of copies sold (after trade discounts, if any) among the total number of publisher's copyrights in the publication (the said 10% is increased by 0.5% for each additional song over 25). Where publisher grants license to a licensee, the royalty to be paid to the writer is that proportion of 50% of the gross amount the publisher receives from the licensee, as the number of uses of the composition under the license and during the period, bears to the total number of uses of the copyrighted musical compositions under the license and during the license period.	Either a one-time sum ranging from $10 to $25 for use of song or a prorated share equal to 10% of the wholesale selling price divided by the number of songs in the folio (if issued by the publisher).
Professional material and free copies	No royalty shall be payable to writer. Free copies of lyrics shall not be distributed except as follows: (1) with the writer's written consent; or (2) in limited numbers for charitable, religious, or governmental purposes; or (3) when authorized for use in a book, magazine, or other periodical where such use is incidental to a novel or story (must bear writer credit and copyright notice; or (4) when distributed solely for the purpose of exploiting the song.	No royalty payable to writer; publisher unrestricted with respect to distribution of such material.
Mechanicals, electrical transcriptions, synchronization, and all other rights	Negotiated percentages, but in no case less than 50% of gross receipts of publisher with maximum deductions stipulated for an agent's (i.e., mechanical rights agency) commission as follows: 5% of gross license fee for phonorecords, 10% of gross license fee for electrical transcriptions, and 10% of gross license fee or $150 (whichever is less) for synchronization.	Writer receives 50% of all net sums actually received.
Foreign advance/royalties	Writer receives minimum of 50% of any advances and not less than 50% of all net sums received by publisher.	Writer receives 50% of any advance and 50% of all net sums actually received.

Songwriter/Music Publisher Contracts: An Analysis of Terms by Comparing the AGAC Contract with a Publisher-Oriented Contract *(cont'd)*

Term	AGAC Contract	Publisher-Oriented Contract
Other income	Before the song may be used in a way new or hereafter known, publisher must give written notice to writer and negotiate the terms and conditions of any such disposition. (Note: Other uses may include commercial broadcasts, videocassettes, video discs, etc.)	Writer entitled to royalties only from sources specified in contract.
Royalty statements and payments	Must be rendered either semiannually or quarterly and not more than 45 days after the end of optioned period.	On a semiannual basis, with 45 days to prepare and deliver to writer.
Writer's consent to changes, additions and uses	No provision granting such rights.	Writer consents to changes, dramatizations, adaptations, editing, and arrangements as the publisher deems desirable.
Trust for writer	Any portion of receipts due writer from license fees shall if not payable immediately be held in trust for the writer until payment is made.	Not likely a publisher would include such a provision.
Right to audit	Upon written demand by writer or his representative, such party may audit publisher's books relating to the composition during business hours.	Limited in number of times audit may be conducted (usually one per year); sometimes no such provision.
Assignment of copyright	Subject to consent of writer unless included in a voluntary bona fide sale of publisher's business.	Publisher has right to assign the contract to any other person, firm, or entity.
Derivative works	No derivative work of the song may be utilized by the publisher or any other party after the contract terminates.	Publisher may authorize derivative works of the song at any time, without the consent of the writer.
Arbitration	Any dispute arising out of contract shall be submitted to arbitration under the prevailing rules of the American Arbitration Association and the parties shall abide by judgment rendered in such arbitration.	Arbitration shall take place in the city in which the publisher has its principal place of business; sometimes no such provision.
Advertising and promotion expenses and demo costs	No provision charging such costs against songwriter's royalties.	Recoupable against songwriter's royalties.

Songwriter/Music Publisher Contracts: An Analysis of Terms by Comparing the AGAC Contract with a Publisher-Oriented Contract   *(cont'd)*

Term	AGAC Contract	Publisher-Oriented Contract
Default in payment or prevention of examination	If publisher shall fail or refuse within 60 days after written demand to furnish or cause to be furnished such statements, books, records, or documents, or to permit inspection thereof, or within 30 days after written demand to make the payment of any royalties due under the contract, then writer shall be entitled upon 10 days' written notice to terminate the contract. However, if publisher within the 10-day period serves on the writer a written notice demanding arbitration and submits to arbitration its claim that it has complied with its obligation to furnish statements, books, records, or documents or permitted inspection thereof, or to pay royalties, as the case may be, or both, and thereafter comply with any award of the arbitrator in 10 days after such award or within such time as the arbitrator specifies, then the contract continues in full force and effect. If the publisher fails to comply with such provisions, then the contract is deemed to have been terminated as of the date of the writer's notice of termination.	Not likely a publisher would include such a provision.

songs writen by the songwriter during the contract term and any option periods, if exercised, are to be assigned to the publisher. A music publisher may request a songwriter to enter into such a contract when the publisher feels that the writer is talented and can steadily create commercial songs. An exclusive songwriter contract may be in the form of an exclusive agreement or an addendum to a regular contract providing for the transfer of rights of an individual musical composition. An exclusive songwriter contract in any form will contain basic terms normally found in a songwriting contract (discussed above) and additional terms relating to the special arrangement between the parties. Such additional terms may relate to the following:

Duration of Contract. The duration of exclusive songwriter contracts varies. They usually run for an initial period with an option for renewal by the publisher (e.g., an initial period of 52 weeks with an option to extend the contract for an additional period of 52 weeks under the same terms). Writers may safeguard themselves with respect to publisher options on extensions by negotiating certain stipulations, e.g., that the publisher cause a minimum number of compositions created under the agreement to be commercially released as recordings, that their royalties equal or supersede their collective advances, that they be granted a bonus, or that the amount of the writer's weekly or monthly advance increase.

Advances. Virtually all bona fide exclusive agreements provide for nonreturnable compensation paid in consideration of delivery of a minimum number of songs during the term of the agreement. Such compensations are considered advances and it is customary for all advances to be recoupable against all royalties earned by all compositions applicable under the contract. Advances are usually paid on a weekly or monthly basis.

Recapture Rights. A "recapture" right refers to the right of the songwriter to automatically reacquire (recapture) the rights to his song if the publisher has not caused a commercial recording of it by a specified time. If an exclusive contract provides for the assignment of songs written prior to the signing of the agreement, it is incumbent upon the songwriter to request that those songs which have not been recorded and released during the term of the agreement revert to him at the expiration of such agreement.

Demo Costs. It is common for exclusive agreements to provide that the songwriter assume all costs for the making of demos of his songs (i.e., demo costs are recoupable against royalties) or for the publisher and writer to split such costs. Thus it is to the writer's advantage to participate in the making of the demos, not only to see that his tunes are accurately recorded but to make sure that costs are kept reasonable.

Songwriters' Hall of Fame and Museum.

The Songwriters' Hall of Fame was established in 1968 by songwriters Johnny Mercer and Abe Olman and publisher Howard Richmond to honor the creators of the American popular song. A board of directors prepared the necessary qualifications for induction and a list of eligible songwriters. The general membership subsequently elected the first songwriters into the Hall of Fame.

To differentiate between members of the Hall of Fame and the general membership, a parent organization, the National Academy of Popular Music, was set up in 1973 to act as the sponsor of the Hall of Fame. In 1975, the Academy's president, Sammy Cahn, and folksinger Oscar Brand began planning a museum and archive. These were realized in 1977, when there opened in New York City a museum whose displays include plaques honoring songwriters elected to the Hall of Fame, musical memorabilia, rare sheet music, curios, and other mementos commemorating songwriters, popular music, and entertainment in America.

To be eligible for election to the Hall of Fame, a songwriter must have a substantial catalog of hit songs and have published his or her first hit song at least 20 years earlier. Songwriters are elected by the Academy's general membership.

The roster of living writers follows:[*]

Louis Alter	John Green
Harold Arlen	Sheldon Harnick
Burt Bacharach	Edward Heyman
Alan Bergman	Burton Lane
Marilyn Bergman	Jack Lawrence
Irving Berlin	Alan Jay Lerner
Leonard Bernstein	Jay Livingston
Jerry Bock	Jerry Livingston
Irving Caesar	Frederick Loewe
Sammy Cahn	Herb Magidson
Hoagy Carmichael	Johnny Marks
Cy Coleman	Joseph Meyer
Betty Comden	Mitchell Parish
J. Fred Coots	Leo Robin
Sam Coslow	Arthur Schwartz
Hal David	Pete Seeger
Mack David	Carl Sigman
Howard Dietz	Stephen Sondheim
Edward Eliscu	Jule Styne
Ray Evans	Jimmy Van Heusen
Sammy Fain	Harry Warren
Ira Gershwin	Paul Francis Webster
Adolph Green	Jack Yellen
Bud Green	

[*]Current as of 1981.

Deceased members of the Hall of Fame are:[*]

Harold Adamson
Milton Ager
Fred Ahlert
Ernest Ball
Katherine Lee Bates
William Becket
William Billings
James Bland
Carrie Jacobs Bond
James Brockman
Lew Brown
Nacio Herb Brown
Alfred Bryan
Joe Burke
Johnny Burke
Anne Caldwell
Harry Carroll
Sidney Clare
Will D. Cobb
George M. Cohan
Con Conrad
Hart P. Danks
Benny Davis
Reginald De Koven
Peter De Rose
Buddy De Sylva
Mort Dixon
Walter Donaldson
Paul Dresser
Dave Dreyer
Al Dubin
Vernon Duke
Gus Edwards
Raymond B. Egan
Duke Ellington
Daniel Decatur Emmet
Dorothy Fields
Ted Fio Rito
Fred Fisher
Stephen Foster
Arthur Freed
Rudolf Friml
George Gershwin

L. Wolfe Gilbert
Haven Gillespie
Patrick S. Gilmore
Mack Gordon
Ferde Grofé
Woody Guthrie
Oscar Hammerstein II
Lou Handman
W. C. Handy
James F. Hanley
Otto Harbach
E. Y. Harburg
Charles K. Harris
Lorenz Hart
Ray Henderson
Victor Herbert
William J. (Billy) Hill
Joseph E. (Joe)
   Howard
Julia Ward Howe
Howard Johnson
James P. Johnson
James Weldon Johnson
Arthur Johnston
Isham Jones
Scott Joplin
Irving Kahal
Gus Kahn
Bert Kalmar
Jerome Kern
Francis Scott Key
Ted Koehler
Huddie Ledbetter
Edgar Leslie
Sam Lewis
Frank Loesser
Ballard MacDonald
Edward Madden
Joseph McCarthy
Jimmy McHugh
Johnny Mercer
George W. Meyer
Jimmy Monaco

Neil Moret
Theodore Morse
Lewis F. Muir
Ethelbert Nevin
Jack Norworth
Chauncey Olcott
John Howard Payne
J. S. Pierpont
Lou Pollack
Cole Porter
Ralph Rainger
Andy Razaf
Harry Revel
Eben E. Rexford
Jimmie Rodgers
Richard Rodgers
Sigmund Romberg
George F. Root
Billy Rose
Vincent Rose
Harry Ruby
Bob Russell
Jean Schwartz
Seymour Simons
Harry B. Smith
Samuel Francis Smith
Ted Snyder

John Philip Sousa
Andrew B. Sterling
Harry A. Tierney
Charles Tobias
Roy Turk
Egbert Van Alstyne
Albert Von Tilzer
Harry Von Tilzer
Fats Waller
Samuel A. Ward
Ned Washington
Mabel Wayne
Kurt Weill
Percy Wenrich
Richard Whiting
Clarence Williams
Hank Williams
Spencer Williams
Septimus Winner
Harry MacGregor
   Woods
Henry C. Work
Allie Wrubel
Vincent Youmans
Joe Young
Rida Johnson Young
Victor Young

Soul Music. *See* POPULAR MUSIC.

Sound-Alike Album. An album containing the same selections as a previously released album (usually one that is very successful) and whose cover may mislead the public into believing that it is the original product even though performed by a different artist. In a sense, these are cover versions of albums, but they usually emphasize the material and not the new artist. They may even bear the original artist's name or picture on their covers to further imply it is his performance, or contain an illustration simulating a likeness found on the original al-

---

[*]Current as of 1981.

bum cover. Examples of sound-alikes include recordings of songs from a Broadway show, theatrical motion picture, or the hits of a popular recording artist contained on one album, recorded by a studio or unknown artist. These recordings are legal if the producer obtains a direct or compulsory license to manufacture and distribute discs and tapes embodying the compositions and does not seek to pass it off as the work of the original artist.

A spurious sound-alike recording may actually be a reproduction of a legitimate sound recording with a particular variation or variations to hide its true nature. For example, the sound-alike may be a slightly speeded up or slowed down version of the original recording, giving it a somewhat altered frequency and pitch; or it may embody a new track containing the sounds of an additional instrument, such as a tambourine or conga; or it may be any combination of these or contain other variations to make it appear to be a "new" recording. This type of spurious sound-alike recording has been made by record and tape pirates as a means of seeking to avoid criminal prosecution or an infringement action, but courts have uniformly held that these are illegal reproductions and offenders are subject to copyright infringement and/or unfair competition suits as well as criminal prosecution.

Sound Effects Recording. Sound effects are often used in commercial recordings and films, the latter including theatrical motion pictures, industrial, and documentary films, and films for television, educational, and cable TV. Producers commonly obtain the particular sound effect they want from special dealers who make and sell recorded sound effects.

A typical seller of sound effects will carry a large catalog containing airplane and automobile noises, applause, baby sounds, bird calls, crowd sounds, gun and cannon noises, clock tickings, animal noises, waterfall and whistle sounds, etc.

Sound effects recordings are normally sold outright for use in audio recordings or films without the need for permission or royalty payments for public performances. However, certain sound effects, such as calliope or carnival music, may be copyrighted and require specific permission from the copyright owner for synchronization purposes.

Sound effects recordings are sold by the album or by the "needle drop" (*see* SOUND TRACK LIBRARY). Albums commonly contain 10 to 20 sound effects per side, the effects ranging in length from a few seconds to over two minutes.

Sound Recording. Term used in the copyright law that refers to a certain type of work of authorship.

Definition. "Sound recordings" is defined in the 1976 Copyright Act (Section 101) as "works that result from the fixation of a series of musical, spoken, or other sounds, but not including the sounds accompanying a motion picture or other audiovisual work, regardless of the nature of the material objects, such as disks, tapes, or other phonorecords, in which they are embodied."

Example. At a recording session, a number of instrumentalists and vocalists perform and record their parts onto a multi-track tape. The sounds are mixed and a "master" tape is derived containing all the sounds blended together as desired. The total amount and arrangement of sounds produced in the final form is the "sound recording" and is a copyrightable work of authorship. Records or tapes that may be manufactured from the "master" tape are material objects that embody the sound recording and are referred to in the copyright law as PHONORECORDS.

Copyright Registration. A sound recording is a work of authorship and it may also embody another work of authorship—the underlying musical, dramatic, or literary work. The Copyright Office permits a claimant registering a sound recording for copyright to register the musical, dramatic, or literary work on the same application if he is the owner of that work also.

Authorship/Copyright Duration. Under the statute, the duration of copyright protection in a work created on or after January 1, 1978, is based upon wxether the AUTHOR is an individual identified in the Copyright Office records or if there are two or more authors or whether it is an anonymous work, a pseudonymous work, or a work made for hire. Most commercial music recordings contain sounds contributed by a number of individuals and this might cause confusion as to who the "author" of the work is. The copyright law does not provide a mechanism to determine the authorship of a sound recording but leaves this to individual bargaining.

Most recordings issued by record manufacturers are created under WORK MADE FOR HIRE agreements, in which case the manufacturer would be considered the "author" under copyright law. In other cases, it would be the individual record producer. It is important that the authorship be established, as this fixes the method for determining the term of COPYRIGHT DURATION.

History of Copyright Protection for Sound Recordings. A copyright in sound recordings was not originally provided for under the Copyright Act of 1909. This law was designed to provide protection only for certain categories of creative works, and sound recordings were not deemed to fit any of these. After intensive lobbying efforts by trade industry groups and revelations of the huge volume of pirate recordings as well as involvement in piracy of organized crime elements, the copyright law was amended on October 15, 1971, to provide federal copyright protection for all sound recordings "fixed" and published on or after February 15, 1972. With the enactment of the Copyright Act of 1976, a copyright in both published and unpublished sound record-

ings was created. This provides statutory copyright protection against unauthorized duplications of sound recordings—i.e., PIRACY. (BOOTLEGGING and COUNTERFEITING involve other prohibited activities.)

Recordings fixed prior to Februrary 15, 1972, may be protected under an individual state's antipiracy statute.° (In addition, federal prosecutions have been had of pre-1972 recordings on the basis of infringement of the underlying compositions protected by their individual copyrights.) The 1976 Copyright Act limits the duration of state law protection, however, and provides that states may only protect sound recordings fixed before February 15, 1972, until February 15, 2047. While a COPYRIGHT NOTICE is required for protection of a sound recording fixed on or after February 15, 1972, there is no requirement for a notice to appear on a sound recording fixed prior to this date.

See also COPYRIGHT PROTECTION AND NATIONAL ORIGIN; COPYRIGHT REGISTRATION OF A SOUND RECORDING.

Sound Track. The music heard in motion pictures is frequently made available to the public in the form of record and tape albums, commonly called *sound tracks*. The music in album sound tracks is usually somewhat different in form than it was in the film. The music may be edited, remixed, or altered in sequence, so as to be more appropriate for listening pleasure or to accommodate the limitations of the configuration. Motion picture producers license rights to their films' music sound tracks to record companies, which in some cases are affiliates of the motion picture company.

Sound Track Library. A collection of prerecorded background-music pieces from which

---

°At this writing, Vermont does not have an antipiracy statute.

individual compositions may be selected and used in sound tracks for films or to accompany other types of productions. Compositions vary in length to fit most needs—from a few-second spot to a complete score. Recordings are available on audio tape (full track in 7½ or 15 ips) and LPs (33⅓ rpm).

Suppliers/Users. Recordings in a sound track library are made and supplied by a production company. Users of these tracks include film producers, broadcasters, corporations, advertisers, and government agencies.

Library music is used by an entity whose budget for a production is not large enough to include the making and recording of original music. A prerecorded sound track can be an attractive alternative, offering a readily available and relatively inexpensive assortment of musical selections to fit most needs. The cutting, editing, and synchronizing of prerecorded library music for a film, for example, can make an inexpensive production appear costly and professional.

Productions. Library music is commonly used in the following types of productions: industrial films, corporate sales training presentations (on film, slides, or cassettes), travelogues, documentaries, cable and educational television presentations, radio and TV spots, and fashion shows.

Selections. A production company's music library normally contains selections that are suitable for a wide variety of uses. Categories, moods, and applications of prerecorded music include the following types: marches; dances; music to fit all types of foreign nationality moods; music adaptable for battles, chases, mysteries, sports, and fashion shows, and newsreels; national anthems; historical period music; electronic, religious, romantic, and topical music, fanfares. Compositions are recorded at the production company's expense. They are performed by groups ranging in size from a small ensemble to a large orchestra.

Licenses. The compositions supplied by sound track libraries are usually copyrighted arrangements of public domain compositions, but include original works. Since the owner of a copyrighted musical composition has certain exclusive rights (*see* COPYRIGHT OWNER), the user of copyrighted library music must obtain from the copyright proprietor a license if he wishes to use the work in a motion picture or utilize it in certain other ways.

Rates. Production companies usually charge to use library music in one of the following ways:

Needle drop basis—An LP containing one or various selections is played and there is a certain fee for each "drop" of the needle. The lifting of the needle to use another part or selection or placing the same music in a different section of the film is considered an additional needle drop.

Per film or production basis—This is the unlimited use of library music in a film or production for one flat fee. Fees are based on the length of the film or production and other factors.

Annual agreement basis—This is the unlimited use of library music for a one-time yearly fee. Fees vary as to the type of productions done. They may also be scaled according to the type of usage (cable TV, industrial, theatrical, etc.), and the geographical territory of exhibition (U.S., U.S. and Canada, foreign, or worldwide).

Standard. A song whose popularity continues to such degree after its initial introduction that it remains part of the regular musical repertoire of a society years later. Also called an "evergreen," a standard is generally characterized by the following:

- It is familiar to or well liked by the general public (despite how long ago it initially became popular).
- It has a universal lyric or theme and is timeless.
- It is highly melodic.
- It has been recorded by many artists and may continue to be, in new or updated arrangements.

- It is played from time to time on the radio after its initial success (this decreases as the length of such interval increases, unless there is a new, "updated" recording of the song).
- It is often performed in venues such as nightclubs and bars; at affairs such as weddings and bar mitzvahs; at political, civic, and fraternal functions; at concerts or on television. It is often part of the repertory of dance bands, combos, and cocktail pianists and is also used by singers for auditions.
- It is a song that stands up on its own, without the need for elaborate arrangement or production (a standard, however, may find itself arranged or produced to conform to the music style currently in vogue).
- It is singable by the average person.
- It continually sells well in sheet music and is constantly used in various printed music editions—fakebooks, songbooks, folios, and arrangements for band, choral groups, and the various musical instruments (the basic costs for these have previously been covered; it is just a matter of reprinting a work).
- It is a continual source of income for its publisher, composer, and lyricist (until it falls into the public domain).

The chances of a song becoming a standard are indeed slim. The primary means of exposing new songs today (and for several years now) has been from radio airplay of recordings. First, therefore, a song has to be chosen for recording, an arrangement made, and a commercial recording produced. Records have to be pressed, the label has to schedule a release date, a marketing campaign must be devised, and the record has to be promoted to radio stations. Most contemporary-music radio stations, however, have tight playlists. The situation is further complicated by the fact that at any one time, there is a multitude of new records competing for the few slots open to new records each week. And once a record does get on, it competes with all those already on, as well as with future releases. Consequently the chart life of even popular records is ephemeral. A song generally needs constant and widespread initial exposure to at least have a chance to become a standard. If it re-

ceives this, one can only hope it evokes such strong public reaction that not only is the public unlikely to forget it but there will always be a demand for it, which will be continually satisfied by record companies and others.

Examples of standards of the 20th century include the following (decades listed are those during which the songs were written):

1900–09: "Bill Bailey, Won't You Please Come Home," "Take Me Out to the Ball Game," "By the Light of the Silvery Moon"

1910–19: "Oh, You Beautiful Doll," "When Irish Eyes are Smiling," "Till We Meet Again"

1920–29: "April Showers," "Tea for Two," "Stardust"

1930–39: "Smoke Gets in Your Eyes," "Stormy Weather," "My Funny Valentine"

1940–49: "When You Wish Upon a Star," "The More I See You," "Some Enchanted Evening"

1950–59: "Love and Marriage," "More," "Climb Every Mountain"

1960–69: "Moon River," "People," "Somewhere My Love (Lara's Theme)"

Standard music also refers to concert or symphonic works.

State of the Art. Denotes the most modern and advanced technology or equipment used in an industry or that which has the best performance standards at that particular time. The term is often used to describe equipment used for recording and disc mastering or the latest recording process. In the late 1950s, stereo recording was considered state of the art in recording technology; in the late 1970s, digital recording.

Statutory Copyright. *See* COPYRIGHT.

Stereophonic Recording. A stereophonic recording has two individual channels or tracks, each with separate information. Stereo sound, which is reproduced from two or more speakers, permits a three-dimensional representation of the original recorded event. Such an effect offers the listener depth and direction as to the location of the instruments and voices, a more accurate reproduction of the ambience in which the original performance took place, and a closer facsimile of sounds performed "live." Since the late 1960s, most records and tapes released commercially have been stereophonic recordings; some have been quadraphonic (these enjoyed a brief popularity and heavy promotion in the early 1970s), and some older monaural recordings have been released in simulated stereo.

History of Stereo Sound. The first reproduction of stereophonic sound was reported in 1919. Two engineers placed a microphone in front of each member of a five-piece band (performing in San Francisco) and reproduced their sound via loudspeakers on the floor above, each placed in the position corresponding to that of the performer.

In 1933, Bell Telephone Laboratories demonstrated stereophonic reproduction when it transmitted over telephone lines the sound of the Philadelphia Orchestra playing in Philadelphia and reproduced it over three loudspeakers in Washington, D.C. In 1940, Bell demonstrated stereophonic reproduction on film: at Carnegie Hall in New York City, stereo sound emanated across the stage, but without a picture. With Walt Disney's release of *Fantasia* later that year, stereophonic reproduction first became demonstrable to the overall public. This marked the first commercial utilization of stereophonic sound by an entertainment industry (radio broadcasting in stereo was introduced in the 1920s, but only on an experimental basis). The record industry was impeded from commercially releasing stereo records for decades because it lacked the technology.

Successful experiments with reproducing sounds in stereo were conducted in the early 1930s by engineer A. D. Blumlein of Electrical

and Musical Industries Ltd. (EMI) in England. Blumlein filed for and was granted patents covering all aspects of the modern-day stereophonic disc, including 45/45 engraving of separate information on the two walls of a single groove. These ideas never took shape, however (Blumlein died during World War II), and it became the goal of other scientists to develop a single-groove stereo recording technique (it should be noted that by 1950, stereo tape recording was available).

In the early and mid 1950s, Emory Cook, based in Connecticut, experimented with "binaural" recording. On Cook's binaural phonograph record were an outer and an inner band, for the left and the right channels. Sound was reproduced with a Y-shaped tone arm developed by Ched Smiley of New Jersey. However, sound reproduction was never perfectly synchronized, as it was highly unlikely that the styli would drop exactly into matching grooves. Other techniques were developed by other scientists and companies, but for one reason or another, were mostly abandoned. Western Electric's Westrex subsidiary eventually developed a successful method for inscribing both stereo channels into a single record groove. This technique was demonstrated to record companies in New York in October 1957. Shortly afterward, Columbia in America and Decca in England also demonstrated stereo records, but to avoid an industry with different technical standards for stereo records, record company representatives met and decided to adopt the Westrex system. In 1958, stereo phonograph records with a single groove, as we know them today, became a commercial reality—Audio Fidelity, a small label, released a single-groove stereo disc for which the newly introduced Westrex 45/45 cutting head had been used to cut the master lacquer.

When stereo records were first released, consumers of course did not own the equipment on which to play them. But stereo records were designed to be compatible (thanks in part to Peter C. Goldmark) and could therefore be played either on monaural systems (although the sounds would be reproduced by the system in mono) or on stereophonic equipment, able to extract the stereo information from the record. Stereo enjoyed immediate popularity, but it was nearly a decade before labels eliminated production of mono records and consequent duplication of repertoire for the retail market.

Reproducing Stereo Sound on a Record Player. After performances are recorded in a studio on a multi-track master tape, the sounds are mixed down to a 2-track stereo format, with right and left channels. Stereo discs are then made, with a single groove. When a record is cut, the information from one channel is inscribed on one wall of the groove and information from the other channel is engraved on the opposite wall. When the record is played on a stereo system, the needle and cartridge pick up the audio from one groove wall and feed it through the amplification system to one of the speakers, while the audio from the opposite groove wall is fed through the audio system to the other speaker. Thus stereophonic sound is reproduced.

Stock Company (Theater). There are basically two types of stock companies: resident stock and unit (touring) stock companies. A resident stock company is a company of actors under one management organized to present consecutive productions of different plays at a theater with no layoff or hiatus between productions. A unit stock company is put together by a producer who packages a production and tours it. Stars often headline unit stock productions.

Studio. *See* RECORDING STUDIO.

Subdistributor (Records and Tapes). Company that buys records and tapes from distrib-

utors (manufacturers' branches and independent distributors) and resells these products to retailers. Subdistributors thus function as "middlemen" between distributors and retailers. Rack jobbers and one-stops are subdistributors.

See also DISTRIBUTOR (RECORDS AND TAPES); WHOLESALER (RECORDS AND TAPES).

Subpublisher. *See* INTERNATIONAL SUBPUBLISHING AGREEMENT.

Supporting Act. Bands that perform at concerts are often classified as *featured act* (also referred to as the *star act* or *headliner*) or *supporting act*. The supporting act opens the concert and functions to arouse the audience's spirit for the headliner. But more important, perhaps, they are put on the bill to help sell tickets, as the extra attraction some people need.

Supporting acts range from new (or "baby") to "medium" acts. The exposure a supporting act gets from appearing before audiences drawn to see the featured act can enable the group to expand its audience and build its record sales. New acts often obtain employment "supporting" well-established ones in concerts because they are under contract to the same agency, personal manager, or label.

Symphony Orchestra. In the United States, there are symphony orchestras in most major metropolitan areas and in many less populated cities. Symphony orchestras provide a wide range of musical entertainment for the public. Their repertoires range from classical symphonic literature to the so-called pops. Their concert programs include regular home subscription series, individual home concerts, subscription series in other cities, children/youth series, individual children/youth concerts, tour concerts, summer series, and individual summer concerts.

Classifications. U.S. and Canadian orches-

Symphony orchestras entertain the public with a broad range of musical literature, from classical to avant garde. Here Zubin Mehta conducts the New York Philharmonic Orchestra.

tras are classified by the AMERICAN SYMPHONY ORCHESTRA LEAGUE (ASOL). ASOL's classifications, as set forth in its *Resource Guide*, are based primarily on the orchestra's annual income or expense budget,° but it makes further distinctions, as described in the following:

Major orchestras (musicians employed full time for a contracted number of weeks per year, this being their major source of income), *regional orchestras* (musicians engaged from 15 to 36 weeks per year), *metropolitan orchestras* (musicians generally trained professionally, but such employment is not their main source of income), *urban orchestras* (conductor and manager usually employed on a full-time basis, musicians on a per-service basis); *community orchestras* (conductors and managers may be hired on a full-time or avocational basis; musicians range from students to professionals); *college orchestras* (comprised of faculty and students of a university or college), *youth orchestras* (comprised of junior high, high school, and college-age students from a particular geographical area but not from an individual educational institution).

Managers of major orchestras have defined a major symphony orchestra as an institution operated by a nonprofit corporation duly recognized by the Internal Revenue Service and/ or appropriate governmental agencies, for the purpose of serving its community by the presentation of orchestral concerts. Such orchestras shall (1) be in continuous existence for a minimum of three years prior to the year of membership, (2) employ professional musicians, employed on a weekly basis, whose principal employment shall be that orchestra,

(3) be able to perform the full range of symphonic repertoire with its regular personnel, and (4) have annual operating income of at least: for membership in December 1979— $1.5 million in 1977–78 and $2 million in 1978–79; for membership in December 1980—$2 million in 1978–79 and $2.25 million in 1979–80; for membership in December 1981—$2.25 million in 1979–80 and $2.5 million in 1980–81.

U.S. and Canadian Major Symphony Orchestras†

Atlanta Symphony Orchestra
Baltimore Symphony Orchestra
Boston Symphony Orchestra
Buffalo Philharmonic Orchestra
Chicago Symphony Orchestra
Cincinnati Symphony Orchestra
Cleveland Orchestra
Dallas Symphony Orchestra
Denver Symphony Orchestra
Detroit Symphony Orchestra
Honolulu Symphony Orchestra
Houston Symphony Orchestra
Indianapolis Symphony Orchestra
Kansas City Philharmonic
Los Angeles Philharmonic Orchestra
Milwaukee Symphony Orchestra
Minnesota Orchestra
Montreal Symphony Orchestra
National Symphony Orchestra
New Jersey Symphony Orchestra
New Orleans Philharmonic Symphony Orchestra
New York Philharmonic Orchestra
North Carolina Symphony Orchestra
Philadelphia Orchestra
Pittsburgh Symphony Orchestra
Rochester Philharmonic Orchestra

° Under ASOL's classifications in 1979, annual incomes for the different groups were as follows: major orchestra, in excess of $2 million; regional orchestra, $500,000—$2 million; metropolitan orchestra, $100,000–$500,000. An urban orchestra had a budget between $50,000 and $100,000 per year; a community orchestra, less than $50,000 per year. Classifications in subsequent years for most categories are to be based in part upon increased annual incomes.

---

† ASOL classifications, 1979. In 1978–79, major symphony orchestras had an annual operating income of at least $2 million; regional orchestra classifications include symphony orchestras with audited annual incomes of $500,000 to $2 million. Source: *American Symphony Orchestra League Resource Guide.*

Saint Louis Symphony Orchestra
San Antonio Symphony Orchestra
San Diego Symphony Orchestra
San Francisco Symphony Orchestra
Seattle Symphony Orchestra
Syracuse Symphony Orchestra
Toronto Symphony Orchestra
Utah Symphony Orchestra
Vancouver Symphony Orchestra

U.S. and Canadian Regional Symphony Orchestras

American Symphony Orchestra
Birmingham Symphony Orchestra
Calgary Philharmonic Orchestra
Charlotte Symphony Orchestra
Columbus Symphony Orchestra
Edmonton Symphony Orchestra
Flint Symphony Orchestra
Florida Philharmonic Orchestra
Florida Symphony Orchestra
Fort Worth Symphony Orchestra
Grand Rapids Symphony Orchestra
Hartford Symphony Orchestra
Hudson Valley Philharmonic Orchestra
Jacksonville Symphony Orchestra
Long Beach Symphony Orchestra
The Louisville Orchestra
Memphis Symphony Orchestra
Nashville Symphony Orchestra
Oakland Symphony Orchestra
Oklahoma Symphony Orchestra
Omaha Symphony Orchestra
Oregon Symphony Orchestra
Phoenix Symphony Orchestra
Puerto Rico Symphony Orchestra
Quebec Symphony Orchestra
Richmond Symphony Orchestra
Saint Paul Chamber Orchestra
San Jose Symphony Orchestra
Toledo Symphony Orchestra
Tulsa Philharmonic Orchestra
Victoria Symphony Orchestra
Wichita Symphony Orchestra
Winnipeg Symphony Orchestra

Administration. The management and administration of both business and creative operations of symphony orchestras may be complex, particularly for those with large annual incomes or budgets. Major symphony orchestras employ full-time staffs which handle these affairs. Staff positions vary somewhat from orchestra to orchestra, but on page 413 is a general listing of the positions of a major symphony orchestra.

The following are general descriptions of these various positions:

Board of directors—Sets policies, oversees budget, and makes major financial decisions, hires important personnel (including the music director) and delegates powers to each office, and is the liaison between community and orchestra.

Managing director—Carries out policies of the board, oversees financial stability, sees that the orchestra serves the community's cultural needs, and is involved in long-range planning and budgeting, labor negotiations, fund raising, engaging guest artists, publicity, and other activities of the orchestra. Also known as the orchestra manager, president, executive director, or chief administrator.

Orchestra manager—assists managing director in management operations; also involved in arranging concert tours and supervising staff activities. Also called assistant manager.

Director of development—Supervises orchestra's endowment program, is responsible for annual fund-raising campaigns (will attempt to raise money through such means as mail drives and personal calls), and is involved in long-term fund raising.

Director of public relations—Promotes orchestra's concerts and special events through a publicity/advertising campaign in the various media; maintains a liaison with music critics and supplies them with press releases and other information.

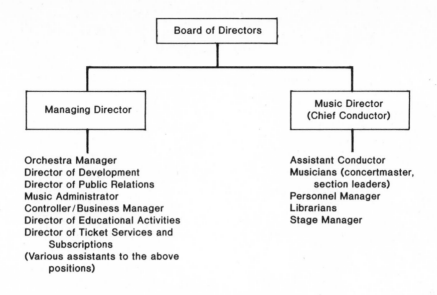

Board of Directors

Managing Director

Orchestra Manager
Director of Development
Director of Public Relations
Music Administrator
Controller/Business Manager
Director of Educational Activities
Director of Ticket Services and
    Subscriptions
(Various assistants to the above
    positions)

Music Director
(Chief Conductor)

Assistant Conductor
Musicians (concertmaster,
    section leaders)
Personnel Manager
Librarians
Stage Manager

Music administrator—Assists the conductor in coordinating the musical season by setting up the subscription concerts and engaging guest soloists and artists.

Controller/business manager—Checks expenditures and administers financial activities, including payroll.

Director of educational activities—Plans young people's concerts, coordinates reduced ticket price programs for students, and sees that schools receive information regarding the orchestra's youth concerts.

Director of ticket services and subscriptions—Coordinates subscription campaigns for concert programs by finding new subscribers and sending renewals to current or previous subscribers (subscriptions are the main source of income for ticket sales).

Music director—Is responsible for orchestra's artistic operations and development, plans musical season, selects repertoire and guest conductors and artists, is involved in final auditions for potential new members, makes public appearances for fund-raising drives, helps develop orchestra's public image.

The music director is usually the chief conductor. He or she reports to the board of directors.

Concertmaster—Leads and coordinates playing of string section, may determine bowings and fingerings of first violin section, tunes the orchestra, plays many solos passages, and may be a featured soloist.

Section leaders—Are responsible for the playing of their sections, assign individual parts within sections, may supervise sectional rehearsals. The section leaders may be involved in preliminary auditions of prospective members. Some orchestras have string committees, woodwind committees, etc., for this. Section leaders are also called principal players.

Librarian—Rents or purchases printed music (i.e., selections to be performed by the orchestra), sees that these are complete and legible when they arrive, compares parts to the conductor's score (for markings) and makes necessary adjustments, enters bowings for individual parts as concertmaster indicates, distributes parts at rehearsals and performances, files music, and returns rented editions.

Stage manager—Sets up the players' chairs, music stands, and lights for rehearsals and concert performances, puts the podium in place, maintains backstage areas, may oversee rental and transport of rented percussion instruments, controls who enters stage area, and directs stagehands (if employed).

Personnel manager—Makes known the orchestra's audition schedule to musicians (often through media advertisements and notices to colleges), hires substitutes when musicians are absent, oversees musicians' attendance and punctuality.

Labor Contracts. Orchestra musicians are generally members of the AMERICAN FEDERATION OF MUSICIANS OF THE UNITED STATES AND CANADA (AFM); concert soloists are members of the AMERICAN GUILD OF MUSICAL ARTISTS (AGMA). Unions negotiate on behalf of orchestra musicians for minimum wages with respect to rehearsals, concert engagements, and recording sessions, as well as other terms of employment.

Income. A symphony orchestra's income may come from various sources including the following:

Concerts—Various types of series (e.g., subscription)

Grants (tax supported)—Various governmental agencies

Grants (other)—Various business and union funding

Other—Contributions from patrons, investment and interest income, various fund-raising projects, recording royalties, etc.

Expenses. A symphony orchestra's expenses include the following:

Artistic personnel—Salaries, fees and honorariums.

Concert production—Costs of music (purchase and rentals), venue costs, copyright license fees, cartage of instruments, all miscellaneous expenses akin to the running of a business, such as insurance and advertising.

Fund raising.

Other—Stationery and printing, sound system rental.

Administrative—miscellaneous expenses.

Recording Contracts. Some symphony orchestras have agreements with record companies which provide for them to record a certain number of albums a year during the term of their contract. Usually all recording costs° are absorbed by the record company. The orchestra receives a royalty based on record sales. The "standard" royalty rate for those orchestras under contract to a recozding company would be: (1) for works in the public domain—20% of the wholesale price, on 90% of sales; (2) for copyrighted works—12% of the wholesale price, on 90% of sales. The rates may be slightly higher or lower, depending upon the reputation of the orchestra and its conductor. The orchestra may split its royalties with the conductor, based on its arrangements with him.

If soloists are involved in a recording, they usually have an agreement directly with the recording company and receive a portion of the 20% or 12% available, which reduces the orchestra's royalties accordingly. The orchestra's contract might specify that its royalties cannot be reduced by more than one third, one half, etc., in the event a soloist is involved.

Record companies that have actively released recordings by symphony orchestras include CBS (Masterworks), RCA (Red Seal), Deutsche Grammophon, Capitol/EMI (Angel), London, and Philips.

Synchronization Right. Recording music onto the sound track of a motion picture film or videotape is known as *synchronization*. Under the copyright law, the copyright owner of a musical composition has the exclusive right to reproduce or authorize the reproduction of the

---

°AFM union scale payments to the musicians, AFM pension fund and health and welfare payments, hall rental, music hire, engineering costs, etc.

work in COPIES, which includes motion pictures. In essence, then, the *synchronization right* is the exclusive right granted in the U.S. Copyright Act to copyright owners to authorize the recording of a musical work onto the sound track of a motion picture.

Consequently a producer who wishes to use a musical composition in his motion picture must obtain a license for the synchronization right. Licenses for rights are negotiated directly with the copyright owner or its representative, such as a MECHANICAL RIGHTS AGENCY.

The license to use a musical composition in a motion picture sound track is known as a *synchronization license*. If the license covers U.S. theatrical exhibition, the producer must also obtain the PERFORMING RIGHT. The copyright law does not provide a compulsory license for the use of music in conjunction with theatrical motion pictures. However, synchronization rights for PUBLIC BROADCASTING are subject to compulsory license under an established schedule of fees and conditions.

See also MOTION PICTURE MUSIC; TELEVISION.

T

Take. A *take* may refer to either of the following:

1. An attempt at putting down a track (that is, recording a vocal and/or instrumental performance). ("Let's try another take".)

2. An acceptable rendition of a performance, an instrumental or a vocal selection, that has been recorded ("After three tries, the singer finally did a take").

In laying down the basic tracks of a multitrack recording, there may be several takes (attempts at recording a particular segment of music or song) before one is deemed acceptable. Several takes of a selection are often made to afford the producer a choice—that is, to permit him to evaluate each and either use the best take or splice together parts from each take to achieve a satisfactory overall performance.

During the recording of the basic tracks the engineer or assistant records each take on a track sheet and writes down on the log any pertinent information (such as markings on the score for editing or differences in performance) regarding a particular take. When a new take is being recorded, the engineer will announce the name of the selection and the number of the take before the performers restart at an agreed place in the score. The announcement onto the tape is known as *slating*. Some engineers also include a low-frequency tone which enables the takes to be easily located on the tape during rewinding or fast-forwarding.

Television. Music is an integral part of television entertainment. It is found to one degree or another in nearly all programming, including variety and music shows, talk shows, situation comedies, game shows, dramas, documentaries, specials, cartoons, sports telecasts, and television films. Consequently television is important as a working medium and source of income for singers, instrumentalists, composers, arrangers, orchestrators, conductors, music directors and coordinators, copyists, and recording engineers. Performers are represented by the UNIONS that have jurisdiction in television, and stations are licensed by performing rights organizations for the right to broadcast nondramatic performances of copyrighted music. For many participants, the television industry serves as both an employer and a promoter of musical talent.

Licenses. To use a musical composition in a television film or videotape the producer will obtain from the copyright owner a synchronization license (*see* SYNCHRONIZATION RIGHT). Television synchronization licenses typically run for a period of from three to five years and permit unlimited television exhibition of the film or videotape embodying the musical composition within the confines of the license (i.e., it may be limited to certain territories). Fees are based on a number of factors including the length of the license, the importance of the composition to the show, and whether it is performed by someone visually.

The PERFORMING RIGHT in the composition must also be obtained for its broadcast on television. Copyright owners are represented by performing rights organizations for the licensing of performing rights in their music copyrights. Performing rights organizations license the nondramatic performing rights in musical works to broadcasters (i.e., local stations and networks). Music publishers and songwriters will collect from their performing rights organizations royalties for performances of their compositions on television. Methodology used to determine royalties from television performances payable by ASCAP, BMI, and SESAC is explained in the respective entries.

Copyright Ownership of Original Music. Original music composed for television, such as a theme song for a weekly series or a score for a made-for-television movie, is customarily written under a WORK MADE FOR HIRE agreement. Composers with strong credits, who are consequently in a strong bargaining position, may be able to negotiate full or part ownership of the copyrights.

Regulation of Television. In the United States, the FEDERAL COMMUNICATIONS COMMISSION (FCC) regulates interstate and foreign communication by television. The FCC is legally prohibited from censoring programs, but the NATIONAL ASSOCIATION OF BROADCASTERS (NAB) administers television (and radio) "codes" governing programming and advertising practices, with which stations may voluntarily comply. The FCC may revoke a station's license for repeated violations of its regulations. Networks are not licensed by the FCC—the commission licenses only individual stations.

See also EMMY AWARDS.

Theatre Authority, Inc. Nonprofit organization set up by various performers' unions and related guilds to protect professional entertainers from exploitation in benefits, telethons, and other charitable functions at which they are asked to appear or donate their talents. Theatre Authority makes sure the event is le-

gitimate, sets the terms and conditions under which the entertainer may appear, and provides an insurance policy for injuries sustained in connection with appearances.

While Theatre Authority permits "star" performers to donate their services, it requires that "non-star" performers (determination of status to be made by TA) receive the applicable union scale (any "star" or "non-star" has the right to be paid his or her usual fee, if it is so desired). Where a performer donates his or her services, TA requires the sponsoring organization to make a contribution to a fund, which is later allocated to needy members of its participating organizations, including Actors Fund, Catholic Actors Guild, Episcopal Actors Guild, Jewish Theatrical Guild, Negro Actors Guild, Authors League, League of New York Theaters, and five actors' unions—Actors' Equity Association, American Guild of Variety Artists, American Federation of Television and Radio Artists, American Guild of Musical Artists, and Screen Actors Guild. In Hollywood, the Association of Motion Picture and Television Producers is a member.

Theatre Authority, Inc., provides its member organizations with information about clearance agreements. Individual performers may call their unions or TA offices for such information. Theatre Authority was founded in 1934 and operates nationwide, with main offices in Hollywood and New York.

Theatrical Productions, Investing in. *See* LIMITED PARTNERSHIPS (FOR INVESTMENTS IN THEATRICAL PRODUCTIONS).

Titles of Musical Compositions. Basically, titles do not meet the requirements of the law, which extends copyright protection only to a substantial amount of original authorship (*see* COPYRIGHTABLE WORKS). Therefore, titles of musical compositions (and other works) are not copyrightable.

Some titles may be subject to protection by courts, however, under the laws relating to UNFAIR COMPETITION. For a title to qualify for such protection, it has to have acquired a "secondary meaning"—having, by sufficient usage, become embedded in the public's mind so as to identify that title as connected to the work and distinguish it from others.

In determining whether a title has acquired a secondary meaning, courts will examine the length of time the title has been used (it must be a sufficient time), public response to the title over the years, and whether the public has been or is likely to be deceived by the use of the same title with a different work.

Thus the mere use or adoption of a title may be insufficient to safeguard it under the laws of unfair competition and render it protectible. It must have acquired a secondary meaning as determined by a court of law. Furthermore, such public recognition must continue in order for protection under unfair competition to subsist. The consistent nonuse of even a title that has previously acquired a secondary meaning would probably cause a reversion of it to the public.

A purely descriptive or common title would probably not receive protection under the theory of unfair competition. Common titles, such as "You," "Runaway," or "You Belong to Me," are probably subject to use by multiple users without infringement.

It is even not uncommon for identically titled songs to become successive hits. For example, two songs titled "Best of My Love" became hits within two years of each other—an Asylum release of the Eagles recording in 1975 and a 1977 recording by the Emotions on Columbia. "Lady" became a hit for the recording group Styx in 1975, and another "Lady" enjoyed widespread popularity in a Kenny Rogers recording in 1980. However, an unusual title that is closely associated with an immensely popular song, such as "Rudolph the Red-Nosed Reindeer," would probably be determined by a court of law to have acquired a secondary meaning and enjoy protection under the laws of unfair competition.

Tony Awards. Prizes of merit given annually in the United States by the American Theatre Wing to honor the achievements of professionals in the Broadway theater. The awards, first presented in 1947, are officially called the Antoinette Perry Awards, having been named in honor of the actress, producer, and director, who died in 1946. Miss Perry was a member of the American Theatre Wing's first board of directors.

Since the inception of the awards, the categories have changed from season to season. The criterion that persons eligible to vote follow is "distinguished achievement in the theatre" (as opposed to "best"). There may therefore be two or more winners in a particular category. This happened, for example, in 1960, when both *Fiorello!* and *The Sound of Music* received Tonys in the Musical category.

Over the years, the scope of voting eligibility has been enlarged. As of 1980, persons eligible to vote for the Tony Awards are the board of directors of the American Theatre Wing, the membership of the League of New York Theatres and Producers, members of the governing boards of Actors' Equity Association, the Dramatists Guild, the Society of Stage Directors and Choreographers, and United Scenic Artists, and individuals whose names appear on the first- and second-night press lists. Legitimate theatrical productions eligible for Tony Awards are those opening in an eligible Broadway theater (as specified by the Tony Administration Committee of the League of New York Theatres and Producers, Inc.) or previewing in a Broadway theater between specified eligibility dates. The Tony Nominating Committee determines which

Broadway productions are eligible for awards.

The American Theatre Wing is an organization that evolved from the Stage Women's War Relief, a group formed in 1917 by members of the theater world (a counterpart men's committee formed in 1920). The organization's present name was adopted in 1941.

Activities of the American Theatre Wing include sponsorship of scholarship and grant programs, annual seminars for students of the theater, and bringing professional theatrical productions to hospitals, schools, and institutions.

See also Appendix I.

Top 40. Radio station format. The programming associated with top 40 is perhaps the most popular type of radio station format in the United States.

Top 40 programming is characterized by the following: a high rotation of the current pop "hit" singles (with the biggest hits in this group receiving the highest rotation), a light rotation of up-and-coming hits and recurrents (recent or declining hits), and an occasional playing of an oldie. This format is also characterized by bouncy jingles and station IDs, repeatedly aired; ebullient DJ "personality" patter; contests, promotions, and giveaways; and hourly news/sports/weather reports. The target audience of this format is generally teen to 24 years old. A top 40 station determines which records are the current "hits" from national and local sales reports, trade charts, research, and programming on competitive stations. This information is sometimes supplied by record company promotion representatives.

When the top 40 format was developed (see below), its playlist consisted of approximately the top 40 best-selling singles. Over the years, the number of records on the playlist has been reduced. Top 40 playlists actually range (depending on the station) from as few as 15 to over 60 records. The decision of how many records to have on a playlist is based upon various factors, including the station owner's and program director's aims, the "sound" wanted, the station's market, its target audience, and the quality of the current selections of records. The number of records on the playlist will vary even in the same station from time to time. There is a tendency for top 40 stations in large (primary) markets to have the smallest playlists.

Development of Top 40 Format. The person generally credited with developing the top 40 format is Todd Storz. The concept of repeatedly playing the current top hits, however, was actually not new to radio—the weekly *Hit Parade,* for example, preceded it. But Storz's adaptation of a daily rotation of the forty best-selling singles and repeatedly aired jingles, station IDs, and special effects into one format created a "sound," sparked much excitement, and was widely accepted by other stations. Storz launched this programming at KOWH in Omaha in 1952, then in 1953 brought his format to WTIX in New Orleans, where it met with great success. The top 40 format eventually spread to radio stations throughout the country and has enjoyed mass popularity. "Top 40" has actually been replaced in the radio industry by the term "contemporary hit radio," which more accurately describes today such a station's programming content.

The term "top 40" is also used to describe a song, recording, or artist having strong commercial potential or appeal.

Topical Song. Song whose lyric pertains to a matter of current or limited interest (as opposed to a universal subject, such as love). Songs whose themes deal with a particular event, social issue, political campaign, or holiday, for example, would probably be considered topical songs.

Topical songs that deal with specific (timely) events have to be recorded and publicly distributed before interest in the event subsides. Christmas songs, for example, are normally recorded during the months of June, July, and August, to allow adequate time for the label to manufacture records and tapes, devise marketing and promotion campaigns, and get the product to wholesalers and retailers. Today, radio station program directors begin to program Christmas songs just after Thanksgiving.

In general, topical songs are not very COMMERCIAL and consequently are not usually successful in terms of record and sheet music sales and performance royalties. However, there are exceptions to this which are indeed extraordinary. Two of the all-time best-selling records, for example, are holiday songs: "White Christmas" (Irving Berlin) and "Rudolph the Red-Nosed Reindeer" (Johnny Marks). These perennial Christmastime classics also have enormous sheet music sales and have earned considerable sums from uses in other areas, such as films and music boxes.

Another topical song became so popular and was performed so often that in its period of statutory copyright protection, most people erroneously believed it was in the public domain. Consequently the song was often used in public without a license and was the subject of many a copyright infringement case. The song was "Happy Birthday," originally published as "Good Morning to All" (Mildred and Patty Hall) in 1893.

Tour, Concert. A concert tour is an extremely important means for an artist to gain exposure to a broad segment of the public. This may result in the artist's expanding his audience, increasing his popularity, and promoting sales of his records and tapes. While a concert tour is not necessarily a major profit center in and of itself, it is often imperative, particularly in the case of a new artist seeking to gain national recognition or an established artist trying to sustain his career.

Putting It Together. A concert tour involves the planning, work, and cooperation of several industry people. After the artist and personal manager make the decision to tour, the artist's agent will try to interest concert promoters in booking his client in the various cities. Concert promoters in turn contact the managers of various halls, arenas, and other venues to make arrangements to use the facilities for a particular night (a more detailed explanation of booking a concert appears under AGENT). Acts frequently travel with entourages that include—in addition to a road manager and road crew—spouses, children, relatives, friends, and companions. Business managers sometimes accompany star or superstar artists or other clients who draw large audiences.

Record Company Operations. For most acts, tours are planned to promote the release of a new album. Consequently various departments of the RECORD COMPANY are closely involved with the tour so as to maximize potential record sales. Briefly, these departments usually work in the following way: the artist development department, in conjunction with the act's personal manager and agency, plans the tour; the publicity department invites local media to the concerts to review them; the promotion department uses the concerts as a means to get local radio stations involved—via airplay, interviews with the artist, and giveaway promotions (of concert tickets and albums); and the sales department and distribution branches get the act's records into the stores in the markets where it is performing. A local distribution branch may also be involved in advertising the concert on key radio stations and in the press, setting up in-store displays at local record/tape retailers and arranging for promotional appearances there by the artist, and having the artist meet with local program directors, DJs, and press.

Promotional concert tours commonly commence a short period, such as one month, after an album's release. TOUR SUPPORT may be provided to acts that cannot afford the high costs of touring.

Itinerary. The length of a tour and the number of engagements and cities played depend on such criteria as the act's popularity, status of its current product, finances, willingness to play, schedule, and public demand. Superstar acts may play as many as 80 or more engagements on a single tour (most of them in different cities). Tours may range from a few weeks or less for a regional tour to 5 months or more for a nationwide U.S. tour, and may even exceed 9 months for an international tour (including the U.S.).

Following is a sample itinerary for a nationwide U.S. tour. (Note: Such a tour would typically encompass a few dates in Canada; intervals between dates means there were no engagements for those days.)

Expenses. Expenses incurred by the touring artist may include the following:

Salaries—Background musicians and vocalists, tour manager, road manager, road crew (set-up workers, electricians, sound technicians, and carpenters), accountant, security personnel, wardrobe person, personal assis-

tants, and concessionaires. Depending on the group's means of transportation, a salary may also be paid to a bus driver, truck driver, or pilot.

Equipment—Musical instruments (owned or rented) and related accessories, sound and lighting equipment; repair of instruments and equipment.

Transportation—Airplanes, trains, limousines, taxis. Some acts own buses, trucks, or airplanes; others may rent them. Where these are owned or rented, there are also the costs of maintenance and gasoline.

Wardrobe.

Insurance—Instruments, equipment. vehicles, wardrobe.

Living—Lodging, meals, telephone, entertainment.

Miscellaneous—There may also be expenses for rehearsal studios and fees to the arranger, copyist, set designer, lighting and sound specialists, and choreographer.

Expenses, which can easily run a million dollars or more for an extensive nationwide tour, are usually paid for out of the act's gross earnings for performing engagements. (From such income, commissions are also paid to the personal manager and booking agent.) The ex-

---

Sample Engagement Schedule for Nationwide U.S. Concert Tour*

Day	City	Day	City	Day	City
1	Fort Worth, Tex.	25	Madison, Wis.	53	Buffalo, N.Y.
2	Austin, Tex.	26	Indianapolis, Ind.	54	Cincinnati, Ohio
3	Houston, Tex.	28	Pontiac, Mich.	57	Cleveland, Ohio
5	Denver, Colo.	30	Chicago, Ill.	61	Philadelphia, Pa.
6	Salt Lake City, Utah	32	Kansas City, Kans.	64	Washington, D.C.
8	San Diego, Cal.	33	Tulsa, Okla.	66	Norfolk, Va.
10	Los Angeles, Cal.	34	Oklahoma City, Okla.	68	Birmingham, Ala.
13	Oakland, Cal.	37	New Haven, Conn.	69	Atlanta, Ga.
16	Seattle, Wash.	38	Providence, R.I.	72	Greensboro, N.C.
18	Vancouver, B.C.	41	Toronto, Ont.	73	Columbia, S.C.
20	Portland, Ore.	42	Montreal, Que.	74	Jacksonville, Fl.
21	St. Paul, Minn.	45	Pittsburgh, Pa.	76	Miami, Fla.
24	Ames, Iowa	46–48	New York, N.Y.		

---

* Based on the Bee Gees' 1979 North American tour.

orbitant expenses often necessitate and justify the high cost of tickets and the act's demand for a high percentage of the ticket receipts.

AFM Regulations. AFM members touring in the United States and Canada may be responsible for paying "Work Dues" [*see* AMERICAN FEDERATION OF MUSICIANS OF THE UNITED STATES AND CANADA (AFM].

Foreign Tours. When a U.S. act tours abroad, certain arrangements must be made so the members may legally enter and work in each foreign country. Immigration laws vary from country to country. Each member should at least have a valid passport well in advance of the tour.

Nontouring Periods. During periods when an act is not touring or has no current releases, it is beneficial for it to maintain visibility in the media. This will impress the public as to its importance, maintain or enhance its image, and remind consumers of its existing product. Publicity may be obtained through interviews and press releases. Information may be conveyed about a new album being recorded, a new direction the act is taking, future tour plans, or the personal lives of its members. What an act does while *not* touring and how its interests are served may have a strong influence upon its future.

Tour Support. The exposure to large audiences as a result of a concert tour may substantially increase the sale of an act's records and tapes. Therefore it is beneficial to both the label and the act for the latter to give concerts before as much of the public as possible. The costs of touring, however, can be so high as to exceed the income received from concert engagements, and therefore prohibit the group from touring. In view of this, some record companies provide financial assistance to an act to enable it to make a concert tour. Such financial assistance is referred to as *tour support*.

Record companies most often allocate tour support to those groups that need it most—new ("baby") and developing acts. In the entry TOUR, CONCERT are listed many of the expenses incurred while doing a tour. In recent years, due to the economics of the business, some labels have reduced or eliminated tour support for their acts, but the practice does still exist.

Some record companies provide tour support gratis, others recoup all or a portion of it from the artist's recording royalties, and some even share in the revenue earned from the artist's tour dates. If income is shared, it is applied against the moneys (tour support) advanced to the attraction.

Track. A term that has several different meanings, a "track" may refer to any of the following:

1. A channel of a multi-track recording ("Put the saxophone on track 7").

2. An overdub ("Let's record the saxophone track again").

3. A musical performance—individual or group ("Did you hear the playback of the saxophone track?" "The band laid down a great track").

4. A selection on an album ("I like the first track on the B side best").

Trade Associations. The music business, in its entirety, comprises various industries—music publishing, recording, and record/tape retailing to name but a few. Companies within these industries commonly join together to form organizations that represent their collective interests to the public, the government, the press, and allied industries. These organizations are known as *trade associations* and they are normally *national, nonprofit,* and *voluntary.* While individual companies belonging to a trade association may be competitors in the same field, they all share common goals that are usually best served by the association.

Objectives. Basically, the objectives of a trade association are to advance, guide, protect, and encourage the interests of the industry it represents.

Programs and Activities of a General Nature. To achieve its objectives, a trade association sponsors various programs and activities, all attuned to the problems, needs, and goals of its members and its industry. While many of these relate specifically to the industry, they also include the following of a general nature:

- To act as collective voice, spokesman, and information and public relations arm for the industry.
- To aid its members in every possible way.
- To encourage practices that will strengthen the industry and uphold sound business ethics.
- To sponsor market research and specialized studies and promulgate the results of these to its members.
- To sponsor educational programs for its members, related industries, and consumers or users of its products. These educational activities might take many shapes, including seminars and symposia.

- To foster relationships with other industry organizations.
- To act as liaison between the industry and government agencies.
- To support the enactment of legislation beneficial to the industry on federal, state, and local levels and to oppose the enactment of legislation that is detrimental to the industry.
- To hold regular membership meetings, conventions, and/or banquets.
- To recognize achievements of its members and others who support the industry or cause it to prosper.
- To distribute newsletters or bulletins reporting its activities to members.

Directorship. A trade association is normally run by a board of directors and officers elected by the membership for a specified term.

Dues. Membership dues are normally required and are payable on an annual basis. Dues are used to run the association and administer its programs and activities.

The following table gives the major U.S.

Major U.S. Trade Associations in or Related to the Music Business

Name*	Industry Represented
Amusement and Music Operators Association (AMOA)	Coin-operated music and amusement (jukebox)
Electronic Industries Association/ Consumer Electronics Group (EIA/CEG)	Consumer electronics hardware manufacturing
International Tape Association (ITA)	Audio and video tape manufacturing
Music Publishers' Association of the U.S. (MPA)	Music publishing (educational, standard)
National Association of Broadcasters (NAB)	Radio and television broadcasting
National Association of Music Merchants (NAMM)	Music retailing
National Association of Recording Merchandisers (NARM)	Record/tape retailing and wholesaling
National Music Publishers' Association	Music publishing
Recording Industry Association of America (RIAA)	Recording manufacturing

* There also exist smaller yet nevertheless beneficial trade associations in or related to the music business, which are not included here either because they have not been in existence long enough or because their membership is regional or local. The exclusion of a trade association here is by no means a reflection on its merit or position.

trade associations in, or closely related to, the music business.

See also PROFESSIONAL ASSOCIATIONS AND EDUCATIONAL ORGANIZATIONS.

Trademarks. A "trademark" is a word, name, device, or symbol, or any combination of these, adopted and used by a merchant or manufacturer to identify goods made or sold by him and to distinguish them from goods made or sold by others. A "service mark" (see below) is a mark that identifies the source of a service, rather than of goods.

A trademark and a service mark (hereinafter called "a trademark") serve various functions. A trademark: (1) identifies the product or service; (2) serves as a guarantee that the particular product or service is genuinely that of the business enterprise; (3) serves to make the customer aware of the quality of the product or service; and (4) serves as an advertisement.

As in other industries, trademarks are used in the music business to protect, identify, and distinguish company products and services. They include brand names, logos, and slogans. Some more well known registered trademarks include the following: "Columbia," "RCA," "WB Records," "Capitol," "Elektra," "Epic," "Atlantic," and "MCA Records." A slogan may serve as a trademark, but only if it is identified with the user by the public—i.e., has required "distinctiveness" or "secondary meaning." One example of this is "The Greatest Show on Earth" (Ringling Bros. and Barnum & Bailey Circus). A service mark is used to identify and distinguish entertainment services, and may include the name of, for example, a performing group.

How Trademark Rights Are Established. Rights in a trademark are acquired only by adoption and actual use of the mark, and the use must continue if those rights are to be preserved. Registration is not necessary, but it is

desirable. In order for a trademark to be eligible for federal registration, goods bearing the mark° must have been sold or shipped in interstate commerce or other commerce that can be regulated by Congress. A trademark for goods must be placed in some manner on the goods, on their containers, or on tags or labels affixed thereto. A service mark is usually displayed in advertisements or other promotional materials. A trademark differs from the commercial and trade names that companies use to identify their businesses. Commercial and trade names are not subject to registration unless actually used as trademarks or service marks, and not just as corporate names.

An application for registration of a mark may be filed at any time after trademark rights have been obtained through use; that is, after the mark has been placed on the product and the product has been shipped or used in commerce which may be lawfully regulated by Congress. An individual, company, partnership, corporation, union, association, or other organization may adopt and own a trademark.

Principal Register and the Supplemental Register of the U.S. Patent and Trademark Office. A mark may qualify for registration on the Principal Register if it distinguishes the applicant's goods from those of others, and if it is coined, arbitrary, fanciful, or suggestive (these are referred to as "technical marks") or, through extensive use, has acquired secondary meaning signifying origin in one source. Common English or foreign-language words may be technical trademarks so long as they do not describe the goods—e.g., "Mustang" for automobiles.

Those marks that do not qualify for the Principal Register because they are, for example, descriptive, but that are nonetheless capa-

---

° The term "mark" means any trademark or service mark, whether registered or not.

ble of distinguishing an applicant's products, may be registered on the Supplemental Register if they have been lawfully used in commerce for at least one year. A mark registered on the Supplemental Register may consist of any symbol, name, word, slogan, phrase, geographical name, or device or any combination of these, even if descriptive of the goods, so long as it is capable of distinguishing one source from another—e.g., "Le Car" for automobiles.

Legal Effects. There are certain benefits for registration on the Principal Register (which are not available to unregistered marks): (1) it is "constructive notice," or notice inferred by law, so that no one may in good faith lawfully adopt a mark previously registered; (2) it is prima facie evidence of the registrant's ownership, of the validity of the registration, and, if it becomes incontestable, of the exclusive right of the registrant to use the mark in commerce on the goods or services for which registration has issued; (3) it entitles the registrant to sue in the United States courts; and (4) it entitles the registrant to deposit a copy of the certificate with customs officials to prevent the importation into the U.S. of goods bearing an infringing mark. With certain exceptions, a mark registered on the Principal Register and used continuously and extensively for 5 years after registration becomes incontestable if an appropriate affidavit is filed.

The important privileges given to marks on the Principal Register are not available to marks registered on the Supplemental Register. For example, a certificate issued under the Supplemental Register is not prima facie evidence of ownership. While protection is limited, however, it can prevent another party from registering the mark.

Registration and Examination of Applications. Registration of a trademark is handled by the U.S. Patent and Trademark Office; an application must be filed with the office in the name of the owner of the mark. Filing and prosecution of the application for registration may be made by the owner, his attorney, or other person authorized to practice in trademark matters. Application forms are available upon request from the Commissioner of Patents and Trademarks, Washington, D.C. 20231.

The application for registration of a trademark comprises: (1) a written application; (2) a drawing of the mark; (3) five specimens (e.g., labels, hang tags, record jackets, etc.) or facsimiles of the trademark actually used; and (4) the required filing fee.

Applications are examined by a trademark examiner. If the trademark is found allowable by the examiner and no opposition is filed, a certificate is issued. If the examiner finds that the mark is not entitled to registration for any reason, the applicant is notified and advised of the reasons and of any formal objections or requirements. The applicant has 6 months from the date of mailing to respond to the examiner's objections. After such response, the application is reconsidered or reexamined. Upon further refusal of the registration, the applicant may appeal to the Trademark Trial and Appeal Board. All applications for registration of marks on the Principal Register, after being allowed by the examiner, are published in the *Official Gazette* of the Patent and Trademark Office and are subject to opposition by any person who believes he would be damaged by such registration on the Principal Register. Opposition must be made within 30 days after publication. Marks registered on the Supplemental Register are not subject to opposition.

Foreign Applicants. Applicants not domiciled in the United States must, in addition to the above, appoint by an instrument in writing filed in the Patent and Trademark Office the name and address of a United States resident on whom may be served notices or process in proceedings affecting the mark and to whom all official communications will be addressed.

A foreign applicant may apply for registration in the same manner as U.S. residents if the mark is used in commerce that may be regulated by Congress. If the mark is not used in commerce with the U.S., the applicant may base the registration upon one that has been previously secured in the country of origin and is in full force and effect. Such application, however, must be accompanied by a certification or certificate issued by the trademark office of the foreign country, showing that the mark has been registered in that country, along with a translation of the foreign certificate of registration.

Term of Registration and Renewals. Trademarks last as long as they are used. A registration becomes subject to automatic cancellation unless, in the sixth year following registration, an affidavit is filed stating that the mark is still in use. If the affidavit is filed, the trademark registration remains in effect for 20 years and may be renewed by the filing of a renewal application for additional periods of 20 years, so long as it remains in use in commerce. A mark not used in commerce may also be eligible for renewal if its nonuse is due to special circumstances which excuse the nonuse and is not due to any intention to abandon the mark.

Notice of Trademark Registration. After a registration has been made, notice should be given. The symbol ® or the words "Registered in U.S. Patent and Trademark Office," or its abbreviation "Reg. U.S. Pat. and Tm. Off.," should appear on merchandise near the mark.

Selecting a Trademark. New companies or established ones seeking names and trademarks must be sure not to select one that infringes upon the rights of another. With the abundance of companies owning registered and unregistered marks, it may be difficult to select a name or mark that is clear of others' rights.

A number of sources should be investigated: the records of the Patent and Trademark Office, trade directories, lists, telephone directories, and reference books. Also, performing and mechanical rights organizations as well as AFM and AFTRA may be able to provide information regarding existing names, and the services of trademark search bureaus may be engaged. Adopting a mark that infringes upon someone else's prior right may result in a lawsuit after much money has been spent advertising it. Prior registered marks may be cited by a trademark examiner against applications to register a trademark.

Service, Certification, and Collective Marks. Under the Trademark Act of 1946, service marks, certification marks, and collective marks may be registered. A "service mark" includes titles, names, symbols, slogans, and character names and distinctive features of radio and television programs used in the sale or advertising of services to identify them. A "certification mark" refers to a mark used in connection with the products or services by those other than the owner of the mark to certify origin or quality, such as work by members of a union. A "collective mark" is a trademark or service mark used by members of a cooperative, association, or other collective group and indicates membership.

An application for registration of the name of a recording act or performing group would be a service mark application, as it is considered that such person or group of persons is rendering an entertainment service. The requirement is that, before an application can be filed, the service mark must have been used in performances in at least two states, under the name he/they are registering. Use is established by advertising or by a sign at the place where performance occurs.

Five specimens or facsimiles of a mark must accompany an application for registration. In the case of service marks not used in printed or written form (such as a radio series), it is acceptable to submit three single-face, unbreakable disc recordings, so long as the speed at which the recordings are to be played is specified thereon. If the applicant is unable to furnish recordings of the required type, the Patent and Trademark Office may arrange, at the applicant's expense, to have the necessary disc recordings made from any type of recording the applicant submits. For TV programs and films, film strips of the title frames may be used.

U.S. Trademark Statutes. The federal law that currently protects trademarks is the Trademark Act of 1946, as amended. The 1946 Act, Public Law 489, commonly known as the Lanham Act, became effective on July 5, 1947, and superseded the Trademark Acts of 1920 and 1905. The 1905 act, the first comprehensive U.S. trademark law, was based upon the theory that ownership of a trademark is acquired by adoption and use. The first federal statute in the United States providing for registration of trademarks was the Federal Trade-Mark Act of 1870, which was superseded by the act of 1881.

Trademark Laws in Foreign Countries. Some record companies have subsidiaries or license masters in foreign countries. Owners of trademarks having business or prospective business in foreign countries should investigate the trademark laws in those countries in which they wish to protect their marks.

Trademark laws are strictly national in scope and vary from country to country. In many, a resident may obtain a registration of a trademark without having used it in commerce, and such a registration may be used to bar the importation into that country of products bearing the mark. The duration of certificates of registration also varies with the domestic laws in foreign countries. In some foreign countries, a domestic registration enables the owner to secure registration before actually using the mark there.

International Trademark Laws. International treaties pertaining to protection of trademark rights include the Convention of Paris in 1883 and the Arrangement of Madrid in 1891. The Paris Convention provides citizens of party nations the same protection in each contracting country that the nationals of that country enjoy if they have complied with the trademark requirements of the country. Under the Madrid Arrangement, a trademark registered in any one country may qualify for registration in all signatory countries. Neither the United States nor the United Kingdom are signatories to the Madrid Arrangement of 1891.

State Registration of Marks. A registration of a mark at the state level (prior to a federal registration) secures state jurisdiction over trademark infringements. Liability for infringement varies from state to state; trademark infringement in some states is treated as a crime, giving rise to fine and/or imprisonment. In all states there is also civil liability (damages and/or injunction) for trademark infringement. State registration is of evidentiary value and constitutes prima facie evidence of ownership in the state. Federal registration, however, ordinarily provides proper protection and renders unnecessary the registration of a trademark under the statute of a state. For marks in interstate commerce, the principal advantages of state registration are the threat of criminal prosecution where available and the right to invoke the anti-dilution statutes to prevent watering down the distinctiveness of a strong or well-known mark. Not every state has an anti-dilution statute.

As previously stated, a trademark endures as long as it is in use. The terms of state trademark registrations vary from state to state (e.g., the term in New York is for 10 years from the date of registration, with renewable successive periods of 10 years).

Common Law Protection. The common law of the states protects trademarks and trade names from infringement and unfair competi-

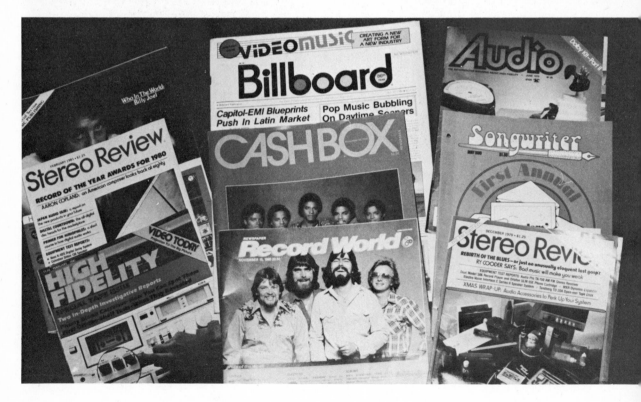

tion even where a registration has not issued. The evidentiary advantages inherent in a federal registration are not available in an action on an unregistered trademark or trade name.

See Logo.

Trades. Publications issued regularly that report the latest news, developments, and activities of an industry, trade, or profession.

Three trades dominate in the coverage of the music industry: *Billboard, Cash Box,* and *Record World.* Published weekly, they report on the activities of record companies, wholesalers, retailers, artists, music publishers, songwriters, recording studios, unions, trade associations, performing and mechanical rights licensing organizations, personal and business managers, agents, concert promoters, and others.

Other fields covered in the trades (as they relate to the music industry) include radio, television, electronics, advertising, public relations, educction, and banking. There is also legal reporting, such as on copyright and trademark laws, piracy, bootlegging, counterfeiting, and antitrust statutes. The trades are both domestic and international in scope, though international coverage is limited. *Billboard, Cash Box,* and *Record World* also contain reviews of new singles and albums and news on radio programming. One of the most important features of the trades is their Charts. Advertising, usually abundant in the trades, is another way in which record companies promote their product to wholesalers, retailers, and broadcasters. *Billboard* publishes various annual directories, which are useful guides and sources of information to the industry (e.g., *International Buyer's Guide* and *International Talent Directory*).

Variety is another important trade publication, though its coverage of the music/record business is not as extensive as the trades discussed above, since it covers the entire entertainment industry, including motion pictures, television, radio, legitimate theater, and talent. *Variety* is published weekly (it publishes an annual "Anniversary Edition"). There is also a *Daily Variety* issued Monday through Friday.

There are various "tip sheets" (often in newsletter format) that are useful to broadcasters. Tip sheets report on: records receiving heavy airplay on radio stations of various formats, records being added to or dropped from the playlists of stations around the country, and trends in the industry. They also select "picks" and "sleepers" from new releases. Tip sheets are used by many contemporary-music radio stations as a guide in their programming. Notable tip sheets include *The Gavin Report, Friday Morning Quarterback,* and *Radio and Records.*

There are numerous trades that serve specific industries such as record/tape retailing, broadcasting, and recording studios. There are also many educational music magazines and journals as well as consumer-oriented trades and mass consumer publications that cover news of the music business. Some examples of the preceding include *ASCAP in Action, Audio, Country Music Magazine, Creem, Down Beat, Guitar Player, High Fidelity, Hit Parader, Hollywood Reporter, International Musician, The Many Worlds of Music (BMI), Modern Recording, Music Retailer, Musical America, Rolling Stone, Songwriter,* and *Stereo Review.*

Translations. American popular songs will normally not find a market in non-English-speaking countries unless the lyrics are first translated. As a matter of fact, a mere translation will usually not suffice, lyrics requiring adaptation to idioms, sentiments, and expressions of the secondary language.

The right to change a musical composition's lyrics from one language to another is an exclusive right of the copyright owner, from whom permission must be obtained to legally translate the work. It is customary for U.S.

music publishers in making INTERNATIONAL SUBPUBLISHING AGREEMENTS to grant to the foreign publisher the right to translate works included in the agreement and also to make title changes. The subpublisher thus may engage a local lyricist to write new lyrics to compositions that it feels would be commercially acceptable for the market if they had local-language lyrics. However, the original publisher may reserve the right to approve the translation, particularly where its agreement with the original writers provides for them to approve any translations.

With respect to royalties earned from translated versions of a work, the composer normally receives 50% of the writer's share and the original lyricist and the translator each receive 25% of the writer's share for uses of the translated version. The publisher's share for the translated version is normally divided equally between original publisher and subpublisher, but this may vary somewhat in subpublication agreements.

It is the policy and practice of many foreign performing rights societies, with respect to allocating writer's royalties for local performances of a work, to credit the local (foreign) lyricist or translator with 25% or more of the writer's share of performance royalties. This amount may be deducted from the moneys transmitted to the original writers even on renditions where the local language lyric was not performed. Consequently the original writer may not receive full payments for performances of the American version in the territory.

It is also the practice of certain societies to pay the local "sublyricist" a performance royalty, regardless of an agreement providing for no financial participation in the work by such person. When a U.S. recording is released abroad then, and it is anticipated that the bulk of performances of the song will be from the American version, it may be advisable for the U.S. publisher to retain translation rights, unless it is believed that the subpublishers will successfully generate local-language covers.

Until the mid 1970s, there used to be a problem involving what is commonly called "secondary lyrics." This was where the translated version of the original work found its way back to the original territory and became a hit and the translator was not paid for performances in the original territory. This happened in the case of a number of European songs that were translated into English by American lyricists and later became hits in their original country. Rules were modified by foreign societies, however, to provide for a translator to participate in a share of the performance royalties in such a situation.

Turntable Hit. Trade jargon for a single that receives substantial airplay but whose sales are not anywhere commensurate with such activity. Such a record may enter and climb the bottom portions of the charts (where airplay often is the determining factor) but only rise so far (positions at the top of the charts are weighted heavily by sales).

TV Album Marketer. *See* RECORD MERCHANDISING COMPANY.

U

Unfair Competition. General term applied to practices in trade and commerce of imitating the title, name, appearance, color, shape, or design of the goods of another so as to cause confusion, or to deceive the public into buying the goods made by imitation, thus resulting in economic injury to the party being imitated. Such conduct is actionable whether dishonest and fraudulent or innocent.

The laws of unfair competition are used to prevent and restrain the passing off of one's goods as those of a competitor. Much of the law of unfair competition is judge-made or common law. However, many states have statutes against unfair competition, as does the federal government [Section 43(a) of the Lanham Trade-Mark Act]. There are various applications of the laws of unfair competition, including protection of the following:

1. Titles of songs that have acquired secondary meaning (titles cannot be copyrighted).
2. Sound recordings. Those not protected by federal law (i.e., fixed prior to February 15, 1972) may in some circumstances be protected against unauthorized duplication.
3. Trademarks. In the absence of a federal trademark registration, users of marks have sought common-law relief under the state laws relating to this doctrine.
4. Names of artists. Names may not be copyrighted but in certain cases may be eligible for protection as "service marks." Again, in the absence of a registration of a mark or where such names are not eligible for trademark registration, protection from wrongdoers has been obtained under the unfair competi-

tion doctrine. Also, individual artists in some cases have a "right of publicity" and can prevent exploitation of their names under that theory.
5. The distinctive appearance of album covers.

Union Scale. Minimum wage paid to a union member for a particular engagement. Scales vary for the different fields of work—recordings, television, motion pictures, club dates, etc. The scale for engagements in the same field of work may be uniform throughout the country, or vary from locality to locality—this depends on whether or not a union has a national labor agreement with employers in a particular field of work. Union scale does not set a limit on what the performer can earn for a particular job; he is free to negotiate a rate of compensation over scale (*See* OVERSCALE ARTIST).

Union scale for AFM musicians is uniform throughout the United States (although different in Canada) in certain fields of work, including phonograph records, commercial announcements, network radio and televison, and theatrical motion pictures. Thus a musician working in any of these fields would earn the same scale whether the job took place in Los Angeles, New York, Nashville, or elsewhere. The scales in these media are determined through COLLECTIVE BARGAINING between the International Union of the AFM and employers. Local AFM unions, however, have jurisdiction over wages and working conditions in local areas of employment, such as clubs, hotels, and local television. Hence scale for these engagements normally varies. AF-TRA's scale for making phonograph recordings is also uniform throughout the United States.

Unions. There are various labor unions in the entertainment business that represent professional performers. An artist's union affiliation depends upon his field of actual or promised employment. Fields of work include phonograph recordings, radio, television, opera, le-gitimate theater, theatrical motion pictures, nightclubs, circuses, etc.

Unions serve as the exclusive COLLECTIVE BARGAINING representative of their members for the purpose of dealing, negotiating, and contracting with employers with respect to terms and conditions of employment, engagement, and performance of work. Unions negotiate for minimum wages (*See* UNION SCALE) and overtime compensation, pension and welfare fund contributions, and various working

Major U.S. Entertainment Unions

Union	Members	Medium and/or Jurisdiction of Representation
Actors' Equity Association (AEA or Equity)	Stage performers (actors, vocalists, dancers, etc.), stage managers	Legitimate theater, including Broadway, Off Broadway, musical comedy, light opera, stock, dinner theater, children's theater. touring companies, repertory theater, etc.
American Federation of Musicians (AFM)	Instrumentalists, leaders, contractors, copyists, arrangers, orchestrators, group musicians	Phonograph recordings, videodiscs, videocassettes, commercial announcements, network radio and TV, TV videotape, educational TV, electrical transcriptions, theatrical motion pictures, TV films, industrial films, Broadway and Off Broadway shows, concert and theatrical productions including opera and symphonies, cafés, clubs, discos, hotels
American Federation of Television and Radio Artists (AFTRA)	Singers, actors, announcers, narrators, newspersons, sportscasters, sound effects artists	Phonograph recordings, videodiscs, videotaped TV programs and commercials, radio
American Guild of Musical Artists (AGMA)	"Musical artists" (including vocalists, solo instrumentalists, narrators, dancers, dance groups), stage directors, stage managers	Grand opera, ballet, dance, concert, recital, oratorio
American Guild of Variety Artists (AGVA)	Singers, dancers, comedians, skaters, jugglers, magicians	Nightclubs, cabarets, mountain and seashore resorts, banquets, fairs, carnivals, burlesque, vaudeville, etc.
Screen Actors Guild (SAG)	Actors and actresses (including singers)	Motion pictures (theatrical, industrial, and educational), filmed television programs, filmed television commercials

conditions. Additionally, unions represent members when individual disputes arise with employers, and work for the passage of legislation beneficial for their members and their professions.

Entertainment unions are affiliated with the AMERICAN FEDERATION OF LABOR AND CONGRESS OF INDUSTRIAL ORGANIZATIONS (AFL-CIO). Several receive their jurisdictional charters from ASSOCIATED ACTORS AND ARTISTES OF AMERICA (FOUR A's). The American Federation of Musicians is not a branch of Four A's, although it is affiliated with AFL-CIO.

Artists often perform in more than one field and therefore become members of more than one union. Four A's unions have reciprocal arrangements whereby a performer in good standing in one union may become a member of another Four A's union by paying an initiation fee and dues at a reduced rate. For such individuals, the parent union is the first union joined and the sister union would be any other Four A's union joined afterward. The following example illustrates a multifaceted artist and his union affiliations: A vocalist makes phonograph recordings (AFTRA), performs on Broadway (Equity), and sings in grand opera (AGMA) and on television (AFTRA or SAG). In each case, the regulations of the union having jurisdiction over that medium as indicated prevail, even though there is only one "parent" union for the performer.

The table contains essential information on the major unions that represent professional performers. The jurisdiction for each of these extends throughout the United States, and for some, into other territories, including Canada. More detailed information is found in their respective entries. Not included are smaller or related industry unions, such as the following Four A's affiliates: Hebrew Actors Union (HAU), Italian Actors Union (IAU), and Asociación Puertorriqueña de Artistas e Technicos del Espectaculo (APATE) (whose juris-

diction, while limited to Puerto Rico, covers all areas of entertainment within the scope of Four A's). Other unions include International Alliance of Theatrical Stage Employees (IATSE), Theatrical Wardrobe Attendants Union (TWAU), Association of Theatrical Press Agents and Managers (ATPAM), and National Association of Broadcast Employees and Technicians (NABET).

Conflict of Jurisdiction. It is sometimes problematic as to which union exercises jurisdiction over a basically theatrical production. In general, operatic productions are covered by AGMA, Broadway musicals by Equity, and nightclub performances by AGVA.

With regard to jurisdiction over musicians, AGMA is the exclusive bargaining agent for all solo concert artists, including instrumentalists, in the concert fields, although such musicians may be members of AFM and be under such jurisdiction for other types of work. For instance, a solo violinist giving a recital at a concert hall would be under AGMA jurisdiction, while members of an orchestra playing in an opera would be under AFM jurisdiction.

In television, a program made for TV on *film* normally comes under the jurisdiction of SAG; if *live* or made on *videotape*, AFTRA generally prevails.

See also NATIONAL LABOR RELATIONS BOARD; THEATRE AUTHORITY, INC.

Unit. A standard of measurement. One unit means a quantity of one of the item being measured. In the record business, the term "units" is most commonly used in reference to measuring quantities of records and tapes (i.e., LPs, singles prerecorded cassettes, or 8-track tapes) that are manufactured, ordered, shipped, or sold. Multi-record sets and twin-pack tapes are regarded as one unit. The term may also be used in reference to the sales of an "album" (combined disc and tape counterparts) in all its collective configurations (the "album" amassed a sale of 1 million *units* by selling 500,000 LPs, 300,000 8-track tapes, and 200,000 cassettes).

Universal Copyright Convention. *See* INTERNATIONAL COPYRIGHT RELATIONS.

Universal Product Code (UPC). *See* BAR CODING.

Unpublished Work. An unpublished WORK is protected by the federal copyright law once it is "fixed" in a tangible form, whether or not a registration has been made for the work at the Copyright Office. This is because the 1976 Copyright Act provides a single system of statutory protection for all copyrightable works, whether published or unpublished. This grant of statutory protection is made without regard to the nationality or domicile of the author (as opposed to published works, where certain conditions with respect to national origin must be met to secure statutory protection).

Works that were not published or registered for copyright prior to 1978 were subject to perpetual protection under common law. All such works that are "fixed" (written or recorded) have automatically come under the protection of the federal copyright law. The duration of these copyrights varies but the statute provides that in no case will any such copyright enter the public domain before December 31, 2002.

See also PUBLICATION.

V

Videocassettes and Videodiscs. Home equipment providing audio and audiovisual entertainment has undergone marked changes over the years. Technologies introduced to the public have included cylinder recordings, one-sided discs, two-sided discs, radio, open-reel tape recorders, television, LPs, stereo sound, audio tape cartridges, cassettes, and quad, among others. Most recently, new video technologies have been ushered in that offer a wide range of home-entertainment and learning possibilities. There are two basic systems: the videocassette recorder and the videodisc player.

Descriptions. A *videocassette recorder*, or VCR, is a machine that both records and plays audiovisual programs. The insertion of a blank cassette into the machine can record for later viewing anything that comes through the TV set. Prerecorded tapes offer a wide variety of fare and can be purchased or rented at various outlets. The machine transmits the program recorded on magnetic videotape to a television screen, where it can be viewed. A VCR attaches by a cable to the terminals of the television set. Connection of a VCR does not impede normal TV reception when the VCR is not in operation. Consumer VCR hardware and software are presently of two standard formats: Beta and VHS.

A *videodisc* system consists of a player unit and discs. The player transmits encoded information on the disc to a television screen, where the audiovisual program can be viewed. The player is attached by a cable to the antenna connections of the television set. Again, connection of a videodisc player to a TV set does not interfere with normal reception of broadcast TV programs. There are in 1981 two prevailing formats on the market:° one uses an optical system in which a laser beam "reads" the contents of an ungrooved disc, and the other, a mechano-electrical system, utilizes a grooved disc, a phonograph-like turntable, and a stylus. It is important to note that unlike a VCR, a videodisc player cannot record; it can only play back.

Music Aspects. The income sources available to owners of copyrighted music embodied in videocassettes/discs are similar to a synchronization use and a mechanical use. A producer of videocassette/disc programs containing copyrighted music must obtain these rights from the copyright proprietor to use the composition. A user may not acquire these rights under the compulsory license of the copyright law. The compulsory license is limited to making and distributing phonorecords and is not available to audiovisual devices.

There is no statutory guidance with regard to royalty payments for software sales. This is a matter of individual negotiation between the software producer and the copyright proprietor. While it is likely that a standard computation will evolve to determine software royalty payments, at this writing no precedent has been set as the standard.

° Matsushita/JVC (Japanese Victor Company) have another noncompatible videodisc format, but its projected introduction into the marketplace is not until late 1981; therefore, the ultimate impact in the market is not possible to predict.

The various approaches that have been suggested for licensing musical compositions for reproduction in video software include the following: (1) a flat fee; (2) a percentage of the suggested retail or wholesale price (with escalation provisions); (3) a multiple of the statutory rate for phonorecords; (4) a flat fee plus a royalty on copies sold; and (5) a percentage of the gross fees from the rental or lease of software. Whether all rights are included under one license, such as an existing synchronization license, is a matter of determination by the parties.

In 1981, THE HARRY FOX AGENCY, INC. (HFA) sent a letter to its affiliated publishers listing various criteria that may be considered in arriving at a licensing fee for use of musical compositions in videocassettes and videodiscs. They are as follows:

1. Nature of video product (such as motion picture, video record of concert, or other non-dramatic rendition)

2. Type of use of composition (such as background or feature, instrumental or vocal)

3. a) Length of time of entire production; b) Length of time of music in production and total number of compositions used; c) Length of time of use of particular composition being licensed

4. Duration of license requested

5. Whether any rights regarding the composition have been previously licensed in connection with production to appear on video product (is this a new production or an existing production being transferred to video product)

6. Budget for production, including costs of particular items (such as artist payments)

7. Manner of distribution (such as sale or rental for home use)

8. Estimated number of units to be manufactured

9. Territory of distribution

10. a) Wholesale price and suggested retail list price of units; b) Rental prices and marketing arrangements of units.

11. Estimated profit margins

A producer of video software may manufacture and offer for sale motion pictures that through inadvertence have fallen into the public domain. Such a producer may therefore believe he has no license obligation. The film, however, may contain a score of musical compositions still under copyright protection, and where such supplier does not obtain a license to use the music from each copyright proprietor, he may be an infringer of copyright for each selection and the publishers may bring legal action against him.

Videocassettes. The manufacture and marketing of a home entertainment system that reproduces audiovisual programs from magnetic tape had long been a goal of American and foreign consumer electronics industries. As technology for this was developing during the 1960s, manufacturers devised various types of videotape systems, but for the most part ran into technical and financial problems before even bringing their products to the marketplace. In 1970, Sony Corporation demonstrated a home videocassette recorder, although the unit wasn't ready for commercial marketing. In 1972, a system called Cartvision, manufactured by a company of the same name, was put on the market but also failed to gain acceptance, as did subsequent introductions.

It was not until late 1975, when Sony introduced its Betamax VCR, that a practical machine for video recording and playback was available for consumer use. The success of Sony's Betamax (of the Beta format, as its name implies) prompted other manufacturers to expedite their research and manufacturing programs to have competitive equipment on the market. Within a few years, units under several different brand names were available in the United States. Beta-format videocassette recorders have been sold under the brand names of Sony, Zenith, Sanyo, Toshiba, and

Sears. The remaining manufacturers (RCA, Sharp, Panasonic Quasar, GE, etc.) market VCRs using the VHS format. Mechanically, the difference between the two formats is in the outside dimensions of the cassette, since both formats use half-inch video-tape for the actual recording. Beta- as well as VHS-format blank videocassettes have been issued by all major blank-type manufacturers. In addition, almost all prerecorded videocassettes are released simultaneously in both formats.

Videodiscs. During the 1970s, manufacturers raced to produce and market practical videodisc systems. The early years of the decade promised videodisc players shortly, but manufacturers were besieged by mechanical problems. In August 1971, a videodisc system called TED, developed jointly by Telefunken in West Germany and Decca in England, was marketed in Western Europe, but without much success.

By the end of the decade, the first videodisc player and library of feature-length discs was marketed in the United States: the "Magnavision" system, developed by Philips of the Netherlands and MCA, Inc., in the U.S. This system debuted in Atlanta on December 15, 1978, the players having been manufactured by Magnavox and the discs by Disco-Vision, a subsidiary of MCA, Inc.

The Philips-MCA and U.S. Pioneer machines use optical technology. Video programs are recorded on a reflective disc protected by a sturdy smooth-surfaced plastic coat. This is played on the machine's phonograph-like turntable. A laser beam scans the disc and is reflected by indentations impressed in the disc's inner surface. The resulting reflections

pass to a photoelectric sensor, which "reads" (interprets) the pattern and converts it to audio and video electronic signals that are played on the attached television set. The optical video-disc has stereophonic capability and is supplied with audio outputs for connection to a standard stereo system. Since scanning by a laser beam offers no physical contact with its recorded program, there is no record or stylus wear. The Magnavision system permits frames to be viewed separately, in reverse, or in slow motion, and has a numerical index to find an exact frame or point in any program.

RCA has a capacitance player that utilizes grooved records and a diamond stylus to pick up sound and images. The disc has encoded information impressed on it which is traced by the stylus and converted into video and audio signals. The RCA system, unlike the optical system, presently has a monaural sound track only, but is scheduled to have stereo sound availability in the near future. RCA's videodisc system is called "SelectaVision." As protection from damage by dirt and scratches, the discs come in special plastic "caddies" which are inserted into the machine rather than placed by hand on a turntable.

Other videodisc systems and equipment have been developed by companies including Sony, JVC, and Matsushita. One advantage videodisc systems have over videocassette systems is cost—both hardware and software of videodisc systems cost substantially less than their cassette counterparts. A disadvantage is that a consumer cannot record on it. A detriment to both systems is the incompatibility of the different formats—software of one format cannot be played on hardware of another.

W

Wholesaler (Records and Tapes). Company that sells records and tapes to subdistributors and/or retailers for resale. A wholesaler, which itself may be a SUBDISTRIBUTOR, does not sell directly to consumers.

Wholesalers in the music business are of the following types: (1) distribution branches (of "major" record companies); (2) independent distributors; (3) rack jobbers; (4) one-stops; (5) importers; (6) exporters; and (7) cut-out vendors.

Wild Spot. *See* RESIDUAL (TV AND RADIO COMMERCIALS AND TV PROGRAMS).

Work. Term used in the copyright law that refers to a copyrightable intellectual property. Examples of a "work" include a musical composition, an opera, a ballet, a motion picture, a sound recording, and the liner notes, artwork, or photographs that appear on album covers.

"Work" Distinguished from "Copies" and "Phonorecords." The copyright law draws a sharp distinction between a "work" and "any material object in which the work is embodied." A work can be embodied in two types of material objects: COPIES and PHONORECORDS. Basically, "copies" are those material objects from which the work can be read or visually perceived; "phonorecords" are those objects which embody the fixation of sounds but not those in which the sounds accompany a motion picture or other audiovisual work. Thus a song is a *work* of authorship that can be reproduced in *copies* (sheet music and films) or *phonorecords* (phonograph discs and cassette tapes).

See also COPYRIGHTABLE WORKS.

Work Made for Hire. In the music industry, certain types of works are commonly created or prepared under employment or special contract to an individual, corporation, organization, or other entity. Such an agreement is generally referred to as a "work made for hire" or "employee for hire" agreement. Theatrical and television motion picture scores and songs, sound recordings, arrangements for recordings and printed editions of music, advertising music, and serious musical compositions are all frequently prepared under "work made for hire" agreements.

Copyright Law Provisions. The federal copyright statute recognizes the concept of a work made for hire and contains various provisions regarding this. These include copyright ownership, COPYRIGHT DURATION, and others which may vary from those prescribed for a work created independently by an author.

Definition. Under the 1976 Copyright Act (Section 101), a "work made for hire" is defined as "(1) a work prepared by an employee within the scope of his or her employment; or (2) a work specially ordered or commissioned for use as a contribution to a collective work, as a part of a motion picture or other audiovisual work, as a translation, as a supplementary work, as a compilation, as an instructional text, as a test, as answer material for a test, or as an atlas, if the parties expressly agree in a written instrument signed by them that the work shall be considered a work made for hire."

Ownership/Authorship. The statute provides that unless there is a written agreement to the contrary signed by both parties, all rights comprised in the copyright of a work made for hire are owned by the employer or other person for whom the work was created or prepared. Thus the employer or other copyright proprietor is able to secure copyright in his name and is considered the "author" of the work. (Oral agreements are not enforceable in litigation.)

Renewal/Termination. For a work made for hire that was copyrighted before 1978, renewal is made in the name of the employer or the other copyright owner to whom the rights have been transferred, and not by the actual author of the work. (There is no renewal term for works created on or after January 1, 1978.) Termination rights are not applicable to works made for hire, regardless of whether they are created before or after 1978.

Commercial Practice. Works made for hire in an employee/employer situation are normally characterized by an express, written contract and a salary, fee, or advance against future royalties. For example, a composer employed by a motion picture producer might score films and be compensated in the form of a weekly salary, an arranger might write charts for a recording session for a one-time fee, and a record producer might produce a recording in exchange for an advance against future royalties. In all these situations, ownership of copyright vests in the employer. The work is created at the request, expense, risk, control, and, often, direction of the employer. The employer, likewise, benefits most from financial gains derived as a result of the work.

Courts have held that works created or prepared outside the normal scope of employment are owned by the employee. Therefore, it is imperative that agreements specify what, in terms of specific duties, types of works, and regular working hours, is considered the normal scope of employment. Works created before a "work made for hire" agreement is effected, and after it is terminated, are not considered to be within the normal scope of employment and ownership rights vest in the actual author.

Sometimes there is confusion over who owns the rights to a work that was created by special order or commission (such as a serious musical composition). A specially commissioned or ordered work is considered made for hire only if two conditions are met: (1) there must be a written agreement signed by both parties stating the work shall be considered a work made for hire and (2) such work must be of a certain kind (i.e., it must fit into one of the nine categories designated by the law as stated in the definition above). Although there is no specific category out of the nine for musical compositions, a commissioned work can fit a category depending upon how it is used and for what use it was commissioned. The statute does provide, however, that a "supplementary work," which is one prepared for publication as a secondary adjunct to a work by another author for the purpose of assisting in the use of the other work, includes musical arrangements.

Appendixes

A. Acronyms and Abbreviations

AEA: Actors' Equity Association
AFL-CIO: American Federation of Labor and Congress of Industrial Organizations
AFM: American Federation of Musicians of the United States and Canada
AFTRA: American Federation of Television and Radio Artists
AGAC: American Guild of Authors and Composers
AGMA: American Guild of Musical Artists
AGVA: American Guild of Variety Artists
AMC: American Music Conference
AMOA: Amusement and Music Operators Association
AMRA: American Mechanical Rights Association
AOR: album-oriented rock
A & R: artists and repertoire
ARB: Arbitron
ASCAP: American Society of Composers, Authors and Publishers
ASOL: American Symphony Orchestra League
ATPAM: Association of Theatrical Press Agents and Managers
BIEM: Bureau International des Sociétés gérant les Droits d'Enregistrement et de Reproduction Mécanique
BMA: Black Music Association
BMI: Broadcast Music, Inc.
CATV: Cable Television or Community Antenna TV
CISAC: International Confederation of Societies of Authors and Composers
CLGA: Composers and Lyricists Guild of America
CMA: Country Music Association
CSB: Copyright Service Bureau Ltd.
C & W: country and western
demo: demonstration recording
DJ: disc jockey
FCC: Federal Communications Commission
FTC: Federal Trade Commission
Four A's: Associated Actors and Artistes of America

GMA: Gospel Music Association
HFA: The Harry Fox Agency
IATSE: International Alliance of Theatrical Stage Employees and Moving Picture Machine Operators of U.S. and Canada
IFPI: International Federation of Producers of Phonograms and Videograms
ips: inches per second
MENC: Music Educators National Conference
MOR: middle of the road
NAB: National Association of Broadcasters
NAIRD: National Association of Independent Record Distributors
NAJE: National Association of Jazz Educators
NAMM: National Association of Music Merchants
NARAS: National Academy of Recording Arts and Sciences
NARM: National Association of Recording Merchandisers
NLRB: National Labor Relations Board
NMC: National Music Council
NMPA: National Music Publishers' Association
NSAI: Nashville Songwriters Association, International
PD: program director; public domain
R & B: rhythm and blues
RIAA: Recording Industry Association of America, Inc.
rpm: revolutions per minute
SAG: Screen Actors Guild
SAMPAC: Society of Advertising Music Producers, Arrangers & Composers
SASE: self-addressed stamped envelope
SESAC: *formerly* The Society of European Stage Authors and Composers
TWAU: Theatrical Wardrobe Attendants Union
UCC: Universal Copyright Convention
VCR: video cassette recorder
VTR: video tape recorder

FORM PA

UNITED STATES COPYRIGHT OFFICE

B. Application for Copyright Registration of a Musical Composition on Form PA as Filed by a Songwriter

REGISTRATION NUMBER
PA   PAU

EFFECTIVE DATE OF REGISTRATION

. . . .
(Month)   (Day)   (Year)

DO NOT WRITE ABOVE THIS LINE. IF YOU NEED MORE SPACE, USE CONTINUATION SHEET (FORM PA/CON)

(1) Title

TITLE OF THIS WORK:

MONOTUNE

NATURE OF THIS WORK: (See instructions)

PREVIOUS OR ALTERNATIVE TITLES:

---

(2) Author(s)

IMPORTANT: Under the law, the "author" of a "work made for hire" is generally the employer, not the employee (see instructions). If any part of this work was "made for hire" check "Yes" in the space provided, give the employer (or other person for whom the work was prepared) as "Author" of that part, and leave the space for dates blank.

1

NAME OF AUTHOR: Chivas Silver

Was this author's contribution to the work a "work made for hire"?   Yes . . . . .   No. **X** . . .

DATES OF BIRTH AND DEATH:
Born 1954   Died . . . .
(Year)   (Year)

AUTHOR'S NATIONALITY OR DOMICILE:
Citizen of . . . . USA . . . . } or { Domiciled in . . . .
(Name of Country)   (Name of Country)

WAS THIS AUTHOR'S CONTRIBUTION TO THE WORK:
Anonymous?   Yes . . . . . .   No . . . . . .
Pseudonymous?   Yes . . . . .   No . . . . . .
If the answer to either of these questions is "Yes," see detailed instructions attached.

AUTHOR OF: (Briefly describe nature of this author's contribution)
words and music

2

NAME OF AUTHOR:

Was this author's contribution to the work a "work made for hire"?   Yes . . . . . .   No. . . . . .

DATES OF BIRTH AND DEATH:
Born . . . .   Died . . . .
(Year)   (Year)

AUTHOR'S NATIONALITY OR DOMICILE:
Citizen of . . . . } or { Domiciled in . . . .
(Name of Country)   (Name of Country)

WAS THIS AUTHOR'S CONTRIBUTION TO THE WORK:
Anonymous?   Yes . . . . . .   No . . . . . .
Pseudonymous?   Yes . . . . .   No . . . . . .
If the answer to either of these questions is "Yes," see detailed instructions attached.

AUTHOR OF: (Briefly describe nature of this author's contribution)

3

NAME OF AUTHOR:

Was this author's contribution to the work a "work made for hire"?   Yes . . . . . .   No. . . . . .

DATES OF BIRTH AND DEATH:
Born . . . .   Died . . . .
(Year)   (Year)

AUTHOR'S NATIONALITY OR DOMICILE:
Citizen of . . . . } or { Domiciled in . . . .
(Name of Country)   (Name of Country)

WAS THIS AUTHOR'S CONTRIBUTION TO THE WORK:
Anonymous?   Yes . . . . . .   No . . . . . .
Pseudonymous?   Yes . . . . .   No . . . . . .
If the answer to either of these questions is "Yes," see detailed instructions attached.

AUTHOR OF: (Briefly describe nature of this author's contribution)

---

(3) Creation and Publication

YEAR IN WHICH CREATION OF THIS WORK WAS COMPLETED:

Year 1981 . . . .

(This information must be given in all cases.)

DATE AND NATION OF FIRST PUBLICATION:

Date . . . .
(Month)   (Day)   (Year)

Nation . . . .
(Name of Country)

(Complete this block ONLY if this work has been published.)

---

(4) Claimant(s)

NAME(S) AND ADDRESS(ES) OF COPYRIGHT CLAIMANT(S):

Chivas Silver
1001 35th Street
Pomona, Washington

TRANSFER: (If the copyright claimant(s) named here in space 4 are different from the author(s) named in space 2, give a brief statement of how the claimant(s) obtained ownership of the copyright.)

- *Complete all applicable spaces (numbers 5-9) on the reverse side of this page*
- *Follow detailed instructions attached*   • *Sign the form at line 8*

DO NOT WRITE HERE

Page 1 of . . . . pages

	EXAMINED BY:	APPLICATION RECEIVED:	
	CHECKED BY:		FOR COPYRIGHT OFFICE USE ONLY
	CORRESPONDENCE: ☐ Yes	DEPOSIT RECEIVED:	
	DEPOSIT ACCOUNT FUNDS USED: ☐	REMITTANCE NUMBER AND DATE:	

DO NOT WRITE ABOVE THIS LINE. IF YOU NEED ADDITIONAL SPACE, USE CONTINUATION SHEET (FORM PA/CON)

PREVIOUS REGISTRATION:

⑤ Previous Registration

- Has registration for this work, or for an earlier version of this work, already been made in the Copyright Office? Yes .... No . X ....

- If your answer is "Yes," why is another registration being sought? (Check appropriate box)

  ☐ This is the first published edition of a work previously registered in unpublished form.
  ☐ This is the first application submitted by this author as copyright claimant.
  ☐ This is a changed version of the work, as shown by line 6 of the application.

- If your answer is "Yes," give: Previous Registration Number .... Year of Registration ....

COMPILATION OR DERIVATIVE WORK: (See instructions)

⑥ Compilation or Derivative Work

PREEXISTING MATERIAL: (Identify any preexisting work or works that the work is based on or incorporates.)

....
....
....

MATERIAL ADDED TO THIS WORK: (Give a brief, general statement of the material that has been added to this work and in which copyright is claimed.)

....
....
....

DEPOSIT ACCOUNT: (If the registration fee is to be charged to a Deposit Account established in the Copyright Office, give name and number of Account.)

Name: ....

Account Number: ....

CORRESPONDENCE: (Give name and address to which correspondence about this application should be sent.)

Name: .... Chivas Silver

Address: .... 1001 35th Street,
(Apt.)

.... Pomona, WA 90000
(City)   (State)   (ZIP)

⑦ Fee and Correspondence

CERTIFICATION: ✱ I, the undersigned, hereby certify that I am the: (Check one)

☒ author ☐ other copyright claimant ☐ owner of exclusive right(s) ☐ authorized agent of: ....
(Name of author or other copyright claimant, or owner of exclusive right(s))

of the work identified in this application and that the statements made by me in this application are correct to the best of my knowledge.

Handwritten signature: (X) *Chivas Silver*

Typed or printed name.... Chivas Silver   Date .. 3-4-81

⑧ Certification (Application must be signed)

MAIL CERTIFICATE TO

(Certificate will be mailed in window envelope)

CHIVAS SILVER
(Name)
.... 1001 35th Street ....
(Number, Street and Apartment Number)
POMONA   WA   90000
(City)   (State)   (ZIP code)

⑨ Address For Return of Certificate

✱ 17 U.S.C. §506(e) FALSE REPRESENTATION – Any person who knowingly makes a false representation of a material fact in the application for copyright registration provided for by section 409, or in any written statement filed in connection with the application, shall be fined not more than $2,500.
☆ U.S. GOVERNMENT PRINTING OFFICE: 1980-311-425/12

Aug. 1980—50,000

FORM PA

UNITED STATES COPYRIGHT OFFICE

C. Application for Copyright Registration of a Musical Composition on Form PA as Filed by a Music Publisher

REGISTRATION NUMBER

PA   PAU

EFFECTIVE DATE OF REGISTRATION

....
(Month)   (Day)   (Year)

DO NOT WRITE ABOVE THIS LINE. IF YOU NEED MORE SPACE, USE CONTINUATION SHEET (FORM PA/CON)

(1) Title

TITLE OF THIS WORK:

WANDERING THROUGH TIME

NATURE OF THIS WORK: (See instructions)

PREVIOUS OR ALTERNATIVE TITLES:

---

(2) Author(s)

IMPORTANT: Under the law, the "author" of a "work made for hire" is generally the employer, not the employee (see instructions). If any part of this work was "made for hire" check "Yes" in the space provided, give the employer (or other person for whom the work was prepared) as "Author" of that part, and leave the space for dates blank.

1
NAME OF AUTHOR:
Chivas Silver
Was this author's contribution to the work a "work made for hire"? Yes....... No... X
DATES OF BIRTH AND DEATH:
Born .... Died ....
(Year)   (Year)

AUTHOR'S NATIONALITY OR DOMICILE:
Citizen of ... US .... } or { Domiciled in ....
(Name of Country)   (Name of Country)

WAS THIS AUTHOR'S CONTRIBUTION TO THE WORK:
Anonymous? Yes...... No......
Pseudonymous? Yes...... No......
If the answer to either of these questions is "Yes," see detailed instructions attached.

AUTHOR OF: (Briefly describe nature of this author's contribution)
words and music

2
NAME OF AUTHOR:
Was this author's contribution to the work a "work made for hire"? Yes....... No......
DATES OF BIRTH AND DEATH:
Born .... Died ....
(Year)   (Year)

AUTHOR'S NATIONALITY OR DOMICILE:
Citizen of .... } or { Domiciled in ....
(Name of Country)   (Name of Country)

WAS THIS AUTHOR'S CONTRIBUTION TO THE WORK:
Anonymous? Yes...... No......
Pseudonymous? Yes...... No......
If the answer to either of these questions is "Yes," see detailed instructions attached.

AUTHOR OF: (Briefly describe nature of this author's contribution)

3
NAME OF AUTHOR:
Was this author's contribution to the work a "work made for hire"? Yes....... No......
DATES OF BIRTH AND DEATH:
Born .... Died ....
(Year)   (Year)

AUTHOR'S NATIONALITY OR DOMICILE:
Citizen of .... } or { Domiciled in ....
(Name of Country)   (Name of Country)

WAS THIS AUTHOR'S CONTRIBUTION TO THE WORK:
Anonymous? Yes...... No......
Pseudonymous? Yes...... No......
If the answer to either of these questions is "Yes," see detailed instructions attached.

AUTHOR OF: (Briefly describe nature of this author's contribution)

---

(3) Creation and Publication

YEAR IN WHICH CREATION OF THIS WORK WAS COMPLETED:

Year. 1981

(This information must be given in all cases.)

DATE AND NATION OF FIRST PUBLICATION:

Date.......... January 31 1981 ....
(Month)   (Day)   (Year)

Nation .... US ....
(Name of Country)

(Complete this block ONLY if this work has been published.)

---

(4) Claimant(s)

NAME(S) AND ADDRESS(ES) OF COPYRIGHT CLAIMANT(S):

Upfront Music Publishing Company
1234 Sheridan Street
Navasota, Texas

TRANSFER: (If the copyright claimant(s) named here in space 4 are different from the author(s) named in space 2, give a brief statement of how the claimant(s) obtained ownership of the copyright.)
by contract

- *Complete all applicable spaces (numbers 5-9) on the reverse side of this page*
- *Follow detailed instructions attached*   • *Sign the form at line 8*

DO NOT WRITE HERE

Page 1 of .... pages

EXAMINED BY:	APPLICATION RECEIVED:	
CHECKED BY:		FOR COPYRIGHT OFFICE USE ONLY
CORRESPONDENCE: ☐ Yes	DEPOSIT RECEIVED:	
DEPOSIT ACCOUNT FUNDS USED: ☐	REMITTANCE NUMBER AND DATE:	

DO NOT WRITE ABOVE THIS LINE. IF YOU NEED ADDITIONAL SPACE, USE CONTINUATION SHEET (FORM PA/CON)

PREVIOUS REGISTRATION:

- Has registration for this work, or for an earlier version of this work, already been made in the Copyright Office? Yes . . . . No . **X** . . . .

- If your answer is "Yes," why is another registration being sought? (Check appropriate box)

  ☐ This is the first published edition of a work previously registered in unpublished form.
  ☐ This is the first application submitted by this author as copyright claimant.
  ☐ This is a changed version of the work, as shown by line 6 of the application.

- If your answer is "Yes," give: Previous Registration Number . . . . Year of Registration . . . .

(5) Previous Registration

COMPILATION OR DERIVATIVE WORK: (See instructions)

PREEXISTING MATERIAL: (Identify any preexisting work or works that the work is based on or incorporates.)
. . . .
. . . .
. . . .

MATERIAL ADDED TO THIS WORK: (Give a brief, general statement of the material that has been added to this work and in which copyright is claimed.)
. . . .
. . . .
. . . .

(6) Compilation or Derivative Work

DEPOSIT ACCOUNT: (If the registration fee is to be charged to a Deposit Account established in the Copyright Office, give name and number of Account.)

Name: . . . .

Account Number: . . . .

CORRESPONDENCE: (Give name and address to which correspondence about this application should be sent.)

Name: Richard Dukes, Upfront Publishing Co.

Address: 1234 Sheridan Street   (Apt.)

Navasota   TX   77000
(City)   (State)   (ZIP)

(7) Fee and Correspondence

CERTIFICATION: ✱ I, the undersigned, hereby certify that I am the: (Check one)

☐ author ☐ other copyright claimant ☐ owner of exclusive right(s) ☑ authorized agent of: Upfront Music Publishing Company
(Name of author or other copyright claimant, or owner of exclusive right(s))

of the work identified in this application and that the statements made by me in this application are correct to the best of my knowledge.

Handwritten signature: (X)   *Richard Dukes*

Typed or printed name. . . . Richard Dukes . . . . Date . . 3-4-81 . . . . .

(8) Certification (Application must be signed)

| UPFRONT MUSIC PUBLISHING COMPANY .... (Name) 1234 Sheridan Street .... (Number, Street and Apartment Number) NAVASOTA   TX   77000 (City)   (State)   (ZIP code) | **MAIL CERTIFICATE TO** (Certificate will be mailed in window envelope) | **(9) Address For Return of Certificate** |

✱ 17 U.S.C. §506(e) FALSE REPRESENTATION – Any person who knowingly makes a false representation of a material fact in the application for copyright registration provided for by section 409 or in any written statement filed in connection with the application, shall be fined not more than $2,500.

☆ U.S. GOVERNMENT PRINTING OFFICE: 1980-311-425/12

Aug. 1980—50,000

FORM PA

UNITED STATES COPYRIGHT OFFICE

D. Application for Copyright Registration of a Derivative Work on Form PA as Filed by a Songwriter

This application shows registration of a derivative work and shows how individual titles in an unpublished collection of songs being registered for copyright can be listed on the continuation sheet. But to get the individual titles catalogued in the Copyright Office, one needs to file Form CA or file a basic registration for each work.

REGISTRATION NUMBER

PA   PAU

EFFECTIVE DATE OF REGISTRATION

....
(Month)   (Day)   (Year)

DO NOT WRITE ABOVE THIS LINE. IF YOU NEED MORE SPACE, USE CONTINUATION SHEET (FORM PA/CON)

(1) Title

TITLE OF THIS WORK:

A DREAM IN SONG

NATURE OF THIS WORK: (See instructions)

Words, music, arrangement

PREVIOUS OR ALTERNATIVE TITLES:

(2) Author(s)

IMPORTANT: Under the law, the "author" of a "work made for hire" is generally the employer, not the employee (see instructions). If any part of this work was "made for hire" check "Yes" in the space provided, give the employer (or other person for whom the work was prepared) as "Author" of that part, and leave the space for dates blank.

1

NAME OF AUTHOR: Agnes Dubin

Was this author's contribution to the work a "work made for hire"? Yes...... No. **X**

DATES OF BIRTH AND DEATH:
Born 1942.. Died ....
(Year)   (Year)

AUTHOR'S NATIONALITY OR DOMICILE:
Citizen of **USA** .... } or { Domiciled in ....
(Name of Country)   (Name of Country)

WAS THIS AUTHOR'S CONTRIBUTION TO THE WORK:
Anonymous? Yes...... No. **X**
Pseudonymous? Yes...... No. **X**

If the answer to either of these questions is "Yes," see detailed instructions attached.

AUTHOR OF: (Briefly describe nature of this author's contribution)
Words, music, and arrangement

2

NAME OF AUTHOR:

Was this author's contribution to the work a "work made for hire"? Yes...... No......

DATES OF BIRTH AND DEATH:
Born .... Died ....
(Year)   (Year)

AUTHOR'S NATIONALITY OR DOMICILE:
Citizen of .... } or { Domiciled in ....
(Name of Country)   (Name of Country)

WAS THIS AUTHOR'S CONTRIBUTION TO THE WORK:
Anonymous? Yes...... No......
Pseudonymous? Yes...... No......

If the answer to either of these questions is "Yes," see detailed instructions attached.

AUTHOR OF: (Briefly describe nature of this author's contribution)

3

NAME OF AUTHOR:

Was this author's contribution to the work a "work made for hire"? Yes...... No......

DATES OF BIRTH AND DEATH:
Born .... Died ....
(Year)   (Year)

AUTHOR'S NATIONALITY OR DOMICILE:
Citizen of .... } or { Domiciled in ....
(Name of Country)   (Name of Country)

WAS THIS AUTHOR'S CONTRIBUTION TO THE WORK:
Anonymous? Yes...... No......
Pseudonymous? Yes...... No......

If the answer to either of these questions is "Yes," see detailed instructions attached.

AUTHOR OF: (Briefly describe nature of this author's contribution)

(3) Creation and Publication

YEAR IN WHICH CREATION OF THIS WORK WAS COMPLETED:

Year. 1981..

(This information must be given in all cases.)

DATE AND NATION OF FIRST PUBLICATION:

Date......................................
(Month)   (Day)   (Year)

Nation...................................
(Name of Country)

(Complete this block ONLY if this work has been published.)

(4) Claimant(s)

NAME(S) AND ADDRESS(ES) OF COPYRIGHT CLAIMANT(S):

Agnes Dubin
2181 Wickford Road
Havertown, Pa. 19131

TRANSFER: (If the copyright claimant(s) named here in space 4 are different from the author(s) named in space 2, give a brief statement of how the claimant(s) obtained ownership of the copyright.)

• *Complete all applicable spaces (numbers 5-9) on the reverse side of this page*
• *Follow detailed instructions attached*   • *Sign the form at line 8*

DO NOT WRITE HERE

Page 1 of .... pages

	EXAMINED BY:	APPLICATION RECEIVED:	
	CHECKED BY:		FOR COPYRIGHT OFFICE USE ONLY
	CORRESPONDENCE: ☐ Yes	DEPOSIT RECEIVED:	
	DEPOSIT ACCOUNT FUNDS USED: ☐	REMITTANCE NUMBER AND DATE:	

DO NOT WRITE ABOVE THIS LINE. IF YOU NEED ADDITIONAL SPACE, USE CONTINUATION SHEET (FORM PA/CON)

PREVIOUS REGISTRATION:

⑤
Previous Registration

- Has registration for this work, or for an earlier version of this work, already been made in the Copyright Office?   Yes . . . .   No **X** . . . .

- If your answer is "Yes," why is another registration being sought?   (Check appropriate box)

  ☐ This is the first published edition of a work previously registered in unpublished form.
  ☐ This is the first application submitted by this author as copyright claimant.
  ☐ This is a changed version of the work, as shown by line 6 of the application.

- If your answer is "Yes," give: Previous Registration Number . . . . Year of Registration . . . .

COMPILATION OR DERIVATIVE WORK: (See instructions)

⑥
Compilation or Derivative Work

PREEXISTING MATERIAL: (Identify any preexisting work or works that the work is based on or incorporates.)

. . . . Lord, Dismiss Us With Thy Blessing (a hymn in the
. . . . public domain)
. . . .

MATERIAL ADDED TO THIS WORK: (Give a brief, general statement of the material that has been added to this work and in which copyright is claimed.)

. . . . Additional words, music, and arrangement
. . . .
. . . .

DEPOSIT ACCOUNT: (If the registration fee is to be charged to a Deposit Account established in the Copyright Office, give name and number of Account.)

Name: . . . .

Account Number: . . . .

CORRESPONDENCE: (Give name and address to which correspondence about this application should be sent.)

Name: . . . . . **Agnes Dubin**

Address: . . . **2181 Wickford Road**
. . . . (Apt.)

. . . . . **Havertown, Pa.** **19131**
(City) . . . . (State) . . . . (ZIP)

⑦
Fee and Correspondence

CERTIFICATION: ✱ I, the undersigned, hereby certify that I am the: (Check one)

⑧
Certification (Application must be signed)

☒ author ☐ other copyright claimant ☐ owner of exclusive right(s) ☐ authorized agent of: . . . .
. . . . (Name of author or other copyright claimant, or owner of exclusive right(s))

of the work identified in this application and that the statements made by me in this application are correct to the best of my knowledge.

☞   Handwritten signature: (X) . . . *Agnes Dubin* . . . .

Typed or printed name. . . . . . . **Agnes Dubin** . . . . Date **10/25/81**

MAIL CERTIFICATE TO

. . . . **Agnes Dubin** . . . .
. . . . (Name)
. . . . . . **2181 Wickford Road** . . . .
. . . . (Number, Street and Apartment Number)
. . . . **Havertown, Pa. 19131** . . . .
. . . . (City) . . . . . . (State) . . . . . . (ZIP code)

(Certificate will be mailed in window envelope)

⑨
Address For Return of Certificate

✱ 17 U.S.C. §506(e) FALSE REPRESENTATION—Any person who knowingly makes a false representation of a material fact in the application for copyright registration provided for by section 409, or in any written statement filed in connection with the application, shall be fined not more than $2,500.

U.S. GOVERNMENT PRINTING OFFICE:1979—281-421/10

July 1979—125,000

CONTINUATION SHEET FOR FORM PA

FORM PA/CON

UNITED STATES COPYRIGHT OFFICE

- If at all possible, try to fit the information called for into the spaces provided on Form PA.
- If you do not have space enough for all of the information you need to give on Form PA, use this continuation sheet and submit it with Form PA.
- If you submit this continuation sheet, leave it attached to Form PA. Or, if it becomes detached, clip (do not tape or staple) and fold the two together before submitting them.
- **PART A** of this sheet is intended to identify the basic application. **PART B** is a continuation of Space 2. **PART C** is for the continuation of Spaces 1, 4, or 6. The other spaces on Form PA call for specific items of information, and should not need continuation.

REGISTRATION NUMBER
PA   PAU
EFFECTIVE DATE OF REGISTRATION
....
(Month)   (Day)   (Year)
CONTINUATION SHEET RECEIVED
Page _____ of _____ pages

DO NOT WRITE ABOVE THIS LINE. FOR COPYRIGHT OFFICE USE ONLY

(A)

Identification of Application

IDENTIFICATION OF CONTINUATION SHEET: This sheet is a continuation of the application for copyright registration on Form PA, submitted for the following work:

- TITLE: (Give the title as given under the heading "Title of this Work" in Space 1 of Form PA.)

  A Dream In Song

- NAME(S) AND ADDRESS(ES) OF COPYRIGHT CLAIMANT(S): (Give the name and address of at least one copyright claimant as given in Space 4 of Form PA.)

  Agnes Dubin, 2181 Wickford Road, Havertown, Pa. 19131

(B)

Continuation of Space 2

NAME OF AUTHOR:

Was this author's contribution to the work a "work made for hire"? Yes...... No......

DATES OF BIRTH AND DEATH:
Born .... Died ....
(Year)   (Year)

AUTHOR'S NATIONALITY OR DOMICILE:

Citizen of .... } or { Domiciled in ....
(Name of Country)   (Name of Country)

WAS THIS AUTHOR'S CONTRIBUTION TO THE WORK:
Anonymous? Yes...... No......
Pseudonymous? Yes...... No......

AUTHOR OF: (Briefly describe nature of this author's contribution)

If the answer to either of these questions is "Yes," see detailed instructions attached.

NAME OF AUTHOR:

Was this author's contribution to the work a "work made for hire"? Yes...... No......

DATES OF BIRTH AND DEATH:
Born .... Died ....
(Year)   (Year)

AUTHOR'S NATIONALITY OR DOMICILE:

Citizen of .... } or { Domiciled in ....
(Name of Country)   (Name of Country)

WAS THIS AUTHOR'S CONTRIBUTION TO THE WORK:
Anonymous? Yes...... No......
Pseudonymous? Yes...... No......

AUTHOR OF: (Briefly describe nature of this author's contribution)

If the answer to either of these questions is "Yes," see detailed instructions attached.

NAME OF AUTHOR:

Was this author's contribution to the work a "work made for hire"? Yes...... No......

DATES OF BIRTH AND DEATH:
Born .... Died ....
(Year)   (Year)

AUTHOR'S NATIONALITY OR DOMICILE:

Citizen of .... } or { Domiciled in ....
(Name of Country)   (Name of Country)

WAS THIS AUTHOR'S CONTRIBUTION TO THE WORK:
Anonymous? Yes...... No......
Pseudonymous? Yes...... No......

AUTHOR OF: (Briefly describe nature of this author's contribution)

If the answer to either of these questions is "Yes," see detailed instructions attached.

(C)

Continuation of Other Spaces

CONTINUATION OF (Check which): ☒ Space 1   ☐ Space 4   ☐ Space 6

1. Hope On, Forever!
2. Little Barefoot Girl
3. The Nightingale and the Forest
4. Reflections and Recollections
5. Summer Day, Wintry Night

FORM SR

UNITED STATES COPYRIGHT OFFICE

E. Application for Copyright Registration of a Sound Recording on Form SR as Filed by an Artist/Musician

REGISTRATION NUMBER

SR · SRU

EFFECTIVE DATE OF REGISTRATION

. . . .
(Month)　　　(Day)　　　(Year)

DO NOT WRITE ABOVE THIS LINE. IF YOU NEED ADDITIONAL SPACE, USE CONTINUATION SHEET (FORM SR/CON)

① Title

TITLE OF THIS WORK:

RESTORATION BLUES

Catalog number of sound recording, if any: . . . .

PREVIOUS OR ALTERNATIVE TITLES:

NATURE OF MATERIAL RECORDED:
(Check Which)

☒ Musical　　☐ Musical-Dramatic
☐ Dramatic　　☐ Literary
☐ Other: . . . .
. . . .
. . . .

② Author(s)

IMPORTANT: Under the law, the "author" of a "work made for hire" is generally the employer, not the employee (see instructions). If any part of this work was "made for hire," check "Yes" in the space provided, give the employer (or other person for whom the work was prepared) as "Author" of that part, and leave the space for dates blank.

1

NAME OF AUTHOR: Chivas Silver

Was this author's contribution to the work a "work made for hire"? Yes...... No.. **X**

AUTHOR'S NATIONALITY OR DOMICILE:
Citizen of US.......... { or } { Domiciled in ....
(Name of Country)　　　　　　　　　　(Name of Country)

AUTHOR OF: (Briefly describe nature of this author's contribution)
words, music and performance

DATES OF BIRTH AND DEATH:
Born............ Died............
(Year)　　　　(Year)

WAS THIS AUTHOR'S CONTRIBUTION TO THE WORK:
Anonymous? Yes........ No......
Pseudonymous? Yes........ No......
If the answer to either of these questions is "Yes," see detailed instructions attached.

2

NAME OF AUTHOR:

Was this author's contribution to the work a "work made for hire"? Yes...... No......

AUTHOR'S NATIONALITY OR DOMICILE:
Citizen of .... { or } { Domiciled in ....
(Name of Country)　　　　　　　　　　(Name of Country)

AUTHOR OF: (Briefly describe nature of this author's contribution)

DATES OF BIRTH AND DEATH:
Born............ Died............
(Year)　　　　(Year)

WAS THIS AUTHOR'S CONTRIBUTION TO THE WORK:
Anonymous? Yes........ No......
Pseudonymous? Yes........ No......
If the answer to either of these questions is "Yes," see detailed instructions attached.

3

NAME OF AUTHOR:

Was this author's contribution to the work a "work made for hire"? Yes...... No......

AUTHOR'S NATIONALITY OR DOMICILE:
Citizen of .... { or } { Domiciled in ....
(Name of Country)　　　　　　　　　　(Name of Country)

AUTHOR OF: (Briefly describe nature of this author's contribution)

DATES OF BIRTH AND DEATH:
Born............ Died............
(Year)　　　　(Year)

WAS THIS AUTHOR'S CONTRIBUTION TO THE WORK:
Anonymous? Yes........ No......
Pseudonymous? Yes........ No......
If the answer to either of these questions is "Yes," see detailed instructions attached.

③ Creation and Publication

YEAR IN WHICH CREATION OF THIS WORK WAS COMPLETED:

Year 1981
(This information must be given in all cases.)

DATE AND NATION OF FIRST PUBLICATION:

Date..........................
(Month)　　　(Day)　　　(Year)

Nation..........................
(Name of Country)
(Complete this block ONLY if this work has been published.)

④ Claimant(s)

NAME(S) AND ADDRESS(ES) OF COPYRIGHT CLAIMANT(S):

Chivas Silver
1001 35th Street
Pomona, Washington

TRANSFER: (If the copyright claimant(s) named here in space 4 is different from the author(s) named in space 2, give a brief statement of how the claimant(s) obtained ownership of the copyright.)

• Complete all applicable spaces (numbers 5-9) on the reverse side of this page
• Follow detailed instructions attached
• Sign the form at line 8

DO NOT WRITE HERE

Page 1 of .... pages

EXAMINED BY:	APPLICATION RECEIVED:	
CHECKED BY:		FOR COPYRIGHT OFFICE USE ONLY
CORRESPONDENCE: ☐ Yes	DEPOSIT RECEIVED:	
DEPOSIT ACCOUNT FUNDS USED: ☐	REMITTANCE NUMBER AND DATE:	

DO NOT WRITE ABOVE THIS LINE. IF YOU NEED ADDITIONAL SPACE, USE CONTINUATION SHEET (FORM SR/CON)

PREVIOUS REGISTRATION:

- Has registration for this work, or for an earlier version of this work, already been made in the Copyright Office? Yes. . . . . No. . . . .

- If your answer is "Yes," why is another registration being sought? (Check appropriate box)
  ☐ This is the first published edition of a work previously registered in unpublished form.
  ☐ This is the first application submitted by this author as copyright claimant.
  ☐ This is a changed version of the work, as shown by line 6 of the application.

- If your answer is "Yes," give: Previous Registration Number. . . . . Year of Registration . . . .

⑤ Previous Registration

COMPILATION OR DERIVATIVE WORK: (See instructions)

PREEXISTING MATERIAL: (Identify any preexisting work or works that the work is based on or incorporates.)

. . . .
. . . .
. . . .

MATERIAL ADDED TO THIS WORK: (Give a brief, general statement of the material that has been added to this work and in which copyright is claimed.)

. . . .
. . . .
. . . .
. . . .

⑥ Compilation or Derivative Work

DEPOSIT ACCOUNT: (If the registration fee is to be charged to a Deposit Account established in the Copyright Office, give name and number of Account.)

Name: . . . .

Account Number: . . . .

CORRESPONDENCE: (Give name and address to which correspondence about this application should be sent.)

Name: Chivas Silver

Address: 1001 35th St. (Apt.)

Pomona, Washington
(City)   (State)   (ZIP)

⑦ Fee and Correspondence

CERTIFICATION: ✱ I, the undersigned, hereby certify that I am the: (Check one)
☑ author ☐ other copyright claimant ☐ owner of exclusive right(s) ☐ authorized agent of: . . . .
(Name of author or other copyright claimant, or owner of exclusive right(s))
of the work identified in this application and that the statements made by me in this application are correct to the best of my knowledge.

Handwritten signature: (X) *Chivas Silver*

Typed or printed name: Chivas Silver   Date: 3-4-81

⑧ Certification (Application must be signed)

CHIVAS SILVER
(Name)
1001 35th Street
(Number, Street and Apartment Number)
Pomona, Washington   90000
(City)   (State)   (ZIP code)

MAIL CERTIFICATE TO

(Certificate will be mailed in window envelope)

⑨ Address for Return of Certificate

✱ 17 U.S.C. § 506(e): FALSE REPRESENTATION—Any person who knowingly makes a false representation of a material fact in the application for copyright registration provided for by section 409, or in any written statement filed in connection with the application, shall be fined not more than $2,500.

☆ U.S. GOVERNMENT PRINTING OFFICE: 1980: 311-425/7

Jan. 1980—50,000

FORM SR
UNITED STATES COPYRIGHT OFFICE

F. Application for Copyright Registration of a Sound Recording on Form SR as Filed by a Record Company

REGISTRATION NUMBER

SR   SRU

EFFECTIVE DATE OF REGISTRATION

....
(Month)   (Day)   (Year)

DO NOT WRITE ABOVE THIS LINE. IF YOU NEED ADDITIONAL SPACE, USE CONTINUATION SHEET (FORM SR/CON)

(1) Title

TITLE OF THIS WORK:

DISCO ISN'T DEAD

Catalog number of sound recording, if any GR-8979

PREVIOUS OR ALTERNATIVE TITLES:

NATURE OF MATERIAL RECORDED: (Check Which)

☒ Musical   ☐ Musical Dramatic
☐ Dramatic   ☐ Literary
☐ Other ....

(2) Author(s)

IMPORTANT: Under the law, the "author" of a "work made for hire" is generally the employer, not the employee (see instructions). If any part of this work was "made for hire," check "Yes" in the space provided, give the employer (or other person for whom the work was prepared) as "Author" of that part, and leave the space for dates blank.

1

NAME OF AUTHOR:
Bullet Record Company Inc.
Was this author's contribution to the work a "work made for hire"? Yes **X** No ......

AUTHOR'S NATIONALITY OR DOMICILE:
Citizen of ..... US ..... } or { Domiciled in ....
(Name of Country)   (Name of Country)

AUTHOR OF: (Briefly describe nature of this author's contribution)
sound recording

DATES OF BIRTH AND DEATH:
Born .... Died ....
(Year)   (Year)

WAS THIS AUTHOR'S CONTRIBUTION TO THE WORK:
Anonymous? Yes ...... No ......
Pseudonymous? Yes ...... No ......
If the answer to either of these questions is "Yes," see detailed instructions attached

2

NAME OF AUTHOR:

Was this author's contribution to the work a "work made for hire"? Yes ...... No ......

AUTHOR'S NATIONALITY OR DOMICILE:
Citizen of .... } or { Domiciled in ....
(Name of Country)   (Name of Country)

AUTHOR OF: (Briefly describe nature of this author's contribution)

DATES OF BIRTH AND DEATH:
Born .... Died ....
(Year)   (Year)

WAS THIS AUTHOR'S CONTRIBUTION TO THE WORK:
Anonymous? Yes ...... No ......
Pseudonymous? Yes ...... No ......
If the answer to either of these questions is "Yes," see detailed instructions attached

3

NAME OF AUTHOR:

Was this author's contribution to the work a "work made for hire"? Yes ...... No ......

AUTHOR'S NATIONALITY OR DOMICILE:
Citizen of .... } or { Domiciled in ....
(Name of Country)   (Name of Country)

AUTHOR OF: (Briefly describe nature of this author's contribution)

DATES OF BIRTH AND DEATH:
Born .... Died ....
(Year)   (Year)

WAS THIS AUTHOR'S CONTRIBUTION TO THE WORK:
Anonymous? Yes ...... No ......
Pseudonymous? Yes ...... No ......
If the answer to either of these questions is "Yes," see detailed instructions attached

(3) Creation and Publication

YEAR IN WHICH CREATION OF THIS WORK WAS COMPLETED:
Year 1981
(This information must be given in all cases.)

DATE AND NATION OF FIRST PUBLICATION:
Date February 1 1981
     (Month) (Day) (Year)
Nation US
     (Name of Country)
(Complete this block ONLY if this work has been published.)

(4) Claimant(s)

NAME(S) AND ADDRESS(ES) OF COPYRIGHT CLAIMANT(S):

Bullet Record Company, Inc.
4567 Main Street
Ojai, California

TRANSFER: (If the copyright claimant(s) named here in space 4 is different from the author(s) named in space 2, give a brief statement of how the claimant(s) obtained ownership of the copyright.)

• Complete all applicable spaces (numbers 5-9) on the reverse side of this page
• Follow detailed instructions attached
• Sign the form at line 8

DO NOT WRITE HERE

Page 1 of .... pages

EXAMINED BY:	APPLICATION RECEIVED:	
CHECKED BY:		FOR COPYRIGHT OFFICE USE ONLY
CORRESPONDENCE: ☐ Yes	DEPOSIT RECEIVED:	
DEPOSIT ACCOUNT FUNDS USED: ☐	REMITTANCE NUMBER AND DATE:	

DO NOT WRITE ABOVE THIS LINE. IF YOU NEED ADDITIONAL SPACE, USE CONTINUATION SHEET (FORM SR/CON)

PREVIOUS REGISTRATION:

⑤ Previous Registration

- Has registration for this work, or for an earlier version of this work, already been made in the Copyright Office? Yes . . . . No **X** . . .

- If your answer is "Yes," why is another registration being sought? (Check appropriate box)
  - ☐ This is the first published edition of a work previously registered in unpublished form.
  - ☐ This is the first application submitted by this author as copyright claimant.
  - ☐ This is a changed version of the work, as shown by line 6 of the application.

- If your answer is "Yes," give: Previous Registration Number . . . . Year of Registration . . . .

COMPILATION OR DERIVATIVE WORK: (See instructions)

⑥ Compilation or Derivative Work

PREEXISTING MATERIAL: (Identify any preexisting work or works that the work is based on or incorporates.)
. . . .
. . . .
. . . .

MATERIAL ADDED TO THIS WORK: (Give a brief, general statement of the material that has been added to this work and in which copyright is claimed.)
. . . .
. . . .
. . . .

DEPOSIT ACCOUNT: (If the registration fee is to be charged to a Deposit Account established in the Copyright Office, give name and number of Account.)

⑦ Fee and Correspondence

Name: . . . .

Account Number: . . . .

CORRESPONDENCE: (Give name and address to which correspondence about this application should be sent.)

Name: Ms. J. Singleton, Bullet Records

Address: 4567 Main Street . . . . (Apt.)

Ojai . . . . CA . . . . 93899 . . . .
(City)   (State)   (ZIP)

CERTIFICATION: ✱ I, the undersigned, hereby certify that I am the: (Check one)
☐ author ☐ other copyright claimant ☐ owner of exclusive right(s) ☒ authorized agent of Bullet Record Co., Inc.
(Name of author of other copyright claimant, or owner of exclusive right(s))
of the work identified in this application and that the statements made by me in this application are correct to the best of my knowledge.

⑧ Certification (Application must be signed)

Handwritten signature: (X) *Jane Singleton*

Typed or printed name: Jane Singleton . . . . Date: 3-4-81 . . . . . .

MAIL CERTIFICATE TO

(Certificate will be mailed in window envelope)

⑨ Address for Return of Certificate

BULLET RECORD COMPANY, INC. . . . .
(Name)
4567 Main Street
. . . .
Ojai . . . (Number, Street and Apartment Number) . . . CA . . . . 93899 . . . .
(City)   (State)   (ZIP code)

✱ 17 U.S.C. § 506(e): FALSE REPRESENTATION—Any person who knowingly makes a false representation of a material fact in the application for copyright registration provided for by section 409, or in any written statement filed in connection with the application, shall be fined not more than $2,500.

☆U.S. GOVERNMENT PRINTING OFFICE: 1980: 311-425/7

Jan. 1980—50,000

G. Academy Award Winners*

1934   **Best Song**
"The Continental" from *The Gay Divorcee*, RKO Radio. Music by Con Conrad; lyrics by Herb Magidson.
Best Score
One Night of Love, Columbia Studio Music Dept. Louis Silvers, Head. Thematic music by Victor Schertzinger and Gus Kahn.†

1935   **Best Song**
"Lullaby of Broadway" from *Gold Diggers of 1935*, Warner Bros. Music by Harry Warren; lyrics by Al Dubin.
Best Score
The Informer, RKO Radio Studio Music Dept. Max Steiner, Head. Score by Max Steiner.†

1936   **Best Song**
"The Way You Look Tonight" from *Swing Time*, RKO Radio. Music by Jerome Kern; lyrics by Dorothy Fields.
Best Score
Anthony Adverse, Warner Bros. Studio Music Dept. Leo Forbstein, Head. Score by Erich Wolfgang Korngold.†

1937   **Best Song**
"Sweet Leilani" from *Waikiki Wedding*, Paramount. Music and lyrics by Harry Owens.
Best Score
One Hundred Men and a Girl, Universal Studio Music Dept. Charles Previn, Head. Score: No composer credit.†

1938   **Best Song**
"Thanks for the Memory" from *Big Broadcast of 1938*, Paramount. Music by Ralph Rainger; lyrics by Leo Robin.
Best Score
Alexander's Ragtime Band, 20th Century-Fox. Alfred Newman.
Original Score
The Adventures of Robin Hood, Warner Bros. Erich Wolfgang Korngold.

1939   **Best Song**
"Over the Rainbow" from *The Wizard of Oz*, Metro-Goldwyn-Mayer. Music by Harold Arlen; lyrics by E. Y. Harburg.

Best Score
Stagecoach, Walter Wanger, UA. Richard Hageman, Frank Harling, John Leipold and Leo Shuken.
Original Score
The Wizard of Oz, Metro-Goldwyn-Mayer. Herbert Stothart.

1940   **Best Song**
"When You Wish Upon a Star" from *Pinocchio*, Disney, RKO Radio. Music by Leigh Harline; lyrics by Ned Washington.
Best Score
Tin Pan Alley, 20th Century-Fox. Alfred Newman.
Original Score
Pinocchio, Disney, RKO Radio. Leigh Harline, Paul J. Smith and Ned Washington.

1941   **Best Song**
"The Last Time I Saw Paris" from *Lady Be Good*, Metro-Goldwyn-Mayer. Music by Jerome Kern; lyrics by Oscar Hammerstein II.
Scoring of a Dramatic Picture
All That Money Can Buy, RKO Radio. Bernard Herrmann.
Scoring of a Musical Picture
Dumbo, Disney, RKO Radio. Frank Churchill and Oliver Wallace.

1942   **Best Song**
"White Christmas" from *Holiday Inn*, Paramount. Music and lyrics by Irving Berlin.
Scoring of a Dramatic or Comedy Picture
Now, Voyager, Warner Bros. Max Steiner.
Scoring of a Musical Picture
Yankee Doodle Dandy, Warner Bros. Ray Heindorf and Heinz Roemheld.

1943   **Best Song**
"You'll Never Know" from *Hello, Frisco, Hello*, 20th Century-Fox. Music by Harry Warren; lyrics by Mack Gordon.
Scoring of a Dramatic or Comedy Picture
The Song of Bernadette, 20th Century-Fox. Alfred Newman.
Scoring of a Musical Picture
This Is the Army, Warner Bros. Ray Heindorf.

1944   **Best Song**
"Swinging on a Star" from *Going My Way*, Paramount. Music by James Van Heusen; lyrics by Johnny Burke.

---

* Courtesy: Academy of Motion Picture Arts and Sciences.
† Scoring awards from 1934 to 1937 were presented to the departmental head of the studio rather than the composer as this was a Music Department Achievement.

1944 Best Song *(cont'd)*

Scoring of a Dramatic or Comedy Picture
Since You Went Away, Selznick, UA. Max Steiner.

Scoring of a Musical Picture
Cover Girl, Columbia. Carmen Dragon and Morris Stoloff.

1945 Best Song
"It Might As Well Be Spring" from *State Fair*, 20th Century-Fox. Music by Richard Rodgers; lyrics by Oscar Hammerstein II.

Scoring of a Dramatic or Comedy Picture
Spellbound, Selznick, UA. Miklos Rozsa.

Scoring of a Musical Picture
Anchors Aweigh, Metro-Goldwyn-Mayer. Georgie Stoll.

1946 Best Song
"On the Atchison, Topeka and Santa Fe" from *The Harvey Girls*, Metro-Goldwyn-Mayer. Music by Harry Warren; lyrics by Johnny Mercer.

Scoring of a Dramatic or Comedy Picture
The Best Years of Our Lives, Goldwyn, RKO Radio. Hugo Friedhofer.

Scoring of a Musical Picture
The Jolson Story, Columbia. Morris Stoloff.

1947 Best Song
"Zip-A-Dee-Doo-Dah" from *Song of the South*, Disney-RKO Radio. Music by Allie Wrubel; lyrics by Ray Gilbert.

Scoring of a Dramatic or Comedy Picture
A Double Life, Kanin, U-I. Miklos Rozsa.

Scoring of a Musical Picture
Mother Wore Tights, 20th Century-Fox. Alfred Newman.

1948 Best Song
"Buttons and Bows" from *The Paleface*, Paramount. Music and lyrics by Jay Livingston and Ray Evans.

Scoring of a Dramatic or Comedy Picture
The Red Shoes, Rank-Archers-Eagle-Lion (British). Brian Easdale.

Scoring of a Musical Picture
Easter Parade, Metro-Goldwyn-Mayer. Johnny Green and Roger Edens.

1949 Best Song
"Baby, It's Cold Outside" from *Neptune's Daughter*, Metro-Goldwyn-Mayer. Music and lyrics by Frank Loesser.

Scoring of a Dramatic or Comedy Picture
The Heiress, Paramount. Aaron Copland.

Scoring of a Musical Picture
On the Town, Metro-Goldwyn-Mayer. Roger Edens and Lennie Hayton.

1950 Best Song
"Mona Lisa" from *Captain Carey, USA*, Paramount. Music and lyrics by Ray Evans and Jay Livingston.

Scoring of a Dramatic or Comedy Picture
Sunset Boulevard, Paramount. Franz Waxman.

Scoring of a Musical Picture
Annie Get Your Gun, Metro-Goldwyn-Mayer. Adolph Deutsch and Roger Edens.

1951 Best Song
"In the Cool, Cool, Cool of the Evening" from *Here Comes the Groom*, Paramount. Music by Hoagy Carmichael; lyrics by Johnny Mercer.

Scoring of a Dramatic or Comedy Picture
A Place in the Sun, Paramount. Franz Waxman.

Scoring of a Musical Picture
An American in Paris, Metro-Goldwyn-Mayer. Johnny Green and Saul Chaplin.

1952 Best Song
"High Noon" ("Do Not Forsake Me, Oh My Darlin' ") from *High Noon*, Kramer, UA. Music by Dimitri Tiomkin; lyrics by Ned Washington.

Scoring of a Dramatic or Comedy Picture
High Noon, Kramer, UA. Dimitri Tiomkin.

Scoring of a Musical Picture
With a Song in My Heart, 20th Century-Fox. Alfred Newman.

1953 Best Song
"Secret Love" from *Calamity Jane*, Warner Bros. Music by Sammy Fain; lyrics by Paul Francis Webster.

Scoring of a Dramatic or Comedy Picture
Lili, Metro-Goldwyn-Mayer. Bronislau Kaper.

Scoring of a Musical Picture
Call Me Madam, 20th Century-Fox. Alfred Newman.

1954 Best Song
"Three Coins in the Fountain" from *Three Coins in the Fountain*, 20th Century-Fox. Music by Jule Styne; lyrics by Sammy Cahn.

Scoring of a Dramatic or Comedy Picture
The High and the Mighty, Wayne-Fellows Prods., Inc., Warner Bros. Dimitri Tiomkin.

Scoring of a Musical Picture
Seven Brides for Seven Brothers, Metro-Goldwyn-Mayer. Adolph Deutsch and Saul Chaplin.

1955 Best Song
"Love Is a Many-Splendored Thing" from *Love Is a Many-Splendored Thing*, 20th Century-Fox. Music by Sammy Fain; lyrics by Paul Francis Webster.

Scoring of a Dramatic or Comedy Picture
Love Is a Many-Splendored Thing, 20th Century-Fox. Alfred Newman.

Scoring of a Musical Picture
Oklahoma!, Rodgers & Hammerstein Pictures, Inc., Magna Theatre Corp. Robert Russell Bennett, Jay Blackton and Adolph Deutsch.

1956 **Best Song**
"Whatever Will Be, Will Be" ("Que Sera, Sera") from *The Man Who Knew Too Much*, Filwite Prods., Inc., Paramount. Music and lyrics by Jay Livingston and Ray Evans.
Scoring of a Dramatic or Comedy Picture
Around the World in 80 Days, The Michael Todd Co., Inc., UA. Victor Young.
Scoring of a Musical Picture
The King and I, 20th Century-Fox. Alfred Newman and Ken Darby.

1957 **Best Song**
"All the Way" from *The Joker Is Wild*, A.M.B.L. Prod., Paramount. Music by James Van Heusen; lyrics by Sammy Cahn.
Scoring of a Dramatic or Comedy Picture
The Bridge On The River Kwai, A Horizon Picture, Columbia. Malcolm Arnold.

1958 **Best Song**
"Gigi" from *Gigi*, Arthur Freed Prods., Inc., M-G-M. Music by Frederick Loewe; lyrics by Alan Jay Lerner.
Scoring of a Dramatic or Comedy Picture
The Old Man and the Sea, Leland Hayward, Warner Bros. Dimitri Tiomkin.
Scoring of a Musical Picture
Gigi, Arthur Freed Prods., Inc., M-G-M. Andre Previn.

1959 **Best Song**
"High Hopes" from *A Hole in the Head*, Sincap Prods., UA. Music by James Van Heusen; lyrics by Sammy Cahn.
Scoring of a Dramatic or Comedy Picture
Ben-Hur, Metro-Goldwyn-Mayer. Miklos Rozsa.
Scoring of a Musical Picture
Porgy and Bess, Samuel Goldwyn Prods., Columbia. Andre Previn and Ken Darby.

1960 **Best Song**
"Never on Sunday" from *Never on Sunday*, Melinafilm Prod., Lopert Pictures Corp. (Greek). Music and lyrics by Manos Hadjidakis.
Scoring of a Dramatic or Comedy Picture
Exodus, Carlyle-Alpina S.A. Prod., UA. Ernest Gold.
Scoring of a Musical Picture
Song Without End (The Story of Franz Liszt), Goetz-Vidor Pictures Prod., Columbia. Morris Stoloff and Harry Sukman.

1961 **Best Song**
"Moon River" from *Breakfast at Tiffany's*, Jurow-Shepherd Prod., Paramount. Music by Henry Mancini; lyrics by Johnny Mercer.
Scoring of a Dramatic or Comedy Picture
Breakfast at Tiffany's, Jurow-Shepherd Prod., Paramount. Henry Mancini.
Scoring of a Musical Picture
West Side Story, Mirisch Pictures, Inc. and B

and P Enterprises, Inc., UA. Saul Chaplin, Johnny Green, Sid Ramin and Irwin Kostal.

1962 **Best Song**
"Days of Wine and Roses" from *Days of Wine and Roses*, Martin Manulis-Jalem Prod., Warner Bros. Music by Henry Mancini; lyrics by Johnny Mercer.
Music Score—substantially original
Lawrence of Arabia, Horizon Pictures (G.B.), Ltd.-Sam Spiegel-David Lean Prod., Columbia. Maurice Jarre.
Scoring of Music—adaptation or treatment
Meredith Willson's *The Music Man*, Warner Bros. Ray Heindorf.

1963 **Best Song**
"Call Me Irresponsible" from *Papa's Delicate Condition*, Amro Prods., Paramount. Music by James Van Heusen; lyrics by Sammy Cahn.
Music Score—substantially original
Tom Jones, Woodfall Prod., UA-Lopert Pictures. John Addison.
Scoring of Music—adaptation or treatment
Irma La Douce, Mirisch-Phalanx Prod., UA. Andre Previn.

1964 **Best Song**
"Chim Chim Cher-ee" from *Mary Poppins*, Walt Disney Prods. Music and lyrics by Richard M. Sherman & Robert B. Sherman.
Music Score—substantially original
Mary Poppins, Walt Disney Prods. Richard M. Sherman and Robert B. Sherman.
Scoring of Music—adaptation or treatment
My Fair Lady, Warner Bros. Andre Previn.

1965 **Best Song**
"The Shadow of Your Smile" from *The Sandpiper*. Filmways-Venice Prod., M.G.M. Music by Johnny Mandel; lyrics by Paul Francis Webster.
Music Score—substantially original
Doctor Zhivago, Sostar S.A.-Metro-Goldwyn-Mayer British Studios, Ltd. Prod., M-G-M. Maurice Jarre.
Scoring of Music—adaptation or treatment
The Sound of Music, Argyle Enterprises Prod., 20th Century-Fox. Irwin Kostal.

1966 **Best Song**
"Born Free" from *Born Free*, Open Road Films, Ltd.-Atlas Films, Ltd. Prod., Columbia. Music by John Barry; lyrics by Don Black.
Original Music Score
Born Free, Open Road Films, Ltd.-Atlas Films, Ltd. Prod., Columbia. John Barry.
Scoring of Music—adaptation or treatment
A Funny Thing Happened on the Way to the Forum, Melvin Frank Prod., United Artists. Ken Thorne.

1967 **Best Song**
"Talk to the Animals" from *Doctor Dolittle*, Apjac Prods., 20th Century-Fox. Music and lyrics by Leslie Bricusse.
Original Music Score
Thoroughly Modern Millie, Ross Hunter-Universal Prod., Universal. Elmer Bernstein.
Scoring of Music—adaptation or treatment
Camelot, Warner Bros.-Seven Arts. Alfred Newman and Ken Darby.

1968 **Best Song**
"The Windmills of Your Mind" from *The Thomas Crown Affair*, Mirisch-Simkoe-Solar Prod., United Artists. Music by Michel Legrand; lyrics by Alan and Marilyn Bergman.
Best Original Score—for a motion picture (not a musical)
The Lion in Winter, Haworth Prods., Ltd., Avco Embassy. John Barry.
Best Score of a Musical Picture—(original or adaptation)
Oliver!, Romulus Films, Columbia. Adapted by John Green.

1969 **Best Song**
"Raindrops Keep Fallin' on My Head" from *Butch Cassidy and the Sundance Kid*, George Roy Hill-Paul Monash Prod., 20th Century-Fox. Music by Burt Bacharach; lyrics by Hal David.
Best Original Score—for a motion picture (not a musical)
Butch Cassidy and the Sundance Kid, George Roy Hill-Paul Monash Prod., 20th Century-Fox. Burt Bacharach.
Best Score of a Musical Picture—(original or adaptation)
Hello, Dolly!, Chenault Prods., 20th Century-Fox. Adapted by Lennie Hayton and Lionel Newman.

1970 **Best Song**
"For All We Know" from *Lovers and Other Strangers*, ABC Pictures Prod., Cinerama. Music by Fred Karlin; lyrics by Robb Royer and James Griffin aka Robb Wilson and Arthur James.
Best Original Score
Love Story, The Love Story Company Prod., Paramount. Francis Lai.
Best Original Song Score
Let It Be, Beatles-Apple Prod., UA. Music and lyrics by The Beatles.

1971 **Best Song**
"Theme from Shaft" from *Shaft*, Shaft Prods., Ltd., M-G-M. Music and lyrics by Isaac Hayes.
Best Original Dramatic Score
Summer of '42, A Robert Mulligan-Richard Alan Roth Prod., Warner Bros. Michel Legrand.

Best Scoring: Adaptation and Original Song Score
Fiddler on the Roof, Mirisch-Cartier Prods., UA. Adapted by John Williams.

1972 **Best Song**
"The Morning After" from *The Poseidon Adventure*, An Irwin Allen Production, 20th Century-Fox. Music and lyrics by Al Kasha and Joel Hirschhovn.
Best Original Dramatic Score
Limelight, A Charles Chaplin Prod., Columbia. Charles Chaplin, Raymond Rasch and Larry Russell.
Best Scoring: Adaptation and Original Song Score
Cabaret, An ABC Pictures Prod., Allied Artists. Adapted by Ralph Burns.

1973 **Best Song**
"The Way We Were" from *The Way We Were*, Rastar Prods., Columbia. Music by Marvin Hamlisch; lyrics by Alan and Marilyn Bergman.
Best Original Dramatic Score
The Way We Were, Rastar Prods., Columbia. Marvin Hamlisch.
Best Scoring: Original Song Score and/or Adaptation
The Sting, A Universal-Bill/Phillips-George Roy Hill Film Prod., Zanuck/Brown Presentation, Universal. Adapted by Marvin Hamlisch.

1974 **Best Song**
"We May Never Love Like This Again" from *The Towering Inferno*, An Irwin Allen Production, 20th Century-Fox/Warner Bros. Music and lyrics by Al Kasha and Joel Hirschhorn.
Best Original Dramatic Score
The Godfather Part II, A Coppola Company Prod., Paramount. Nino Rota and Carmine Coppola.
Best Scoring: Original Song Score and/or Adaptation
The Great Gatsby, A David Merrick Prod., Paramount. Adapted by Nelson Riddle.

1975 **Best Song**
"I'm Easy" from *Nashville*, An ABC Entertainment-Jerry Weintraub-Robert Altman Production, Paramount. Music and lyrics by Keith Carradine.
Best Original Score
Jaws, A Universal-Zanuck/Brown Production, Universal. John Williams.
Best Scoring: Original Song Score and/or Adaptation
Barry Lyndon, A Hawk Films, Ltd. Production, Warner Bros. Adapted by Leonard Rosenman.

1976 **Best Song**
"Evergreen" ("Love Theme from A Star Is

1976 Best Song *(cont'd)*

Born") from *A Star Is Born*, A Barwood/Jon Peters Production, First Artists Presentation, Warner Bros. Music by Barbra Streisand; lyrics by Paul Williams.

Best Original Score

The Omen, 20th Century-Fox Productions, Ltd., 20th Century-Fox. Jerry Goldsmith.

Best Original Song Score and Its Adaptation or Best Adaptation Score

Bound for Glory, The Bound For Glory Company Production, United Artists. Adapted by Leonard Rosenman.

1977 Best Song

"You Light Up My Life" from *You Light Up My Life*, The Session Company Production, Columbia. Music and lyrics by Joseph Brooks.

Best Original Score

Star Wars, A Lucasfilm, Ltd. Production, Twentieth Century-Fox. John Williams.

Best Original Song Score and Its Adaptation or Best Adaptation Score

A Little Night Music, A Sascha-Wien Film Production in association with Elliott Kastner, New World Pictures. Adapted by Jonathan Tunick.

1978 Best Song

"Last Dance" from *Thank God It's Friday*, A Casablanca-Motown Production, Columbia. Music and lyrics by Paul Jabara.

Best Original Score

Midnight Express, A Casablanca Filmworks Production, Columbia. Giorgio Moroder.

Best Adaptation Score

The Buddy Holly Story, An Innovisions-ECA Production, Columbia. Adaptation score by Joe Renzetti.

1979 Best Song

"It Goes Like It Goes" from *Norma Rae*, A Twentieth Century-Fox Production, Twentieth Century-Fox. Music by Davis Shire; lyrics by Norman Gimbel.

Best Original Score

A Little Romance, A Pan Arts Associates Production, Orion Pictures Company. Georges Delerue.

Best Original Song Score and Its Adaptation or Best Adaptation Score

All That Jazz, A Columbia/Twentieth Century-Fox Production, Twentieth Century-Fox. Adaptation Score by Ralph Burns.

1980 Best Original Song

"Fame" from *Fame*, A Metro-Goldwyn-Mayer Production, Metro-Goldwyn-Mayer, Music by Michael Gore, Lyric by Dean Pitchford.

Best Original Score

Fame. A Metro-Goldwyn-Mayer Production, Metro-Goldwyn-Mayer. Michael Gore.

H. Grammy Winners*

1958

Record of the Year
"Nel Blu Dipinto Di Blu (Volare)," Domenico Modugno (Decca)

Album of the Year
The Music from Peter Gunn, Henry Mancini (RCA)

Song of the Year
"Nel Blu Dipinto Di Blu (Volare)," Domenico Modugno (Decca)

Best Vocal Performance, Female
Ella Fitzgerald Sings the Irving Berlin Song Book, Ella Fitzgerald (Verve)

Best Vocal Performance, Male
"Catch a Falling Star," Perry Como (RCA-Victor)

Best Performance by an Orchestra
Billy May's Big Fat Brass, Billy May (Capitol)

Best Performance by a Dance Band
Basie, Count Basie (Roulette)

Best Performance by a Vocal Group or Chorus
"That Old Black Magic," Louis Prima and Keely Smith (Capitol)

Best Jazz Performance, Individual
Ella Fitzgerald Sings the Duke Ellington Song Book, Ella Fitzgerald (Verve)

Best Jazz Performance, Group
Basie, Count Basie (Roulette)

Best Comedy Performance
"The Chipmunk Song," David Seville (Liberty)

Best Country and Western Performance
"Tom Dooley," The Kingston Trio (Capitol)

Best Rhythm and Blues Performance
"Tequila," The Champs (Challenge)

Best Arrangement
The Music from Peter Gunn, Arranged by Henry Mancini (RCA)

Best Engineered Record, Classical
Duets with a Spanish Guitar, (Laurindo Almeida & Salli Terri);

Engineer: Sherwood Hall, III (Cap.)

Best Engineered Record, Other Than Classical
"The Chipmunk Song" (David Seville); Engineer: Ted Keep (Liberty)

Best Album Cover
Only the Lonely (Frank Sinatra); Art Director: Frank Sinatra (Cap.)

Best Musical Composition First Recorded and Released in 1958 (over 5 minutes)
Cross Country Suite; Composer, Nelson Riddle (Dot)

Best Original Cast Album, Broadway or TV
The Music Man—Original Broadway Cast, Meredith Willson (Capitol)

Best Sound Track Album, Dramatic Picture Score or Original Cast
Gigi—Sound Track; Andre Previn (MGM)

Best Performance, Documentary, Spoken Word
The Best of the Stan Freberg Shows, Stan Freberg (Capitol)

Best Recording for Children
"The Chipmunk Song," David Seville (Liberty)

Best Classical Performance, Orchestral
Gaiete Parisienne—Felix Slatkin cond.; Hollywood Bowl Symphony Orch. (Cap.)

Best Classical Performance, Instrumental (with Concerto Scale Accompaniment)
Tchaikovsky: Concerto No. 1, in B-Flat Minor, Op. 23—Van Cliburn, Pianist; Symphony Orch., Kiril Kondrashin (RCA)

Best Classical Performance, Instrumentalist (Other than Concerto Scale)
Segovia Golden Jubilee, Andres Segovia (Decca)

Best Classical Performance, Chamber Music (Including Chamber Orchestra)

Beethoven Quartet 130, Hollywood String Quartet (Cap.)

Best Classical Performance—Vocal Soloist (with or without Orchestra)
Operatic Recital, Renata Tebaldi (London)

Best Classical Perf.—Operatic/Choral
Virtuoso, Roger Wagner Chorale (Cap.)

1959

Record of the Year
"Mack the Knife," Bobby Darin (Atco)

Album of the Year
Come Dance with Me, Frank Sinatra (Cap.)

Song of the Year
"The Battle of New Orleans"; Composer, Jimmy Driftwood (Col.)

Best Vocal Performance, Female
"But Not for Me," Ella Fitzgerald (Verve)

Best Vocal Performance, Male
Come Dance with Me, Frank Sinatra (Cap.)

Best Performance by a Dance Band
Anatomy of a Murder, Duke Ellington (Col.)

Best Performance by an Orchestra
"Like Young," David Rose and his orchestra with André Previn (MGM)

Best Performance by a Chorus
"Battle Hymn of the Republic," Mormon Tabernacle Choir; Richard Condie, Conductor (Col.)

Best Jazz Performance, Soloist
Ella Swings Lightly, Ella Fitzgerald (Verve)

Best Jazz Performance, Group
I Dig Chicks, Jonah Jones (Cap.)

Best Classical Performance, Orchestra
Debussy: *Images for Orchestra*, Boston Symphony Orch., Charles Munch, conductor (RCA)

Best Classical Performance—Concer-

* Courtesy: National Academy of Recording Arts & Sciences.

1959 *(cont'd)*
to or Instrumental Soloist (Full Orchestra)

Rachmaninoff: *Piano Concerto No. 3*, Van Cliburn, Pianist; Kiril Kondrashin conducting Symphony of the Air (RCA)

Best Classical Performance—Opera Cast or Choral

Mozart: *The Marriage of Figaro*, Erich Leinsdorf conducting Vienna Philharmonic Orchestra (RCA)

Best Classical Performance—Vocal Soloist (with or without Orchestra)

Bjoerling in Opera, Jussi Bjoerling (London)

Best Classical Performance, Chamber Music (including Chamber Orchestra)

Beethoven: *Sonata No. 21, in C, Op. 53* (Waldstein); *Sonata No. 18, in E-Flat, Op. 31, No. 3*, Artur Rubinstein, Pianist (RCA)

Best Classical Performance—Instrumental Soloist (Other Than Full Orchestral Accompaniment)

Beethoven: *Sonata No. 21, in C, Op. 53* (Waldstein); *Sonata No. 18, in E-Flat, Op. 31, No. 3*, Artur Rubinstein, Pianist (RCA)

Best Musical Composition First Recorded and Released in 1959 (5 Minutes)

Anatomy of a Murder; Composer, Duke Ellington (Col.)

Best Sound Track Album—Background Score from Motion Picture or TV

Anatomy of a Murder (Motion Picture), Duke Ellington (Col.)

Best Sound Track Album, Original Cast, Motion Picture or Television

Porgy and Bess—Motion Picture Cast, Andre Previn and Ken Darby (Col.)

Best Broadway Show Album

Gypsy, Ethel Merman (Col.)
Redhead, Gwen Verdon (RCA)

Best Comedy Performance—Spoken Word

Inside Shelley Berman, Shelley Berman (Verve)

Best Comedy Performance—Musical

The Battle of Kookamonga, Homer and Jethro (RCA)

Best Performance—Documentary or Spoken Word (Other Than Comedy)

A Lincoln Portrait, Carl Sandburg (Col.)

Best Performance by "Top 40" Artist

Midnight Flyer, Nat "King" Cole (Cap.)

Best Country and Western Performance

"The Battle of New Orleans," Johnny Horton (Col.)

Best Rhythm and Blues Performance

"What a Diff'rence a Day Makes," Dinah Washington (Mercury)

Best Performance—Folk

The Kingston Trio at Large, The Kingston Trio (Cap.)

Best Recording for Children

Peter and the Wolf, Peter Ustinov, Narr., Herbert von Karajan cond. Philharmonia Orch. (Angel)

Best Arrangement

Come Dance with Me (Frank Sinatra); Arranged by Billy May (Cap.)

Best Engineering Contribution—Classical Recording

Victory at Sea, Vol. I (Robert Russell Bennett); Engineer: Lewis W. Layton (RCA)

Best Engineering Contribution—Novelty Recording

Alvin's Harmonica (David Seville); Engineer: Ted Keep (Liberty)

Best Engineering Contribution—Other Than Classical or Novelty

Belafonte at Carnegie Hall; Engineer: Robert Simpson (RCA)

Best Album Cover

Shostakovich *Symphony No. 5* (Howard Mitchell); Art Dir.: Robert M. Jones (RCA)

Best New Artist of 1959

Bobby Darin (Atco)

1960
Record of the Year

"Theme from *A Summer Place*," Percy Faith (Col.)

Album of the Year

Button Down Mind, Bob Newhart (W.B.)

Song of the Year

"Theme from *Exodus*"; Composer, Ernest Gold

Best Vocal Performance Single Record or Track—Female

"Mack the Knife," Ella Fitzgerald (Verve)

Best Vocal Performance—Album—Female

Mack the Knife—Ella in Berlin,

Ella Fitzgerald (Verve)

Best Vocal Performance Single Record or Track—Male

"Georgia on My Mind," Ray Charles (ABC)

Best Vocal Performance—Album—Male

Genius of Ray Charles, Ray Charles (ABC)

Best Performance by a Band for Dancing

Dance with Basie; Count Basie (Roulette)

Best Arrangement

"Mr. Lucky," Henry Mancini (RCA)

Best Performance by an Orchestra

"Mr. Lucky," Henry Mancini (RCA)

Best Performance by a Vocal Group

We Got Us, Eydie Gorme/Steve Lawrence (ABC)

Best Performance by a Chorus

Songs of the Cowboy, Norman Luboff Choir (Col.)

Best Jazz Performance Solo or Small Group

West Side Story, Andre Previn (Contempo)

Best Jazz Performance Large Group

Blues and the Beat, Henry Mancini (RCA)

Best Classical Performance Orchestra

Bartok: *Music for Strings, Percussion and Celeste*, Fritz Reiner, Cond. Chicago Sym. (RCA)

Best Classical Performance Vocal or Instrumental Chamber Music

Conversations with the Guitar, Laurindo Almeida (Cap.)

Best Classical Performance Concerto or Instrumental Soloist

Brahms: *Piano Concerto No. 2 in B-Flat*, Sviatoslav Richter (Leinsdorf cond. Chicago Sym.) (RCA)

Best Classical Performance Instrumental Soloist or Duo (Other Than Orchestral)

The Spanish Guitars of Laurindo Almeida, Laurindo Almeida (Cap.)

Best Classical Performance Vocal Soloist

A Program of Song, Leontyne Price (RCA)

Best Classical Opera Production

Puccini: *Turandot*—Erich Leinsdorf, Rome Opera Hse. Chorus & Orch. (Tebaldi, Nilsson, Bjoerling, Tozzi) (RCA)

1960 *(cont'd)*

Best Contemporary Classical Composition
> *Orchestral Suite from Tender Land Suite*, Aaron Copland, Comp. (RCA)

Best Classical Performance Choral (including Oratorio)
> Handel: *The Messiah*, Sir Thomas Beecham cond. Royal Philharmonic Orch. & Chorus (RCA)

Best Sound Track Album or Recording of Music Score from Motion Picture or Television
> *Exodus*, Ernest Gold, Comp. (RCA)

Best Sound Track Album or Recording of Original Cast from Motion Picture or Television
> *Can Can* (Frank Sinatra, Original Cast), Cole Porter, Comp. (Cap.)

Best Show Album (Original Cast)
> *The Sound of Music* (Mary Martin), Comps: Richard Rodgers, Oscar Hammerstein (Col.)

Best Comedy Performance (Spoken Word)
> *Button Down Mind Strikes Back*, Bob Newhart (W.B.)

Best Comedy Performance (Musical)
> *Jonathan and Darlene Edwards in Paris*, Jonathan and Darlene Edwards (Jo Stafford and Paul Weston) (Col.)

Best Performance—Documentary or Spoken Word (Other Than Comedy)
> *F.D.R. Speaks* (Franklin D. Roosevelt), Robert Bialek, A&R Prod. (Wash.)

Best Performance by a Pop Single Artist
> "Georgia on My Mind," Ray Charles (ABC)

Best Country and Western Performance
> "El Paso," Marty Robbins (Col.)

Best Rhythm and Blues Performance
> "Let the Good Times Roll," Ray Charles (Atl.)

Best Performance—Folk
> "Swing Dat Hammer," Harry Belafonte (RCA)

Best Album Created for Children
> *Let's All Sing with the Chipmunks*, David Seville (Ross Bagdasarian) (Lib.)

Best Engineering Contribution Classical Records
> *Spanish Guitars of Laurindo Almeida*; Engineer: Hugh Davies (Cap.)

Best Engineering Contribution Popular Recording
> *Ella Fitgerald Sings the George and Ira Gershwin Song Book*; Engineer: Luis P. Valentin (Vrv.)

Best Engineering Contribution Novelty
> *The Old Payola Roll Blues* (Stan Freberg); Engineer: John Kraus (Cap.)

Best Album Cover
> *Latin à la Lee* (Peggy Lee); Art Dir: Marvin Schwartz (Cap.)

Best New Artist of 1960
> Bob Newhart (W.B.)

Best Jazz Composition of More Than Five Minutes Duration
> *Sketches of Spain*, Miles Davis and Gil Evans (Col.)

1961

Record of the Year
> "Moon River," Henry Mancini (RCA)

Album of the Year
> *Judy at Carnegie Hall*, Judy Garland (Cap.)

Album of the Year, Classical
> *Stravinsky Conducts, 1960: Le Sacre du Printemps; Petrouchka*, Igor Stravinsky cond. Columbia Symphony (Col.)

Song of the Year
> "Moon River," Comps: Henry Mancini and Johnny Mercer (RCA)

Best Instrumental Theme or Instrumental Version of Song
> "African Waltz," Comp: Galt MacDermott (Roulette)

Best Solo Vocal Performance, Female
> *Judy at Carnegie Hall* (Album), Judy Garland (Cap.)

Best Solo Vocal Performance, Male
> "Lollipops and Roses" (single), Jack Jones (Kapp)

Best Jazz Performance—Soloist or Small Group (Instrumental)
> *Andre Previn Plays Harold Arlen*, Andre Previn (Contemporary)

Best Jazz Performance—Large Group
> *West Side Story*, Stan Kenton (Cap.)

Best Original Jazz Composition
> "African Waltz," Comp: Galt MacDermott (Roulette)

Best Performance by an Orchestra—for Dancing
> "Up a Lazy River," Si Zentner (Lib.)

Best Performance by an Orchestra—for Other Than Dancing
> *Breakfast at Tiffany's*, Henry Mancini (RCA)

Best Arrangment
> "Moon River," Henry Mancini, Arranger (RCA)

Best Performance by a Vocal Group
> *High Flying*, Lambert, Hendricks and Ross (Col.)

Best Performance by a Chorus
> *Great Band with Great Voices*, Johnny Mann Singers (Si Zentner Orch.) (Lib.)

Best Sound Track Album or Recording of Score from Motion Picture or Television
> *Breakfast at Tiffany's*, Henry Mancini (RCA)

Best Sound Track Album or Recording of Original Cast from Motion Picture or Television
> *West Side Story*, Johnny Green, Saul Chaplin, Sid Ramin and Irwin Kostal (Col.)

Best Original Cast Show Album
> *How to Succeed in Business Without Really Trying*, Comp: Frank Loesser (RCA)

Best Comedy Performance
> *An Evening with Mike Nichols and Elaine May*, Mike Nichols and Elaine May (Merc.)

Best Documentary or Spoken Word Recording (Other Than Comedy)
> *Humor in Music*, Leonard Bernstein cond. New York Philharmonic Orch. (Col.)

Best Engineering Contribution—Popular Recording
> *Judy at Carnegie Hall* (Judy Garland); Engineer: Robert Arnold (Cap.)

Best Engineering Contribution—Novelty Recording
> *Stan Freberg Presents The United States of America*; Engineer: John Kraus (Cap.)

Best Album Cover
> *Judy at Carnegie Hall* (Judy Garland); Art Dir: Jim Silke (Cap.)

Best Recording for Children
> Prokofiev: *Peter And The Wolf*, Leonard Bernstein cond. New York Philharmonic Orch. (Col.)

Best Rock and Roll Recording

1961 *(cont'd)*

"Let's Twist Again," Chubby Checker (Parkway)

Best Country and Western Recording

"Big Bad John," Jimmy Dean (Col.)

Best Rhythm and Blues Recording

"Hit the Road Jack," Ray Charles (Am-Par)

Best Folk Recording

Belafonte Folksingers at Home and Abroad, Belafonte Folk Singers (RCA)

Best Gospel or Other Religious Recording

Everytime I Feel the Spirit, Mahalia Jackson (Col.)

Best New Artist of 1961

Peter Nero (RCA)

Best Classical Performance—Orchestra

Ravel: *Daphnis et Chloe*, Charles Munch cond. Boston Symphony Orch. (RCA)

Best Classical Perf.—Chamber Music

Beethoven: *Serenade, Op. 8;* Kodály: *Duo for Violin and Cello, Op. 7*, Jascha Heifetz, Gregor Piatigorsky, William Primrose (RCA)

Best Classical Performance—Instrumental Soloist (With Orchestra)

Bartok: *Concerto No. 1 for Violin and Orchestra*, Isaac Stern (Ormandy cond. Philharmonic Orch.) (Col.)

Best Classical Perf.—Instrumental Soloist or Duo Without Orchestra

Reverie for Spanish Guitars, Laurindo Almeida (Cap.)

Best Opera Recording

Puccini: *Madama Butterfly*, Gabriele Santini cond. Rome Opera Chorus & Orch. (Angel)

Best Classical Performance, Choral

Bach: *B Minor Mass*, Robert Shaw Chorale, Robert Shaw cond. (RCA)

Best Classical Performance—Vocal Soloist

The Art of the Prima Donna, Joan Sutherland (Molinari-Pradelli cond. Royal Opera House Orch.) (London)

Best Contemporary Classical Composition

Discantus; Comp: Laurindo Almeida (Cap.)

Movements for Piano and Orchestra; Comp: Igor Stravinsky (Col.)

Best Album Cover—Classical

Puccini: *Madama Butterfly*, (Santini cond. Rome Opera Chorus & Orchestra); Art Dir: Marvin Schwartz (Angel)

Best Engineering Contribution Classical Recording

Ravel: *Daphnis et Chloe*, (Munch cond. Boston Sym.); Engineer: Lewis W. Layton (RCA)

1962

Record of the Year

"I Left My Heart in San Francisco," Tony Bennett (Col.)

Album of the Year

The First Family, Vaughn Meader (Cadence)

Album of the Year, Classical

Columbia Records Presents *Vladimir Horowitz*, Vladimir Horowitz (Col.)

Song of the Year

"What Kind of Fool Am I;" Comps: Leslie Bricusse and Anthony Newley (London)

Best Instrumental Theme

"A Taste of Honey"; Comps: Bobby Scott and Ric Marlow (Reprise)

Best Solo Vocal Performance, Female

Ella Swings Brightly with Nelson Riddle, Ella Fitzgerald (album) (Verve)

Best Solo Vocal Performance, Male

"*I Left My Heart in San Francisco*," Tony Bennett (album) (Col.)

Best Jazz Performance—Soloist or Small Group (Instrumental)

Desafinado, Stan Getz (Verve)

Best Jazz Performance—Large Group Instrumental

Adventures in Jazz, Stan Kenton (Cap.)

Best Original Jazz Composition

"Cast Your Fate to the Winds"; Comp: Vince Guaraldi (Fantasy)

Best Performance by an Orchestra—for Dancing

Fly Me to the Moon Bossa Nova, Joe Harnell (Kapp)

Best Performance by an Orchestra or Instrumentalist with Orchestra—Not for Jazz or Dancing

The Colorful Peter Nero, Peter Nero (RCA)

Best Instrumental Arrangement

"Baby Elephant Walk" (Mancini & Orch.); Arranger: Henry Mancini (RCA)

Best Background Arrangement

"I Left My Heart in San Francisco," (Tony Bennett); Arr: Marty Manning (Col.)

Best Performance by a Vocal Group

"If I Had a Hammer," Peter, Paul and Mary (W.B.)

Best Performance by a Chorus

Presenting The New Christy Minstrels, The New Christy Minstrels (Col.)

Best Original Cast Show Album

No Strings (Original Broadway Cast); Comp: Richard Rodgers (Cap.)

Best Classical Performance, Orch.

Stravinsky: *The Firebird Ballet*, Igor Stravinsky, Columbia Sym. (Col.)

Best Classical Perf.—Chamber Music

The Heifetz—Piatigorsky Concerts With Primrose, Pennario and Guests, Jascha Heifetz, Gregor Piatigorsky, William Primrose (RCA)

Best Classical Perf.—Instrumental Soloist(s) (with Orchestra)

Stravinsky: *Concerto in D for Violin*, Isaac Stern (Stravinsky cond. Columbia Symphony) (Col.)

Best Classical Perf.—Instrumental Soloist or Duo (without Orchestra)

Columbia Records Presents *Vladimir Horowitz*, Vladimir Horowitz (Col.)

Best Opera Recording

Verdi: *Aïda*, Georg Solti cond. Rome Opera House Orch. & Chorus (Price, Vickers, Gorr, Merrill, Tozzi) (RCA)

Best Classical Perf.—Choral

Bach: *St. Matthew Passion*, Philharmonia Choir, Wilhelm Pitz, Choral Dir./Otto Klemperer cond. Philharmonic Orch. (Angel)

Best Classical Performance—Vocal Soloist With or Without Orchestra

Wagner: *Gotterdamerung—Brunnhilde's Immolation Scene/Wesendonck Songs*, Eileen Farrell (Bernstein cond. New York Philharmonic) (Col.)

Best Classical Composition by Contemporary Composer

The Flood; Comp: Igor Stravinsky (Col.)

Best Engineering Contribution—Classical

Strauss: *Also Sprach Zarathustra Op. 30*, (Reiner cond. Chicago

1962 *(cont'd)*
Symphony); Engineer: Lewis W. Layton (RCA)

Best Album Cover, Classical
The Intimate Bach, (Almeida, Majewski, De Rosa) Art Dir: Marvin Schwartz (Cap.)

Best Comedy Performance
The First Family, Vaughn Meader (Cadence)

Best Documentary or Spoken Word Recording (Other Than Comedy)
The Story-Teller: A Session with Charles Laughton, Charles Laughton (Cap.)

Best Engineering Contribution—Other Than Novelty or Classical
Hatari! (Henry Mancini); Engineer: Al Schmitt (RCA)

Best Engineering Contribution—Novelty
The Civil War, Vol. 1 (Fennell); Engineer: Robert Fine (Merc.)

Best Album Cover
Lena . . . Lovely and Alive (Lena Horne); Art Dir: Robert Jones (RCA)

Best Recording for Children
Saint-Saens: Carnival of the Animals/Britten: Young Person's Guide to the Orchestra, Leonard Bernstein (Col.)

Best Rock and Roll Recording
"Alley Cat," Bent Fabric (Atco)

Best Country and Western Recording
"Funny Way of Laughin'," Burl Ives (Decca)

Best Rhythm and Blues Recording
"I Can't Stop Loving You," Ray Charles (ABC)

Best Folk Recording
"If I Had a Hammer," Peter, Paul and Mary (W.B.)

Best Gospel or Other Religious Recording
Great Songs of Love and Faith, Mahalia Jackson (Col.)

Best New Artist of 1962
Robert Goulet (Col.)

1963

Record of the Year
"The Days of Wine and Roses," Henry Mancini (RCA)

Album of the Year
The Barbra Streisand Album, Barbra Streisand (Col.)

Album of the Year, Classical
Britten: *War Requiem*, Benjamin Britten, Cond. London Sym. Orch. & Chorus (London)

Song of the Year
"The Days of Wine and Roses"; Comps: Henry Mancini and Johnny Mercer (RCA)

Best Instrumental Theme
"More" (Theme from *Mondo Cane*); Comps: Norman Newell, Nino Oliviero, and Riz Ortolani (U.A.)

Best Vocal Performance, Female
The Barbra Streisand Album, Barbra Streisand (Col.)

Best Vocal Performance, Male
"Wives and Lovers" (single), Jack Jones (Kapp)

Best Instrumental Jazz Performance—Soloist or Small Group
"Conversations with Myself," Bill Evans (Verve)

Best Instrumental Jazz Performance—Large Group
Encore: Woody Herman, 1963, Woody Herman Band (Philips)

Best Original Jazz Composition
"Gravy Waltz"; Comps: Steve Allen, Ray Brown

Best Performance by an Orchestra—for Dancing
This Time by Basie! Hits of the 50's and 60's, Count Basie (Reprise)

Best Performance by an Orch. or Instrumentalist with Orch.—Not Jazz/Dancing
"Java," Al Hirt (RCA)

Best Instrumental Arrangement
"I Can't Stop Loving You" (Count Basie); Arranger: Quincy Jones (Reprise)

Best Background Arrangement
"The Days of Wine and Roses" (Mancini); Arranger: Henry Mancini (RCA)

Best Performance by a Vocal Group
"Blowin' in the Wind," Peter, Paul and Mary (W.B.)

Best Performance by a Chorus
Bach's Greatest Hits, The Swingle Singers (Philips)

Best Original Score from a Motion Picture or Television Show
Tom Jones (John Addison cond.); Comp: John Addison (U.A.)

Best Score from an Original Cast Show Album
She Loves Me (Original Cast); Comps: Jerry Bock, Sheldon Harnick (MGM)

Best Classical Performance, Orch.
Bartok: *Concerto for Orchestra*, Erich Leinsdorf, Boston Sym. Orch. (RCA)

Best Classical Performance—Chamber Music
Evening of Elizabethan Music, Julian Bream Consort (RCA)

Best Classical Performance—Instrumental Soloist(s) (With Orchestra)
Tchaikovsky: *Concerto No. 1 in B-flat Minor for Piano & Orchestra*, Artur Rubinstein (Leinsdorf cond. Boston Symphony Orch.) (RCA)

Best Classical Performance—Instrumental Soloist or Duo (Without Orch.)
The Sound of Horowitz, Vladimir Horowitz (Col.)

Best Opera Recording
Puccini: *Madama Butterfly*, Erich Leinsdorf cond. RCA Italiana Opera Orch. & Chorus (Price, Tucker, Elias) (RCA)

Best Classical Performance, Choral
Britten: *War Requiem*—David Willcocks, Dir. Bach Choir/Edward Chapman, Dir. Highgate School Choir/Benjamin Britten cond. London Sym. Orch. & Chorus (Lndn)

Best Classical Performance—Vocal Soloist (With/Without Orchestra)
Great Scenes From Gershwin's Porgy and Bess, Leontyne Price (RCA)

Best Classical Composition by Contemporary Composer
War Requiem; Comp: Benjamin Britten (London)

Best Engineered Recording, Classical
Puccini: *Madama Butterfly* (Leinsdorf); Engineer: Lewis Layton (RCA)

Best Album Cover, Classical
Puccini: *Madama Butterfly* (Leinsdorf); Art Dir: Robert Jones (RCA)

Most Promising New Classical Recording Artist
Andre Watts (Pianist) (Col.)

Best Comedy Performance
"Hello Mudduh, Hello Faddah," Allan Sherman (W.B.)

Best Documentary, Spoken Word or Drama Recording (Other Than Comedy)
Who's Afraid of Virginia Woolf?, Edward Albee (W.B.)

1963 *(cont'd)*

Best Engineered Recording—Other Than Classical
"Charade" (Mancini Orch. & Chorus); Engineer: James Malloy (RCA)

Best Engineered Recording—Special or Novel Effects
Civil War Vol. II (Frederick Fennell); Engineer: Robert Fine (Merc.)

Best Album Cover—Other Than Classical
The Barbra Streisand Album; Art Dir: John Berg (Col.)

Best Album Notes
The Ellington Era (Duke Ellington); Stanley Dance, Leonard Feather (Col.)

Best Recording for Children
Bernstein Conducts for Young People, Leonard Bernstein, N.Y. Phil. (Col.)

Best Rock and Roll Recording
"Deep Purple," Nino Tempo & April Stevens (Atco)

Best Country and Western Recording
"Detroit City," Bobby Bare (RCA)

Best Rhythm and Blues Recording
"Busted," Ray Charles (ABC/Para)

Best Folk Recording
"Blowin' in the Wind," Peter, Paul and Mary (W.B.)

Best Gospel or Other Religious Recording (Musical)
"Dominique," Soeur Sourire (The Singing Nun) (Philips)

Best New Artist of 1963
Swingle Singers (Philips)

1964

Record of the Year
"The Girl from Ipanema," Stan Getz, Astrud Gilberto (Verve)

Album of the Year
Getz/Gilberto, Stan Getz, Joao Gilberto (Verve)

Album of the Year, Classical
Bernstein: *Symphony No. 3 (Kaddish),* Leonard Bernstein cond. New York Philharmonic Orch. (Col.)

Song of the Year
"Hello, Dolly!"; Comp: Jerry Herman (Kapp)

Best Instrumental Composition (Other Than Jazz)
"The Pink Panther Theme"; Comp: Henry Mancini (RCA)

Best Vocal Performance, Female
"People" (single), Barbra Streisand (Col.)

Best Vocal Performance, Male
"Hello, Dolly!" (single), Louis Armstrong (Kapp)

Best Instrumental Jazz Performance—Small Group or Soloist with Small Group
Getz/Gilberto, Stan Getz, Joao Gilberto (Verve)

Best Instrumental Jazz Performance—Large Group or Soloist with Large Group
Guitar from Ipanema, Laurindo Almeida (Cap.)

Best Original Jazz Composition
"The Cat"; Comp: Lalo Schifrin (Verve)

Best Instrumental Performance, Non-Jazz
"Pink Panther," Henry Mancini (RCA)

Best Instrumental Arrangement
"Pink Panther" (Henry Mancini); Arranger: Henry Mancini (RCA)

Best Accompaniment Arrangement for Vocalist(s) or Instrumentalist(s)
"People" (Barbra Streisand); Arranger: Peter Matz (Col.)

Best Performance by a Vocal Group
A Hard Day's Night, The Beatles (Cap.)

Best Performance by a Chorus
The Swingle Singers Going Baroque, The Swingle Singers (Philips)

Best Original Score Written for a Motion Picture or TV Show
Mary Poppins (Andrews, Van Dyke); Comps: Richard M. and Robert B. Sherman (Buena Vista)

Best Score from an Original Cast Show Album
Funny Girl (Streisand, Orig. Cast); Comps: Jule Styne and Bob Merrill (Cap.)

Best Comedy Performance
I Started Out as a Child, Bill Cosby (W.B.)

Best Documentary, Spoken Word or Drama Recording (Other Than Comedy)
BBC Tribute to John F. Kennedy, "That Was the Week That Was" Cast (Decca)

Best Engineered Recording
Getz/Gilberto (Stan Getz, Joao Gilberto); Engineer: Phil Ramone (Verve)

Best Engineered Recording—Special or Novel Effects
The Chipmunks Sing the Beatles; Engineer: Dave Hassinger (Lib.)

Best Album Cover
People (Barbra Streisand); Art Dir: Robert Cato; Photographer: Don Bronstein (Col.)

Best Recording for Children
Mary Poppins, Julie Andrews, Dick Van Dyke (Buena Vista)

Best Rock and Roll Recording
"Downtown," Petula Clark (W.B.)

Best Rhythm and Blues Recording
"How Glad I Am," Nancy Wilson (Cap.)

Best Folk Recording
"We'll Sing in the Sunshine," Gale Garnett (RCA)

Best Gospel or Other Religious Recording (Musical)
Great Gospel Songs, Tennessee Ernie Ford (Cap.)

Best New Artist of 1964
The Beatles (Cap.)

Best Country and Western Single
"Dang Me," Roger Miller (Smash)

Best Country and Western Album
Dang Me/Chug-a-Lug, Roger Miller (Smash)

Best Country and Western Vocal Performance, Female
"Here Comes My Baby" (single), Dottie West (RCA)

Best Country and Western Vocal Performance, Male
"Dang Me" (single), Roger Miller (Smash)

Best Country and Western Song
"Dang Me"; Comp: Roger Miller (Smash)

Best New Country and Western Artist of 1964
Roger Miller (Smash)

Best Album Notes
Mexico (Legacy Collection) (Chavez), Stanton Catlin, Carleton Beals (Col.)

Best Performance, Orchestra
Mahler: *Symphony No. 5 in C-Sharp Minor;* Berg: "*Wozzeck*" *Excerpts,* Erich Leinsdorf, Boston Sym. (RCA)

Best Chamber Performance, Instrumental
Beethoven: *Trio No. 1 in E Flat, Op. 1, No. 1* (Jacob Lateiner, pi-

1964 *(cont'd)*

ano, Jascha Heifetz, Gregor Piatigorsky) (RCA)

Best Chamber Music Performance, Vocal

It Was a Lover and His Lass (Morley, Byrd & Others), New York Pro Musica, Noah Greenberg, cond. (Decca)

Best Performance—Instrumental Soloist(s) (With Orchestra)

Prokofieff: *Concerto No. 1 in D Major for Violin* (Ormandy cond. Phil. Orch.); Isaac Stern (Col.)

Best Performance—Instrumental Soloist (Without Orchestra)

Vladimir Horowitz Plays Beethoven, Debussy, Chopin (Beethoven: *Sonata No. 8 "Pathetique"*; Debussy: *Preludes*; Chopin: *Etudes & Scherzos 1 Thru 4*), Vladimir Horowitz (Col.)

Best Opera Recording

Bizet: *Carmen*, Von Karajan cond. Vienna Philharmonic Orch. & Cho. (Price, Corelli, Merrill, Freni) (RCA)

Best Choral Performance (Other Than Opera)

Britten: *A Ceremony of Carols*, Robert Shaw, Robert Shaw Chorale (RCA)

Best Vocal Soloist Performance (With or Without Orchestra)

Berlioz: *Nuits d'Eté (Song Cycle)*/Falla: *El Amor Brujo*, (Reiner cond. Chicago Sym.) Leontyne Price (RCA)

Best Composition by a Contemporary Composer

Piano Concerto; Comp: Samuel Barber (Col.)

Best Engineered Recording, Classical

Britten: *Young Person's Guide to the Orchestra* (Giulini, Philharmonia); Engineer: Douglas Larter (Angel)

Best Album Cover, Classical

Saint-Saens: *Carnival of the Animals*/Britten: *Young Person's Guide to the Orchestra* (Fiedler, Boston Pops); Art Dir: Robert Jones; Graphic Artist: Jan Balet (RCA)

Most Promising New Recording Artist

Marilyn Horne (London)

1965

Record of the Year

"A Taste of Honey," Herb Alpert & the Tijuana Brass; A&R Prod: Herb Alpert and Jerry Moss (A&M)

Album of the Year

September of My Years, Frank Sinatra; A&R Prod: Sonny Burke (Reprise)

Album of the Year—Classical

Horowitz at Carnegie Hall—An Historic Return, (Vladimir Horowitz); A&R Prod: Thomas Frost (Col.)

Song of the Year

"The Shadow of Your Smile" (Love Theme from *The Sandpiper*); Comps: Paul Francis Webster and Johnny Mandel (Merc.)

Best Vocal Performance—Female

My Name is Barbra (Album), Barbra Streisand (Col.)

Best Vocal Performance—Male

"It Was a Very Good Year" (Single), Frank Sinatra (Reprise)

Best Instrumental Performance, Non-Jazz

"A Taste of Honey," Herb Alpert & the Tijuana Brass (A&M)

Best Performance by a Vocal Group

We Dig Mancini, Anita Kerr Singers (RCA)

Best Performance by a Chorus

Anyone for Mozart?, The Swingle Singers (Philips)

Best Original Score Written for a Motion Picture or TV Show

The Sandpiper (Robert Armbruster Orch.), Comp: Johnny Mandel (Merc.)

Best Score from an Original Show Album

On a Clear Day; Comps: Alan Lerner, Burton Lane (RCA)

Best Comedy Performance

Why Is There Air?, Bill Cosby (W.B.)

Best Spoken Word or Drama Recording

John F. Kennedy—As We Remember Him, Goddard Lieberson, Prod. (Col.)

Best New Artist

Tom Jones (Parrot)

Best Recording For Children

Dr Suess Presents Fox in Sox—Green Eggs and Ham, Marvin Miller (RCA—Camden)

Best Album Notes

September of My Years (Frank Sinatra); Stan Cornyn (Reprise)

Best Instrumental Jazz Performance—Small Group or Soloist w/ Small Group

"The 'In' Crowd," Ramsey Lewis Trio (Cadet)

Best Instrumental Jazz Performance—Large Group or Soloist w/ Large Group

"Ellington '66," Duke Ellington Orchestra (Reprise)

Best Original Jazz Composition

"Jazz Suite on the Mass Texts"; Comp: Lalo Schifrin (RCA)

Best Instrumental Arrangement

"A Taste of Honey" (Alpert & Tijuana Brass); Arranger: Herb Alpert (A&M)

Best Arrangement Accompanying a Vocalist or Instrumentalist

"It Was a Very Good Year" (Frank Sinatra); Arranger: Gordon Jenkins (Reprise)

Best Contemporary (R & R) Single

"King of the Road," Roger Miller (Smash)

Best Contemporary (R & R) Vocal Performance—Female

"I Know a Place" (Single), Petula Clark (W.B.)

Best Contemporary (R & R) Vocal Performance—Male

"King of the Road," Roger Miller (Smash)

Best Contemporary (R & R) Performance Group (Vocal or Instrumental)

"Flowers on the Wall" (Single), The Statler Brothers (Col.)

Best Rhythm and Blues Recording

"Papa's Got a Brand New Bag," James Brown (King)

Best Folk Recording

"An Evening with Belafonte/Makeba," Harry Belafonte, Miriam Makeba (RCA)

Best Gospel or Other Religious Recording (Musical)

"Southland Favorites," George Beverly Shea and the Anita Kerr Singers (RCA)

Best Country and Western Single

"King of the Road," Roger Miller (Smash)

Best Country and Western Album

The Return of Roger Miller, Roger Miller (Smash)

Best Country and Western Vocal Performance—Female

"Queen of the House," Jody Miller (Cap.)

Best Country and Western Vocal

1965 *(cont'd)*

Performance—Male
"King of the Road," Roger Miller (Smash)

Best Country and Western Song
"King of the Road"; Songwr: Roger Miller (Smash)

Best New Country and Western Artist
Statler Brothers (Col.)

Best Engineered Recording
"A Taste of Honey" (Alpert & Tijuana Brass); Engineer: Larry Levine (A&M)

Best Engineered Recording, Classical
Horowitz at Carnegie Hall—An Historic Return (Vladimir Horowitz); Engineer: Fred Plaut (Col.)

Best Album Cover—Photography
Jazz Suite on the Mass Texts (Paul Horn); Art Dir: Bob Jones; Photographer: Ken Whitmore (RCA)

Best Album Cover—Graphic Arts
Bartok: *Concerto No. 2 for Violin/* Stravinsky: *Concerto for Violin* (Silverstein, Leinsdorf, Boston Sym.); Art Dir: George Estes; Graphic: James Alexander (RCA)

Best Classical Performance, Orchestra
Ives: *Symphony No. 4,* Leopold Stokowski cond. American Sym. Orch. (Col.)

Best Classical Chamber Music Perf. Instrumental or Vocal
Bartok: *The Six String Quartets,* Juilliard String Quartet (Col.)

Best Classical Performance—Instrumental Soloist(s) (with Orchestra)
Beethoven: *Concerto No. 4 in G Major for Piano and Orchestra,* Artur Rubinstein (Leinsdorf cond. Boston Symphony) (RCA)

Best Classical Performance—Instrumental Soloist (without Orchestra)
Horowitz at Carnegie Hall—An Historic Return, Vladimir Horowitz (Col.)

Best Opera Recording
Berg: *Wozzeck,* Karl Bohm cond. Orch. of German Opera, Berlin (Fisher-Dieskau, Lear, Wunderlich) (DGG)

Best Choral Perf. (Other than Opera)
Stravinsky: *Symphony of Psalms/* Poulenc: *Gloria,* Robert Shaw cond. Robert Shaw Chorale, RCA Victor Sym. Orch. (RCA)

Best Vocal Perf.—with/without Orchestra

Strauss: *Salome (Dance of the Seven Veils, Interlude, Final Scene), The Egyptian Helen (Awakening Scene),* Leontyne Price (RCA)

Best Composition by a Contemporary Classical Composer
Symphony No. 4; Comp: Charles Ives (Col.)

Most Promising New Recording Artist
Peter Serkin, Pianist (RCA)

1966

Record of the Year
"Strangers in the Night," Frank Sinatra; A&R Prod: Jimmy Bowen (Reprise)

Album of the Year
Sinatra—A Man and His Music, Frank Sinatra; A&R Prod: Sonny Burke (Reprise)

Song of the Year
"Michelle," Songwrs: John Lennon, Paul McCartney (Cap.)

Best Instrumental Theme
"*Batman* Theme"; Comp: Neal Hefti (RCA)

Best Vocal Performance—Female
"If He Walked into My Life" (Single), Eydie Gorme (Col.)

Best Vocal Performance—Male
"Strangers in the Night," Frank Sinatra (Reprise)

Best Instrumental Performance (Other Than Jazz)
"What Now My Love," Herb Alpert & the Tijuana Brass (A&M)

Best Performance by a Vocal Group
A Man and a Woman, Anita Kerr Singers (W.B.)

Best Performance by a Chorus
"Somewhere, My Love" (Lara's Theme from *Dr. Zhivago*), Ray Coniff & Singers (Col.)

Best Original Score Written for a Motion Picture or TV Show
Dr. Zhivago; Comp: Maurice Jarre (MGM)

Best Score from an Original Cast Show Album
Mame; Comp: Jerry Herman (Col.)

Best Comedy Performance
Wonderfulness, Bill Cosby (W.B.)

Best Spoken Word, Documentary or Drama Recording
Edward R. Murrow—A Reporter Remembers, Vol. I, The War Years, Edward R. Murrow (Col.)

Best Recording for Children

Dr. Seuss Presents: If I Ran the Zoo and Sleep Book, Marvin Miller (RCA—Camden)

Best Album Notes
Sinatra at The Sands, Stan Cornyn (Reprise)

Best Instrumental Jazz Performance Group or Soloist with Group
"Goin' Out of My Head," Wes Montgomery (Verve)

Best Original Jazz Composition
In the Beginning God; Comp: Duke Ellington (RCA)

Best Contemporary (R & R) Recording
"Winchester Cathedral," New Vaudeville Band (Fontana)

Best Contemporary (R & R) Solo Vocal Performance—Male or Female
"Eleanor Rigby" (Single), Paul McCartney (Cap.)

Best Contemporary (R & R) Group Performance—Vocal or Instrumental
"Monday, Monday" (Single), The Mamas & The Papas (Dunhill)

Best Rhythm & Blues Recording
"Crying Time," Ray Charles (ABC-Par)

Best Rhythm & Blues Solo Vocal Performance—Male or Female
"Crying Time" (Single), Ray Charles (ABC-Par)

Best Rhythm & Blues Group—Vocal or Instrumental
"Hold It Right There" (Single), Ramsey Lewis (Cadet)

Best Folk Recording
"Blues in the Street," Cortelia Clark (RCA)

Best Sacred Recording (Musical)
Grand Old Gospel, Porter Wagoner & The Blackwood Bros. (RCA)

Best Country and Western Recording
"Almost Persuaded," David Houston (Epic)

Best Country and Western Vocal Performance—Female
"Don't Touch Me" (Single), Jeannie Seely (Monument)

Best Country and Western Vocal Performance—Male
"Almost Persuaded" (single), David Houston (Epic)

Best Country and Western Song
"Almost Persuaded"; Songwr: Billy Sherrill, Glenn Sutton (Epic)

Best Instrumental Arrangement
"What Now My Love" (Alpert & Tijuana Brass); Arranger: Herb Alpert (A&M)

1966 *(cont'd)*

Best Arrangement Accompanying a Vocalist or Instrumentalist

"Strangers in the Night" (Frank Sinatra); Arranger: Ernie Freeman (Reprise)

Best Engineered Recording

"Strangers in the Night" (Frank Sinatra); Engineers: Eddie Brackett, Lee Herschberg (Reprise)

Best Engineered Recording, Classical

Wagner: *Lohengrin* (Leindorf cond. Boston Sym., Pro Musica Chorus); Engineer: Anthony Salvatore (RCA)

Best Album Cover, Photography

Confessions of a Broken Man (Porter Wagoner); Art Dir: Robert Jones; Photographer: Les Leverette (RCA)

Best Album Cover, Graphic Arts

Revolver (The Beatles); Graphic Art: Klaus Voormann (Cap.)

Album of the Year, Classical

Ives: *Symphony No. 1 in D Minor*, Morton Gould cond. Chicago Sym.; A&R: Howard Scott (RCA)

Best Classical Performance, Orchestra

Mahler: *Symphony No. 6 in A Minor*, Erich Leinsdorf cond. Boston Sym. (RCA)

Best Chamber Music Performance—Instrumental or Vocal

Boston Symphony Chamber Players, Boston Symphony Chamber Players (RCA)

Best Performance—Instrumental Soloist(s) (With or Without Orchestra)

Baroque Guitar, Julian Bream (RCA)

Best Opera Recording

Wagner: *Die Walkure*, Georg Solti cond. Vienna Philharmonic (Nilsson, Crespin, Ludwig, King, Hotter) (London)

Best Classical Choral Performance (Other Than Opera)

Handel: *Messiah*, Robert Shaw cond. Robert Shaw Chorale and Orch. (RCA)

Ives: *Music For Chorus* (Gen. Wm. Booth Enters Into Heaven, Serenity, The Circus Band, etc.), Gregg Smith cond. Columbia Chamber Orch., Gregg Smith Singers, Ithaca College Concert Choir/George Bragg cond. Texas Boys Choir (Col.)

Best Classical Vocal Soloist Perf.

(With or Without Orchestra)

Prima Donna, Leontyne Price (Molinari-Pradelli cond. RCA Italiana Opera Orch.) (RCA)

1967

Record of the Year

"Up, Up and Away," 5th Dimension; A&R Prods: Marc Gordon, Johnny Rivers (Soul City)

Album of the Year

Sgt. Pepper's Lonely Hearts Club Band, The Beatles; A&R Prod: George Martin (Cap.)

Song of the Year

"Up, Up and Away," Songwr: Jim Webb (Soul City)

Best Instrumental Theme

"*Mission: Impossible* Theme," Comp: Lalo Schifrin (Dot)

Best Vocal Performance, Female

"Ode to Billie Joe" (Single), Bobbie Gentry (Cap.)

Best Vocal Performance, Male

"By the Time I Get to Phoenix" (Single), Glen Campbell (Cap.)

Best Instrumental Performance

Chet Atkins Picks the Best, Chet Atkins (RCA)

Best Performance by a Vocal Group (Two to Six Persons)

"Up, Up and Away," 5th Dimension (Soul City)

Best Performance by a Chorus (Seven or More Persons)

"Up, Up and Away," Johnny Mann Singers (Lib.)

Best Original Score Written for a Motion Picture or TV Show

Mission: Impossible; Comp. Lalo Schifrin (Dot)

Best Score from an Original Cast Show Album

Cabaret; Comps: Fred Ebb & John Kander; A&R Prod: Goddard Lieberson (Col.)

Best Comedy Recording

Revenge, Bill Cosby (WB-7 Arts)

Best New Artist

Bobbie Gentry (Cap.)

Best Instrumental Jazz Performance Small Group or Soloist w/small Group

Mercy, Mercy, Mercy, Cannonball Adderley Quintet (Cap.)

Best Instrumental Jazz Performance Large Group or Soloist w/large Group

Far East Suite, Duke Ellington (RCA)

Best Contemporary Single

"Up, Up and Away," 5th Dimension; A&R Prods: Marc Gordon, Johnny Rivers (Soul City)

Best Contemporary Album

Sgt. Pepper's Lonely Hearts Club Band; The Beatles; A&R Prod: George Martin (Cap.)

Best Contemporary Female Solo Vocal Performance

"Ode to Billie Joe," Bobbie Gentry (Cap.)

Best Contemporary Male Solo Vocal Performance

"By the Time I Get to Phoenix," Glen Campbell (Cap.)

Best Contemporary Group Performance Vocal or Instrumental

"Up, Up and Away," 5th Dimension (Soul City)

Best Rhythm and Blues Recording

"Respect," Aretha Franklin; A&R Prod: Jerry Wexler (Atl.)

Best Rhythm and Blues Solo Vocal Performance—Female

"Respect," Aretha Franklin (Atl.)

Best Rhythm and Blues Solo Vocal Performance—Male

"Dead End Street," Lou Rawls (Cap.)

Best Rhythm and Blues Group Performance Vocal or Instrumental (2 or more)

"Soul Man," Sam & Dave (Stax)

Best Sacred Performance

How Great Thou Art, Elvis Presley (RCA)

Best Gospel Performance

More Grand Old Gospel, Porter Wagoner & The Blackwood Bros. (RCA)

Best Folk Performance

"Gentle on My Mind," John Hartford (RCA)

Best Country and Western Recording

"Gentle on My Mind," Glen Campbell; A&R Prod: Al de Lory (Cap.)

Best Country and Western Solo Vocal Performance—Female

"I Don't Wanna Play House," Tammy Wynette (Epic)

Best Country and Western Solo Vocal Performance—Male

"Gentle on My Mind," Glen Campbell (Cap.)

Best Country and Western Performance Duet, Trio or Group (Vocal or Inst.)

1967 *(cont'd)*

Jackson, Johnny Cash, June Carter (Col.)

Best Country and Western Song
"Gentle on My Mind," Songwr: John Hartford (RCA)

Best Spoken Word, Documentary or Drama Recording
Gallant Men, Sen. Everett M. Dirksen (Cap.)

Best Recording for Children
Dr. Seuss: *How the Grinch Stole Christmas,* Boris Karloff (MGM)

Best Instrumental Arrangement
"Alfie" (Bacharach Orch.); Arranger: Burt Bacharach (A&M)

Best Arrangement Accompanying Vocalist(s) or Instrumentalist(s)
"Ode to Billie Joe" (Bobbie Gentry); Arranger: Jimmie Haskell (Cap.)

Best Engineered Recording
Sgt. Pepper's Lonely Hearts Club Band (Beatles); Eng: G. E. Emerick (Cap.).

Best Engineered Recording, Classical
The Glorious Sound of Brass, (Phil. Brass Ensemble); Eng: Edward T. Graham (Cap.)

Best Album Cover—Photography
Bob Dylan's Greatest Hits, Art Dirs: John Berg & Bob Cato; Photographer: Roland Scherman (Col.)

Best Album Cover, Graphic Arts
Sgt. Pepper's Lonely Hearts Club Band; Art Dirs: Peter Blake & Jann Haworth (Cap.)

Best Album Notes
Suburban Attitudes in Country Verse; John D. Loudermilk (RCA)

Album of the Year, Classical
Berg: *Wozzeck,* Pierre Boulez, Paris Nat'l Opera; A&R Prod: Thomas Shepard (Col.)
Mahler: *Symphony No. 8 in E Flat Major (Symphony of a Thousand),* Leonard Bernstein, London Sym. Orch.; A&R Prod: John McClure (Col.)

Best Classical Performance, Orch.
Stravinsky: *Firebird and Petrouchka Suites,* Igor Stravinsky, Columbia Sym. (Col.)

Best Chamber Music Performance
West Meets East, Ravi Shankar & Yehudi Menuhin (Angel)

Best Classical Performance—Instr. Soloist(s) (with/without Orchestra)
Horowitz in Concert, Vladimir Horowitz (Col.)

Best Opera Recording
Berg: *Wozzeck,* Pierre Boulez & Paris Nat'l Opera (Berry, Strauss, Uhl, Doench); A&R: Thomas Shepard (Col.)

Best Classical Choral Performance
Mahler: *Symphony No. 8 in E Flat Major,* Leonard Bernstein, London Sym. Orch. (Col.)
Orff: *Catulli Carmina,* Robert Page cond. Temple Univ. Chorus, Eugene Ormandy cond. Philadelphia Orch. (Col.)

Best Classical Vocal Soloist Perf.
Prima Donna, Volume 2, Leontyne Price (Molinari-Pradelli cond. RCA Italiana Opera Orch.) (RCA)

1968

Record of the Year
"Mrs. Robinson," Simon & Garfunkel; A&R Prods: Paul Simon, Art Garfunkel, Roy Halee (Col.)

Album of the Year
By the Time I Get to Phoenix, Glen Campbell; A&R Prod: Al de Lory (Cap.)

Song of the Year
"Little Green Apples"; Songwr: Bobby Russell (Col.)

Best New Artist of 1968
Jose Feliciano (RCA)

Best Instrumental Arrangement
"Classical Gas" (Mason Williams); Arranger: Mike Post (W.B.)

Best Arrangement Accompanying Vocalist(s)
"MacArthur Park" (Richard Harris); Arranger: Jim Webb (Dunhill)

Best Engineered Recording
"Wichita Lineman" (Glen Campbell); Engrs: Joe Polito, Hugh Davies (Cap.)

Best Album Cover
Underground (Thelonius Monk); Art Dirs: John Berg, Richard Mantel; Photography: Horn/Griner Studio (Col.)

Best Album Notes
Johnny Cash at Folsom Prison; Annotator: Johnny Cash (Col.)

Best Contemporary—Pop Vocal Performance, Female
"Do You Know the Way to San Jose" (Single); Dionne Warwicke (Scepter)

Best Contemporary—Pop Vocal Performance, Male
"Light My Fire" (Single), Jose Feliciano (RCA)

Best Contemporary—Pop Performance Vocal, Duo or Group
"Mrs. Robinson," Simon & Garfunkel (Col.)

Best Contemporary—Pop Performance Chorus
Mission Impossible/Norwegian Wood (medley), Alan Copeland Singers (ABC)

Best Contemporary—Pop Performance, Instrumental
"Classical Gas," Mason Williams (WB-7 Arts)

Best Rhythm and Blues Vocal Performance, Female
"Chain of Fools" (Single), Aretha Franklin (Atl.)

Best Rhythm and Blues Vocal Performance, Male
"(Sittin' on) The Dock of the Bay" (Single), Otis Redding (Volt)

Best Rhythm and Blues Performance by a Duo or Group, Vocal or Instrumental
"Cloud Nine," The Temptations (Soul/Gordy)

Best Rhythm and Blues Song
"(Sittin' on) The Dock of the Bay"; Songwrs: Otis Redding, Steve Cropper (Volt)

Best Country Vocal Perf., Female
"Harper Valley P.T.A." (Single), Jeannie C. Riley (Plantation)

Best Country Vocal Perf., Male
"Folsom Prison Blues" (Single), Johnny Cash (Col.)

Best Country Perf., Duo or Group Vocal or Instrumental
"Foggy Mountain Breakdown," Flatt & Scruggs (Col.)

Best Country Song
"Little Green Apples"; Songwr: Bobby Russell (Smash)

Best Sacred Performance
Beautiful Isle of Somewhere, Jake Hess (RCA)

Best Gospel Performance
The Happy Gospel of the Happy Goodmans, The Happy Goodman Family (Word)

Best Soul Gospel Performance
"The Soul of Me," Dottie Rambo (Heartwarming)

Best Folk Performance
"Both Sides Now," Judy Collins (Elektra)

Best Instrumental Theme
"Classical Gas"; Comp: Mason Williams (WB-7 Arts)

Best Original Score Written for a

1968 *(cont'd)*

Motion Picture or a TV Special
The Graduate; Songwr: Paul Simon; Add'l Music: Dave Grusin (Col.)

Best Score from an Original Cast Show Album
Hair; Comps: Gerome Ragni, James Rado, Galt MacDermott; A&R Prod: Andy Wiswell (RCA)

Best Comedy Recording
To Russell, My Brother, Whom I Slept With, Bill Cosby (WB-7 Arts)

Best Spoken Word Recording
Lonesome Cities (Album); Rod McKuen (WB-7 Arts)

Best Instrumental Jazz Performance Small Group or Soloist w/Small Group
Bill Evans at the Montreux Jazz Festival; Bill Evans Trio (Verve)

Best Instrumental Jazz Performance Large Group or Soloist w/Large Group
And His Mother Called Him Bill, Duke Ellington (RCA)

Best Classical Performance—Orchestra
Boulez Conducts Debussy, New Phil. Orch., Pierre Boulez, cond. (Col.)

Best Chamber Music Performance
Gabrieli: *Canzoni for Brass, Winds, Strings and Organ,* E. Power Biggs with Edward Tarr Ensemble & Gabrieli Consort, Vittorio Negri, cond. (Col.)

Best Opera Recording
Mozart: *Cosi Fan Tutte,* Erich Leinsdorf cond. New Philharmonia Orch. & Ambrosian Opera Chorus (Price, Raskin, Troyanos, Milnes, Shirley, Flagello); A&R: Richard Mohr (RCA)

Best Performance—Instrumental Soloist(s) (with/without Orch.)
Horowtiz on Television, Vladimir Horowitz (Col.)

Best Choral Perf. (Other Than Opera)
The Glory of Gabrieli, Vittorio Negri cond./Gregg Smith Singers/Texas Boys Choir, George Bragg, Dir./Edward Tarr Ensemble (with E. Power Biggs) (Col.)

Best Classical Vocal Soloist Perf.
Rossini Rarities, Montserrat Caballe (Cillario cond. RCA Italiana Opera Orch. & Chorus) (RCA)

Best Engineered Recording—Classical
Mahler: *Symphony No. 9 in D Major* (Solti cond. London Symphony Orch.); Eng: Gordon Parry (London)

1969

Record of the Year
"Aquarius/Let the Sunshine in," 5th Dimension; A&R Prod: Bones Howe (Soul City)

Album of the Year
Blood, Sweat and Tears, Blood, Sweat & Tears; A&R Prod: James Guercio (Col.)

Song of the Year
"Games People Play"; Songwr: Joe South

Best New Artist of 1969
Crosby, Stills & Nash (Atl.)

Best Instrumental Arrangement
"Love Theme from *Romeo and Juliet*" (Mancini); Arranger: Henry Mancini (RCA)

Best Arrangement Accompanying Vocalist(s)
"Spinning Wheel" (Blood, Sweat & Tears); Arranger: Fred Lipsius (Col.)

Best Engineered Recording
Abbey Road (The Beatles); Engrs: Geoff Emerick & Phillip McDonald (Apple)

Best Album Cover
America the Beautiful (Gary McFarland); Painting: Evelyn J. Kelbish; Graphics: David Stahlberg

Best Album Notes
Nashville Skyline (Bob Dylan); Annotator: Johnny Cash (Col.)

Best Contemporary Vocal Perf., Female
"Is That All There Is" (Single), Peggy Lee (Cap.)

Best Contemporary Vocal Perf., Male
"Everybody's Talkin'," Harry Nilsson (U.A.)

Best Contemporary Vocal Performance by a Group
"Aquarius/Let the Sunshine in," 5th Dimension (Soul City)

Best Contemporary Perf. by a Chorus
"Love Theme from *Romeo and Juliet*," Percy Faith Orchestra & Chorus (Col.)

Best Contemporary Instrumental Perf.

Variations on a Theme by Eric Satie, Blood, Sweat & Tears (Col.)

Best Contemporary Song
"Games People Play"; Songwr: Joe South

Best Rhythm and Blues Vocal Performance Female
"Share Your Love with Me" (Single), Aretha Franklin (Atl.)

Best Rhythm and Blus Vocal Perf., Male
"The Chokin' Kind" (Single), Joe Simon (Sound Stage 7)

Best Rhythm and Blues Vocal Perf., by a Group or Duo
"It's Your Thing," The Isley Brothers (T-Neck)

Best Rhythm and Blues Instrumental Performance
"Games People Play," King Curtis (Atco)

Best Rhythm and Blues Song
"Color Him Father"; Songwr: Richard Spencer

Best Soul Gospel
"Oh Happy Day," Edwin Hawkins Singers (Buddah)

Best Country Vocal Perf., Female
Stand By Your Man (Album), Tammy Wynette (Epic)

Best Country Vocal Perf., Male
"A Boy Named Sue" (Single), Johnny Cash (Col.)

Best Country Performance by a Due or Group
"MacArthur Park," Waylon Jennings & The Kimberleys (RCA)

Best Country Instrumental Perf.
The Nashville Brass Featuring Danny Davis Play More Nashville Sounds, Danny Davis & The Nashville Brass (RCA)

Best Country Song
"A Boy Named Sue"; Songwr: Shel Silverstein

Best Sacred Performance
Ain't That Beautiful Singing, Jake Hess (RCA)

Best Gospel Performance
In Gospel Country, Porter Wagoner & the Blackwood Bros. (RCA)

Best Folk Performance
Clouds, Joni Mitchell (W.B.)

Best Instrumental Theme
"Midnight Cowboy"; Comp: John Barry

Best Original Score Written for a Motion Picture or TV Special
Butch Cassidy and the Sundance

1969 *(cont'd)*

Kid; Comp: Burt Bacharach (A&M)

Best Score from an Original Cast Show Album

Promises, Promises; Comps: Burt Bacharach & Hal David; A&R Prods: Henry Jerome, Phil Ramone (Lib./U.A.)

Best Recording for Children

Peter, Paul and Mommy, Peter, Paul & Mary (W.B.)

Best Comedy Recording

Bill Cosby, Bill Cosby (Uni)

Best Spoken Word Recording

We Love You, Call Collect, Art Linkletter & Diane (Word/Cap)

Best Instrumental Jazz Perf., Small Group or Soloist with Small Group

Willow Weep for Me, Wes Montgomery (Verve)

Best Instrumental Jazz Perf., Large Group or Soloist with Large Group

Walking in Space, Quincy Jones (A&M)

Album of the Year, Classical

Switched-on Bach, Walter Carlos; A&R Prod: Rachel Elkind (Col.)

Best Classical Performance, Orchestra

Boulez Conducts Debussy, Vol. 2 *Images Pour Orchestre,* Pierre Boulez, Cleveland Orch. (Col.)

Best Chamber Music Performance

Gabrieli: *Antiphonal Music of Gabrieli (Canzoni for Brass Choirs),* The Philadelphia, Cleveland and Chicago Brass Ensembles (Col.)

Best Performance—Instrumental Soloist(s) (With or Without Orchestra)

Switched-on Bach, Walter Carlos (Col.)

Best Opera Recording

Wagner: *Siegfried,* Herbert von Karajan cond. Berlin Philharmonic (Solos: Thomas, Stewart, Stolze, Dernesch, Keleman, Dominguez, Gayer, Ridderbusch); A&R: Otto Gerdes (DGG)

Best Choral Perf. (Other Than Opera)

Berio: *Sinfonia,* Swingle Singers, Ward Swingle, Choral Master/New York Philharmonic, Luciano Berio, cond. (Col.)

Best Vocal Soloist Perf., Classical

Barber: Two Scenes from *Antony and Cleopatra/*Knoxville: *Summer of 1915,* Leontyne Price (Schippers cond. New Philharmonia) (RCA)

Best Engineered Recording, Classical

Switched-on Bach (Walter Carlos); Eng: Walter Carlos (Col.)

1970

Record of the Year

"Bridge Over Troubled Water," Simon & Garfunkel; A&R Prods: Paul Simon, Arthur Garfunkel, Roy Halee (Col.)

Album of the Year

Bridge Over Troubled Water, Simon & Garfunkel; A&R Prods: Paul Simon, Arthur Garfunkel, Roy Halee (Col.)

Song of the Year

"Bridge Over Troubled Water," Songwr: Paul Simon (Col.)

Best New Artist of the Year

Carpenters (A&M)

Best Instrumental Arrangement

Theme from Z (Henry Mancini), Arranger: Henry Mancini (RCA)

Best Arrangement Accompanying Vocalist(s)

"Bridge Over Troubled Water" (S&G), Arrangers: Paul Simon, Arthur Garfunkel, Jimmie Haskell, Ernie Freeman, Larry Knechtel (Col.)

Best Engineered Recording

"Bridge Over Troubled Water" (Simon & Garfunkel), Eng: Roy Halee (Col.)

Best Album Cover

Indianola Mississippi Seeds (B.B. King), Cover Design: Robert Lockart; Photography: Ivan Nagy (ABC)

Best Album Notes

The World's Greatest Blues Singer (Bessie Smith), Ann: Chris Albertson (Col.)

Best Contemporary Vocal Perf., Female

I'll Never Fall in Love Again, Dionne Warwicke (Album) (Scepter)

Best Contemporary Vocal Perf., Male

"Everything Is Beautiful," Ray Stevens (Single) (Barnaby)

Best Contemporary Vocal Performance by a Group

"Close To You," Carpenters (A&M)

Best Contemporary Instrumental Perf.

Theme from Z and Other Film Music, Henry Mancini (RCA)

Best Contemporary Song

"Bridge Over Troubled Water," Songwr: Paul Simon (Col.)

Best Rhythm and Blues Vocal Performance, Female

"Don't Play That Song," Aretha Franklin (Single) (Atl.)

Best Rhythm and Blues Vocal Performance, Male

"The Thrill Is Gone," B. B. King (Single) (ABC)

Best Rhythm and Blues Vocal Performance by a Duo or Group

"Didn't I (Blow Your Mind This Time)," The Delfonics (Philly Groove)

Best Rhythm and Blues Song

"Patches," Songwrs: Ronald Dunbar and General Johnson (Atl.)

Best Soul Gospel Performance

"Every Man Wants to Be Free," Edwin Hawkins Singers (Buddah)

Best Country Vocal Perf., Female

"Rose Garden," Lynn Anderson (Single) (Col.)

Best Country Vocal Perf., Male

"For the Good Times," Ray Price (Single) (Col.)

Best Country Performance by a Duo or Group

"If I Were a Carpenter," Johnny Cash and June Carter (Col.)

Best Country Instrumental Perf.

"Me & Jerry," Chet Atkins & Jerry Reed (RCA)

Best Country Song

"My Woman, My Woman, My Wife," Songwr: Marty Robbins (Col.)

Best Sacred Performance

"Everything Is Beautiful," Jake Hess (RCA)

Best Gospel Performance (Other Than Soul Gospel)

"Talk About the Good Times," Oak Ridge Boys (Heart Warming)

Best Ethnic or Traditional Recording

"Good Feelin'," T-Bone Walker (Polydor)

Best Instrumental Composition

"Airport Love Theme," Comp: Alfred Newman (Decca)

Best Original Score Written for a Motion Picture or TV Special

Let It Be, Comps: John Lennon, Paul McCartney, George Harrison, Ringo Starr (Apple)

Best Score from an Original Cast Show Album

Company, Comp: Stephen Sond-

1970 *(cont'd)*
heim; A&R Prod: Thomas Z. Shepard (Col.)

Best Recording for Children
Sesame Street, Joan Cooney, Producer (Col.)

Best Comedy Recording
The Devil Made Me Buy This Dress, Flip Wilson (Little David)

Best Spoken Word Recording
Why I Oppose the War in Vietnam, Dr. Martin Luther King, Jr. (Black Forum)

Best Jazz Perf., Small Group or Soloist with Small Group
Alone, Bill Evans (MGM)

Best Jazz Perf., Large Group or Soloist with Large Group
Bitches Brew, Miles Davis (Col.)

Album of the Year, Classical
Berlioz: *Les Troyens*, Colin Davis, Royal Opera Hse. Orch.; A&R Prod: Erik Smith (Philips)

Best Classical Performance, Orchestra
Stravinsky: *Le Sacre du Printemps*, Pierre Boulez, Cleveland Orch. (Col.)

Best Classical Perf., Instrumental Soloist(s) (With or Without Orch.)
Brahms: *Double Concerto (Concerto in A Minor for Violin and Cello)*, David Oistrakh & Mstislav Rostropovich (Angel)

Best Chamber Music Performance
Beethoven: *The Complete Piano Trios*, Eugene Istomin, Isaac Stern, Leonard Rose (Col.)

Best Opera Recording
Berlioz: *Les Troyens*, Colin Davis cond. Royal Opera House Orch. & Chorus (Vickers, Veasey, Lindholm); A&R: Erik Smith (Philips)

Best Vocal Soloist Perf., Classical
Schubert: *Lieder*, Dietrich Fischer-Dieskau (DGG)

Best Choral Perf. (Other Than Opera)
(Ives) *New Music of Charles Ives*, Gregg Smith cond. Gregg Smith Singers & Columbia Chamber Ensemble (Col.)

Best Engineered Recording, Classical
Stravinsky: *Le Sacre du Printemps* (Boulez cond. Cleveland Orch.), Engs: Fred Plaut, Ray Moore, Arthur Kendy (Col.)

1971
Record of the Year
"It's Too Late," Carole King; Prod: Lou Adler (Ode)

Album of the Year
Tapestry, Carole King; Prod: Lou Adler (Ode)

Song of the Year
"You've Got a Friend," Songwr: Carole King (Ode)

Best New Artist of the Year
Carly Simon (Elektra)

Best Instrumental Arrangement
Theme from *Shaft*, Arrangers: Isaac Hayes and Johnny Allen (Enterprise)

Best Arrangement Accompanying Vocalist(s)
"Uncle Albert/Admiral Halsey" (Paul and Linda McCartney), Arranger: Paul McCartney (Apple)

Best Engineered Recording
Theme from *Shaft* (Isaac Hayes), Engineers: Dave Purple, Ron Capone, Henry Bush (Enterprise)

Best Album Cover
Pollution (Pollution), Album Design: Dean O. Torrance; Art Director: Gene Brownell (Prophesy)

Best Album Notes
Sam, Hard and Heavy (Sam Samudio), Annotator: Sam Samudio (Atl.)

Best Pop Vocal Performance, Female
Tapestry (Album), Carole King (Ode)

Best Pop Vocal Performance, Male
"You've Got a Friend" (Single), James Taylor (W.B.)

Best Pop Vocal Performance by a Group
Carpenters (Album), Carpenters (A&M)

Best Pop Instrumental Performance
Smackwater Jack (Album), Quincy Jones (A&M)

Best Rhythm and Blues Vocal Performance, Female
"Bridge Over Troubled Water" (Single), Aretha Franklin (Atl.)

Best Rhythm and Blues Vocal Performance, Male
"A Natural Man" (Single), Lou Rawls (MGM)

Best Rhythm and Blues Vocal Performance by a Group
"Proud Mary" (Single), Ike and Tina Turner (U.A.)

Best Rhythm and Blues Song
"Ain't No Sunshine," Songwr: Bill Withers (Sussex)

Best Soul Gospel Performance
"Put Your Hand in the Hand of the Man from Galilee," Shirley Caesar (Hob)

Best Country Vocal Performance, Female
"Help Me Make It Through the Night," Sammi Smith (Single) (Mega)

Best Country Vocal Performance, Male
"When You're Hot, You're Hot," Jerry Reed (Single) (RCA)

Best Country Vocal Performance by a Group
"After the Fire Is Gone" (Single), Conway Twitty and Loretta Lynn (Decca)

Best Country Instrumental Performance
"Snowbird" (Single), Chet Atkins (RCA)

Best Country Song
"Help Me Make It Through the Night," Songwr: Kris Kristofferson

Best Sacred Performance
Did You Think to Pray, Charley Pride (RCA)

Best Gospel Performance (Other Than Soul Gospel)
Let Me Live, Charley Pride (RCA)

Best Ethnic or Traditional Recording
They Call Me Muddy Waters, Muddy Waters (Chess)

Best Instrumental Composition
"Theme from *Summer of '42*," Composer: Michel Legrand (W.B.)

Best Original Score Written for a Motion Picture
Shaft, Composer: Isaac Hayes (Enterprise)

Best Score from an Original Cast Show Album
Godspell, Composer: Stephen Schwartz; Producer: Stephen Schwartz (Bell)

Best Recording for Children
Bill Cosby Talks to Kids about Drugs, Bill Cosby (Uni)

Best Comedy Recording
This Is a Recording, Lily Tomlin (Polydor)

Best Spoken Word Recording
Desiderata, Les Crane (W.B.)

Best Jazz Performance by a Soloist
The Bill Evans Album, Bill Evans (Col.)

Best Jazz Performance by a Group
The Bill Evans Album, Bill Evans Trio (Col.)

Best Jazz Performance by a Big Band
New Orleans Suite, Duke Ellington (Atl.)

Album of the Year, Classical

1971 *(cont'd)*

Horowitz Plays Rachmaninoff, Vladimir Horowitz; Prods: Richard Killough, Thomas Frost (Col.)

Best Classical Performance—Orchestra

Mahler: *Sym. No. 1 in D Major,* Carlo Maria Giulini cond. Chicago Symphony Orchestra (Angel)

Best Classical Performance—Instrumental Soloist or Soloists (with Orchestra)

Villa-Lobos: *Concerto for Guitar,* Julian Bream (Previn cond. London Symphony) (RCA)

Best Classical Performance—Instrumental Soloist or Soloists (without Orchestra)

Horowitz Plays Rachmaninoff, Vladimir Horowitz (Col.)

Best Chamber Music Performance

Debussy: *Quartet in G Minor/Ravel: Quartet in F Major,* Juilliard Quartet (Col.)

Best Opera Recording

Verdi: *Aida,* Erich Leinsdorf cond. London Symphony Orchestra (Price, Domingo, Milnes, Bumbry, Raimondi); Producer: Richard Mohr (RCA)

Best Classical Vocal Soloist Performance

Leontyne Price Sings Robert Schumann, Leontyne Price (RCA)

Best Choral Performance, Classical (Other Than Opera)

Berlioz: *Requiem,* Colin Davis cond. London Symphony Orch.; Russell Burgess cond. Wandsworth School Boys Choir; Arthur Oldham cond. London Symphony Chorus (Philips)

Best Engineered Recording, Classical

Berlioz: *Requiem* (Davis cond. London Sym. Orch.; Burgess cond. Wandsworth School Boys Choir; Oldham cond. London Sym. Chorus); Engineer: Vittorio Negri (Philips)

1972

Record of the Year

"The First Time Ever I Saw Your Face," Roberta Flack; Prod: Joel Dorn (Atlantic)

Album of the Year

The Concert for Bangla Desh, George Harrison, Ravi Shankar, Bob Dylan, Leon Russell, Ringo Starr, Billy Preston, Eric Clapton, Klaus Voormann; Prods: George Harrison, Phil Spector (Apple)

Song of the Year

"The First Time Ever I Saw Your Face," Songwr: Ewan MacColl

Best New Artist of the Year

America (W.B.)

Best Instrumental Arrangement

"Theme from *The French Connection*" (Don Ellis), Arranger: Don Ellis (Col.)

Best Arrangement Accompanying Vocalist

"What Are You Doing the Rest of Your Life" (Sarah Vaughn), Arranger: Michel Legrand (Mainstream)

Best Engineered Recording

Moods (Neil Diamond), Engineer: Armin Steiner (UNI)

Best Album Cover

The Siegel Schwall Band, Art Director: Acy Lehman; Artist: Harvey Dinnerstein (Wooden Nickel)

Best Album Notes

Tom T. Hall's Greatest Hits, Annotator: Tom T. Hall (Mercury)

Best Jazz Performance by a Soloist

Alone at Last, Gary Burton (Atlantic)

Best Jazz Performance by a Group

First Light, Freddie Hubbard (CTI)

Best Jazz Performance by a Big Band

Toga Brava Suite, Duke Ellington (U.A.)

Best Pop Vocal Performance, Female

"I Am Woman" (Single), Helen Reddy (Capitol)

Best Pop Vocal Performance, Male

"Without You" (Single), Harry Nilsson (RCA)

Best Pop Vocal Performance by a Duo, Group or Chorus

"Where Is the Love" (Single), Roberta Flack, Donny Hathaway (Atl.)

Best Pop Instrumental Performance by an Instrumental Performer

"Outa-Space" (Single), Billy Preston (A&M)

Best Pop Instrumental Performance by an Arranger, Composer, Orchestra and/or Choral Leader

Black Moses (Album), Isaac Hayes (Enterprise)

Best Rhythm and Blues Vocal Performance, Female

Young, Gifted & Black (Album), Aretha Franklin (Atlantic)

Best Rhythm and Blues Vocal Performance, Male

"Me & Mrs. Jones" (Single), Billy Paul (Phil. Int.)

Best Rhythm and Blues Vocal Performance by a Duo, Group or Chorus

"Papa Was a Rolling Stone" (Single), The Temptations (Gordy Motown)

Best Rhythm and Blues Instrumental Performance

"Papa Was a Rolling Stone" (Single), The Temptations; Cond: Paul Riser (Gordy Motown)

Best Rhythm and Blues Song

"Papa Was a Rolling Stone," Songwrs: Barrett Strong, Norman Whitfield (Single)

Best Soul Gospel Performance

"Amazing Grace" Aretha Franklin (Atlantic)

Best Country Vocal Performance, Female

"Happiest Girl in the Whole U.S.A.," Donna Fargo (Single) (Dot)

Best Country Vocal Performance, Male

Charley Pride Sings Heart Songs, Charley Pride (Album) (RCA)

Best Country Vocal Performance by a Duo or Group

"Class of '57" (Single), The Statler Bros. (Mercury)

Best Country Instrumental Performance

Charlie McCoy/The Real McCoy, Charlie McCoy (Album) (Monument)

Best Country Song

"Kiss an Angel Good Mornin'," Songwr: Ben Peters

Best Inspirational Performance

He Touched Me, Elvis Presley (RCA)

Best Gospel Performance

Love, Blackwood Bros. (RCA)

Best Ethnic or Traditional Recording

The London Muddy Waters Session, Muddy Waters (Chess)

Best Recording for Children

The Electric Company, Project Director: Christopher Cerf, Lee Chamberlin, Bill Cosby

Best Comedy Recording

FM & AM, George Carlin (Little David)

Best Spoken Word Recording

Lenny, Prod: Bruce Botnick (Blue Thumb)

1972 *(cont'd)*

Best Instrumental Composition
"Brian's song," Michel Legrand

Best Original Score Written for a Motion Picture or a Television Special
The Godfather, Composer: Nino Rota (Paramount)

Best Score from an Original Cast Show Album
Don't Bother Me, I Can't Cope, Composer: Micki Grant; Prod: Jerry Ragavoy (Polydor)

Album of the Year, Classical
Mahler: *Symphony No. 8*, Georg Solti conducting Chicago Symphony Orchestra, Vienna Boys Choir, Vienna State Opera Chorus, Vienna Singverein Chorus & Soloists; Prod: David Harvey (London)

Best Classical Performance—Orchestra
Mahler: *Symphony No. 7*, Georg Solti Conducting Chicago Symphony Orchestra (London)

Best Opera Recording
Berlioz: *Benvenuto Cellini*, Colin Davis conducting BBC Symphony, Chorus of Covent Garden; Prod: Erik Smith (Philips)

Best Choral Performance
Mahler: *Symphony No. 8*, Georg Solti Conducting (London)

Best Chamber Music Performance
Julian & John, Julian Bream, John Williams (RCA)

Best Instrumental Soloist Performance (with Orchestra)
Brahms: *Concerto No. 2*, Artur Rubinstein (RCA)

Best Instrumental Soloist Performance (Without Orchestra)
Horowitz Plays Chopin, Vladimir Horowitz (Col.)

Best Vocal Soloist Performance
Brahms: *Die Schone Magelone*, Dietrich Fischer-Dieskau (Angel)

Best Album Notes
Vaughn Williams: *Symphony No. 2*, Annotator: James Lyons (RCA)

Best Engineered Recording
Mahler: *Symphony No. 8*, Engineers: Gordon Parry, Kenneth Wilkinson (London)

1973

Record of the Year
"Killing Me Softly with His Song," Roberta Flack; Prod: Joel Dorn (Atlantic)

Album of the Year
Innervisions, Stevie Wonder; Prod: Stevie Wonder (Tamla/Motown)

Song of the Year
"Killing Me Softly with His Song," Songwr: Norman Gimbel, Charles Fox

Best New Artist of the Year
Bette Midler (Atlantic)

Best Instrumental Arrangement
"Summer in the City" (Quincy Jones), Arranger: Quincy Jones (A&M)

Best Arrangement Accompanying Vocalist
"Live and Let Die" (Paul McCartney & Wings); Arranger: George Martin (Apple)

Best Engineered Recording (non-classical)
Innervisions (Stevie Wonder), Engineers: Robert Margouleff & Malcolm Cecil (Tamla/Motown)

Best Album Package
Tommy (London Symphony Orchestra/Chambre Choir), Art Director: Wilkes & Braun, Inc. (Ode)

Best Album Notes
God Is in the House (Art Tatum), Annotator: Dan Morgenstern (Onyx)

Best Jazz Performance by a Soloist
God Is in the House (Album), Art Tatum (Onyx)

Best Jazz Performance by a Group
Supersax Plays Bird (Album); Supersax (Capitol)

Best Jazz Performance by a Big Band
Giant Steps (Album), Woody Herman (Fantasy)

Best Pop Vocal Performance, Female
"Killing Me Softly with His Song" (Single), Roberta Flack (Atlantic)

Best Pop Vocal Performance, Male
"You Are the Sunshine of My Life" (Single), Stevie Wonder (Tamla/Motown)

Best Pop Vocal Performance by a Duo, Group or Chorus
"Neither One of Us (Wants to Be the First to Say Goodbye)" (Single), Gladys Knight & The Pips (Soul/Motown)

Best Pop Instrumental Performance
"Also Sprach Zarathustra (2001)" (Single), Eumir Deodato (CTI)

Best Rhythm and Blues Vocal Performance, Female
"Master of Eyes" (Single), Aretha Franklin (Atlantic)

Best Rhythm and Blues Vocal Performance, Male
"Superstition" (Track), Stevie Wonder (Tamla/Motown)

Best Rhythm and Blues Vocal Performance by a Duo, Group or Chorus
"Midnight Train to Georgia" (Single), Gladys Knight & The Pips (Buddah)

Best Rhythm and Blues Instrumental Performance
"Hang on Sloopy" (Single), Ramsey Lewis (Columbia)

Best Rhythm and Blues Song
"Superstition," Songwr: Stevie Wonder

Best Soul Gospel Performance
"Loves Me Like a Rock" (Single), Dixie Hummingbirds (ABC)

Best Country Vocal Performance, Female
"Let Me Be There" (Single), Olivia Newton-John (MCA)

Best Country Vocal Performance, Male
"Behind Closed Doors" (Single), Charlie Rich (Epic/Col.)

Best Country Vocal Performance by a Duo or Group
"From the Bottle to the Bottom" (Track), Kris Kristofferson, Rita Coolidge (A&M)

Best Country Instrumental Performance
"Dueling Banjos" (Track), Eric Weissberg, Steve Mandell (W.B.)

Best Country Song
"Behind Closed Doors," Songwriter: Kenny O'Dell

Best Inspirational Performance
Let's Just Praise the Lord (Album), Bill Gaither Trio (Impact)

Best Gospel Performance
Release Me (from My Sin) (Album), Blackwood Brothers (Skylite)

Best Ethnic or Traditional Recording
Then and Now (Album), Doc Watson (U.A.)

Best Recording for Children
Sesame Street Live (Album), Sesame Street Cast, Joe Raposo, Producer (Columbia)

Best Comedy Recording
Los Cochinos (Album), Cheech & Chong (Ode)

Best Spoken Word Recording

1973 *(cont'd)*
Jonathan Livingston Seagull (Album), Richard Harris (Dunhill/ABC)
Best Instrumental Composition
"Last Tango in Paris," Composer: Gato Barbieri
Album of Best Original Score Written for a Motion Picture
Jonathan Livingston Seagull, Composer: Neil Diamond (Col.)
Best Score from the Original Cast Show Album
A Little Night Music, Composer: Stephen Sondheim; Producer: Goddard Lieberson (Col.)
Album of the Year, Classical
Bartok: *Concerto for Orchestra*, Pierre Boulez conducting New York Philharmonic Orchestra; Prod: Thomas Z. Shepard (Col.)
Best Classical Performance, Orchestra
Bartok: *Concerto for Orchestra*, Pierre Boulez conducting New York Philharmonic Orchestra (Col.)
Best Opera Recording
Bizet: *Carmen*, Leonard Bernstein conducting Metropolitan Opera Orchestra, Manhattan Opera Chorus (Horne, McCracken, Maliponte, Krause); Prod: Thomas W. Mowrey (D.G.)
Best Choral Performance, Classical
Walton: *Belshazzar's Feast*, Andre Previn conducting London Symphony Orchestra, Arthur Oldham conducting London Symphony Orchestra Chorus (Angel)
Best Chamber Music Performance
Joplin: *The Red Back Book*, Gunther Schuller & New England Conservatory Ragtime Ensemble (Angel)
Best Classical Performance, Instrumental Soloist (with Orchestra)
Beethoven: *Concerti (5) for Piano and Orchestra*, Vladimir Ashkenazy (Solti conducting Chicago Symphony) (London)
Best Classical Performance, Instrumental Soloist (without Orchestra)
(Scriabin) *Horowitz Plays Scriabin*, Vladimir Horowitz (Columbia)
Best Classical Vocal Soloist Performance
Puccini: *Heroines* (La Bohème, La Rondine, Tosca, Manon Lescaut),

Leontyne Price (Downes conducting New Philharmonia) (RCA)
Best Album Notes, Classical
Hindemith: *Sonatas for Piano (Complete)*, Annotator: Glenn Gould (Columbia)
Best Engineered Recording, Classical
Bartok: *Concerto for Orchestra* (Boulez cond. New York Philharmonic), Engineers: Edward T. Graham, Raymond Moore (Columbia)

1974
Record of the Year
"I Honestly Love You," Olivia Newton-John; Prod: John Farrar (MCA)
Album of the Year
Fulfillingness' First Finale, Stevie Wonder; Prod: Stevie Wonder (Tamla/Motown)
Song of the Year
"The Way We Were," Songwriters: Marilyn & Alan Bergman, Marvin Hamlisch
Best New Artist of the Year
Marvin Hamlisch (MCA)
Best Instrumental Arrangement
"Threshold" (Pat Williams), Arranger: Pat Williams (Capitol)
Best Arrangement Accompanying Vocalists
"Down to You" (Joni Mitchell), Arrangers: Joni Mitchell & Tom Scott (Asylum)
Best Engineered Recording (nonclassical)
Band On The Run (Paul McCartney & Wings) (Album), Engineer: Geoff Emerick (Apple/Capitol)
Best Album Package
Come and Gone (Mason Proffit), Art Directors: Ed Thrasher & Christopher Whorf (Warner Bros.)
Best Album Notes (A Tie)
For the Last Time (Bob Wills and His Texas Playboys), Annotator: Charles R. Townsend (United Artists)
The Hawk Flies (Coleman Hawkins), Annotator: Dan Morgenstern (Milestone)
Best Producer of the Year
Thom Bell
Best Jazz Performance by a Soloist
First Recordings! (Album), Charlie Parker (Onyx)
Best Jazz Performance by a Group

The Trio (Album), Oscar Peterson, Joe Pass, Niels Pedersen (Pablo)
Best Jazz Performance by a Big Band
Thundering Herd (Album), Woody Herman (Fantasy)
Best Pop Vocal Performance, Female
"I Honestly Love You" (Single), Olivia Newton-John (MCA)
Best Pop Vocal Performance, Male
Fulfillingness' First Finale (Album), Stevie Wonder (Tamla/Motown)
Best Pop Vocal Performance by a Duo, Group or Chorus
"Band on the Run" (Single), Paul McCartney & Wings (Apple/Capitol)
Best Pop Instrumental Performance
"The Entertainer" (Single), Marvin Hamlisch (MCA)
Best Rhythm and Blues Vocal Performance, Female
"Ain't Nothing Like the Real Thing" (Single), Aretha Franklin (Atlantic)
Best Rhythm and Blues Vocal Performance, Male
"Boogie on Reggae Woman" (Track), Stevie Wonder (Tamla/Motown)
Best Rhythm and Blues Vocal Performance by a Duo, Group or Chorus
"Tell Me Something Good" (Single), Rufus (ABC)
Best Rhythm and Blues Instrumental Performance
"TSOP (The Sound of Philadelphia)" (Single), MFSB (Philadelphia Intl./Epic)
Best Rhythm and Blues Song
"Living for the City," Songwriter: Stevie Wonder
Best Soul Gospel Performance
In the Ghetto (Album), James Cleveland and the Southern California Community Choir (Savoy)
Best Country Vocal Performance, Female
Love Song (Album), Anne Murray (Capitol)
Best Country Vocal Performance, Male
"Please Don't Tell Me How the Story Ends" (Single), Ronnie Milsap (RCA)
Best Country Vocal Performance by a Duo or Group
"Fairytale" (Track), The Pointer Sisters (Blue Thumb)

1974 *(cont'd)*

Best Country Instrumental Perform.
The Atkins-Travis Traveling Show (Album), Chet Atkins & Merle Travis (RCA)

Best Country Song
"A Very Special Love Song," Songwriters: Norris Wilson & Billy Sherrill

Best Inspirational Performance
"How Great Thou Art" (Track), Elvis Presley (RCA)

Best Gospel Performance
"The Baptism of Jesse Taylor" (Single), Oak Ridge Boys (Columbia)

Best Ethnic or Traditional Recording
Two Days in November (Album), Doc & Merle Watson (United Artists)

Best Recording for Children
Winnie the Pooh and Tigger Too (Album), Sebastian Cabot, Sterling Holloway, Paul Winchell (Disneyland)

Best Comedy Recording
That Nigger's Crazy (Album), Richard Pryor (Partee/Stax)

Best Spoken Word Recording
Good Evening (Album), Peter Cook & Dudley Moore (Island)

Best Instrumental Composition
"Tubular Bells" (Theme from *The Exorcist*), Composer: Mike Oldfield

Album of Best Original Score Written for a Motion Picture or a Television Special
The Way We Were, Composers: Marvin Hamlisch, Alan & Marilyn Bergman (Columbia)

Best Score from the Original Cast Show Album
Raisin, Composers: Judd Woldin & Robert Brittan; Producer: Thomas Z. Shepard (Columbia)

Album of the Year, Classical
Berlioz: *Symphonie Fantastique*, Georg Solti Conducting Chicago Symphony; Producer: David Harvey (London)

Best Classical Performance—Orchestra
Berlioz: *Symphonie Fantastique*, Georg Solti Conducting Chicago Symphony (London)

Best Opera Recording
Puccini: *La Bohème*, Conductor: Georg Solti; Producer: Richard Mohr (RCA)

Best Choral Performance Classical (Other than Opera)
Berlioz: *The Damnation of Faust*, Conductor: Colin Davis (Philips)

Best Chamber Music Performance
Brahms and Schumann Trios, Artur Rubinstein, Henryk Szeryng & Pierre Fournier (RCA)

Best Classical Performance Instrumental Soloist or Soloists (with Orchestra)
Shostakovich: *Violin Concerto No. 1*, David Oistrakh (Angel)

Best Classical Performance Instrumental Soloist or Soloists (without Orchestra)
Albeniz: *Iberia*, Alicia de Larrocha (London)

Best Classical Vocal Soloist Performance
Leontyne Price Sings Richard Strauss, Leontyne Price (RCA)

Best Album Notes—Classical
The Classic Erich Wolfgang Korngold, Annotator: Rory Guy (Angel)

Best Engineered Recording—Classical
Berlioz: *Symphonie Fantastique*, Engineer: Kenneth Wilkinson (London)

1975

Record of the Year
"Love Will Keep Us Together," Captain & Tennille; Prod: Daryl Dragon (A&M)

Album of the Year
Still Crazy After All These Years, Paul Simon; Prod: Paul Simon & Phil Ramone (Columbia)

Song of the Year
"Send in the Clowns," Songwriter: Stephen Sondheim

Best New Artist of the Year
Natalie Cole (Capitol)

Best Instrumental Arrangement
"The Rockford Files" (Mike Post), Arranger: Mike Post, Pete Carpenter (MGM)

Best Arrangement Accompanying Vocalists
"Misty" (Ray Stevens), Arranger: Ray Stevens (Barnaby)

Best Engineered Recording (non-classical)
Between the Lines (Janis Ian), Engineer: Brooks Arthur, Larry Alexander & Russ Payne (Columbia)

Best Album Package

Honey (Ohio Players), Art Director: Jim Ladwig (Mercury)

Best Album Notes (non-classical)
"Blood on the Tracks" (Bob Dylan), Annotator: Pete Hamill (Columbia)

Best Producer of the Year
Arif Mardin

Best Jazz Performance by a Soloist
Oscar Peterson and Dizzy Gillespie (Album), Dizzy Gillespie (solo) (Pablo)

Best Jazz Performance by a Group
No Mystery (Album), Chick Corea and Return to Forever (Polydor)

Best Jazz Performance by a Big Band
Images (Album), Phil Woods with Michel Legrand & His Orchestra (Gryphon/RCA)

Best Pop Vocal Performance, Female
"At Seventeen" (Single), Janis Ian (Columbia)

Best Pop Vocal Performance, Male
Still Crazy After All These Years (Album), Paul Simon (Columbia)

Best Pop Vocal Performance by a Duo, Group or Chorus
"Lyin' Eyes" (Single), Eagles (Asylum)

Best Pop Instrumental Performance
"The Hustle" (Single), Van McCoy and the Soul City Symphony (AVCO)

Best Rhythm and Blues Vocal Performance, Female
"This Will Be" (Single), Natalie Cole (Capitol)

Best Rhythm and Blues Vocal Performance, Male
"Living for the City" (Single), Ray Charles (Crossover)

Best Rhythm and Blues Vocal Perform. by a Duo, Group or Chorus
"Shining Star" (Single), Earth, Wind & Fire (Columbia)

Best Rhythm and Blues Instrumental Performance
"Fly, Robin, Fly" (Single), Silver Convention (Midland/RCA)

Best Rhythm and Blues Song
"Where Is The Love," Songwriters: Harry Wayne Casey, Richard Finch, Willie Clarke, Betty Wright

Best Soul Gospel Performance
Take Me Back (Album), Andrae Crouch and the Disciples (Light)

Best Country Vocal Performance, Female
"I Can't Help It (If I'm Still in

1975 *(cont'd)*

Love with You)" (Single), Linda Ronstadt (Capitol)

Best Country Vocal Performance, Male

"Blue Eyes Crying in the Rain" (Single), Willie Nelson (Columbia)

Best Country Vocal Performance by a Duo or Group

"Lover Please" (Single), Kris Kristofferson & Rita Coolidge (Monument)

Best Country Instrumental Performance

"The Entertainer" (Track), Chet Atkins (RCA)

Best Country Song

"(Hey Won't You Play) Another Somebody Done Somebody Wrong Song," Songwriters: Chips Moman & Larry Butler

Best Inspirational Performance

Jesus, We Just Want to Thank You (Album), The Bill Gaither Trio (Impact)

Best Gospel Performance

No Shortage (Album), Imperials (Impact)

Best Ethnic or Traditional Recording

The Muddy Waters Woodstock Album, Muddy Waters (Chess)

Best Latin Recording

Sun of Latin Music (Album), Eddie Palmieri (Coco)

Best Recording for Children

The Little Prince (Album), Richard Burton, narrator (PIP)

Best Comedy Recording

Is It Something I Said? (Album), Richard Pryor (Reprise)

Best Spoken Word Recording

Give 'em Hell Harry (Album), James Whitmore (U.A.)

Best Instrumental Composition

"Images," Composer: Michel Legrand

Album of Best Original Score Written for a Motion Picture or a Television Special

Jaws, Composer: John Williams (MCA)

Best Cast Show Album

The Wiz, Composer: Charlie Smalls; Producer: Jerry Wexler (Atlantic)

Album of the Year, Classical

Beethoven: *Symphonies (9) Complete,* Sir Georg Solti conducting the Chicago Symphony Orch.; Prod: Ray Minshull (London)

Best Classical Performance, Orchestra

Ravel: *Daphnis et Chloe* (Complete Ballet), Pierre Boulez conducting New York Philharmonic (Columbia)

Best Opera Recording

Mozart: *Cosi Fan Tutte,* Colin Davis conducting Royal Opera House, Covent Garden; Prin. Solos: Caballe, Baker, Gedda, Ganzarolli, Van Allan, Cotrubas; Prod: Erik Smith (Philips)

Best Choral Performance, Classical

Orff: *Carmina Burana,* Robert Page directing Cleveland Orchestra Chorus & Boys Choir; Michael Tilson Thomas conducting Cleveland Orchestra; Soloists: Blegen, Binder, Riegel (Columbia)

Best Chamber Music Performance

Schubert: *Trios Nos. 1 in B Flat Maj., Op. 99 & 2 in E Flat Major, Op. 100 (The Piano Trios),* Artur Rubinstein, Henryk Szeryng, Pierre Fournier (RCA)

Best Classical Performance, Instrumental Soloist (with Orchestra)

Ravel: *Concerto for Left Hand & Concerto for Piano in G Major/* Faure: *Fantaisie for Piano & Orchestra,* Alicia de Larrocha (De Burgos and Foster conducting London Philharmonic) (London)

Best Classical Performance, Instrumental Soloist (without Orchestra)

Bach: *Sonatas & Partitas for Violin Unaccompanied,* Nathan Milstein (DG)

Best Classical Vocal Soloist Performance

Mahler: *Kindertotenlieder,* Janet Baker (Bernstein conducting Israel Philharmonic) (Columbia)

Best Album Notes, Classical

Footlifters (Schuller conducting All-Star Band), Annotator: Gunther Schuller (Columbia)

Best Engineered Recording, Classical

Ravel: *Daphnis et Chloe* (Complete Ballet) (Boulez conducting New York Philharmonic), Engineers: Bud Graham, Ray Moore & Milton Cherin (Columbia)

1976

Record of the Year

"This Masquerade" George Benson; Prod: Tommy Lipuma (Warner Bros.)

Album of the Year

Songs in the Key of Life, Stevie Wonder (Tamla/Motown)

Song of the Year

"I Write the Songs," Songwriter: Bruce Johnston

Best New Artist of the Year

Starland Vocal Band (Windsong/ RCA)

Best Instrumental Arrangement

"Leprechaun's Dream" (Chick Corea), Arranger: Chick Corea (Polydor)

Best Arrangement Accompanying Vocalists

"If You Leave Me Now" (Chicago), Arrangers: Jimmie Haskell & James William Guercio (Columbia)

Best Arrangement for Voices

"Afternoon Delight" (Starland Vocal Band), Arrangers: Starland Vocal Band (Windsong/RCA)

Best Engineered Recording (nonclassical)

Breezin' (George Benson), Engineer: Al Schmitt (Warner Bros.)

Best Album Package

Chicago X (Chicago), Art Director: John Berg (Columbia)

Best Album Notes

The Changing Face of Harlem, The Savoy Sessions (Various), Annotator: Dan Morgenstern (Savoy)

Best Producer of the Year

Stevie Wonder

Best Jazz Vocal Performance

Fitzgerald & Pass . . . Again (Album), Ella Fitzgerald (Vocal) (Pablo)

Best Jazz Performance by a Soloist

Basie & Zoot (Album), Count Basie (solo) (Pablo)

Best Jazz Performance by a Group

The Leprechaun (Album), Chick Corea (Poldyor)

Best Jazz Performance by a Big Band

The Ellington Suites (Album), Duke Ellington (Pablo)

Best Pop Vocal Performance, Female

Hasten Down the Wind (Album), Linda Ronstadt (Asylum)

Best Pop Vocal Performance, Male

Songs in the Key of Life (Album), Stevie Wonder (Tamla/Motown)

Best Pop Vocal Performance by a Duo, Group or Chorus

"If You Leave Me Now" (Single), Chicago (Columbia)

Best Pop Instrumental Performance

1976 *(cont'd)*
Breezin' (Album), George Benson (Warner Bros.)

Best Rhythm and Blues Vocal Performance, Female
"Sophisticated Lady (She's a Different Lady)" (Single), Natalie Cole (Capitol)

Best Rhythm and Blues Vocal Performance, Male
"I Wish" (Track), Stevie Wonder (Tamla/Motown)

Best Rhythm and Blues Vocal Performance by a Duo, Group or Chorus
"You Don't Have to Be a Star (To Be in My Show)" (Single), Marilyn McCoo, Billy Davis, Jr. (ABC)

Best Rhythm and Blues Instrumental Performance
"Theme from *Good King Bad*" (Track), George Benson (CTI)

Best Rhythm and Blues Song
"Lowdown," Songwriters: Boz Scaggs, David Paich

Best Soul Gospel Performance
How I Got Over (Album), Mahalia Jackson (Columbia)

Best Country Vocal Performance, Female
Elite Hotel (Album), Emmylou Harris (Reprise/W.B.)

Best Country Vocal Performance, Male
"(I'm a) Stand By My Woman Man" (Single), Ronnie Milsap (RCA)

Best Country Vocal Performance by a Duo or Group
"The End Is Not in Sight (The Cowboy Tune)" (Single), Amazing Rhythm Aces (ABC)

Best Country Instrumental Performance
Chester & Lester (Album), Chet Atkins, Les Paul (RCA)

Best Country Song
"Broken Lady," Songwriter: Larry Gatlin

Best Inspirational Performance
The Astonishing, Outrageous, Amazing, Incredible, Unbelievable, Different World of Gary S. Paxton (Album), Gary S. Paxton (Newpax)

Best Gospel Performance
"Where the Soul Never Dies" (Single), Oak Ridge Boys (Columbia)

Best Ethnic or Traditional Recording
Mark Twang (Album), John Hartford (Flying Fish)

Best Latin Recording
Unfinished Masterpiece (Album), Eddie Palmieri (Coco)

Best Recording for Children
Prokofiev: *Peter and the Wolf/* Saint Saens: *Carnival of the Animals*, Hermione Gingold, Karl Bohm, conductor (D.G.)

Best Comedy Recording
Bicentennial Nigger (Album), Richard Pryor (Warner Bros.)

Best Spoken Word Recording
Great American Documents (Album), Orson Welles, Henry Fonda, Helen Hayes, James Earl Jones (CBS)

Best Instrumental Composition
"Bellavia," Composer: Chuck Mangione

Album of Best Original Score Written for a Motion Picture or a Television Special
Car Wash, Composer: Norman Whitfield (MCA)

Best Cast Show Album
Bubbling Brown Sugar, Various Composers; Prod: Hugo & Luigi (H & L)

Album of the Year, Classical
Beethoven: *Five Piano Concertos*, Artur Rubinstein, Daniel Barenboim conducting London Philharmonic; Prod: Max Wilcox (RCA)

Best Classical Orchestral Performance
Strauss: *Also Sprach Zarathustra*, Sir Georg Solti conducting the Chicago Symphony; Prod: Ray Minshull (London)

Best Opera Recording
Gershwin: *Porgy and Bess*, Lorin Maazel conducting the Cleveland Orchestra & Chorus; Prod: Michael Woolcock (London)

Best Choral Performance, Classical
Rachmaninoff: *The Bells*, Arthur Oldham, Chorus Master of London Symphony Chorus; Andre Previn conducting London Symphony Orchestra (Angel)

Best Chamber Music Performance
The Art of Courtly Love, David Munrow conducting the Early Music Consort of London (Seraphim)

Best Classical Performance, Instrumental Soloist (With Orchestra)
Beethoven: *The Five Piano Concertos*, Artur Rubinstein (Barenboim conducting London Philharmonic) (RCA)

Best Classical Performance, Instrumental Soloist (Without Orchestra)
Horowitz Concerts 1975/76, Vladimir Horowitz (RCA)

Best Classical Vocal Soloist Performance
(Herbert) *Music of Victor Herbert*, Beverly Sills (Angel)

Best Engineered Recording, Classical
Gershwin: *Rhapsody in Blue* (Michael T. Thomas conducting Columbia Jazz Band), Engineers: Edward Graham, Ray Moore, Milton Cherin (Columbia)

1977

Record of the Year
"Hotel California," Eagles; Prod: Bill Szymczyk (Asylum)

Album of the Year
Rumours, Fleetwood Mac; Prods: Fleetwood Mac, Richard Dashut & Ken Caillat (Warner Bros)

Song of the Year
"Love Theme from *A Star Is Born*" ("Evergreen"), Songwriters: Barbra Streisand & Paul Williams
"You Light Up My Life," Songwriter: Joe Brooks

Best New Artist of the Year
Debby Boone (Warner Bros/Curb)

Best Instrumental Arrangement
"Nadia's Theme" (*The Young and the Restless*) (Barry De Vorzon), Arrangers: Harry Betts, Perry Botkin, Jr. & Barry De Vorzon (Arista)

Best Arrangement Accompanying Vocalist(s)
"Love Theme from *A Star Is Born*" ("Evergreen") (Barbra Streisand), Arranger: Ian Freebairn-Smith (Columbia)

Best Arrangement for Voices
"New Kid in Town" (Eagles), Arrangers: Eagles (Asylum)

Best Engineered Recording (non-classical)
AJA (Steely Dan), Engineers: Roger Nichols, Elliot Scheiner, Bill Schnee & Al Schmitt (ABC)

Best Album Package
Simple Dreams (Linda Ronstadt), Art Director: Kosh (Asylum)

Best Album Notes
Bing Crosby: A Legendary Performer, Annotator: George T. Simon (RCA)

Best Producer of the Year
Peter Asher

1977 (cont'd)

Best Jazz Vocal Performance
Look to the Rainbow (Album), Al Jarreau (Warner Bros)

Best Jazz Performance by a Soloist
The Giants (Album), Oscar Peterson (Pablo)

Best Jazz Performance by a Group
The Phil Woods Six–Live from the Showboat (Album), Phil Woods (RCA)

Best Jazz Performance by a Big Band
Prime Time (Album), Count Basie and his Orchestra (Pablo)

Best Pop Vocal Performance, Female
"Love Theme from *A Star Is Born*" ("Evergreen") (Single), Barbra Streisand (Columbia)

Best Pop Vocal Performance, Male
"Handy Man" (Single), James Taylor (Columbia)

Best Pop Vocal Performance by a Duo, Group or Chorus
"How Deep Is Your Love" (Single), Bee Gees (RSO)

Best Pop Instrumental Performance
Star Wars (Album), John Williams conducting London Symphony Orchestra (20th Century)

Best Rhythm and Blues Vocal Performance, Female
"Don't Leave Me This Way" (Single), Thelma Houston (Motown)

Best Rhythm and Blues Vocal Performance, Male
Unmistakably Lou (Album), Lou Rawls (PIR/Epic)

Best Rhythm and Blues Vocal Performance by a Duo, Group or Chorus
"Best of My Love" (Track), Emotions (Columbia)

Best Rhythm and Blues Instrumental Performance
"Q" (Track), Brothers Johnson (A & M)

Best Rhythm and Blues Song
"You Make Me Feel Like Dancing," Songwriters: Leo Sayer & Vini Poncia

Best Gospel Performance, Contemporary or Inspirational
Sail On (Album), Imperials (Dayspring/Word)

Best Gospel Performance, Traditional
"Just a Little Talk with Jesus" (Track), Oak Ridge Boys (Rockland Road)

Best Soul Gospel Performance, Contemporary
Wonderful! (Album), Edwin Hawkins & The Edwin Hawkins Singers (Birthright)

Best Soul Gospel Performance, Traditional
James Cleveland Live at Carnegie Hall (Album), James Cleveland (Savoy)

Best Inspirational Performance
Home Where I Belong (Album), B. J. Thomas (Myrrh/Word)

Best Country Vocal Performance, Female
"Don't It Make My brown Eyes Blue" (Single), Crystal Gayle (United Artists)

Best Country Vocal Performance, Male
"Lucille" (Single), Kenny Rogers (United Artists)

Best Country Vocal Performance by a Duo or Group
"Heaven's Just a Sin Away" (Single), The Kendalls (Ovation)

Best Country Instrumental Performance
Country Instrumentalist of the Year (Album), Hargus "Pig" Robbins (Elektra)

Best Country Song
"Don't It Make My Brown Eyes Blue," Songwriter: Richard Leigh

Best Ethnic or Traditional Recording
Hard Again (Album), Muddy Waters (Blue Sky/CBS)

Best Latin Recording
Dawn (Album), Mongo Santamaria (Vaya)

Best Recording for Children
Aren't You Glad You're You (Album), Christopher Cerf and Jim Timmens (Sesame Street)

Best Comedy Recording
Let's Get Small (Album), Steve Martin (Warner Bros)

Best Spoken Word Recording
The Belle of Amherst (Album), Julie Harris (Credo)

Best Instrumental Composition
"Main Title from *Star Wars*," Composer: John Williams

Best Original Score Written for a Motion Picture or a Television Special
Star Wars, Composer: John Williams (20th Century)

Best Cast Show Album
Annie, Composers: Charles Strouse & Martin Charnin; Producers: Larry Morton & Charles Strouse (Columbia)

Album of the Year, Classical
Concert of the Century, Leonard Bernstein, Vladimir Horowitz, Isaac Stern, Mstislav Rostropovich, Dietrich Fischer-Dieskau, Yehudi Menuhin and Lyndon Woodside; Producer: Thomas Frost (Columbia)

Best Classical Orchestral Performance
Mahler: *Symphony No. 9*, Carlo Maria Giulini conducting the Chicago Symphony Orchestra; Producer: Gunther Breest (DG)

Best Opera Recording
Gershwin: *Porgy and Bess*, John De Main conducting Sherwin M. Goldman/Houston Grand Opera production, Prin. Solos: Albert, Dale, Smith, Shakesnider, Lane, Brice, Smalls; Producer: Thomas Z. Shepard (RCA)

Best Choral Performance, Classical (Other Than Opera)
Verdi: *Requiem*, Sir Georg Solti conducting the Chicago Symphony Orchestra, Margaret Hillis, Choral Director of the Chicago Symphony Chorus (RCA)

Best Chamber Music Performance
Schoenberg: *Quartets for Strings*, Juilliard Quartet (Columbia)

Best Classical Performance Instrumental Soloist or Soloists (With Orchestra)
Vivaldi: *The Four Seasons*, Itzhak Perlman, Violin (Perlman conducting the London Philharmonic Orchestra) (Angel)

Best Classical Performance Instrumental Soloist or Soloists (Without Orchestra)
Beethoven: *Sonata for Piano No. 18;* Schumann: *Fantasiestucke;* Artur Rubinstein, Piano (RCA)

Best Classical Vocal Soloist Performance
Bach: *Arias*, Janet Baker (Marriner conducting Academy of St. Martin-in-the-Fields) (Angel)

Best Engineered Recording, Classical
Ravel: *Bolero*, Solti conducting the Chicago Symphony; Engineer: Kenneth Wilkinson (London)

1978

Record of the Year
"Just the Way You Are," Billy Joel; Prod: Phil Ramone (Columbia)

1978 *(cont'd)*

Album of the Year
Saturday Night Fever, Bee Gees, David Shire, Yvonne Elliman, Tavares, Kool & The Gang, K. C. & The Sunshine Band, MFSB, Trammps, Walter Murphy, Ralph MacDonald; Prod: Bee Gees, Karl Richardson, Albhy Galuten, Freddie Perren, Bill Oakes, David Shire, Arif Mardin, Thomas J. Valentino, Ralph MacDonald, W. Salter, K. G. Productions, H. W. Casey, Richard Finch, Bobby Martin, Broadway Eddie, Ron Kersey (RSO)

Song of the Year
"Just the Way You Are," Songwriter: Billy Joel

Best New Artist of the Year
A Taste of Honey (Capitol)

Best Pop Vocal Performance, Female
"You Needed Me" (Single), Anne Murray (Capitol)

Best Pop Vocal Performance, Male
"Copacabana (At the Copa)" (Single), Barry Manilow (Arista)

Best Pop Vocal Performance by a Duo, Group or Chorus
Saturday Night Fever (Album), Bee Gees (RSO)

Best Pop Instrumental Performance
Children of Sanchez (Album), Chuck Mangione Group (A&M)

Best R & B Vocal Performance, Female
"Last Dance" (Single), Donna Summer (Casablanca)

Best R & B Vocal Performance, Male
"On Broadway" (Single), George Benson (W.B.)

Best R & B Vocal Performance by a Duo, Group or Chorus
All 'n All (Album), Earth, Wind & Fire (Columbia)

Best R & B Instrumental Performance
"Runnin'" (Track), Earth, Wind & Fire (Columbia)

Best Rhythm & Blues Song
"Last Dance," Songwriter: Paul Jabara

Best Country Vocal Performance, Female
Here You Come Again (Album), Dolly Parton (RCA)

Best Country Vocal Performance, Male
"Georgia on My Mind" (Single), Willie Nelson (Columbia)

Best Country Vocal Performance by a Duo or Group
"Mamas Don't Let Your Babies Grow Up to Be Cowboys" (Single) Waylon Jennings & Willie Nelson (RCA)

Best Country Instrumental Performance
"One O'clock Jump" (Track), Asleep At The Wheel (Capitol)

Best Country Song
"The Gambler," Songwriter: Don Schlitz

Best Gospel Performance, Contemporary or Inspirational
"What a Friend" (Track), Larry Hart (Genesis)

Best Gospel Performance, Traditional
Refreshing (Album), The Happy Goodman Family (Canaan)

Best Soul Gospel Performance, Contemporary
Live in London (Album), Andrae Crouch & The Disciples (Light)

Best Soul Gospel Performance, Traditional
Live and Direct (Album), Mighty Clouds of Joy (ABC)

Best Inspirational Performance
Happy Man (Album), B. J. Thomas (Myrrh)

Best Ethnic or Traditional Recording
I'm Ready (Album), Muddy Waters (Blue Sky)

Best Latin Recording
Homenaje A Beny More (Album), Tito Puente (Tico)

Best Recording for Children
The Muppet Show (Album), Jim Henson (Arista)

Best Comedy Recording
A Wild and Crazy Guy (Album), Steve Martin (W.B.)

Best Spoken Word Recording
Citizen Kane (Motion Picture Soundtrack), Orson Welles (Mark 56)

Best Instrumental Composition
"Theme from *Close Encounters of the Third Kind*," Composer: John Williams

Best Album of Original Score Written for a Motion Picture or a Television Special
Close Encounters of the Third Kind, Composer: John Williams (Arista)

Best Cast Show Album
Ain't Misbehavin', Prod: Thomas Z. Shepard (RCA RedSeal)

Best Jazz Vocal Performance
All Fly Home (Album), Al Jarreau (W.B.)

Best Jazz Instrumental Performance, Soloist
Montreux '77—Oscar Peterson Jam (Album), Oscar Peterson (Pablo)

Best Jazz Instrumental Performance, Group
Friends (Album), Chick Corea (Polydor)

Best Jazz Instrumental Performance, Big Band
Live in Munich (Album), Thad Jones and Mel Lewis (Horizon/A&M)

Best Instrumental Arrangement
"Main Title from 'Overture Part One,'" (*The Wiz* Original Soundtrack), Arrangers: Quincy Jones and Robert Freedman (MCA)

Best Arrangement Accompanying Vocalist(s)
"Got to Get You into My Life" (Earth, Wind & Fire), Arranger: Maurice White (RSO)

Best Arrangement for Voices
"Stayin' Alive" (The Bee Gees), Arranger: the Bee Gees (RSO)

Best Album Package
Boys in the Trees (Carly Simon), Art Directors: Johnny Lee & Tony Lane (Elektra)

Best Album Notes
A Bing Crosby Collection, Vols. I & II, Annotator: Michael Brooks (Columbia)

Best Historical Repackage Album
Lester Young Story Vol. 3, Producer: Michael Brooks (Columbia)

Best Engineered Recording
FM (No Static at All) (Steely Dan) (Track), Engineers: Roger Nichols and Al Schmitt (MCA)

Best Producer of the Year
Bee Gees, Albhy Galuten & Karl Richardson

Album of the Year, Classical
Brahms: *Concerto for Violin in D Major*, Itzhak Perlman with Carlo Maria Giulini (cond. Chicago Symphony); Prod: Christopher Bishop (Angel)

Best Classical Orchestral Performance
Beethoven: *Symphonies (9)* (Complete), Herbert von Karajan cond. Berlin Philharmonic; Prod: Michel Glotz (DG)

1978 *(cont'd)*

Best Opera Recording
Lehar: *The Merry Widow*, Julius Rudel (cond. New York City Opera Orchestra & Chorus—Prin. Solos: Sills, Titus); Prods: George Sponhaltz & John Coveney (Angel)

Best Choral Performance, Classical (Other Than Opera)
Beethoven: *Missa Solemnis*, Sir Georg Solti, cond.; Margaret Hillis, Choral Director (Chicago Sym. Orchestra & Chorus) (London)

Best Chamber Music Performance
Beethoven: *Sonatas for Violin and Piano* (Complete), Itzhak Perlman & Vladimir Ashkenazy (London)

Best Classical Performance Instrumental Soloist(s) (with Orchestra)
Rachmaninoff: *Concerto No. 3 in D Minor for Piano (Horowitz Golden Jubilee)*, Vladimir Horowitz (Ormandy cond. Philadelphia Orch.) (RCA)

Best Classical Performance Instrumental Soloist(s) (Without Orchestra)
The Horowitz Concerts 1977/78, Vladimir Horowitz (RCA)

Best Classical Vocal Soloist Performance
Luciano Pavarotti—Hits From Lincoln Center, Luciano Pavarotti (London)

Best Engineered Recording, Classical
Varese: *Ameriques/Arcana/Ionisation (Boulez Conducts Varese)*, Boulez cond. New York Philharmonic; Engineers: Bud Graham, Arthur Kendy & Ray Moore (Columbia)

1979

Record of the Year
(Grammys to the Artist and Producer) "What a Fool Believes," The Doobie Brothers; Ted Templeman, Producer (W. B.)

Album of the Year
(Grammys to the Artist and Producer) *52nd Street*, Billy Joel; Phil Ramone, Producer (Columbia)

Song of the Year
(A Songwriter's Award) "What a Fool Believes," Kenny Loggins, Michael McDonald, Songwriters

Best New Artist
Rickie Lee Jones (W. B.)

Best Pop Vocal Performance, Female
"I'll Never Love This Way Again," Dionne Warwick (Single) (Arista)

Best Pop Vocal Performance, Male
52nd Street, Billy Joel (Album) (Columbia)

Best Pop Vocal Performance by a Duo, Group or Chorus
Minute by Minute, The Doobie Brothers (Album) (W. B.)

Best Pop Instrumental Performance
"Rise," Herb Alpert (Single) (A & M)

Best Rock Vocal Performance, Female
"Hot Stuff," Donna Summer (Single) (Casablanca)

Best Rock Vocal Performance, Male
"Gotta Serve Somebody," Bob Dylan (Single) (Columbia)

Best Rock Vocal Performance by a Duo or Group
"Heartache Tonight," Eagles (Single) (Asylum)

Best Rock Instrumental Performance
"Rockestra Theme," Wings (Track) (Columbia)

Best R & B Vocal Performance, Female
"Deja Vu," Dionne Warwick (Track) (Arista)

Best R & B Vocal Performance, Male
"Don't Stop 'til You Get Enough," Michael Jackson (Single) (Epic)

Best R & B Vocal Performance by a Duo, Group or Chorus
"After the Love Has Gone," Earth, Wind & Fire (Track) (ARC-CBS)

Best R & B Instrumental Performance
"Boogie Wonderland (Instrumental)," Earth, Wind & Fire (Single) (ARC-CBS)

Best Rhythm & Blues Song
(A Songwriter's Award) "After the Love Has Gone," David Foster, Jay Graydon, Bill Champlin, Songwriters

Best Disco Recording
(Grammy to the Artist and Producer) "I Will Survive," Gloria Gaynor; Dino Fekaris, Freddie Perren, Producers (Single) (Polydor)

Best Country Vocal Performance, Female
Blue Kentucky Girl, Emmylou Harris (Album) (W. B.)

Best Country Vocal Performance, Male
"The Gambler," Kenny Rogers (Single) (U. A.)

Best Country Vocal Performance by a Duo or Group
"The Devil Went Down to Georgia," Charlie Daniels Band (Single) (Epic)

Best Country Instrumental Performance
"Big Sandy/Leather Britches," Doc & Merle Watson (Track) (U. A.)

Best Country Song
(A Songwriter's Award) "You Decorated My Life," Rob Morrison, Debbie Hupp, Songwriters

Best Gospel Performance, Contemporary or Inspirational
Heed the Call, Imperials (Album) (Dayspring)

Best Gospel Performance, Traditional
Lift Up the Name of Jesus, The Blackwood Brothers (Album) (Skylite)

Best Soul Gospel Performance, Contemporary
I'll Be Thinking of You, Andrae Crouch (Album) (Light)

Best Soul Gospel Performance, Traditional
Changing Times, Mighty Clouds of Joy (Album) (Epic)

Best Inspirational Performance
You Gave Me Love (When Nobody Gave Me a Prayer), B. J. Thomas (Album) (Myrrh)

Best Ethnic or Traditional Recording
Muddy "Mississippi" Waters Live, Muddy Waters (Album) (Blue Sky/CBS)

Best Latin Recording
Irakere, Irakere (Album) (Columbia)

Best Recording for Children
The Muppet Movie, Jim Henson, Creator; Paul Williams, Producer (Album) (Atlantic)

Best Comedy Recording
Reality . . . What a Concept, Robin Williams (Album) (Casablanca)

Best Spoken Word, Documentary or Drama Recording
Ages of Man (Readings from Shakespeare), Sir John Gielgud (Album) (Caedmon)

Best Instrumental Composition
(A Composer's Award) Main Title Theme from *Superman*, John Williams, Composer

Best Album of Original Score Written for a Motion Picture or a Television Special

1979 *(cont'd)*

(A Composer's Award) *Superman,* John Williams, Composer (W. B.)

Best Cast Show Album

[Awards to the Composer(s), Lyricist(s) and Album Producer(s)] *Sweeney Todd,* Stephen Sondheim, Composer/Lyricist; Thomas Z. Shepard, Producer (RCA)

Best Jazz Fusion Performance, Vocal or Instrumental

8:30, Weather Report (Album) (ARC-CBS)

Best Jazz Vocal Performance

Fine and Mellow, Ella Fitzgerald (Album) (Pablo)

Best Jazz Instrumental Performance, Soloist

Jousts, Oscar Peterson (Album) (Pablo)

Best Jazz Instrumental Performance, Group

Duet, Gary Burton & Chick Corea (Album) (ECM/W.B.)

Best Jazz Instrumental Performance, Big Band

At Fargo, 1940 Live, Duke Ellington (Album) (Book-of-the-Month Records)

Best Instrumental Arrangement

(An Arranger's Award) "Soulful Strut," Claus Ogerman, Arranger (W. B.)

Best Arrangement Accompanying Vocalist(s)

(An Arranger's Award) "What a Fool Believes," Michael McDonald, Arranger (W. B.)

Best Album Package

(An Art Director's Award) *Breakfast in America,* Mike Doud, Art Director (A & M); Mick Haggerty, Co-Art Director

Best Album Notes

(An Annotator's Award) *Charlie Parker: The Complete Savoy Sessions,* Bob Porter & James Patrick, Annotators (Savoy)

Best Historical Reissue

[Grammy to the Reissue Album Producer(s) *Billie Holiday* (*Giants of Jazz*)] Jerry Korn, Michael Brooks, Producers (Time-Life)

Best Engineered Recording (Non-Classical)

(An Engineer's Award) *Breakfast in America,* Peter Henderson, Engineer (Album) (A & M)

Producer of the Year (Non-Classical) Larry Butler

Best Classical Album

(Grammys to the Artist and Producer) Brahms: *Symphonies Complete,* Sir Georg Solti, cond. Chicago Symphony Orchestra; James Mallinson, Producer (London)

Best Classical Orchestral Recording

(Grammys to the Conductor and Producer) Brahms: *Symphonies Complete,* Sir Georg Solti, cond. Chicago Symphony Orchestra; James Mallinson, Producer (London)

Best Opera Recording

(Grammys to the Conductor and Producer) Britten: *Peter Grimes,* Colin Davis (cond. Orchestra & Chorus of the Royal Opera House, Covent Garden—Prin. Solos: Vickers, Harper, Summers); Vittorio Negri, Producer (Philips)

Best Choral Performance, Classical (Other Than Opera)

(Grammys to the Conductor and Choral Director) Brahms: *A German Requiem,* Sir Georg Solti, Cond.; Margaret Hillis, Choral Dir. (Chicago Symphony Chorus & Orchestra) (London)

Best Chamber Music Performance

Copland: *Appalachian Spring,* Dennis Russell Davies, cond. St. Paul Chamber Orchestra (Sound 80)

Best Classical Performance—Instrumental Soloist or Soloists (With Orchestra)

Bartok: *Concertos For Piano Nos. 1 & 2,* Maurizio Pollini (Abbado cond. Chicago Symphony Orchestra) (DG)

Best Classical Performance—Instrumental Soloist or Soloists (Without Orchestra)

The Horowitz Concerts 1978/79, Vladimir Horowitz (RCA)

Best Classical Vocal Soloist Performance

"O Sole Mio," Luciano Pavarotti (Bologna Orchestra) (London)

Best Engineered Recording, Classical

(An Engineer's Award) Sondheim: *Sweeney Todd,* Anthony Salvatore, Engineer (RCA)

Classical Producer of the Year James Mallinson

1980

Record of the Year

(Grammys to the Artist and Producer) "Sailing," Christopher Cross; Michael Omartian, Producer (W.B.)

Album of the Year

(Grammys to the Artist and Producer) *Christopher Cross,* Christopher Cross; Michael Omartian, Producer (W.B.)

Song of the Year

(A Songwriter's Award) "Sailing," Christopher Cross, Songwriter

Best New Artist

Christopher Cross (W.B.)

Best Pop Vocal Performance, Female,

"The Rose," Bette Midler (Single) (Atlantic)

Best Pop Vocal Performance, Male

"This Is It," Kenny Loggins (Track) (Columbia)

Best Pop Vocal Performance by a Duo or Group with Vocal

"Guilty," Barbra Streisand & Barry Gibb (Track) (Columbia)

Best Pop Instrumental Performance

One on One, Bob James & Earl Klugh (Album) (Columbia)

Best Rock Vocal Performance, Female

Crimes of Passion, Pat Benatar (Album) (Chrysalis)

Best Rock Vocal Performance, Male

Glass Houses, Billy Joel (Album) (Columbia)

Best Rock Performance by a Duo or Group with Vocal

Against the Wind, Bob Seger & The Silver Bullet Band (Album) (Capitol)

Best Rock Instrumental Performance

"Reggatta de Blanc," Police (Track) (A&M)

Best R & B Vocal Performance, Female

"Never Knew Love Like This Before," Stephanie Mills (Single) (20th Century)

Best R & B Vocal Performance, Male

Give Me the Night, George Benson (Album) (W.B./QWest)

Best R & B Performance by a Duo or Group with Vocal

"Shining Star," Manhattans (Single) (Columbia)

Best R & B Instrumental Performance

"Off Broadway," George Benson (Track) (W.B./QWest)

Best Rhythm & Blues Song

(A Songwriter's Award) "Never

1980 *(cont'd)*

Knew Love Like This Before," Reggie Lucas & James Mtume, Songwriters

Best Jazz Fusion Performance, Vocal or Instrumental

"Birdland," Manhattan Transfer (Single) (Atlantic)

Best Country Vocal Performance, Female

"Could I Have This Dance," Anne Murray (Single) (Capitol)

Best Country Vocal Performance, Male

"He Stopped Loving Her Today," George Jones (Single) (Epic)

Best Country Performance by a Duo or Group with Vocal

"That Lovin' You Feelin' Again," Roy Orbison & Emmylou Harris (Single) (W.B.)

Best Country Instrumental Performance

"Orange Blossom Special/Hoedown," Gilley's "Urban Cowboy" Band (Track) (Full Moon/Asylum)

Best Country Song

(A Songwriter's Award) "On the Road Again," Willie Nelson, Songwriter

Best Gospel Performance, Contemporary or Inspirational

The Lord's Prayer, Reba Rambo, Dony McGuire, B. J. Thomas, Andrae Crouch, the Archers, Walter & Tramaine Hawkins, Cynthia Clawson (Album) (Light)

Best Gospel Performance, Traditional

We Came to Worship, Blackwood Brothers (Album) (Voice Box)

Best Soul Gospel Performance, Contemporary

Rejoice, Shirley Caesar (Album) (Myrrh)

Best Soul Gospel Performance, Traditional

Lord, Let Me Be an Instrument, James Cleveland & The Charles Fold Singers (Album) (Savoy)

Best Inspirational Performance

With My Song I Will Praise Him, Debby Boone (Album) (Lamb & Lion)

Best Ethnic or Traditional Recording

Rare Blues (Dr. Isaiah Ross, Maxwell Street Jimmy, Big Joe Williams, Son House, Rev. Robert Wilkins, Little Brother Montgomery, Sunnyland Slim), Norman

Dayron, Producer (Album) (Takoma)

Best Latin Recording

La Onda Va Bien, Cal Tjader (Album) (Concord Jazz)

Best Recording For Children

In Harmony/A Sesame Street Record (The Doobie Brothers, James Taylor, Carly Simon, Bette Midler, Muppets, Al Jarreau, Linda Ronstadt, Wendy Waldman, Libby Titus & Dr. John, Livingston Taylor, George Benson & Pauline Wilson, Lucy Simon, Kate Taylor & The Simon/Taylor Family), Lucy Simon & David Levine, Producers (Album) (Sesame St./WB)

Best Comedy Recording

No Respect, Rodney Dangerfield (Album) (Casablanca)

Best Spoken Word, Documentary or Drama Recording

Gertrude Stein, Gertrude Stein, Gertrude Stein, Pat Carroll (Album) (Caedmon)

Best Instrumental Composition

(A Composer's Award) "The Empire Strikes Back," John Williams, Composer

Best Album of Original Score Written for a Motion Picture or a Television Special

(A Composer's Award) *The Empire Strikes Back*, John Williams, Composer (RSO)

Best Cast Show Album

(Awards to the Composer, Lyricist, and Album Producers) *Evita (Premier American Recording)*, Andrew Lloyd Webber, Composer; Tim Rice, Lyrics; Andrew Lloyd Webber, Tim Rice, Producers (MCA)

Best Jazz Vocal Performance, Female

A Perfect Match/Ella & Basie, Ella Fitzgerald (Album) (Pablo)

Best Jazz Vocal Performance, Male

"Moody's Mood," George Benson (Track) (W.B./QWest)

Best Jazz Instrumental Performance, Soloist

I Will Say Goodbye, Bill Evans (Album) (Fantasy)

Best Jazz Instrumental Performance, Group

We Will Meet Again, Bill Evans (Album) (W.B.)

Best Jazz Instrumental Performance, Big Band

On the Road, Count Basie and Orchestra (Album) (Pablo)

Best Instrumental Arrangement

(An Arranger's Award) "Dinorah, Dinorah," Quincy Jones & Jerry Hey, Arrangers (W.B.)

Best Arrangement Accompanying Vocalist(s)

(An Instrumental Arranger's Award) "Sailing," Michael Omartian & Christopher Cross, Arrangers (W.B.)

Best Arrangement for Voices

(A Vocal Arranger's Award) "Birdland," Janis Siegel, Vocal Arranger (Atlantic)

Best Album Package

(An Art Director's Award) *Against the Wind*, Roy Kohara, Art Director (Capitol)

Best Album Notes

(An Annotator's Award) *Trilogy: Past, Present & Future*, David McClintick, Annotator (Reprise)

Best Historical Reissue Album

(Grammy to the Reissue Album Producer) *Segovia—The EMI Recordings 1927–39*, Keith Hardwick, Producer (Angel)

Best Engineered Recording (Non-Classical)

(An Engineer's Award) *The Wall*, James Guthrie, Engineer (Album) (Columbia)

Producer of the Year (Non-Classical)

(A Producer's Award) Phil Ramone

Best Classical Album

(Grammys to the Artist and Producers) Berg: *Lulu* (Complete Version), Pierre Boulez cond. Orchestre de l'Opera de Paris/Principal Soloists: Teresa Stratas, Yvonne Minton, Franz Mazura, Toni Blankenheim; Guenther Breest, Michael Horwarth, Producers (DG)

Best Classical Orchestral Recording

(Grammys to the Conductor and Producer) Bruckner: *Symphony No. 6 in A Major*, Sir Georg Solti cond. Chicago Symphony Orchestra; Ray Minshull, Producer (London)

Best Opera Recording

(Grammys to the Conductor and Producers) Berg: *Lulu* (Complete Version), Pierre Boulez cond. Orchestre de l'Opera de Paris/Principal Soloists: Teresa Stratas, Yvonne Minton, Franz Mazura, Toni Blan-

1980 *(cont'd)*

kenheim; Guenther Breest, Michael Horwarth, Producers (DG)

Best Choral Performance, Classical (Other Than Opera)

(Grammys to the Conductor and Choral Director) Mozart: *Requiem,* Carlo Maria Giulini, Conductor; Norbert Balatsch, Chorus Master; Philharmonia Chorus & Orchestra (Angel)

Best Chamber Music Performance

Music For Two Violins (Moszkowski: *Suite For Two Violins*/ Shostakovich: *Duets*/Prokofiev: *Sonata For Two Violins*), Itzhak Perlman, Pinchas Zukerman (Angel)

Best Classical Performance—Instrumental Soloist or Soloists (With Orchestra)

° Berg: *Concerto for Violin and Orchestra*/Stravinsky: *Concerto in D Major for Violin and Orchestra,* Itzhak Perlman (Seiji Ozawa cond. Boston Symphony Orchestra) (DG)

° Brahms: *Concerto in A Minor for Violin and Cello* (*Double Concerto*), Itzhak Perlman & Mstislav Rostropovich (Bernard Haitink cond. Concertgebouw Orchestra) (Angel)

Best Classical Performance—Instru-

———————————

° *A Tie*

mental Soloist or Soloists (Without Orchestra)

The Spanish Album, Itzhak Perlman (Angel)

Best Classical Vocal Soloist Performance

Prima Donna, Volume 5—Great Soprano Arias from Handel to Britten, Leontyne Price (Henry Lewis cond. Philharmonia Orchestra) (RCA)

Best Engineered Recording, Classical (An Engineer's Award) Berg: *Lulu* (Complete Version), Karl-August Naegler, Engineer (DG)

Classical Producer of the Year

(A Producer's Award) Robert Woods

I. Tony Awards*

1949
Musical: *Kiss Me Kate*
Authors (Musical): Bella and Samuel Spewack, *Kiss Me Kate*
Composer and Lyricist: Cole Porter, *Kiss Me Kate*
Producers (Musical): Saint-Subber and Lemuel Ayers, *Kiss Me Kate*
Actor (Musical): Ray Bolger, *Where's Charley?*
Actress (Musical): Nanette Fabray, *Love Life*
Choreographer: Gower Champion, *Lend An Ear*
Conductor and Musical Director: Max Meth, *As the Girls Go*

1950
Musical: *South Pacific*
Authors (Musical): Oscar Hammerstein II and Joshua Logan, *South Pacific*
Composer: Richard Rodgers, *South Pacific*
Producers (Musical): Richard Rodgers, Oscar Hammerstein II, Leland Hayward and Joshua Logan, *South Pacific*
Actor (Musical): Ezio Pinza, *South Pacific*
Actress (Musical): Mary Martin, *South Pacific*
Actor, Supporting or Featured (Musical): Myron McCormick, *South Pacific*
Actress, Supporting or Featured (Musical): Juanita Hall, *South Pacific*
Choreographer: Helen Tamiris, *Touch and Go*
Conductor and Musical Director: Maurice Abravanel, *Regina*

1951
Musical: *Guys and Dolls*
Authors (Musical): Jo Swerling and Abe Burrows, *Guys and Dolls*
Composer and Lyricist: Frank Loesser, *Guys and Dolls*
Producers (Musical): Cy Feuer and Ernest H. Martin, *Guys and Dolls*
Actor (Musical): Robert Alda, *Guys and Dolls*
Actress (Musical): Ethel Merman, *Call Me Madam*
Actor, Supporting or Featured (Musical): Russell Nype, *Call Me Madam*
Actress, Supporting or Featured (Musical): Isabel Bigley, *Guys and Dolls*
Choreographer: Michael Kidd, *Guys and Dolls*
Conductor and Musical Director: Lehman Engel, *The Consul*

1952
Musical: *The King & I*
Actor (Musical): Phil Silvers, *Top Banana*
Actress (Musical): Gertrude Lawrence, *The King & I*
Actor, Supporting or Featured (Musical): Yul Brynner, *The King & I*
Actress, Supporting or Featured (Musical): Helen Gallagher, *Pal Joey*
Choreographer: Robert Alton, *Pal Joey*
Conductor and Musical Director: Max Meth, *Pal Joey*

1953
Musical: *Wonderful Town*
Authors (Musical): Joseph Fields and Jerome Chodorov, *Wonderful Town*
Composer: Leonard Bernstein, *Wonderful Town*
Producer (Musical): Robert Fryer, *Wonderful Town*
Actor (Musical): Thomas Mitchell, *Hazel Flagg*
Actress (Musical): Rosalind Russell, *Wonderful Town*
Actor, Supporting or Featured (Musical): Hiram Sherman, *Two's Company*
Actress, Supporting or Featured (Musical): Sheila Bond, *Wish You Were Here*
Choreographer: Donald Saedler, *Wonderful Town*
Conductor and Musical Director: Lehman Engel, *Wonderful Town* and Gilbert and Sullivan Season

1954
Musical: *Kismet*
Author (Musical): Charles Lederer and Luther Davis, *Kismet*
Composer: Alexander Borodin, *Kismet*
Producer (Musical): Charles Lederer, *Kismet*
Actor (Musical): Alfred Drake, *Kismet*
Actress (Musical): Dolores Gray, *Carnival in Flanders*
Actor, Supporting or Featured (Musical): Harry Belafonte, *John Murray Anderson's Almanac*
Actress, Supporting or Featured (Musical): Gwen Verdon, *Can-Can*
Choreographer: Michael Kidd, *Can-Can*
Musical Conductor: Louis Adrian, *Kismet*

1955
Musical: *The Pajama Game*
Authors (Musical): George Abbott and Richard Bissell, *The Pajama Game*
Composer and Lyricist: Richard Adler and Jerry Ross, *The Pajama Game*
Producers (Musical): Frederick Brisson, Robert Griffith and Harold S. Prince, *The Pajama Game*
Actor (Musical): Walter Slezak, *Fanny*
Actress (Musical): Mary Martin, *Peter Pan*

---

* Courtesy: American Theatre Wing.

1955 *(cont'd)*

Actor, Supporting or Featured (Musical): Cyril Ritchard, *Peter Pan*

Actress, Supporting or Featured (Musical): Carol Haney, *The Pajama Game*

Choreographer: Bob Fosse, *The Pajama Game*

Conductor and Musical Director: Thomas Schippers, *The Saint of Bleecker Street*

1956

Musical: *Damn Yankees*

Authors (Musical): George Abbott and Douglass Wallop, *Damn Yankees*

Composer and Lyricist: Richard Adler and Jerry Ross, *Damn Yankees*

Producers (Musical): Frederick Brisson, Robert Griffith, Harold S. Prince in association with Albert B. Taylor, *Damn Yankees*

Actor (Musical): Ray Walston, *Damn Yankees*

Actress (Musical): Gwen Verdon, *Damn Yankees*

Actor, Supporting or Featured (Musical): Russ Brown, *Damn Yankees*

Actress, Supporting or Featured (Musical): Lotte Lenya, *The Threepenny Opera*

Choreographer: Bob Fosse, *Damn Yankees*

Conductor and Musical Director: Hal Hastings, *Damn Yankees*

1957

Musical: *My Fair Lady*

Author (Musical): Alan Jay Lerner, *My Fair Lady*

Composer: Frederick Loewe, *My Fair Lady*

Producer (Musical): Herman Levin, *My Fair Lady*

Actor (Musical): Rex Harrison, *My Fair Lady*

Actress (Musical): Judy Holiday, *Bells Are Ringing*

Actor, Supporting or Featured (Musical): Sydney Chaplin, *Bells Are Ringing*

Actress, Supporting or Featured (Musical): Edith Adams, *Li'l Abner*

Choreographer: Michael Kidd, *Li'l Abner*

Conductor and Musical Director: Franz Allers, *My Fair Lady*

1958

Musical: *The Music Man*

Author (Musical): Meredith Willson and Franklin Lacey, *The Music Man*

Composer and Lyricist: Meredith Willson, *The Music Man*

Producer (Musical): Kermit Bloomgarden, Herbert Greene, Frank Productions, *The Music Man*

Actor (Musical): Robert Preston, *The Music Man*

Actress (Musical): Thelma Ritter, *New Girl in Town* Gwen Verdon, *New Girl In Town*

Actor, Supporting or Featured (Musical): David Burns, *The Music Man*

Actress, Supporting or Featured (Musical): Barbara Cook, *The Music Man*

Choreographer: Jerome Robbins, *West Side Story*

Conductor and Musical Director: Herbert Greene, *The Music Man*

1959

Musical: *Redhead*

Authors (Musical): Herbert and Dorothy Fields, Sidney Sheldon and David Shaw, *Redhead*

Composer: Albert Hague, *Redhead*

Producers (Musical): Robert Fryer and Lawrence Carr, *Redhead*

Actor (Musical): Richard Kiley, *Redhead*

Actress (Musical): Gwen Verdon, *Redhead*

Actor, Supporting or Featured (Musical): Russell Nype, *Goldilocks*

Cast of *La Plume de Ma Tante*

Actress, Supporting or Featured (Musical): Pat Stanley, *Goldilocks*

Cast of *La Plume de Ma Tante*

Choreographer: Bob Fosse, *Redhead*

Conductor and Musical Director: Salvatore Dell'Isola, *Flower Drum Song*

1960

Musical: *Fiorello! The Sound of Music*

Authors (Musical): Jerome Weidman and George Abbott, *Fiorello!* Howard Lindsay and Russel Crouse, *The Sound of Music*

Composers: Jerry Bock, *Fiorello!* Richard Rodgers, *The Sound of Music*

Producer (Musical): Robert Griffith and Harold Prince, *Fiorello!* Leland Hayward and Richard Halliday, *The Sound of Music*

Director (Musical): George Abbott, *Fiorello!*

Actor (Musical): Jackie Gleason, *Take Me Along*

Actress (Musical): Mary Martin, *The Sound of Music*

Actor, Supporting or Featured (Musical): Tom Bosley, *Fiorello!*

Actress, Supporting or Featured (Musical): Patricia Neway, *The Sound of Music*

Choreographer: Michael Kidd, *Destry Rides Again*

Scenic Designer (Musical): Oliver Smith, *The Sound of Music*

Conductor and Musical Director: Frederick Dvonch, *The Sound of Music*

1961

Musical: *Bye, Bye Birdie*

Author (Musical): Michael Stewart, *Bye, Bye Birdie*

Producer (Musical): Edward Padula, *Bye, Bye Birdie*

Director (Musical): Gower Champyon, *Bye, Bye Birdie*

Actor (Musical): Richard Burton, *Camelot*

Actress (Musical): Elizabeth Seal, *Irma la Douce*

Actor, Supporting or Featured (Musical): Dick Van Dyke, *Bye, Bye Birdie*

Actress, Supporting or Featured (Musical): Tammy Grimes, *The Unsinkable Molly Brown*

Choreographer: Gower Champion, *Bye, Bye Birdie*

Scenic Designer (Musical): Oliver Smith, *Camelot*

Conductor and Musical Director: Franz Allers, *Camelot*

1962

Musical: *How to Succeed in Business Without Really Trying*
Author (Musical): Abe Burrows, Jack Weinstock and Willie Gilbert, *How to Succeed* . . .
Composer: Richard Rodgers, *No Strings*
Producer (Musical): Cy Feuer and Ernest Martin, *How to Succeed* . . .
Director (Musical): Abe Burrows, *How to Succeed* . . .
Actor (Musical): Robert Morse, *How to Succeed* . . .
Actress (Musical): Anna Maria Alberghetti, *Carnival*, Diahann Carroll, *No Strings*
Actor, Supporting or Featured (Musical): Charles Nelson Reilly, *How to Succeed* . . .
Actress, Supporting or Featured (Musical): Phyllis Newman, *Subways Are for Sleeping*
Choreographer: Agnes de Mille, *Kwamina*, Joe Layton, *No Strings*
Conductor and Musical Director: Elliot Lawrence, *How to Succeed* . . .

1963

Musical: *A Funny Thing Happened on the Way to the Forum*
Author (Musical): Burt Shevelove and Larry Gelbart, *A Funny Thing Happened on the Way to the Forum*
Composer and Lyricist: Lionel Bart, *Oliver!*
Producer (Musical): Harold Prince, *A Funny Thing Happened on the Way to the Forum*
Director (Musical): George Abbott, *A Funny Thing Happened on the Way to the Forum*
Actor (Musical): Zero Mostel, *A Funny Thing Happened on the Way to the Forum*
Actress (Musical): Vivien Leigh, *Tovarich*
Actor, Supporting or Featured (Musical): David Burns, *A Funny Thing Happened on the Way to the Forum*
Actress, Supporting or Featured (Musical): Anna Quayle, *Stop the World—I Want to Get Off*
Choreographer: Bob Fosse, *Little Me*
Conductor and Musical Director: Donald Pippin, *Oliver!*

1964

Musical: *Hello, Dolly!*
Author (Musical): Michael Stewart, *Hello, Dolly!*
Composer and Lyricist: Jerry Herman, *Hello, Dolly!*
Producer (Musical): David Merrick, *Hello, Dolly!*
Director (Musical): Gower Champion, *Hello Dolly!*
Actor (Musical): Bert Lahr, *Foxy*
Actress (Musical): Carol Channing, *Hello, Dolly!*
Actor, Supporting or Featured (Musical): Jack Cassidy, *She Loves Me*
Actress, Supporting or Featured (Musical): Tessie O'Shea, *The Girl Who Came to Supper*
Choreographer: Gower Champion, *Hello, Dolly!*
Conductor and Musical Director: Shepard Coleman, *Hello, Dolly!*

1965

Musical: *Fiddler On The Roof*
Author (Musical): Joseph Stein, *Fiddler On The Roof*
Composer and Lyricist: Jerry Bock and Sheldon Harnick, *Fiddler On The Roof*
Producer (Musical): Harold Prince, *Fiddler On The Roof*
Director (Musical): Jerome Robbins, *Fiddler On The Roof*
Actor (Musical): Zero Mostel, *Fiddler On The Roof*
Actress (Musical): Liza Minelli, *Flora, the Red Menace*
Actor, Supporting or Featured (Musical): Victor Spinetti, *Oh, What A Lovely War*
Actress, Supporting or Featured (Musical): Maria Karnilova, *Fiddler On The Roof*
Choreographer: Jerome Robbins, *Fiddler On The Roof*

1966

Musical: *Man of La Mancha*
Composer and Lyricist: Mitch Leigh and Joe Darion, *Man of La Mancha*
Director (Musical): Albert Marre, *Man of La Mancha*
Actor (Musical): Richard Kiley, *Man of La Mancha*
Actress (Musical): Angela Lansbury, *Mame*
Actor, Supporting or Featured (Musical): Frankie Michaels, *Mame*
Actress, Supporting or Featured (Musical): Beatrice Arthur, *Mame*
Choreographer: Bob Fosse, *Sweet Charity*

1967

Musical: *Cabaret*
Composer and Lyricist: John Kander and Fred Ebb, *Cabaret*
Director (Musical): Harold Prince, *Cabaret*
Actor (Musical): Robert Preston, *I Do! I Do!*
Actress (Musical): Barbara Harris, *The Apple Tree*
Actor, Supporting or Featured (Musical): Joel Grey, *Cabaret*
Actress, Supporting or Featured (Musical): Peg Murray, *Cabaret*
Choreographer: Ronald Field, *Cabaret*

1968

Musical: *Hallelujah, Baby!*
Composer and Lyricist: Jule Styne, Betty Comden and Adolph Green, *Hallelujah, Baby!*
Producer (Musical): Albert Selden, Hal James, Jane C. Nusbaum and Harry Rigby, *Hallelujah, Baby!*
Director (Musical): Gower Champion, *The Happy Time*
Actor (Musical): Robert Goulet, *The Happy Time*
Actress (Musical): Patricia Routledge, *Darling of the Day* Leslie Uggams, *Hallelujah, Baby!*
Actor, Supporting or Featured (Musical): Hiram Sherman, *How Now, Dow Jones*
Actress, Suppporting or Featured (Musical): Lillian Hayman, *Hallelujah, Baby!*
Choreographer: Gower Champion, *The Happy Time*

1969

Musical: *1776*
Director (Musical): Peter Hunt, *1776*
Actor (Musical): Jerry Orbach, *Promises, Promises*
Actress (Musical): Angela Lansbury, *Dear World*

1969 *(cont'd)*
Actor, Supporting or featured (Musical): Ronald Holgate, *1776*
Actress, Supporting or Featured (Musical): Marian Mercer, *Promises, Promises*
Choreographer: Joe Layton, *George M!*

1970
Musical: *Applause*
Director (Musical): Ron Field, *Applause*
Actor (Musical): Cleavon Little, *Purlie*
Actress (Musical): Lauren Bacall, *Applause*
Actor, Supporting or Featured (Musical): Rene Auberjonois, *Coco*
Actress, Supporting or Featured (Musical): Melba Moore, *Purlie*
Choreographer: Ron Field, *Applause*

1971
Musical: *Company*
Book (Musical): George Furth, *Company*
Lyrics (Musical): Stephen Sondheim, *Company*
Score (Musical): Stephen Sondheim, *Company*
Producer (Musical): Harold Prince, *Company*
Director (Musical): Harold Prince, *Company*
Actor (Musical): Hal Linden, *The Rothschilds*
Actress (Musical): Helen Gallagher, *No, No, Nanette*
Actor, Supporting or Featured (Musical): Keene Curtis, *The Rothschilds*
Actress, Supporting or Featured (Musical): Patsy Kelly, *No, No, Nanette*
Choreographer: Donald Saddler, *No, No, Nanette*

1972
Musical: *Two Gentlemen of Verona*
Book (Musical): *Two Gentlemen of Verona* by John Guare and Mel Shapiro
Score: *Follies.* Composer: Stephen Sondheim
    Lyricist: Stephen Sondheim
Director (Musical): Harold Prince and Michael Bennett, *Follies*
Actor (Musical): Phil Silvers, *A Funny Thing Happened on the Way to the Forum* (Revival)
Actress (Musical): Alexis Smith, *Follies*
Actor, Supporting or Featured (Musical): Larry Blyden, *A Funny Thing Happened on the Way to the Forum* (Revival)
Actress, Supporting or Featured (Musical): Linda Hopkins, *Inner City*
Choreographer: Michael Bennett, *Follies*

1973
Musical: *A Little Night Music*
Book (Musical): *A Little Night Music* by Hugh Wheeler
Score (Musical): *A Little Night Music.* Music and lyrics: Stephen Sondheim
Director (Musical): Bob Fosse, *Pippin*
Actor (Musical): Ben Vereen, *Pippin*
Actress (Musical): Glynis Johns, *A Little Night Music*

Actor, Supporting or Featured (Musical): George S. Irving, *Irene*
Actress, Supporting or Featured (Musical): Patricia Elliot, *A Little Night Music*
Choreographer: Bob Fosse, *Pippin*

1974
Musical: *Raisin*
Book (Musical): *Candide* by Hugh Wheeler
Score: *Gigi.* Music: Frederick Loewe
    Lyrics: Alan Jay Lerner
Director (Musical): Harold Prince, *Candide*
Actor (Musical): Christopher Plummer, *Cyrano*
Actress (Musical): Virginia Capers, *Raisin*
Actor, Supporting or Featured (Musical): Tommy Tune, *Seesaw*
Actress, Supporting or Featured (Musical): Janie Sell, *Over Here!*
Choreographer: Michael Bennett, *Seesaw*

1975
Musical: *The Wiz*
Book (Musical): *Shenandoah*
Score: *The Wiz*
Director (Musical): Geoffrey Holder, *The Wiz*
Actor (Musical): John Cullum, *Shenandoah*
Actress (Musical): Angela Lansbury, *Gypsy*
Actor, Supporting or Featured (Musical): Ted Ross, *The Wiz*
Actress, Supporting or Featured (Musical): Dee Dee Bridgewater, *The Wiz*
Choreographer: George Faison, *The Wiz*

1976
Musical: *A Chorus Line*
Book (Musical): *A Chorus Line*
Score: *A Chorus Line*
Director (Musical): Michael Bennett, *A Chorus Line*
Actor (Musical): George Rose, *My Fair Lady*
Actress (Musical): Donna McKechnie, *A Chorus Line*
Actor, Featured role (Musical): Sammy Williams, *A Chorus Line*
Actress, Featured role (Musical): Carole Bishop, *A Chorus Line*
Choreographer: Michael Bennett and Bob Avian, *A Chorus Line*

1977
Musical: *Annie*
Book (Musical): *Annie*
Score: *Annie*
Director (Musical): Gene Saks, *I Love My Wife*
Actor (Musical): Barry Bostwick, *The Robber Bridegroom*
Actress (Musical): Dorothy Loudon, *Annie*
Actor, Featured role (Musical): Lenny Baker, *I Love My Wife*
Actress, Featured role (Musical): Delores Hall, *Your Arm's Too Short To Box With God*
Choreographer: Peter Gennaro, *Annie*

1978
Musical: *Ain't Misbehavin'*
Book (Musical): *On The Twentieth Century*
Score: *On The Twentieth Century*
Director (Musical): Richard Maltby, Jr., *Ain't Misbehavin'*
Actor (Musical): John Cullum, *On The Twentieth Century*
Actress (Musical): Liza Minnelli, *The Act*
Actor, Featured role (Musical): Kevin Kline, *On The Twentieth Century*
Actress, Featured role (Musical): Nell Carter, *Ain't Misbehavin'*
Choreographer: Bob Fosse, *Dancin'*

1979
Musical: *Sweeney Todd*
Book (Musical): *Sweeney Todd*
Score: *Sweeney Todd*
Director (Musical): Harold Prince, *Sweeney Todd*
Actor (Musical): Len Cariou, *Sweeney Todd*

Actress (Musical): Angela Lansbury, *Sweeney Todd*
Actor, Featured role (Musical): Henderson Forsythe, *The Best Little Whorehouse In Texas*
Actress, Featured role (Musical): Carlin Glynn, *The Best Little Whorehouse In Texas*
Choreographer: Michael Bennett and Bob Avian, *Ballroom*

1980
Musical: *Evita*
Book (Musical): *Evita*
Score: *Evita*
Director (Musical): Harold Prince, *Evita*
Actor (Musical): Jim Dale, *Barnum*
Actress (Musical): Patti LuPone, *Evita*
Actor, Featured role (Musical): Mandy Patinkin, *Evita*
Actress, Featured role (Musical): Priscilla Lopez, *A Day in Hollywood/A Night in the Ukraine*
Choreographer: Tommy Tune and Thommie Walsh, *A Day in Hollywood/A Night in the Ukraine*

J. Gold Record Awards*

ALBUMS

1958
Oklahoma, Gordon MacRae (Capitol)

1959
Hymns, Ernie Ford (Capitol)
Johnny's Greatest Hits, Johnny Mathis (Columbia)
Music Man—Original Cast (Capitol)
Sing Along With Mitch, Mitch Miller (Columbia)
South Pacific, Rodgers & Hammerstein (RCA Victor)
Peter Gunn, Henry Mancini (RCA Victor)

1960
Student Prince, Mario Lanza (RCA Victor)
60 Years of Music—Honoring 30 Great Artists (RCA Victor)
Elvis, Elvis Presley (RCA Victor)
Pat's Great Hits, Pat Boone (Dot)
Kingston Trio at Large, Kingston Trio (Capitol)
Kingston Trio, Kingston Trio (Capitol)
More Sing Along with Mitch, Mitch Miller (Columbia)
Heavenly, Johnny Mathis (Columbia)
Warm, Johnny Mathis (Columbia)
Love Is the Thing, Nat King Cole (Capitol)
Here We Go Again, Kingston Trio (Capitol)
From the Hungry i, Kingston Trio (Capitol)
Sound of Music—Original Cast (Columbia)
Merry Christmas, Johnny Mathis (Columbia)
Christmas Sing Along, Mitch Miller (Columbia)
Still More! Sing Along, Mitch Miller (Columbia)

1961
Calcutta Album, Lawrence Welk
Come Dance with Me, Frank Sinatra (Capitol)
Sold Out, Kingston Trio (Capitol)
Glenn Miller Story, Glenn Miller Orch. (RCA Victor)
Christmas Carols, Mantovani (London)
Theatre Land, Mantovani (London)
Film Encores Vol. I, Mantovani (London)
Gems Forever, Mantovani (London)
Strauss Waltzes, Mantovani (London)
Spirituals, Ernie Ford (Capitol)
Elvis' Golden Records, Elvis Presley (RCA Victor)
Belafonte at Carnegie Hall, Harry Belafonte (RCA Victor)
Tchaikovsky Concerto, Van Cliburn (RCA Victor)
Encore—Golden Hits, The Platters (Mercury)
Blue Hawaii, Elvis Presley (RCA Victor)

*Courtesy: Recording Industry Association of America, Inc. (RIAA).

1962
Holiday Sing Along with Mitch, Mitch Miller (Columbia)
Party Sing Along with Mitch, Mitch Miller (Columbia)
More Johnny's Greatest Hits, Johnny Mathis (Columbia)
West Side Story—Original Cast (Columbia)
Camelot—Original Cast (Columbia)
Flower Drum Song—Original Cast (Columbia)
Theme from a Summer Place, Billy Vaughn (Dot)
Blue Hawaii, Billy Vaughn (Dot)
Sail Along Silvery Moon, Billy Vaughn (Dot)
Bob Newhart Button Down Mind, Bob Newhart (Warner Bros.)
Saturday Night Sing Along With Mitch, Mitch Miller (Columbia)
Memories Sing Along With Mitch, Mitch Miller (Columbia)
Sentimental Sing Along With Mitch, Mitch Miller (Columbia)
Star Carol, Ernie Ford (Capitol)
Nearer the Cross, Ernie Ford (Capitol)
Frank Sinatra Sings For Only The Lonely, Frank Sinatra (Capitol)
Nice'N'Easy, Frank Sinatra (Capitol)
Songs for Swingin' Lovers, Frank Sinatra (Capitol)
String Along, Kingston Trio (Capitol)
Music, Martinis and Memories, Jackie Gleason (Capitol)
Music For Lovers Only, Jackie Gleason (Capitol)
Judy At Carnegie Hall, Judy Garland (Capitol)
Happy Times Sing Along, Mitch Miller (Columbia)
Memories Are Made of This, Ray Coniff (Columbia)
Concert in Rhythm, Ray Conniff (Columbia)
'S Marvelous, Ray Conniff (Columbia)
Modern Sounds in Country & Western Music, Ray Charles (ABC-Paramount)
Breakfast at Tiffany's, Henry Mancini (RCA Victor)
This is Sinatra, Frank Sinatra (Capitol)
Bouquet, Percy Faith Strings (Columbia)
So Much In Love, Ray Conniff (Columbia)
Faithfully, Johnny Mathis (Columbia)
Swing Softly, Johnny Mathis (Columbia)
Open Fire, Two Guitars, Johnny Mathis (Columbia)
Peter, Paul and Mary, Peter, Paul and Mary (Warner Bros.)
My Son The Folk Singer, Allan Sherman (Warner Bros.)
The First Family, Vaughn Meader (Cadence)

1963
West Side Story—Original Soundtrack (Columbia)
Glorious Sound of Christmas, Eugene Ormandy—The Philadelphia Orch. (Columbia)
1812 Overture—Tchaikovsky, Antal Dorati and the Minneapolis Symphony (Mercury)

1963 *(cont'd)*
Exodus—Original Soundtrack (RCA Victor)
Calypso, Harry Belafonte (RCA Victor)
G.I. Blues, Elvis Presley (RCA Victor)
Season's Greetings from Perry Como, Perry Como (RCA Victor)
VIVA, Percy Faith (Columbia)
The Music Man—Soundtrack (Warner Bros.)
Time Out, Dave Brubeck Quartet (Columbia)
I Left My Heart in San Francisco, Tony Bennett (Columbia)
Elvis' Christmas Album, Elvis Presley (RCA Victor)
Girls, Girls, Girls, Elvis Presley (RCA Victor)
Belafonte Returns to Carnegie Hall, Harry Belafonte (RCA Victor)
Belafonte, Harry Belafonte (RCA Victor)
Jump-Up-Calypso, Harry Belafonte (RCA Victor)
Moving, Peter, Paul and Mary (Warner Bros.)
Exodus, Mantovani (London)
Days of Wine and Roses, Andy Williams (Columbia)
Moon River And Other Great Movie Themes, Andy Williams (Columbia)
Handel's Messiah, Eugene Ormandy—The Philadelphia Orch. (Columbia)
Christmas with Conniff, Ray Conniff (Columbia)
The Lord's Prayer, Mormon Tabernacle Choir (Columbia)
Porgy and Bess—Original Soundtrack (Columbia)
Folk Song Sing Along, Mitch Miller (Columbia)
In The Wind, Peter, Paul and Mary (Warner Bros.)
Singing Nun, Soeur Sourire (Philips)

1964
My Fair Lady—Original Cast
John Fitzgerald Kennedy—A Memorial Album (Premier Albums)
Carousel—Motion Picture Soundtrack (Capitol)
The King and I—Motion Picture Soundtrack (Capitol)
Ramblin' Rose, Nat King Cole (Capitol)
Meet The Beatles! The Beatles (Capitol)
Honey in the Horn, Al Hirt (RCA Victor)
The Beatles' Second Album, The Beatles (Capitol)
The Second Barbra Streisand Album, Barbra Streisand (Columbia)
Hello, Dolly!—Original Cast (RCA Victor)
Hello, Dolly!, Louis Armstrong (Kapp)
The Wonderful World of Andy Williams, Andy Williams (Columbia)
Christmas Hymns and Carols, Robert Shaw (RCA Victor)
Victory at Sea, Volume I, Robert Russell Bennett (RCA Victor)
Something New, The Beatles (Capitol)
The Best of the Kingston Trio, Kingston Trio (Capitol)
Unforgettable, Nat King Cole (Capitol)
Funny Girl—Original Cast (Capitol)
Ramblin, New Christy Minstrels (Columbia)
The Barbra Streisand Album, Barbra Streisand (Columbia)

Johnny Horton's Greatest Hits, Johnny Horton (Columbia)
Cotton Candy, Al Hirt (RCA Victor)
The Andy Williams Christmas Album, Andy Williams (Columbia)
Call Me Irresponsible, Andy Williams (Columbia)
My Fair Lady—Movie Soundtrack (Columbia)
Beatles '65, The Beatles (Capitol)
The Beatles' Story, The Beatles (Capitol)
Mary Poppins—Movie Soundtrack (Vista)

1965
Glad All Over, The Dave Clark Five (Epic)
Peter, Paul and Mary in Concert, Peter, Paul and Mary (Warner Bros.)
Everybody Loves Somebody, Dean Martin (Reprise)
Wonderland of Golden Hits, Andre Kostelanetz (Columbia)
Barbra Streisand/The Third Album, Barbra Streisand (Columbia)
Ring of Fire, Johnny Cash (Columbia)
Beach Boys in Concert, The Beach Boys (Capitol)
All Summer Long, The Beach Boys (Capitol)
Sugar Lips, Al Hirt (RCA Victor)
People, Barbra Streisand (Columbia)
The Sound of Music—Movie Soundtrack (RCA Victor)
Trini Lopez at PJ's, Trini Lopez (Warner Bros.)
Getz/Gilberto, Stan Getz (Verve)
Beatles VI, The Beatles (Capitol)
Dear Heart, Andy Williams (Columbia)
Help!, The Beatles (Capitol)
Introducing Herman's Hermits, Herman's Hermits (MGM)
Herman's Hermits on Tour, Herman's Hermits (MGM)
More Encore of Golden Hits, The Platters (Mercury)
Return of Roger Miller, Roger Miller (Smash)
Great Songs From My Fair Lady, Andy Williams (Columbia)
Gunfire Ballads & Trail Songs, Marty Robbins (Columbia)
Look At Us, Sonny and Cher (Atco)
The Beach Boys Today, The Beach Boys (Capitol)
The Pink Panther, Henry Mancini (RCA Victor)
Out of Our Heads, The Rolling Stones (London)
Fiddler On The Roof—Original Cast (RCA Victor)
Surfer Girl, The Beach Boys (Capitol)
Surfin' USA, The Beach Boys (Capitol)
Sinatra's Sinatra, Frank Sinatra (Reprise)
Welcome to the LBJ Ranch (Capitol)
My Name is Barbra, Barbra Streisand (Columbia)
The Door is Still Open to My Heart, Dean Martin (Warner Bros.)
Going Places, Herb Alpert and the Tijuana Brass (A&M)
Whipped Cream & Other Delights, Herb Alpert and the Tijuana Brass (A&M)
Rubber Soul, The Beatles (Capitol)

1966
My Name is Barbra, Two, Barbra Streisand (Columbia)

1966 *(cont'd)*

The Best of Herman's Hermits, Herman's Hermits (MGM)

December's Children, Rolling Stones (London)

Joan Baez, Vol. 2, Joan Baez (Vanguard)

Joan Baez, Joan Baez (Vanguard)

Joan Baez in Concert, Joan Baez (Vanguard)

September of My Years, Frank Sinatra (Reprise)

A Man and His Music, Frank Sinatra (Reprise)

Summer Days, The Beach Boys (Capitol)

Golden Hits, Roger Miller (Smash)

Ballads of the Green Berets, SSGT. Barry Sadler (RCA Victor)

Ray Orbison's Greatest Hits, Roy Orbison (Monument)

Living Language Spanish (Young People's)

Living Language French, (Young People's)

Color Me Barbra, Barbra Streisand (Columbia)

I'm The One Who Loves You, Dean Martin (Reprise)

Big Hits (High Tide and Green Grass), Rolling Stones (London)

Oliver—Original Cast (RCA Victor)

South of the Border, Herb Alpert and the Tijuana Brass (A & M)

The Lonely Bull, Herb Alpert and the Tijuana Brass (A & M)

What Now My Love, Herb Alpert and the Tijuana Brass (A & M)

Herb Alpert's Tijuana Brass Volume 2, Herb Alpert and the Tijuana Brass (A & M)

My World, Eddy Arnold (RCA Victor)

South Pacific—Original Cast (Columbia)

If You Can Believe Your Eyes and Ears. The Mama's and the Papa's (ABC/Dunhill)

Yesterday and Today, The Beatles (Capitol)

The Best of Jim Reeves, Jim Reeves (RCA Victor)

The Best of The Animals, The Animals (M-G-M)

Dang Me, Roger Miller (Smash)

Gold Vault of Hits, Four Seasons (Philips)

Aftermath, Rolling Stones (London)

Dr. Zhivago—Soundtrack (M-G-M)

Think Ethnic, Smothers Brothers (Mercury)

Strangers in the Night, Frank Sinatra (Reprise)

Revolver, The Beatles (Capitol)

The Dave Clark Five's Greatest Hits, Dave Clark Five (Epic)

Somewhere My Love, Ray Conniff (Columbia)

The Shadow of Your Smile, Andy Williams (Columbia)

The Best of Al Hirt, Al Hirt (RCA Victor)

I Started Out as a Child, Bill Cosby (Warner Bros.)

Wonderfulness, Bill Cosby (Warner Bros.)

Why Is There Air?, Bill Cosby (Warner Bros.)

Bill Cosby Is a Very Funny Fellow, Right?, Bill Cosby (Warner Bros.)

Jeanette MacDonald and Nelson Eddy Favorites, Jeanette MacDonald and Nelson Eddy (RCA Victor)

Perry Como Sings Merry Christmas Music, Perry Como (Camden)

The Monkees, The Monkees (Colgems)

Elvis Presley, Elvis Presley (RCA Victor)

Elvis' Gold Records, Vol 2, Elvis Presley (RCA Victor)

Elvis' Golden Records, Vol. 3, Elvis Presley (RCA Victor)

Dean Martin Sings Again, Dean Martin (Reprise)

Boots, Nancy Sinatra (Reprise)

Soul and Inspiration, Righteous Brothers (Verve)

The Mamas and the Papas, Mamas and the Papas (ABC-Dunhill)

Bobby Vinton's Greatest Hits, Bobby Vinton (Epic)

Little Deuce Coupe, The Beach Boys (Capitol)

Shut Down—Vol. 2, The Beach Boys (Capitol)

Winchester Cathedral, New Vaudeville Band (Fontana)

Spanish Eyes, Al Martino (Capitol)

1967

Just Like Us, Paul Revere & The Raiders (Columbia)

More of The Monkees, The Monkees (Colgems)

S. R. O., Herb Alpert and the Tijuana Brass (A&M)

Got Live If You Want It, The Rolling Stones (London)

Till, Roger Williams (Kapp)

Songs of the Fabulous Fifties Part 1, Roger Williams (Kapp)

Songs of the Fabulous Fifties Part 2, Roger Williams (Kapp)

Roger Williams' Greatest Hits, Roger Williams (Kapp)

Yakety Sax, Boots Randolph (Monument)

That's Life, Frank Sinatra (Reprise)

Lou Rawls Live! Lou Rawls (Capitol)

The Two Sides of the Smothers Brothers, Smothers Brothers (Mercury)

Between the Buttons, The Rolling Stones (London)

Midnight Ride, Paul Revere & The Raiders (Columbia)

Thoroughly Modern Millie—Original Soundtrack (Decca)

The Best of Mancini, Henry Mancini (RCA Victor)

An Evening with Belafonte, Harry Belafonte (RCA Victor)

Best of The Beach Boys, The Beach Boys (Capitol)

Winchester Cathedral, Lawrence Welk (Dot)

Spirit of '67, Paul Revere & The Raiders (Columbia)

The Mamas and the Papas Deliver, The Mamas and the Papas (Dunhill)

Born Free, Roger Williams (Kapp)

Mame—Original Cast (Columbia)

Headquarters, The Monkees (Colgems)

My Cup Runneth Over, Ed Ames (RCA Victor)

Stranger on the Shore, Mr. Acker Bilk (Atco)

I Never Loved A Man The Way I Love You, Aretha Franklin (Atlantic)

Seargent Pepper's Lonely Hearts Club Band, Beatles (Capitol)

Man of La Mancha—Original Cast (Kapp)

Revenge, Bill Cosby (Warner Bros.)

Parsley, Sage, Rosemary & Thyme, Simon & Garfunkel (Columbia)

Born Free, Andy Williams (Columbia)

The Best of the Lovin' Spoonful, Lovin' Spoonful (Kama Sutra)

Themes for Young Lovers, Percy Faith & his Orchestra (Columbia)

I Walk the Line, Johnny Cash (Columbia)

Surrealistic Pillow, Jefferson Airplane (RCA Victor)

1967 *(cont'd)*
Flowers, The Rolling Stones (London)
A Man and A Woman—Soundtrack (United Artists)
Ebb Tide, Earl Grant (Decca)
Blue Midnight, Bert Kaempfert (Decca)
Sounds Like, Herb Alpert & the Tijuana Brass (A&M)
Sergio Mendes and Brasil '66, Sergio Mendes & Brasil '66 (A&M)
Sounds of Silence, Simon & Garfunkel (Columbia)
Paul Revere & The Raiders Greatest Hits, Paul Revere & the Raiders (Columbia)
Blonde on Blonde, Bob Dylan (Columbia)
Highway 61, Bob Dylan (Columbia)
Bringing It All Back Home, Bob Dylan (Columbia)
The Doors, Doors (Elektra)
2nd Vault of Golden Hits, Four Seasons (Philips)
Ode to Billie Joe, Bobbie Gentry (Capitol)
Tony Bennett's Greatest Hits Volume III, Tony Bennett (Columbia)
Pisces, Aquarius, Capricorn and Jones Ltd., Monkees ((Colgems)
Sinatra at The Sands, Frank Sinatra (Reprise)
Along Comes The Association, The Association (Warner Bros.)
Their Satanic Majesty's Request, The Rolling Stones (London)
Release Me, Engelbert Humperdinck (Parrot)
Herb Alpert's Ninth, Herb Alpert & the Tijuana Brass (A&M)
Magical Mystery Tour, The Beatles (Capitol)
Merry Christmas to All, Ray Conniff (Columbia)
The Button-Down Mind Strikes Back, Bob Newhart (Warner Bros.)
Insight Out, The Association (Warner Bros.)

1968
Jim Nabors Sings, Jim Nabors (Columbia)
Bob Dylan's Greatest Hits, Bob Dylan (Columbia)
Strange Days, Doors (Elektra)
Dream With Dean, Dean Martin (Reprise)
Guantanamera, The Sandpipers (A&M)
Farewell To The First Golden Era, The Mamas and the Papas (Dunhill)
How Great Thou Art, Elvis Presley (RCA Victor)
Distant Drums, Jim Reeves (RCA Victor)
Blooming Hits, Paul Mauriat and Orchestra (Philips)
Best of Buck Owens, Buck Owens (Capitol)
Doctor Doolittle—Original Soundtrack (20th Century Fox)
The Byrd's Greatest Hits, The Byrds (Columbia)
Welcome to My World, Dean Martin (Reprise)
Houston, Dean Martin (Reprise)
Are You Experienced, Jimi Hendrix (Reprise)
John Wesley Harding, Bob Dylan (Columbia)
The Graduate—Soundtrack (Columbia)
The Best of Eddy Arnold, Eddy Arnold (RCA Victor)
The Great Caruso, Mario Lanza (RCA Victor)
Modern Sounds in Country and Western Music, Vol. 2, Ray Charles (ABC)
Greatest Hits, Ray Charles (ABC)

Loving You, Elvis Presley (RCA Victor)
Turtles' Greatest Hits, The Turtles (White Whale)
The Birds, The Bees and the Monkees, The Monkees (Colgems)
Gigi—Soundtrack (MGM)
Bookends, Simon & Garfunkel (Columbia)
Somewhere There's a Someone, Dean Martin (Reprise)
Persuasive Percussion, Enoch Light (Command)
Songs I Sing On The Jackie Gleason Show, Frank Fontaine (ABC)
Love, Andy, Andy Williams (Columbia)
Doris Day's Greatest Hits, Doris Day (Columbia)
Disraeli Gears, Cream (Atco)
Merry Christmas, Andy Williams (Columbia)
Glenn Miller and His Orchestra, Glenn Miller (RCA Victor)
To Russell, My Brother, Whom I Slept With, Bill Cosby (Warner Bros.)
The Beat of the Brass, Herb Alpert and the Tijuana Brass (A&M)
Wheels of Fire, Cream (Atco)
Groovin', The Rascals (Atlantic)
Vanilla Fudge, Vanilla Fudge (Atco)
Collections, The Rascals (Atlantic)
Somewhere My Love, Roger Williams. (Kapp)
Waiting For The Sun, The Doors (Elektra)
The Good, the Bad and the Ugly—Original Soundtrack (United Artists)
A Man and His Soul, Ray Charles (ABC)
Lady Soul, Aretha Franklin (Atlantic)
Look Around, Sergio Mendes & Brasil '66 (A&M)
The Young Rascals, The Rascals (Atlantic)
Time Peace—The Rascals Greatest Hits, The Rascals (Atlantic)
Camelot—Original Soundtrack (Warner Bros.)
Feliciano, Jose Feliciano (RCA Victor)
Axis: Bold as Love, Jimi Hendrix (Reprise)
Cheap Thrills, Janis Joplin With Big Brother and the Holding Company (Columbia)
By the Time I Get to Phoenix, Glen Campbell (Capitol)
Gentle On My Mind, Glen Campbell (Capitol)
My Love Forgive Me, Robert Goulet (Columbia)
Johnny Cash at Folsom Prison, Johnny Cash (Columbia)
Honey, Andy Williams (Columbia)
Purple Onion, Smothers Brothers (Mercury)
Wichita Lineman, Glen Campbell (Capitol)
Electric Ladyland, Jimi Hendrix (Reprise)
The Kinks Greatest Hits, The Kinks (Reprise)
Honey, Bobby Goldsboro (United Artists)
Dean Martin Christmas Album, Dean Martin (Reprise)
Steppenwolf, Steppenwolf (Dunhill)
Aretha Now, Aretha Franklin (Atlantic)
In-A-Gadda-Da-Vida, Iron Butterfly (Atco)
Fresh Cream, Cream (Atco)
The Time Has Come, Chambers Brothers (Columbia)
Walt Disney Presents The Jungle Book—Original soundtrack (Disneyland)
The Beatles, The Beatles (Apple)
The Christmas Album, Herb Alpert and the Tijuana Brass (A & M)

1968 *(cont'd)*
Harper Valley PTA, Jeannie C. Riley (Plantation)
Funny Girl—motion picture soundtrack (Columbia)
Beggars Banquet, The Rolling Stones (London)
The Sea, The San Sebastian Strings (Warner Bros.)

1969
Walt Disney Presents The Story of Mary Poppins—Story-teller LP (Disneyland)
Hey Little One, Glen Campbell (Capitol)
The Christmas Song, Nat King Cole (Capitol)
The Lettermen!!!...and "Live," The Lettermen (Capitol)
Wildflowers, Judy Collins (Elektra)
Album 1700, Peter, Paul and Mary (Warner Bros.)
Gentry/Campbell, Bobbie Gentry and Glen Campbell (Capitol)
Dean Martin's Greatest Hits, Volume I, Dean Martin (Reprise)
Yellow Submarine, The Beatles (Apple)
Steppenwolf the Second, Steppenwolf (Dunhill)
Who Will Answer? Ed Ames (RCA)
Boots With Strings, Boots Randolph (Monument)
Dionne Warwick's Greatest Hits, Dionne Warwick (Scepter)
A Man Without Love, Engelbert Humperdinck (Parrot)
The Last Waltz, Engelbert Humperdinck (Parrot)
The Association's Greatest Hits, The Association (Warner Bros.)
Wednesday Morning 3 A.M., Simon & Garfunkel (Columbia)
Wonderland by Night, Bert Kaempfert (Decca)
Bert Kaempfert's Greatest Hits, Bert Kaempfert (Decca)
Drummer Boy, Harry Simeone (20th Century Fox)
200 MPH, Bill Cosby (Warner Bros.)
Hair—Original Cast (RCA)
It Must Be Him, Ray Conniff (Columbia)
Young Girl, Union Gap (Columbia)
His Hand In Mine, Elvis Presley (RCA)
Blood, Sweat and Tears, Blood, Sweat and Tears (Columbia)
Galveston, Glen Campbell (Capitol)
Freedom Suite, The Rascals (Atlantic)
Goodbye, Cream (Atco)
Donovan's Greatest Hits, Donovan (Epic)
2001: A Space Odyssey—Soundtrack (MGM)
Soulin', Lou Rawls (Capitol)
Best of The Lettermen, The Lettermen (Capitol)
Nashville Skyline, Bob Dylan (Columbia)
Fever Zone, Tom Jones (Parrot)
Help Yourself, Tom Jones (Parrot)
Equinox, Sergio Mendez & Brasil '66 (A & M)
A Day In The Life, Wes Montgomery (A&M)
Fool On The Hill, Sergio Mendes & Brasil '66 (A&M)
The Righteous Brothers Greatest Hits, The Righteous Brothers (Verve)
This Is Tom Jones, Tom Jones (Parrot)
H. William's Greatest Hits, Hank Williams (MGM)
The Very Best of Connie Francis, Connie Francis (MGM)

How the West Was Won—Soundtrack (MGM)
Your Cheatin' Heart, Hank Williams (MGM)
The Best of Herman's Hermits Vol. II, Herman's Hermits (MGM)
The Stripper and Other Fun Songs For the Family, David Rose and Orchestra (MGM)
There's a Kind of Hush All Over the World, Herman's Hermits (MGM)
Romeo & Juliet—Soundtrack (Capitol)
Tom Jones Live! Tom Jones (Parrot)
The Age of Aquarius, 5th Dimension (Soul City)
Elvis TV Special, Elvis Presley (RCA)
Ball, Iron Butterfly (Atco)
Led Zeppelin, Led Zeppelin (Atlantic)
Johnny Cash's Greatest Hits, Johnny Cash (Columbia)
Oliver—Soundtrack (Colgems)
The Soft Parade, The Doors (Elektra)
Johnny Cash at San Quentin, Johnny Cash (Columbia)
Switched On Bach, Walter Carlos (Columbia)
Three Dog Night, Three Dog Night (Dunhill)
Tommy, The Who (Decca)
Blind Faith, Blind Faith (Atco)
Happy Heart, Andy Williams (Columbia)
Gentle On My Mind, Dean Martin (Reprise)
Through the Past, Darkly, The Rolling Stones (London)
The Good, the Bad and the Ugly, Hugo Montenegro (RCA)
A Warm Shade of Ivory, Henry Mancini (RCA)
Glen Campbell—"Live," Glen Campbell (Capitol)
Alice's Restaurant, Arlo Guthrie (Reprise)
Realization, Johnny Rivers (Imperial)
Golden Greats, Gary Lewis (Liberty)
Crosby, Stills & Nash, Crosby, Stills & Nash (Atlantic)
Who Knows Where The Time Goes, Judy Collins (Elektra)
Golden Instrumentals, Billy Vaughn and Orchestra
Jimi Hendrix Smash Hits, Jimi Hendrix (Reprise)
Abbey Road, The Beatles (Apple)
Tom Jones—Live at Las Vegas, Tom Jones (Parrot)
Best of Cream, Cream (Atco)
Best of The Bee Gees, The Bee Gees (Atco)
Led Zeppelin II, Led Zeppelin (Atlantic)
Green Green Grass, Tom Jones (Parrot)
Let It Bleed, Rolling Stones (London)
The Band, The Band (Capitol)
Santana, Santana (Columbia)
The Child Is Father To The Man, Blood, Sweat & Tears (Columbia)
Kozmic Blues, Janis Joplin (Columbia)
Stand! Sly and the Family Stone (Epic)
Suitable for Framing, Three Dog Night (Dunhill)
Cycles, Frank Sinatra (Reprise)
Hot Buttered Soul, Isaac Hayes (Enterprise)
From Vegas to Memphis, Elvis Presley (RCA)
Chicago Transit Authority, Chicago Transit Authority (Columbia)
Buddy Holly Story, Buddy Holly and The Crickets (Decca)
Honey, Ray Conniff (Columbia)

1970

Engelbert, Engelbert Humperdinck (Parrot)
Engelbert Humperdinck, Engelbert Humperdinck
  (Parrot)
Captured Live At the Forum, Three Dog Night (Dunhill)
Easy Rider—Soundtrack (Dunhill)
The Best of Charley Pride, Charley Pride (RCA)
Volunteers, Jefferson Airplane (RCA)
Crown of Creation, Jefferson Airplane (RCA)
From Elvis in Memphis, Elvis Presley (RCA)
Hello, I'm Johnny Cash, Johnny Cash (Columbia)
See What Tomorrow Brings, Peter, Paul and Mary
  (Warner)
Alive Alive-O! Jose Feliciano (RCA)
Bridge over Troubled Water, Simon & Garfunkel
  (Columbia)
Bobby Sherman, Bobby Sherman (Metromedia)
Mantovani's Golden Hits, Mantovani (London)
Try a Little Kindness, Glen Campbell (Capitol)
Get Together, Andy Williams (Columbia)
Morrison Hotel, The Doors (Elektra)
Goin' Out Of My Head, The Lettermen (Capitol)
Hey Jude, The Beatles (Apple)
My Way, Frank Sinatra (Reprise)
The Plastic Ono Band—Live Peace in Toronto, The
  Plastic Ono Band (Apple)
Monster, Steppenwolf (Dunhill)
Feliciano/10 to 23, Jose Feliciano (RCA)
Deja Vu, Crosby, Stills, Nash and Young (Atlantic)
Up, Up and Away, Fifth Dimension (Soul City)
Warm, Herb Alpert and The Tijuana Brass (A & M)
A Gift From a Flower to a Garden, Donovan (Epic)
*Don't Come Home a Drinkin' (With Lovin' On Your
  Mind)*, Loretta Lynn (Decca)
Chicago, Chicago (Columbia)
Tammy's Greatest Hits, Tammy Wynette (Epic)
Claudine, Claudine Longet (A & M)
Joe Cocker, Joe Cocker (A & M)
Tom, Tom Jones (Parrot)
A Song Will Rise, Peter, Paul and Mary (Warner)
McCartney, Paul McCartney (Apple)
Midnight Cowboy—Soundtrack (United Artists)
The Fifth Dimension—Greatest Hits, 5th Dimension
  (Soul City)
Butch Cassidy and the Sundance Kid, Burt Bacharach
  (A & M)
The Ventures Play Telstar, The Lonely Bull and Others.
  The Ventures (Dolton)
Golden Greats, The Ventures (Liberty)
American Woman, The Guess Who (RCA)
Let It Be, The Beatles (Apple)
Woodstock (Cotillion)
Band of Gypsys, Jimi Hendrix (Capitol)
Hurt So Bad, Lettermen (Capitol)
Self Portrait, Bob Dylan (Columbia)
Grand Funk, Grand Funk Railroad (Capitol)
Here Comes Bobby, Bobby Sherman (Metromedia)
Blood, Sweat and Tears 3, Blood, Sweat and Tears
  (Columbia)
Live Steppenwolf, Steppenwolf (Dunhill)

Golden Grass, Grass Roots (Dunhill)
It Ain't Easy, Three Dog Night (Dunhill)
Raindrops Keep Fallin' on My Head, B.J. Thomas (Scep-
  ter)
To Our Children's Children's Children, Moody Blues
  (Threshold)
The Devil Made Me Buy This Dress, Flip Wilson (Little
  David)
Absolutely Live, Doors (Elektra)
Live at Leeds, The Who (Decca)
Here Where There Is Love, Dionne Warwick (Scepter)
Valley of the Dolls, Dionne Warwick (Scepter)
Closer to Home, Grand Funk Railroad (Capitol)
Mountain Climbing, Climbing (Windfall)
Mad Dogs & Englishmen, Joe Cocker (A&M)
Days of Future Passed, Moody Blues (Deram)
On the Threshold of a Dream, Moody Blues (Deram)
Okie From Muskogee, Merle Haggard and The Strangers
  (Capitol)
Led Zeppelin III, Led Zeppelin (Atlantic)
Edizione D'Oro, Four Seasons (Philips)
On Time, Grand Funk Railroad (Capitol)
Everybody Knows This Is Nowhere, Neil Young with
  Crazy Horse (Reprise)
Best of Peter, Paul and Mary (Ten) Years Together,
  Peter, Paul and Mary (Warner)
Sweet Baby James, James Taylor (Warner)
Stage Fright, The Band (Capitol)
Paint Your Wagon—Sountrack (Paramount)
Abraxas, Santana (Columbia)
Sesame Street—Original Cast (Columbia)
With Love, Bobby, Bobby Sherman (Metromedia)
Get Yer Ya-Ya's Out!, The Rolling Stones (London)
The Question of Balance, The Moody Blues (Threshold)
Jimi Hendrix/Otis Redding at Monterey—Monterey
  Pop Soundtrack (Reprise)
After the Gold Rush, Neil Young (Reprise)
Make It Easy On Yourself, Burt Bacharach (A&M)
Close to You, The Carpenters (A&M)
Reach Out, Burt Bacharach (A&M)
With a Little Help From My Friends, Joe Cocker
  (A&M)
Gold, Neil Diamond (UNI)
Benefit, Jethro Tull (Reprise)
Merry Christmas, Bing Crosby (Decca)
Share The Land, The Guess Who (RCA)
Sly & The Family Stone's Greatest Hits, Sly & The Fam-
  ily Stone (Epic)
Nancy & Lee, Nancy Sinatra and Lee Hazlewood
  (Reprise)
Frank Sinatra's Greatest Hits, Frank Sinatra (Reprise)
Live Album, Grand Funk Railroad (Capitol)
Stephen Stills, Stephen Stills (Atlantic)
Jim Nabors' Christmas Album, Jim Nabors (Columbia)
Super Session, Bloomfield/Kooper/Stills (Columbia)
Touching You, Touching Me, Neil Diamond (UNI)
In Search of the Lost Chord, The Moody Blues (Deram)
New Morning, Bob Dylan (Columbia)
Cosmo's Factory, Creedence Clearwater Revival
  (Fantasy)

1970 *(cont'd)*

Willy and the Poor Boys, Creedence Clearwater Revival (Fantasy)

Green River, Creedence Clearwater Revival (Fantasy)

Bayou Country, Creedence Clearwater Revival (Fantasy)

Creedence Clearwater Revival, Creedence Clearwater Revival (Fantasy)

All Things Must Pass, George Harrison (Apple)

The Partridge Family Album, The Partridge Family (Bell)

Pendulum, Creedence Clearwater Revival (Fantasy)

The Freewheelin' Bob Dylan, Bob Dylan (Columbia)

John Barleycorn Must Die, Traffic (United Artists)

We Made It Happen, Engelbert Humperdinck (Parrot)

Jesus Christ Superstar, Various Artists (Decca)

Ladies of the Canyon, Joni Mitchell (Reprise)

Dean Martin's Greatest Hits Vol. II, Dean Martin (Reprise)

Portrait, 5th Dimension (Bell)

In My Life, Judy Collins (Elektra)

1971

I Who Have Nothing, Tom Jones (Parrot)

Taproot Manuscript, Neil Diamond (UNI)

Plastic Ono Band, John Lennon (Apple)

Love Story—Soundtrack (Paramount)

Chicago III, Chicago (Columbia)

The Worst of Jefferson Airplane, Jefferson Airplane (RCA)

Elton John, Elton John (UNI)

On Stage February 1970, Elvis Presley (RCA)

Charley Pride's 10th Album, Charley Pride (RCA)

Just Plain Charley, Charley Pride (RCA)

Charley Pride in Person, Charley Pride (RCA)

Pearl, Janis Joplin (Columbia)

For the Good Times, Ray Price (Columbia)

The Fightin' Side of Me, Merle Haggard and the Strangers (Capitol)

Gary Puckett and the Union Gap's Greatest Hits, Gary Puckett and the Union Gap (Columbia)

Tumbleweed Connection, Elton John (UNI)

Love Story, Andy Williams (Columbia)

Rose Garden, Lynn Anderson (Columbia)

Up To Date, Partridge Family (Bell)

The Cry of Love, Jimi Hendrix (Reprise)

Woodstock II (Cotillion)

Friends, Elton John (Paramount)

Whales & Nightingales, Judy Collins (Elektra)

If I Could Only Remember My Name, David Crosby (Atlantic)

Naturally, Three Dog Night (ABC/Dunhill)

Steppenwolf 7, Steppenwolf (ABC/Dunhill)

Golden Bisquits, Three Dog Night (ABC/Dunhill)

Steppenwolf Gold, Steppenwolf (ABC/Dunhill)

Greatest Hits, Herb Alpert and The Tijuana Brass (A & M)

Four Way Street, Crosby, Stills, Nash, & Young (Atlantic)

Stoney End, Barbra Streisand (Columbia)

Survival, Grand Funk Railroad (Capitol)

Mud Slide Slim and The Blue Horizon, James Taylor (Warner Bros.)

Greatest Hits, Barbra Streisand (Columbia)

Paranoid, Black Sabbath (Warner Bros.)

Sticky Fingers, Rolling Stones (Rolling Stones)

Tea For The Tillerman, Cat Stevens (A & M)

Sweetheart, Engelbert Humperdinck (Parrot)

Nantucket Sleigh Ride, Mountain (Windfall)

Love's Lines Angels and Rhymes, Fifth Dimension (Bell)

Carpenters, The Carpenters (A & M)

Tapestry, Carole King, (Ode)

Ram, Paul and Linda McCartney (Apple)

Black Sabbath, Black Sabbath (Warner Bros.)

If You Could Read My Mind, Gordon Lightfoot (Warner/Reprise)

The Best of The Guess Who, The Guess Who (RCA)

Hawaii 5-0, The Ventures (UA/Liberty)

Aqualung, Jethro Tull (Reprise)

Aretha Franklin at the Fillmore West, Aretha Franklin (Atlantic)

Burt Bacharach, Burt Bacharach (A & M)

L. A. Woman, The Doors (Elektra)

Every Picture Tells A Story, Rod Stewart (Mercury)

Emerson, Lake & Palmer, Emerson, Lake & Palmer (Cotillion)

B. S. & T. 4, Blood Sweat and Tears (Columbia)

Layla, Derek & The Dominos (Atco)

Chapter Two, Roberta Flack (Atlantic)

Stephen Stills 2, Stephen Stills (Atlantic)

Songs for Beginners, Graham Nash (Atlantic)

Tarkus, Emerson, Lake & Palmer (Cotillion)

Bark, Jefferson Airplane (Grunt)

Every Good Boy Deserves Favour, Moody Blues (Threshold)

Osmonds, The Osmond Bros. (MGM)

Andy Williams' Greatest Hits, Andy Williams (Columbia)

Poems, Prayers and Promises, John Denver (RCA)

Who's Next, The Who (Decca)

Master of Reality, Black Sabbath (Warner Bros.)

Sound Magazine, Partridge Family (Bell)

Imagine, John Lennon (Apple)

Santana, Santana (Columbia)

Harmony, Three Dog Night (ABC/Dunhill)

Fiddler on the Roof—Soundtrack (United Artists)

Teaser & The Firecat, Cat Stevens (A & M)

The Allman Brothers Band At Fillmore East, The Allman Brothers (Capricorn)

James Gang Rides Again, James Gang (ABC/Dunhill)

A Partridge Family Christmas Card, The Partridge Family (Bell)

There's a Riot Goin' On, Sly & The Family Stone (Epic)

Live at Carnegie Hall, Chicago (Columbia)

Blue, Joni Mitchell (Reprise)

Grateful Dead, Grateful Dead (Warner Bros.)

Led Zeppelin, Led Zeppelin (Atlantic)

E Pluribus Funk, Grand Funk Railroad (Capitol)

Barbra Joan Streisand, Barbra Streisand (Columbia)

Rainbow Bridge, Jimi Hendrix (Reprise)

A Space in Time, Ten Years After (Columbia)

1971 *(cont'd)*
Carole King Music, Carole King (Ode)
Candles In The Rain, Melanie (Buddah)
All In The Family—Original Cast (Atlantic)
The Donny Osmond Album, Donny Osmond (MGM)
Live, Fifth Dimension (Bell)
The World of Johnny Cash, Johnny Cash (Columbia)
Dionne Warwicke Story—Decade of Gold, Dionne Warwicke (Scepter)

1972
American Pie, Don McLean (United Artists)
Bob Dylan's Greatest Hits, Vol. II, Bob Dylan (Columbia)
The Concert for Bangla Desh, George Harrison & Friends (Apple)
Aerie, John Denver (RCA)
She's A Lady, Tom Jones (Parrot)
Wildlife, Wings (Apple)
Meaty, Beaty, Big & Bouncy, The Who (Decca)
Stones, Neil Diamond (UNI)
Loretta Lynn's Greatest Hits, Loretta Lynn (Decca)
Homemade, Osmonds (MGM)
Hot Rocks, Rolling Stones (London)
To You With Love, Donny Osmond (MGM)
Killer, Alice Cooper (Warner Bros.)
Blessed Are, Joan Baez (Vanguard)
Any Day Now, Joan Baez (Vanguard)
Leon Russell & the Shelter People, Leon Russell (Shelter)
A Nod Is as Good as a Wing . . . To A Blind Horse, Faces (Warner Bros.)
Low Spark of High Heeled Boys, Traffic (Island)
Charley Pride Sings Heart Songs, Charley Pride (RCA)
Harvest, Neil Young (Warner/Reprise)
Madman Across The Water, Elton John (UNI)
Rockin' The Fillmore, Humble Pie (A & M)
Paul Simon, Paul Simon (Columbia)
Nilsson Schmilsson, Nilsson (RCA)
Baby I'm A Want You, Bread (Elektra)
America, America (Warner Bros.)
Fragile, Yes (Atlantic)
Tom Jones Live at Caesars Palace, Tom Jones (Parrot)
Another Time, Another Place, Engelbert Humperdinck (Parrot)
Eat a Peach, Allman Bros. Band (Capricorn)
Cher, Cher Bono (Kapp)
Pictures At An Exhibition, Emerson, Lake & Palmer (Atlantic)
First Take, Roberta Flack (Atlantic)
Quiet Fire, Roberta Flack (Atlantic)
Young, Gifted and Black, Aretha Franklin (Atlantic)
Let's Stay Together, Al Green (Hi)
All I Ever Need Is You, Sonny & Cher (Kapp)
Blood Sweat & Tears Greatest Hits, Blood, Sweat and Tears (Columbia)
Glen Campbell's Greatest Hits, Glen Campbell (Capitol)
Hello Darlin', Conway Twitty (Decca)
Partridge Family Shopping Bag, Partridge Family (Bell)
Thick As A Brick, Jethro Tull (Warner/Reprise)

Hendrix In The West, Jimi Hendrix (Warner/Reprise)
Phase III, The Osmonds (MGM)
Exile on Main Street, Rolling Stones (Rolling Stones)
Graham Nash & David Crosby, Graham Nash & David Crosby (Atlantic)
Manassas, Stephen Stills (Atlantic)
Mark, Don & Mel, Grand Funk Railroad (Capitol)
Mardi Gras, Creedence Clearwater Revival (Fantasy)
Gather Me, Melanie (Neighborhood)
13, The Doors (Elektra)
Joplin in Concert, Janis Joplin (Columbia)
All Day Music, War (United Artists)
Live in Concert, James Gang, (ABC/Dunhill)
Cherish, David Cassidy (Bell)
Simon & Garfunkel's Greatest Hits, Simon & Garfunkel (Columbia)
School's Out, Alice Cooper (Warner Bros.)
A Song For You, The Carpenters (A & M)
Thirds, James Gang (ABC/Dunhill)
History of Eric Clapton, Eric Clapton (Atco)
Amazing Grace, Aretha Franklin (Atlantic)
Roberta Flack & Donny Hathaway, Roberta Flack & Donny Hathaway (Atlantic)
Honky Chateau, Elton John (UNI)
Sonny & Cher Live, Sonny & Cher (Kapp)
Seven Separate Fools, Three Dog Night (ABC/Dunhill)
Never A Dull Moment, Rod Stewart (Mercury)
Cheech & Chong, Cheech & Chong (Ode)
Chicago V, Chicago (Columbia)
Elvis as Recorded at Madison Square Garden, Elvis Presley (RCA)
Carlos Santana & Buddy Miles 'Live', Carlos Santana and Buddy Miles
Their Sixteen Greatest Hits, The Grassroots (ABC/Dunhill)
Donny Hathaway Live, Donny Hathaway (Atco)
Big Bambu, Cheech & Chong (Ode)
Procol Harum 'Live' in Concert with the Edmonton Symphony Orchestra, Procol Harum (A & M)
Love Theme from "The Godfather," Andy Williams (Columbia)
Moods, Neil Diamond (UNI)
Trilogy, Emerson, Lake & Palmer (Cotillion)
Still Bill, Bill Withers (Sussex)
Super Fly (Original motion picture soundtrack), Curtis Mayfield (Curtom)
Smokin', Humble Pie (A & M)
What You Hear Is What You Get, Ike and Tina Turner (United Artists)
Carney, Leon Russell (Shelter)
FM & AM, George Carlin (Little David)
Phoenix, Grand Funk Railroad (Capitol)
Catch Bull At Four, Cat Stevens (A & M)
The Best of Charley Pride, Charley Pride (RCA)
Easy Loving, Freddie Hart (Capitol)
The London Chuck Berry Session, Chuck Berry (Chess)
Demons and Wizards, Uriah Heep (Mercury)
Close to the Edge, Yes (Atlantic)
Rhymes & Reasons, Carole King (Ode)
The Best of Merle Haggard, Merle Haggard (Capitol)

1972 *(cont'd)*

Rock of Ages, The Band (Capitol)

Machine Head, Deep Purple (Warner Bros.)

Black Sabbath—Vol. IV, Black Sabbath (Warner Bros.)

Love It To Death, Alice Cooper (Warner Bros.)

Stand Up, Jethro Tull (Warner/Reprise)

Living In The Past, Jethro Tull (Chrysalis)

Caravanserai, Santana (Columbia)

Guitar Man, Bread (Elektra)

Seventh Sojourn, Moody Blues (Threshold)

It's A Beautiful Day, It's A Beautiful Day (Columbia)

I'm Still In Love With You, Al Green (Hi)

Chilling, Thrilling Sounds of The Haunted House—Soundtrack (Disneyland)

No Secrets, Carly Simon (Elektra)

Greatest Hits On Earth, Fifth Dimension (Bell)

Godspell—Original Cast (Bell)

The Partridge Family At Home With Their Greatest Hits, Partridge Family (Bell)

Tommy, London Symphony Orch. and Chamber Choir with Guest Soloists (Ode)

The World Is A Ghetto, War (United Artists)

Summer Breeze, Seals & Crofts (Warner Bros.)

Europe '72, Grateful Dead (Warner Bros.)

One Man Dog, James Taylor (Warner Bros.)

Homecoming, America (Warner Bros.)

Summer of '42, Peter Nero (Columbia)

An Anthology, Duane Allman (Capricorn)

Manna, Bread (Elektra)

On The Waters, Bread (Elektra)

For The Roses, Joni Mitchell (Asylum)

Hot August Night, Neil Diamond (MCA)

Portrait of Donny, Donny Osmond (MGM)

The Osmonds 'Live', The Osmonds (MGM)

Son of Schmilsson, Nilsson (RCA)

Rocky Mountain High, John Denver (RCA)

1973

Long John Silver, Jefferson Airplane (Grunt)

More Hot Rocks (Big Hits and Fazed Cookies), Rolling Stones (London)

The Magician's Birthday, Uriah Heep (Mercury)

Crazy Horses, Osmonds (MGM)

Too Young, Donny Osmond (MGM)

Creedence Gold, Creedence Clearwater Revival (Fantasy)

The Happiest Girl in the Whole U.S.A., Donna Fargo (Dot)

Loggins & Messina, Loggins & Messina (Columbia)

360 Degrees of Billy Paul, Billy Paul (Phila. Intl.)

Don't Shoot Me I'm Only the Piano Player, Elton John (MCA)

World Wide 50 Gold Award Hits, Vol. I, Elvis Presley (RCA)

Elvis—Aloha From Hawaii Via Satellite, Elvis Presley (RCA)

Live Concert at the Forum, Barbra Streisand (Columbia)

The Stylistics, The Stylistics (Avco)

Around the World With Three Dog Night, Three Dog Night (ABC/Dunhill)

I Am Woman, Helen Reddy (Capitol)

Shoot Out at the Fantasy Factory, Traffic (Island)

Dueling Banjos—motion picture soundtrack from *Deliverance*, as performed by Eric Weissberg & Steve Mandel (Warner Bros.)

Baby Don't Get Hooked on Me, Mac Davis (Columbia)

Wattstax—The Living Word—Various Artists (Stax)

In Concert, Derek & the Dominos (RSO)

Billion Dollar Babies, Alice Cooper (Warner Bros.)

Kenny Rogers & The First Edition Greatest Hits, Kenny Rogers & The First Edition (Warner Reprise)

Houses of the Holy, Led Zeppelin (Atlantic)

The Best of Bread, Bread (Elektra)

Who Do We Think We Are!, Deep Purple (Warner Bros.)

The Beatles 1962–1966, The Beatles (Apple)

The Beatles 1966–1970, The Beatles (Apple)

The Dark Side of the Moon, Pink Floyd (Harvest)

The Divine Miss M, Bette Midler (Atlantic)

They Only Come Out At Night, Edgar Winter Group (Epic)

Back Stabbers, The O'Jays (Phila. Intl.)

Sittin's In, Loggins & Messina (Columbia)

Yessongs, Yes (Atlantic)

The Yes Album, Yes (Atlantic)

Red Rose Speedway, Paul McCartney & Wings (Apple)

William E. McEuen Presents Will the Circle Be Unbroken, The Nitty Gritty Dirt Band (United Artists)

Can't Buy A Thrill, Steely Dan (ABC Dunhill)

Made in Japan, Deep Purple (Warner Bros.)

Living in the Material World, George Harrison (Apple)

Curtis, Curtis Mayfield (Curtom)

Back to the World, Curtis Mayfield (Curtom)

Now & Then, The Carpenters (A & M)

Class Clown, George Carlin (Little David)

The Sensational Charley Pride, Charley Pride (RCA)

From Me To You, Charley Pride (RCA)

The Country Way, Charley Pride (RCA)

Round 2, The Stylistics (Avco)

There Goes Rhymin' Simon, Paul Simon (Columbia)

Moving Waves, Focus (Sire)

Diamond Girl, Seals & Crofts (Warner Bros.)

Fantasy, Carole King, (Ode)

Lone Live, Leon Russell (Shelter)

Elvis—That's the Way It Is, Elvis Presley (RCA)

Live at the Sahara Tahoe, Isaac Hayes (Stax)

The Captain and Me, Doobie Brothers (Warner Bros.)

Call Me, Al Green (London)

Spinners, Spinners (Atlantic)

Chicago VI, Chicago (Columbia)

Dick Clark: 20 Years of Rock'N Roll—Original Artists (Buddah)

A Passion Play, Jethro Tull (Chrysalis)

Foreigner, Cat Stevens (A & M)

Cabaret—Original Soundtrack (ABC Dunhill)

Fresh, Sly & The Family Stone (Epic)

We're An American Band, Grand Funk Railroad (Capitol)

Brothers and Sisters, Allman Bros. Band (Capricorn)

Toulouse Street, Doobie Brothers

Killing Me Softly, Roberta Flack (Atlantic)

Farewell Andromeda, John Denver (RCA)

1973 *(cont'd)*
Jesus Christ Superstar—Original Movie Soundtrack (MCA)
Anticipation, Carly Simon (Elektra)
Deliver the Word, War (United Artists)
Bloodshot, J. Geils Band (Atlantic)
My Best to You, Donny Osmond (Kolob)
Love Devotion Surrender, Carlos Santana and Mahavishnu John McLaughlin (Columbia)
Long Hard Climb, Helen Reddy (Capitol)
Beginnings, Allman Brothers Band (Atco)
Goats Head Soup, Rolling Stones (Rolling Stones)
Focus 3, Focus (Sire)
Los Cochinos, Cheech & Chong (Ode)
Goodbye Yellow Brick Road, Elton John (MCA)
Cyan, Three Dog Night (ABC/Dunhill)
Sing It Again Rod, Rod Stewart (Mercury)
Uriah Heep Live, Uriah Heep (Mercury)
Angel Clare, Art Garfunkel (Columbia)
Quadrophenia, The Who (MCA)
Meddle, Pink Floyd (Harvest)
Jonathan Livingston Seagull—Neil Diamond/Original Soundtrack (Columbia)
The Golden Age of Rock'N Roll, Sha Na Na (Kama Sutra)
Life and Times, Jim Croce (ABC)
The Smoker You Drink, The Player You Get, Joe Walsh (ABC/Dunhill)
Imagination, Gladys Knight & The Pips (Buddah)
I've Got So Much to Give, Barry White (20th Century)
Head to the Sky, Earth, Wind & Fire (Columbia)
Ringo, Ringo Starr (Apple)
The Silver Tongued Devil and I, Kris Kristofferson (Monument)
3 + 3, Isley Brothers (T-Neck)
You Don't Mess around with Jim, Jim Croce (ABC/Dunhill)
Behind Closed Doors, Charlie Rich (Epic)
Joy, Isaac Hayes (Stax)
Welcome, Santana (Columbia)
Jesus Was A Capricorn, Kris Kristofferson (Monument)
Mind Games, John Lennon (Apple)
I Got A Name, Jim Croce (ABC/Dunhill)
The Joker, Steve Miller Band (Capitol)
Muscle of Love, Alice Cooper (Warner Bros.)
Full Sail, Loggins & Messina (Columbia)
Time Fades Away, Neil Young (Warner-Reprise)
Band on the Run, Paul McCartney & Wings (Apple)
John Denver's Greatest Hits, John Denver (RCA)
The Singles 1969–1973, The Carpenters (A & M)
Brain Salad Surgery, Emerson, Lake & Palmer (Manticore)
Bette Midler, Bette Midler (Atlantic)
Snowbird, Anne Murray (Capitol)
Dylan, Bob Dylan (Columbia)
American Graffiti—Movie Soundtrack (MCA)

1974
The Early Beatles, The Beatles (Apple)
The Lord's Prayer, Jim Nabors (Columbia)
Ship Ahoy, The O'Jays (Phila. Intl.)

Livin' for You, Al Green (Hi)
Eagles, Eagles (Asylum)
Colors of the Day, Judy Collins (Elektra)
Hot Cakes, Carly Simon (Elektra)
Planet Waves, Bob Dylan (Asylum)
Johnny Winter Live, Johnny Winter (Columbia)
The Pointer Sisters, The Pointer Sisters (Blue Thumb)
Alone Together, Dave Mason (Blue Thumb)
Under the Influence of Love Unlimited, Love Unlimited (20th Century)
Stone Gon', Barry White (20th Century Fox)
Live—Full House, J. Geils Band (Atlantic)
Tales from Topographic Oceans, Yes (Atlantic)
The Way We Were, Barbra Streisand (Columbia)
Court and Spark, Joni Mitchell (Asylum)
Ummagumma, Pink Floyd (Harvest)
Half Breed, Cher (MCA)
Sweet Freedom, Uriah Heep (Warner Bros.)
Laid Back, Greg Allman (Capricorn)
Unborn Child, Seals & Crofts (Warner Bros.)
War Live, War (United Artists)
The Payback, James Brown (Polydor)
Chicago VII, Chicago (Columbia)
Burn, Deep Purple (Warner Bros.)
Sabbath, Bloody Sabbath, Black Sabbath (Warner Bros.)
Tubular Bells, Mike Oldfield (Virgin)
Shinin' On, Grand Funk Railroad (Capitol)
What Were Once Vices Are Now Habits, Doobie Brothers (Warner Bros.)
Buddha and The Chocolate Box, Cat Stevens (A & M)
Love Is the Message, MFSB (Phila. Intl.)
Hard Labor, Three Dog Night (ABC/Dunhill)
The Sting—Original Motion Picture Soundtrack (MCA)
Very Special Love Songs, Charlie Rich (Epic)
Head Hunters, Herbie Hancock (Columbia)
Rhapsody in White, Love Unlimited Orchestra (20th Century)
The Best of the Best of Merle Haggard, Merle Haggard (Capitol)
Bachman-Turner Overdrive II, Bachman-Turner Overdrive (Mercury)
Wild and Peaceful, Kool & The Gang (De-Lite)
Maria Muldaur, Maria Muldaur (Warner-Reprise)
Open Our Eyes, Earth, Wind & Fire (Columbia)
Pretzel Logic, Steely Dan (ABC)
The Way We Were—Original Soundtrack Recording (Columbia)
Mighty Love, The Spinners (Atlantic)
Tres Hombres, Z. Z. Top (London)
Sundown, Gordon Lightfoot (Reprise)
It's Been A Long Time, The New Birth (RCA)
On the Border, Eagles (Asylum)
Love Song for Jeffrey, Helen Reddy (Capitol)
Claudine—Motion Picture Soundtrack, Gladys Knight & The Pips (Buddah)
Live Rhymin', Paul Simon (Columbia)
Ziggy Stardust, David Bowie (RCA)
On Stage, Loggins & Messina (Columbia)
Back Home Again, John Denver (RCA)
Skin Tight, Ohio Players (Mercury)
Caribou, Elton John (MCA)

1974 *(cont'd)*

The Great Gatsby—Original Soundtrack Recording (Paramount)

Before the Flood, Bob Dylan & The Band (Asylum)

Workingman's Dead, The Grateful Dead (Warner Bros.)

American Beauty, The Grateful Dead (Warner Bros.)

Shock Treatment, The Edgar Winter Group (Epic)

That's A Plenty, The Pointer Sisters (Blue Thumb)

Diamond Dogs, David Bowie (RCA)

461 Ocean Boulevard, Eric Clapton (RSO)

Let's Put It All Together, The Stylistics (Avco)

Endless Summer, The Beach Boys (Capitol)

Not Fragile, Bachman-Turner Overdrive (Mercury)

Journey to the Centre of the Earth, Rick Wakeman (A & M)

Rags to Rufus, Rufus (ABC)

If You Love Me, Let Me Know, Olivia Newton-John (MCA)

His 12 Greatest Hits, Neil Diamond (MCA)

Bridge of Sighs, Robin Trower (Chrysalis)

Can't Get Enough, Barry White (20th Century Fox)

So Far, Crosby, Stills, Nash & Young (Atlantic)

Welcome Back, My Friends, To The Show That Never Ends—Ladies and Gentlemen, Emerson, Lake & Palmer (Manticore)

Bad Company, Bad Company (Swan Song)

Moontan, Golden Earring (MCA)

Second Helping, Lynyrd Skynyrd (MCA)

Desperado, Eagles (Asylum)

The Souther-Hillman-Furay Band, The Souther-Hillman-Furay Band (Asylum)

Stop and Smell the Roses, Mac Davis (Columbia)

On the Beach, Neil Young (Reprise)

Santana's Greatest Hits, Santana (Columbia)

The Beach Boys in Concert, The Beach Boys (Reprise)

Black Oak Arkansas, Black Oak Arkansas (Atco)

Body Heat, Quincy Jones (A & M)

Cheech and Chong's Wedding Album, Cheech & Chong (Ode)

Bachman-Turner Overdrive, Bachman-Turner Overdrive (Mercury)

Let Me Be There, Olivia Newton-John (MCA)

Alice Cooper's Greatest Hits, Alice Cooper (Warner Bros.)

Wrap Around Joy, Carole King, (Ode)

Photographs and Memories, His Greatest Hits, Jim Croce (ABC)

Walls and Bridges, John Lennon (Apple)

There Won't Be Anymore, Charlie Rich (RCA)

Serenade, Neil Diamond (Columbia)

Holiday, America (Warner Bros.)

It's Only Rock'N' Roll, The Rolling Stones (Rolling Stones)

Live It Up, The Isley Brothers (T-Neck)

When the Eagle Flies, Traffic (Island)

David Live, David Bowie (RCA)

Small Talk, Sly & the Family Stone (Epic)

War Child, Jethro Tull (Chrysalis)

Greatest Hits, Elton John (MCA)

I Feel A Song, Gladys Knight & The Pips (Buddah)

Anka, Paul Anka (United Artists)

Mother Lode, Loggins & Messina (Columbia)

Miles of Aisles, Joni Mitchell (Asylum)

I Don't Know How To Love Him, Helen Reddy (Capitol)

This Is the Moody Blues, Moody Blues (Threshold)

Here's Johnny . . . Magic Moments from The Tonight Show—Various Artists (Casablanca)

Melodies of Love, Bobby Vinton (ABC)

Odds and Sods, The Who (MCA)

Goodnight Vienna, Ringo Starr (Apple)

Fire, Ohio Players (Mercury)

Dark Horse, George Harrison (Apple)

Verities and Balderdash, Harry Chapin (Elektra)

Me and Bobby McGee, Kris Kristofferson (Monument)

Roadwork, Edgar Winter (Epic)

New and Improved, The Spinners (Atlantic)

Relayer, Yes (Atlantic)

Free and Easy, Helen Reddy (Capitol)

All The Girls In The World Beware!!!, Grand Funk Railroad (Capitol)

Pronounced Leh-nerd Skin-nerd, Lynyrd Skynyrd (MCA)

Late For The Sky, Jackson Browne (Asylum)

The Best of Bread: Vol. II, Bread (Elektra)

Rufusized, Rufus (ABC)

1975

Butterfly, Barbra Streisand (Columbia)

Elvis—A Legendary Performer, Vol. I, Elvis Presley (RCA)

Did You Think To Pray, Charley Pride (RCA)

Stormbringer, Deep Purple (Warner Bros.)

Al Green Explores Your Mind, Al Green (Hi)

Average White Band, Average White Band (Atlantic)

Joy To The World—Their Greatest Hits, Three Dog Night (ABC/Dunhill)

So What, Joe Walsh (ABC/Dunhill)

Caught Up, Millie Jackson (Spring)

Heart Like a Wheel, Linda Ronstadt (Capitol)

Dawn's New Ragtime Follies, Dawn (Bell)

Blood On The Tracks, Bob Dylan (Columbia)

An Evening With John Denver, John Denver (RCA)

Dragon Fly, Jefferson Starship (Grunt)

I'm Leaving It All Up To You, Marie & Donny Osmond (MGM)

Have You Never Been Mellow, Olivia Newton-John (MCA)

Something/Anything?, Todd Rundgren (Bearsville)

Energized, Foghat (Bearsville)

Together for the First Time, Bobby Bland/B. B. King (ABC/Dunhill)

Physical Graffiti, Led Zeppelin (Swan Song)

Do It ('Til You're Satisfied), B. T. Express (Scepter)

A Touch of Gold Volume II, Johnny Rivers (Imperial)

Johnny Rivers' Golden Hits, Johnny Rivers (Imperial)

Tommy—(Original Soundtrack Recording) Various Artists (Polydor)

Perfect Angel, Minnie Riperton (Epic)

Chicago VIII, Chicago (Columbia)

1975 *(cont'd)*

Tuneweaving, Tony Orlando & Dawn (Bell)

White Gold, Love Unlimited Orchestra (20th Century)

Just Another Way To Say I Love You, Barry White (20th Century)

That's The Way of the World, Earth, Wind & Fire (Columbia)

Phoebe Snow, Phoebe Snow (MCA)

Get Your Wings, Aerosmith (Columbia)

Spirit of America, The Beach Boys (Capitol)

Styx II, Styx (Wooden Nickel)

Eldorado, The Electric Light Orchestra (United Artists)

Nightbirds, La Belle (Epic)

Straight Shooter, Bad Company (Swan Song)

Katy Lied, Steely Dan (ABC)

Sun Goddess, Ramsey Lewis (Columbia)

Capt. Fantastic and the Brown Dirt Cowboy, Elton John (MCA)

Four Wheel Drive, Bachman-Turner Overdrive (Mercury)

Stampede, The Doobie Brothers (Warner Bros.)

Welcome To My Nightmare, Alice Cooper (Atlantic)

Venus & Mars, Wings (Capitol)

Survival, The O'Jays (Phila. Intl.)

Janis Joplin's Greatest Hits, Janis Joplin (Columbia)

Hearts, America (Warner Bros.)

Horizon, Carpenters (A & M)

Live In London, The O'Jays (Phila. Intl.)

Fandango, Z. Z. Top (London)

Nuthin' Fancy, Lynyrd Skynyrd (MCA)

One Of These Nights, Eagles (Asylum)

The Heat Is On, The Isley Brothers Featuring Fight The Power (T-Neck)

To Be True, Harold Melvin & The Blue Notes Featuring Theodore Pendergrass (Phila. Intl.)

Young Americans, David Bowie (RCA)

Chocolate Chip, Isaac Hayes (ABC)

Barry Manilow II, Barry Manilow (Bell)

Cut The Cake, Average White Band (Atlantic)

Why Can't We Be Friends?, War (United Artists)

Fire on the Mountain, The Charlie Daniels Band (Kama Sutra)

Love Will Keep Us Together, Captain & Tennille (A & M)

Made In The Shade, The Rolling Stones (Rolling Stone)

Toys In The Attic, Aerosmith (Columbia)

The Marshall Tucker Band, The Marshall Tucker Band (Capricorn)

Cat Stevens Greatest Hits, Cat Stevens (A & M)

Honey, Ohio Players (Mercury)

Light of Worlds, Kool & The Gang (De-Lite)

Red Octopus, Jefferson Starship (Grunt)

Don't Cry Now, Linda Ronstadt (Asylum)

Before the Next Teardrop Falls, Freddy Fender (ABC-Dot)

Funny Lady (Original Soundtrack Recording)—Barbra Streisand and James Caan (Arista)

Aerosmith, Aerosmith (Columbia)

Between the Lines, Janis Ian (Columbia)

Gorilla, James Taylor (Warner Bros.)

Wish You Were Here, Pink Floyd (Columbia)

Pick of the Litter, Spinners (Atlantic)

Windsong, John Denver (RCA)

Tony Orlando & Dawn's Greatest Hits, Tony Orlando & Dawn (Arista)

Clearly Love, Olivia Newton-John (MCA)

I'll Play For You, Seals & Crofts (Warner Bros.)

Is It Something I Said?, Richard Pryor (Warner/Reprise)

Win, Lose or Draw, The Allman Bros. Band (Capricorn)

Prisoner in Disguise, Linda Ronstadt (Asylum)

For Everyman, Jackson Browne (Asylum)

Blow by Blow, Jeff Beck (Epic)

Born to Run, Bruce Springsteen (Columbia)

Ain't No 'Bout-A-Doubt It, Graham Central Station (Warner Bros.)

Kris & Rita Full Moon, Kris Kristofferson and Rita Coolidge (A & M)

The Six Wives of Henry VIII, Rick Wakeman (A&M)

Rock of the Westies, Elton John (MCA)

Rocky Mountain Christmas, John Denver (RCA)

Raunch 'N Roll, Black Oak Arkansas (Atco)

Where We All Belong, The Marshall Tucker Band (Capricorn)

Wind On The Water, David Crosby & Graham Nash (ABC Records/Atlantic Tape)

Foghat, Foghat (Bearsville)

Extra Texture, George Harrison (Apple)

Sedaka's Back, Neil Sedaka (Rocket)

Diamonds and Rust, Joan Baez (A & M)

Piano Man, Billy Joel (Columbia)

Minstrel In The Gallery, Jethro Tull (Chrysalis)

Still Crazy After All These Years, Paul Simon (Columbia)

Blue Sky—Night Thunder, Michael Murphey (Epic)

Chicago IX—Chicago's Greatest Hits, Chicago (Columbia)

Sheer Heart Attack, Queen (Elektra)

Judith, Judy Collins (Elektra)

History—America's Greatest Hits, America (Warner Bros.)

Helen Reddy's Greatest Hits, Helen Reddy (Capitol)

Alive! Kiss (Casablanca)

The Hissing of Summer Lawns, Joni Mitchell (Asylum)

Seals & Crofts Greatest Hits, Seals & Crofts (Warner Bros.)

Fleetwood Mac, Fleetwood Mac (Warner Reprise)

Breakaway, Art Garfunkel (Columbia)

Gratitude, Earth, Wind & Fire (Columbia)

Family Reunion, O'Jays (Epic)

Save Me, Silver Convention (RCA/Midland International)

The Who By Numbers, The Who (MCA)

The Best of Carly Simon, Carly Simon (Elektra)

The Hungry Years, Neil Sedaka (Rocket)

Atlantic Crossing, Rod Stewart (Warner Bros.)

Head On, Bachman-Turner Overdrive (Mercury)

Main Course, Bee Gees (RSO)

Trying To Get The Feeling, Barry Manilow (Arista)

Rhinestone Cowboy, Glen Campbell (Capitol)

Bay City Rollers, Bay City Rollers (Arista)

1976

High On the Hog, Black Oak Arkansas (Atco)

Wake Up Everybody, Harold Melvin & The Blue Notes (Phila. Intl.)

Rufus—Featuring Chaka Khan, Rufus Featuring Chaka Khan (ABC)

Desire, Bob Dylan (Columbia)

Numbers, Cat Stevens (A & M)

Mona Bone Jakon, Cat Stevens (A & M)

Love to Love You Baby, Donna Summer (Oasis)

No Way to Treat a Lady, Helen Reddy (Capitol)

A Christmas Album, Barbra Streisand (Columbia)

Face the Music, Electric Light Orchestra (United Artists)

Black Bear Road, C. W. McCall (MGM)

Searchin' for a Rainbow, The Marshall Tucker Band (Capricorn)

Bare Trees, Fleetwood Mac (Warner/Reprise)

Run With the Pack, Bad Company (Swan Song)

Inseparable, Natalie Cole (Capitol)

Eagles—Their Greatest Hits 1971-1975, Eagles (Asylum)

M.U.—The Best of Jethro Tull, Jethro Tull (Chrysalis)

Station to Station, David Bowie (RCA)

Frampton Comes Alive!, Peter Frampton (A & M)

The Dream Weaver, Gary Wright (Warner Bros.)

Barry White's Greatest Hits, Barry White (20th Century)

Will O' the Wisp, Leon Russell (Shelter)

A Night at the Opera, Queen (Elektra)

Song of Joy, Captain & Tennille (A & M)

Red Headed Stranger, Willie Nelson (Columbia)

Fool for the City, Foghat (Bearsville)

Bustin' Out, Pure Prairie League (RCA)

Thoroughbred, Carole King (Ode)

Wings at the Speed of Sound, Paul McCartney & Wings (Capitol)

The Outlaws, The Outlaws—Waylon Jennings, Willie Nelson, Jessi Colter, Tompall Glaser (RCA)

Brass Construction, Brass Construction (United Artists)

Presence, Led Zeppelin (Swan Song)

Eargasm, Johnnie Taylor (Columbia)

Apostrophe', Frank Zappa (Discreet)

Hair of the Dog, Nazareth (A & M)

City Life, Blackbyrds (Fantasy)

2nd Anniversary, Gladys Knight & The Pips (Buddah)

Lazy Afternoon, Barbra Streisand (Columbia)

Destroyer, Kiss (Casablanca)

Black and Blue, The Rolling Stones (Rolling Stone)

Mothership Connection, Parliament (Casablanca)

Come on Over, Olivia Newton-John (MCA)

You've Never Been This Far Before/Baby's Gone, Conway Twitty (MCA)

Here and There, Elton John (MCA)

Takin' It to the Streets, Doobie Brothers (Warner Bros.)

Look Out For #1, Brothers Johnson (A & M)

Bitches Brew, Miles Davis (Columbia)

Hideaway, America (Warner Bros.)

Rocks, Aerosmith (Columbia)

Souvenirs, Dan Fogelberg (Epic)

All the Love in the World, Mac Davis (Columbia)

Desolation Boulevard, Sweet (Capitol)

Harvest for the World, The Isley Brothers (T-Neck)

Breezin', George Benson (Warner Bros.)

Contradiction, Ohio Players (Mercury)

Amigos, Santana (Columbia)

Rock 'N' Roll Music, The Beatles (Capitol)

Twelve Dreams of Dr. Sardonicus, Spirit (Columbia)

Olé ELO, The Electric Light Orchestra (United Artists)

Chicago X, Chicago (Columbia)

Beautiful Noise, Neil Diamond (Columbia)

Love Trilogy, Donna Summer (Oasis)

Spitfire, Jefferson Starship (Grunt)

Natalie, Natalie Cole (Capitol)

Sparkle, Aretha Franklin (Atlantic)

Second Childhood, Phoebe Snow (Columbia)

All-Time Greatest Hits, Johnny Mathis (Columbia)

A Kind of Hush, The Carpenters (A & M)

Silk Degrees, Boz Scaggs (Columbia)

Ted Nugent, Ted Nugent (Epic)

Fly Like an Eagle, Steve Miller Band (Capitol)

Changesonebowie, David Bowie (RCA)

Music, Music, Helen Reddy (Capitol)

Soul Searching, Average White Band (Atlantic)

This One's for You, Barry Manilow (Arista)

Spirit, John Denver (RCA)

Native Sons, Loggins & Messina (Columbia)

All Things in Time, Lou Rawls (Phila. Intl.)

War's Greatest Hits, War (United Artists)

Get Closer, Seals & Crofts (Warner Bros.)

Hasten Down the Wind, Linda Ronstadt (Asylum)

15 Big Ones, The Beach Boys (Warner-Reprise)

Dreamboat Annie, Heart (Mushroom)

Wild Cherry, Wild Cherry (Epic Sweet City)

Frampton, Peter Frampton (A & M)

Wired, Jeff Beck (Epic)

Royal Scam, Steeley Dan (ABC)

Children of the World, Bee Gees (RSO)

Best of BTO (So Far), Bachman-Turner Overdrive (Mercury)

Hard Rain, Bob Dylan (Columbia)

Abandoned Luncheonette, Daryl Hall & John Oates (Atlantic)

Spirit, Earth, Wind & Fire (Columbia)

Dave Mason, Dave Mason (Columbia)

The Manhattans, The Manhattans (Columbia)

Happiness Is Being With the Spinners, The Spinners (Atlantic)

Whistling Down the Wire, David Crosby & Graham Nash (ABC Atlantic Tape)

The Clones of Dr. Funkenstein, Parliament (Casablanca)

In the Pocket, James Taylor (Warner Bros.)

A Night on the Town, Rod Stewart (Warner Bros.)

Message in the Music, O'Jays (Phila. Intl.)

Barry Manilow I, Barry Manilow (Arista)

A New World Record, The Electric Light Orchestra (United Artists)

One More For From the Road, Lynyrd Skynyrd (MCA)

Agents of Fortune, Blue Oyster Cult (Columbia)

Boston, Boston (Epic)

A Fifth of Beethoven, The Walter Murphy Band (Private Stock)

1976 (cont'd)
Summertime Dream, Gordon Lightfoot (Warner/Reprise)
Free to Be . . . You and Me, Marlo Thomas and Friends (Arista Bell)
Blue Moves, Elton John (MCA/Rocket)
For Earth Below, Robin Trower (Chrysalis)
The Song Remains the Same, Led Zeppelin (Swan Song)
Firefall, Firefall (Atlantic)
Bigger than Both of Us, Daryl Hall & John Oates (RCA)
Rock and Roll Outlaws, Foghat (Bearsville)
Mystery to Me, Fleetwood Mac (Warner/Reprise)
Over-Nite Sensation, The Mothers (Discreet)
Rock and Roll Over, Kiss (Casablanca)
Four Seasons of Love, Donna Summer (Oasis)
Free for All, Ted Nugent (Epic)
Brass Construction II, Brass Construction (United Artists)
The Pretender, Jackson Browne (Asylum)
Times of Your Life, Paul Anka (United Artists)
Jackson Browne, Jackson Browne (Asylum)
Ol' Blue Eyes is Back, Frank Sinatra (Warner/Reprise)
Moondanke, Van Morrison (Warner Bros.)
Best of The Doobies, Doobie Brothers (Warner Bros.)
Alice Cooper Goes to Hell, Alice Cooper (Warner Bros.)
And I Love You So, Perry Como (RSA)
Nights Are Forever, England Dan & John Ford Coley (Big Tree)
Bicentennial Nigger, Richard Pryor (Warner Bros.)
Don't Stop Believin', Olivia Newton-John (MCA)
Greatest Hits, Linda Ronstadt (Asylum)
That Christmas Feeling, Glen Campbell (Capitol)
Best of the Beach Boys Volume 2, Beach Boys (Capitol)
Hotel California, Eagles (Asylum)
Long Misty Days, Robin Trower (Chrysalis)
Wings Over America, Wings (Capitol)
Daryl Hall & John Oates, Daryl Hall & John Oates (RCA)
Dr. Buzzard's Original Savannah Band, Dr. Buzzard's Original Savannah Band (RCA)
Car Wash—Original Motion Picture Soundtrack—Rose Royce (MCA)
James Taylor's Greatest Hits, James Taylor (Warner Bros.)
Live Bullet, Bob Seger & the Silver Bullet Band (Capitol)
Hejira, Joni Mitchell (Asylum)
A Star Is Born, Barbra Streisand and Kris Kristofferson (Columbia)
Donny and Marie Featuring Songs From Their Television Show, Donny and Marie Osmond (Polydor)
Occupation: Foole, George Carlin (Little David)
A Day at the Races, Queen (Elektra)
The Best of Leon Russell, Leon Russell (Shelter)
Greatest Hits, ABBA (Atlantic)

1977
After the Lovin', Engelbert Humperdinck (Columbia)
Long May You Run, Stills & Young Band (Warner/Reprise)
Year of the Cat, Al Stewart (GRT/Janus)
Tejas, Z.Z. Top (London)

Thirty-Three & ⅓, George Harrison (Warner/Dark Horse)
Ohio Players Gold, Ohio Players (Phonogram/Mercury)
Leftoverture, Kansas (Columbia/Kirshner)
Night Moves, Bob Seger & the Silver Bullet Band (Capitol)
Flowers, Emotions (Columbia)
Ask Rufus, Rufus-featuring Chaka Khan (ABC)
You Are My Starship, Norman Connors (Buddah)
Night Shift, Foghat (Warner/Bearsville)
Animals, Pink Floyd (Columbia)
Rumours, Fleetwood Mac (Warner Bros.)
The Best of George Harrison, George Harrison (Capitol)
Songs From The Wood, Jethro Tull (Chrysalis)
Lost Without Your Love, Bread (Elektra)
Southern Comfort, Crusaders (ABC/Blue Thumb)
I Hope We Get To Love In Time, Marilyn McCoo & Billy Davis, Jr.
. . . Roots, Quincy Jones (A & M)
Dressed to Kill, Kiss (Casablanca)
Love At The Greek, Neil Diamond (Columbia)
24 Greatest Hits, Hank Williams (Polydor/MGM)
Unpredictable, Natalie Cole (Capitol)
This Is Niecy, Deniece Williams (Columbia)
The Best Of The Statler Brothers, Statler Brothers (Phonogram/Mercury)
Burnin' Sky, Bad Company (Atlantic/Swan Song)
In Flight, George Benson (Warner Bros.)
Dreaming My Dreams, Waylon Jennings (RCA)
Queen, Queen (Elektra)
Works, Vol. I, Emerson, Lake & Palmer (Atlantic)
In the Court Of The Crimson King/An Observation, King Crimson (Atlantic)
John Denver's Greatest Hits, Vol. II, John Denver (RCA)
Arrival, ABBA (Atlantic)
The Roaring Silence, Manfred Mann's Earth Band (Warner Bros.)
The Jacksons, The Jacksons (Epic)
Come In from the Rain, Captain & Tennille (A & M)
A Rock and Roll Alternative, Atlanta Rhythm Section (Polydor)
Unfinished Business, The Blackbyrds (Fantasy)
Montrose, Montrose (Warner Bros.)
Ahh . . . The Name Is Bootsy, Baby, Bootsy's Rubber Band (Warner Bros.)
Go For Your Guns, Isley Brothers (T-Neck)
Gord's Gold, Gordon Lightfoot (Warner/Reprise)
Rocky—Original soundtrack (United Artists)
Endless Flight, Leo Sayer (Warner Bros.)
Festival, Santana (Columbia)
The Wild, The Innocent, And The E Street Shuffle, Bruce Springsteen (Columbia)
The Beatles At The Hollywood Bowl, The Beatles (Capitol)
The Best of Friends, Loggins & Messina (Columbia)
Book Of Dreams, Steve Miller Band (Capitol)
Foreigner, Foreigner (Atlantic)
Toledo Window Box, George Carlin (Warner/Little David)
Person to Person, Average White Band (Atlantic)

1977 *(cont'd)*

Teddy Pendergrass, Teddy Pendergrass (Phila. Intl.)
Right on Time, Brothers Johnson (A & M)
Little Queen, Heart (Columbia/Portrait)
Ain't That A Bitch, Johnny Guitar Watson (DJM)
A Real Mother For Ya, Johnny Guitar Watson (DJM)
Carolina Dreams, Marshall Tucker Band (Warner/Reprise)
Kiss, Kiss (Casablanca)
Parliament Live/P Funk Earth Tour, Parliament (Casablanca)
Izitso, Cat Stevens (A & M)
I'm In You, Peter Frampton (A & M)
Ol' Waylon, Waylon Jennings (RCA)
Slave, Slave (Atlantic/Cotillion)
Barry Manilow Live, Barry Manilow (Arista)
Changes in Latitudes, Changes in Attitudes, Jimmy Buffett (ABC)
Superman, Barbra Streisand (Columbia)
Hotter Than Hell, Kiss (Casablanca)
Here At Last . . . Bee Gees . . . Live, Bee Gees (RSO)
Melissa, Melissa Manchester (Arista)
CSN, Crosby, Stills & Nash (Atlantic)
Love Gun, Kiss (Casablanca)
J.T., James Taylor (Columbia)
Unmistakably Lou, Lou Rawls (Phila. Intl.)
Beethoven: The 9 Symphonies, Berlin Philharmonic Orchestra (Polydor/Deutsche Grammophon)
Cat Scratch Fever, Ted Nugent (Epic)
Rejoice, Emotions (Columbia)
Travelin' At The Speed Of Thought, The O'Jays (Columbia)
Even in the Quietest Moments . . ., Supertramp (A & M)
I Remember Yesterday, Donna Summer (Casablanca)
On Your Feet Or On Your Knees, Blue Oyster Cult (Columbia)
Star Wars—Original soundtrack (20th Century)
Alleluia—Praise Gathering for Believers—Various Artists (Benson/Impact)
The Floaters, The Floaters (ABC)
Are You Ready For The Country, Waylon Jennings (RCA)
Maze, Featuring Frankie Beverly, Maze (Capitol)
Going For The One, Yes (Atlantic)
Crime Of The Century, Supertramp (A & M)
Nether Lands, Dan Fogelberg (Epic)
You Get What You Play For, REO Speedwagon (Epic)
Shaun Cassidy, Shaun Cassidy (Warner Bros.)
Kenny Rogers, Kenny Rogers (United Artists)
Platinum Jazz, War (United Artists-Blue Note)
A New Life, Marshall Tucker Band (Warner Bros.)
It's A Game, Bay City Rollers (Arista)
Anytime . . . Anywhere, Rita Coolidge (A & M)
A Place In The Sun, Pablo Cruise (A & M)
Equinox, Styx (A & M)
Ozark Mountain Daredevils, Ozark Mountain Daredevils (A & M)
Pure Gold, Elvis Presley (RCA)
Livin' On The Fault Line, Doobie Brothers (Warner Bros.)

I Robot, Alan Parsons (Arista)
Chicago XI, Chicago (Columbia)
Beauty On A Back Street, Daryl Hall & John Oates (RCA)
Simple Dreams, Linda Ronstadt (Asylum)
Celebrate Me Home, Kenny Loggins (Columbia)
The Outlaws, The Outlaws (Arista)
Barry White Sings for Someone You Love, Barry White (20th Century)
Simple Things, Carole King (Capitol)
Star Wars and Other Galactic Funk, Meco (Millennium)
Elton John's Greatest Hits, Vol. II, Elton John (MCA)
Welcome To My World, Elvis Presley (RCA)
Luna Sea, Firefall (Atlantic)
Love You Live, Rolling Stones (Atlantic/Rolling Stones)
Aja, Steely Dan (ABC)
In Full Bloom, Rose Royce (Warner/Whitfield)
Southern Nights, Glen Campbell (Capitol)
From Elvis Presley Boulevard, Memphis, Tennessee, Elvis Presley (RCA)
Too Hot to Handle, Heatwave (Epic)
Point of Know Return, Kansas (CBS/Kirshner)
Foghat Live, Foghat (Warner/Bearsville)
American Stars 'n' Bars, Neil Young (Warner/Bearsville)
The Grand Illusion, Styx (A & M)
Jailbreak, Thin Lizzy (Phonogram/Mercury)
Greatest Hits, Olivia Newton-John (MCA)
Love Songs, The Beatles (Capitol)
Elvis—A Legendary Performer, Vol. II, Elvis Presley (RCA)
The Johnny Cash Portrait/His Greatest Hits, Vol. II, Johnny Cash (Columbia)
You Light Up My Life, Debby Boone (Warner Bros.)
Rock & Roll Love Letter, Bay City Rollers (Arista)
Eric Carmen, Eric Carmen (Arista)
Street Survivors, Lynyrd Skynyrd (MCA)
You Light Up My Life—Original Soundtrack (Arista)
Captured Angel, Dan Fogelberg (Epic)
Let It Flow, Dave Mason
Elvis Sings The Wonderful World of Christmas, Elvis Presley (RCA)
Anthology, Steve Miller Band (Capitol)
Something To Love, L.T.D. (A & M)
We Must Believe In Magic, Crystal Gayle (United Artists)
Out Of The Blue, Electric Light Orchestra (United Artists/Jet)
News Of The World, Queen (Elektra)
2112, Rush (Phonogram)
A Farewell To Kings, Rush (Phonogram)
All The World's A Stage, Rush (Phonogram)
I'm Glad You're Here With Me Tonight, Neil Diamond (Columbia)
All 'N All, Earth, Wind & Fire (Columbia)
Down Two Then Left, Boz Scaggs (Columbia)
Greatest Hits, Etc., Paul Simon (Columbia)
In City Dreams, Robin Trower (Chrysalis)
Saturday Night Fever—Original Soundtrack (RSO)
Flowing Rivers, Andy Gibb (RSO)
Foot Loose & Fancy Free, Rod Stewart (Warner Bros.)

1977 *(cont'd)*
Born Late, Shaun Cassidy (Warner Bros.)
Dedication, Bay City Rollers (Arista)
Kiss Alive II, Kiss (Casablanca)
Galaxy, War (MCA)
The Turning Point, John Mayall (Polydor)
Let's Get Small, Steve Martin (Warner Bros.)
Moonflower, Santana (Columbia)
The Stranger, Billy Joel (Columbia)
I Want To Live, John Denver (RCA)
His Hand in Mine, Elvis Presley (RCA)
Elvis Country, Elvis Presley (RCA)
The Story of Star Wars—Original Cast With Narration
    by Roscoe Lee Browne (20th Century)
Bay City Rollers/Greatest Hits, Bay City Rollers (Arista)
Draw The Line, Aerosmith (Columbia)
French Kiss, Bob Welch (Capitol)
Once Upon A Time, Donna Summer (Casablanca)
Friends & Strangers, Ronnie Laws (United Artists/Blue
    Note)
Greatest Hits, Captain & Tennille (A & M)
Tupelo Honey, Van Morrison (Warner Bros.)
Daytime Friends, Kenny Rogers (United Artists)
Viva Terlingua, Jerry Jeff Walker (MCA)
Masque, Kansas (Columbia/Kirshner)
A Chorus Line—Original Cast (Columbia)
Feelin' Bitchy, Millie Jackson (Spring)
Thankful, Natalie Cole (Capitol)
Here You Come Again, Dolly Parton (RCA)
Action, Blackbyrds (Fantasy)
Running On Empty, Jackson Browne (Asylum)
Works, Vol. II, Emerson, Lake & Palmer (Atlantic)
Besto of Z.Z. Top, Z.Z. Top (London)

1978
Bee Gees Gold, Volume I, Bee Gees (Polydor/RSO)
Brass Construction III, Brass Construction (United Art-
    ists)
Close Encounters Of The Third Kind—Original Sound-
    track (Arista)
Diamantina Cocktail, Little River Band (Capitol/Har-
    vest)
Funkentelechy vs. The Placebo Syndrome, Parliament
    (Casablanca)
New Season, Donny & Marie Osmond (Polydor)
Waylon Live, Waylon Jennings (RCA)
Reach For It, George Duke (Epic)
Spectres, Blue Oyster Cult (Columbia)
Little Criminals, Randy Newman (Warner Bros.)
Slowhand, Eric Clapton (RSO)
Leif Garrett, Leif Garrett (Atlantic)
Waylon & Willie, Waylon Jennings and Willie Nelson
    (RCA)
It Was Almost Like A Song, Ronnie Milsap (RCA)
Don Juan's Reckless Daughter, Joni Mitchell (Asylum)
Double Live Gonzo, Ted Nugent (Epic)
When You Hear Lou, You've Heard It All, Lou Rawls
    (Phila. Intl.)
Even Now, Barry Manilow (Arista)

Ten Years of Gold, Kenny Rogers (United Artists)
Street Player, Rufus (ABC)
Blue Lights In The Basement, Roberta Flack (Atlantic)
A Weekend in L.A., George Benson (Warner Bros.)
Earth, Jefferson Starship (RCA/Grunt)
Watermark, Art Garfunkel (Columbia)
Countdown To Ecstasy, Steely Dan (ABC)
Bootsy? Player of the Year, Bootsy's Rubber Band
    (Warner Bros.)
The Album, ABBA (Atlantic)
It Feels So Good, Manhattans (Columbia)
Golden Time of Day, Maze (Capitol)
Longer Fuse, Dan Hill (20th Century)
London Town, Paul McCartney & Wings (Capitol)
Feels So Good, Chuck Mangione (A & M)
Emotion, Samantha Sang (Private Stock)
Chic, Chic (Atlantic)
Carole King . . . Her Greatest Hits, Carole King (CBS/
    Ode)
Son of a Son of a Sailor, Jimmy Buffett (ABC)
Central Heating, Heatwave (Epic)
Showdown, Isley Brothers (Columbia/T-Neck)
Champagne Jam, Atlanta Rhythm Section (Polydor)
Excitable Boy, Warren Zevon (Asylum)
Heavy Horses, Jethro Tull (Chrysalis)
FM, Original Soundtrack (MCA)
Player, Player (RSO)
Endless Wire, Gordon Lightfoot (Warner Bros.)
Rock'n'Roll Animal, Lou Reed (RCA)
Grease, Original Soundtrack (Polydor-RSO)
You Light Up My Life, Johnny Mathis (Columbia)
So Full of Love, O'Jays (Phila. Intl.)
Together Forever, Marshall Tucker Band (Capricorn)
Infinity, Journey (Columbia)
The Sound In Your Mind, Willie Nelson (Columbia)
Flying High on Your Love, Bar-Kays (Polydor-Mercury)
Secrets, Con Funk Shun (Polydor/Mercury)
Boys In The Trees, Carly Simon (Elektra)
Warmer Communications, Average White Band (Atlan-
    tic)
Double Platinum, Kiss (Casablanca)
Thank God It's Friday, Original Soundtrack (Casablanca)
Menagerie, Bill Withers, (Columbia)
Bat Out of Hell, Meat Loaf (CBS/Cleveland Intl.)
Van Halen, Van Halen (Warner Bros.)
The Best of Rod Stewart, Rod Stewart (Polydor/Mer-
    cury)
City to City, Gerry Rafferty (United Artists)
Shadow Dancing, Andy Gibb (Polydor/RSO)
Stranger in Town, Bob Seger and The Silver Bullet Band
    (Capitol)
And Then There Were Three, Genesis (Atlantic)
Songbird, Barbra Streisand (Columbia)
Disco Inferno, Tramps (Atlantic)
But Seriously, Folks, Joe Walsh (Asylum)
Magazine, Heart (Mushroom)
Greatest Stories—Live, Harry Chapin (Elektra)
Don't Let Me Be Misunderstood, Santa Esmeralda star-
    ring Leroy Gomez (Casablanca)
The Best Of Dolly Parton, Dolly Parton (RCA)

1978 *(cont'd)*

Some Girls, The Rolling Stones (Atlantic/Rolling Stones)

Life Is A Song Worth Singing, Teddy Pendergrass (CBS/Phila. Intl.)

Darkness On The Edge of Town, Bruce Springsteen (Columbia)

Octave, Moody Blues (London)

Double Vision, Foreigner (Atlantic)

Send It, Ashford & Simpson (Warner Bros.)

Love Me Again, Rita Coolidge (A & M)

Worlds Away, Pablo Cruise (A & M)

Stone Blue, Foghat (Bearsville)

Sounds . . . And Stuff Like That, Quincy Jones (A & M)

Togetherness, L.T.D. (A & M)

You Can Tune A Piano, But You Can't Tuna Fish, REO Speedwagon (Epic)

Street Legal, Bob Dylan (Columbia)

It's A Heartache, Bonnie Tyler (RCA)

Eddie Money, Eddie Money (Columbia)

You're Gonna Get It, Tom Petty and the Heartbreakers (ABC/Shelter)

Natalie Live, Natalie Cole (Capitol)

Sgt. Pepper's Lonely Hearts Club Band, Original Soundtrack (Polydor/RSO)

That's What Friends Are For, Johnny Mathis and Deniece Williams (Columbia)

Stardust, Willie Nelson (Columbia)

Pyramid, Alan Parsons Project (Arista)

Elite Hotel, Emmylou Harris (Warner Bros./Reprise)

Blam, Brothers Johnson (A & M)

Under Wraps, Shaun Cassidy (Warner Bros.)

A Taste of Honey, A Taste of Honey (Capitol)

Macho Man, Village People (Casablanca)

Heartbreaker, Dolly Parton (RCA)

Reaching For The Sky, Peabo Bryson (Capitol)

Natural High, Commodores (Motown)

Come Get It, Rick James (Motown)

Who Are You, The Who (MCA)

Don't Look Back, Boston (Epic)

Loveshine, Con Funk Shun (Polydor/Mercury)

Get It Out'Cha System, Millie Jackson (Polydor/Spring)

Sleeper Catcher, Little River Band (Capitol/Harvest)

Smooth Talk, Evelyn "Champagne" King (RCA)

Skynyrd's First And . . . Last, Lynyrd Skynyrd (MCA)

Do What You Wanna Do, Dramatics (ABC)

Sunbeam, Emotions (Columbia/ARC)

Nightwatch, Kenny Loggins (Columbia)

Mariposa De Oro, Dave Mason (Columbia)

Live and More, Donna Summer (Casablanca)

When I Dream, Crystal Gayle (United Artists)

Love or Something Like It, Kenny Rogers (United Artists)

Village People, Village People (Casablanca)

Flat as a Pancake, Head East (A & M)

Rose Royce Strikes Again, Rose Royce (Warner Bros./Whitfield)

Raydio, Raydio (Arista)

Living in the U.S.A., Linda Ronstadt (Asylum)

I've Always Been Crazy, Waylon Jennings (RCA)

Dog and Butterfly, Heart (CBS/Portrait)

Twin Sons of Different Mothers, Dan Fogelberg and Tim Weisberg (CBS/Full Moon)

Bursting Out, Jethro Tull (Chrysalis)

The Wiz, Original Soundtrack (MCA)

Kiss—Peter Criss, Peter Criss (Casablanca)

Kiss—Ace Frehley, Ace Frehley (Casablanca)

Kiss—Gene Simmons, Gene Simmons (Casablanca)

Kiss—Paul Stanley, Paul Stanley (Casablanca)

One Nation Under A Groove, Funkadelic (Warner Bros.)

Sunburn, Sun (Capitol)

Is It Still Good to Ya, Ashford & Simpson (Warner Bros.)

Hot Streets, Chicago (Columbia)

Images, Crusaders (ABC/Blue Thumb)

Mixed Emotions, Exile (Warner/Curb)

Children of Sanchez, Chuck Mangione (A & M)

Pieces of Eight, Styx (A & M)

Tormato, Yes (Atlantic)

Let's Keep It That Way, Anne Murray (Capitol)

Only One Love In My Life, Ronnie Milsap (RCA)

Cruisin', Village People (Casablanca)

The Cars, Cars (Elektra)

Elan, Firefall (Atlantic)

Danger Zone, Player (Polydor/RSO)

52nd Street, Bill Joel (Columbia)

A Single Man, Elton John (MCA)

Along The Red Ledge, Daryl Hall & John Oates (RCA)

Time Passages, Al Stewart (Arista)

What Ever Happened to Benny Santini? Cris Rea (United Artists)

Inner Secrets, Santana (Columbia)

Weekend Warriors, Ted Nugent (Epic)

Marshall Tucker Band's Greatest Hits, Marshall Tucker Band (Capricorn)

Live Bootleg, Aerosmith (Columbia)

A Wild And Crazy Guy, Steve Martin (Warner Bros.)

Goin' Coconuts, Donny & Marie Osmond (Polydor)

Brother to Brother, Gino Vannelli (A & M)

Feel the Need, Leif Garrett (Atlantic/Scotti Bros.)

Songs Of Kristofferson, Kris Kristofferson (Columbia)

You Had To Be There, Jimmy Buffett (ABC)

Crystal Ball, Styx (A & M)

A Retrospective, Linda Ronstadt (Capitol)

Backless, Eric Clapton (Polydor/RSO)

Chaka, Chaka Khan (Warner Bros./Tattoo)

Totally Hot, Olivia Newton-John (MCA)

Two For The Show, Kansas (CBS/Kirshner)

Barbra Streisand's Greatest Hits, Volume II, Barbra Streisand (Columbia)

In the Night-Time, Michael Henderson (Arista/Buddah)

Sesame Street Fever, The Muppets and Robin Gibb (Sesame Street)

Greetings from Asbury Park, New Jersey, Bruce Springsteen (Columbia)

Comes A Time, Neil Young (Warner/Reprise)

Greatest Hits, Barry Manilow (Arista)

The Steve Miller Band's Greatest Hits 1974-78, Steve Miller Band (Capitol)

C'est Chic, Chic (Atlantic)

Jazz, Queen (Elektra)

The Gambler, Kenny Rogers (United Artists)

1978 *(cont'd)*
Wings Greatest, Wings (Capitol)
Bish, Stephen Bishop (ABC)
You Don't Bring Me Flowers, Neil Diamond (Columbia)
The Best of Earth, Wind & Fire,—Volume I, Earth, Wind & Fire (Columbia/ARC)
Steely Dan's Greatest Hits, Steely Dan (ABC)
Toto, Toto (Columbia)
Motor-Booty Affair, Parliament (Casablanca)
Blondes Have More Fun, Rod Stewart (Warner Bros.)
Hemispheres, Rush (Mercury)
Tanya Tucker's Greatest Hits, Tanya Tucker (Columbia)
Take This Job and Shove It, Johnny Paycheck (Epic)
A Legendary Performer—Elvis, Volume 3, Elvis Presley (RCA)
Entertainers . . . On And Off The Record, Statler Brothers (Mercury)
Briefcase Full of Blues, Blues Brothers (Atlantic)
Barry White, The Man, Barry White (20th Century)
Minute By Minute, Doobie Brothers (Warner Bros.)
The Last Farewell And Other Hits, Roger Whittaker (RCA)

1979
Heaven Tonight, Cheap Trick (Epic)
Spark of Love, Lenny Williams (ABC)
10th Anniversary of Golden Piano Hits, Ferrante & Teicher (United Artists/Liberty)
John Denver, John Denver (RCA)
Life for the Taking, Eddie Money (Columbia)
Love Beach, Emerson, Lake & Palmer (Atlantic)
Spirits Having Flown, Bee Gees (RSO)
Love Tracks, Gloria Gaynor (Polydor)
New Kind of Feeling, Anne Murray (Capitol)
Sanctuary, J. Geils Band (Capitol/EMI)
Gold, Jefferson Starship (RCA/Grunt)
Willie & Family Live, Willie Nelson (Columbia)
Energy, Pointer Sisters (Plant/EA)
Step II, Sylvester (Fantasy)
2 Hot, Peaches & Herb (Polydor)
Dire Straits, Dire Straits (Warner Bros.)
Armed Forces, Elvis Costello (Columbia)
TNT, Tanya Tucker (MCA)
Three Hearts, Bob Welch (Capitol)
Knock on Wood, Amii Stewart (Ariola America)
Crosswinds, Peabo Bryson (Capitol)
Nicolette, Nicolette Larson (Warner Bros.)
Cheryl Lynn, Chery Lynn (Columbia)
Enlightened Rogues, Allman Brothers Band (Capricorn)
Wanted Live in Concert, Richard Pryor (Warner Bros.)
Livin' Inside Your Love, George Benson (Warner Bros.)
Live at Budokan, Cheap Trick (Epic)
Destiny, The Jacksons (Epic)
Desolation Angels, Bad Company (Swan Song)
I Love You So, Natalie Cole (Capitol)
Van Halen II, Van Halen (Warner Bros.)
Go West, Village People (Casablanca)
Parallel Lines, Blondie (Chrysalis)
Breakfast in America, Supertramp (A & M)
We Are Family, Sister Sledge (Cotillion)

Evolution, Journey (Columbia)
Legend, Poco (MCA)
Music Box Dancer, Frank Mills (Polydor)
Instant Funk, Instant Funk (Salsoul)
Music Box, Evelyn "Champagne" King (RCA)
Inspiration, Maze featuring Frankie Beverly (Capitol)
Disco Nights, G.Q. (Arista)
George Harrison, George Harrison (Dark Horse)
Flag, James Taylor (Columbia)
Greatest Hits, Waylon Jennings (RCA)
Hair, Original Soundtrack (Various Artists/RCA)
Take Me Home, Cher (Cassablanca)
Rickie Lee Jones, Rickie Lee Jones (Warner Bros.)
The Message Is Love, Barry White
Sooner or Later, Rex Smith (Columbia)
Night Owl, Gerry Rafferty (United Artists)
Dynasty, Kiss (Casablanca)
Teddy, Teddy Pendergrass (Phila. Intl.)
Underdog, Atlanta Rhythm Section (Polydor)
Monolith, Kansas (Kirshner)
Back To The Egg, Wings (Columbia)
Annie, Original Cast Album (Columbia)
The Kids Are Alright, Movie Soundtrack, The Who (MCA)
Communique, Dire Straits (Warner Bros.)
Best of Nat King Cole, Nat King Cole (Capitol)
Million Mile Reflections, Charlie Daniels (Epic)
Molly Hatchet, Molly Hatchet (Epic)
Classics, Kenny Rogers & Dottie West (United Artists)
Where I Should Be, Peter Frampton (A & M)
Get the Knack, Knack (Capitol)
Music Band, War (MCA)
Waiting For Columbus, Little Feat (Warner Bros.)
Hot Property, Heatwave (Epic)
Candy-O, The Cars (Elektra)
Queen Live Killers, Queen (Elektra)
Reality . . . What a Concept, Robin Williams (Casablanca)
One For The Road, Willie Nelson and Leon Russell (Columbia)
Decade, Neil Young (Reprise)
Bustin' Loose, Chuck Brown & The Soul Searchers (Source)
In Color, Cheap Trick (Epic)
Rock-On, Raydio (Arista)
Street Life, Crusaders (MCA)
McFadden & Whitehead, McFadden and Whitehead (Phila. Intl.)
What 'Cha Gonna Do with My Lovin'? Stephanie Mills (20th Century)
A Night At Studio 54—Various Artists (Casablanca)
Candy, Con Funk Shun (Mercury)
Rust Never Sleeps, Neil Young (Reprise)
Morning Dance, Spyro Gyra (Infinity)
Look Sharp, Joe Jackson (A & M)
Dionne, Dionne Warwick (Arista)
Pleasure & Pain, Dr. Hook (Capitol)
The Main Event, Original Soundtrack Recording (CBS)
Bring It Back Alive, The Outlaws (Arista)
Ronnie Milsap Live, Ronnie Milsap (RCA)

1979 *(cont'd)*

The Joy of Christmas, Mormon Tabernacle Choir (CBS)
Devotion, LTD (A & M)
Great Balls of Fire, Dolly Parton (RCA)
Voulez-Vouz, ABBA (Atlantic)
Adventures of Panama Red, New Riders Of The Purple Sage (Columbia)
First Under the Wire, Little River Band (Capitol)
Secret Omen, Cameo (Casablanca)
Nine Lives, REO Speedwagon (CBS)
Highway to Hell, AC/DC (Atlantic)
The Muppet Movie, Original Soundtrack Recording (Atlantic)
Chicago XIII, Chicago (Columbia)
Off the Wall, Michael Jackson (CBS)
Stay Free, Ashford & Simpson (Warner Bros.)
Slow Train Coming, Bob Dylan (CBS)
Home Free, Dan Fogelberg (CBS)
Give Me Your Love For Christmas, Johnny Mathis (CBS)
Identify Yourself, O'Jays (Phila. Intl.)
Volcano, Jimmy Buffett (MCA)

1980

Head Games, Foreigner (Atlantic)
Low Budget, Kinks (Arista)
In Through The Out Door, Led Zeppelin (Atlantic)
Miss the Mississippi, Crystal Gayle (Columbia)
Flirtin' With Disaster, Molly Hatchet (Epic)
Don't Let Go, Isaac Hayes (Polydor)
Ladies Night, Kool and the Gang (Phonogram)
Uncle Jam Wants You, Funkadelic (Warner Bros.)
Kenny, Kenny Rogers (Capitol)
Comedy Is Not Pretty, Steve Martin (Warner Bros.)
Strikes, Blackfoot (Atco)
Live & Sleazy, Village People (Casablanca)
One Voice, Barry Manilow (Arista)
Eat To The Beat, Blondie (Chrysalis)
A Christmas Together, John Denver & The Muppets (RCA)
A Long Run, Eagles (Asylum)
Stormwatch, Jethro Tull (Chrysalis)
Rise, Herb Alpert (A & M)
Cornerstone, Styx (A & M)
Dream Police, Cheap Trick (Epic)
Keep The Fire, Kenny Loggins (Columbia)
We Sold Our Soul For Rock N' Roll, Black Sabbath (Warner Bros.)
Twice The Fire, Peaches & Herb (Polydor)
I'll Always Love You, Anne Murray (Capitol)
Eve, The Alan Parsons Project (Arista)
Tusk, Fleetwood Mac (Warner Bros.)
Injoy, Bar-Kays (Mercury)
Prince, Prince (Warner Bros.)
Wet, Barbra Streisand (Columbia)
Damn The Torpedos, Tom Petty & Heartbreakers (MCA)
Bee Gees' Greatest Hits, Bee Gees (RSO)
Rod Stewart's Greatest Hits Volume I & II, Rod Stewart (Warner Bros.)

What Goes Around, Waylon Jennings (RCA)
Deguello, ZZ Top (Warner Bros.)
Willie Nelson Sings Kristofferson, Willie Nelson (Columbia)
Hydra, Toto (Columbia)
Classic Crystal, Crystal Gayle (United Artists)
Freedom At Point Zero, Jefferson Starship (Grunt)
Gloryhallastoopid, Parliament (Casablanca)
Masterjam, Rufus & Chaka (MCA)
Live Rust, Neil Young & Crazy Horse (Warner Bros.)
Night In The Ruts, Arrowsmith (Columbia)
September Morn, Neil Damond (Columbia)
ELO Greatest Hits, Electric Light Orchestra (Jet)
The Wall, Pink Floyd (Columbia)
Phoenix, Dan Fogelbert (Epic)
Teddy Live! Coast To Coast, Teddy Pendergrass (Phila. Intl.)
The Best of "Skeletons From The Closet", The Grateful Dead (Warner Bros.)
Richard Pryor's Greatest Hits, Richard Pryor (Warner Bros.)
Permanent Wave, Rush (Mercury)
The Whispers, The Whispers (Solar)
Y'all Come Back Saloon, The Oak Ridge Boys (MCA)
In The Heat Of The Night, Pat Benatar (Chrysalis)
Gold & Platinum, Lynyrd Skynyrd (MCA)
Ray, Goodman & Brown, Ray, Goodman & Brown (Polydor)
Big Fun, Shalamar (Solar)
American Gigolo, Original Soundtrack (Polydor)
The Rose, Original Soundtrack, Bette Midler (Atlantic)
Mickey Mouse Disco, Mickey Mouse (Disneyland)
. . . but the little girls understand, The Knack (Capitol)
Gap Band II, Gap Band (Mercury)
Love Stinks, J. Geils Band (EMI/America)
Greatest Hits, Volume 2, Abba (Atlantic)
Light Up The Night, Brothers Johnson (A & M)
Fun And Games, Chuck Mangione (A & M)
Against The Wind, Bob Seger & The Silver Bullet Band (Capitol)
Bebe Le Strange, Heart (Epic)
Glass Houses, Billy Joel (Columbia)
Departure, Journey (Columbia)
Christopher Cross, Christopher Cross (Warner Bros.)
Chapter Two, Roberta Flack (Atlantic)
After Dark, Andy Gibb (RSO)
Mad Love, Linda Ronstadt (Asylum)
The Sinatra Christmas Album, Frank Sinatra (MCA)
Partners In Crime, Rupert Holmes (Infinity)
Mouth To Mouth, Lipps, Inc. (Casablanca)
Turnstiles, Billy Joel (Columbia)
Ridin' The Storm Out, REO Speedwagon (Epic)
Gideon, Kenny Rogers (United Artists)
Women & Children First, Van Halen (Warner Bros.)
Pretenders, Pretenders (Warner Bros.)
Roberta Flack Featuring Donny Hathaway, Roberta Flack & Donny Hathaway (Atlantic)
Go All The Way, The Isley Brothers (T-Neck)
Middle Man, Boz Scaggs (Columbia)
Straight Ahead, Larry Gatlin (Columbia)

1980 *(cont'd)*
Song For America, Kansas (Kirshner)
Sweet Sensation, Stephanie Mills (20th Century)
Just One Night, Eric Clapton (RSO)
Star Wars—The Empire Strikes Back, Original Soundtrack, Various Artists (RSO)
Spirit Of Love, Con Funk Shun (Mercury)
Two Places At The Same Time, Ray Parker Jr. & Raydio (Arista)
Some Enchanted Evening, Blue Oyster Cult (Columbia)
Electric Horseman, Original Soundtrack, Various Artists (Columbia)
After Midnight, The Manhattans (CBS Masterworks)
Urban Cowboy, Original Soundtrack, Various Artists (Asylum)
Best of R. Whittaker, Roger Whittaker (RCA)
Cameosis, Cameo (Chocolate City)
The Boss, Diana Ross (Motown)
Move It On Over, George Thorogood & The Destroyers (Rounder)
Duke, Genesis (Atlantic)
Scream Dream, Ted Nugent (Epic)
McCartney II, Paul McCartney (Columbia)
Unmasked, Kiss (Casablanca)
Make Your Move, Captain & Tennille (Casablanca)
Hot Box, Fatback Band (Spring)
S.O.S., S.O.S. Band (Tabu)
Empty Glass, Pete Townshend (Atco)
Fame, Original Soundtrack, Various Artists (RSO)
Anytime, Anyplace, Anywhere, Rossington Collins Band (MCA)
Xanadu, Original Soundtrack, Olivia Newton-John & Electric Light Orchestra (MCA)
Music Man, Waylon Jennings (RCA)
The Oak Ridge Boys Have Arrived, The Oak Ridge Boys (MCA)
The Blues Brothers, Original Soundtrack, The Blues Brothers (Atlantic)
Weird Scenes Inside The Gold Mine, The Doors (Elektra)
The Game, Queen (Elektra)
No Nukes, Various Artists (Asylum)
Give Me The Night, George Benson (Warner Bros.)
One In A Million You, Larry Graham (Warner Bros.)
21 At 33, Elton John (MCA)
Full Moon, Charlie Daniels (Epic)
TP, Teddy Pendergrass (Phila. Intl.)
Lost In Love, Air Supply (Arista)
Best Of Don Williams Volume II, Don Williams (MCA)
Together, The Oak Ridge Boys (MCA)
Back In Black, AC/DC (Atlantic)
Let There Be Rock, AC/DC (Atco)
If You Want Blood You've Got It, AC/DC (Atlantic)
Chipmunk Punk, The Chipmunks (Pickwick Intl.)
One Trick Pony, Paul Simon (Warner Bros.)
Panorama, The Cars (Elektra)
Honeysuckle Rose, Original Soundtrack, Willie Nelson & Family (Columbia)
Crimes Of Passion, Pat Benatar (Chrysalis)
The Glow Of Love, Change (RFC/Warner Bros.)

Horizon, Eddie Rabbitt (Elektra)
The Best of Eddie Rabbitt, Eddie Rabbitt (Elektra)
Sweet Forgiveness, Bonnie Raitt (Warner Bros.)
Beatin' The Odds, Molly Hatchet (Epic)
Greatest Hits, Anne Murray (Capitol)
Alive, Kenny Loggins (Columbia)
The B-52's, B-52's (Warner Bros.)
Zapp, Zapp (Warner Bros.)
One Step Closer, Doobie Brothers (Warner Bros.)
Suite For Flute & Jazz Piano, Claude Bolling & Jean-Pierre Rampal (CBS Masterworks)
Suite For Flute & Jazz Piano, Jean-Pierre Rampal & Claude Bolling (CBS Masterworks)
Freedom Of Choice, Devo (Warner Bros.)
Greatest Hits, Kenny Rogers (Liberty)
I Believe In You, Don Williams (MCA)
Linda Ronstadt's Greatest Hits, Volume II, Linda Ronstadt (Asylum) .
One For The Road, Kinks (Arista)
Triumph, The Jacksons (Epic)
Paris, Supertramp (A & M)
Audio Visions, Kansas (Kirshner)
Zenyatta Mondatta, The Police (A & M)
The River, Bruce Springsteen (Columbia)
The Wanderer, Donna Summer (Geffen)
Celebrate, Kool and the Gang (Phonogram)
Conquistador, Maynard Ferguson (Columbia)
Touchdown, Bob James (Columbia)
Streetlife Serenade, Billy Joel (Columbia)
All Shook Up, Cheap Trick (Epic)
Greatest Hits, The Doors (Elektra)
Feelings, Johnny Mathis (Columbia)

SINGLES

1958
"Catch a Falling Star," Perry Como (RCA Victor)
"He's Got the Whole Wornd In His Hands," Laurie London (Capitol)
"Hard Headed Woman," Elvis Presley (RCA Victor)
"Patricia," Perez Prado (RCA Victor)

1959
"Tom Dooley," Kingston Trio (Capitol)

1961
"Calcutta," Lawrence Welk (Dot)
"Big Bad John," Jimmy Dean (Columbia)

1962
"The Lion Sleeps," The Tokens (RCA Victor)
"Can't Help Falling in Love," Elvis Presley (RCA Victor)
"I Can't Stop Loving You," Ray Charles (ABC/Paramount)
"Roses Are Red," Bobby Vinton (Epic)
"Theme From a Summer Place," Percy Faith (Columbia)

1963
"Hey Paula," Paul and Paula (Philips)
"Sugar Shack," Jim Gilmer and the Fireballs (Dot)

1964

"I Want to Hold Your Hand," The Beatles (Capitol)
"Can't Buy Me Love," The Beatles (Capitol)
"Everybody Loves Somebody," Dean Martin (Reprise)
"Rag Doll," The 4 Seasons (Philips)
"A Hard Day's Night," The Beatles (Capitol)
"Oh, Pretty Woman," Roy Orbison (Monument)
"I Feel Fine," The Beatles (Capitol)

1965

"Downtown," Petula Clark (Warner Bros.)
"King of the Road," Roger Miller (Smash)
"Mrs. Brown You've Got A Lovely Daughter," Herman's Hermits (MGM)
"(I Can't Get No) Satisfaction," The Rolling Stones (London)
"Wooly Bully," Sam the Sham and the Pharoahs (MGM)
"I'm Henry VIII, I Am," Herman's Hermits (MGM)
"Help!" The Beatles (Capitol)
"Eight Days A Week," The Beatles (Capitol)
"I Got You Babe," Sonny and Cher (Atco)
"Yesterday," The Beatles (Capitol)
"A Lover's Concerto," The Toys (Dynovoice)

1966

"We Can Work It Out," The Beatles (Capitol)
"Ballad of the Green Berets," SSGT. Barry Sadler (RCA Victor)
"Sounds of Silence," Simon & Garfunkel (Columbia)
"These Boots Are Made for Walkin'," Nancy Sinatra (Reprise)
"Lightnin' Strikes," Lou Christie (MGM)
"No Where Man," The Beatles (Capitol)
"Soul and Inspiration," Righteous Brothers (Verve)
"California Dreamin'," Mamas and the Papas (ABC/Dunhill)
"Monday, Monday," Mamas and the Papas (ABC/Dunhill)
"Paperback Writer," The Beatles (Capitol)
"When a Man Loves a Woman," Percy Sledge (Atlantic)
"Lil' Red Riding Hood," Sam the Sham and the Pharoahs (MGM)
"Hanky Panky," Tommy James and the Shondells (Roulette)
"Yellow Submarine," The Beatles (Capitol)
"Summer in the City," Lovin' Spoonful (Kama Sutra)
"Sunny," Bob Hebb (Philips)
"Cherish," Association (Valiant)
"Last Train to Clarksville," The Monkees (Colgems)
"96 Tears,"? (Question mark) and The Mysterians (Cameo)
"I'm A Believer," The Monkees (Colgems)
"Winchester Cathedral," New Vaudeville Band (Fontana)
"Battle of New Orleans," Johnny Horton (Columbia)
"Good Vibrations," Beach Boys (Capitol)

1967

"Snoopy vs. The Red Baron," The Guardsmen (Laurie)
"Mellow Yellow," Donovan (Epic)

"A Little Bit Me, A Little Bit You," The Monkees (Colgems)
"Penny Lane," The Beatles (Capitol)
"Sugartown," Nancy Sinatra (Reprise)
"There's a Kind of Hush (All Over the Land)," Herman's Hermits (MGM)
"Somethin' Stupid," Frank and Nancy Sinatra (Reprise)
"This Diamond Ring," Gary Lewis (Liberty)
"Ruby Tuesday," The Rolling Stones (London)
"Happy Together," The Turtles (White Whale)
"Respect," Aretha Franklin (Atlantic)
"Green Onions," Booker T. & The MG's (Stax)
"Stranger on the Shore," Mr. Acker Bilk (Atco)
"I Never Loved a Man the Way I Love You," Aretha Franklin (Atlantic)
"Groovin'," The Young Rascals (Atlantic)
"Sweet Soul Music," Arthur Conley (Atco)
"Pleasant Valley Sunday," The Monkees (Colgems)
"Windy," Association (Warner Bros.)
"Little Bit O'Soul," Music Explosion (Laurie)
"Georgy Girl," The Seekers (Capitol)
"Baby I Love You," Aretha Franklin (Atlantic)
"Ode to Billie Joe," Bobby Gentry (Capitol)
"All You Need Is Love," The Beatles (Capitol)
"Light My Fire," The Doors (Elektra)
"Can't Take My Eyes Off You," Frankie Valli (Philips)
"The Letter," The Box Tops (Mala)
"Come Back When You Grow Up," Bobby Vee and The Strangers (Liberty)
"To Sir with Love," Lulu (Epic)
"Daydream Believer," The Monkees (Colgems)
"Soul Man," Sam and Dave (Stax)
"Never My Love," The Association (Warner Bros.)
"Hello Goodbye," The Beatles (Capitol)
"Incense and Peppermints," Strawberry Alarm Clock (UNI)
"The Rain, the Park and Other Things," The Cowsills (MGM)

1968

"Chain of Fools," Aretha Franklin (Atlantic)
"Skinny Legs and All," Joe Tex (Dial)
"Judy in Disguise With Glasses," John Fred and the Playboys (Paula)
"Bend Me, Shape Me," American Breed (Acta)
"Woman, Woman," The Union Gap (Columbia)
"Green Tambourine," The Lemon Pipers (Buddah)
"I Say A Little Prayer," Dionne Warwick (Scepter)
"Valleri," The Monkees (Colgems)
"Love Is Blue," Paul Mauriat (Philips)
"Simon Says," 1910 Fruitgum Co. (Buddah)
"(Sittin' On) The Dock of the Bay," Otis Redding (Volt)
"Since You've Been Gone," Aretha Franklin (Atlantic)
"Honey," Bobby Goldsboro (United Artists)
"Young Girl," Union Gap (Columbia)
"Lady Madonna," The Beatles (Capitol)
"Cry Like A Baby," Box Tops (Mala)
"Cowboys to Girls," The Intruders (Gamble)
"Tighten Up," Archie Bell and The Drells (Atlantic)
"Mrs. Robinson," Simon & Garfunkel (Columbia)

1968 *(cont'd)*

"Yummy, Yummy, Yummy," Ohio Express (Buddah)
"Beautiful Morning," The Rascals (Atlantic)
"Grazing in the Grass," Hugh Masekela (UNI)
"Lady Willpower," Gary Puckett and The Union Gap (Columbia)
"This Guy's In Love With You," Herb Alpert (A & M)
"Think," Aretha Franklin (Atlantic)
"The Horse," Cliff Nobles & Co. (Phil.—L.A. Soul)
"People Got To Be Free," The Rascals (Atlantic)
"Harper Valley PTA," Jeannie C. Riley (Plantation)
"Hello, I Love You," The Doors (Electra)
"Slip Away," Clarence Carter (Atlantic)
"Hey Jude," The Beatles (Capitol)
"Stoned Soul Picnic," The 5th Dimension (Liberty)
"Born To Be Wild," Steppenwolf (Dunhill)
"1, 2, 3, Red Light," 1910 Fruitgum Co. (Buddah)
"Turn Around, Look At Me," The Vogues (Reprise)
"Sunshine of Your Love," Cream (Atco)
"I Say A Little Prayer," Aretha Franklin (Atlantic)
"Little Green Apples," O. C. Smith (Columbia)
"Who's Making Love," Johnnie Taylor (Stax)
"Those Were The Days," Mary Hopkin (Apple)
"Girl Watcher," The O'Kaysions (ABC)
"Midnight Confession," Grassroots (Dunhill)
"Fire," Crazy World of Arthur Brown (Atlantic)
"I Love How You Love Me," Bobby Vinton (Epic)
"Over You," Union Gap (Columbia)

1969

"Chewy, Chewy," Ohio Express (Buddah)
"Abraham, Martin & John," Dion (Laurie)
"See Saw," Aretha Franklin (Atlantic)
"Soulful Strut," Young Holt Limited (Brunswick)
"Wichita Lineman," Glen Campbell (Capitol)
"Touch Me," The Doors (Elektra)
"Everyday People," Sly & The Family Stone (Epic)
"The Worst That Can Happen," The Brooklyn Bridge (Buddah)
"Can I Change My Mind," Tyrone Davis (Dakar)
"Hooked On A Feeling," B.J. Thomas (Scepter)
"Too Weak To Fight," Clarence Carter (Atlantic)
"Stormy," Classics IV (Imperial)
"Build Me Up Buttercup," The Foundations (UNI)
"Dizzy," Tommy Roe (ABC)
"Magic Carpet Ride," Steppenwolf (Dunhill)
"Sheila," Tommy Roe (ABC)
"Sweet Pea," Tommy Roe (ABC)
"Indian Giver," 1910 Fruitgum Co. (Buddah)
"It's Your Thing," Isley Brothers (T-Neck)
"Time of the Season," The Zombies (Date)
"Hair," The Cowsills (MGM)
"Only The Strong Survive," Jerry Butler (Mercury)
"Aquarius/Let the Sunshine In," 5th Dimension (Soul City)
"This Magic Moment," Jay and the Americans (United Artists)
"Get Back," The Beatles with Billy Preston (Apple)
"Oh Happy Day," Edwin Hawkins' Singers (Pavilion)

"You Make Me So Very Happy," Blood, Sweat and Tears (Columbia)
"The Chokin' Kind," Joe Simon (Sound Stage 7)
"Gitarzan," Ray Stevens (Monument)
"Grazin' in the Grass," Friends of Distinction (RCA)
"In the Ghetto," Elvis Presley (RCA)
"Love Theme from Romeo & Juliet," Henry Mancini (RCA)
"These Eyes," The Guess Who (RCA)
"In the Year 2525," Zager & Evans (RCA)
"Love Can Make You Happy," Mercy (Sundi)
"Ballad of John & Yoko," The Beatles (Capitol)
"Spinning Wheel," Blood, Sweat and Tears (Columbia)
"One," Three Dog Night (Dunhill)
"Color Him Father," The Winstons (Metromedia)
"A Boy Named Sue," Johnny Cash (Columbia)
"Sweet Caroline," Neil Diamond (UNI)
"Honky Tonk Women," The Rolling Stones (London)
"Sugar, Sugar," The Archies (Calendar)
"Put a Little Love in Your Heart," Jackie DeShannon (Imperial)
"I'll Never Fall in Love Again," Tom Jones (Parrot)
"Little Woman," Bobby Sherman (Metromedia)
"Get Together," Youngbloods (RCA)
"Jean," Oliver (CGC)
"Galveston," Glen Campbell (Capitol)
"Baby, I Love You," Andy Kim (Steed)
"Something," The Beatles (Apple)
"Laughing," The Guess Who (RCA)
"Suspicious Minds," Elvis Presley (RCA)
"Rudolph, The Red Nosed Reindeer," Gene Autry (Columbia)
"Wedding Bell Blues," The 5th Dimension (Soul City)
"Na Na Hey Hey Kiss Him Goodbye," Steam (Fontana)
"Take A Letter Maria," R. B. Greaves (Atco)
"Going in Circles," Friends of Distinction (RCA)
"Smile a Little Smile For Me," Flying Machine (Congress)
"Raindrops Keep Falling on My Head," B. J. Thomas (Scepter)
"Back Field in Motion," Mel & Tim (Bamboo)
"Jet Plane," Peter, Paul & Mary (Warner Bros.)
"That'll Be the Day," Buddy Holly and the Crickets (Coral)
"Holly Holy," Neil Diamond (UNI)

1970

"And When I Die," Blood Sweat and Tears (Columbia)
"Jam Up and Jelly Tight," Tommy Roe (ABC)
"La La La (If I Had You)," Bobby Sherman (Metromedia)
"Don't Cry Daddy," Elvis Presley (RCA)
"Venus," The Shocking Blue (Colossus)
"Jingle Jangle," Archies (Kirshner)
"Thank You (Falettinme Be Mice Elf Again)," Sly & the Family Stone (Epic)
"Without Love," Tom Jones (Parrot)
"Bridge Over Troubled Water," Simon & Garfunkel (Columbia)

1970 *(cont'd)*

"Hey There Lonely Girl," Eddie Holman (ABC)

"Let It Be," The Beatles (Apple)

"Didn't I (Blow Your Mind This Time)," The Delfonics (Philly Groove)

"Rainy Night in Georgia," Brook Benton (Cotillion)

"The Rapper," Jaggerz (Kama Sutra)

"Easy Come, Easy Go," Bobby Sherman (Metromedia)

"Whole Lotta Love," Led Zeppelin (Atlantic)

"Arizona," Mark Lindsay (Columbia)

"Love Grows (Where My Rosemary Goes)," Edison Lighthouse (Bell)

"Spirit in the Sky," Norman Greenbaum (Reprise)

"House of the Rising Son," Frijid Pink (Parrot)

"Turn Back the Hands of Time," Tyrone Davis (Dakar)

"Give Me Just a Little More Time," Chairmen of the Board (Invictus)

"American Women," The Guess Who (RCA)

"Love on a Two-Way Street," The Moments (Stang)

"Cecilia," Simon & Garfunkel (Columbia)

"Which Way You Goin' Billy," Poppy Family (London)

"Everything Is Beautiful," Ray Stevens (Barnaby)

"Hitchin' a Ride," Vanity Fair (Page One)

"Mama Told Me (Not to Come)," Three Dog Night (Dunhill)

"Band of Gold," Freda Payne (Invictus)

"Ride Captain Ride," Blues Image (Atco)

"Make It with You," Bread (Elektra)

"O-O-H Child," The Stairsteps (Buddah)

"(They Long to Be) Close to You," The Carpenters (A & M)

"The Wonder of You," Elvis Presley (RCA)

"In The Summertime," Mungo Jerry (Janus)

"Julie, Do Ya Love Me," Bobby Sherman (Metromedia)

"Patches," Clarence Carter (Atlantic)

"Spill the Wine," Eric Burdon and War (MGM)

"Candida," Dawn (Bell)

"Don't Play That Song," Aretha Franklin (Atlantic)

"Cracklin' Rosie," Neil Diamond (UNI)

"I Think I Love You," The Partridge Family (Bell)

"Groovy Situation," Gene Chandler (Mercury)

"We've Only Just Begun," The Carpenters (A & M)

"Snowbird," Anne Murray (Capitol)

"Somebody Has Been Sleeping In My Bed," 100 Proof (Hot Wax)

"One Less Bell to Answer," 5th Dimension (Bell)

"Instant Karma," John Ono Lennon (Apple)

"My Sweet Lord," George Harrison (Apple)

"Down on the Corner," Creedence Clearwater Revival (Fantasy)

"Travelin' Band," Creedence Clearwater Revival (Fantasy)

"Bad Moon Rising," Creedence Clearwater Revival (Fantasy)

"Up Around the Bend," Creedence Clearwater Revival (Fantasy)

"Lookin' Out My Back Door," Creedence Clearwater Revival (Fantasy)

"Knock Three Times," Dawn (Bell)

1971

"Groove Me," King Floyd (Chimneyville)

"Gypsy Woman," Brian Hyland (UNI)

"Rose Garden," Lynn Anderson (Columbia)

"One Bad Apple," The Osmonds (MGM)

"Precious, Precious," Jackie Moore (Atlantic)

"Doesn't Somebody Want to Be Wanted," The Partridge Family (Bell)

"Have You Ever Seen the Rain," Creedence Clearwater Revival (Fantasy)

"Don't Let the Green Grass Fool You," Wilson Pickett (Atlantic)

"She's A Lady," Tom Jones (Parrot)

"Amos Moses," Jerry Reed (RCA)

"Lonely Days," Bee Gees (Atco)

"Joy to the World," Three Dog Night (ABC/Dunhill)

"For All We Know," The Carpenters (A & M)

"The Battle Hymn of Lt. Calley," Terry Nelson (Plantation)

"Help Me Make It through the Night," Sammi Smith (Mega)

"Put Your Hand in the Hand," Ocean (Kama Sutra)

"Proud Mary," Ike and Tina Turner (Liberty)

"Bridge Over Troubled Water," Aretha Franklin (Atlantic)

"Want Ads," Honey Cone (Hot Wax)

"Stay Awhile," The Bells (Polydor)

"Don't Knock My Love," Wilson Pickett (Atlantic)

"Indian Reservation," The Raiders (Columbia)

"Rainy Days & Mondays," The Carpenters (A & M)

"It's Too Late," Carole King (Ode)

"Treat Her Like a Lady," Cornelius Brothers & Sister Rose (United Artists)

"It Don't Come Easy," Ringo Starr (Apple)

"Don't Pull Your Love," Hamilton, Joe Frank and Reynolds (ABC/Dunhill)

"Take Me Home, Country Roads," John Denver (RCA)

"How Can You Mend a Broken Heart," Bee Gees (Atco)

"Spanish Harlem," Aretha Franklin (Atlantic)

"Bring the Boys Home," Freda Payne (Invictus)

"Sweet and Innocent," Donny Osmond (MGM)

"Signs," Five Man Electrical Band (Lionel)

"You've Got a Friend," James Taylor (Warner Bros.)

"She's Not Just Another Woman," The 8th Day (Invictus)

"Uncle Albert/Admiral Halsey," Paul & Linda McCartney (Apple)

"Ain't No Sunshine," Bill Withers (Sussex)

"Stick-Up," Honey Cone (Hot Wax)

"Maggie May," Rod Stewart (Mercury)

"Go Away Little Girl," Donny Osmond (MGM)

"Superstar," The Carpenters (A & M)

"The Night They Drove Old Dixie Down," Joan Baez (Vanguard)

"Tired of Being Alone," Al Green (Hi)

"Thin Line Between Love and Hate," The Persuaders (Atco)

"Yo-Yo," The Osmonds (MGM)

"Gypsys, Tramps & Thieves," Cher (Kapp)

"Easy Loving," Freddie Hart (Capitol)

"Family Affair," Sly & the Family Stone (Epic)

1971 *(cont'd)*

"Trapped by a Thing Called Love," Denise LaSalle (Westbound)

"Scorpio," Dennis Coffey and The Detroit Guitar Band (Sussex)

"Rock Steady," Aretha Franklin (Atlantic)

"Cherish," David Cassidy (Bell)

"Brand New Key," Melanie (Neighborhood)

"An Old Fashioned Love Song," Three Dog Night (ABC/Dunhill)

"Clean Up Woman," Betty Wright (Alston)

1972

"You Are Everything," The Stylistics (Avco)

"American Pie," Don McLean (United Artists)

"Drowning in the Sea of Love," Joe Simon (Spring)

"Let's Stay Together," Al Green (Hi)

"Baby I'm A Want You," Bread (Elektra)

"Sunshine," Jonathan Edwards (Capricorn)

"I'd Like to Teach the World to Sing," The New Seekers (Elektra)

"Precious and Few," Climax (Carousel)

"Hurting Each Other," The Carpenters (A & M)

"Without You," Nilsson (RCA)

"Day after Day," Badfinger (Apple)

"Kiss an Angel Good Mornin'," Charley Pride (RCA)

"The Lion Sleeps Tonight," Robert John (Atlantic)

"I Gotcha," Joe Tex (Dial)

"Jungle Fever," The Chakachas (Polydor)

"Puppy Love," Donny Osmond (MGM)

"A Horse with No Name," America (Warner Bros.)

"Down by the Lazy River," The Osmonds (MGM)

"Ain't Understanding Mellow," Jerry Butler and Brenda Lee Eager (Mercury)

"Betcha By Golly, Wow," The Stylistics (Avco)

"The First Time Ever I Saw Your Face," Roberta Flack (Atlantic)

"Day Dreaming," Aretha Franklin (Atlantic)

"Heart of Gold," Neil Young (Warner Bros.)

"Look What You've Done for Me," Al Green (Hi)

"Lean on Me," Bill Withers (Sussex)

"Nice to Be With You," Gallery (Sussex)

"Outa-Space," Billy Preston (A & M)

"Slippin' into Darkness," War (United Artists)

"Troglodyte," The Jimmy Castor Bunch (RCA)

"Last Night I Didn't Get to Sleep at All," Fifth Dimension (Bell)

"Daddy Don't You Walk So Fast," Wayne Newton (Chelsea)

"Walking In The Rain With The One I Love," Love Unlimited (UNI)

"Song Sung Blue," Neil Diamond (UNI)

"Hey Girl," Donny Osmond (MGM)

"Sylvia's Mother," Dr. Hook & the Medicine Show (Columbia)

"How Do You Do," Mouth & MacNeal (Philips)

"Too Late to Turn Back Now," Cornelius Bros. & Sister Rose (United Artists)

"Brandy," Looking Glass (Epic)

"Alone Again (Naturally)," Gilbert O'Sullivan (MAM)

"Candy Man," Sammy Davis, Jr. (MGM)

"The Happiest Girl in the Whole U.S.A.," Donna Fargo (Dot)

"Power of Love," Joe Simon (Polydor)

"I'm Still in Love With You," Al Green (Hi)

"Back Stabbers," The O'Jays (Phila. Intl.)

"Where is the Love," Roberta Flack and Donny Hathaway (Atlantic)

"Long Cool Woman (In A Black Dress)," The Hollies (Epic)

"Ding-a-Ling," Chuck Berry (Chess)

"Get On The Good Foot," James Brown (Polydor)

"Everybody Plays the Fool," The Main Ingredient (RCA)

"Baby Don't Get Hooked on Me," Mac Davis (Columbia)

"Black and White," Three Dog Night (ABC/Dunhill)

"Use Me," Bill Withers (Sussex)

"Burning Love," Elvis Presley (RCA)

"I'll Be Around," The Spinners (Atlantic)

"Freddies Dead (Theme from Super Fly)," Curtis Mayfield (Curtom)

"Go All the Way," Raspberries (Capitol)

"Saturday in the Park," Chicago (Columbia)

"I Can See Clearly Now," Johnny Nash (Epic)

"If You Don't Know Me by Now," Harold Melvin & the Blue Notes (Phila. Intl.)

"Garden Party," Rick Nelson (Decca)

"I'd Love You to Want Me," Lobo (Big Tree)

"Mr. and Mrs. Jones," Billy Paul (Phila. Int'l.)

"I'm Stone in Love With You," The Stylistics (Avco)

"You Ought to Be With Me," Al Green (Hi)

"Nights In White Satin," Moody Blues (Deram)

"I Am Woman," Helen Reddy (Capitol)

1973

"Funny Face," Donna Fargo (Dot)

"You're So Vain," Carly Simon (Elektra)

"It Never Rains in Southern California," Albert Hammond (Mums)

"Super Fly," Curtis Mayfield (Curtom)

"Rockin' Pneumonia & The Boogie Flu," Johnny Rivers (United Artists)

"Crocodile Rock," Elton John (MCA)

"Love Jones," Brighter Side of Darkness (20th Century)

"Love Train," The O'Jays (Phila. Int'l.)

"Could It Be I'm Falling in Love," The Spinners (Atlantic)

"Harry Hippie," Bobby Womack and Peace (United Artists)

"Killing Me Softly With His Songs," Roberta Flack (Atlantic)

"The World Is a Ghetto," War (United Artists)

"Cisco Kid," War (United Artists)

"Your Mama Don't Dance," Loggins & Messina (Columbia)

"Dueling Banjos," Eric Weissberg (Warner Bros.)

"Last Song," Edward Bear (Capitol)

"Clair," Gilbert O'Sullivan (MAM)

"Ain't No Woman," Four Tops (ABC/Dunhill)

"The Night the Lights Went Out in Georgia," Vicki Lawrence (Bell)

1973 *(cont'd)*

"Tie A Yellow Ribbon Round The Old Oak Tree," Dawn (Bell)

"The Cover of Rolling Stone," Dr. Hook & the Medicine Show (Columbia)

"Break Up To Make Up," The Stylistics (Avco)

"Call Me (Come Back Home)," Al Green (Hi)

"Little Willy," The Sweet (Bell)

"Funky Worm," Ohio Players (Westbound)

"Sing," The Carpenters (A & M)

"Pillow Talk," Sylvia (Vibration)

"Leaving Me," Independents (Wand)

"I'm Gonna Love You Just A Little More Baby," Barry White (20th Century)

"Frankenstein," Edgar Winter Group (Epic)

"Will It Go Round In Circles," Billy Preston (A & M)

"Playground in My Mind," Clint Holmes (Epic)

"Drift Away," Dobie Gray (Decca)

"My Love," Paul McCartney & Wings (Apple)

"One of a Kind (Love Affair)," Spinners (Atlantic)

"Natural High," Bloodstone (London)

"Doin' It To Death," Fred Wesley and the JB's (People)

"Shambala," Three Dog Night (ABC/Dunhill)

"Bad Bad Leroy Brown," Jim Croce (ABC/Dunhill)

"Give Your Baby a Standing Ovation," The Dells (Cadet)

"Yesterday Once More," The Carpenters (A & M)

"The Morning After," Maureen McGovern (20th Century)

"Brother Louie," Stories (Kama Sutra)

"Monster Mash," Bobby Pickett (Parrot)

"Here I Am (Come and Take Me)," Al Green (Hi)

"Smoke on the Water," Deep Purple (Warner Bros.)

"Delta Dawn," Helen Reddy (Capitol)

"Live and Let Die," Paul McCartney & Wings (Apple)

"Behind Closed Doors," Charlie Rich (Epic)

"If You Want Me to Stay," Sly & The Family Stone (Epic)

"Twelfth of Never," Donny Osmond (Kolob)

"Get Down," Gilbert O'Sullivan (MAM)

"That Lady," Isley Brothers (T-Neck)

"We're An American Band," Grand Funk Railroad (Capitol)

"Loves Me Like a Rock," Paul Simon (Columbia)

"Say, Has Anybody Seen My Sweet Gypsy Rose," Dawn (Bell)

"Half-Breed," Cher (MCA)

"Midnight Train to Georgia," Gladys Knight & The Pips (Buddah)

"I Believe in You (You Believe in Me)," Johnny Taylor (Stax)

"Heart Beat—It's a Lovebeat," The DeFranco Family featuring Tony DeFranco (20th Century)

"Why Me," Kris Kristofferson (Monument)

"Angie," Rolling Stones (Rolling Stone)

"Paper Roses," Marie Osmond (Kolob)

"The Most Beautiful Girl," Charlie Rich (Epic)

"Top of the World," The Carpenters (A & M)

"Show and Tell," Al Wilson (Rocky Road)

"Space Race," Billy Preston (A & M)

"If You're Ready," Staple Singers (Stax)

"The Love I Lost," Harold Melvin & The Blue Notes (Phila. Int'l.)

"Photograph," Ringo Starr (Apple)

1974

"Just You and Me," Chicago (Columbia)

"Time in a Bottle," Jim Croce (ABC)

"Goodbye Yellow Brick Road," Elton John (MCA)

"Americans," Byron MacGregor (Westbound)

"Leave Me Alone (Ruby Red Dress)," Helen Reddy (Capitol)

"The Joker," Steve Miller Band (Capitol)

"Smokin' in the Boys Room," Brownsville Station (Big Tree)

"I Have Got to Use My Imagination," Gladys Knight & The Pips (Buddah)

"You're Sixteen," Ringo Starr (Apple)

"The Way We Were," Barbra Streisand (Columbia)

"Never, Never, Gonna Give Ya Up," Barry White (20th Century)

"Love's Theme," Love Unlimited Orchestra (20th Century)

"Let Me Be There," Olivia Newton-John (MCA)

"Seasons in the Sun," Terry Jacks (Bell)

"Until You Come Back to Me," Aretha Franklin (Atlantic)

"Jungle Boogie," Kool & the Gang (De-Lite)

"Spiders and Snakes," Jim Stafford (MGM)

"Dark Lady," Cher (MCA)

"Rock On," David Essex (Columbia)

"Hooked on a Feeling," Blue Swede (EMI)

"Sunshine on My Shoulder," John Denver (RCA)

"TSOP," MFSB (Phila. Int'l.)

"The Lord's Prayer," Sister Janet Mead (A & M)

"Lookin' for a Love," Bobby Womack (United Artists)

"Bennie and the Jets," Elton John (MCA)

"The Best Thing That Ever Happened to Me," Gladys Knight & The Pips (Buddah)

"The Payback," James Brown (Polydor)

"Come and Get Your Love," Redbone (Epic)

"The Streak," Ray Stevens (Barnaby)

"The Loco-Motion," Grand Funk Railroad (Capitol)

"Just Don't Want to Be Lonely," The Main Ingredient (RCA)

"Mockingbird," Carly Simon and James Taylor (Elektra)

"The Show Must Go On," Three Dog Night (Dunhill)

"You Make Me Feel Brand New," The Stylistics (Avco)

"Be Thankful for What You Got," William DeVaughn (Roxbury)

"Band on the Run," Paul McCartney & Wings (Apple)

"Billy Don't Be a Hero," Bo Donaldson & the Heywoods (Dunhill)

"The Entertainer," Original Motion Picture Soundtrack from *The Sting* (MCA)

"For the Love of Money," The O'Jays (Phila. Int'l.)

"Sundown," Gordon Lightfoot (Reprise)

"Hollywood Swinging," Kool & the Gang (De-Lite)

"Rock the Boat," The Hues Corporation (RCA)

"On and On," Gladys Knight & The Pips (Buddah)

"Annie's Song," John Denver (RCA)

1974 *(cont'd)*

"If You Love Me (Let Me Know)," Olivia Newton-John (MCA)

"Feel Like Makin' Love," Roberta Flack (Atlantic)

"Tell Me Something Good," Rufus (ABC)

"The Night Chicago Died," Paper Lace (Mercury)

"(You're) Having My Baby," Paul Anka (United Artists)

"Sideshow," Blue Magic (Atco)

"The Air That I Breathe," The Hollies (Epic)

"Don't Let the Sun Go Down on Me," Elton John (MCA)

"Can't Get Enough of Your Love, Babe," Barry White (20th Century Fox)

"I Shot the Sheriff," Eric Clapton (RSO)

"I'm Leaving It (All) Up to You," Donny & Marie Osmond (MGM)

"Rock Me Gently," Andy Kim (Capitol)

"Then Came You," Dionne Warwick & The Spinners (Atlantic)

"I Honestly Love You," Olivia Newton-John (MCA)

"Nothing from Nothing," Billy Preston (A & M)

"Skin Tight," Ohio Players (Mercury)

"Do It ('Til You're Satisfied)," B. T. Express (Scepter)

"Kung Fu Fighting," Carl Douglas (20th Century)

"I Can Help," Billy Swan (Monument)

"My Melody of Love," Bobby Vinton (ABC)

"When Will I See You Again," Three Degrees (Phila. Int'l.)

"You Ain't Seen Nothing Yet," Bachman-Turner Overdrive (Mercury)

"You're The First, The Last, My Everything," Barry White (20th Century)

"Cat's In The Cradle," Harry Chapin (Elektra)

1975

"Back Home Again," John Denver (RCA)

"Angie Baby," Helen Reddy (Capitol)

"Sha-La-La (Make Me Happy)," Al Green (Hi)

"Fire," Ohio Players (Mercury)

"Lucy in the Sky with Diamonds," Elton John (MCA)

"Mandy," Barry Manilow (Bell)

"Please Mr. Postman," Carpenters (A & M)

"Have You Never Been Mellow," Olivia Newton-John (MCA)

"Pick Up the Pieces," Average White Band (Atlantic)

"Lady Marmalade," LaBelle (Epic)

"My Eyes Adored You," Frankie Valli (Private Stock)

"Lovin' You," Minnie Riperton (Epic)

"Black Water," Doobie Brothers (Warner Bros.)

"Philadelphia Freedom," The Elton John Band (MCA)

"Chevy Van," Sammy Johns (GRC)

"Before the Next Teardrop Falls," Freddy Fender (ABC/Dot)

"(Hey Won't You Play) Another Somebody Done Somebody Wrong Song," B. J. Thomas (ABC)

"He Don't Love You (Like I Love You)," Tony Orlando & Dawn (Elektra)

"Shining Star," Earth, Wind & Fire (Columbia)

"Love Won't Let Me Wait," Major Harris (Atlantic)

"Thank God I'm a Country Boy," John Denver (RCA)

"The Hustle," Van McCoy and The Soul City Symphony (Avco)

"Love Will Keep Us Together," Captain & Tennille (A & M)

"Wildfire," Michael Murphey (Epic)

"Express," B. T. Express (Scepter)

"Magic," Pilot (Capitol)

"Why Can't We Be Friends?" War (United Artists)

"Jive Talkin'," Bee Gees (RSO)

"Listen to What the Man Said," Paul McCartney & Wings (Capitol)

"Rhinestone Cowboy," Glen Campbell (Capitol)

"Someone Saved My Life Tonight," Elton John (MCA)

"Fight the Power Part I," Isley Bros. (T-Neck)

"Fallin' in Love," Hamilton, Joe Frank & Reynolds (Playboy)

"Please Mister Please," Olivia Newton-John (MCA)

"Wasted Days and Wasted Nights," Freddy Fender (ABC-Dot)

"Mr. Jaws," Dickie Goodman (Private Stock)

"Fame," David Bowie (RCA)

"Feelings," Morris Albert (RCA)

"They Just Can't Stop It (Games People Play)," Spinners (Atlantic)

"Do It Anyway You Wanna," Peoples Choice (Phila. Int'l.)

"I'm Sorry," John Denver (RCA)

"Let's Do It Again," The Staple Singers (Curtom)

"Bad Blood," Neil Sedaka (Rocket)

"Fly, Robin, Fly," Silver Convention (RCA/Midland International)

"Island Girl," Elton John (MCA)

"Saturday Night," Bay City Rollers (Arista)

"The Way I Want to Touch You," Captain & Tennille (A & M)

"Convoy," C. W. McCall (MGM)

1976

"Love Rollercoaster," Ohio Players (Mercury)

"I Write the Songs," Barry Manilow (Arista)

"I Love Music," O'Jays (Phila. Int'l.)

"You Sexy Thing," Hot Chocolate (Big Tree)

"Proud Mary," Creedence Clearwater Revival (Fantasy)

"Theme from S.W.A.T.," Rhythm Heritage (ABC)

"Love to Love You Baby," Donna Summer (Oasis)

"Fox on the Run," Sweet (Capitol)

"Singasong," Earth, Wind & Fire (Columbia)

"Sweet Thing," Rufus featuring Chaka Khan (ABC)

"Disco Lady," Johnnie Taylor (Columbia)

"50 Ways to Leave Your Lover," Paul Simon (Columbia)

"December, 1963 (Oh, What a Night)," Four Seasons (Warner Bros.)

"Lonely Night (Angel Face)," Captain & Tennille (A & M)

"Love Hurts," Nazareth (A & M)

"Boogie Fever," The Sylvers (Capitol)

"Dream Weaver," Gary Wright (Warner Bros.)

"All By Myself," Eric Carmen (Arista)

"Right Back Where We Started From," Maxine Nightingale (United Artists)

1976 *(cont'd)*

"Only Sixteen," Dr. Hook (Capitol)

"Welcome Back," John Sebastian (Warner/Reprise)

"I. O. U.," Jimmy Dean (GRT/Casino)

"Bohemian Rhapsody," Queen (Elektra)

"Get Up and Boogie," Silver Convention (Midland International)

"Silly Love Songs," Wings (Capitol)

"Kiss and Say Goodbye," The Manhattans (Columbia)

"Shannon," Henry Gross (Lifesong)

"Fooled Around and Fell in Love," Elvin Bishop (Capricorn)

"Sara Smile," Daryl Hall & John Oates (RCA)

"Afternoon Delight," Starland Vocal Band (Windsong)

"Shop Around," Captain & Tennille (A & M)

"Don't Go Breaking My Heart," Elton John & Kiki Dee (MCA/Rocket)

"You'll Never Find Another Love Like Mine," Lou Rawls (Phila. Int'l.)

"Play That Funky Music," Wild Cherry (Epic/Sweet City)

"A Fifth of Beethoven," Walter Murphy & The Big Apple Band (Private Stock)

"Summer," War (United Artists)

"You Should Be Dancing," Bee Gees (RSO)

"Heaven Must Be Missing An Angel," Tavares (Capitol)

"More, More, More," Andrea True Connection (Buddah)

"Disco Duck," Rick Dees & His Cast of Idiots (RSO)

"I'd Really Love to See You Tonight," England Dan & John Ford Coley (Big Tree)

"Tear the Roof Off the Sucker," Parliament (Casablanca)

"Devil Woman," Cliff Richard (MCA/Rocket)

"Let 'Em In," Wings (Capitol)

"If You Leave Me Now," Chicago (Columbia)

"Getaway," Earth, Wind & Fire (Columbia)

"Lowdown," Boz Scaggs (Columbia)

"Teddy Bear," Red Sovine (Gusto/Starday)

"You Don't Have to Be a Star (To Be in My Show)," Marilyn McCoo & Billy Davis, Jr. (ABC)

"Tonight's the Night (Gonna be Alright)," Rod Stewart (Warner Bros.)

"The Rubberband Man," The Spinners (Atlantic)

"Muskrat Love," Captain & Tennille (A & M)

"Car Wash," Rose Royce (MCA)

"You Make Me Feel Like Dancing," Leo Sayer (Warner Bros.)

"Love So Right," Bee Gees (RSO)

1977

"Hot Line," The Sylvers (Capitol)

"Beth," Kiss (Casablanca)

"I'll Be Good to You," Brothers Johnson (A & M)

"Nadia's Theme ('The Young & the Restless')," Barry DeVorzon and Perry Botkin, Jr. (A & M)

"Stand Tall," Burton Cummings (CBS/Portrait)

"Sorry Seems to Be the Hardest Word," Elton John (MCA)

"Enjoy Yourself," Jacksons (Epic)

"Torn Between Two Lovers," Mary MacGregor (Capitol/Ariola America)

"After The Lovin'," Engelbert Humperdinck (Epic)

"Blinded By the Light," Manfred Mann's Earth Band (Warner Bros.)

"I Like Dreamin'," Kenny Nolan (20th Century)

"New Kid in Town," Eagles (Asylum)

"Dancing Queen," Abba (Atlantic)

"Evergreen (Theme from *A Star Is Born*)," Barbra Streisand (Columbia)

"Rich Girl," Daryl Hall & John Oates (RCA)

"I Never Cry," Alice Cooper (Warner Bros.)

"Don't Give Up On Us," David Soul (Private Stock)

"I've Got Love On My Mind," Natalie Cole (Capitol)

"The Things We Do for Love," 10CC (Phonogram/Mercury)

"Fly Like An Eagle," Steve Miller Band (Capitol)

"Southern Nights," Glen Campbell (Capitol)

"Tryin' To Love Two," William Bell (Phonogram/Mercury)

"When I Need You," Leon Sayer (Warner Bros.)

"Hotel California," Eagles (Elektra/Asylm)

"Ain't Gonna Bump No More," Joe Tex (Epic)

"Lucille," Kenny Rogers (United Artists)

"Undercover Angel," Alan O'Day (Atlantic)

"Gonna Fly Now (Theme from *Rocky*)," Bill Conti (United Artists)

"Angel In Your Arms," Hot (Atlantic/Big Tree)

"Da Doo Ron Ron," Shaun Cassidy (Warner Bros.)

"Best Of My Love," Emotions (Columbia)

"I Just Want to Be Your Everything," Andy Gibb (Polydor/RSO)

"Travelin' Man," Rick Nelson (United Artists/Imperial)

"Do You Wanna Make Love," Peter McCann (20th Century)

"Float On," The Floaters (ABC)

"(Your Love Has Lifted Me) Higher and Higher," Rita Coolidge (A & M)

"Looks Like We Made It," Barry Manilow (Arista)

"The King Is Gone," Ronnie McDowell (GRT)

"Way Down," Elvis Presley (RCA)

"Dreams," Fleetwood Mac (Warner Bros.)

"Telephone Line," Electric Light Orchestra (United Artists/Jet)

"*Star Wars* Theme/Cantina Band," Meco (Millennium)

"That's Rock 'n' Roll," Shaun Cassidy (Warner Bros.)

"Boogie Nights," Heatwave (Epic)

"It's Ecstasy When You Lay Down Next to Me," Barry White (20th Century)

"Strawberry Letter 23," Brothers Johnson (A & M)

"You Light Up My Life," Debby Boone (Warner Bros.)

"Telephone Man," Meri Wilson (GRT)

"Nobody Does It Better," Carly Simon (Elektra)

"I Feel Love," Donna Summer (Casablanca)

"Don't It Make My Brown Eyes Blue," Crystal Gayle (United Artists)

"Swayin' to the Music," Johnny Rivers (Atlantic/Big Tree)

"Heaven on the 7th Floor," Paul Nicholas (Polydor/RSO)

"How Deep Is Your Love," Bee Gees (Polydor/RSO)

"(Every Time I Turn Around) Back in Love Again," L.T.D. (A & M)

1978

"Baby Come Back," Player (Polydor/RSO)
"My Way," Elvis Presley (RSA)
"Hey Deanie," Shaun Cassidy (Warner Bros.)
"Blue Bayou," Lind Ronstadt (Asylum)
"Short People," Randy Newman (Warner Bros.)
"We Are the Champions," Queen (Elektra)
"Stayin' Alive," Bee Gees (Polydor/RSO)
"Here You Come Again," Dolly Parton (RCA)
"We're All Alone," Rita Coolidge (A & M)
"You're in My Heart," Rod Stewart (Warner Bros.)
"Emotion," Samantha Sang (Private Stock)
"Dance, Dance, Dance," Chic (Atlantic)
"Love Is Thicker than Water," Andy Gibb (Polydor/RSO)
"Night Fever," Bee Gees (Polydor/RSO)
"Sometimes When We Touch," Dan Hill (20th Century)
"Just the Way You Are," Billy Joel (Columbia)
"Always And Forever," Heatwave (Epic)
"Our Love," Natalie Cole (Capitol)
"Can't Smile without You," Barry Manilow (Arista)
"You're the One That I Want," John Travolta and Olivia Newton-John (Polydor/RSO)
"Lay Down Sally," Eric Clapton (Polydor/RSO)
"Flash Light," Parliament (Casablanca)
"Jack and Jill," Raydio (Arista)
"The Closer I Get to You," Roberta Flack and Donny Hathaway (Atlantic)
"If I Can't Have You," Yvonne Elliman (Polydor/RSO)
"Too Much, Too Little, Too Late," Johnny Mathis and Deniece Williams (Columbia)
"Shadow Dancing," Andy Gibb (Polydor/RSO)
"Use Ta Be My Girl," O'Jays (Phila. Int'l.)
"It's A Heartache," Bonnie Tyler (RCA)
"Dust in the Wind," Kansas (CBS/Kirshner)
"The Groove Line," Heatwave (Epic)
"Baker Street," Gerry Rafferty (United Artists)
"Last Dance," Donna Summer (Casablanca)
"Two Out of Three Ain't Bad," Meat Loaf (Cleveland Intl.)
"Miss You," Rolling Stones (Atlantic/Rolling Stones)
"Grease," Frankie Valli (Polydor/RSO)
"Take A Chance On Me," ABBA (Atlantic)
"Boogie Oogie Oogie," A Taste of Honey (Capitol)
"Shame," Evelyn "Champagne" King (RCA)
"An Everlasting Love," Andy Gibb (Polydor/RSO)
"King Tut," Steve Martin (Warner Bros.)
"Hopelessly Devoted to You," Olivia Newton-John (RSO)
"Summer Nights," John Travolta & Olivia Newton-John (Polydor/RSO)
"Copacabana," Barry Manilow (Arista)
"Hot Blooded," Foreigner (Atlantic)
"Got to Get You Into My Life," Earth Wind & Fire (Columbia/ARC)
"Hot Child in the City," Nick Gilder (Chrysalis)
"Kiss You All Over," Exile (Warner/Curb)
"Close the Door," Teddy Pendergrass (Phila. Int'l.)
"You Needed Me," Anne Murray (Capitol)
"MacArthur Park," Donna Summer (Casablanca)
"Macho Man," Village People (Casablanca)

"Magnet and Steel," Walter Egan (Columbia)
"Double Vision," Foreigner (Atlantic)
"Le Freak," Chic (Atlantic)
"You Don't Bring Me Flowers," Barbra Streisand and Neil Diamond (Columbia)
"One Nation Under a Groove," Funkadelic (Warner Bros.)
"Too Much Heaven," Bee Gees (Polydor/RSO)
"I Love the Night Life," Alicia Bridges (Polydor)
"YMCA," Village People (Casablanca)

1979

"(Our Love) Don't Throw It All Away," Andy Gibb (Polydor/RSO)
"Got To Be Real," Cheryl Lynn (Columbia)
"My Life," Billy Joel (Columbia)
"September," Earth, Wind & Fire (Columbia/ARC)
"Instant Replay," Dan Hartman (CBS/Blue Sky)
"Da Ya Think I'm Sexy," Rod Stewart (Warner Bros.)
"Every 1's a Winner," Hot Chocolate (Infinity)
"Tragedy," Bee Gees (RSO)
"Fire," Pointer Sisters (Planet/EA)
"I Will Survive," Gloria Gaynor (Polydor)
"A Little More Love," Olivia Newton-John (MCA)
"Hold the Line," Toto (Columbia)
"Shake Your Groove Thing," Peaches & Herb (Polydor)
"I Don't Know if It's Right," Evelyn "Champagne" King (RCA)
"I Want Your Love," Chic (Atlantic)
"Heaven Knows," Donna Summer With Brooklyn Dreams (Casablanca)
"Bustin' Loose," Chuck Brown & The Soul Searchers (MCA/Source)
"In The Navy," Village People (Casablanca)
"Knock On Wood," Amii Stewart (Ariola America)
"Music Box Dancer," Frank Mills (Polydor)
"I Got My Mind Made Up (You Can Get It Girl)," Instant Funk (RCA/Salsoul)
"Livin' It Up," Bell & James (A & M)
"Heart of Glass," Blondie (Chrysalis)
"Reunited," Peaches & Herb (Polydor)
"Love You Inside Out," Bee Gees (RSO)
"Shake Your Body," The Jacksons (Epic)
"What a Fool Believes," Doobie Bros. (Warner Bros.)
"Hot Stuff," Donna Summer (Casablanca)
"Disco Nights (RockFreak)," G. Q. (Arista)
"Take Me Home," Cher (Casablanca)
"Ain't No Stopping Us Now," McFadden & Whitehead (Phila. Int'l.)
"Good Night Tonight," Wings (Columbia)
"Boogie Wonderland," Earth, Wind & Fire with the Emotions (ARC/Columbia)
"Stumblin' In," Suzi Quatro with Chris Norman (RSO)
"We Are Family," Sister Sledge
"Bad Girls," Donna Summer (Casablanca)
"Good Times," Chic (Atlantic)
"You Take My Breath Away," Rex Smith (Columbia)
"Makin' It," David Naughton (RSO)
"Just When I Needed You Most," Randy Vanwarmer (Bearsville/Warner Bros.)

1979 *(cont'd)*

"She Believes in Me," Kenny Rogers (United Artists)

"I Want You To Want Me," Cheap Trick (Epic)

"My Sharona," The Knack (Capitol)

"I Was Made For Lovin' You," Kiss (Casablanca)

"Mama Can't Buy You Love," Elton John (MCA)

"The Devil Went Down to Georgia," Charlie Daniels (Epic)

"When You're in Love With a Beautiful Woman," Dr. Hook (Capitol)

"You Gonna Make Me Love Somebody Else," The Jones Girls (Phila. Int'l.)

"Main Event," Barbra Streisand (Columbia)

"Sad Eyes," Robert John (EMI)

"Lead Me On," Maxine Nightingale (RCA)

"Rise," Herb Alpert (A & M)

"I'll Never Love This Way Again," Dionne Warwicke (Arista)

"Born to Be Alive," Patrick Hernandez (CBS)

"After the Love Has Gone," Earth, Wind & Fire (CBS)

"Don't Stop Till You Get Enough," Michael Jackson (CBS)

"Don't Bring Me Down," Electric Light Orchestra (Jet/ CBS)

"Pop Muzik," M (Warner Bros.)

"Ladies' Night," Kool & the Gang (Phonogram)

"Dim All the Lights," Donna Summer (Casablanca)

1980

"Escape (The Pina Colada Song)," Rupert Holmes (MCA)

"Babe," Styx (A & M)

"Heartache Tonight," The Eagles (Asylum)

"Second Time Around," Shalamar (Solar)

"No More Tears (Enough Is Enough)," Barbra Streisand (Columbia)

"No More Tears (Enough Is Enough)," Donna Summer (Casablanca)

"Do That To Me One More Time," Captain & Tennille (Casablanca)

"Rock With You," Michael Jackson (Epic)

"Coward Of The County," Kenny Rogers (United Artists)

"On The Radio," Donna Summer (Casablanca)

"And The Beat Goes On," The Whispers (Solar)

"I Wanna Be Your Lover," Prince (Warner Bros.)

"Yes, I'm Ready," Teri De Sario & KC (Casablanca)

"Another Brick In The Wall (Part II)," Pink Floyd (Columbia)

"Call Me," Blondie (Chrysalis)

"Workin' My Way Back To You," The Spinners (Atlantic)

"Crazy Little Thing Called Love," Queen (Elektra)

"Special Lady," Ray, Goodman & Brown (Polydor)

"Funky Town," Lipps, Inc. (Casablanca)

"Take Your Time (Do It Right)," S.O.S. Band (Tabu)

"The Rose," Bette Midler (Columbia)

"Sexy Eyes," Dr. Hook (Capitol)

"I'm Alive," Electric Light Orchestra (MCA)

"Magic," Olivia Newton-John (MCA)

"Shining Star," The Manhattans (Columbia)

"Coming Up," Paul McCartney (Columbia)

"It's Still Rock 'N Roll To Me," Billy Joel (Columbia)

"Little Jeannie," Elton John (MCA)

"The Breaks," Kurtis Blow (Phonogram) (12-inch)

"One In A Million You," Larry Graham (Warner Bros.)

"Another One Bites The Dust," Queen (Elektra)

"All Out Of Love," Air Supply (Arista)

"Woman In Love," Barbra Streisand (Columbia)

"Lookin' For Love," Johnny Lee (Asylum)

"He's So Shy," Pointer Sisters (Elektra)

"Lady," Kenny Rogers (Liberty)

"The Wanderer," Donna Summer (Warner Bros.)

"Jessie," Carly Simon (Warner Bros.)

"Theme From The Dukes of Hazzard," Waylon Jennings (RCA)

"Whip It," Devo (Warner Bros.)

"Starting Over," John Lennon (Warner Bros.)

"More Than I Can Say," Leo Sayer (Warner Bros.)

K. Platinum Record Awards

ALBUMS

1976

Eagles—Their Greatest Hits, Eagles (Asylum)
Desire, Bob Dylan (Columbia)
Framptom Comes Alive!, Peter Framptom (A & M)
Presence, Led Zeppelin (Swan Song)
Wings at the Speed of Sound, Wings (Capitol)
Rock 'N' Roll Music, The Beatles (Capitol)
Black and Blue, The Rolling Stones (Rolling Stone)
Rocks, Aerosmith (Columbia)
Breezin', George Benson (Warner Bros.)
Look Out for #1, Brothers Johnson (A & M)
Chicago X, Chicago (Columbia)
Mothership Connection, Parliament (Casablanca)
Beautiful Noise, Neil Diamond (Columbia)
Silk Degrees, Boz Scaggs (Columbia)
Song of Joy, Captain & Tennille (A & M)
Fly Like An Eagle, Steve Miller Band (Capitol)
Spitfire, Jefferson Starship (Grunt)
Spirit, John Denver (RCA)
Spirit, Earth, Wind & Fire (Columbia)
Hasten Down the Wind, Linda Ronstadt (Asylum)
Dreamboat Annie, Heart (Mushroom)
Destroyer, Kiss (Casablanca)
The Song Remains the Same, Led Zeppelin (Swan Song)
Boston, Boston (Epic)
A Night on the Town, Rod Stewart (Warner Bros.)
The Outlaws, The Outlaws—Waylon Jennings, Willie Nelson, Jessi Colter, Tompall Glaser (RCA)
Run With the Pack, Bad Company (Swan Song)
A New World Record, Electric Light Orchestra (United Artists)
Blue Moves, Elton John (MCA/Rocket)
Brass Construction, Brass Construction (United Artists)
Hotel California, Eagles (Asylum)
Wild Cherry, Wild Cherry (Epic/Sweet City)
Wings Over America, Wings (Capitol)
Best of the Doobies, Doobie Brothers (Warner Bros.)
Children of the World, Bee Gees (RSO)
One More For From the Road, Lynyrd Skynyrd (MCA)
Soul Searching, Average White Band (Atlantic)

1977

Rock And Roll Over, Kiss (Casablanca)
Greatest Hits, War (United Artists)
This One's For You, Barry Manilow (Arista)
Greatest Hits, Linda Ronstadt (Asylum)
A Star Is Born, Barbra Streisand and Kris Kristofferson
All Things In Time, Lou Rawls (Phila. Int'l.)
Rumours, Fleetwood Mac (Warner Bros.)

Animals, Pink Floyd (Columbia)
Leftoverture, Kansas (Columbia/Kirshner)
Year of the Cat, Al Stewart (GRT/Janus)
Night Moves, Bob Seger & The Silver Bullet Band (Capitol)
The Pretender, Jackson Browne (Elektra/Asylum)
Ask Rufus, Rufus featuring Chaka Khan (ABC)
After The Lovin', Engelbert Humperdinck (Epic)
Go For Your Guns, Isley Brothers (Columbia/T-Neck)
Book of Dreams, Steve Miller Band (Capitol)
I'm In You, Peter Framptom (A & M)
Barry Manilow Live, Barry Manilow (Arista)
Rocky—Original Soundtrack (United Artists)
Love Gun, Kiss (Casablanca)
Love at the Greek, Neil Diamond (Columbia)
Little Queen, Heart (Columbia/Portrait)
Right on Time, Brothers Johnson (A & M)
Superman, Barbra Streisand (Columbia)
Foreigner, Foreigner (Atlantic)
Unpredictable, Natalie Cole (Capitol)
The Beatles At The Hollywood Bowl, The Beatles (Capitol)
Star Wars—Original Soundtrack (20th Century)
CSN, Crosby, Stills & Nash (Atlantic)
Rejoice, Emotions (Columbia)
J.T., James Taylor (Columbia)
Moody Blue, Elvis Presley (RCA)
Endless Flight, Leo Sayer (Warner Bros.)
Shaun Cassidy, Shaun Cassidy (Warner Bros.)
Cat Scratch Fever, Ted Nugent (Epic)
Free For All, Ted Nugent (Epic)
In Flight, George Benson (Warner Bros.)
The Floaters, The Floaters (ABC)
Ol' Waylon, Waylon Jennings (RCA)
Chicago XI, Chicago (Columbia)
Simple Dreams, Linda Ronstadt (Asylum)
In Concert, Elvis Presley (RCA)
Anytime . . . Anywhere, Rita Coolidge (A & M)
Elton John's Greatest Hits, Vol. II, Elton John (MCA)
Out Of The Blue, Electric Light Orch. (United Artists/Jet)
Barry White Sings for Someone You Love, Barry White (20th Century)
James Taylor's Greatest Hits, James Taylor (Warner Bros.)
Here at Last . . . Bee Gees . . . Live, Bee Gees (Polydor/RSO)
Kiss Alive II, Kiss (Casablanca)
Point of Know Return, Kansas (Columbia/Kirshner)
Elvis Sings the Wonderful World of Christmas, Elvis Presley (RCA)
In Full Bloom, Rose Royce (Warner Bros./Whitfield)

1977 *(cont'd)*
Down Two Then Left, Boz Scaggs (Columbia)
All 'N' All, Earth, Wind & Fire (Columbia)
Street Survivors, Lynyrd Skynyrd (MCA)
I'm Glad You're Here With Me Tonight, Neil Diamond (Columbia)
Draw the Line, Aerosmith (Columbia)
You Light Up My Life, Debby Boone (Warner Bros.)
Born Late, Shaun Cassidy (Warner Bros.)
Changes in Latitudes, Changes in Attitudes, Jimmy Buffett (ABC)
Greatest Hits, Olivia Newton-John (MCA)
'Live' Bullet, Bob Seger & The Silver Bullet Band (Capitol)
Foghat Live, Foghat (Warner/Bearsville)
Foot Loose & Fancy Free, Rod Stewart (Warner Bros.)
Too Hot to Handle, Heatwave (Epic)
The Grand Illusion, Styx (A & M)
Aja, Steely Dan (ABC)
News of the World, Queen (Elektra)

1978
Saturday Night Fever, Bee Gees (Polydor/RSO)
The Stranger, Billy Joel (Columbia)
Greatest Hits, Etc., Paul Simon (Columbia)
We Must Believe in Magic, Crystal Gayle (United Artists)
Even Now, Barry Manilow (Arista)
Slowhand, Eric Clapton (RSO)
London Town, Paul McCartney & Wings (Capitol)
Waylon & Willie, Waylon Jennings and Willie Nelson (RCA)
Here You Come Again, Dolly Parton (RCA)
French Kiss, Bob Welch (Capitol)
Weekend in L.A., George Benson (Warner Bros.)
Showdown, Isley Brothers (CBS/T-Neck)
M.U.—The Best of Jethro Tull, Jethro Tull (Chrysalis)
Earth, Jefferson Starship (RCA/Grunt)
Funkentelechy vs. The Placebo Syndrome, Parliament (Casablanca)
Grease—Original soundtrack (Polydor/RSO)
Let's Get Small, Steve Martin (Warner Bros.)
FM—Original Soundtrack (MCA)
Son of a Son of a Sailor, Jimmy Buffett (ABC)
I Want to Live, John Denver (RCA)
Double Platinum, Kiss (Casablanca)
Feels So Good, Chuck Manigione (A & M)
Carolina Dreams, Marshal Tucker Band (Capricorn)
Stranger in Town, Bob Seger & The Silver Bullet Band (Capitol)
So Full of Love, O'Jays (Phila. Int'l.)
Magazine, Heart (Mushroom)
Star Wars And Other Galactic Funk, Meco (Millenium)
Thank God It's Friday—Original Soundtrack (Casablanca)
Shadow Dancing, Andy Gibb (Polydor/RSO)
City to City, Gerry Rafferty (United Artists)
Thankful, Natalie Cole (Capitol)
Central Heating, Heatwave (Epic)
Teddy Pendergrass, Teddy Pendergrass (Phila. Int'l.)

Double Vision, Foreigner (Atlantic)
Some Girls, Rolling Stones (Atlantic/Rolling Stones)
Darkness on the Edge of Town, Bruce Springsteen (Columbia)
You Light Up My Life, Johnny Mathis (Columbia)
Agents of Fortune, Blue Oyster Cult (Columbia)
Sgt. Pepper's Lonely Hearts Club Band—Original Soundtrack (Polydor/RSO)
Greatest Hits, Abba (Atlantic)
Double Live Gonzo, Ted Nugent (Epic)
Ten Years of Gold, Kenny Rogers (United Artists)
Takin' It to the Streets, Doobie Brothers (Warner Bros.)
Flowing Rivers, Andy Gibb (Polydor/RSO)
Boys in the Trees, Carly Simon (Elektra)
But Seriously, Folks, Jow Walsh (Asylum)
The Album, Abba (Atlantic)
Natural High, Commodores (Motown)
Don't Look Back, Boston (Epic)
Running on Empty, Jackson Browne (Asylum)
Bat Out of Hell, Meat Loaf (CBS/Cleveland Int'l.)
Life Is a Song Worth Singing, Teddy Pendergrass (Phila. Int'l.)
Songbird, Barbra Streisand (Columbia)
Worlds Away, Pablo Cruise (A & M)
Blam, Brothers Johnson (A & M)
Togetherness, L.T.D. (A & M)
Who Are You, The Who (MCA)
(Living in the U.S.A., Linda Ronstadt (Asylum)
Champagne Jam, Atlanta Rhythm Section (Polydor)
Kiss—Peter Criss, Peter Criss (Casablanca)
Kiss—Ace Frehley, Ace Frehley (Casablanca)
Kiss—Gene Simmons, Gene Simmons (Casablanca)
Kiss—Paul Stanley, Paul Stanley (Casablanca)
A Taste of Honey, A Taste of Honey (Capitol)
Pieces of Eight, Styx (A & M)
Under Wraps, Shaun Cassidy (Warner/Curb)
Infinity, Journey (Columbia)
Van Halen, Van Halen (Warner Bros.)
Nightwatch, Kenny Loggins (Columbia)
Live and More, Donna Summer (Casablanca)
52nd Street, Billy Joel (Columbia)
I Robot, Alan Parsons Project (Arista)
Hot Streets, Chicago (Columbia)
Dog and Butterfly, Heart (Portrait)
Tormato, Yes (Atlantic)
Sounds . . . And Stuff Like That, Quincy Jones (A & M)
Skynyrd's First And . . . Last, Lynyrd Skynyrd (MCA)
Backless, Eric Clapton (Polydor/RSO)
A Single Man, Elton John (MCA)
Weekend Warriors, Ted Nugent (Epic)
Barbra Streisand's Greatest Hits, Volume II, Barbra Streisand (Columbia)
A Wild & Crazy Guy, Steve Martin (Warner Bros.)
Greatest Hits, Barry Manilow (Arista)
The Steve Miller Band's Greatest Hits 1974-78, Steve Miller Band (Capitol)
Jazz, Queen (Elektra)
Totally Hot, Olivia Newton-John (MCA)
Wings Greatest, Wings (Capitol)
You Don't Bring Me Flowers, Neil Diamond (Columbia)

1978 *(cont'd)*
The Best of Earth, Wind & Fire, Volume I, Earth, Wind & Fire (Columbia/ARC)
Steely Dan's Greatest Hits, Steely Dan (ABC)
Twin Sons of Different Mothers, Dan Fogelberg and Tim Weisberg (CBS/Full Moon)
Cruisin', Village People (Casablanca)
You Get What You Play For, REO Speedwagon (Epic)
One Nation Under a Groove, Funkadelic (Warner Bros.)
Let's Keep It That Way, Anne Murray (Capitol)
Barry White, The Man, Barry White (20th Century)
Live Bootleg, Aerosmith (Columbia)
Stardust, Willie Nelson (Columbia)
Macho Man, Village People (Casablanca)
The Cars, Cars (Elektra)
C'est Chic, Chic (Atlantic)
Blondes Have More Fun, Rod Stewart (Warner Bros.)

1979
Briefcase Full of Blues, Blues Brothers (Atlantic)
Elan, Firefall (Atlantic)
Brother To Brother, Gino Vanelli (A & M)
Toto, Toto (Columbia)
Octave, Moody Blues (London)
Spirits Having Flown, Bee Gees (RSO)
The Gambler, Kenny Rogers (United Artists)
Minute by Minute, Doobie Bros. (Warner Bros.)
Two for the Show, Kansas (CBS/Kirshner)
Time Passages, Al Stewart (Arista)
Dire Straits, Dire Straits (Warner Bros.)
Love Tracks, Gloria Gaynor (Polydor)
2 Hot! Peaches & Herb (Polydor)
Go West, Village People (Casablanca)
Desolation Angels, Bad Company (Swan Song)
Bad Girls, Donna Summer (Casablanca)
Destiny, The Jacksons (Epic)
Breakfast in America, Supertramp (A & M)
Van Halen II, Van Halen (Warner Bros.)
Sleeper Catcher, Little River Band (Harvest)
Live at Budokan, Cheap Trick (Epic)
We Are Family, Sister Sledge (Atlantic)
Parallel Lines, Blondie (Chrysalis)
I Am, Earth, Wind & Fire (ARC)
Back to the Egg, Wings (CBS)
Discovery, Electric Light Orchestra (Jet/CBS)
Dynasty, Kiss (Casablanca)
Teddy, Teddy Pendergrass (Phila. Int'l.)
Get The Knack, The Knack (Capitol)
Candy-O, Cars (Elektra)
Rickie Lee Jones, Rickie Lee Jones (Warner Bros.)
Million Mile Reflection, Charlie Daniels Band (Epic)
Greatest Hits, Waylon Jennings (RCA)
The Kids Are Alright—Movie Soundtrack, The Who (MCA)
Disco Nights, G.Q. (Arista)
Evolution, Journey (CBS)
Eddie Money, Eddie Money (CBS)
First Under the Wire, Little River Band (Capitol)
Risque, Chic (Atlantic)

Off The Wall, Michael Jackson (CBS)
Nether Lands, Dan Fogelberg (Epic)
Identify Yourself, O'Jays (Phila. Int'l.)

1980
Head Games, Foreigner (Atlantic)
In Through The Out Door, Led Zeppelin (Atlantic)
Kenny, Kenny Rogers (Capitol)
Ladies Night, Kool and the Gang (Phonogram)
One Voice, Barry Manilow (Arista)
A Christmas Together, John Denver and The Muppets (RCA)
The Long Run, The Eagles (Asylum)
Rise, Herb Alpert (A & M)
Cornerstone, Styx (A & M)
Dream Police, Cheap Trick (Epic)
Summertime Dream, Gordon Lightfoot (Reprise)
Rust Never Sleeps, Neil Young (Warner Bros.)
Tusk, Fleetwood Mac (Warner Bros.)
Prince, Prince (Warner Bros.)
On The Radio, Volumes I & II, Donna Summer (Casablanca)
Flirtin' With Disaster, Molly Hatchet (Epic)
Wet, Barbra Streisand (Columbia)
Bee Gees' Greatest, Bee Gees (RSO)
Rod Stewart's Greatest Hits, Rod Stewart (Warner Bros.)
Damn The Torpedoes, Tom Petty & The Heartbreakers (MCA)
Willie Nelson & Family Live, Willie Nelson (Columbia)
Dionne, Dionne Warwick (Arista)
Phoenix, Dan Fogelberg (Epic)
The Wall, Pink Floyd (Columbia)
Highway To Hell, AC/DC (Atlantic)
The Whispers, The Whispers (Solar)
Gold And Platinum, Lynyrd Skynyrd (MCA)
A Place In The Sun, Pablo Cruise (A & M)
Against The Wind, Bob Seger & The Silver Bullet Band (Capitol)
Glass Houses, Billy Joel (Columbia)
September Morn, Neil Diamond (Columbia)
Slow Train Coming, Bob Dylan (Columbia)
Mad Love, Linda Ronstadt (Asylum)
Gideon, Kenny Rogers (United Artists)
Mickey Mouse Disco, Mickey Mouse (Disneyland)
Women And Children First, Van Halen (Warner Bros.)
Go All The Way, The Isley Brothers (T-Neck)
The Rose, Original Soundtrack, Bette Midler (Atlantic)
Departure, Journey (Columbia)
Eat To The Beat, Blondie (Chrysalis)
Urban Cowboy, Original Soundtrack, Various Artists (Asylum)
Christopher Cross, Christopher Cross (Warner Bros.)
"Xanadu"—Original Motion Picture Soundtrack, Olivia Newton-John & Electric Light Orchestra (MCA)
Emotional Rescue, The Rolling Stones (Atlantic)
Hold Out, Jackson Browne (Elektra)
Light Up The Night, Brothers Johnson (A & M)
The Game, Queen (Elektra)
Back In Black, AC/DC (Atlantic)
Give Me The Night, George Benson (Warner Bros.)

1980 *(cont'd)*
Panorama, The Cars (Elektra)
ELO's Greatest Hits, Electric Light Orchestra (Jet)
Crimes Of Passion, Pat Benatar (Chrysalis)
Full Moon, The Charlie Daniels Band (Epic)
You Can Tune A Piano, But You Can't Tuna Fish, REO
   Speedwagon (Epic)
*"Honeysuckle Rose"—Original Motion Picture Sound-
   track,* Willie Nelson & Family (Columbia)
TP, Teddy Pendergrass (Xhila. Intl.)
One Step Closer, Doobie Brothers (Warner Bros.)
Guilty, Barbra Streisand (Columbia)
Greatest Hits, Anne Murray (Capitol)
Greatest Hits, Kenny Rogers (Liberty)
In The Heat Of The Night, Pat Benatar (Chrysalis)
Triumph, The Jacksons (Epic)
The River, Bruce Springsteen (Columbia)
Annie, Original Cast Album (Columbia)
Celebrate Me Home, Kenny Loggins (Columbia)
Molly Hatchet, Molly Hatchet (Epic)

SINGLES

1976
"Disco Lady," Johnnie Taylor (Columbia)
"Kiss and Say Goodbye," The Manhattans (Columbia)
"Play That Funky Music," Wild Cherry (Epic/Sweet
   City)
"Disco Duck," Rick Dees & His Cast of Idiots (RSO)

1977
"Car Wash," Rose Royce (MCA)
"You Light Up My Life," Debby Boone (Warner Bros.)
"Boogie Nights," Heatwave (Epic)

1978
"Stayin' Alive," Bee Gees (Polydor/RSO)
"Emotion," Samantha Sang (Private Stock)
"We Are the Champions," Queen (Elektra)
"Night Fever," Bee Gees (Polydor/RSO)
"Star Wars Theme/Cantina Band," Meco (Millenium)
"Shadow Dancing," Andy Gibb (Polydor/RSO)
"You're the One That I Want," (John Travolta & Olivia
   Newton-John (Polydor/RSO)
"Boogie Oogie Oogie," A Taste of Honey (Capitol)
"Grease," Frankie Valli (Polydor/RSO)
"Le Freak," Chic (Atlantic)

1979
"Hot Child in the City," Nick Gilder (Chrysalis)
"YMCA," Village People (Casablanca)
"Too Much Heaven," Bee Gees (RSO)
"Da Ya Think I'm Sexy," Rod Stewart (Warner Bros.)
"I Will Survive," Gloria Gaynor (Polydor)
"Reunited," Peaches & Herb (Polydor)
"Tragedy," Bee Gees (RSO)
"Shake Your Body," The Jacksons (Epic)
"Ain't No Stoppin' Us Now," McFadden & Whitehead
   (Phila. Intl.)
"Knock on Wood," Amii Stewart (Ariola America)
"Hot Stuff," Donna Summer (Casablanca)
"Bad Girls," Donna Summer (Casablanca)

1980
"Funkytown," Lipps, Inc. (Casablanca)
"Take Your Time (Do It Right)", S.O.S. Band (Tabu)
"Another One Bites The Dust," Queen (Elektra)

PHOTO CREDITS

374–375. All photos courtesy of Music Retailer.

410. Photo by Marianne Barcellona. Copyright © 1980 by Marianne Barcellona. All rights reserved. Courtesy, New York Philharmonic Orchestra and Marianne Barcellona.

428. Photographed by Steven M. Rachlin.